TRUSTS, TRUSTEES AND EXECUTORS

by

W. A. WILSON

M.A., LL.B.

Lord President Reid Professor of Law
University of Edinburgh

and

A. G. M. DUNCAN

M.A., LL.B., W.S.

Senior Lecturer in Scots Law
University of Edinburgh

with a chapter on Judicial Variation of Trusts

by

W. A. ELLIOTT

M.C., Q.C., B.L.

Published under the auspices of
THE SCOTTISH UNIVERSITIES LAW INSTITUTE

EDINBURGH
W. GREEN & SON LTD.
1975

First published in 1975

ISBN 0 414 00566 X

Printed in Great Britain
by
The Eastern Press Ltd.
of London and Reading

PREFACE

THIS is one of two volumes which together will cover the field of Trusts, Trustees, Executors and Judicial Factors. The other, on Judicial Factors, by Sheriff N. M. L. Walker, has already been published.

In this volume, Mr. Duncan is responsible for Chapters 15 to 19 and part of Chapter 20; Professor Wilson is responsible for the remainder with the exception of Chapter 12 on the Judicial Variation of Trusts which Mr. W. A. Elliott, Q.C., kindly agreed to contribute.

Professor Wilson wishes to thank the Hon. Lord Mackintosh, who was convener of the Scottish Universities Law Institute's Advisory Committee in the early years of the project; the Hon. Lord Mackenzie Stuart, who succeeded Lord Mackintosh as convener and was good enough to read and comment upon a substantial part of the manuscript; Mr. A. E. McRae, until recently Depute Commissary Clerk, Edinburgh, who kindly read over Chapter 29; Mr. W. D. H. Sellar, who also read part of the manuscript; Professor T. B. Smith, until recently Director of the Scottish Universities Law Institute, for his advice and encouragement; Dr. G. R. Thomson of W. Green & Son Ltd. for his advice and consummate patience over many years; Mrs. M. Wedderburn and Miss E. A. Mozolowski for assistance with proof-reading; and Mr. James Farrell, Advocate, who prepared the tables of cases and statutes.

The law is stated at June 1, 1973. Mr. Elliott, however, wishes it to be noted that, if the proposals set forth in the recent White Paper on Capital Transfer Tax are implemented, many of the references to taxation in Chapter 12 will be superseded.

Edinburgh,
October 1974.

CONTENTS

CONTENTS

PART III—EXECUTORS

APPENDIX

TABLE OF CASES

ix

TABLE OF STATUTES

AUTHORITIES CITED AND ABBREVIATIONS THEREOF

Bankton   Andrew McDouall, Lord Bankton, *Institute of the Laws of Scotland in Civil Rights*, 3 vols., 1751–3.

Bell, *Comm.*   Professor G. J. Bell, *Commentaries on the Law of Scotland and the Principles of Mercantile Jurisprudence*, 7th ed., 1870.

Bell, *Prin.*   Professor G. J. Bell, *Principles of the Law of Scotland*, 10th ed., 1899.

Candlish Henderson   *The Principles of Vesting in the Law of Succession*, 2nd ed., 1938.

Currie   *The Confirmation of Executors in Scotland*, by J. G. Currie, 7th ed., by A. E. McRae, 1973.

Dykes   D. O. Dykes, Supplement to McLaren, *Law of Wills and Succession*, 1934.

Encyc.   *Encyclopaedia of the Laws of Scotland*, 18 vols., 1926–52.

Ersk.   Professor John Erskine of Carnock, *An Institute Of the Law of Scotland*, 8th ed., 2 vols., 1871.

Forsyth   C. Forsyth, *The Principles and Practice of the Law of Trusts and Trustees in Scotland*, 1844.

Gloag & Henderson   *Introduction to the Law of Scotland*, by W. M. Gloag and R. C. Henderson, 7th ed., by A. M. Johnston and Others, 1968.

Howden   C. R. A. Howden, *Trusts, Trustees and the Trusts Acts in Scotland*, 1893.

Hume, *Lect.*   Baron David Hume, *Lectures on the Law of Scotland*, 6 vols. (Stair Socy.), 1939–58.

Judicial Factors   *Judicial Factors*, by N.M.L. Walker, 1974.

Lewin   *Lewin on Trusts*, 16th ed., by W. J. Mowbray, 1964.

Mackenzie Stuart   *The Law of Trusts*, by A. Mackenzie Stuart, 1932.

McLaren   John, Lord McLaren, *Law of Wills and Succession,* 3rd ed., 1894; Supplement by Dykes, 1934.

Meston   *The Succession (Scotland) Act 1964*, by M. C· Meston, 2nd ed., 1969.

Pettit   P. H. Pettit, *Equity and the Law of Trusts*, 2nd ed., 1970.

R.C.   Rules of the Court of Session 1965.

Stair   Sir James Dalrymple, Viscount Stair, *Institutions of the Law of Scotland*, 5th ed., 2 vols., 1832.

Tudor   *Tudor on Charities*, 6th ed., by Douglas H. McMullen, Spencer G. Maurice and David B. Parker, 1967.

Underhill   *Underhill's Law Relating to Trusts and Trustees,* 12th ed., by R. T. Oerton, 1970.

Walker   *Principles of Scottish Private Law,* by D. M. Walker, 1970.

STATUTES

"the 1823 Act" . Confirmation of Executors (Scotland) Act 1823.

"the 1858 Act" . Confirmation of Executors (Scotland) Act 1858.

"the 1900 Act" . Executors (Scotland) Act 1900.

"the 1921 Act" . Trusts (Scotland) Act 1921.

"the 1961 Act" . Trusts (Scotland) Act 1961.

"T.I.A. 1961" . Trustee Investments Act, 1961.

"the 1964 Act" . Succession (Scotland) Act 1964.

PART I—TRUSTS

PART I—TRUSTS

CHAPTER 1

THE NATURE OF A TRUST

CRAIG,[1] in his treatment of conditions in feudal charters, describes trusts under the heading *Fideicommissariae Conditiones*. Stair also compares trusts to *fidei commissa*[2] and he uses " fideicommissary " in relation to the duties of the executor to the legatees and creditors of the deceased.[3] There are isolated references to *fidei commissa* in case law,[4] and it has been suggested by several writers that the Scottish entail was derived from *fidei commissa*.[5]

Nevertheless, when the trust first appears in the law of Scotland it is an *inter vivos* bilateral transaction [6]: " the Thing intrusted is in the custody of the person intrusted, to the behove of the intruster." [7] A conveys property to B to be used for the benefit of A. Stair emphasises that in a proper trust there is no back-bond, declaration or reversion. His definition of trust is " the stating a Right so far in the Person of the Trustee, as it can hardly be recovered from him, but by his faithfulness in following that, which he knows to be the true Design of the Truster." [8] The law can be conveniently examined by considering the various problems to which the trust relationship gave rise.

Recovery of property

The first type of situation which caused difficulty was that in which the truster wished to recover his property. This was largely a question of proof and a solution was attempted by the Blank Bonds and Trusts Act 1696.[9]

Bona fide third party

The second question which arose was whether the truster could recover the property from a third party to whom the trustee had conveyed it in breach of trust. In *King* v. *Douglas*,[10] where a disposition by a mother to

---

[1] *Ius Feudale*, 2. 5. 9.
[2] IV, 6, 2; IV, 45, 21.
[3] III, 8, 30; III, 8, 71. See also Ersk. III, 9, 5; III, 9, 42; Hume, *Lect.* V, 208; *Tait* v. *Kay* (1779) Mor. 3142; *Bell* v. *Campbell* (1781) Mor. 3861.
[4] *e.g. Fothringhame* v. *Mauld* (1679) Mor. 16179; *Seton* v. *Pitmedden* (1717) Mor. 4425.
[5] Mackenzie, *Treatise of Tailies* (Coll. Wks., Vol. II, 484); Bankton, II, 3, 135; Kames, *Principles of Equity*, 244; Sandford, *Law of Entails in Scotland*, 2nd ed., 13; Smith, *Studies Critical and Comparative* (1962), 203–205. For an interesting comparison, see Hahlo " The Trust in South African Law " (1961) 78 S.A.L.J. 195. See also *Abdul Hameed Sittee Kadija* v. *De Saram* [1946] A.C. 209.
[6] *Williamson* v. *Law* (1623) Durie 54; *Lady Stanipath* (1624) Durie 141.
[7] Stair, I, 13, 7.
[8] IV, 6, 2. See also I, 13, 7; IV, 45, 21; Ersk. III, 1, 32.
[9] See Chap. 4.
[10] (1636) Durie 820.

3

her son of a liferent of a sum was qualified by a bond granted by the son in favour of the mother and the son subsequently assigned the sum to his sister, it was found that the back-bond could not affect the sister but only the granter thereof. In *Workman* v. *Crawford*,[11] an unusually clear decision, the pursuer sought to reduce a disposition which had been granted by the trustee to a third party, the trust being evidenced by a back-bond. It was found to be a relevant defence that the third party had acquired for onerous causes and without knowledge of the back-bond.

In *Gordon* v. *Crawford*,[12] a back-bond was found effectual against a singular successor. Stair [13] states that if the thing intrusted is transmitted to a singular successor, taking bona fide, the successor is secure " and the trustee is only liable personally upon the trust."

In *Thomson* v. *Douglas Heron & Co.*,[14] lands were disponed to the disponer's man of business to sell them and apply the proceeds for the disponer's behoof, a qualification which did not appear in the record. The disponee conveyed the lands to a third party in security of a debt due by him: thereafter other creditors adjudged the lands but did not take infeftment. It was decided that a heritable creditor was in the same position as a bona fide purchaser who could have effectually acquired the property from the disponee. But, as adjudgers took *tantum et tale*, the disponer was preferred to them.

The question was finally settled by the House of Lords in *Redfearn* v. *Somervail*.[15] A share in a company which was held in trust was fraudulently assigned for value by the trustee to a third party who acted in good faith and without knowledge of the trust. The assignation was duly intimated to the company, which had no notice of the trust. In a competition between the assignee and the beneficiary in the trust, the Court of Session found for the beneficiary on the principle *assignatus utitur jure auctoris*—the third party could not obtain a title better than the trustee had. This decision was eventually reversed by the House of Lords. The argument founded on *assignatus utitur jure auctoris* was rejected. Both speeches in the House of Lords demonstrated very clearly that the maxim applies only in questions between the assignee and the debtor whose debt has been assigned.[16]

Lord Eldon pointed out that the maxim created no hardship for the assignee because he could always apply to the known debtor to ascertain how the debt stood. He could not, however, ascertain the existence of secret trusts. The beneficiary could be in no better position than an assignee without intimation. It was accordingly held that an intimated assignation for onerous cause could not be defeated by a latent equity.

[11] (1672) Mor. 10208.
[12] (1676) 2 Stair Dec. 440. See Elchies, *Annotations on Stair's Institutions*, 72.
[13] I, 13, 7. See also Stair, II, 10, 5.
[14] (1786) Mor. 10229.
[15] (1813) 1 Dow's Appeals 50; 1 Pat.App. 707.
[16] See Elchies, *Annotations*, 72.

Redfearn was followed in *Burns* v. *Lawrie's Trs.*,[17] the facts of which were slightly different in that the share was assigned in security of a prior debt and not upon an immediate advance of money. Although Lord Medwyn expressed doubt and was inclined to attach significance to the distinction in that it placed the case between the bankruptcy cases of *Dingwall* and *Gordon* on the one hand,[18] and *Redfearn* on the other, the majority opined that, if the assignation was granted for an onerous cause, and was taken in good faith, that was sufficient to protect it against a latent equity.

Diligence

The third question which arose was whether the trust property was subject to the diligence of the trustee's creditors. In *Livingston and Shaw* v. *Lord Forrester and the Creditors of Grange* [19] it was decided that a creditor adjudged under burden of the back-bond because he proceeded on a personal right. Similarly it was held in *Mackenzie* v. *Watson and Stuart* [20] that the back-bond was good against an arrestment by a creditor of the trustee. The same result was reached in *Brugh* v. *Forbes*,[21] where it was said " it is hard to tie purchasers who pay an adequate price by back-bonds that may be latent; but arresters and adjudgers only affect the subject as their debtor has it in his person with its qualities." It was again held in *Preston* v. *Earl of Dundonald's Creditors* [22] that a back-bond affects adjudgers.

One early case [23] is inconsistent with this line of authority. Boylstoun gave Makelwood money to buy cloth for him. Makelwood employed Palmer to buy the cloth which was left in the hands of Robertson. It was then arrested by Makelwood's creditors. The decision was that, as the cloth had been bought in Makelwood's name, the property was in the person of Makelwood and not in the person of Boylstoun, " albeit he had a Mandate or Trust from him, which is but a personal Obligment; but Property or Dominion is only constitute or transmitted by Possession, and Boylstoun had got no possession of the Linen-Cloath, either by himself or by any in his name to his use." It may be that cases of this type were regarded as falling in a different chapter from the decisions concerned with heritage and a back-bond. In any event the decision was later regarded as erroneous.[24]

Trustee's bankruptcy

The fourth question, which caused somewhat greater difficulty than the others, was whether the trust property, on the bankruptcy of the trustee,

---

[17] (1840) 2 D. 1348. See also *Attwood* v. *Kinnears* (1832) 10 S. 817.
[18] See, *infra*, p. 6.
[19] (1664) Mor. 10200.
[20] (1678) Mor. 10188.
[21] (1715) Mor. 10213.
[22] (1805) Mor. " Personal and Real," App. No. 2.
[23] *Boylstoun* v. *Robertson and Fleming* (1672) 2 Stair Dec. 54.
[24] See *Heirs of Robert Selby* v. *Jollie* (1795) Mor. 13438.

was available to his creditors. The first occasion on which the question was
considered fully seems to have been *Wylie* v. *Duncan* in 1803.[25] Infeftment
was taken on an absolute and irredeemable conveyance of heritage but the
disponee granted a missive narrating the sale and engaging to resell the
property at the same price on six months' notice. The disponer continued
to possess the subjects. The disponee was later sequestrated. In a competition between the disponer and the trustee in the sequestration, the Lord
Ordinary preferred the disponer on the ground that the trustee took
tantum et tale. The trustee reclaimed and the finding was reversed. The
Lords " considered the burden as personal, and not good against the
creditors." From the report contained in Ross's *Leading Cases*,[26] it
appears that the result would not have been different if the obligation had
had the character of a trust. Lord Meadowbank noted: " Court unani-
mous that a trustee on a bankrupt estate is not affected by personal declarations even of trust, unless contained in the deed of conveyance of the
heritable subjects." In *Dingwall* v. *McCombie*,[27] however, it was held that
creditors were affected by a latent trust on the ground that the trustee's
creditors could not stand in a better position than the trustee.

The matter was fully explored in *Gordon* v. *Cheyne*,[28] where a share
stood in the books of a company in the bankrupt's name but he had
granted an acknowledgment that it was the property of another. The
trustee in the sequestration relied on *Redfearn*. The truster argued that
that decision was not relevant. Creditors were not in the same position as
bona fide purchasers or assignees because " creditors trust to the personal
credit of their debtor, while purchasers advance their money for the
specific subject itself, trusting nothing to his credit." It was held that
Redfearn did not apply to the general body of creditors who took the right
tantum et tale as it stood in the person of the bankrupt.

Finally, the problem reached the House of Lords in *Heritable Reversionary Co. Ltd.* v. *Millar*.[29] This was an action of declarator of trust
against the trustee on the sequestrated estates of an individual who held an
unqualified feudal title but had granted a declaration that he held the
subjects in trust for the pursuers. In the Court of Session the majority
thought that the creditors of the trustee were not affected by a qualification
which did not appear in the title.

> " It appears to me that there is a principle in the law of Scotland
> which affirms that where a party has a legal title in writing, whether he
> be disponee or assignee, and that title has been perfected by sasine in
> the one case and intimation of the assignation in the other, the title is
> not defeasible by reference to any latent equities." [30]

Some reliance was placed on *Wylie* v. *Duncan* and *Redfearn* v. *Somervail*.

---

[25] (1803) Mor. 10269.　　　　　　　　　　　　　　[26] III, 134.
[27] (1822) 1 S. 501.　　　　　　　　　　　　　　　　[28] Feb. 5, 1824, F.C.
[29] (1891) 18 R. 1166; (1892) 19 R.(H.L.) 43. For a trenchant criticism by Professor Goudy of
the Court of Session's judgment, see (1891) 3 J.R. 365.
[30] *Per* L.P. Inglis, 18 R. 1181.

In the House of Lords the decision of the Court of Session was reversed. Lord Herschell and Lord Watson stated that *Wylie* v. *Duncan* was not in point because the personal right there arose from a *pactum de retrovendendo* and there was a distinction between heritable property held on latent trust of which the owner is a bare trustee and heritable property of which the owner has come under some contractual obligation. As has been already indicated, there is evidence that the *ratio* of *Wylie* v. *Duncan* did extend to property held on trust and it has been suggested that *Wylie* would have been decided differently if it had occurred after *Heritable Reversionary Co. Ltd.*[31]

Redfearn v. *Somervail* was disposed of on the ground that it rested on personal bar, a view which, as has been pointed out, is not supported by an analysis of the speeches. Lord Watson said of *Redfearn* [32]:

" It must, however, be kept in view that the validity of a right acquired in such circumstances by a bona fide disponee for value does not rest upon the recognition of any power in the trustee which he can lawfully exercise, because breach of trust duty and wilful fraud can never be in themselves lawful, but upon the well-known principle that a true owner who chooses to conceal his right from the public, and to clothe his trustee with all the *indicia* of ownership, is thereby barred from challenging rights acquired by innocent third parties for onerous considerations under contracts with his fraudulent trustee."

The reasoning of the House of Lords was that what passed to the trustee in the sequestration under section 102 of the Bankruptcy (Scotland) Act 1856 was the " property " of the bankrupt and heritage held in trust was not property.

" An apparent title to land or personal estate, carrying no real right of property with it, does not, in the ordinary or in any true legal sense, make such land or personal estate the property of the person who holds the title." [33] " No one in ordinary parlance would speak of land or funds held only in trust for another as the property of the trustee." [34]

The principle of *Millar* was applied to an *ex facie* absolute assignation of a bond and disposition in security qualified by a back-letter in *Forbes's Trs.* v. *Macleod* [35]; and it has been held that the principle is not restricted to cases in which the property has been conveyed to the trustee by a third party but extends to the situation where the beneficial ownership was originally in the trustee and he has undertaken to hold it in trust for the beneficiary.[36]

[31] *Hinkelbein* v. *Craig* (1905) 13 S.L.T. 84.
[32] p. 47.
[33] *Per* Lord Watson at p. 49.
[34] *Per* Lord Macnaghten at p. 53.
[35] (1898) 25 R. 1012.
[36] *Hinkelbein* v. *Craig* (1905) 13 S.L.T. 84.

In his dissenting opinion in *Millar*,[37] in the Court of Session, Lord McLaren relied on Lord Westbury's dictum in *Fleeming* v. *Howden* [38]:

" The right of a trustee under a sequestration is very different from the right of a singular successor, for it is a rule common both to English and Scotch bankrupt law that the trustee or assignee takes the property of the bankrupt subject to all the rights and equities that affected it at the time of the bankruptcy. But the singular successor is not bound by a trust or duty of which he had no notice. The trustee under a sequestration is in the same position as a gratuitous alienee. He takes such estate or interest only as the bankrupt can lawfully convey."

Although this statement is obviously too widely expressed and has been criticised on that ground,[39] it does correctly answer the question raised in the *Millar* type of case.

Trust and contract

From the foregoing discussion it is obvious that the distinction between a contractual right and the right of the beneficiary against the trustee is crucial to the analysis of the concept of trust.[40] Some confusion has been created by the celebrated dictum of Lord Westbury that " an obligation to do an act with respect to property creates a trust." [41] It is important to notice the context in which this statement was made. The obligation referred to was a statutory duty to create a valid entail of certain land by recording a deed in the Register of Tailzies. The bankrupt and his predecessors had failed to do this and the dictum continues:

" and if a fiar bound to fulfil an obligation acquires or retains, by means of his neglect of that duty, a greater estate than he would otherwise have had, he is a trustee of such excess of interest for the benefit of the persons who would have been entitled to it if the obligation had been duly fulfilled."

The obligation accordingly was not a contractual one and the dictum seems partly to be founded on the doctrine of constructive trust. In the latter part of his speech, in which he set forth an alternative ground of judgment, Lord Westbury repeated the observation with reference to an obligation contained in a clause of devolution which was set forth in the recorded title of the bankrupt. The trust was patent on the face of the title. It is therefore clear that the dictum is too widely expressed and it has been the subject of adverse comment.[42]

[37] 18 R. 1174.
[38] 6 M. (H.L.) 113, 121.
[39] *Per* L.P. Inglis, 18 R. 1183; *per* Lord Watson, 19 R.(H.L.) 49.
[40] See the review by W. Hunter of the first edition of Menzies (1893) 5 J.R. 179.
[41] *Fleeming* v. *Howden* (1868) 6 M. (H.L.) 113, 121.
[42] *Heritable Reversionary Co. Ltd.* v. *McKay's Tr.* (1891) 18 R. 1166, 1183, *per* L.P. Inglis; *Bank of Scotland* v. *Liquidators of Hutchison Main & Co. Ltd.*, 1914 S.C.(H.L.) 1, 7, *per* Lord Kinnear. Both comments are directed to the alternative ground of judgment although the dictum under discussion was delivered in the earlier part of the speech. Lord Shaw's

In *Bank of Scotland* v. *Liquidators of Hutchison Main & Co. Ltd.*[43] a company, A, made an arrangement with a bank whereby it was agreed, *inter alia*, that the company would then obtain from B, an English company, a secured debenture which would be assigned to the bank in lieu of certain assets which the bank held in security of a debt due by A and which were to be surrendered to A. The undertaking by A's agents was in the following terms:

> " We are authorised by the directors . . . to procure from Mr. Johnson a debenture or floating charge over the whole of his assets in the name of the company for the amount required to secure the debt due by Mr. Johnson to our clients. So soon as that debenture reaches our hands we have instructions to make it available to the Bank of Scotland as further and additional security for the repayment by our clients of their indebtedness to the bank."

The assets were surrendered and A obtained the debenture from B but before it was assigned to the bank, A went into liquidation. The bank claimed the debenture on the ground that it had been held by A as a trustee or agent and *Heritable Reversionary Co. Ltd.* v. *Millar* was applicable. Support was also sought from Lord Westbury's dictum that an obligation to do an act with respect to property creates a trust. The House of Lords, affirming the judgment of the Second Division of the Court of Session, held that the bank was in the position of a mere personal creditor who held no complete security for its debt and it was not entitled to a preference in respect of the debenture.

The agency argument was rejected on the ground that there were no averments to suggest that A procured the debenture as agent for the bank; *Heritable Reversionary Co. Ltd.* v. *Millar* was clearly distinguishable in that " the trust so established was declared in express terms, and directly affected the constitution of the real right " [44]; Lord Westbury's dictum was too widely expressed and did not affect " the well-settled principle that a contractual obligation with regard to property, which has not effectually and actually brought about either a security upon it or a conveyance of it, is not *per se* the foundation of a trust or of a declarator of trust." [45]

The distinction between trust and contract arose in a different way in *Govan New Bowling-Green Club* v. *Geddes.*[46] The bowling-club had no capital with which to buy the ground which it used and twenty-two members of the club bought the property with their own money. The ground was disponed to two persons in trust for themselves and the twenty other persons each to the extent of one twenty-second *pro indiviso* share. There

---

criticism in the *Bank of Scotland* case at p. 17 is difficult to follow. See also *Bank of Scotland* v. *Liquidators of Hutchison Main & Co. Ltd.*, 1913 S.C. 255, 262, *per* Lord Salvesen, p. 264, *per* Lord Guthrie.

[43] 1914 S.C.(H.L.) 1. See Lorimer, " *Tantum et Tale* in Scots Bankruptcy Law," (1914) 26 J.R. 429.

[44] *Per* Lord Kinnear at p. 7.

[45] *Per* Lord Shaw at p. 17.

[46] (1898) 25 R. 485.

was an agreement that when the club was able to raise the necessary sum, and repaid the purchase price to the twenty-two persons, it could demand a conveyance of the ground. The club raised an action for declarator that it was entitled to a conveyance in terms of the agreement and a question was raised as to whether this was a declarator of trust falling under the 1696 Act. It was held that the averments did not disclose a case of trust. The twenty-two persons did not hold an authority from the club to make the purchase and they were not under an obligation to convey to the club or to hold in trust for the club when they did so. The twenty-two had the beneficial ownership of the property qualified only by a contractual obligation to sell in a certain event. " In any case, the result of the agreement is sufficiently averred, but that is not a trust; it is an obligation undertaken by the owners of the estate to another body of persons who never were the owners of the estate, and who could not declare a trust regarding it." [47]

The ex facie absolute disposition

The distinction between a personal obligation and a trust can be seen quite clearly in the *Bank of Scotland* case.[48] The question becomes much more acute when the *ex facie* absolute disposition qualified by a back-letter is considered. The back-letter seems to be near to a mere personal obligation or a *pactum de retrovendendo*.

In *Robertson* v. *Duff*,[49] Lord Fullerton treated a security created by *ex facie* absolute disposition as a trust. On the other hand, in *Campbell* v. *Bertram*,[50] Lord Curriehill decided that the right of reversion was " a mere personal *pactum de retrovendendo*." In *National Bank of Scotland Ltd.* v. *Union Bank of Scotland Ltd.*[51] Lord President Inglis criticised Lord Fullerton's view as being " scientifically inaccurate " and opined that

" what is left in the debtor is not a real right of any kind, is not a right of property of any kind, not even a right of redemption or reversion in any proper sense, but a mere personal right to enforce a *pactum de retrovendendo*, or, in other words, to demand a reconveyance of the estate upon tendering to the infeft proprietor payment of everything that is due to him at the date of the demand."

In the House of Lords,[52] Lord Watson agreed that the transaction did not fall " within the category of proper trusts " but thought that it was not " in substance or in form a *pactum de retrovendendo*." He went on to opine that the disponer's right was a personal right consisting *in obligatione*, a *jus actionis*, which was of precisely the same quality as the right of a beneficiary under a proper trust.

47 *Per* Lord McLaren at p. 492.
48 It is also clear in *National Bank of Scotland Glasgow Nominees Ltd.* v. *Adamson*, 1932 S.L.T. 492, where the contention that a contract for the sale of shares made the seller a trustee for the buyer was firmly rejected. The facts were widely different from *Stevenson* v. *Wilson*, 1907 S.C. 445, where a constructive trust was held to exist (see *infra*, p. 80).
49 (1840) 2 D. 279, 291.
50 (1865) 4 M. 23, 28.
51 (1885) 13 R. 380, 413.
52 (1886) 14 R.(H.L.) 1, 4.

It is to be noted that the disponee's obligation [53] did not include the word " trust." The subjects were to be held " in security " and were to be reconveyed on repayment of the advances. *Heritable Reversionary Co. Ltd.* v. *Millar*, on the other hand, was not a typical case of the security transaction because the deed executed by the disponee did include the words " I hold the said subjects in trust." [54]

Agency

It seems to be accepted that where an agent procures property on behalf of his principal, he holds the property in trust for the principal.

" When an agent obtains money for the specific purpose of purchasing a property for his client and takes the title in his own name, and becomes bankrupt, it is clear that in such a case the law will get behind the apparent title to the beneficial and the real title, and that— always granted that the interests of third parties who have bought upon the faith of the records have not arisen—the property will, in the event of bankruptcy, be correctly treated as never having been *in bonis* of the debtor, but always of the client. Lord McLaren explains this with clarity in *Forbes's Trs.* v. *Macleod.*[55] Or when a property is acquired by a company with the company's money and put for convenience' sake in the name of the company's manager, then upon the occasion of the manager's bankruptcy the same result happens. The apparent title and the beneficial and real title are in conflict, not on account of the existence of any promise on the part of the manager to transfer it to the company, but on account of the fact that the property all along never was the manager's but was the company's. It would be, therefore, contrary to the truth of the case to permit that property to enter the assets of the manager, to whom it never in truth belonged. The company stands accordingly preferred to the property in the distribution of his assets." [56]

It seems that, in the end of the day, the distinction between contractual obligation and trust can be a mere matter of words and the form can be decisive. " I promise to convey the property " results in a mere personal obligation, whereas " I acknowledge that I hold the property in trust " creates a trust. It seems that if the trust is expressly declared in this way the matter is concluded and the nature of the transaction need not, and cannot, be further examined. It is not necessary that there should have been a conveyance of the property to the trustee; he can declare a trust of subjects which were vested beneficially in him at the time of the declara-

---

[53] See (1885) 13 R. 380. The back-letter in *Forbes's Trs.* v. *Macleod* (1898) 25 R. 1012 was in broadly the same terms.
[54] See 18 R. 1167. See also the terms of the back-letter in *Aberdeen Trades Council* v. *Shipconstructors and Shipwrights Association*, 1948 S.C. 94; 1949 S.C.(H.L.) 45.
[55] (1898) 25 R. 1012.
[56] *Bank of Scotland* v. *Liquidators of Hutchison Main & Co. Ltd.*, 1914 S.C.(H.L.) 1, 15, *per* Lord Shaw of Dunfermline. See also Bankton, I, 18, 12; Bell, *Comm.* I, 287; *Dunn* v. *Pratt* (1898) 25 R. 461.

tion. This point arose in *Hinkelbein* v. *Craig*,[57] where X, who was infeft in heritable property, entered into partnership with Y and the heritage was thereafter occupied by the firm. Both X and the firm were later sequestrated and one of X's creditors sought a declarator that the heritage fell to be attributed to X's estate and not to that of the firm. The trustee on the sequestrated estate of the firm contended that the heritage had been made over to the firm and was held by X in trust for the firm notwithstanding that he had not executed a declaration of trust. The pursuer argued that there was a distinction between " a latent trust of what had been the trustee's own property and a latent trust of what had been somebody else's property " and that " so long as the original owner remained infeft his obligation remained only an obligation to convey, and without conveyance could not be transmuted into an obligation to hold in trust." Lord Johnston, however, rejected this argument and opined that *Heritable Reversionary Co.* v. *Millar* could apply to a case of this kind. Moreover, he noted the pursuer's concession that a recorded declaration of trust by the original owner " without the circuity of a precedent conveyance to himself " would have been effectual.

The form of words cannot, however, be decisive in every case because the wording of the normal back-bond cannot easily be distinguished from the wording of what has been held to be a mere contractual obligation or a *pactum de retrovendendo*. The transaction must be examined and if there is disclosed what Lord Shaw described as [58] " the familiar case " of " a disposition of heritable property entering the record, but granted concurrently with a back bond which acknowledges that the transaction, although giving the title to the disponee, was truly a security transaction," there is a form of trust. The category is not clearly defined because Lord Shaw went on to say: " Nor do I question that the same result could be achieved in a less formal manner."

Again, in agency cases, there may be no use of " trust " or similar wording and indeed there may not be a document at all, but if on an examination of the transaction it appears that X was authorised by Y to acquire property on his behalf and to take the title thereto in his own name, then it will be held that X holds the property in trust for Y.

Trust as a contract

Trust cannot satisfactorily be defined in terms of contract. Attempts have been made. Stair places trust " amongst mandates or commissions " [59] and then qualifies this by saying that it may be referred to depositation " seeing the Right is in custody of the person intrusted." Erskine's definition is: " A trust is also of the nature of depositation by which a proprietor transfers to another the property of the subject intrusted, not that it should remain with him, but that it may be applied to

---

[57] (1905) 13 S.L.T. 84. See also *Allan's Trs.* v. *Inland Revenue*, 1971 S.L.T. 62.
[58] *Bank of Scotland* v. *Liqrs. of Hutchison Main & Co. Ltd.*, 1914 S.C.(H.L.) 1, 16.
[59] I, 12, 17. See also I, 13, 7; IV, 6, 3; Bankton, I, 15, 9, 14; Elchies, *Annotations*, 69.

certain uses for the behoof of a third party." [60] In *Gordon* v. *Gordon's Trs.*,[61] Lord Barcaple said: " In Scotland the law of trusts has always been treated as part of the general law of contracts, and the obligations upon the trustee, and the rights of the truster and the beneficiaries as against him, have been given effect to on the ground of contracts." Lord President Inglis in *Cuningham* v. *Montgomerie* [62] said:

> " Scientifically considered, the position of trustees under such a deed is this, that they are depositaries of the trust-estate and mandataries for its administration. This is a combination of two well-known contracts in the civil law, and the character and quality of these contracts is perfectly well fixed both in the civil law and in modern jurisprudence."

The contract theory later fell from favour. Lord Kincairney pointed out that the trustee's obligation contained an element of discretion which is not present in a contractual obligation.[63] McLaren preferred to regard trust as a *quasi*-contract, " distinct from mandate, but closely allied to it " because the duties of a trustee differed in many respects from those of a mandatary.[64] Finally, in *Allen* v. *McCombie's Trs.*[65] Lord President Dunedin, in discussing Lord President Inglis's dictum, said:

> " It is quite true that the origin of trust may very well be taken to be a combination of these two contracts. In the older works, for instance, Mr. Erskine's work, written at a time when trust law was as one may say exceedingly unfamiliar, trust is treated as a branch of deposit. But, although that is historically true, I do not think that trust can be treated as deposit and mandate and the rule of these two contracts applied and no other. Nor do I think that breach of trust can be treated merely as breach of contract."

He went on to doubt as to whether all actions could be divided into the two categories of breach of contract and *quasi*-delict. Lord McLaren accepted that the relationship between truster and trustee might be contractual but denied the existence of a contract between the trustee and the beneficiary although the latter had a *jus quaesitum* for the enforcement of the trust. Lord Kinnear said [66]:

> " For practical purposes I agree with your Lordship that there can be no doubt that we have derived the law of trust as now administered much more directly, through the aid of decisions of the House of Lords, from the equitable administration of trusts by the Court of Chancery in England, than by any logical deduction from the strictly

---

[60] III, 1, 32.
[61] (1866) 4 M. 501, 535.
[62] (1879) 6 R. 1333, 1337. See *Croskery* v. *Gilmour's Trs.* (1890) 17 R. 697, 700 to the same effect. See also More, *Lectures*, I, 187.
[63] *Carruthers* v. *Carruthers' Tr.* (1895) 22 R. 775, 778.
[64] II, 825.
[65] 1909 S.C. 710, 716.
[66] p. 720.

legal conception of the contracts to which the Lord Ordinary refers. But whatever be the origin of the legal conception of trust it has wider consequences in the fiduciary relation which it creates than can be referred to contract."

The property

The idea that the trustee holds an estate of one kind and the beneficiary an estate of another kind has received little acceptance in Scotland although Lord McLaren did refer in one case to " the owners of the legal and the owners of the beneficial estate." [67] Confusion was created by Lord Westbury's dictum that " the *jus crediti* is no more than another denomination of what may be called the estate of a beneficiary, or an equitable estate." [68]

The preponderance of authority is to the effect that the property is vested in the trustee—" the property of the thing intrusted, be it Land or Moveables, is in the person of the Intrusted, else it is not proper Trust " [69]—and the beneficiary has merely a right of action against the trustee.

> " The right of the beneficiary has never in Scotland been acknowledged as a positive, vested, equitable and co-existent right, as distinguished from the legal right of the trustee, as in England; but merely as a personal right of action against the trustee, to fulfil an obligation undertaken for behoof of him, the beneficiary; the actual right of property being in the trustee alone, but for the purposes declared in the trust-deed." [70]

In *Inland Revenue* v. *Clark's Trs.*[71] Lord President Normand, after pointing out that there is no action by which a beneficiary as such can vindicate for himself the trust property, described the beneficiary's right as " nothing more than a personal right to sue the trustees and to compel them to administer the trust in accordance with the directions which it contains." [72] Lord Moncrieff disapproved McLaren's description of the beneficiary's right as " a personal right of property in the estate which is the subject of the disposition " [73] and said:

> " In my view, the right of property in the estate of the trust is vested in the trustees to the exclusion of any competing right of property, and the right of the beneficiary . . . is merely a right *in personam* against the trustees to enforce their performance of the trust. It is true that, in the assertion of that right, a beneficiary will in certain cases obtain

---

[67] *Govan New Bowling-Green Club* v. *Geddes* (1898) 25 R. 485, 492. See also *Hay's Trs.* v. *Hay* (1890) 17 R. 961, 964; *Cameron's Trs.* v. *Cameron*, 1907 S.C. 407, 415, *per* Lord Kyllachy.

[68] *Buchanan* v. *Angus* (1862) 4 Macq. 374, 378.

[69] Stair, I, 13, 7. See also IV, 6, 1, and *De Robeck* v. *Inland Revenue*, 1928 S.C.(H.L.) 34, 40, *per* Lord Dunedin—" The trustees were owners of the lands—in trust, no doubt, but still owners."

[70] Forsyth, 12. See also Bell, *Comm.* I, 34; *Prin.*, ss. 1482, 1996; *Hetherington's Trs.* v. *Lord Advocate*, 1954 S.C.(H.L.) 19, 36, *per* Lord Reid.

[71] 1939 S.C. 11. Approved by Lord Keith, *Parker* v. *Lord Advocate*, 1960 S.C.(H.L.) 29, 41.

[72] p. 22.

[73] McLaren, II, 832.

the aid of the Court to enable him to use the names of the trustees, but it is only as representing the trustees in such a case that he can attach or assert any property right over the assets of the trust." [74]

Unfortunately, the cases relating to the *ex facie* absolute disposition reveal a different view. In *Union Bank* v. *National Bank*,[75] Lord Watson stated that " apart from considerations of feudal law " the disponer " had the radical right, in this sense, that according to the reality of the transaction she was the only person who had a proprietary interest in the subjects of the security." In *Heritable Reversionary Co. Ltd.* v. *Millar* the same eminent judge declared that the trustee, although he had the legal title, was the apparent owner while the beneficiary was the " true owner." [76] Lord Herschell regarded the beneficiaries as " the true and beneficial owners of the property." [77] In *Bank of Scotland* v. *Liqrs. of Hutchison Main & Co. Ltd.*[78] Lord Shaw distinguished the " apparent title " and " the beneficial and the real title " and opined that the essential feature of the security type of transaction was that " the question of property itself in what I have ventured to call a real and beneficial sense is settled adversely to the debtor—settled, that is to say, in this way, that the property does not belong to him but belongs to someone else." [79]

These decisions also assert that although a trustee can give a good title to a *bona fide* purchaser for value, that is not because the property is vested in the trustee but because the true owner of the property, who chose to conceal his right, is personally barred from challenging the right acquired by the third party.[80]

It may be that this problem, like many others in Scots law, is one of semantics and that these *dicta* referred to " property " as used in the Bankruptcy Acts. Moreover, it has already been indicated [81] that the reasoning in *Redfearn* v. *Somervail*, which is the authority as to the *bona fide* third party's title, was not founded on the doctrine of personal bar. It must be accepted that the property in the normal sense is vested in the trustee.

Another difficulty which must be mentioned arises from *Parker* v. *Lord Advocate*,[82] where Lord Patrick, in describing the legal situation in a trust after the capital had vested and was immediately payable to the beneficiaries, said: " Each child then owned the corpus of one-third of the trust fund." [83] Lord Mackintosh described the beneficiary's right as " a

---

[74] p. 26.
[75] 14 R.(H.L.) 1, 4.
[76] 19 R.(H.L.) 43, 46. See also the dicta quoted at p. 7 *supra*.
[77] p. 43.
[78] 1914 S.C.(H.L.) 1, 15.
[79] p. 16. " Debtor " presumably refers to the bankrupt disponee.
[80] *Heritable Reversionary Co. Ltd.* v. *Millar*, *supra*, at p. 44, *per* Lord Herschell; p. 47 *per* Lord Watson. *Bank of Scotland* v. *Liquidators of Hutchison Main & Co. Ltd.*, *supra*, at p. 6, *per* Lord Kinnear.
[81] See *supra*, p. 7.
[82] 1958 S.C. 426.
[83] p. 435.

jus in re, a real right in the trust fund." [84] These statements were, however, made in attempts to contrast the position after the date of vesting with the child's previous position as a liferenter with a contingent right to the fee and were probably not meant to imply that the property of the fund was vested in the beneficiary. In the House of Lords,[85] Lord Cohen adopted the passage of Lord Patrick's opinion in which the sentence quoted above occurred but Viscount Simonds said: " The beneficial interest which then arose or accrued to each child was an absolute interest in one-third of the *corpus,* subject to the expenses of administration and distribution and duties, if any." [86]

The beneficiary's right

As McLaren argues,[87] *jus crediti* is not a completely accurate description of the right. The beneficiary's right may be only a right of action but it is more than " the right which is vested in the creditor in any personal obligation " [88] because the trust estate can be vindicated on the sequestration of the trustee. McLaren suggests *jus ad rem* as a right lying between a mere *jus crediti* and a *jus in re* but the nomenclature is in such a state of confusion that it is probably better to describe it merely as a type of personal right.[89]

Radical right

The doctrine of resulting trust [90] is that where a trust has been constituted without such a declaration of purposes as disposes of the trust property in the events which happen the property is held in trust for the granter and his heirs. It is sometimes said that the truster has therefore a radical right or a radical beneficial interest in the trust estate. In some types of trust, however, a radical proprietary title remains vested in the truster. The commonest example is the trust for creditors. If the estate transferred to the trustee is not exhausted when the trust purposes have been fulfilled, no reconveyance from the trustee is required to vest in the granter either the title or the beneficial interest in the surplus assets.[91] The trust is merely a burden on the granter's proprietary right.[92] The principle is derived from the feudal law and one of its effects in the former law was that the granter's heir could not complete title by a conveyance from the trustee and had to serve to the granter.[93]

[84] p. 437.
[85] 1960 S.C.(H.L.) 29.
[86] p. 36.
[87] II, 832. See Smith, *Studies Critical and Comparative* (1962) 221–223.
[88] *Encyc.* VIII, s.v. " Jus Crediti," 1342.
[89] See *Edmond* v. *Gordon* (1858) 3 Macq. 116, 122, *per* Lord Cranworth, p. 129, *per* Lord Wensleydale.
[90] See *infra,* p. 73.
[91] *Campbell* v. *Edderline* (1801) Mor. " Adjudication " App. No. 11; *McMillan* v. *Campbell* (1831) 9 S. 551; (1834) 7 W. & S. 441; *Herries, Farquhar & Co.* v. *Brown* (1838) 16 S. 948; *Lindsay* v. *Giles* (1844) 6 D. 771; *Marquis of Huntly* v. *Earl of Fife* (1885) 14 R. 1091.
[92] *Kinmond, Luke & Co.* v. *James Finlay & Co.* (1904) 6 F. 564.
[93] *Gilmour* v. *Gilmours* (1873) 11 M. 853.

There is little authority as to the extension of the doctrine beyond trusts for creditors. In *Smith* v. *Stuart*,[94] Lord McLaren said:

" It is true that the decisions which establish the principle of a radical right in a truster depending on his original title are decisions relating to what are termed ' voluntary trusts,' *i.e.*, trusts which are intended to create a security over the estate for the benefit of the truster's creditors. But the principle does not depend at all on the particular purposes of the trust, but on the conception that the trust purposes do not exhaust the estate, and that in certain events the estate, or a part of it, reverts to the truster, and may be claimed by him as undisposed of. I do not see why the operation of this principle should be confined to trusts constituted for the benefit of ordinary creditors, or why a father who has come under obligations to his wife and children, and who conveys property to trustees in fulfilment of these obligations, should be held to have divested himself unconditionally and irrevocably. The true view would seem to be that, in the case of the dissolution of the marriage without issue surviving, the trust stands recalled, and that no reconveyance is necessary."

Definitions of trust

It may be that, as Mr. W. Hunter said in reviewing the first edition of Menzies, " the nature of trust is of too anomalous a character to admit of definition." [95]

Definitions propounded by English writers [96] are of little assistance because they include the word " equitable." [97]

According to Bell [98] the doctrine of trust depends on the following principles:

" 1. That a full legal estate is created in the person of the trustee, to be held by him against all adverse parties and interests, for the accomplishment of certain ends and purposes.

2. That the uses and purposes of the trust operate as qualifications of the estate in the trustee, and as burdens on it preferable to all who may claim through him.

3. That those purposes and uses are effectually declared by directions in the deed, or by a reservation of power to declare in future, and a declaration made accordingly.

4. And that the reversionary right, so far as the estate is not exhausted by the uses and purposes, remains with the truster, available to him, his heirs and creditors."

The first two of these principles are features of a trust but the other two are not applicable to all examples of the trust relationship.

---

[94] (1894) 22 R. 130, 136.
[95] (1893) 5 J.R. 180. For an analysis of the difficulties, see Smith, *Studies Critical and Comparative*, 219–221.
[96] Lewin, 3; Underhill, 3.
[97] See the opinions of Lords Normand and Moncrieff in *Inland Revenue* v. *Clark's Trs.*, 1939 S.C. 11. [98] *Prin.* s. 1991.

In the English case of *Camille and Henry Dreyfus Foundation Incorporated* v. *Inland Revenue*,[99] Lord Normand propounded, as a description rather than a definition of a " typical trust according to Scots law,"—

> " a fund is held as their property in law by persons who are directed to hold it, subject to purposes which operate as a qualification of their rights and constitute a burden on the property preferable to all claims by or through them, and subject also to a reversionary right remaining with the truster, his heirs and assignees, so far as the estate is not exhausted by the purposes."

This is a satisfactory description but it is too narrow as a definition.

McLaren's definition is " an interest created by the transfer of property to a trustee, in order that he may carry out the truster's directions respecting its management and disposal." [1] This is narrow in that a trust can exist although there has been no transfer to the trustee and there are no directions by the truster.

Menzies' attempt is unsatisfactory—" Wherever a proprietary title is burdened with an obligation attached to, or arising out of, the acquisition of such title, and limiting the beneficial use of the property by the holder of the title, he is, in so far as his beneficial use is thus limited, a trustee." [2] This could cover a number of legal relationships which are not trusts.

The American Law Institute's Restatement suggests " a fiduciary relationship with respect to property, subjecting the person by whom the property is held to equitable duties to deal with the property for the benefit of another person, which arises as a result of a manifestation of an intention to create it."

It seems that any definition must be founded upon the peculiar character of the obligation owed by the trustee to the beneficiary; " the very name ' trust ' or ' trustee ' implies a duty or obligation to someone else." [3] That duty is fiduciary in character. " A fiduciary duty is one which must be discharged with a good conscience and, regardless of personal interests and prejudices, for the benefit of another." [4] A trust then is a legal relationship in which property is vested in one person, the trustee, who is under a fiduciary obligation to apply the property to some extent for the benefit of another person, the beneficiary, the obligation being a qualification of the trustee's proprietary right and preferable to all claims of the trustee or his creditors.

Trusts not corporations

It has been said that " the trust has thus something of a corporate character incident to it " [5] but this was founded merely on the point that,

[99] 1955 S.L.T. 335, 337; [1956] A.C. 39, 48.
[1] II, 825.
[2] p. 1.
[3] *Barrie* v. *Barrie's Tr.*, 1933 S.C. 132, 141, *per* L.J.-C. Alness.
[4] *Board of Management for Dundee General Hospitals* v. *Bell's Trs.*, 1952 S.C.(H.L.) 78, 88, *per* Lord Normand.
[5] *Lumsden* v. *Buchanan* (1865) 3 M.(H.L.) 89, 95, *per* Lord Cranworth.

as the law then stood, trust property, on the death of the last surviving trustee, did not pass to his representatives. It is clear that a trust is not a corporation.

"Corporations, properly so called, are public bodies created for definite purposes by royal charters or by public law, and this is equally true of *quasi* corporations, or bodies having some, but not all, of the incidents of corporations. But if the constitution of any private trust could in law have a similar effect, every individual would be able, for purposes and upon conditions of his own choice, without any restraint or regulation by public law, to invest himself or others with a corporate character, and so to limit and subdivide, by mere operation of law, what would otherwise be the effect of his and their engagements." [6]

An entity created by statute may, of course, be called a " trust " or " trustees " and be a corporate body—*e.g.* the Church of Scotland General Trustees,[7] the Scottish Hospital Trust [8]; and, of course, a body corporate can be a trustee.

The trust title

The legal title of trustees in the trust estate is that of joint owners.[9] " They cannot take it *pro indiviso*, each having a portion of it, and yet manage the whole as one body for the benefit of those who are beneficially interested." [10] In a conveyance in trust, the condition of survivorship is implied and consequently, on the death of one, the title which was in him passes to those surviving.[11] Testamentary trustees who had entered into a deed of copartnership with another party were held collectively to constitute one partner and the argument that each trustee was a separate partner was rejected.[12]

Legislation

The principal statute affecting trusts is the Trusts (Scotland) Act 1921. Therein a " trust " means and includes any trust constituted by any deed or other writing, or by private or local Act of Parliament, or by Royal Charter, or by resolution of any corporation or public or ecclesiastical body.[13] It also includes the appointment of any tutor, curator or judicial factor by deed, decree or otherwise. A " judicial factor " means any per-

---

6 *Muir* v. *City of Glasgow Bank* (1879) 6 R.(H.L.) 21, 39, *per* Lord Selborne. See also *Martin* v. *Wight* (1841) 3 D. 485.
7 Church of Scotland (General Trustees) Order Confirmation Act 1921. See *Church of Scotland General Trustees*, 1931 S.C. 704.
8 Hospital Endowments (Scotland) Act 1971.
9 *Gracie* v. *Gracie*, 1910 S.C. 899, 904, *per* Lord Kinnear.
10 *Gillespie* v. *City of Glasgow Bank* (1879) 6 R.(H.L.) 104, 111, *per* Lord Blackburn.
11 *Gordon's Trs.* v. *Eglinton* (1851) 13 D. 1381, *per* L.J.-C. Hope; *Findlay* (1855) 17 D. 1014; *Oswald's Trs.* v. *City of Glasgow Bank* (1879) 6 R. 461; *Mags. of Banff* v. *Ruthin Castle Ltd.*, 1944 S.C. 36.
12 *Beveridge* v. *Beveridge* (1872) 10 M.(H.L.) 1.
13 1921 Act, s. 2. See *Edinburgh Royal Infirmary Board of Management*, 1959 S.C. 393.

son holding a judicial appointment as a factor or curator on another person's estate.[14] A " trust deed " means and includes any deed or other writing, private or local Act of Parliament, Royal Charter, or resolution of any corporation or ecclesiastical body constituting any trust and any decree, deed or other writing appointing a tutor, curator or judicial factor.[13] " Trustee " means and includes any trustee under any trust whether nominated, appointed, judicially or otherwise, or assumed, whether sole or joint, and whether entitled or not to receive any benefit under the trust or any remuneration as trustee for his services, and includes any trustee *ex officio*, executor nominate, tutor, curator and judicial factor.[13] The same meanings can be attached to these expressions in the Trusts (Scotland) Act 1961 [15] and the Trustee Investments Act 1961.[16]

[14] 1961 Act, s. 3.
[15] 1961 Act, s. 6 (1).
[16] T.I.A. 1961, s. 17 (5).

CHAPTER 2

THE CONSTITUTION OF A TRUST

Capacity to create a trust

As a general rule, anyone who can competently alienate property in his possession can create a trust. So pupils and persons of unsound mind cannot create a trust. A minor can create an *inter vivos* trust with the consent of his curator if he has one or without his consent if he has no curator.[1] Such a deed may, however, be subject to reduction on the ground of minority and lesion. There is no restriction on a minor's power to create a testamentary trust.[2] No disability now attaches to married women,[3] bastards, aliens [4] or criminals. A bankrupt can create a trust of the reversion of his estate.

The Crown can convey property in trust [5] as can a corporation unless there is something in its constitution to restrain it. Any conveyance or assignment by a company registered under the Companies Acts of all its property to trustees for the benefit of all its creditors is void to all intents.[6]

A firm can create a trust.

The conveyance

The question of whether a conveyance by one person to another constitutes a trust is decided by reference to the intention of the granter which is ascertained by a construction of the deed.[7] It is not necessary that the word " trust " should be used.

> " My Lords, there is no magic, as was admitted at the bar, in the use of the word ' trust.' There may be half a dozen words in the English language which would bring about the same result as the use of the word ' trust,' and it appears to me that words which say that one person holds property ' on behalf of ' or ' for behoof of ' another, are words which come up to and satisfy the idea of the word ' trust,' just as much as the word ' trust ' itself, if the circumstances of the case are consistent with that interpretation." [8] " If there is an appointment of a beneficiary, and if some person is charged with the administration of the funds beneficially destined, we have the essentials of a trust." [9]

1 Howden, 56.
2 Succession (Scotland) Act 1964, s. 28.
3 Married Women's Property (Scotland) Act 1920.
4 Status of Aliens Act 1914, s. 17.
5 Crown Private Estates Act 1862, s. 6. See Lewin, 9; Howden, 55.
6 Companies Act 1948, s. 320 (2).
7 *Wilson* v. *Lindsay* (1878) 5 R. 539, 541, *per* L.P. Inglis.
8 *Gillespie, etc.* v. *City of Glasgow Bank* (1879) 6 R.(H.L.) 104, 107, *per* Lord Cairns L.C.; see also *Johnston* (1880) 18 S.L.R. 60, 61, *per* Lord Gifford.
9 *Macpherson* v. *Macpherson's C.B.* (1894) 21 R. 386, 387, *per* Lord McLaren.

21

It is clearly established that a conveyance to " A for behoof of B " will, in the absence of indications to the contrary result, be construed as the constitution of a trust for B.[10] The nature of the beneficial right conferred depends on a construction of the deed and it is not necessarily a right of property.[11] Similarly, where there was a bequest " to A for the benefit of herself and of her sister B," it was held that each sister had a vested beneficial right in fee to one-half of the bequest but that A was bound to hold B's share during their joint lives as a trustee.[12]

In some cases it has been argued that the terms of the deed merely imposed a personal obligation on the disponee. This argument was advanced where the testator bequeathed his whole estate to his wife " under the obligation of her paying all my just and lawful debts, and bringing up and educating my children and I appoint her sole guardian and curator of my children, and I grant her full power of sale of said estate, and I appoint X to be law-agent on the said estate." It was held that the collocation of the obligation to pay debts and the obligation to bring up the children, the appointment of another person as executor to act with the widow, the conferring of a power of sale and the appointment of a law-agent all pointed to the constitution of a trust.[13]

Again, where a testator disponed to the residuary legatee of his moveable estate the whole residue of his heritable estate " always with and under the conditions and provisions hereinafter inserted " and thereafter directed the disponee to dispose of the heritage within a certain period and invest the proceeds for certain persons in liferent and their representatives in fee, it was held that the disponee was a trustee and was not beneficially entitled to the rents of the property while it remained unsold.[14]

In *Romanes* v. *Romanes' Trs.*,[15] a testatrix bequeathed two legacies absolutely to her nieces and in a letter of later date addressed to the nieces wrote:

> " I think it simpler just to make you and Bella the Trustees of the money you are to have the interest of during your life. If the longest liver has any need of all the money during her life, she can keep her sister's share as well as her own, but if she had no need of it, the sister's share can go to A, B and C."

The Lord Ordinary expressed the opinion that if the letter had had testamentary effect it would have restricted the bequests to a liferent and imposed a trust for behoof of A, B and C.

A disposition of property to X as " a free gift " could not make X a trustee for a third party.[16] A legacy stated to be for a purpose which

---

10 *Gilpin* v. *Martin* (1869) 7 M. 807; *Michie's Exors.* v. *Michie* (1905) 7 F. 509.
11 *Leitch* v. *Leitch*, 1927 S.C. 823. For a comment on the defects of this decision, see Mackenzie Stuart, 31.
12 *Macpherson* v. *Macpherson's C.B.*, *supra*.
13 *Urquhart's Exors.* v. *Abbott* (1899) 1 F. 1149. *Cf. Rigg* (1905) 13 S.L.T. 144; *Gow's Trs.* v. *Gow*, 1912, 2 S.L.T. 256.
14 *Johnston, supra*.
15 1933 S.N. 112.
16 *Mags. of Banff* v. *Ruthin Castle Ltd.*, 1944 S.C. 36.

benefits only the donee does not impose an obligation to use it for that purpose.[17] A gift to an institution for a specified purpose may, of course, create a trust.

Trusts for maintenance

In a situation in which the trustees are directed to pay income to X, it is possible to have a subsidiary trust under which X is a trustee obliged to apply the money for the benefit of a third party.[18]

In *Jack* v. *Marshall*,[19] the income of a fund was to be paid to a beneficiary " for the maintenance of himself and the maintenance and education of his children." The testator added: " And I desire my trustees to secure that the said children receive a good education suitable to their station in life." The " liferent provision " in favour of the beneficiary was declared to be alimentary. It was held that as the trustees had no power to control the beneficiary in the application of the money the provision was nothing more than a liferent and was not a trust for the education of the children. That decision was followed in *Chalmers' J.F.* v. *Chalmers*,[20] which concerned surplus income which was to be paid over to the beneficiary " for the education and support of his children." Although certain of the features of the provision in *Jack* did not appear in the deed in this case, it was again held that there was no trust for the children.

Precatory trusts [21]

A question may arise as to whether an expression used by the testator which is not in imperative form is to be given effect as a precatory trust or treated as a mere wish or request. It seems that there is a distinction between the expression of a wish directed to an executor and one directed to a beneficiary. " It is quite possible to constitute a precatory trust which is binding upon an executor; but if estate is left to a person not as an executor but as a beneficiary, then it must be left with a clearly expressed condition in order to bind him." [22]

> " What I take the rule now to be is, that words of request are given their ordinary meaning, and not treated as being imperative, unless it appears that it was the intention of the testator so to use them. A trust may still be constituted by precatory words but in each case it is a question of construction whether the testator did, or did not, intend to impose an obligation. . . ." [23]

Where a wife left a testamentary writing addressed to her husband in which she said: " I wish to leave everything that may be considered mine,

---

[17] *Ross* v. *Thomson* (1896) 4 S.L.T. 155.
[18] *Dunsmure's Trs.* v. *Dunsmure*, 1920 S.C. 147.
[19] (1879) 6 R. 543.
[20] (1903) 5 F. 1154 (Lord Moncreiff's dissenting opinion is cogent).
[21] For the English law, see Lewin, 42–43; Underhill, 38–43.
[22] *Garden's Exor.* v. *More*, 1913 S.C. 285, 288, *per* L.P. Dunedin. See *Walker's Exor.* v. *Walker*, 1953 S.L.T.(Notes) 59.
[23] *Walker's Exor.* v. *Walker*, 1953 S.L.T.(Notes) 59, 60, *per* Lord Sorn.

money or personal property, entirely at your disposal, knowing that you will do as I wish with it," the argument that the husband was a mere trustee was rejected and it was held that the estate had been transferred absolutely to him under burden of payment of certain special legacies bequeathed in other sentences of the writing.[24] The imposition on the recipient of an obligation to test in a certain way does not affect the recipient's power to dispose of the property *inter vivos*.[25]

The expression of an " anxious desire " and a " hope " that the legatee would make certain testamentary dispositions was held to impose no obligation on the legatee.[26] If the testator does not state with certainty the amount or the objects of the gift to be given, this is a factor indicating mere wish rather than precatory trust.[27] " I would prefer " has been construed as a polite form of command when addressed to trustees.[28]

Powers

A power of disposal may be proprietary or fiduciary.[29] A proprietary power enables the donee to convey the property to himself if it can be exercised *inter vivos*, or to his own executor or to another party if it is exercisable *mortis causa*. A fiduciary power is in the nature of a trust in the person of the donee. A fiduciary power cannot be delegated and the description of the class to be benefited must be sufficiently certain. A power conferred on a trustee or executor is prima facie fiduciary; one conferred on a person not described as a trustee or executor is prima facie proprietary. The same person may be the donee of both types of power.

Where the testator directed that his whole property was to be " placed entirely under control " of his daughter " to allocate to the members of my family as she thinks proper," it was held that the daughter had an absolute beneficial right to the property and the reference to allocation was no more than a wish or a hope.[30]

Subjects

Broadly, any property which can be alienated can be the subject of a trust. A right to a peerage cannot be the subject of a trust.[31] A trust of foreign land is invalid if the *lex loci situs* does not give effect to trusts.[32]

Objects

Any person, legal or natural, can be the beneficiary. A beneficiary can be *incapax*. The trust can be in favour of persons who are not yet born,[33]

24   *Wilson* v. *Lindsay, supra. Cf. Hamilton's Trs.* v. *Hamilton* (1901) 4 F. 266.
25   *Murray* v. *Macfarlane's Trs.* (1895) 22 R. 927.
26   *Barclay's Exor.* v. *McLeod* (1880) 7 R. 477. See also *Campbell's Trs.* v. *Kinsey-Morgan's Trs.*, 1915 S.C. 298.
27   *Reddie's Trs.* v. *Lindsay* (1890) 17 R. 558.
28   *Reid's Trs.* v. *Dawson*, 1915 S.C.(H.L.) 47.
29   *Bannerman's Trs.* v. *Bannerman*, 1915 S.C. 398.
30   *Miller* v. *Miller* (1906) 13 S.L.T. 770.
31   *The Buckhurst Peerage* (1876) 2 App.Cas. 1.
32   *Brown's Trs.* v. *Gregson*, 1920 S.C.(H.L.) 87. See also *Re Piercy* [1895] 1 Ch. 83.
33   But see Chap. 10.

or who are unascertained or who belong to a prescribed class [34] or who are to be selected from a prescribed class. [35]

A witness to the trust deed can be a beneficiary. [36]

If a beneficiary is misnamed, extrinsic evidence can be led to prove the person intended by the testator. [37]

Discretionary trusts

There is little Scottish authority on the subject of the discretionary trust—*i.e.* a trust for a certain period of the income of property for a class of persons fulfilling certain qualifications, the persons who are to share from time to time and the amounts which they respectively take being in the discretion of the trustees. The class of persons must be defined with sufficient certainty. [38] There is authority on the way in which the discretion is to be exercised. [39] In England, the right of the beneficiary under a discretionary trust has been described as follows:

" He has a right to be considered as a potential recipient of benefit by the trustees and a right to have his interest protected by a court of equity. Certainly that is so, and when it is said that he has a right to have the trustees exercise their discretion ' fairly ' or ' reasonably ' or ' properly ' that indicates clearly enough that some objective consideration (not stated explicitly in declaring the discretionary trust, but latent in it) must be applied by the trustees and that the right is more than a mere spes." [40]

A beneficiary may renounce his right, and thereby cease to be an object of the trust. [41] The right may not be capable of effectual assignation. [42]

Truster as trustee

In *Allan's Trs.* v. *Inland Revenue* [43] Lord Reid said that the idea that a person can make himself the trustee of his own property " is something of a novelty in the law of Scotland and there is little authority as to whether this is possible or as to how it can be done." He went on to point out that McLaren apparently did not contemplate that a person could make himself the trustee and to note that the earliest reference which counsel were able to discover was at page 30 of *Menzies on Trustees*, which was published in 1913. After referring to Mackenzie Stuart at pages 8 and 12, Lord Reid said: " I think that we can now accept the position as a reason-

[34] See Chap. 6.
[35] See *ibid.*
[36] *Simson* v. *Simson* (1883) 10 R. 1247.
[37] *Cathcart's Trs.* v. *Bruce*, 1923 S.L.T. 722.
[38] See *infra*, p. 82.
[39] See *infra*, pp. 334–338, 372.
[40] *Gartside* v. *I.R.C.* [1968] A.C. 553, 617, *per* Lord Wilberforce.
[41] *Re Gulbenkian's Settlements* (*No.* 2) [1970] Ch. 408.
[42] *Re Coleman* (1888) 39 Ch.D. 443, C.A. *Cf. Re Smith* [1928] Ch. 915; *Re Nelson* [1928] Ch. 920.
[43] 1971 S.L.T. 62.

able development of the law, that a person can make himself a trustee of his own property provided that he also does something equivalent to delivery or transfer of the trust fund." [44]

Lord Guest thought that the notion that the truster could constitute himself sole trustee had crept into Scots law from English law, that the first evidence of this anglicisation was to be found in Menzies and that the doctrine was fairly established when Professor Mackenzie Stuart wrote in 1932.

There are, however, earlier authorities which contemplate the possibility. In *University of Aberdeen* v. *Magistrates of Aberdeen* [45] Lord Deas declared that the Act 1696, c. 25, relating to proof of trust, could not apply " where the same parties were both trusters and trustees." Again, in *Hinkelbein* v. *Craig*,[46] Lord Johnston discusses an attempted distinction between a latent trust of what had been the trustee's own property and a latent trust of what had been somebody else's property. He noted a concession by one party that a trust could be constituted by " a recorded declaration of trust by the original owner without the circuity of a precedent conveyance to himself." Thirdly, in his dissenting opinion in *Cameron's Trs.* v. *Cameron*,[47] Lord Kyllachy said:

> " I know of no principle of trust law which prevents the constitution or bars the subsistence of a trust in which the truster is (or becomes) himself the *sole* trustee. . . . It has never, I think, been doubted that an owner either of an estate in land or of a heritable security may, either by a separate declaration of trust, or by a declaration of trust inserted *in gremio* of his title, create a trust in his own person quite as effectual as if he had executed a disposition and assignation in favour of independent trustees."

THE TRUST PURPOSES

The purposes of the trust must be set forth in the conveyance to the trustee or in some identified writing " legally declared by the granter." [48] A verbal or secret trust is not recognised by Scots law.[49] The purposes may be stated by reference to another deed [50]; or may be disclosed to the trustee at some time after the conveyance.[51] If no purposes are declared, the estate is held in a resulting trust for the truster and his representatives.[52]

[44] p. 63.
[45] (1876) 3 R. 1087, 1102.
[46] (1905) 13 S.L.T. 84.
[47] 1907 S.C. 407, 415.
[48] Menzies, *Lectures on Conveyancing*, 4th ed., 503–504; *Willoch* v. *Auchterlony* (1769) Mor. 5539; 1 Ross L.C. 401; *Banff Mags.* v. *Ruthin Castle Ltd.*, 1944 S.C. 36, 51, *per* Lord Mackay.
[49] *Shaw's Trs.* v. *Greenock Medical Aid Society*, 1930 S.L.T. 39.
[50] *Murray* v. *Matheson's Trs.* (1898) 6 S.L.T. 149.
[51] *Edmond* v. *Lord Provost of Aberdeen* (1898) 1 F. 154.
[52] *Sutherland's Trs.* v. *Sutherland's Tr.* (1893) 20 R. 925; *Edmond* v. *Lord Provost of Aberdeen* (1898) 1 F. 154, 163, *per* Lord Young.

The trust may be *inter vivos* or *mortis causa*: " the disposal by a man voluntarily of his estate after his death among those whom he means to take it." [53] A trust is said to be simple if the trustee's duty is merely to hold the trust estate and make it over to the person entitled to it when called upon to do so.

Trusts for administration

A person may convey his estate to trustees for the administration of his affairs in his lifetime, including the payment of his debts. This is known as a trust for administration.[54] The granter retains the radical beneficial interest in the estate and can revoke the trust at his pleasure.[55]

Executory trusts

" Every trust where an act is to be done, or a common conveyance to be executed, is an executory trust, no doubt, in a sense; but not in the sense in which lawyers speak of it. That is a trust executed, but a trust executory means, not simply a trust under which an act is to be done, which applies to every case, but one in which there is something to be performed which is not defined by the original settlor where he has expressed an intention in general words which is to be carried out in a complete and legal form by the persons who are entrusted with the estate." [56]

Trusts for creditors

" A debtor who knows himself to be insolvent may, with a view to the equal distribution of his funds, convey them to a trustee for the benefit of all his creditors." [57] The trust purposes may be stated *in gremio* of the conveyance or in a separate deed. The essential clauses are the conveyance in trust for behoof of creditors and the declaration that the purposes of the trust are to be the realisation of the estate and its proportional division among the creditors. There are usually other clauses dealing with the mode of administration of the estate. " A trust for a family purpose, or a testamentary purpose, or both, does not become a trust for the payment of creditors, merely because the deed constituting it contains a direction to pay the maker's debts." [58] If the trust is to be effectual possession must follow on the deed and intimation must be made.[59]

The trustee is a " trustee " under the Trusts Acts.[60] Any conveyance or

[53] *Edmond* v. *Lord Provost of Aberdeen* (1898) 1 F. 154, 163, *per* Lord Young. See *Denny's Trs.* v. *Dumbarton Mags.*, 1945 S.C. 147; *City of Edinburgh* v. *Wright* (1902) 9 S.L.T. 318.
[54] See *Byres' Trs.* v. *Gemmell* (1895) 23 R. 332; *Bertram's Trs.* v. *Bertram*, 1909 S.C. 1238; *Scott* v. *Scott*, 1930 S.C. 903.
[55] See Chap. 10.
[56] *Graham* v. *Stewart* (1855) 2 Macq. 295, 324, *per* Lord St. Leonards. See also *Sandys* v. *Bain's Trs.* (1897) 25 R. 261, 267, *per* Lord Kinnear; *Brash's Trs.* v. *Phillipson*, 1916 S.C. 271.
[57] Bell, *Comm.* II, 382.
[58] *Globe Insurance Co.* v. *McKenzie* (1850) 7 Bell's App.Cas. 296, 321, *per* Lord Brougham.
[59] *Mess* v. *Sime's Tr.* (1898) 25 R. 398; *Doughty* v. *Wells* (1906) 14 S.L.T. 299.
[60] 1921 Act, s. 2; *Royal Bank of Scotland* (1893) 20 R. 741.

assignment by a company of all its property to trustees for the benefit of all its creditors is void to all intents.[61]

The trustee is accountable to the creditors, who have a *jus crediti*. The trust cannot be revoked by the granter and the trustee must hold adversely to him.[62] On the other hand, in what is sometimes called a " family " trust, a trust for benefit of the truster or his family, there is no direct relationship between the trustee and the creditors of the truster and the trustee is accountable, not to the creditors, but to the truster. The remedy of the creditors is to go against the truster himself.[63]

The position is quite different where there is a trust of the *universitas* of the estate, either a testamentary trust or a trust for creditors. The creditors there have a direct right against the trustee. A creditor, whether he accedes or not, cannot obtain a preference by arrestment in the hands of the trustee,[64] but a non-acceding creditor can recover his share of the estate by a direct action against the trustee.[65] He cannot ask the court to take the place of the trustee by raising a multiplepoinding.[66] The trust deed is superseded by the sequestration of the granter and the trustee must denude in favour of the trustee in the sequestration.[67] This is so even where the debtor himself applies for and obtains sequestration.[68] The trust created by the trust deed is not destroyed but it is suspended until the sequestration process is completed.[69] The debtor has a radical right to call on the trustee to denude in his favour when the purposes of the trust have been carried out.[70]

Marriage-contract trusts

The object of an antenuptial marriage-contract is the settlement of provisions in favour of the spouses and children and the protection of these against the diligence of the creditors of the spouses. Where there is a trust, its object is to divest the spouses of the fee so that the estate of the fiars is protected absolutely and the wife can obtain an alimentary provision out of the estate which belonged to herself from which her own and her husband's creditors are excluded.[71] In general, if the spouse and children have to have a preference over the husband's creditors and not merely a *jus crediti* entitling them to rank along with the creditors, or a *spes successionis*, it is necessary to constitute a trust.

It is essential to the constitution of an effectual marriage-contract trust that at least one of the trustees should be a neutral person. It has been

[61] Companies Act 1948, s. 320 (2).
[62] Bell, *Comm*. II, 383.
[63] *Lucas' Trs.* v. *Beresford's Trs.* (1892) 19 R. 943.
[64] *Henderson* v. *Henderson's Tr.* (1882) 10 R. 185.
[65] *Ogilvie and Son* v. *Taylor* (1887) 14 R. 399.
[66] *Kyd* v. *Waterson* (1880) 7 R. 884.
[67] Bell, *Comm*. II, 391; *Nicolson* v. *Johnstone and Wright* (1872) 11 M. 179.
[68] *McAlister* v. *Swinburne & Co.* (1874) 1 R. 958.
[69] *Salaman* v. *Rosslyn's Trs.* (1900) 3 F. 298.
[70] Bell, *Comm*. II, 392; *Gilmour* v. *Gilmour* (1873) 11 M. 853; *Ritchie* v. *McIntosh* (1881) 8 R. 747. See *supra*, p. 16.
[71] *Mackie* v. *Gloag's Trs.* (1884) 11 R.(H.L.) 10, 16, *per* Lord Watson.

said that a trust in which the spouses are the sole trustees or constitute a majority of the trustees gives no protection to the beneficiaries against the voluntary acts of the spouses and is therefore not effectual against creditors.[72] As Menzies remarks,[73] it is difficult to see why the number or personal character of the trustees can affect the nature of the beneficiary's right as a matter of law although the probability of a misuse of trust funds may be increased.

In *Cooper* v. *Cooper*,[74] Lord Watson opined that a contract signed by the parties immediately after the marriage ceremony was still an antenuptial marriage-contract; Lord Macnaghten doubted whether a contract executed after the status of the contracting party had been definitely altered by marriage could be regarded as an antenuptial contract. A deed which is not in the form of a marriage-contract may nevertheless be held to be equivalent to a marriage-contract.[75]

Construction of conveyance

A general conveyance of a spouse's whole means and estate has been held not to carry a liferent [76] or an annuity.[77] A *spes successionis* has been held to fall within such a conveyance.[78] A conveyance of *acquirenda* has been held not to include a right to elect between legitim and a testamentary provision [79]; a fund over which the truster is subsequently given a power of disposal [80]; income [81]; estate purchased from savings from income [82]; an insurance policy effected by the truster's husband on the life of the truster and expressed to be payable to her representatives [83]; estate acquired after the dissolution of the marriage.[84] Legacies have been held to fall within *acquirenda*.[85]

A conveyance by a husband to marriage-contract trustees of all property " now belonging or which shall belong to him at the time of his decease " does not deprive him of any right in or control over property acquired after the date of the contract and such property is liable for his debts.[86]

---

72 *McCallum* v. *McCulloch's Trs.* (1904) 7 F. 337. See p. 236, *infra*.   73 p. 472.
74 (1888) 15 R.(H.L.) 21.
75 *Wilken's Trs.* v. *Wilken* (1904) 6 F. 655.
76 *Boyd's Trs.* v. *Boyd* (1877) 4 R. 1082; *Young's Trs.* (1885) 12 R. 968; *Neilson's Trs.* v. *Henderson* (1897) 24 R. 1135.
77 *Culcreuch Trs.* v. *Home* (1894) 2 S.L.T. 170.
78 *Wyllie's Trs.* v. *Boyd* (1891) 18 R. 1121; *cf. McEwan's Trs.* v. *Macdonald*, 1909 S.C. 57.
79 *Mackenzie's Trs.* v. *Beveridge's Trs.*, 1908 S.C. 1185.
80 *Montgomerie's Trs.* v. *Alexander's Trs.*, 1911 S.C. 856; *Murray's Trs.* v. *MacGregor's Trs.*, 1931 S.C. 516.
81 *Hunter* v. *More's Trs.* (1896) 4 S.L.T. 28; *Murdoch's Trs.* v. *Stock*, 1923 S.C. 906.
82 *Dunbar Dunbar* v. *Dunbar Dunbar* (1905) 7 F.(H.L.) 92. But see as to the burden of proof, *Young's Trs.* v. *Young's Trs.* (1892) 20 R. 22.
83 *Thomson's Trs.* v. *Thomson* (1879) 6 R. 1227; *Coulson's Trs.* v. *Coulson* (1901) 3 F. 1041; *Constable* v. *Mackenzie*, 1911, 1 S.L.T. 411.
84 *Wardlaw* v. *Wardlaw's Trs.* (1880) 7 R. 1070; *Russell's Trs.* (1887) 14 R. 849; *Morier* v. *Gilmour* (1890) 27 S.L.R. 751; *Boyd's Trs.* v. *Boyd* (1905) 7 F. 576; *Eadie's Trs.* v. *Henderson*, 1919, 1 S.L.T. 253.
85 *Pullar's Trs.* v. *MacOwan* (1879) 16 S.L.R. 806. As to the effect of declarations by the testator, see *Douglas' Trs.* v. *Kay's Trs.* (1879) 7 R. 295; *Simson's Trs.* v. *Brown* (1890) 17 R. 581.
86 *Wyllie's Trs.* v. *Boyd* (1891) 18 R. 1121.

If the trust funds which the husband undertook by the marriage-contract to pay to the trustees have not in fact been paid over, the trustees cannot rank as creditors in the husband's sequestration.[87]

Effect

Provisions in antenuptial marriage-contracts are onerous deeds—" because it is on the faith of suitable provisions secured to the parties in marriage-contracts, that they enter into the married state." [88] As the deed is onerous, it cannot be reduced under the Bankruptcy Act 1621 as a disposition of property to conjunct and confident persons.[89] A woman can in her antenuptial marriage-contract create for herself an alimentary liferent of funds provided by herself.[90] That is an exception to the general rule. The husband cannot create in favour of himself an alimentary liferent of funds contributed by him.[91]

Formerly, it was possible to exclude a child's right to legitim from the estates of the parents by making a provision for it in the antenuptial marriage-contract.[92] The provision was not required to be substantial.[93] It is not possible to do this in contracts executed on or after September 10, 1964 although the child's right may be excluded if it elects to accept in lieu of legitim the provision made in its favour under the contract.[94]

The rights conferred on the children of the marriage are absolute and irrevocable and cannot be revoked by the spouses.[95] An express power of revocation will, however, be given effect.[96] Where there is a destination to persons other than the descendants of the marriage as conditional institutes or substitutes, their right is merely a *spes successionis in destinatione* and can be revoked.[97] It is different if the deed confers on them an immediate and indefeasible right as where they take as institutes.[98]

Where the wife has created in the antenuptial marriage-contract an alimentary liferent for herself, the protection does not continue after the dissolution of the marriage and the wife can renounce the liferent.[99] This is so even although some or all of the trust fund has been provided by the wife's father and he was a party to the deed.[1] The position may be

---

[87] *Mackinnon's Trs.* v. *Dunlop*, 1913 S.C. 232.
[88] Ersk. IV, I, 33; *Callander* v. *Callander's Exor.*, 1972 S.L.T. 209.
[89] *McLay* v. *McQueen* (1899) 1 F. 804.
[90] See *infra*, p. 94.
[91] *Harvey* v. *Ligertwood* (1872) 10 M.(H.L.) 33.
[92] Ersk. III, 9, 23.
[93] *Maitland* v. *Maitland* (1843) 6 D. 244; *Galloway's Trs.* v. *Galloway*, 1943 S.C. 339.
[94] Succession (Scotland) Act 1964, s. 12.
[95] *Mackie* v. *Gloag's Trs.* (1884) 11 R.(H.L.) 10.
[96] *Fowler's Trs.* v. *Fowler* (1898) 25 R. 1034; *Simpson's Trs.* v. *Taylor*, 1912 S.C. 280.
[97] *Barclay's Trs.* v. *Watson* (1903) 5 F. 926; *Lord Advocate* v. *Stewart* (1906) 8 F. 579; *Montgomerie's Trs.* v. *Alexander's Trs.*, 1911 S.C. 856; *Eadie's Trs.* v. *Henderson*, 1919, 1 S.L.T. 253; *Duff's Trs.* v. *Phillips*, 1921 S.C. 287.
[98] *Mackie* v. *Gloag's Trs.* (1884) 11 R.(H.L.) 10; *Allan's Testamentary Trs.* v. *Allan's M-C Trs.* (1907) 15 S.L.T. 73; *Leslie's Trs.* v. *Leslie*, 1921 S.C. 940.
[99] *Dempster's Trs.* v. *Dempster*, 1949 S.C. 92; *Sturgis's Trs.* v. *Sturgis*, 1951 S.C. 637; *Pearson*, 1968 S.C. 8.
[1] *Martin* v. *Bannatyne* (1861) 23 D. 705; *Neame* v. *Neame's Trs.*, 1956 S.L.T. 57; *Strange*, 1966 S.L.T. 59.

different if words are used in the trust deed which clearly and explicitly show that it was intended that the alimentary character of the liferent was to continue after the dissolution of the marriage.[2] An alimentary liferent cannot be renounced *stante matrimonio* once it is being enjoyed [3] but renunciation is competent if the right to the liferent is still contingent.[4]

A liferent which is not alimentary can be renounced *stante matrimonio* [5] and, *a fortiori*, after the dissolution of the marriage.[6]

If the liferent has been effectually renounced the trustees are bound to denude in favour of the wife if there are no trust purposes to be fulfilled, *e.g.*, if the fee was destined to the children of the marriage and there is in fact no issue and cannot be issue.[7] Similarly, if the fee has been irrevocably appointed to the children and they have attained majority, they are entitled to obtain payment from the trustees.[8]

Where there is no trust constituted, the antenuptial marriage-contract is an onerous deed and in certain circumstances may confer a *jus crediti* on the children.[9] On the other hand, the children and their descendants may have only a *spes successionis in obligatione*, a right which the parent cannot defeat by his gratuitous deed.[10]

Postnuptial trusts

A postnuptial marriage-contract trust, if the provision is reasonable in amount, has the same effect *intra familiam* as an antenuptial marriage-contract trust.[11] It cannot be revoked by the spouses jointly if there is a provision for children who may yet be born.[12] The position is different if there is no provision for children.[13] Provisions for children or strangers are protected against creditors and are irrevocable if the granter was solvent at the time the deed was granted and the conveyance was completed.[14] A woman cannot in a postnuptial marriage-contract create in favour of herself an alimentary liferent of funds derived from herself.[15]

[2] *Strange, supra*; *Sutherland*, 1968 S.C. 200. *Cf. Dempster's Trs. v. Dempster, supra.*
[3] *Kennedy* v. *Kennedy's Trs.*, 1953 S.C. 60.
[4] *Douglas-Hamilton* v. *Duke and Duchess of Hamilton's Trs.*, 1961 S.C. 205; *Ford* v. *Ford's Trs.*, 1961 S.C. 122; *Findlay*, 1962 S.C. 210; *Smillie*, 1966 S.L.T. 41.
[5] *Beith's Trs.* v. *Beith*, 1950 S.C. 66. The ratio of *Menzies* v. *Murray* (1875) 2 R. 507, was said to have been superseded.
[6] *Pretty* v. *Newbigging* (1854) 16 D. 667; *McMurdo's Trs.* v. *McMurdo* (1897) 24 R. 458.
[7] *Dempster's Trs.* v. *Dempster, supra*; *Beith's Trs.* v. *Beith, supra*; *Steel's Trs.* v. *Cassels*, 1939 S.C. 502. See also *Burn-Murdoch's Trs.* v. *Tinney*, 1937 S.C. 743; *Adamson's Trs.* v. *Adamson's C.B.*, 1940 S.C. 596.
[8] *Sturgis's Trs.* v. *Sturgis, supra.*
[9] See *Goddard* v. *Stewart's Children* (1844) 6 D. 1018.
[10] *Macdonald* v. *Hall* (1893) 20 R.(H.L.) 88.
[11] *Peddie* v. *Peddie's Trs.* (1891) 18 R. 491; Candlish Henderson, *Vesting*, 2nd ed., 285. Prior to the Married Women's Property (Scotland) Act 1920 a postnuptial settlement was not protected against creditors because it was a donation and therefore revocable; if, however, it could be regarded as a reasonable provision taking effect after the granter's death, it was sustained (*Galloway* v. *Craig* (1861) 4 Macq. 267). The question between donation and provision will still be relevant if the granter is sequestrated within a year and a day of the completion of the settlement (Married Women's Property (Scotland) Act 1920, s. 5). See also *Lawson's Tr.* v. *Lawson*, 1938 S.C. 632, 642, *per* Lord Mackay; Menzies, *Conveyancing*, 2nd ed., 403.
[12] *Allan* v. *Kerr* (1869) 8 M. 34; *Low* v. *Low's Trs.* (1877) 5 R. 185.
[13] *Gillon's Trs.* v. *Gillon* (1903) 5 F. 533.
[14] *Corbidge* v. *Somerville's Trs.*, 1911 S.C. 1326.   [15] *Cargill*, 1965 S.L.T. 193.

Unit trusts

Under the Prevention of Fraud (Investments) Act 1958,[16] a " unit trust scheme " is defined as " any arrangements made for the purpose, or having the effect, of providing facilities for the participation by persons, as beneficiaries under a trust, in profits or income arising from the acquisition, holding, management or disposal of securities or any other property whatsoever."

The legality of a trust of this kind was established by *Smith* v. *Anderson* [17] in which it was held that the beneficiaries were not an association within the meaning of the Companies Act 1862, s. 4, that the management of a trust fund was not the carrying on a business within the meaning of that section and that, if a business was being carried on, it was being carried on only by the trustees and not by the beneficiaries. Such trusts are not within the ambit of the legislation prohibiting the accumulation of income.[18] Unit trust schemes may be authorised under the 1958 Act.[19]

---

[16] s. 26.
[17] (1880) 15 Ch.D. 247.
[18] *Re A.E.G. Unit Trust (Managers) Ltd.'s Deed. Midland Bank Executor and Trustee Co. Ltd.* v. *A.E.G. Unit Trust (Managers) Ltd.* [1957] Ch. 415. See Chap. 8.
[19] s. 17. See *Allied Investors' Trusts Ltd.* v. *Board of Trade* [1956] Ch. 232.

CHAPTER 3

DELIVERY

To make the trust effectual, the estate must be vested in the trustees or in one trustee to be held subject to the acts and directions of the others.[1] Delivery of the trust property to the trustees is therefore essential to the creation of an irrevocable trust except where the Married Women's Policies of Assurance (Scotland) Act 1880 applies.[2] In *Jarvie's Tr.* v. *Jarvie's Trs.*[3] a husband took out in 1870 a policy of insurance in favour of trustees for behoof of his wife and children. The policy was not delivered to the trustees and neither they nor the beneficiaries knew of its existence. It was held that in the absence of delivery no effectual trust had been created.[4]

The case law on this subject is complex and can conveniently be analysed by distinguishing the following situations:

(a) A executes a disposition of property vested in him in favour of B but does not deliver the deed;

(b) A purchases property out of his own funds, takes the disposition in the name of B and retains the deed in his own hands;

(c) A purchases property out of his own funds, takes the disposition in his own name as trustee for B and retains the deed in his own hands;

(d) A purchases property out of his own funds, takes the disposition in the name of B as trustee for C, and retains the deed.

(e) A executes a disposition of property vested in him in favour of B as trustee for C, and retains the deed.

Situations (a) and (b)

Situations (a) and (b) can be conveniently discussed together although there is an important difference between them in that where A grants a disposition in favour of B and retains the deed in his possession, he can destroy it and leave his rights unaffected whereas, if the disposition is by a third party, it is more difficult for A to alter the position.[5]

In situation (a) where A has executed a disposition in favour of B but

---

[1] Bell, *Prin.* s. 1994; Forsyth, 79; *Connell's Trs.* v. *Connell's Tr.*, 1955 S.L.T. 125.
[2] See Chap. 5.
[3] (1887) 14 R. 411.
[4] The effect of the 1880 Act was mentioned in argument.
[5] *Rust* v. *Smith* (1865) 3 M. 378, 382, *per* Lord Deas. There is also the point that a destination taken on A's instructions is not affected by a clause in A's will revoking " prior writings of a testamentary nature " because the title containing the destination is not A's writing—*Murray's Exors.* v. *Geekie*, 1929 S.C. 633, 637, *per* L.P. Clyde. On one view it is also an exception to the rule against nuncupative legacies (*per* Lord Sands, *Dennis* v. *Aitchison*, 1923 S.C. 819, 829).

has not delivered the deed, it is clear that there is no transfer of property.[6] Unilateral deeds, other than ordinary testamentary writings, require for their efficacy that they should be delivered to the grantee or to someone on his behalf.[7] Similarly in situation (b), the fact that A has taken the title to property in the name of B does not constitute *per se* an irrevocable transfer of the property to B.[8]

> " It is well settled that a person does not divest himself of his right of property in the amount contained in a bond simply by taking it payable to another party with whom he enters into no obligatory arrangement and to whom he does not deliver over the bond by way of donation. The money remains his own, although doubtless he may find himself involved in some trouble when he seeks to obtain repayment. It is *a fortiori* of this that a person does not divest himself by taking the bond payable to himself, whom failing to another party. The money remains part of his estate. He is free to deal with it as he pleases, either *inter vivos* or by testamentary deed. Even if he fails to do so and the bond passes on his death to the person designated, it does so as part of his estate vested in him when he died. It is so treated for all Revenue purposes, and, if he be insolvent, in all questions with his creditors." [9] " The mere circumstance that the title was taken in the names of persons other than the owner of the money goes a very short way towards proving that he intended to confer upon these persons an irrevocable right to the investments." [10]

The rule is clearly established although Lord Sands characterised it as " quaint " in view of the fact that the custodier of the deed, because he cannot sue on it as it stands, would require to resort to a declarator in the first instance.[11] Professor Montgomerie Bell remarks upon the risk and inconvenience attendant upon this type of arrangement.[12]

In *Hill* v. *Hill*,[13] a father, having made advances from his own funds, took the bond in favour of his son and retained the deed in his custody. In an action at the instance of the son's executor, the father answered that no *jus quaesitum* had been conferred on the son because there had been no infeftment or intimation which would have constituted legal delivery. The defence was sustained and a distinction was drawn between the case where a man takes a bond for money lent by him in the name of a child *in familia* and the case where a stranger makes a donation to a child and the bond is delivered to the father. In the latter case the presumption is that

---

[6] *Anderson* v. *Robertson* (1867) 5 M. 503.
[7] *Clark's Exor.* v. *Clark*, 1943 S.C. 216, 223, *per* L.J.-C. Cooper.
[8] *Walkers' Exor.* v. *Walker* (1878) 5 R. 965; *Jamieson* v. *McLeod* (1880) 7 R. 1131; *Stewart* v. *Rae* (1883) 10 R. 463; *Lord Advocate* v. *Galloway* (1884) 11 R. 541; *Rose* v. *Cameron's Exor.* (1901) 3 F. 337; Gloag, *Contract*, 68.
[9] *Murray's Exors.* v. *Geekie*, 1929 S.C. 633, 639, *per* Lord Sands. The reference was to moveable bonds issued by a municipal corporation.
[10] *Drysdale's Trs.* v. *Drysdale*, 1922 S.C. 741, 749, *per* Lord Skerrington.
[11] *Inland Revenue* v. *Wilson*, 1927 S.C. 733, 737.
[12] *Lectures*, 108.
[13] (1755) Mor. 11580.

the delivery is to the father as custodier and he has no power of alteration as he has in the former case. In the former case delivery to the father cannot import a delivery for behoof of the child " because the debtor who delivers the bond has no vote in the matter; but must deliver the bond to the father, from whom he got the money." [14] Lord Kames remarked: " It is very commodious that parents should have access to appoint certain subjects to go to certain of their children, reserving still their own power of alteration. This could not be done, at least in the present shape, if the pursuer were well founded in his claim."

In *Balvaird* v. *Latimer*,[15] A purchased a house from his own funds and took the disposition in the name of B, the narrative bearing that B had paid the price. A retained the deed in his custody and later substituted his own name for B's in the narrative but not in the dispositive clause. On A's death he left a general disposition in favour of his widow. B raised an action concluding for declarator that the property in the house was vested in him. It was held by a majority that the general disposition must take effect as A had retained full power over the deed. Lord Balgray, who dissented, took the view that as A had not destroyed the disposition, which he might have done, it was to be considered a delivered evident.

In *Carmichael* v. *Carmichael's Exrx*.[16] a father took out an insurance policy on the life of his pupil son and paid the premiums during the son's minority. The son died after attaining majority but without dealing with the policy in any way. He knew of its existence although it had not been delivered or formally intimated to him. It was held that the proceeds of the policy fell to the son's executrix because, on the evidence, the son had acquired a *jus quaesitum*. The basis of the decision of the House of Lords [17] seems to be that an irrevocable *jus quaesitum* is acquired by a third party only if, on the evidence, it can be inferred that it was intended to confer an irrevocable right upon him. The terms of the contract or document of title are not sufficient evidence *per se* but they form an important piece of evidence. Delivery is not essential and registration or intimation of the deed may provide sufficient additional evidence. There is, however, no general restriction on the kind of evidence which will suffice—" In the end it is a question of evidence." [18]

Registered titles—heritage

It is clearly established, however, that in both situations (a) and (b) there is a distinction between property, the title to which can be registered, such as heritage and shares in limited companies, on the one hand, and property such as bonds and deposit-receipts on the other. Where the title

---

[14] Cited with approval by L.P. Inglis, in *Walker's Exor.* v. *Walker* (1878) 5 R. 965, 968. See also Kames, *Principles of Equity*, II, 66.

[15] Dec. 5, 1816, F.C.

[16] 1919 S.C. 636; 1920 S.C.(H.L.) 195.

[17] See also the speech of Viscount Dunedin in *Inland Revenue* v. *Wilson*, 1928 S.C.(H.L.) 42, 45.

[18] *Per* Lord Dunedin in *Carmichael*, at p. 203.

has been registered in B's name, the transfer may be complete even although the deed has not been delivered to him.

In *Bruce* v. *Bruce*,[19] it was argued that a disposition of an annual rent to a nephew was effectual although it was in the granter's repositories at his death because the sasine had been registered. The Lords found that " though the writs had not been delivered, they were effectual, there being a sasine registrate." Similarly, in *Balvaird*, the Lord President indicated that the result would have been different if infeftment had been taken on the disposition. In *Cameron's Trs.*,[20] which was concerned with a different situation, Lord President Dunedin said:

" Now, if A, infeft in land, dispones gratuitously that land to B, and then registers the disposition in the Register of Sasines, the donation is perfected, not, I think, because of the publication in the register of A's deed, but because by the constructively effected sasine the land itself, the subject of the gift, has been delivered by A to B in the only way in which land can be delivered." [21]

In *Linton* v. *Inland Revenue*,[22] a father, having purchased a farm with his own funds, took the disposition in the names of his pupil children and it was held that the donation was perfected by recording of the deed. However, as the decision proceeded on the basis that the father as tutor acting on behalf of the disponees had accepted delivery of the disposition and authorised its registration, it is not completely in point to the present discussion.

Registered titles—shares

There is authority to the effect that, in the case of shares in a limited company, registration in the company's books has the same result as registration in the Sasine Register in the case of land. In *Lord Advocate* v. *Galloway*,[23] an uncle handed certain of his stock certificates to his nephew and told him to have them transferred to his own name. The nephew gave them to the uncle's law agents who prepared transfers which were duly executed by the uncle and presented for registration. The companies sent notices to the uncle intimating that the transfers had been presented and that, if he did not object thereto, the nephew would be registered as owner. The uncle returned no answer and the transfers were registered. The new certificates were retained by the agents for behoof of the nephew. It was held without difficulty that there had been an effectual donation by the uncle. The decision is frequently cited in discussing whether registration is a substitute for delivery, but it is not of great help because it can easily be regarded as a case in which there was in fact delivery of the deeds to the nephew.

[19] (1675) Mor. 11185.
[20] 1907 S.C. 407.
[21] 1907 S.C. 407, 413; see *infra*, p. 42. See also *Newton* v. *Newton*, 1923 S.C. 15, 22, *per* Lord Hunter.
[22] 1928 S.C. 209.
[23] (1884) 11 R. 541.

In *Inland Revenue* v. *Wilson*,[24] a father purchased from his own funds shares in a limited company in the name of his pupil son. He at first retained the certificates in his own custody but subsequently, after his son had become a minor, he deposited them with his law agents to be held for the son. It was held that the donation of the shares was completed by the retention of the son's name on the company register after his attainment of minority, opinions being reserved as to whether the donation could be complete during the son's pupillarity. Lord Sands said:

" As I have already indicated, donation is not effectually completed by taking a bond payable to the alleged donee. The question therefore arises whether the taking of shares in a limited company is on the same footing. Such taking of shares is of a very different legal character from the taking of a bond or a deposit-receipt. In the former case the donee is made a partner in the company, and all the incidents, statutory and other, of partnership attach to him. Secondly, the ownership of the shares is recorded in a register open to public inspection, and subjected to such inspection for the public protection in view of the privileges accorded to a limited company. Thirdly, the document of title is not in the possession of the donor. The document of title is the register of the company. The share certificate is not a document of title, it is merely an acknowledgment on the part of the officials of the company that the name of the person mentioned in it is duly recorded in the proper document of title, the company's register. This is illustrated by the fact that dividend warrants are issued to the shareholders whose names are on the company's register, without any inquiry or concern as to whether the shareholder is in possession of the share certificate. The register of the company bears, in this aspect, a certain resemblance to the Register of Sasines as regards land. It is not, I think, in dispute that, whereas an effectual donation is not made by causing a disposition in favour of the donor as trustee for another to be recorded in the Register of Sasines, such a donation is made where the sasine is in name and in favour of the donee. The property has effectually passed. For the reasons indicated, I have formed the opinion that a gift is completed where money is applied in acquiring shares in a limited company in the name of the donee . . . and that name is placed upon the register of the company, whereby the donee is made a partner of the company, with the incidents attaching to that position, including the right to receive the dividends, vote at meetings and act as a director." [25]

The judgment of the Court of Session was affirmed by the House of Lords. Viscount Dunedin and Lord Shaw of Dunfermline emphasised that the existence of *animus donandi* was not disputed and Lord Shaw referred with approval to *Lord Advocate* v. *Galloway*.[26]

---

[24] 1927 S.C. 733; 1928 S.C.(H.L.) 42.
[25] 1927 S.C. 737.

[26] *Supra.*

Special destinations

It is at first sight difficult to reconcile what has been said on this subject with some of the cases dealing with special destinations. In *Dennis* v. *Aitchison* [27] a deceased husband had purchased shares in a limited company from his own funds and had taken them in the names of himself and his wife. The share certificates had never been delivered to the wife. It was held that the wife had not acquired a proprietary right, even to the extent of one-half, in the shares during her husband's lifetime, that the whole destination could have only testamentary effect and that, in fact, it had been revoked by a subsequent testamentary writing. Lord President Clyde disapproved a part of the rubric in *Connell's Trs.* v. *Connell's Trs.* [28] which interpreted a passage in Lord Adam's opinion [29] to mean that in such circumstances the wife acquired a proprietary right by *inter vivos* transfer.

The distinction between the special destination cases and the donation cases seems to be that in the latter it was accepted that *animus donandi* existed. In *Inland Revenue* v. *Wilson*,[30] Lord Shaw said:

" Both father and son maintained, and maintain, that there was a donation, and there was no dispute in the Court of Session that such a donation was intended. In those circumstances the case appears to me to fall within the well-known distinction between cases of imperfect or uncompleted tradition—the bank deposit-receipt cases—and those of absolute transfer of shares given effect to upon the register as *per* the intention of parties."

On the other hand, in *Dennis* it was a matter of admission that, apart from the terms of the titles and the subsequent testamentary writings, there was no evidence as to the purpose which the husband had in view when he directed the titles to be expressed.[31]

There seems to be no case where the question arose in relation to heritage. In *Morrison's Trs.* v. *Morrison* [32] it seems to have been assumed that one-half of the heritage vested *inter vivos*. In *Hay's Tr.* v. *Hay's Trs.*,[33] Lord President Cooper carefully stated his assumption that both parties were fully aware of the recording of the disposition containing the special destination " and that such cases as *Cameron's Trs.* are therefore not in point." [34] It may be that the question cannot arise in relation to heritage because the warrant of registration must be signed by or with the authority of the disponees.[35] It could be argued also that it should not

[27] 1923 S.C. 819.
[28] (1886) 13 R. 1175.
[29] p. 1184.
[30] 1928 S.C.(H.L.) 45.
[31] *Per* Lord Skerrington, 1923 S.C. 826.   See also *Drysdale's Trs.* v. *Drysdale*, 1922 S.C. 741.
[32] (1905) 7 F. 810.
[33] 1951 S.C. 329.
[34] p. 332. As to *Cameron's Trs.*, see p. 42 *infra*. The question was whether recording in the Sasine Register constituted delivery.
[35] *Linton* v. *Inland Revenue*, 1928 S.C. 209, 213, *per* L.P. Clyde; p. 215, *per* Lord Sands; p. 217, *per* Lord Ashmore.

arise in relation to shares because a person should not be placed upon the register without his knowledge and consent.

Husband as custodier

In both situations (a) and (b), considerable confusion has been caused by the doctrine that, as a man is the natural custodier of deeds in favour of his wife and children, delivery of such a deed to him or retention of a deed by him has the effect of delivery to the wife or child.

In *Forrest* v. *Wilson*,[36] the circumstances were unusual in that the defender sought to prove payment of a sum of money by founding on a disposition which the pursuer, Forrest, had granted in favour of Forrest's own wife and children. The pursuer argued that the disposition was of no effect because he had retained it in his possession. It was held that the deed was effectual because the pursuer was " the proper custodier of it as a delivered deed, inasmuch as it was the document of Forrest and his wife and family, for whose behoof it was stipulated that it should be granted."

In another case,[37] in which *inter vivos* effect was denied to deposit-receipts which a father had taken in the names of his children but had retained in his possession, Lord Justice-Clerk Moncreiff said that there might be cases in which a father could be held to be the proper custodier for his children in such circumstances. Lord Ormidale said it was a question of intention. Again, in *Smith* v. *Smith's Trs.*,[38] the deceased husband left in his repositories a private cash-book in which there was an account showing sums at credit of his wife. It was held that, as the husband was the proper custodier of the wife's deeds, the account had to be regarded as a delivered document and the wife was entitled to the sums at her credit as a donation. Lord Shand said [39]:

> " The husband is the proper custodier of his wife's papers. There is no doubt a presumption against donation between husband and wife, but I rather think, on the other hand, there is a presumption in favour of delivery. But we may take the case without presumptions, take it simply as a question whether the husband held this book as a delivered document making him the custodier of it as evidence of his wife's and children's rights, or whether he held it as a record of a mere intention which he might destroy at any time ? On that question I give my verdict, without any hesitation, that he held it as a delivered document."

These authorities therefore support the view that the husband's possession of the deed may be equivalent to such delivery to the wife as will complete

---

[36] (1858) 20 D. 1201.

[37] *Miller* v. *Miller* (1874) 1 R. 1107. The case is not a strong one because the documents were in the names of the parents in trust for the children.

[38] (1884) 12 R. 186.

[39] p. 189. See also *Connell's Trs.* v. *Connell's Trs.* (1886) 13 R. 1175, 1187. *Cf. Miller* v. *Miller* (1874) 1 R. 1107, 1109.

an *inter vivos* transfer to her. This seems to have been accepted by the Second Division in *Connell's Trs.* v. *Connell's Tr.*[40]

McLaren's view of the doctrine is that " nothing more is intended by this proposition than that provisions in favour of members of the granter's family, though conceived in the form of deeds *inter vivos*, are effectual if found undelivered in his repositories after his death." [41] The institutional writers [42] when read with the authorities they cite (except one [43]) support this view. It is a corollary of this version of the doctrine that the granter can revoke the provision and that the provision is not effectual against the granter's creditors. In other words, the effect is purely testamentary.

A possible illustration is *Walker's Exor.* v. *Walker*,[44] where a husband advanced his own funds to harbour trustees who granted an assignation in favour of him and his wife and the survivor which he retained in his possession. On the husband's death it was held that, as there had been no delivery to the wife, the fund constituted part of the husband's estate at death; but that the assignation operated as a special destination to convey the fund to the wife on the husband's death.

It should be added that a deposit-receipt does not fall under this rule and has no testamentary effect although, if there is other evidence of *animus donandi*, it may form the foundation of a *donatio mortis causa*.[45] Similarly, a promissory note has no testamentary effect.[46]

The difficulty about McLaren's view is that, in this form, the doctrine has no effect at all because it follows from the case law on special destinations that such provisions are effectual whether they are in favour of the granter's family or not. It is significant that the dictum in *Hill* v. *Hill* quoted above was the foundation of the Lord President's opinion in *Walker's Exor.* v. *Walker* and was stated by Lord Skerrington to be one of the sources of the doctrine of special destinations.[47] Lord President Clyde stated the doctrine of special destination thus:

" if (1) anyone takes the documentary title to property or securities (including shares), which he has acquired in his own right or out of his own means, in favour of some other person (either solely or jointly with himself, and—in the latter case—either with or without a clause of survivorship), and (2) if such title remains in the possession

[40] 1955 S.L.T. 125. But see *Hodge* v. *Morrisons* (1883) 21 S.L.R. 40.

[41] I, 419.

[42] Stair, I, 7, 14; *Bairns of Wallace of Ellerslie* v. *Their Eldest Brother* (1624) Mor. 6344; Ersk. III, 2, 44; *Hamilton of Silvertonhill* v. *His Sisters* (1624) Mor. 4098; *Aikenhead* v. *Aikenhead* (1663) Mor. 16994; *Monro* v. *Monro* (1712) Mor. 5052. See also *Lady Lindoris* v. *Stewart* (1715) Mor. 6126 and Dickson, *Evidence*, s. 921.

[43] *Hamilton* v. *Hamilton* (1741) Mor. 11576.

[44] (1878) 5 R. 965. See also *Buchan* v. *Porteous* (1879) 7 R. 211; *Connell's Trs.* v. *Connell's Trs.* (1886) 13 R. 1175. In *Connell's Trs.* v. *Connell's Tr.*, 1955 S.L.T. 125, Lord Hill Watson regarded *Walker's Exor.* as a case in which there was no *inter vivos* effect because the husband held the deed " in his own right as the party who would be entitled to obtain delivery."

[45] *Crosbie's Trs.* v. *Wright* (1880) 7 R. 823; *Connell's Trs.*, v. *Connell's Trs.*, *supra*; *Lord Advocate* v. *Galloway* (1884) 11 R. 541.

[46] *Miller* v. *Miller* (1874) 1 R. 1107. See also *Stewart's Trs.*, 1953 S.L.T.(Notes) 25 (cheques)

[47] *Duff's Trs.* v. *Phillipps*, 1921 S.C. 287, 298.

of the acquirer undelivered to such other person during the acquirer's lifetime, then such title is held to constitute a valid nomination of such other person as successor of the acquirer in such property or securities —to the extent of the whole, if the title is in favour of such other person solely or as survivor, to the extent of one-half, if the title is a joint one in favour of the acquirer and such other person without a clause of survivorship." [48]

What need, then, is there for a special rule dealing with the cases of husband and wife and parent and child ?

It is submitted that the doctrine has two forms. The first is that already stated, that where a man grants a deed in favour of his wife or child but retains it in his possession it may nevertheless have *inter vivos* effect. As has been indicated this version is supported by some authority but none of the decisions is completely satisfactory. It may have arisen from a misunderstanding of the original form of the doctrine which is found in *Hill* v. *Hill* [49]:

" Hence it is, that when a man lends a sum and takes the bond in name of a child *in familia*, delivery of the bond to the father, has not naturally any other signification than that the bond, which comes in place of the money is to be under his power, as the money formerly was. It cannot import a delivery for behoof of the child; because the debtor who delivers the bond has no vote in the matter; but must deliver the bond to the father from whom he got the money.

A donation to a child by a stranger, and the bond delivered to the father, is a different case. For there the granter of the bond having all under his own power, makes the delivery in order to fix the debt against himself; and as the donation is to the child, the presumption lies that the delivery to the father is as custodier, and not to give him a power of alteration; which in effect would make him creditor and not his child."

Where the deed is not granted or procured by the father, but is a donation by a third party, delivery to the father is treated as delivery to the child.

Situation (c)

The situation in which A takes the disposition in his own name as trustee for B has caused most trouble and has to be considered at some length.

Where there is no possibility of a registered title, it seems that there is no trust without delivery or some equivalent. If A takes out a deposit-receipt in his own name in trust for B there is no legally enforceable trust constituted.[50] Most of the difficulty has arisen when the conveyance has been registered in the Register of Sasines.

[48] *Dennis* v. *Aitchison*, 1923 S.C. 819, 825.
[49] (1755) Mor. 11580. See also *Hamilton* v. *Hamilton* (1741) Mor. 11576.
[50] *Per* Lord Sorn, *Graham's Trs.* v. *Gillies*, 1956 S.C. 437, 455.

In *Gilpin* v. *Martin*,[51] the purchaser of heritage took the disposition in favour of himself for behoof of his three children. The narrative clause did not state explicitly out of whose funds the price had been paid. The deed remained in the purchaser's possession until his death. He executed shortly before his death a disposition and settlement by which he conveyed the subjects to his nephew. One of the children then raised an action to reduce this conveyance on the ground that the father was not *in titulo* to dispose of the property. It was held that an irrevocable trust in favour of the children had been constituted and that the *mortis causa* settlement was an ineffectual attempt to frustrate the trust. It was said that the deed " received all the delivery of which it was susceptible." The opinions proceeded on the basis that it could not safely be assumed that the benefit to the children had been gratuitous. The early decisions of *Balvaird* v. *Latimer* and *Hill* v. *Hill*[52] were distinguished in respect that there the person in whose favour the deed was taken never obtained actual or constructive delivery of it.

Moreover, in *Stewart* v. *Rae*,[53] in which it was held that a husband and wife who had purchased heritage with the wife's funds and had taken the disposition in favour of themselves in liferent and their children, whom failing the wife's heirs, in fee, could revoke the destination to the children, *Gilpin* was distinguished by the Lord Ordinary (Kinnear) and Lord President Inglis on the ground that there the father's only title *ex facie* of the deed was as a trustee and the presumption was that he had not advanced the purchase-money.

In *Cameron's Trs.* v. *Cameron*,[54] a father lent funds belonging to himself on bonds and dispositions in security. One bond, which narrated that the money was derived from funds held by him in trust for his daughter, was taken in favour of himself as trustee for his daughter *nominatim*. It was recorded in the Sasine Register and thereafter retained in the father's custody until his death. Another bond was taken in favour of himself and his brother as trustees for behoof of the father in liferent and his children *nominatim* in fee. It was recorded in the Sasine Register. After the death of the brother, who had no knowledge of the existence of the bond, the loan was repaid to the father, who assigned the bond to a new lender. The children knew nothing of the existence of the bonds. It was admitted that in fact the funds advanced on the bonds belonged to the father. On the father's death it was held by a majority of seven judges that neither bond constituted an effectual trust in favour of the children.

The reasoning in this difficult decision must be analysed in some detail. The argument of the majority can be summarised in the following propositions:

[51] (1869) 7 M. 807.
[52] Dec. 5, 1816, F.C.; (1755) Mor. 11580.
[53] (1883) 10 R. 463.
[54] 1907 S.C. 407.

(1) To perfect a donation of this kind there must be delivery—something which effectually takes the subject out of the control of the donor and puts it into the control of the donee or of somebody else for him.

(2) The father had not effected delivery in this sense because he had uplifted and reinvested the proceeds at his pleasure.

(3) Registration in the Sasine Register is equivalent to delivery of the bond but the delivery was from the borrower to the father and not from the father to the children.

(4) But, in any event, what is said in the older authorities is that infeftment " infers " delivery of a written instrument because infeftment in the old form could not be obtained unless the instrument constituting the warrant had been delivered to the grantee. Under the modern law, however, a deed can be registered by the grantor and then it cannot be inferred that the grantee has accepted delivery of a deed of which he may know nothing.

(5) The question of delivery is one of intention and the father could not have intended to effectuate delivery because he had continued to deal with the bonds as if the funds were his own, which he could not have done without committing a breach of trust if the bonds had been delivered. Moreover, registration did not involve the intention to deliver because the registration had the different purpose of completing the security.

(6) The faith of the records was not affected by the result of the majority view because the object of the Sasine Register is to enable anyone interested in a particular property to ascertain the state of the title to it and the burdens upon it. The public were entitled to rely on the register in so far as it disclosed a valid bond affecting the property but the fact that the bond was granted to the father as trustee was " not a matter which falls within the scope and purpose of the register." [55] Registration is not public intimation to people who have no interest in the land affected by a registered title and no inducement to search the records in order to learn whether a recorded title contains any statement which they may probably have an interest in knowing.

(7) Registration may in certain circumstances amount to intimation but only of a personal right to the subject conveyed—for example to the owner of subjects who was debtor in a personal obligation to convey.

(8) In any event there can be no intimation if there was no proof of knowledge. Constructive knowledge has no application to a case where the argument is that a person is to be presumed to know of the existence of a right in his favour when he is in fact ignorant of it.

---

[55] *Per* Lord Low at p. 425.

(9) In any event, even if the children had in fact known of the registration they would still have had no active title to control the
father's exercise of his legal right. The bonds would merely have
been items of evidence in a declarator of trust—an action which
must have failed on the very absence of delivery.

Gilpin v. *Martin* was distinguished on the ground that the question
there turned on the source of the funds but both Lord President Dunedin
and Lord Kinnear indicated that they preferred the opinion of the Lord
Ordinary (Manor) to the opinions delivered in the Inner House.

Separate consideration was given to the bond in which the father's
brother was named as a co-trustee. It was held that the result was the
same in this case but might have been different if the brother had been the
sole trustee or if the bond had been communicated to him.

Stewart v. *Rae* [56] was referred to only by Lord Kyllachy, who dissented.
It was of some relevance because there the husband and wife had taken
infeftment in the liferent but no infeftment had been taken in the fee. All
three judges based their decision on the point that the fee was still vested
either in the seller or in the wife and it was implied that the result might
have been different had there been infeftment in favour of the children.

Lord Kyllachy, who dissented, argued that, where the title is in the
trustee's name, there must be some " overt extraneous and ostensible act
which involves acceptance of the trust and marks definitely the character
of the trustee's possession "; that this requirement would be satisfied by
intimation of the trust-deed to the beneficiaries or by the trustee's public
actings consistent only with acceptance of the trust; and that registration
of the deed in the Sasine Register constituted both of these elements.
Moreover, if the bonds had been taken in the name of the father as an
individual, and he had thereafter executed separate assignations to himself
as trustee, the recording of these writings would undoubtedly have constituted the trust and it was difficult to see why the result should be
different where there was a single and composite writing recorded as a
whole. Lord Kyllachy's answer to proposition (1) *supra* was that it was
not inconsistent with the constitution of the trust for the trustee to have the
power to uplift and reinvest the funds; in any event the effect of registration was that the beneficiaries could obtain extracts with which they could
enforce their rights. His answer to proposition (6) was " That the Register
of Sasines is concerned merely with the legal estate, and that the registration of deeds therein has no effect except as regards the legal estate, is a
proposition which, so far as I know, is quite novel."

Cameron's Trs. was mentioned incidentally in the House of Lords in
Carmichael v. *Carmichael's Executrix.*[57] Lord Shaw of Dunfermline
indicated that he was in agreement with the opinion of Lord Kyllachy—

[56] *Supra.* This decision was followed in *Kindness* v. *Bruce* (1902) 4 F. 415, where the facts
were similar.
[57] 1920 S.C.(H.L.) 195.

" When Lord Kyllachy says in *Cameron's Trs.* v. *Cameron* that the grantor [58] of the bond and disposition in security there in question ' desired and intended to make, as against himself and everybody concerned, an irrevocable and effective divestiture,' I have no doubt as to the soundness of that. Nor am I able to attach doubt to the further proposition that the recording of the bond in the Register of Sasines for behoof of the grantor as trustee for his daughter was perfectly sufficient to satisfy all the requirements of the law with reference to delivery."

Viscounts Finlay, Haldane and Cave reserved their opinions on this point but Lord Dunedin maintained the view which he had expressed as one of the majority in *Cameron's Trs.*

In two later Revenue cases, *Cameron's Trs.* was carefully distinguished.[59]

Gloag opines that the authority of *Cameron's Trs.* " is perhaps not beyond question; at all events it will not be extended to analogous cases." [60]

It is submitted that *Cameron's Trs.* is an unfortunate decision which should be reconsidered. The reasoning of Lord Kyllachy's dissenting opinion seems irrefragable. It may be said that from a practical point of view it is a hardship to the truster if, to avoid completing the trust right, he must abstain from completing his right against the granter of the disposition. The answer is that if he does not wish to complete the trust at once, he should take the disposition to himself as an individual as the first step.

It seems to be accepted that registration in the Books of Council and Session is in general equivalent to delivery. " It is difficult to see how any act of delivery could put a deed more completely within the power of the grantee than is done by recording it in the books of Council and Session." [61] It is not, however, conclusive—" It may be done, even with the authority of the granter, for a purpose other than that of delivery, and with such evidence as to show that although the granter authorised the recording, he had a design and purpose that it should not thereby be an irrevocable delivered deed." [62]

In *Allan's Trs.* v. *Inland Revenue*,[63] a wealthy woman aged 77 and in failing health had made a will leaving legacies of £20,000 each to B and C and appointing D as her residuary legatee. She became concerned about the amount of estate duty which would become payable on her death and accordingly a scheme was devised to minimise the burden. She revoked the legacies to B and C and took out an endowment policy from an insurance company. In a letter to the insurance company she said: " I

[58] The father was of course the *grantee* of the bond and disposition in security.

[59] *Inland Revenue* v. *Wilson*, 1927 S.C. 733; 1928 S.C.(H.L.) 42; *Linton* v. *Inland Revenue*, 1928 S.C. 209.

[60] *Contract*, p. 74. Gloag states that Lord Hunter followed it in *Drummond* v. *Mathieson*, 1912, 1 S.L.T. 455, but the case was not in point there.

[61] *Per* L.P. Inglis, *Tennent* v. *Tennent's Trs.* (1869) 7 M. 936, 948.

[62] *Ibid.*

[63] 1971 S.L.T. 62. *Cf. Drummond* v. *Mathieson*, 1912, 1 S.L.T. 455.

intend that the policy shall from the moment of its commencement be held upon an irrevocable trust for the benefit of the beneficiary or beneficiaries after mentioned." The sum assured was to be payable to the woman as trustee and it was declared that the policy was to be held in trust for B and C to the extent of £20,000 each and for D to the extent of the remainder. D was aware of the terms of the policy but B and C were not. The question at issue was whether an irrevocable trust had been created in favour of B and C. It was admitted that the intimation to D gave her an irrevocable interest. Both Lord Reid, who spoke for the majority in the House of Lords, and Lord Guest, who dissented, were in agreement that a person could not make himself a trustee of his own property unless there occurred something equivalent to delivery or transfer of the trust fund. Lord Reid said:

> " I think that we can now accept the position, as a reasonable development of the law, that a person can make himself a trustee of his own property provided that he also does something equivalent to delivery or transfer of the trust fund. I reject the argument for the appellants that mere proved intention to make a trust coupled with the execution of a declaration of trust can suffice. If that were so it would be easy to execute such a declaration, keep it in reserve, use it in case of bankruptcy to defeat the claims of creditors, but if all went well and the trustee desired to regain control of the fund simply suppress the declaration of trust." [64]

Their lordships differed as to whether intimation to D was sufficient for irrevocability *quoad* B and C. Lord Guest thought that it was not; that the three benefactions could be treated separately; and that the courts should not " be astute to discover some equivalent to delivery in this highly anomalous situation which was a creation of English law." Lord Reid, with whom Lords Morris of Borth-y-Gest, Upjohn and Donovan concurred, thought that intimation to D sufficed because an inchoate trust could not be set up in part. Lord Reid formulated the requirement for an effective trust as " some bona fide physical act of the truster equivalent to conveyance, transfer or delivery of the subject of the trust." [65]

Lord Reid rejected the partial irrevocability argument on two grounds. First, because, if the trust was declared for X in liferent and Y whom failing Z in fee and intimated only to Y, it would be " unreal " to say that the fund was transferred to the granter as trustee in a question with Y but not in a question with X; the property would have to be held during X's life to ascertain whether Y survived to take a vested interest—" So as the property has been earmarked as trust property I do not see why all the trust purposes should not take effect."

Lord Reid's second reason was that, if partial intimation was not

---

[64] p. 63.
[65] p. 64. The principle adopted by the majority bears some resemblance to the " Perezian exception " of South African law—see Honoré, *The South African Law of Trusts*, 338; *Abeyawardene* v. *West* [1957] A.C. 176.

sufficient, it would be impossible to set up a trust of this kind to benefit persons unborn. Lastly, it has to be borne in mind that the decision depended largely on the fact that the intention to create an irrevocable trust was clearly established.

Lord Reid also discussed *Carmichael* which he described as " in some respects a difficult case to interpret." He regarded it as dealing with the question of how the intention to make an irrevocable contractual provision in favour of a third party can be proved. He thought that such an intention could be established from the terms of the contract alone but that generally other evidence of intention is required. But he went on to opine that *Carmichael* was far removed from the question of whether there had been the equivalent of delivery to constitute a trust. In *Carmichael* the question was whether a third party C could claim payment of a sum due under a contract between A and B; in *Allan's Trs.* the question was whether, on a sum being paid by A to B in terms of the contract, C could obtain payment thereof from B as trustee—" Any benefit to the beneficiaries flowed from the declaration of trust not from the terms of the contract." [65]

In *Clark's Trs.* v. *Inland Revenue* [66] the truster had approached an insurance company with a view to taking out seven separate policies of assurance on his life in favour of his wife and six relatives. He had discussed the matter with a friend of long standing who was a chartered accountant and the approach to the insurance company was made through the accountant. It was initially suggested that the trustees should be the deceased, the accountant and the accountant's partner but the company stated that " for technical reasons " it was considered advisable in trust policies for the life assured to be sole trustee in the first instance and for him to assume any additional trustees thereafter. Accordingly, the truster submitted to the company through the accountant a formal letter of request relative to proposals for seven policies requesting that the proceeds should be payable to the truster as trustee. The letter also contained a request that each of the policies should incorporate a condition that the truster's only interest in the policy was as a trustee and that he would in no circumstances be entitled to any personal benefit thereunder. The first premium was paid on April 25, 1963, when the company was at risk, the policies were issued to the accountant on June 13, 1963, and on August 29, 1963, the truster executed a deed assuming the accountant and his partner as trustees in connection with the trusts created by the policies. Three of the beneficiaries knew nothing of the provision made for their benefit and on the truster's death in 1965 a question arose as to whether he could have revoked the trusts created in the three policies in favour of these beneficiaries between April 1963 and the assumption of the additional trustees in August 1963.

[66] 1972 S.L.T. 189. *Cf. Kerr's Trs.* v. *Inland Revenue*, 1974 S.L.T. 193.

The first argument presented in favour of irrevocability was based on *Allan's Trs.* v. *Inland Revenue.*[67] It was contended that there was only one trust and not seven so that intimation to one or more beneficiaries brought the trust into operation as regards all. There was only one trust because there had been a single scheme to reduce estate duty on the truster's death of which the issue of separate policies was merely part of the mechanics. There had been one proposal form and the premiums had been paid by a single cheque. The Second Division rejected this argument. The letter of request had referred to irrevocable " trusts " in the plural. The policy in favour of the truster's wife constituted a separate trust under the Married Women's Policies of Assurance (Scotland) Act 1880.

The second argument was successful. It was that intimation to the accountant was sufficient. The Second Division somewhat surprisingly accepted that the accountant had been constituted by the truster an agent for the beneficiaries to whom intimation and delivery could be made on behalf of the beneficiaries. This surprising conclusion was reached by inferences from the state of mind of the truster and the accountant. The truster had wished the accountant to be his trustee from the beginning. The accountant had regarded himself as holding the policies for the beneficiaries. It is thought that this decision cannot stand.

Situation (d)

It is clear that where a man instructs his debtor to grant a bond, not in favour of himself, but in favour of trustees for his grandchildren, and the bond is delivered absolutely and unconditionally to the trustees, an irrevocable trust is created. It does not detract from the efficacy of the arrangement that the deed was not executed by the man himself; it is treated as his deed although it is in the form of a bond by his debtor.[68] The difficulty arises where the bond or other deed is not delivered to the trustees but is retained by the truster.

First, it is clear that the doctrine that a man is natural custodier of deeds in favour of his wife and children has no application to this situation.[69] The doctrine is confined to deeds which are directly in favour of the wife or children. It has no application to a deed which constitutes a trust in favour of the wife or children; the trustees are then the persons to whom delivery falls to be made and there is no reason to ascribe the granter's possession of the writ to his position as natural custodier of his family's writs.

It seems to follow from the cases relating to situation (c) and *Connell's Trs.*[70] that in situation (d) there is no irrevocable trust in the absence of delivery. However, in *Cameron's Trs.*,[71] Lord President Dunedin indicated that if the father's brother had been the sole trustee, registration in the

---

[67] *Supra.*
[68] *Collie* v. *Pirie's Trs.* (1851) 13 D. 506.
[69] *Connell's Trs.* v. *Connell's Tr.*, 1955 S.L.T. 125.
[70] 1955 S.L.T. 125. Also *Jarvie's Tr.* v. *Jarvie's Trs.* (1887) 14 R. 411.
[71] 1907 S.C. 413.

Register of Sasines would have been sufficient although it was not effectual where the father and brother were both trustees in the absence of communication to, and acceptance of the trust by, the brother.[72]

Situation (e)

Where A executes a disposition in favour of B as trustee for C it is quite clear that it is of no effect *inter vivos* if it is not delivered. In *Connell's Trs.* v. *Connell's Tr.*[73] the testator in 1879 executed an antenuptial bond of provision by which he bound himself to convey certain property after his death to trustees in trust for his family. The bond remained in the hands of the testator's solicitors and was not delivered to the trustees until after his death. It was held that the bond was invalid for want of delivery.

[72] Lord Kinnear at p. 424.
[73] *Supra.*

CHAPTER 4

PROOF OF TRUST

IT would appear from Stair that prior to 1696 trust could be proved *prout de jure*—" Trust in the right of lands, sums or goods, to the behoof of another, doth frequently occur; and because fraud is ordinarily in it, it is not only probable by writ or oath of the trustee, but sometimes witnesses are examined, *ex officio* to find out the truth." [1] This, however, is not correct. The general principle of the common law was that a written title could not be qualified or explained by parole testimony and an allegation of latent trust did not form an exception to this rule. [2] In the latter part of the seventeenth century there was a deviation from the general rule and in several cases the existence of a latent trust was inferred from facts and circumstances proved by witnesses. [3] This practice is the basis of Stair's statement.

The difficulties created by the deviation came to a head in *Higgins* v. *Callander* [4] where

" The Lords thought the evidences and presumptions of trust very strong; yet, on the other hand, such exorbitant and implicit trusts were not so favourable as to deserve encouragement, being oftentimes used as blinds to intrap and defraud; and, therefore, wished there were an Act for the future, that no trust should be otherwise proveable but by writ or the intrusted party's oath."

The legislature thereafter acted. The preamble to the Act 1696 c. 25, now known as the Blank Bonds and Trusts Act 1696, notes " that the entrusting of persons without any declaration or back bond of trust in writing from the person entrusted, are occasions of fraud, as also of many pleas and contentions." It is then provided

" that no action of declarator of trust shall be sustained as to any deed of trust made for hereafter except upon a declaration or back bond of trust lawfully subscribed by the person alleged to be the trustee and against whom or his heirs or assignees the declarator shall be intented, or unless the same be referred to the oath of party

[1] I, 12, 17; I, 13, 7; IV, 45, 21. See also Ersk. III, 1, 32; Bell, *Comm.* I, 32; Bell, *Prin.* s. 1995.

[2] *Duggan* v. *Wight* (1797) Mor. 12761; see also *per* Lord Braxfield, *Stewart* v. *Bannatyne* (1777) Hailes 762, and *Marshall* v. *Lyell* (1859) 21 D. 514.

[3] *Viscount of Kingston* v. *Fullerton* (1665) Mor. 12749; *Stevenson's Executors* v. *Crawford* (1666) Mor. 12750; *Watson* v. *Bruce* (1673) Mor. 12751; *Leslie* v. *Innernytie* (1685) Mor. 12754; and other cases noted in Brown's Synopsis 1893–1894.

[4] (1696) Mor. 16182. See *Marshall* v. *Lyell, supra*, at p. 524, *per* Lord Cowan. The quotation from the report of *Higgins* in this opinion is inaccurate. " Explicit " should read " implicit," and " interested " should be " intrusted."

50

simpliciter, declaring that this Act shall not extend to the indorsation of bills of exchange, or the notes of any trading company." [5]

The application of the statute has given rise to considerable difficulties and the rigour with which it has been enforced has varied from time to time.[6] Lord Elchies noted, " I observe that their Lordships make pretty bold with that act, and catch at all opportunities to elide it " [7]; on the other hand Lord Justice-Clerk Inglis thought " it would be most unfortunate if any loose construction of the Act 1696 were recognised or encouraged " [8]; while in the present century Lord Sands has expressed a " dislike of the rigidity of the statutory rule " [9] and Lord Justice-Clerk Alness has said, " I am not disposed to extend the operation of the statute beyond the point to which its terms constrain me to go." [10]

Pleading

A defender who wishes to rely on the statute should make express reference to it in his pleas in law.[11] The onus is on the defender to establish that the mode of proof should be limited and the question falls to be decided by an examination of the pursuer's averments.[12]

The question of the mode of proof may not arise if the defender admits on record facts and circumstances sufficient to prove the trust, but the facts and circumstances must be unequivocal and the admissions must be taken with any qualifications attached to them.[13] An averment by the defender that he received the property as a gift from the pursuer does not open the door to parole evidence.[14] Where there are two alleged trustees an admission by one of them of the existence of the trust does not deprive the other of the benefit of the statute.[15]

Form of action

The first requisite for the application of the statute is that the action is in substance a declarator of trust at the instance of the alleged truster or beneficiary or one in his right against the alleged trustee or one in his right.[16] The pursuer cannot avoid the limitation of proof merely by altering the technical form of the action; and if an analysis of his averments discloses what is in substance an allegation of trust the Act applies

---

[5] For the significance of the proviso, see *infra* p. 53.
[6] See, *e.g. Gilmour v. Arbuthnot* (1765) Mor. 12758; *Stewart v. McArthur Stewart* (1777) 5 B.S. 631.
[7] *Annotations on Stair's Institutions*, 76.
[8] *Marshall v. Lyell, supra*, at p. 523.
[9] *Newton v. Newton*, 1923 S.C. 15, 25.
[10] *Galloway v. Galloway*, 1929 S.C. 160, 166.
[11] *McNair's Exrx. v. Litster*, 1939 S.C. 72.
[12] *Galloway v. Galloway*, 1929 S.C. 160.
[13] *Chalmers v. Chalmers* (1845) 7 D. 865; *Leckie v. Leckie* (1854) 17 D. 77.
[14] *Newton v. Newton*, 1923 S.C. 15. The pursuer's argument was based on dicta of Lord Dunedin in *Brownlee's Exrx. v. Brownlee*, 1908 S.C. 232, which seem not to be applicable to cases falling under the statute. See also *Robertson v. Robertson*, 1929 S.L.T. 510; *cf. Grant v. Grant* (1898) 6 S.L.T. 203.
[15] *Seth v. Hain* (1855) 17 D. 1117; *cf.* the opinion of Lord Salvesen, *Cairns v. Davidson*, 1913 S.C. 1054, 1058.
[16] *Marshall v. Lyell* (1859) 21 D. 514; Gloag & Irvine, *Rights in Security*, 147.

even although there is no conclusion for declarator of trust [17] and although the expression " trust " is not used in the pursuer's pleadings.[18] " It is a sacred principle of the law of Scotland, that trust cannot be proved parole, either under a declarator of trust or otherwise." [19]

It is well established that the statute applies to the case where a conveyance has been granted in *ex facie* absolute terms and it is alleged that it was truly granted in security.[20] On the other hand, a contract whereby one party agrees to purchase heritage with his own money and convey it to the other party on the occurrence of certain events is outwith the scope of the Act.[21]

Where the action is not at the instance of the alleged truster or one in his right the Act does not apply.[22] So where the pursuer in an action of defamation sought to establish jurisdiction on the ground that the defender owned heritage in Scotland, the defender was allowed to prove *prout de jure* that the property was held in trust.[23] Similarly, the Act cannot be pleaded by the alleged trustee against the trustee in the truster's sequestration, at least where the trust is a device to defraud the truster's creditors [24]; and where the suspender of a charge on a bill at the instance of the assignee of an indorsee alleged that the assignation was in trust for a party who had discharged the suspender of the debt, it was held that the Act did not restrict the mode of proof.[25]

The statute does not apply where the same party is both truster and trustee.[26]

Deed of trust

The second requisite for the application of the statute is that there is a " deed of trust "—" a deed declaring in absolute terms that a right of property exists in one party, which right is claimed by another." [27] " Wherever written title is necessary, or has been resorted to for the transference of the property, whether heritable or moveable, the rule of the

---

[17] *Anstruther* v. *Mitchell and Cullen* (1857) 19 D. 674; *Tennent* v. *Tennent's Trs.* (1868) 6 M. 840, 846, *per* Lord Barcaple, 874, *per* Lord Ardmillan; *Laird & Co.* v. *Laird and Rutherfurd* (1884) 12 R. 294; *Purnell* v. *Shannon* (1894) 22 R. 74.

[18] *McNair's Exrx.* v. *Litster*, 1939 S.C. 72, 77, *per* Lord Fleming.

[19] *per* Lord Gillies, *Scott* v. *Miller* (1832) 11 S. 21, 29.

[20] *Leckie* v. *Leckie* (1854) 17 D. 77; *Purnell* v. *Shannon* (1894) 22 R. 74.

[21] *Govan New Bowling-Green Club* v. *Geddes* (1898) 25 R. 485; see also *Lindsay* v. *Barmcotte* (1851) 13 D. 718 (joint obligation).

[22] *Lord Elchies' Annotations on Stair's Institutions*, 75; *Lord Elibank* v. *Hamilton* (1827) 6 S. 69; *Scott* v. *Miller* (1832) 11 S. 21, 26, *per* L.P. Hope (Lords Balgray and Gillies *contra*); *Harper* v. *Hume* (1850) 22 Sc.Jur. 577; *Marshall* v. *Lyell* (1859) 21 D. 514, 521, *per* L.J.-C. Inglis; *Lord Advocate* v. *McNeill* (1864) 2 M. 626, 634, *per* Lord Deas; 4 M.(H.L.) 20; *University of Aberdeen* v. *Mags. of Aberdeen* (1876) 3 R. 1087, 1102, *per* Lord Deas; (1877) 4 R.(H.L.) 48. *Liquidators of City of Glasgow Bank* v. *Nicolson's Trs.* (1882) 9 R. 689, 692, *per* L.P. Inglis; *Drynan* v. *Rennie* (1897) 5 S.L.T. 145; *United Collieries* v. *Lord Advocate*, 1950 S.C. 458.

[23] *Hastie* v. *Steel* (1886) 13 R. 843; see also *Murdoch* v. *Wyllie* (1832) 10 S. 445; *Miller* v. *Oliphant* (1843) 5 D. 856; *Stewart* v. *Sutherland* (1868) 7 M. 298.

[24] *Wink* v. *Speirs* (1867) 6 M. 77.

[25] *Middleton* v. *Rutherglen* (1861) 23 D. 526.

[26] *University of Aberdeen* v. *Mags. of Aberdeen*, *supra*, p. 1102, *per* Lord Deas.

[27] *Per* L.P. Inglis, *Laird & Co.* v. *Laird and Rutherfurd* (1884) 12 R. 294, 297.

statute applies." [28] The deed need not have been granted by the person who seeks to have the trust declared. [29]

The property to which the deed relates may be heritable or moveable. [30] The short report of *Lord Strathnaver* v. *McBeath* [31] states that " trust in moveables falls not under the Act 1696." This, however, is not correct [32] and, probably, the true ground of the decision was that, as the Act applies only where there is a " deed of trust," a trust constituted by delivery of moveables without the interposition of writing can be proved by witnesses. Some of the opinions in *McConnachie* v. *Geddes* [33] suggest that proof *prout de jure* is competent even where a moveable right has been constituted in writing, if the writing is not necessary as a legal formality. [34] This was said, however, in the course of a strained attempt to distinguish *Dunn* v. *Pratt*. [35] Perhaps the better point was that as the contract in *McConnachie* did not require to be in writing, the pursuer need not have anticipated that there would be a written contract and therefore did not impliedly consent to the taking of the title in the defender's name.

In *Jackson* v. *Monro*, [36] it appears to have been held that the Act does not apply to bills of exchange because of the final proviso. It has been suggested that the report must be wrong because the exception relates to the first part of the statute prohibiting the execution of writs blank in the name of the creditor and has no relevance to the proof of trust. [37]

The following have been held to constitute a deed of trust: a disposition of heritage [38]; missives for the sale of heritage [39]; letters-patent [40]; an entry in the register of members of a limited company [41]; an assignation of an extract decree [42]; a missive of lease. [43]

A deposit-receipt is not a deed of trust within the meaning of the statute because it is not a document of title forming conclusive evidence of the ownership of the money deposited and, as it is often used to enable an agent to deal with his principal's money, there is no presumption of ownership as there is in the case of a recorded title to land. [44] It has been

---

[28] *Per* Lord Cowan, *Anstruther* v. *Mitchell and Cullen* (1857) 19 D. 674, 688.
[29] *Duggan* v. *Wight* (1797) 3 Pat.App. 610; *Laird & Co.* v. *Laird and Rutherfurd, supra,* at p. 297, *per* Lord Shand; *Anderson* v. *Yorston* (1906) 14 S.L.T. 54.
[30] *Per* Lord McLaren, *Dunn* v. *Pratt* (1898) 25 R. 461, 468; Dickson, *Evidence*, s. 579; McLaren, II, 1065.
[31] (1731) Mor. 12757. The facts are stated at (1731) Mor. 15129.
[32] More's *Notes*, 74; More's *Lectures* I, 187.
[33] 1918 S.C. 391.
[34] Mackenzie Stuart, 15.
[35] (1898) 25 R. 461. See *infra*, p. 56.
[36] (1714) Mor. 16197; see also Erskine, *Principles*, 20th ed., p. 525.
[37] Tait, *Law of Evidence*, 3rd ed., 310; More's *Notes*, 74; More's *Lectures* I, 187; Dickson, *Evidence*, s. 581.
[38] *Adam* v. *Adam*, 1962 S.L.T. 332.
[39] *Dunn* v. *Pratt* (1898) 25 R. 461 but see *infra*, p. 56.
[40] *Laird & Co.* v. *Laird and Rutherfurd, supra.*
[41] *Anderson* v. *Yorston, supra.* As to shares in an English company, see *Thomson* v. *Thomson* (1917) 33 Sh.Ct.Rep. 84 (affmd. by Inner House).
[42] *Purnell* v. *Shannon* (1894) 22 R. 74.
[43] *Seth* v. *Hain* (1855) 17 D. 1117; *McVean* v. *McVean* (1864) 2 M. 1150.
[44] *Cairns* v. *Davidson*, 1913 S.C. 1054; the point was not taken in *National Bank of Scotland* v. *Mackie's Trs.* (1905) 13 S.L.T. 383; 43 S.L.R. 13.

held in an Outer House decision,[45] which purports to apply the reasoning
of Lord Salvesen in *Cairns*, that an entry in the books of the Bank of
England in respect of War Loan (an inscribed stock) is not a " deed of
trust " but it is difficult to reconcile this decision with *Anderson* v. *Yorston* [46] and it is also difficult to see why such an entry is not an absolute
title raising a presumption of ownership. It has been held in the sheriff
court that certificates of War Stock were deeds of trust.[47] *Beveridge* was
distinguished on the ground that inscribed stock was in a different position
from stock transferred by deed.

If there is no " deed of trust," the Act does not apply and the trust can
be proved *prout de jure*.[48] So there is no restriction on proof of a trust
constituted by the delivery of moveables or by a gratuitous deposit of
money.[49] The handing over of bearer bonds is in the same position.[50]

Absolute title

The third requisite for the application of the Act is that the title of the
alleged trustee as embodied in the deed of trust is *ex facie* absolute and has
been taken with the consent of the truster—" it is indispensable that the
true owner of the property should have consented to an absolute title
being taken in the trustee's name." [51] The trustee must have, *ex facie* of
the title, the whole rights of *dominium* and the full *jus disponendi* over the
subjects of the alleged trust. Thus, if the document of title has not been
delivered to the trustee so that he has no effective *jus disponendi* the Act
has no application.[52] The fact that the title is taken in the name of two or
more alleged trustees does not remove the case from the scope of the
statute.[53] If the title is taken in the name of two persons and one of them
avers that he has the sole right to the property, the Act applies.[54]

The Act does not apply if the alleged owner did not consent to the
taking of the title in the name of the alleged trustee. Thus, where a
negotiorum gestor took the title in his own name, it was held that there was
no limitation of proof because the true owner had had no opportunity to
consent to the form of the title.[55]

It follows from what has been said that where the consent is not a true
consent but has been obtained by fraud the statute does not operate—

---

[45] *Beveridge* v. *Beveridge*, 1925 S.L.T. 234; see also *Kennedy* v. *Macrae*, 1946 S.C. 118, 121,
per Lord Keith.
[46] *Supra*.
[47] *Rodger* v. *Paterson* (1937) 53 Sh.Ct.Rep. 328.
[48] *The General Assembly of the General Baptist Churches* v. *Taylor* (1841) 3 D. 1030 as
explained by L.P. Inglis in *Laird & Co.* v. *Laird and Rutherfurd, supra*, at p. 297; *Gardiner*
v. *Cowie* (1897) 4 S.L.T. 256.
[49] *Lord Strathnaver* v. *McBeath* (1731) Mor. 12757; *Taylor* v. *Nisbet* (1901) 4 F. 79; Bankton,
I, 18, 12.
[50] *Newton* v. *Newton*, 1923 S.C. 15, 25, *per* Lord Sands.
[51] *Pant Mawr Quarry Co.* v. *Fleming* (1883) 10 R. 457, 459, *per* L.P. Inglis.
[52] *McNair's Executrix* v. *Litster*, 1939 S.C. 72; see also *Weissenbruch* v. *Weissenbruch*, 1961
S.C. 340.
[53] *Seth* v. *Hain* (1855) 17 D. 1117.
[54] *McVean* v. *McVean* (1864) 2 M. 1150.
[55] *Spruel* v. *Spruel Crawford* (1741) Mor. 16201, explained in *Marshall* v. *Lyell* (1859) 21 D.
514.

" The gates of justice are opened wide in the tracing of fraud." [56] It is, however, necessary to distinguish three different categories of fraud which may be averred. Firstly, there is the allegation of a fraudulent arrangement between the truster and the trustee.[57] The Act does not apply but such cases can be regarded as being outwith the scope of the statute because they involve questions with third parties and not because fraud is alleged. Secondly, many declarators of trust involve an allegation of fraud in that the alleged trustee is fraudulently denying the existence of the trust. Obviously, the objects of the statute would be largely defeated if it did not apply to such cases. The third type of fraud, and that which does elide the operation of the Act, consists of misrepresentations by which the pursuer was induced to consent to the taking of the title in the name of the trustee— fraud in the inception of the transaction.[58] An example can be found in *Galloway* v. *Galloway* [59] where, on one view of the averments, it appeared that the pursuer, having instructed his wife to purchase heritage, consented to the title being taken in her name because she falsely represented to him that the property could not be transferred to him while he was furth of Scotland. Such allegations can be proved *prout de jure*.

In one case it was said that where the true owner allows the absolute title to be taken in the trustee's name on the express condition that a back-letter will be granted at once, and the trustee fraudulently refuses to grant the back-letter, there is a fraud which is outwith the scope of the Act.[60] This seems to take the principle to its limit. In some cases there may be a fraud such as to justify the reduction of the conveyance to the trustee.

Tennent v. *Tennent's Trs.*[61] seems to have involved both a fraudulent arrangement between the truster and the trustees and a fraudulent representation made by the trustees to the truster that the deed would be used only to deceive his creditors. The rubric mentions only the former fraud in relation to the mode of proof but in fact the majority (Lord President Inglis [62] and Lord Ardmillan [63]) seem to have opined that the latter fraud could be proved *prout de jure*. The better view, adopted by Lords Barcaple [64] and Deas,[65] is that an assurance by the grantee that the right will be held by him in trust and used only for a particular purpose is precisely the type of verbal transaction at which the Act was directed and it matters not whether the grantee formed an intention to take advantage of the absolute character of the right before the transaction was entered into or at a later time.

---

[56] *Per* Lord Ardmillan, *Tennent* v. *Tennent's Trs.* (1868) 6 M. 840, 874.
[57] *Lord Elibank* v. *Hamilton* (1827) 6 S. 69; *Wink* v. *Speirs* (1867) 6 M. 77. See p. 52 *supra.*
[58] *Marshall* v. *Lyell* (1859) 21 D. 514.
[59] 1929 S.C. 160.
[60] *Pant Mawr Quarry Co.* v. *Fleming* (1883) 10 R. 457.
[61] (1868) 6 M. 840.
[62] p. 876.
[63] p. 874.
[64] p. 846.
[65] p. 859.

Mandate

Although it has sometimes been said that contracts of mandate are outwith the scope of the statute, in fact the decided cases relating to mandate are consistent with the general principles already stated. Where an agent has been instructed to buy property and to take the title in his own name although truly for behoof of his principal, it is well established that the Act applies.[66] On the other hand, where the agent has not been instructed to take the title in his own name but does so, the statute does not operate because there is not the requisite element of consent on the part of the principal.[67]

> " When it is agreed that rights have been taken as the parties intended, but it is averred that this was done in trust, the Act applies. But when it is alleged that the defender was employed to buy for one party, and took titles in the name of another, that is totally a different case, and no doubt proof *prout de jure* might be allowed." [68]

A difficulty has arisen with regard to missives for the sale of heritable property. In *Dunn* v. *Pratt*,[69] it was averred that the defender, with the pursuer's agreement, entered into missives for the purchase of heritage in his own name " on the understanding and agreement that the disposition by the seller of said property would be granted and taken in the pursuer's name." It was held by a majority that proof must be by writ or oath as the Act applied to the conveyance of a personal right to heritage and the missives constituted a " deed of trust " within the meaning of the statute. It seems that to some extent the decision was founded on the fact that the defender was not a lawyer or other person usually employed as an agent in the purchase of heritage. The Lord President pointed out that the defender had no duty to perform beyond taking the missives in his own name and opined that the result might be different if a law-agent took the missives in his own name and then refused to fulfil his mandate by completing the title in his client's name. Lord McLaren thought that the Act would not apply where the transaction could be referred to " any known category of agency."

This is not a satisfactory distinction.[70] It was made because of the difficulty presented by a number of decisions in which it was specifically said that in the case of a law-agent who had been instructed to purchase heritage the question was one of mandate which could be proved *prout de jure*.[71] As Lord Kinnear pointed out in his cogent dissenting opinion, it is

---

[66] *Duggan* v. *Wight* (1797) 3 Pat.App. 610; Mor. 12761; *Mackay* v. *Ambrose* (1829) 7 S. 699; *Marshall* v. *Lyell* (1859) 21 D. 514; *Anderson* v. *Yorston* (1906) 14 S.L.T. 54. The earlier cases, in the first two of which a different view was adopted, are *Tweedie* v. *Loch*, 5 B.S. 630, *Maxwell* v. *Maxwell*, 5 B.S. 630, and *Alison* v. *Forbes* (1771) Mor. 12760.

[67] *Corbet* v. *Douglas* (1808) Hume 346; *Boswell* v. *Selkrig* (1811) Hume 350; *Horne* v. *Morrison* (1877) 4 R. 977; *Pant Mawr Quarry Co.* v. *Fleming* (1883) 10 R. 457; *McConnachie* v. *Geddes*, 1918 S.C. 391.

[68] Per Lord Glenlee, *Mackay* v. *Ambrose, supra*, at p. 702.

[69] (1898) 25 R. 461.

[70] See Gloag, *Contract*, 2nd ed., 388. Mackenzie Stuart, 16, suggests that the case should be regarded as an exception due to the form of the pleadings.

[71] *Boswell* v. *Selkrig, supra*; *Horne* v. *Morrison, supra*, 979, *per* Lord Deas.

difficult to see why the fact that the defender is a law-agent should be material to the question of law although it might well facilitate proof of the existence of the mandate. The same opinion contains an effective refutation of the other arguments advanced by the majority. It is argued that the result is contrary to the authority of *Corbet*[67] and *Boswell*[67]; that missives of sale cannot with propriety be called a deed and do not vest an absolute right of property in the purchaser; that the pursuer did not propose to cut down or qualify the missives in any way because it is consistent with such a contract that the agent should require the conveyance to be made to his principal; and that the defender was under a duty to demand a conveyance from the seller in favour of the pursuer and if he had taken the title in his own name it could have been reduced on the ground of fraud proved *prout de jure*. It is impossible to read this opinion without feeling the gravest doubt as to the soundness of the decision in *Dunn* and in view of the reservations expressed in *McConnachie*[72] the question obviously requires reconsideration.

Partnership

It has sometimes been said that the Act does not apply to an allegation which is one of partnership and not of trust.[73] Different reasons have been given for this exception. Elchies suggests that " the oblidgement on partners to communicate is equal to a back-bond."[74] In *Jackson* v. *Monro*,[75] it was argued:

" *Ex natura contractus societatis*, there is a mutual trust among all the members of the society, and the deed of one obliges the other; which obligation arises from the nature of the contract itself, and so deeds taken in the name of one of the society do accresce to all."

The exception was allowed in two cases. Where it was averred that a sum of money deposited in a bank in the name of an individual had been so deposited as money belonging to a partnership of which he was a partner, it was held that these averments could be proved *prout de jure*[76]; the opinions proceeded on the view that the statute did not apply to partnership. Where it was alleged that a life insurance policy taken in the name of an individual was the property of two trading companies of which he was a partner it was again held that the Act had no application and that *prout de jure* proof was competent.[77]

However, in *Laird & Co.* v. *Laird and Rutherfurd*[78] the exception was rejected. Letters-patent were taken out in the name of two persons one of

---

[72] *Per* Lord Salvesen, 1918 S.C. 391 at p. 399; see also *Cairns* v. *Davidson*, 1913 S.C. 1054, 1058, *per* Lord Salvesen.
[73] McLaren, II, 1062; Menzies, 33; *Galloway* v. *Galloway*, 1929 S.C. 160, 167, *per* L.J.-C. Alness.
[74] *Annotations on Stair's Institutions*, 74.
[75] (1714) Mor. 16197.
[76] *The General Assembly of the General Baptist Churches* v. *Taylor* (1841) 3 D. 1030.
[77] *Forrester* v. *Robson's Trs.* (1875) 2 R. 755. Lord Gifford expressed doubt on this point and preferred to rest his judgment on the ground that the evidence satisfied the Act.
[78] (1884) 12 R. 294.

whom was a partner of a firm. The action at the instance of the firm was for declarator that the patent was held for behoof of the firm, the names of the two persons having been inserted as patentees only for the purpose of compliance with the Patent Acts. It was held that the 1696 Act applied and that proof was restricted to the writ or oath of the defenders. The Lord Ordinary distinguished *The General Assembly of the General Baptist Churches* and *Forrester* on the ground that in them there was no averment of property held jointly by a partner and an individual who was not a partner. Lord President Inglis distinguished them on the ground that " there was no deed of trust in any of them, there was nothing of the nature of a right granted in favour of an alleged trustee in absolute terms such as we find here." This is true of *The General Assembly of the General Baptist Churches* but it is difficult to see how it applies to *Forrester*. Be that as it may, the balance of authority is in favour of *Laird* and rejects the exception—" a trust does not cease to be a trust because the beneficiary is a firm and the trustee a partner." [79] There would, however, seem to be some ground for reconsideration of the position in the light of section 20 of the Partnership Act 1890.[80]

It is necessary to add that the rejection of the exception does not affect the rule that where a partner, contrary to instructions, takes the title to property in his own name the question is one of mandate and can be expiscated by proof *prout de jure*.[81]

Where the title to heritage stood in the name of a partner before the formation of the partnership, it is competent to prove by parole evidence that the heritage was brought into the partnership estate.[82]

Husband and wife

In *Anderson* v. *Anderson's Tr.*[83] Lord Low held that the Act had no application in a question between husband and wife because it could not apply to a situation in which the truster is a person under a legal disability and the trustee already stands in a fiduciary relation to the truster. In *Galloway* v. *Galloway*,[84] it was argued that *Anderson* was no longer of authority in view of the Married Women's Property (Scotland) Act 1920, which abolished the curatory of a husband and removed the legal disability of a married woman. Two of the judges expressly rejected this contention partly at least on the ground that a wife still could not sue her husband for *quasi*-delict or for debt. The case was, however, decided on other grounds and Outer House judges, fortified by a decision to the

---

[79] Gloag, *Contract*, 388; see also *Adam* v. *Adam*, 1962 S.L.T. 332; J. Bennett Miller, *The Law of Partnership in Scotland*, 382–387. *Cf.* Menzies, 33; Gloag & Irvine, *Rights in Security*, 147.

[80] *Adam* v. *Adam, supra.*

[81] *Horne* v. *Morrison* (1877) 4 R. 977; *Laird & Co.* v. *Laird and Rutherfurd, supra,* at p. 298, *per* Lord Shand.

[82] *Munro* v. *Stein*, 1961 S.C. 362; see also *Hinkelbein* v. *Craig* (1905) 13 S.L.T. 84.

[83] (1898) 6 S.L.T. 204.

[84] 1929 S.C. 160.

effect that a wife can contract with her husband,[85] have recently felt free to hold that the 1696 Act does apply in questions between husband and wife.[86]

Declaration

The " declaration " or " back-bond " required by the Act need not be a formal deed.[87] It need not be probative and it is sufficient that it bears the defender's signature, the authenticity thereof being admitted or proved.[88] Indeed, although the Act requires that the declaration or back-bond is to be " lawfully subscribed," a subscription is not necessary in every case and entries in the books of the alleged trustee have been accepted.[89] In some cases the title of the alleged trustee has been treated as his writ establishing the trust but it is difficult to see why the Act applied at all in such cases as the title was not *ex facie* absolute.[90] The trust can be proved by the tenor of several writs taken together.[91] A letter from the pursuer to the alleged trustee found in the latter's repositories and proved to have been sent at the date of an entry in the books of the alleged trustee, was, together with the book entry, held to be equivalent to the writ of the alleged trustee and sufficient to establish the trust.[92] The date and delivery of the letter were proved by parole evidence. The writ of the alleged trustee's agent may be sufficient but it seems that the agent's authority must be proved by writ.[93]

The document need not contain an express admission of the existence of a trust. It is sufficient if a trust can be inferred from the terms of the document.[94] It has been said that the writings must be " distinct, decided, and unequivocal, and must go directly to the matter of trust " and be " such as not to be capable of being explained in any other way than as an admission that the party holds in trust." [95] This is perhaps to put the test too strictly and the better formulation is Dickson's—a writing " which fairly implies a trust." [96]

If the terms of the writ are ambiguous or exiguous, parole evidence (including evidence as to the circumstances in which it was executed and delivered) may be admitted to explain it [97] but if the document is unam-

---

[85] *Horsburgh* v. *Horsburgh*, 1949 S.C. 227; the Law Reform (Husband and Wife) Act 1962, s. 2 has allowed a wife to sue her husband in respect of delict.

[86] *Inglis* v. *Smyth's Executrix*, 1959 S.L.T.(Notes) 78; *Weissenbruch* v. *Weissenbruch*, 1961 S.C. 340; *Adam* v. *Adam*, 1962 S.L.T. 332.

[87] *McFarlane* v. *Fisher* (1837) 15 S. 978. But it was held in *Kirkwood* v. *Patrick* (1847) 9 D. 1361, that a vitiated deed is not sufficient evidence.

[88] *Taylor* v. *Crawford* (1833) 12 S. 39; *cf. Watson* v. *Forrester* (1708) Mor. 12755.

[89] *Knox* v. *Martin* (1850) 12 D. 719; *Seth* v. *Hain* (1855) 17 D. 1117; *Thomson* v. *Lindsay* (1873) 1 R. 65; see however the opinion of Lord Deas in *Walker* v. *Buchanan, Kennedy & Co.* (1857) 20 D. 259, 269.

[90] *Livingstone* v. *Allan* (1900) 3 F. 233; *National Bank of Scotland* v. *Mackie's Trs.* (1905) 13 S.L.T. 383; 43 S.L.R. 13.

[91] *Seth* v. *Hain, supra; Thomson* v. *Lindsay, supra.*

[92] *Seth* v. *Hain, supra.* See also *Kirkpatrick* v. *Bell* (1864) 36 Sc.Jur. 706.

[93] *Marshall* v. *Lyell* (1859) 21 D. 514.

[94] *Ramsay* v. *Corporation of Butchers in Perth* (1748) Mor. 12757; *Pant Mawr Quarry Co.* v. *Fleming* (1883) 10 R. 457; see Hume, *Lect.*, II, 146.

[95] *Seth* v. *Hain, supra,* at p. 1124, *per* L.J.-C. Hope, p. 1125, *per* Lord Wood.

[96] *Evidence*, s. 583.

[97] *Seth* v. *Hain, supra; Evans* v. *Craig* (1871) 9 M. 801.

biguous or speaks for itself parole evidence is not admissible to qualify or explain it.[98] It is competent to lead parole proof to identify the property to which the document refers [99]; and if the pursuer admits that the writ on which he founds does not correctly set forth the transaction in some respect germane to the issue in the case, parole proof is admissible to ascertain the true agreement.[1]

It has been suggested that the writ must have been in some way delivered to the truster.[2]

It was held in a question between the creditors of the alleged trustee and the creditors of the alleged truster that a document which would have established the trust in a question between the alleged truster and the alleged trustee could be ignored because its terms were not completely clear and it had been granted by the alleged trustee within five days of his bankruptcy to a conjunct and confident person.[3]

It seems that it is not necessary to prove the constitution of a trust at the date of the original conveyance; proof of a trust subsequently emerging is sufficient.[4]

The discharge of a trust obligation can be proved only by writ or oath.[5] Once it has been established that an *ex facie* absolute title was truly granted in security the onus is on the grantee to prove that it was subsequently converted into an absolute title.[6] Where the defender admitted on record that he had received an *ex facie* absolute conveyance of heritage in security of advances made at the time of the conveyance and of future advances, it was held that the advances made after the date of the conveyance must be proved by evidence other than his own oath.[7]

It is competent for the alleged truster to prove by parole evidence that a back-bond was granted and subsequently lost or stolen or fraudulently destroyed.[8] The mere fact that both parties agree that a back-bond existed, but differ as to its contents, does not admit parole proof.[9]

It is incompetent to refer to the trustee's oath after the date of his sequestration.[10]

Where there are several alleged trustees the writ or oath of one does not affect the rights of the others.[11]

It was opined that where a letter by the granter of an *ex facie* absolute disposition stated that the deed was signed only on the faith of a back-bond being prepared without delay and was transmitted to the grantee with the

[98] *Pickard* v. *Pickard*, 1963 S.L.T. 56.
[99] *Pickard* v. *Pickard, supra.*
[1] *Grant's Trs.* v. *Morison* (1875) 2 R. 377; *Pickard* v. *Pickard, supra.*
[2] *Evans* v. *Craig, supra,* at p. 804, *per* Lord Benholme; see also the dissenting opinion of Lord Deas in *Walker* v. *Buchanan, Kennedy & Co.* (1857) 20 D. 259, 269.
[3] *Wallace* v. *Sharp* (1885) 12 R. 687.
[4] *McFarlane* v. *Fisher, supra.*
[5] *Keanie* v. *Keanie*, 1940 S.C. 549.
[6] *Walker* v. *Buchanan, Kennedy & Co., supra.*
[7] *Murray* v. *Wright* (1870) 8 M. 722.
[8] *Kennoway* v. *Ainsley* (1752) Mor. 12438; *Chalmers* v. *Chalmers* (1845) 7 D. 865.
[9] *Chalmers* v. *Chalmers, supra.*
[10] *Mein* v. *Towers* (1829) 7 S. 902.
[11] Menzies, 32.

disposition, the case must be treated as if the back-bond had been granted.[12] It was, however, a " very special case."

The writ of the trustee's executor may suffice.[13] Where the action is against the assignees of the alleged trustee the writ required is that of the trustee.[14]

Trust purposes

Once the existence of the trust has been admitted or proved by writ or oath, the terms and purposes of the trust can be proved by parole evidence.[15]

[12] *Robertson* v. *Duff* (1840) 2 D. 279, 294, *per* Lord Fullerton.
[13] *Montgomery*, Feb. 7, 1811, F.C.
[14] *Govan New-Bowling Club* v. *Geddes* (1898) 25 R. 485, 492, *per* Lord McLaren; Menzies, 32.
[15] *Muir* v. *Gemmell* (1805) Hume 342; *Livingstone* v. *Allan* (1900) 3 F. 233; *National Bank of Scotland* v. *Mackie's Trs.* (1905) 13 S.L.T. 383.

CHAPTER 5

TRUSTS ARISING FROM OPERATION OF LAW

THE FIDUCIARY FEE

IN *Frog's Creditors* v. *His Children*,[1] a decision which was " given with regret, and has been regretted frequently since," [2] it was established that where there is a destination to a person in liferent and to the heirs of his body or children born or to be born, in fee, no heir or child being named, the fee is in the person named and not in his heirs or children; the latter have only a *spes successionis*. This rule, which was later described as an " extraordinary construction " [3] and " the triumph of a legal subtlety over the intention of the maker of the deed," [4] was sometimes said to be a consequence of the maxim *dominium non potest esse in pendente* [5]—" a feudal maxim of Scottish law which forbids the fee to float on poised wing till it finds fitting settlement, and which demands that from the first the fee shall have a local habitation as well as a name " [6]—but Lord Braxfield observed

" that by many decisions, it had been found that the fee was really in the parents, though the destination bore only in liferent to them, and in fee to their children; but that this was not *ex necessitate*, as had sometimes been supposed, lest the fee should be *in pendente*. It was upon the presumed will of the granter, who only meant a *spes successionis* to be in the children." [7]

The doctrine was applied even where all the children to whom the fee was destined were in existence at the date of the disposition [8] and even where there was an ulterior destination [9] but it did not operate where the destination was to the children *nominatim* in fee [10] or to those already in existence *nominatim* and to the other children to be born in fee.[11] Nor did it operate where the property was conveyed to trustees to be held for the parent in liferent and the children *nascituri* in fee.[12]

Doubts subsequently arose as to the necessity and justice of the result

---

[1] (1735) Mor. 4262.
[2] *Per* Lord Ardmillan, *Cumstie* v. *Cumstie's Trs.* (1876) 3 R. 921, 925.
[3] Hume, *Lect.*, IV, 340.
[4] *Per* Lord Ardmillan, *Cumstie* v. *Cumstie's Trs.*, *supra*, at p. 927.
[5] See Stair, III, 5, 50; Dirleton, *Doubts*, Tit. " Fiar "; Ersk. III, 8, 35.
[6] *Per* Lord Ardmillan, *loc. cit.* The theme is developed by L.J.-C. Alness in *Cripps's Trs.* v. *Cripps*, 1926 S.C. 188, 212.
[7] *Gerran* v. *Alexander* (1781) Mor. 4402. See also Ivory's Note in his edition of Erskine, III, 8, 36; Montgomerie Bell, *Lectures*, p. 841.
[8] *Cuthbertson* v. *Thomson* (1781) Mor. 4279.
[9] *Robertson* v. *Duke of Athole*, (1806) Mor. " Fiar, Absolute, Limited " App. No. 1; *Mackintosh* v. *Gordon* (1845) 4 Bell's App. Cas. 105.
[10] *McIntosh* v. *McIntosh*, January 28, 1812, F.C.
[11] *Dykes* v. *Boyd*, June 3, 1813, F.C.
[12] *Seton* v. *Seton's Creditors* (1793) Mor. 4219.

reached in *Frog's Creditors*. " Some remedy was required to sustain intention, to disarm subtlety and to vindicate the essential equity of the law. This remedy was found. A new subtlety was evoked to redress the balance disturbed by the regretted enforcement of the former subtlety." [13] In *Newlands* v. *Newlands' Creditors* [14] the House of Lords affirmed that where the word " liferent " was qualified by the taxative word " *allenarly* " (*pro eius vitali redditu solummodo*) the parent's beneficial right was restricted to a liferent. The " cabalistic " [15] word *allenarly*, a word of " mysterious power and virtue," [16] selected because of " its simplicity and its power," [17] " got the better of all." [16] Although there had been no express decision on the point, the effect of the word is mentioned in Stair's Decisions [18] and had been relied upon by conveyancers.[19] The difficulty of the fee *in pendente* was resolved by the doctrine of the fiduciary fee, that is to say, the concept that a constructive temporary fee was vested in the parent in trust for the children. There is only a " bare trust " created in the liferenter.[20]

> " If the word *allenarly* is added after the words *in liferent for his liferent use*, then a mere liferent takes place in regard to the first disponee, and the *fee* is to be, I cannot tell, according to the argument, distinctly where. It is by implication a fee in the first taker, which gives him some species of interest, coupled with some species of trust for his children, when they come into existence." [21]

It was said in argument that fiduciary fees were common in the laws of Rome and England and that " they are often resorted to in our practice."

> " When I first came to the bar, a disposition to one in liferent for his liferent *use allenarly*, was universally understood to vest merely a liferent, with a fiduciary fee in the liferenter, in compliance with the rule, that a fee cannot be *in pendente*; and it would be most unjust to alter this now, for there are a thousand estates in this country settled in this way, in perfect confidence in this rule, which, had there been a doubt upon the subject, would have been settled on trustees." [22]

The subsequent history [23] of the narrow technical distinction created by *Frog's Creditors* and *Newlands* does not require to be rehearsed because,

---

13 *Per* Lord Ardmillan, *Cumstie* v. *Cumstie's Trs., supra*, at p. 927.
14 (1794) Mor. 4289; 4 Pat.App. 43.
15 *Per* Lord Deas, *Cumstie, supra*, at p. 935.
16 Hume, *Lect.*, IV, 345.
17 *Per* Lord Ardmillan, *Cumstie, supra*, at p. 925.
18 *Thomsons* v. *Lawsons* (1681) 2 Stair Dec. 854, noticed by Lord Chancellor Loughborough in *Newlands* at 4 Pat. App. 54.
19 Hume, *loc. cit.*
20 *Harvey* v. *Donald*, May 26, 1815, F.C.
21 *Per* Lord Loughborough L.C. in *Newlands, supra*, at p. 53.
22 *Per* L.J.-C. Macqueen, 4 Pat. App. 51. There are references to the fiduciary fee in *Lillie* v. *Riddell* (1741) Mor. 4267 and *Mure* v. *Mure* (1786) Mor. 4288 and to " allenarly " in *Crs. of Pringle* v. *Erskine* (1714) Mor. 4261.
23 The rule in *Frog's Creditors* was finally affirmed by the House of Lords in *Ralston* v. *Hamilton (Ferguson's Trs.* v. *Hamilton)* (1862) 4 Macq. 397. Decisions on the distinction are: *Watherstone* v. *Rentons*, 25 Nov. 1801, F.C; *Robertson* v. *Duke of Athole*, 20 Nov. 1806, F.C; *Lindsay* v. *Dott*, 9 Dec. 1807, F.C; *Maxwell* v. *Gracie* (1822) 1 S. 509; *Dundas* v.

after numerous judicial criticisms,[24] section 8 (1) of the Trusts (Scotland)
Act, 1921, provided that

" Where in any deed, whether inter vivos or mortis causa, heritable or
moveable property is conveyed to any person in liferent, and in fee to
persons who, when such conveyance comes into operation, are unborn
or incapable of ascertainment, the person to whom the property is
conveyed in liferent shall not be deemed to be beneficially entitled to
the property in fee by reason only that the liferent is not expressed in
the deed to be a liferent allenarly; and all such conveyances as aforesaid shall, unless a contrary intention appears in the deed, take effect
in the same manner and in all respects as if the liferent were declared
to be a liferent allenarly; provided always that this subsection shall not
apply to any conveyance which has come into operation before the
passing of this Act. For the purposes of this subsection, the date at
which any conveyance in liferent and fee as aforesaid comes into
operation shall be deemed to be the date at which the person to whom
the liferent is conveyed first becomes entitled to receive the rents or
income of the property." [25]

Sheriff Dobie [26] has pointed out two defects in the subsection. First,
it applies only to a direct conveyance or bequest and not to a will directing
trustees to convey property in liferent and fee. This point is not important
because the subsection will apply to the conveyance when it is granted.
Secondly, the subsection does not apply where the fiars are unnamed but
capable of ascertainment—for example, where the fee is destined to the
children of a woman who, at the date the liferent opens, has children but is
past the age of child-bearing; if the liferent is in unqualified terms, *Frog*
will still apply.

Scope of the doctrine

In *Newlands* the fee was destined " to the heirs lawfully to be procreated of his body in fee." The doctrine was subsequently applied to

Lord Dundas (1823) 2 S. 145; *Kennedy* v. *Allan* (1825) 3 S. 554; *Mein* v. *Taylor* (1827) 5 S.
779; 4 W. & S. 22; *Williamson* v. *Cochran* (1828) 6 S. 1035; *Scott* v. *Price* (1837) 15 S. 916;
Mackellar v. *Marquis* (1840) 3 D. 172; *Macintosh* v. *Gordon* (1845) 4 Bell's App.Cas. 105;
Ramsay v. *Beveridge* (1854) 16 D. 764; *Hutton's Trs.* v. *Hutton* (1847) 9 D. 639; *Barstow* v.
Stewart (1858) 20 D. 612; *Ferguson's Trs.* v. *Hamilton* (1862) 24 D.(H.L.) 8; 4 Macq. 397;
Ranken (1870) 8 M. 878; *Grant* v. *Murray* (1872) 44 Sc. Jur. 550; *Henderson's Trs.* v.
Henderson (1876) 3 R. 320; *Cumstie* v. *Cumstie's Trs.* (1876) 3 R. 921; *Dawson* (1876) 4 R.
597; *Beveridge* v. *Beveridge's Trs.* (1878) 5 R. 1116; *Mitchell's Trs.* v. *Smith* (1880) 7 R. 1086;
Studd v. *Cook* (1883) 10 R.(H.L.) 53; *Livingstone* v. *Waddell's Trs.* (1899) 1 F. 831; *McCly-
mont's Exors.* v. *Osborne* (1895) 22 R. 411; *Fraser* (1901) 8 S.L.T. 466; *Gifford's Trs.* v.
Gifford (1903) 5 F. 723; *Millar* v. *Marquess of Lansdowne*, 1910 S.C. 618; *Brash's Trs.* v.
Phillipson, 1916 S.C. 271; *Lockhart's Trs.* v. *Lockhart*, 1921 S.C. 761; *Mearns* v. *Charles*,
1926 S.L.T. 118.

[24] See, for example, *Cumstie* v. *Cumstie's Trs.* (1876) 3 R. 921, 942, *per* L.P. Inglis; *Gifford's
Trs.* v. *Gifford* (1903) 5 F. 723, 731, *per* Lord McLaren, 734, *per* Lord Stormonth Darling.
See also J. A. Clyde " Practice and Procedure in the Court of Session " (1906) 18
J.R. 319, 321.

[25] The subsection does not apply to a conveyance such that the date on which the person to
whom the liferent is conveyed first became entitled to receive the rents or income of the
property fell before August 19, 1921 (See *Dalrymple's Trs.* v. *Watson's Trs.*, 1932 S.L.T.
480).   [26] *Liferent and Fee*, 34.

destinations " to the children procreated or to be procreated," [27] and to the heirs of the marriage.[28] It has also been applied when the destination was to " heirs whomsoever " notwithstanding that they are not *personae praedilectae*.[29] Where there was a gift in " liferent allenarly " and to the " heirs and assignees " of the liferenters in fee, the court remarked on the *prima facie* repugnancy but did not find it necessary to decide whether or not the liferenters were fiduciary fiars.[30]

Where the destination is to the parent for his liferent use allenarly and to his children *nominatim* and any future children he might have and the survivors or survivor of them, the parent takes a fiduciary fee for the children.[31] But if there is no survivorship provision affecting the children named, there is no fiduciary fee and the fee vests in the children named subject to the claims of children subsequently born.[32]

In order to be fiduciary fiar, the liferenter need not be in actual possession of the liferent; it is sufficient if he is a liferenter *in posse*.[33] Where the conveyance is to A in liferent and to B and A's children *nascituri* in fee, the fee is in B *a morte testatoris* and not in A. In the case cited there seems to have been a difference of opinion as to whether B was a fiduciary fiar or whether he had a full right of fee restrictable to a partial right in the event of children coming into existence.[34]

Lord President Inglis thought that there are theoretical difficulties in the situation in which a number of persons are joint fiduciary fiars for the children of all of them as a class.[35] Accordingly, when there was a destination to A and B

" equally between them, and failing either of them without lawful issue, to the survivor of them, the lawful issue of the predeceasor always coming in place of their parent, in liferent, and for their liferent use allenarly, and to their lawful children equally among them share and share alike in fee,"

the effect was held to be that A and B became *pro indiviso* liferenters each to the extent of one-half and were fiduciary fiars in the same proportions, each holding a fiduciary fee for his own children exclusively.[36]

It must be said that Lord McLaren's exposition in *Tristram* [36] of the supposed difficulty of both fiars holding for the children of both is not

[27] *Watherstone* v. *Rentons* (1801) Mor. 4297.
[28] *Maule* (1876) 3 R. 831.
[29] *Cumstie* v. *Cumstie's Trs.* (1876) 3 R. 921.
[30] *Pottie* (1902) 4 F. 876.
[31] *Snell* v. *White* (1872) 10 M. 745.
[32] *Dykes* v. *Boyd*, June 3, 1813 F.C.; *McGowan* v. *Robb* (1862) 1 M. 141 (the Lord Ordinary's judgment was affirmed on a narrower ground); *Martin's Trs.* v. *Milliken* (1864) 3 M. 326, 333, *per* Lord Cowan.
[33] *Cripps's Trs.* v. *Cripps*, 1926 S.C. 188. See also *Snell* v. *White, supra.* Professor Candlish Henderson (*Vesting*, 396) thought that the theory underlying this decision involved a considerable extension of the doctrine and appeared to be not altogether consistent with other decisions.
[34] *Martin's Trs.* v. *Milliken* (1864) 3 M. 326.
[35] *Allen* v. *Flint* (1886) 13 R. 975, 978.
[36] *Tristram* v. *McHaffies* (1894) 22 R. 121.

altogether clear. As Lord Kinnear pointed out,[37] if each was during the joint lives fiduciary fiar as to one-half then on the death of one without issue the survivor could have a liferent and fiduciary fee of the whole. He thought that the theoretical difficulty to which Lord President Inglis had adverted in *Allen* v. *Flint* [35] arose from the joint character of the fiduciary fee and not from the fact that a fiar was holding for persons other than his own children.

Another difficulty has arisen where there are several successive liferents in the destination. On the one hand, it has been said that a situation in which one liferenter was a fiduciary fiar not only for her own children but for a series of liferenters and fiars would be " an entire novelty in the law of Scotland " and not admissible.[38] On the other hand, there is a view that the fiduciary fee is vested in the first of a series of liferenters. This principle was applied by Lord Skerrington in the Outer House in *Campbell* v. *Duncan*.[39] The disposition was to A and B in liferent allenarly and to the heirs of the body of B whom failing to the heirs of the body of A, and there was a declaration that during her lifetime A should enjoy the liferent to the exclusion of B. It was held that A was the sole fiduciary fiar during her lifetime. In the later case of *Cripps's Trs*.[40] in which a liferenter *in posse* was held to be fiduciary fiar, the prior liferent was subject to certain conditions, there was no destination to the children or heirs of the prior liferentrix, and, in any event, the question of a fiduciary fee in the prior liferentrix was not argued.[41]

In both *Campbell* v. *Duncan* and *Cripps's Trs*., the result was that a fiduciary fee was held for persons other than the children or heirs of the fiar. There are earlier *dicta* in which the propriety of this result was questioned. In *Colvile's Trs*. v. *Marindin*, Lord President Dunedin said [42] : " I have never yet heard—and I do not think we ought to extend the doctrine—of the doctrine of a fiduciary fee for somebody who is neither a child nor an heir in any sense of the person in whom the fiduciary fee is created."

In *Devlin* v. *Lowrie*,[43] the destination was to two sisters " in conjunct fee and liferent for their alimentary liferent use allenarly, and the heirs of the survivor " and it was held that the survivor held as fiduciary fiar for her own heirs. It was pointed out in the course of the argument that such a result would imply that during the joint lifetimes of the sisters the two conjunct fiars would hold for the heirs of whichever one survived and that this would be contrary to the *dicta* cited. Lord President Clyde responded to this argument, firstly, by pointing to Lord President Dunedin's words

---

[37] p. 130.
[38] *Per* Lord Adam, *Logan's Trs*. v. *Ellis* (1890) 17 R. 425, 432.
[39] 1913, 1 S.L.T. 260. The principle receives support from *Allardice* v. *Allardice* (1795) 3 Ross's L.C. 655.
[40] *Supra*.
[41] *Per* Lord Ormidale, at p. 206.
[42] 1908 S.C. 911, 919; there are also the dicta relating to joint fiars cited at p. 65 *supra*. *Cf.* *Edmond* v. *Lord Provost of Aberdeen* (1898) 1 F. 154, 159, *per* Lord Low.
[43] 1922 S.C. 255.

" heir *in any sense* of the person in whom the fiduciary fee is created "
and, secondly, by the argument that as the fiduciary fee undoubtedly
existed in the survivor it could not be " called out of the blue " on the
first sister's death and there must therefore have been a fiduciary fee in both
sisters conjunctly while they survived. In *Cripps's Trs.*, Lord Ormidale
expressed the view that the fiduciary fiar could hold not only for his own
children but also for the whole substituted heirs and that this result did not
conflict with Lord Dunedin's observation. The position therefore seems
to be that while the fiduciary fiar cannot hold *only* for persons other than
his own children or heirs he can hold for other persons if he is also holding
for his own children or heirs.[44] In a recent case,[45] Lord Kilbrandon said
that the result of applying *Colvile's Trs.* would have been " discreditable to
the law of Scotland " and that if he had been required to deal with the
question he would have reported the case to the Inner House so that it
could be debated whether, in consequence of the reforms in the doctrine of
fiduciary fee introduced by the 1921 Act, it was still inexpedient that the
doctrine be extended to apply to cases where the unascertained fiars are
other than children, or heirs in any sense, of the liferenter.

The application of section 8 of the 1921 Act is not restricted by reference
to any particular relationship between the liferenter and the fiars. Sheriff
Dobie,[46] however, considers that the question of the classes of beneficiary
for which a fiduciary fee can be held may be an important one in view of
section 8. He argues that if the effect of the section is to make persons,
who would formerly have been fiars, fiduciary fiars in cases where the
beneficial fiars are not of a class for whom a fiduciary fee can be held, the
fee will be undisposed of as it was in *Colvile's Trs.*[47] because the " later
provisions of the section seem limited to supplying machinery for the
administering of an existing and operative fiduciary fee." With respect, it
must be said that this is not so because the application under subsection
(2) [48] may be made by *inter alios* the liferenter " whether or not he would,
according to the existing law, be deemed to be fiduciary fiar " and the
trustee or judicial factor appointed under the subsection is to hold the
property in place of " the liferenter or fiduciary fiar." [49]

Ending of the fiduciary fee

It has been said that " the fiduciary fee is created by the necessity of the
law, and endures only so long as the necessity." [50] Therefore, where the
destination was to the heir of the marriage, the fiduciary fee terminated on
the dissolution of the marriage as the heir was then ascertained.[51] Similarly, where the destination is to the heir-male of the body of X, the

---

[44] See also the opinion of Lord Kinnear in *Tristram* v. *McHaffies* (1894) 22 R. 121, 130.
[45] *Napier* v. *Napiers*, 1963 S.L.T. 143.
[46] *Op. cit.*, pp. 40–41.
[47] 1908 S.C. 911.
[48] See p. 69 *infra*.
[49] See *Napier* v. *Napiers*, 1963 S.L.T. 143, discussed at p. 70 *infra*.
[50] *Per* L.P. Inglis, *Maule* (1876) 3 R. 831.
[51] *Ibid*.

fiduciary fee subsists until X's death because only then can the heir be ascertained.[52] In cases where the destination is to children *nascituri*, it is clearly established that each child at birth acquires a vested *jus crediti* in the fee which is subject to partial defeasance on the birth of subsequent children.[53] It is thought that the fiduciary fee subsists until the fiar's death.[54]

Completion of title

The children take as disponees and not as heirs of the fiduciary fiar. It was held, therefore, that the child's right transmitted to his issue without a service.[55] On the death of the fiduciary fiar, if the fiduciary fee was not feudalised, the children formerly could complete title by service as heirs of provision in general to the fiduciary fiar.[56] The basis of this was that although there was no substantial right in the fiar which could be taken up by special service there was a nominal fee which entitled the children to a general service to the effect of having their propinquity ascertained and their characters as heirs determined. This is merely a declaratory service.[57] If the fiduciary fee was feudalised, the service was a special service. The solution now is that the trustee or factor appointed under section 8 (2) of the 1921 Act can be appointed with warrant to complete title.[58]

Powers

It has been rightly said that the precise position and powers of the fiduciary fiar are uncertain.[59] Lord Fullerton doubted whether a person could " have the powers of a trustee because he is called a fiduciary fiar " and suggested that the sole effect of the doctrine was to take the fee out of the granter of the deed.[60] The fiduciary fiar cannot alienate the trust estate without a petition to the court.[61] In a petition at common law and under section 3 of the Trusts (Scotland) Act 1867, fiduciary fiars were given power to borrow on the security of the trust estate in order to meet extraordinary expenditure and to feu portions of the estate.[62] The fiduciary

---

[52] *Ferguson* v. *Ferguson* (1875) 2 R. 627; *Black* v. *Mason* (1881) 8 R. 497. A statement which suggests a different result is attributed to Lord Braxfield in Ross's report of *Newlands* (3 Ross's L.C. 644) but the accuracy of the note was doubted by the court in *Ferguson*.

[53] *Beattie's Tr.* v. *Cooper's Trs.* (1862) 24 D. 519, 534, *per* Lord Curriehill; *Otto* v. *Weir* (1871) 9 M. 660; *Douglas* v. *Thomson* (1870) 8 M. 374; *Turner* v. *Gaw* (1894) 21 R. 563, 567, *per* Lord McLaren. Sheriff Irvine has remarked that the vesting of the beneficial fee is determined by the same principles as are applicable in determining the vesting of the fee when the estate is held in an express trust for a liferenter and for other persons in fee. (*Encyc. XV* s.v. " Vesting in Succession," 440).

[54] But see Fraser, *Husband and Wife*, 1455.

[55] *Douglas* v. *Thomson* (1870) 8 M. 374.

[56] *Dundas* v. *Dundas* (1823) 2 S. 145; *Peacock* v. *Glen* (1826) 4 S. 749; *Macdougall* (1900) 3 F. 99. See also *Maule, supra,* and T. Lindsay Clark " The Fiduciary Fee in Feudal Conveyancing " (1900) 12 J.R. 25.

[57] Burns, *Conveyancing Practice*, 4th ed., 253–256.

[58] See p. 69 *infra*.

[59] Menzies, *Lectures*, 660; Mackenzie Stuart, 41; Fraser, *Husband and Wife*, 1454.

[60] *Emslie* v. *Fraser* (1850) 12 D. 724, 730.

[61] *Ferguson* v. *Ferguson* (1875) 2 R. 627; *Devlin* v. *Lowrie*, 1922 S.C. 255.

[62] *Pottie* (1902) 4 F. 876. See also *Pettigrew's Exrs.* (1890) 28 S.L.R. 14.

fiar could discharge a bond.[63] It has been held that the fiduciary fiar is entitled to grant a bond and disposition in security over the estate in favour of himself as liferenter as a person who had paid the estate duty.[64]

The administrative difficulties were largely solved by section 8 (2) of the 1921 Act which provides:

" Where under any conveyance, whether coming into operation before or after the passing of this Act, any property is conveyed to one person in liferent and in fee to persons who, when such conveyance comes into operation, are unborn or incapable of ascertainment, it shall be competent to the court, on the application of the liferenter, whether or not he would, according to the existing law, be deemed to be fiduciary fiar, or of any person to whom the fee or any part thereof bears to be presumptively destined, or who may have an interest under such conveyance notwithstanding that such interest is prospective or contingent, or of the Accountant of Court:

(a) To grant authority to the fiduciary fiar to exercise all or such of the powers, or to do all or such of the acts, competent to a trustee at Common Law or under this Act, as to the court may seem fit:

(b) To appoint a trustee or trustees (of whom the liferenter or fiduciary fiar may be one) with all the powers of trustees at Common Law and under this Act, or a judicial factor, to hold the said property in trust in place of the liferenter or fiduciary fiar; and to authorise and ordain the fiduciary fiar to execute and deliver all such deeds as may be necessary for the completion of title to the said property by such trustee or trustees or judicial factor; or otherwise, to grant warrant to such trustee or trustees or judicial factor to complete a title to the said property in the same manner and to the same effect as under a warrant in favour of a trustee or trustees granted in terms of the section of this Act relating to the appointment of new trustees by the court, or a warrant in favour of a judicial factor granted in terms of section twenty-four of the Titles to Land Consolidation (Scotland) Act 1868, or section forty-four of the Conveyancing (Scotland) Act 1874, as the case may be. The expense of completing the title as aforesaid shall, unless the court otherwise directs, be a charge against the capital of the estate."

This provision cannot be applied to an English trust.[65] It is retrospective. As already mentioned,[66] it does not apply where the fiars are unnamed but capable of ascertainment. An application under the section

---

[63] *Moncrieff* v. *Thomson* (1846) 8 D. 548.
[64] *Stuart Menzies* (1903) 10 S.L.T. 636.
[65] *Cripps's Trs.* v. *Cripps*, 1926 S.C. 188.
[66] *Supra*, p. 64.

is competent where the fiduciary fiars hold only part of the property in a fiduciary capacity.[67] It would appear that the petition can be presented after the death of the fiduciary fiar.[67]

It seems that the liferenter or fiduciary fiar cannot be appointed sole trustee.[68] In *Napier* v. *Napiers*,[69] the subsection was applied to a destination of heritage to A in liferent with fee to B if he survive whom failing to C. It was recognised that this was not a fiduciary fee case. A power to sell the trust estate cannot competently be craved in a petition for the appointment of trustees under the subsection. Once the trustees have been appointed and have decided that the power of sale is necessary, they can present a further petition.[70] In *Webb*[67] power to sell was refused as unnecessary.

MARRIED WOMEN'S POLICIES OF ASSURANCE ACT

The Married Women's Policies of Assurance (Scotland) Act 1880,[71] s. 2, provides:

" A policy of assurance effected by any married man on his own life, and expressed upon the face of it to be for the benefit of his wife, or of his children, or of his wife and children, shall, together with all benefit thereof, be deemed a trust for the benefit of his wife for her separate use, or for the benefit of his children, or for the benefit of his wife and children; and such policy, immediately on its being so effected, shall vest in him and his legal representatives in trust for the purpose or purposes so expressed, or in any trustee nominated in the policy, or appointed by separate writing, duly intimated to the assurance office, but in trust always as aforesaid, and shall not otherwise be subject to his control, or form part of his estate, or be liable to the diligence of his creditors, or be revocable as a donation, or reducible on any ground of excess or insolvency; And the receipt of such trustee for the sums secured by the policy, or for the value thereof, in whole or in part, shall be a sufficient and effectual discharge to the assurance office; Provided always, that if it shall be proved that the policy was effected and premiums thereon paid with intent to defraud creditors, or if the person upon whose life the policy is effected shall be made bankrupt within two years from the date of such policy, it shall be competent to the creditors to claim repayment of the premiums so paid from the trustee of the policy out of the proceeds thereof."

The policy must be effected by a " married man." A policy taken out by a man two days before his marriage for the benefit of his intended wife

---

[67] *Webb*, 1934 S.N. 115.
[68] Mackenzie Stuart, 41.
[69] 1963 S.L.T. 143.
[70] *Gibson*, 1967 S.C. 161.
[71] 43 & 44 Vict. c. 26. There are other cases of trusts created by statute, *e.g.* Companies Act 1948, ss. 192, 193. See also the Mortgaging of Aircraft Order 1972 (S.I. 1972/1268) Sched. 2 para. 10; Conveyancing and Feudal Reform (Scotland) Act 1970, s. 27 (1).

was held not to fall under the Act.[72] The Act does apply to a policy effected by a widower for the benefit of his children.[73] Unlike the corresponding English legislation,[74] the statute does not provide for a married woman effecting a policy for the benefit of her husband.

The Act applies only to a policy " expressed upon the face of it to be for the benefit of his wife, or of his children, or of his wife and children." It is not competent to prove by parole evidence that the assured did not intend to effect a policy under the statute.[75] Trusts for the benefit of other persons can be engrafted on to the trust in favour of the wife and children.

There is no definition or limitation in the Act as to the form in which the benefit is to be expressed. An express reference to the Act is not necessary. It is not necessary that the wife or children should be given immediately an absolute vested interest although it is possible to do this.[76] The interest of the wife and children, whatever it may be, receives the protection of the statute and once that interest is defeated the statute ceases to apply to the policy.[77] " It is to the policy that one must go to find the wife's interest or benefit. It is the statute that gives protection, such as the common law would not confer, to the interest or benefit so created." [78]

So the Act applies even if the wife's interest is contingent upon survivance of her husband [79]; even if there is a destination-over to the husband's " heirs executors or assignees " [80]; even if, under an endowment policy, the wife's interest is contingent upon the husband's predeceasing her during the twenty years of the endowment period.[81] Where the policy was " for behoof of the widow " of the assured " in liferent allenarly, and his children or the survivors of them, whom failing his widow, whom all failing his own nearest heirs whomsoever in fee, subject to such declarations as to the terms of payment and vesting " as the assured might appoint by separate writing under his hand, the opinion was expressed that the reference to a " widow " satisfied the requirements of the statute and that the clause as to terms of vesting and payment referred only to the provision for children. As there were no children the argument that the clause reserved to the assured a control over the policy inconsistent with the terms of the statute was not considered.[82] Prima facie a reference to

[72] Coulson's Trs. v. Coulson (1901) 3 F. 1041.
[73] Kennedy's Trs. v. Sharpe (1895) 23 R. 146.
[74] Married Women's Property Act 1882, s. 11.
[75] Dickie's Trs. v. Dickie (1892) 29 S.L.R. 908.
[76] Cousins v. Sun Life Assurance Society [1933] Ch. 126; Sharp's Trs. v. Lord Advocate, 1951 S.C. 442, 461, per Lord Jamieson.
[77] Sharp's Trs. v. Lord Advocate, supra, at p. 448, per L.J.-C. Thomson.
[78] Chrystal's Tr. v. Chrystal, 1912 S.C. 1003, 1008, per Lord Johnston. " The result is that when the policy states the purpose for which the policy has been entered into, the Act creates and declares a trust "—per Lord Hanworth M.R., Cousins v. Sun Life Assurance Society, supra, at p. 133.
[79] Re Fleetwood's Policy [1926] 1 Ch. 48; Walker's Trs. v. Lord Advocate, 1954 S.C. 156, 189, per Lord Mackintosh.
[80] Schumann v. Scottish Widows' Fund Society (1886) 13 R. 678; Dickie's Trs. v. Dickie, supra; Stewart v. Hodge (1901) 8 S.L.T. 436; Sharp's Trs. v. Lord Advocate, supra.
[81] Chrystal's Trs. v. Chrystal, supra.
[82] Dickie's Trs. v. Dickie, supra.

the assured's " wife " means his wife at the time the policy is effected and
not a subsequent wife. The presumption is stronger if there is a destination-
over to his children.[83] It is not decided whether a policy taken out during
the subsistence of one marriage for the benefit of the wife or children of a
subsequent marriage would be protected by the Act. The words " for the
benefit of . . . and his children . . ." are to include a reference to children
adopted by the assured under an adoption order and illegitimate children.[84]

The terms in which the benefit is expressed were considered in two
estate duty decisions in which the question was whether the rights under
policies made under the Act were property in which " the deceased never
had an interest." [85]

In *Haldane's Trs.* v. *Lord Advocate*,[86] the policy was for the benefit of
one of the assured's children if he should be living at the assured's death
but if he were not then living, for the benefit of such of his other two
children as should then be alive " provided always that if, on the said date
[none of the three children] be living the whole benefit of the policy shall
vest absolutely in the last of such children to die. . . ." The Crown argued
that if all three children had predeceased the assured, the trust would no
longer have been for the benefit of the children, the statutory protection
would have flown off and the assured would have been able to revoke the
trust. The Court of Session rejected this contention on the ground that
once there was absolute vesting in the last survivor the statutory protection
must subsist until the date of payment to the exclusion of the truster.

In *Walker's Trs.* v. *Lord Advocate*,[87] the policy was for the benefit of

> " the assured's son A if he shall be alive on the happening of the event
> assured against but if he shall not then be alive then for the benefit in
> equal shares of the assured's son and daughter B and C if they shall
> survive the event assured against and if only one of the said son and
> daughter shall so survive then wholly for the benefit of that one and if
> the assured's said three children shall all predecease the happening of
> the event assured against then for the benefit of the estate of the last
> to die of the three said children."

The Second Division of the Court of Session held that in this case, if
the last surviving child had died intestate, the policy would then have been
held for his heirs *in mobilibus ab intestato* and that, the benefit of these
heirs not being an object which was protected by the statutory trust, the
trust would have been revocable at the will of the assured. The House of
Lords, however, reversed this decision on the ground that holding for the
estate of the deceased child is holding for the benefit of that child. Lord

---

83 *Watson and Others, Ptnrs.*, O.H., July 18, 1944. See Macgillivray, *Insurance Law*, 5th ed.,
      1961, para. 1442.
84 Adoption Act 1958, s. 14 (3); Family Law Reform Act 1969, s. 19 (1).
85 Finance Act 1894, s. 4.
86 1954 S.C. 156.
87 1954 S.C. 156; 1955 S.C.(H.L.) 74.

Reid pointed out that the heirs *ab intestato* would not take by virtue of the destination in the policy but by virtue of a derivative right through the estate of the last surviving child and the proceeds of the policy might have to be used to pay the child's creditors. It is to be noted that although the case was dealt with on the footing that the last surviving child had not taken a vested interest, Lord Reid expressed doubt as to whether this assumption was correct.

At common law, delivery of the trust property to trustees is essential to constitute an irrevocable trust. The trusts created by the 1880 Act are an exception to the general law because the policy vests in the trustees immediately on its being effected and the trust is irrevocable.[88] There is no need to deliver either the deed of trust or the trust property to the trustees.

A policy under the Act can be surrendered at any time by the trustee with the concurrence of the beneficiary.[89] This is clear on principle because if the husband becomes unwilling or unable to pay the annual premiums, which he is not under an obligation to pay and which are not secured, it may be necessary to surrender the policy in order to preserve the trust fund. In any event, the argument against the possibility of surrender was based largely on the decision of *Menzies* v. *Murray* [90] which is no longer authoritative. In the case cited,[91] Lord Shand expressed the opinion that, in terms of the particular policy, the receipt of the trustee alone would have been a sufficient discharge to the insurance company unless there was some notice of contemplated breach of trust.

In two cases [92] it was held that the husband and wife could not validly assign a policy under the Act in security to the husband's creditors. These decisions were, however, derived from *Menzies* v. *Murray* and, as that case is no longer authoritative,[93] assignation with the consent of the beneficiary is now competent.

The trustee in the husband's sequestration has no right to possession of the policy.[94]

RESULTING TRUSTS

A trust results to the truster or his heirs if estate is vested in trustees and there is no effectual disposition of the beneficial interests therein.[95] " When anyone creates a trust and expresses no trust purposes, or the purposes which he expresses fail, then there is a resulting trust for himself

---

[88] *Walker's Trs.* v. *Lord Advocate, supra,* p. 169, *per* L.J.-C. Thomson, p. 182, *per* Lord Patrick.

[89] *Schumann* v. *Scottish Widows' Fund Society* (1886) 13 R. 678.

[90] (1875) 2 R. 507. See *Beith's Trs.* v. *Beith,* 1950 S.C. 66.

[91] 13 R. 683.

[92] *Scottish Life Assurance Co. Ltd.* v. *John Donald Ltd.* (1901) 9 S.L.T. 200; *Edinburgh Life Assurance* v. *Balderston,* 1909, 2 S.L.T. 323. The proposition was conceded in *Pender* v. *Commercial Bank of Scotland Ltd.,* 1940 S.L.T. 306.

[93] *Beith's Trs.* v. *Beith,* 1950 S.C. 66.

[94] *Stewart* v. *Hodge* (1901) 8 S.L.T. 436.

[95] *McLeish's Trs.* v. *McLeish* (1841) 3 D. 914, 924, *per* Lord Moncreiff. There may be a question as to whether the beneficial interest was given to the trustees themselves—see *Anderson* v. *Smoke* (1898) 25 R. 493.

if he continues in life, or if not, for those who after his death come into his place." [96]

" The case resolves into a resulting trust; where funds are conveyed to trustees without such declaration of purposes as disposes of them in all events. The funds fall to the heirs-at-law of the testator, if he has left no other settlement, or into the residue of his estate, if he has left a general settlement." [97]

" In so far as the truster does not dispose of the estate in favour of any third party, it is in trust for the heirs-at-law." [98]

The trust is created by operation of law and the heirs take the estate free from the provisions of the trust deed. [99]

There can be a resulting trust for the testator's heirs even although he expressly or by implication disinherited them. [1] The heirs cannot be deprived of the estate unless it has been effectually and beneficially conveyed to someone else.

No purposes

A resulting trust arises where the truster has not stated any trust purposes—for example, where he has conveyed property to trustees for purposes to be declared later and has failed to make the declaration. " There being no purposes pointed out except to carry out a distribution, the result in law is, that the trust-purposes are undeclared—a case in which trustees must be held to hold for the heir-at-law of the granter." [2]

The failure may be partial—for example, an omission in the will to dispose of the residue of the estate, [3] or, in an antenuptial marriage-contract, of a liferent of part of the fund. [4] If, of course, the fund falls into residue and there is an effectual provision disposing of the residue, there is no resulting trust for the heirs. [5]

In a highly unusual case, [6] a testator conveyed the fee of certain heritage to trustees, the liferent being conferred on his son. The purposes of the trust were to be specified by writing under the testator's hand. In his repositories there was found a sealed envelope on which was indorsed an instruction that it was not to be opened until after the son's death. The son, who was the father's heir-at-law, brought an action against the trustees concluding for declarator that the envelope's contents did not affect the succession to the heritage and that he was entitled to be served

---

[96] *Edmond* v. *Lord Provost of Aberdeen* (1898) 1 F. 154, 164, *per* Lord Young.
[97] *Boyle* v. *Earl of Glasgow's Trs.* (1858) 20 D. 925, 943, *per* the consulted judges.
[98] *Balderston* v. *Fulton* (1856) 28 Sc.Jur. 664, 666, *per* Lord Curriehill.
[99] *Allan* v. *Glasgow's Trs.* (1842) 4 D. 494, 509, *per* Lord Jeffrey.
[1] *Sinclair* v. *Traill* (1840) 2 D. 694; *Cowan* v. *Cowan* (1887) 14 R. 670; *Edmond* v. *Lord Provost of Aberdeen* (1898) 1 F. 154; *McCaig* v. *University of Glasgow*, 1907 S.C. 231; *Aitken's Trs.* v. *Aitken*, 1927 S.C. 374, 380, *per* Lord Sands.
[2] *Thomas* v. *Tennent's Trs.* (1868) 7 M. 114, 119, *per* L.J.-C. Patton.
[3] *Sinclair* v. *Traill* (1840) 2 D. 694.
[4] *Higginbotham's Trs.* v. *Higginbotham* (1886) 13 R. 1016; *Coats' Trs.* v. *Inland Revenue*, 1964 S.L.T. 325; 1965 S.L.T. 145.
[5] Menzies, 672.
[6] *Edmond* v. *Lord Provost of Aberdeen* (1898) 1 F. 154.

heir to the fee. The court accepted that if there were no trust purposes the trustees must hold the heritage in a resulting trust for the pursuer but directed that the envelope should be opened to ascertain if it did contain directions relating to the heritage.

> " To sustain the pursuer's argument would be to use the expression of the truster's wishes that the envelope should not be opened as a reason for defeating the truster's clearly expressed intention that he, the pursuer, should only have a liferent of the estate, and that the fee should be devoted to purposes which may be, and in all probability are, contained in the envelope." [7]

Lord Young opined that a resulting trust should not be declared until all reasonable means have been taken to ascertain whether or not any trust purposes are still subsisting.

> " There is no limit to the reasonable suppositions which may be made as to the time which it may take to ascertain whether there are trust purposes operative and still subsisting—that is to say, which may still be executed—and I should not hesitate to give it as my opinion that if the truster declared in his deed of trust that the estate was to be held by the trustees for purposes which were not to be communicated to them—for purposes declared in a deed which he had entrusted to anyone he chose to name, and which was to be delivered over six months, or six years, or only after the death of the liferenter—we could not say, ' Here is a trust without any purposes at all.' Whether we should give effect to that desire of his, that there should be no communication of the purposes until after the expiry of a longer or shorter period, is another matter, depending upon circumstances." [8]

The envelope did contain directions to the trustees and absolvitor was therefore granted.

Failure of purposes

Except where the doctrine of *cy-près* operates in public trusts, there is a resulting trust where the stated trust purposes fail in whole or in part. A simple example is where the residuary legatee predeceases the testator.[9] A provision may fail because it is inextricable,[10] uncertain,[11] contrary to public policy, or impossible to carry out.[12]

Where a father gave funds to his two daughters with instructions to pay money to his son as they thought proper and, on the son's death, to dispose of any balance " in any way they should think proper," it was held that the direction as to the balance was void from uncertainty and the balance was held in a resulting trust for the father's heirs or residuary

---

[7] *Per* Lord Moncreiff at p. 163.
[8] p. 164.
[9] *Torrie* v. *Mundie* (1832) 10 S. 597; *Berwick's Exor.* (1885) 12 R. 565.
[10] *Mason* v. *Skinner* (1844) 16 Sc.Jur. 422.
[11] See Chaps. 6 and 13.
[12] *McCaig's Trs.* v. *Kirk Session of U.F. Church of Lismore*, 1915 S.C. 426.

legatees.[13] There is also failure where income of the trust estate can no longer be lawfully accumulated and does not fall into residue,[14] and where owing to alteration of circumstances it becomes impossible to continue to carry out the trust purposes.[15]

In public trusts, if a purpose fails, the doctrine of approximation or *cy-près* may be invoked.[16] If, however, that doctrine is not applicable— for example if there is an initial failure and no general charitable intention —then there will be a resulting trust.

Failure of machinery

Failure of the trust machinery will create a resulting trust only where the absence of the machinery makes it impossible to carry out the trust purposes, as where a discretion to select beneficiaries has been committed to trustees who die without having exercised the discretion.[17]

Trusts for creditors

If the trust is for behoof of creditors and there is a surplus after payment of debts, there is in the normal case a resulting trust for the truster. But in *Smith* v. *Cooke* [18] the deed was construed as an absolute disposal of the estate to the creditors so that the creditors had right to the surplus remaining after payment of the debts.

Public subscriptions

Difficulties have frequently arisen where a fund has been raised by public subscription for purposes which do not exhaust the fund or which can no longer be effected and, because of the absence of a general charitable intention, the doctrine of *cy-près* cannot be applied.[19] The terms of the advertisement or other invitation to subscribe can be examined to determine the purpose for which the subscriptions were intended. If there is no room for *cy-près*, the subscribers, under the doctrine of resulting trust, will be entitled to the return of their subscriptions [20] but it must be established that the purpose has failed.[21] If the subscribers cannot be traced, it

---

13 *Anderson* v. *Smoke* (1898) 25 R. 493.
14 *Lord* v. *Colvin* (1865) 3 M. 1083; *Pursell* v. *Elder* (1865) 3 M.(H.L.) 59.
15 *Hedderwick's Trs.* v. *Hedderwick's Exor.*, 1910 S.C. 333.
16 See Chap. 14. Tudor (p. 236) remarks that the doctrine of *cy-près* was settled at a time when the doctrine of resulting trusts was imperfectly understood, and that there is little doubt that, were the subject still open, the court would in the general case hold a trust to result.
17 *Robbie's J.F.* v. *Macrae* (1893) 20 R. 358; *Angus' Exrx.* v. *Batchan's Trs.*, 1949 S.C. 335. See also *New* v. *Bonaker* (1867) L.R. 4 Eq. 655.
18 [1891] A.C. 297. See (1892) 4 J.R. 100. *Cf. Marquess of Queensferry* v. *Scottish Union Assurance Co.* (1839) 1 D. 1203; (1842) 1 Bell's App. Cas. 183.
19 A general charitable intention was found in *Gibson* (1900) 2 F. 1195, *Re Welsh Hospital (Netley) Fund, Thomas* v. *Att.-Gen.* [1921] 1 Ch. 655, and *Re Hillier, Hillier* v. *Att.-Gen.* [1954] 2 All E.R. 59.
20 *Connell* v. *Ferguson* (1857) 19 D. 482, 487, *per* Lord Deas; *Bolton* v. *Ross* (1926) 42 Sh.Ct. Rep. 185. See also *Re Trusts of the Abbott Fund, Smith* v. *Abbott* [1900] 2 Ch. 326; *Re Hobourn Aero Components Ltd's Air Raid Distress Fund* [1946] Ch. 194; *Re Ulverston and District New Hospital Building Trusts* [1956] Ch. 622.
21 *Bain* v. *Black* (1849) 6 Bell's App.Cas. 317, 329, *per* Lord Cottenham L.C.; *Stewart* v. *Colclough* (1900) 8 S.L.T. 236.

appears that the only solution is for the funds to be treated as *bona vacantia*.[22] On the other hand, the subscription may have been intended as an absolute and complete divestiture of the donor's interest. Such a complete divestiture occurred where the fund was raised for the education of the children of a deceased bishop. When the children were grown up a balance remained unexpended and Kekewich J. held that there was no resulting trust for the subscribers and the balance was divisible among the children.[23] If there is a resulting trust for subscribers, the rule in *Clayton's Case* does not apply; the balance is paid to all the subscribers rateably in proportion to their subscriptions and not only to those who subscribed after the date from which the balance accumulated.[24] The fact that the identity of some donors is unascertainable does not affect the existence of the resulting trust.[25]

A related question arises as to the funds contributed by members of a society when the purposes of the society can no longer be carried out. If the society's rules deal with the disposal of the funds they will be given effect.[26] If there are no relevant rules, there may be a resulting trust for the existing members.[27] But it may be held that the members contributed in return for contractual benefits and have no further claim, in which event the funds fall to the Crown as *bona vacantia*.[28] It is, of course, important to distinguish between funds held in trust for the general purposes of the society and funds held in trust for a particular purpose.[29]

When a society has received subscriptions from the public to further public purposes which can no longer be carried out the subscribers are not in the normal case entitled to return of their subscriptions.[30] The subscriptions are gifts under conditions and each subscription does not constitute a separate trust.

It cannot be pretended that the law of Scotland on this whole matter is in a satisfactory state and legislation similar to the Charities Act 1960, s. 14, would be helpful.

CONSTRUCTIVE TRUST

A constructive trust is one created, not by a transaction between the truster and the trustee, but by circumstances. " It is undoubtedly clear

---

22 *Bain* v. *Black, supra*; *Mitchell* v. *Burness* (1878) 5 R. 954, 959, *per* Lord Deas; Menzies, 409.
23 *Re Andrew's Trusts, Carter* v. *Andrew* [1905] 2 Ch. 48.
24 *Re British Red Cross Balkan Fund, British Red Cross Society* v. *Johnson* [1914] 2 Ch. 419.
25 *Re Gillingham Disaster Fund* [1958] Ch. 300.
26 *Gardner* v. *McLintock* (1904) 11 S.L.T. 654; *Leven Penny Savings Bank*, 1948 S.C. 147.
27 *Re Printers and Transferrers Amalgamated Trades Protection Society* [1899] 2 Ch. 184; *Re Customs and Excise Officers' Mutual Guarantee Fund, Robson* v. *Att.-Gen.* [1917] 2 Ch. 18. See also *Wood* (1896) 3 S.L.T. 277.
28 *Cunnack* v. *Edwards* [1896] 2 Ch. 679; *Braithwaite* v. *Att.-Gen.* [1909] 1 Ch. 510; *Re West Sussex Constabulary's Widows, Children and Benevolent* (1930) *Fund Trusts* [1971] Ch. 1.
29 *Bolton* v. *Ross, supra.*
30 *Trs. of Falkirk Certified Industrial School* v. *Ferguson Bequest Fund* (1899) 1 F. 1175; *Anderson's Trs.* v. *Scott*, 1914 S.C. 942, 953; *Moffat* v. *Kirk Session of Canonbie*, 1936 S.C. 209.

that no man can be trustee for another, but by contract; but it is equally clear, that under circumstances, a man may be liable to all the consequences in his own person which a trustee would become liable to by contract." [31]

The situations in which a constructive trust arises fall into two main categories [32]:

(i) Where a person in a fiduciary position gains an advantage by virtue of that position;

(ii) where a person who is a stranger to an existing trust is to his knowledge in possession of property belonging to the trust.

Certain relationships may create a fiduciary duty and the person on whom the duty is imposed has sometimes been called a constructive trustee.

(i) Trustees

The first category arises " where a person clothed with a fiduciary character gains some profit or advantage by availing himself of his position as trustee." [33] This is an aspect of the principle that a trustee must not act as *auctor in rem suam* and is more fully treated under that heading. [34]

The following examples relate to trustees:

(a) where the trustee being as trustee the owner of property acquires a benefit as such owner—

" It is one of the first principles, founded upon no technical rule of law, but upon the highest principles of morality, that wherever a trustee, being ostensibly the owner of a property, acquires any benefits as owner of that property, that benefit cannot be retained by himself, but must be surrendered for the advantage of those who are beneficiaries under the trust " [35];

(b) where the trustee uses the trust funds in trade and makes a profit—

" The law will even presume that the trustee intended that the profits should go to the beneficiary, rather than presume that he intended his own aggrandisement, at the risk or expense of the beneficiary " [36];

(c) where the trustee acquires part of the trust property or a debt due by the trust estate [37]—

---

[31] *York Buildings Co.* v. *Mackenzie* (1795) 3 Pat.App. 378, 393, *per* Lord Thurlow. See the note on this case in *Aberdeen Ry.* v. *Blaikie Bros.* (1853) 1 Macq. 461, 481; Forsyth, 117.

[32] See Pettit, 35; *Selangor United Rubber* v. *Cradock* [1968] 2 All E.R. 1073; *Carl Zeiss Stiftung* v. *Herbert Smith & Co.* [1969] 2 Ch. 276. See, as to a sum payable to an executor, *Beveridge* v. *Beveridge's Exrx.*, 1938 S.C. 160.

[33] McLaren, II, 1045.

[34] See Chap. 23.

[35] *Mags. of Aberdeen* v. *University of Aberdeen* (1877) 5 R.(H.L.) 48, 51, *per* Lord Cairns L.C.

[36] *Laird* v. *Laird* (1858) 20 D. 972, 981, *per* L.P. McNeill. Approved by Lord O'Hagan in *Mags. of Aberdeen* v. *University of Aberdeen, supra,* at p. 55.

[37] *Fraser* v. *Hankey* (1847) 9 D. 415; *Aberdeen Ry.* v. *Blaikie Bros.* (1853) 1 Macq. 461; *Dunn* v. *Chambers* (1897) 25 R. 247 (curator bonis); *Taylor* v. *Hillhouse's Trs.* (1901) 9 S.L.T. 31.

" The law presumes that all the transactions of a trustee in relation to the trust, are made for behoof of the estate; and whatever may be the case where benefit arises to a trustee involuntarily, as by succession to a debt, or otherwise, the law requires every trustee to purify himself by communicating any advantages for which he transacts, or which accrue from his transactions, to his constituents." [38]

The doctrine applies to all persons in a fiduciary relationship— tutors,[39] curators,[40] agents,[41] persons acting in the character of *negotiorum gestor*,[42] trustees for creditors.[43]

(ii) Strangers

A constructive trust arises where the trust funds come into the hands of a third party, either gratuitously or with knowledge of a breach of trust. So where a solicitor who had been given trust funds to invest retained the funds in his own hands, it was held that he was in the position of a trustee and his executrix could not rely on the Statute of Limitations.[44]

" A constructive trust is one which arises when a stranger to a trust already constituted is held by the Court to be bound in good faith and in conscience by the trust in consequence of his conduct and behaviour. Such conduct and behaviour the Court construes as involving him in the duties and responsibilities of a trustee, although but for such conduct and behaviour he would be a stranger to the trust. A constructive trust is therefore, as has been said, ' a trust to be made out of circumstances.' " [45]

A banker who holds money on an account expressly kept as a trust account is a constructive trustee.[46] Where shareholders receive part of the capital of the company as a result of the *ultra vires* actings of the directors, they hold it as constructive trustees for the company.[47]

Fiduciary relationships

The expression " constructive trust " has sometimes been applied to the situation of a person who is under a fiduciary duty arising from a relationship other than an express trust.

A person who agrees to become a director of a company which is to be formed stands in a fiduciary relation to the company and cannot enter into

---

[38] *Hamilton* v. *Wright* (1839) 1 D. 668, 673, *per* Lord Cockburn (his interlocutor as Lord Ordinary was restored by the House of Lords—(1842) 1 Bell's App.Cas. 574).
[39] *Ludquhairn* v. *Haddo* (1632) Mor. 9503.
[40] *Parkhill* v. *Chalmers* (1773) 2 Pat.App. 291.
[41] *Corsan* v. *McGowan* (1736) Mor. 9504.
[42] *Spreul* v. *Crawford* (1741) Elch. " Trust " No. 1; " Adjudication " No. 30.
[43] *Hamilton* v. *Wright* (1839) 1 D. 668; (1842) 1 Bell's App.Cas. 574.
[44] *Soar* v. *Ashwell* [1893] 2 Q.B. 390. See also *Re Eyre Williams, Williams* v. *Williams* [1923] 2 Ch. 533.
[45] *Soar* v. *Ashwell, supra,* at p. 396, *per* Bowen L.J.
[46] Menzies, 814. See also *Barclays Bank Ltd.* v. *Quistclose Investments Ltd.* [1970] A.C. 567.
[47] *Russell* v. *Wakefield Water Works Co.* (1875) L.R. 20 Eq. 474; *Moxham* v. *Grant* [1899] 1 Q.B.88.

a contract for his own benefit with a person who is selling property to the company.[48]

A heritable creditor exercising a power of sale is a trustee for the debtor and for any postponed creditors. Thus if by adopting a mode of sale which is not injurious to him, the highest possible price at the least possible expense may be obtained, he may be under a duty to adopt it.[49]

In rather the same way, the creditor holding a security by *ex facie* absolute disposition, in selling the security subjects, must not act " unfairly and without due regard to the interest of his debtor." [50] McLaren attributes certain of the duties of an agent who acts for both parties in a transaction to his position as a constructive trustee.[51]

If the holder of a power of apportionment acquires the interest in the fund of one of the objects of the power he does so as a trustee for the object. He cannot acquire for himself at an undervalue a reversionary share of a fund which he has the power of increasing or diminishing at pleasure.[52]

If a partner acquires in his own name a renewal of the lease of the business premises and on the termination of the partnership carries on the same business on his own account, he is bound to communicate a share of the profits of the business to his former partner.[53]

The seller of shares in a limited company who received the price and delivered to the buyer a transfer which the directors of the company, as they were entitled to do under the articles, refused to register was held to hold the shares as a quasi-trustee for the buyer and to be bound to pay the dividends as they accrued to the buyer.[54] In a subsequent case, it was said that the seller of shares does not by the making of the contract of sale become a trustee for the buyer.[55]

The person who arrests a ship and brings it to a judicial sale has a fiduciary relationship with the owner. A purchase by him at the sale is therefore illegal and reducible at the instance of the owner.[56]

A solicitor has a fiduciary duty to his clients and in the absence of special agreement cannot appropriate to himself interest on the client's moneys which he has placed on deposit receipt.[57]

[48] *Henderson* v. *The Huntington Copper and Sulphur Company* (1877) 5 R.(H.L.) 1. See also *Edinburgh Northern Tramways Co.* v. *Mann* (1891) 18 R. 1140; *James Young & Sons Ltd.* v. *Gowans* (1902) 10 S.L.T. 85.

[49] *Beveridge* v. *Wilson* (1829) 7 S. 279, 281, cited with approval by L.P. Inglis, *Stewart* v. *Brown* (1882) 10 R. 192, 203.

[50] Bell, *Prin.* s. 912; *Park* v. *Alliance Heritable Security Co.* (1880) 7 R. 546; *Baillie* v. *Drew* (1884) 12 R. 199, 202, *per* L.J.-C. Moncreiff; *Aberdeen Trades Council* v. *Shipconstructors and Shipwrights Association*, 1949 S.C.(H.L.) 45, 65, *per* Lord Reid; *Rimmer* v. *Thomas Usher & Son Ltd.*, 1967 S.L.T. 7.

[51] Paras. 1941–1943.

[52] *McDonald* v. *McGregor* (1874) 1 R. 817.

[53] *McNiven* v. *Peffers* (1868) 7 M. 181.

[54] *Stevenson* v. *Wilson*, 1907 S.C. 445.

[55] *National Bank of Scotland Glasgow Nominees Ltd.* v. *Adamson*, 1932 S.L.T. 492.

[56] *Elias* v. *Block* (1856) 18 D. 1225.

[57] *Brown* v. *Inland Revenue*, 1964 S.C.(H.L.) 180. See now Solicitors (Scotland) Act 1965, s. 4.

CHAPTER 6

THE VALIDITY OF THE TRUST PURPOSES [1]

Perpetuities

The common law of Scotland did not discourage perpetuities.[2] " It is manifest that our law by no means views them with the *abhorrence* in which they are held both in the language of English authorities and in the decisions of the Courts of that country." [3]

" It is the tendency of our law to support trusts; and this opinion receives the strongest sanction from the common practice. Nor is the duration of such trusts restricted by law. There are numerous instances in the cases of mortifications, and of trusts for the foundation and maintenance of schools and hospitals, and for other charitable purposes, which are so constituted as to be calculated to exist to perpetuity; but though these trusts have given rise to much litigation, they have never been challenged on the ground of illegality, because they were to endure to perpetuity." [4]

A trust in which the capital is to be held by the trustees and the income is to be devoted in perpetuity to the upbringing of orphans is therefore valid.[5]

There is some authority to the effect that if a will becomes inextricable or is intended for too distant a contingency it is ineffectual at common law.[6]

It is now not possible to create an entail of land in Scotland.[7]

Uncertainty

The trust purposes must be stated with sufficient certainty. The following directions for distribution were held void from uncertainty: " by my said trustees in such manner as they may think proper " [8]; " at the discretion of my said trustees " [9]; " as my trustees deem wise and pru-

---

[1] The validity of liferent provisions is treated in Chap. 7 and that of accumulation of income in Chap. 8.

[2] *Macnair* v. *Macnair* (1791) Mor. 16210; *Strathmore* v. *Strathmore's Trs.* (1831) 5 W. & S. 170, 193, *per* Lord Brougham L.C.; *Att.-Gen.* v. *National Provincial Bank* [1924] A.C. 262, 266, *per* Viscount Haldane; *Stewart's Trs.* v. *Whitelaw*, 1926 S.C. 701, 716, *per* L.P. Clyde; *Lindsay's Exor.* v. *Forsyth*, 1940 S.C. 568; *Muir's Trs.* v. *Williams*, 1942 S.C. 5, 11, *per* L.J.-C. Cooper.

[3] *Suttie* v. *Suttie's Trs.* (1846) 18 Sc.Jur. 442, 445, *per* L.P. Boyle. .

[4] *Ibid. per* Lord Mackenzie.

[5] *Craig's Trs.* v. *Hunter*, 1956 S.L.T.(Notes) 15. See also *McLeish's Trs.* v. *McLeish* (1841) 3 D. 914; *Maxwell's Trs.* v. *Maxwell* (1877) 5 R. 248; *Trs. of Buchanan Bequest* v. *Dunnett* (1895) 22 R. 602; *Crawford's Trs.* v. *The Working Boys Home* (1901) 8 S.L.T. 371; Forsyth, 393.

[6] Bell, *Comm.* I, 37; *Mason* v. *Skinner* (1844) 16 Sc.Jur. 422; McLaren, I, 306.

[7] Entail Amendment Act 1848, s. 47; Entail (Scotland) Act 1914, s. 8.

[8] *Sutherland's Trs.* v. *Sutherland's Tr.* (1893) 20 R. 925; *Anderson* v. *Smoke* (1898) 25 R. 493; *Dodds* v. *McBain*, 1933 S.N. 16.

[9] *Davidson* v. *Christie* (1896) 3 S.L.T. 231.

dent " [10]; " as my trustees shall deem best." [11]   On the other hand, a
direction to pay to " those whom you know respects me " was upheld.[12]
It was said that the wording " those who respected me " would have been
bad because it gave no workable definition.

Surprisingly, " domestic servants, old personal friends in need, employees not otherwise included in any provision by me, or others whom my
trustees shall consider that I would wish to remember " was also sustained.[13]

Directions to trustees must be stated with sufficient certainty. " The
test is whether a trustee, approaching the matter with proper care and
properly advised, would be able to carry such an instruction out." [14] An
instruction by the testator to his trustees to " see that my house at Row is
carried on as in my lifetime " was held to be void from uncertainty.[15]

Powers of selection

Where the beneficiaries of a private trust have to be selected from a
class, the principles more fully discussed in relation to public trusts
apply.[16] Trustees must be appointed; a power to select must be expressly
or impliedly [17] conferred; the class must be defined with sufficient precision. The following descriptions are sufficiently precise: " my relations " [18] (all who could show a traceable relationship with the testator and
not merely his next-of-kin); " blood relations " [19]; " poorest friends and
relations " [20]; " poor relations " [21]; " poor friends." [22] " Poor acquaintances of mine " [23]; " relations or other persons " [24]; and " dependents " [25]
are not sufficiently precise.[26] The rules as to conjunction and disjunction
of classes apply.[27]

Doubt has been expressed as to whether a truster who has given his
trustees power to apportion a fund among beneficiaries can give the
trustees an option, instead of exercising the power themselves, to convey

---

[10] *Wilson's Trs.* v. *Wilson's Trs.* (1894) 1 S.L.T. 548.
[11] *Shaw's Trs.* (1893) 1 S.L.T. 308.
[12] *Warrender* v. *Anderson* (1893) 1 S.L.T. 304.
[13] *Smellie's Trs.* v. *Glasgow Royal Infirmary* (1905) 13 S.L.T. 450. See also *Macdonald* v.
     Atherton, 1925 S.L.T. 426 (" nearest and most needful relatives on my mother's side ").
[14] *Hood* v. *Macdonald's Tr.*, 1949 S.C. 24, 28, *per* L.J.-C. Thomson.
[15] *Hamilton's Trs.* v. *Hamilton* (1901) 4 F. 266.
[16] See Chap. 13. The dictum of Lord Lyndhurst L.C. quoted on p. 174, *infra* is applicable to
     both private and public trusts.
[17] *Dick* v. *Ferguson* (1758) Mor. 7446; *Macdonald* v. *Atherton, supra.* See *Flockhart's Trs.* v.
     Bourlet, 1934 S.N. 23.
[18] *McCormack* v. *Barber* (1861) 23 D. 398.
[19] *Murray* v. *Fleming* (1729) Mor. 4075.
[20] *Brown* (1762) Mor. 2318.
[21] *Salvesen's Trs.* v. *Wye*, 1954 S.C. 440.
[22] *Ibid. per* Lord Russell at p. 446.
[23] *Ibid.*
[24] *Playfair's Trs.* v. *Playfair* (1900) 2 F. 686.
[25] *Robertson's J.F.* v. *Robertson*, 1968 S.L.T. 32; *Re Ball* [1947] Ch. 228.
[26] As to the law of England, which appears to turn on " narrow and technical distinctions,"
     see *Re Gulbenkian's Settlements* [1970] A.C. 508; *McPhail* v. *Doulton* [1971] A.C. 424;
     Re Baden's Deed Trusts (No. 2) [1971] 3 All E.R. 985; [1972] 3 W.L.R. 250.
[27] *Salvesen's Trs.* v. *Wye, supra.* See *infra*, p. 195.

the fund to other persons, selected by them, to act as trustees for the purpose of apportioning the fund.[28]

Unworkable provisions

Where the directions to the trustees are self-contradictory and unworkable they are held *pro non scripto* and the beneficiary is entitled to the fund if there are no intermediate purposes. An example of this occurred where the direction was to settle the share of one of the testator's daughters in terms similar to the terms of the marriage contracts of her two sisters and the two contracts were not only dissimilar but absolutely repugnant.[29]

Where shares of a partnership were held in trust and the income applied for the benefit of employees of the firm, it was held that the conversion of the business into a limited company made it impossible to carry on the trust and the trust fund reverted to the truster's estate.[30]

Ineffectual provisions

" If we are to sanction the disregard of the testator's directions, on the ground that if carried out they would be ineffectual, then we must be satisfied that this is clearly and incontrovertibly the case. If it admits of any doubt the question must be tried in a proper action with the proper contradictors having interest to try it." [31]

Where trustees were directed to execute a conveyance containing clauses which were null and void by virtue of statute, it was held that the trustees were bound to grant the conveyance with the clauses omitted.[32]

The court will allow a legatee to do directly what may be done indirectly. Where the trustees are directed to purchase a specific subject for a beneficiary and convey it to him in such a way that it will be his absolute property and that no other person has an interest therein, the beneficiary is entitled to require the trustees to pay him the capital sum in cash without making the purchase.[33]

" Wherever a beneficiary totally unfettered by the truster can at once undo what the trustees have done, or what the trustees are directed to do, and wherever there is no limitation of the beneficiary's right, and no restraint imposed upon the beneficiary, but only a direction to trustees, the Court will never insist upon the trustees carrying out the direction, for the only result of this would be to put the beneficiary to the expense, trouble, and inconvenience of undoing in a circuitous way, and entirely at his own pleasure, what the trustees had fruitlessly done." [34]

---

[28] *Potter's Trs.* v. *Allan*, 1918 S.C. 173.
[29] *Murray* v. *Matheson's Trs.* (1898) 6 S.L.T. 149.
[30] *Hedderwick's Trs.* v. *Hedderwick's Exor.*, 1910 S.C. 333.
[31] *Kinnear* v. *Kinnear's Trs.* (1875) 2 R. 765, 768, *per* Lord Neaves.
[32] *Lumsden's Trs.* v. *Lumsden*, 1917 S.C. 579. See also *Kinnear* v. *Kinnear's Trs.* (1875) 2 R. 765; *Sandys* v. *Bain's Trs.* (1897) 25 R. 261; *McFarlane* v. *McFarlane's J.F.*, 1955 S.L.T. (Notes) 68.
[33] *Gordon* v. *Gordon's Trs.* (1866) 4 M. 501.
[34] *Dow* v. *Kilgour's Trs.* (1877) 4 R. 403, 404, *per* Lord Gifford.

" Where there are no parties interested, other than those to whom the funds are left, they are entitled, in the ordinary case, and where no special circumstances exist, to disregard the fetters that have been imposed on the bequest." [35] So where the direction was to purchase for a beneficiary an annuity which was to be alimentary it was held that, as the annuity could not be protected in the absence of a continuing trust,[36] and the beneficiary could thus immediately convert it into a capital sum, the trustees could pay the capital direct to the beneficiary.[37] The court will not supply the deficiency by setting up a trust to protect a legatee against himself.[38]

Objects: morality

A bequest to a company whose objects involve a denial of Christianity is not invalid.[39] As to an annuity bequeathed as a consideration of the annuitant's entering into sexual intercourse with the testator, see the case cited.[40] It is very doubtful whether a testamentary provision in favour of the mistress and illegitimate children of the testator can be challenged as being *contra bonos mores*.[41]

In England, a trust for the future illegitimate children of a named person is contrary to public policy [42] but where the testator created a trust for his son's " children or reputed children " as the son should appoint, and the son appointed the fund to persons named and described as his " children or reputed children " it was held that the power was valid and had been validly exercised.[43]

Public policy

A direction to hold a house for twenty years with most of the rooms bricked up was held to be ineffectual because it did not confer a benefit on anyone.[44]

Conditions

If trustees are directed under certain conditions to convey property to a beneficiary the conditions attach to the gift. " Whatever conditions are adjected to that direction, or whatever qualities are necessarily implied in it, necessarily become conditions and qualities of the gift itself." [45]

---

[35] *Kippen* v. *Kippen's Trs.* (1871) 10 M. 134, 139, *per* Lord Cowan.
[36] See *infra*, p. 94.
[37] *Tod* v. *Tod's Trs.* (1871) 9 M. 728; *Murray* v. *Macfarlane's Trs.* (1895) 22 R. 927; *Kennedy's Trs.* v. *Warren* (1901) 3 F. 1087. See also *infra*, p. 99.
[38] *Murray* v. *Macfarlane's Trs.*, *supra*, at p. 941, *per* Lord McLaren.
[39] *Bowman* v. *Secular Society Ltd.* [1917] A.C. 406.
[40] *Johnstone* v. *McKenzie's Exors.* (1835) 14 S. 106. See also *Young* v. *Johnson and Wright* (1880) 7 R. 760.
[41] *Troussier* v. *Matthew*, 1922 S.L.T. 670. See also *Johnstone* v. *McKenzie's Exors.* (1835) 14 S. 106; *Young* v. *Johnson and Wright* (1880) 7 R. 760. It may be different if there is an averment of an *inter vivos* agreement under which continued intercourse is the consideration for the bequest.
[42] *Occleston* v. *Fullalove* (1874) L.R. 9 Ch. 147.
[43] *Re Hyde* [1932] 1 Ch. 95.
[44] *Brown* v. *Burdett* (1882) 21 Ch.D. 667. See also *infra*, p. 171.
[45] *Per* L.J.-C. Inglis, *Donaldson's Trs.* v. *Macdougall* (1860) 22 D. 1527, 1541, a dissenting opinion sustained on appeal *sub nom. Young* v. *Robertson* (1862) 4 Macq. 314. See also Candlish Henderson, *Vesting*, 24.

Accordingly, a bequest in the form of a direction to convey subject to conditions is not a bequest of a vested absolute and unqualified right of fee.[46]

It is a question of construction whether the testator has imposed a condition or merely declared a purpose to which he desired the legacy to be applied. Where a legacy was given " to help him to come out for a doctor if he choose that profession " it was held that the legatee took it unconditionally.[47] Such expressions as " my wife " or " my fiancée," used to describe the legatee, are not to be treated as importing a condition into the bequest unless there is some further indication of the testator's intention to do this.[48]

Where the fulfilment of the condition depends on an act within the power of the legatee the condition may be held as satisfied if the legatee has done his best to fulfil it.[49] If the condition is in favour of a third party, it is held to be fulfilled when the third party voluntarily renders its fulfilment impossible.[50] If the testator, by imposing the condition, intended to put the beneficiary to an election, the terms of the bequest must be intimated to the beneficiary to give him an opportunity of electing.[51] If there is a bona fide dispute as to the validity of the condition, the beneficiary cannot be required to elect until the dispute is determined.[52]

Conditions: vagueness

A condition may be too vague to receive effect. To be effectual, it must be expressed in terms sufficiently determinate to advertise the beneficiary and the court of the general course of conduct which has been enjoined.[53] It must be capable of legal construction or interpretation. There is no difference between suspensive and resolutive conditions in respect of the standard of precision required. The standard required by English law may be higher.[54]

Conditions: public policy

Conditions in restraint of marriage may be *contra bonos mores*. In principle, an absolute and general prohibition against the legatee's

---

[46] *Gore-Browne-Henderson's Trs.* v. *Grenfell*, 1968 S.L.T. 237.

[47] *Ross* v. *Thomson* (1896) 4 S.L.T. 155.

[48] *Henderson's J.F.* v. *Henderson*, 1930 S.L.T. 743; *Pirie's Trs.* v. *Pirie*, 1962 S.C. 43; *Ormiston's Exor.* v. *Laws*, 1966 S.C. 47; *Towse's Trs.* v. *Towse*, 1924 S.L.T. 465. See also *Hood* v. *Macdonald's Tr.*, 1949 S.C. 24 (" my present manager ").

[49] *Simpson* v. *Roberts*, 1931 S.C. 259; *Munro's Trs.* v. *Monson*, 1965 S.L.T. 314; *Cumming's Trs.*, 1960 S.L.T.(Notes) 96.

[50] *Pirie* v. *Pirie* (1873) 11 M. 941.

[51] *Rodger's Trs.* v. *Allfrey*, 1910 S.C. 1015.

[52] *Balfour's Trs.* v. *Johnston*, 1936 S.C. 137.

[53] *Wemyss* v. *Wemyss's Trs.*, 1921 S.C. 30 (" that X shall never allow the said Y to reside at W "—valid); *Balfour's Trs.* v. *Johnston*, 1936 S.C. 137 (" that she will never hold any communication with, nor take any interest whatsoever in, a child known as D "—valid); *Beaton's J.F.* v. *Beaton and Others*, 1950 S.L.T.(Notes) 63 (" provided she remains true to my memory and does not marry again nor have any association whatever with any other man "—invalid as to the latter part); *Veitch's Exor.* v. *Veitch and Others*, 1947 S.L.T. 17 (" that X continues to occupy the house at Inchbonny "—valid).

[54] *Sifton* v. *Sifton* [1938] A.C. 656; *Veitch's Exor.* v. *Veitch, supra.*

marriage is inoperative. But a liferent provision terminating on the marriage of a daughter or the remarriage of a surviving spouse is effectual [55]; and a condition that a legacy is to fall if the legatee is married at the date of the testator's death will be given effect because it does not restrain the legatee's choice.[56] A condition that the legatee shall not marry a particular individual is valid.[57]

A condition that two persons should be living together as man and wife at the testator's death was held not to be *contra bonos mores* even although the wife was at the relevant date in a home for treatment of drug addiction.[58]

A condition that a child legatee shall not reside with his or her parents against whose character no allegation is made is *contra bonos mores* and is held *pro non scripto*.[59] A prohibition against the legatee communicating with or taking an interest in a child to whom she was not related was upheld.[60]

The opinion has been expressed that it would be *contra bonos mores* for trustees to exact from a legatee a promise to remain a Protestant in the future as a condition of payment of a legacy by them.[61]

A condition that the legatee must denude himself of all right in lands on succeeding to a peerage is not contrary to public policy.[62]

Securities over land

It is impossible to create, after November 29, 1970, a security over land by way of an *ex facie* absolute disposition.

A grant of any right over an interest in land for the purpose of securing any debt by way of a heritable security can be effected at law only if it is embodied in a standard security.[63] A deed which is not in the form of a standard security and which, for the purpose of constituting a heritable security, contains a disposition or assignation of an interest in land is to that extent void and unenforceable. If the deed has been recorded, the creditor in the purported security may be required, by any person having an interest, to grant any deed which may be appropriate to clear the Register of Sasines of that security.[64]

[55] *Sturrock* v. *Rankin's Trs.* (1875) 2 R. 850; *Kidd* v. *Kidds* (1863) 2 M. 227.
[56] *Aird's Exrs.* v. *Aird*, 1949 S.C. 154.
[57] *Forbes* v. *Forbes' Trs.* (1882) 9 R. 675.
[58] *Barker* v. *Watson's Trs.*, 1919 S.C. 109.
[59] *Fraser* v. *Rose* (1849) 11 D. 1466; *Grant's Trs.* v. *Grant* (1898) 25 R. 929; see also *Wemyss* v. *Wemyss's Trs.*, 1921 S.C. 30.
[60] *Balfour's Trs.* v. *Johnston*, 1936 S.C. 137.
[61] *Innes' Trs.* v. *Innes and Others*, 1963 S.L.T. 353, 358, *per* Lord Carmont.
[62] *Earl of Caithness* v. *Sinclair*, 1912 S.C. 79.
[63] Conveyancing and Feudal Reform (Scotland) Act 1970, s. 9 (3).
[64] s. 9 (4).

CHAPTER 7

LIFERENTS AND ANNUITIES

A LIFERENT is " a right that one has to use and enjoy a subject during life, without destroying or wasting its substance." [1] " The person entitled to such enjoyment for life is called the Liferenter; the person whose property is burdened with the liferent is called the Fiar; and the reversionary right of use and enjoyment, after the liferent has expired, is called the Fee." [2]

It is possible to create a liferent without disposing of the fee or while making an ineffectual attempt to dispose of the fee.[3] It is not possible to create an anomalous interest, intermediate between a liferent and a fee, in the form of a right of sale, administration and consumption.[4] It is possible to constitute an interest similar to a liferent terminating on marriage [5] or when a third party attains majority.[6] A condition that a liferent will be forfeited if the liferenter sells or otherwise disposes of his interest will be valid.[7]

Whether a bequest is in liferent or in fee is a question of construction.[8] There may be a question as to whether a gift is intended to be to A in liferent and B in fee or merely to create a substitution of B to A as institute.[9] In relation to heritage a liferent has to be distinguished from a mere right of occupation.[10] In some cases a direction to pay the income of a fund has been construed as a bequest of the fee.[11]

[1] Ersk. II. 9, 39.
[2] Bell, *Prin.* s. 1037.
[3] *Cumstie* v. *Cumstie's Trs.* (1876) 3 R. 921, 942, *per* L.P. Inglis; *Spinks's Exors.* v. *Simpson* (1894) 21 R. 551; *Carruthers* v. *Crawford,* 1945 S.C. 82.
[4] *Cochrane's Exrx.* v. *Cochrane,* 1947 S.C. 134 (overruling *Denholm's Trs.* v. *Denholm's Trs.,* 1907 S.C. 61, 1908 S.C. 255; *Heavyside* v. *Smith,* 1929 S.C. 68); *Innes's Trs.* v. *Innes,* 1948 S.C. 406.
[5] *Kidd* v. *Kidds* (1863) 2 M. 227; *Carruthers* v. *Crawford,* 1945 S.C. 82.
[6] *Hill* v. *Hill's Tutors* (1866) 5 M. 12. See *Parker* v. *Lord Advocate,* 1958 S.C. 426, 437, *per* Lord Mackintosh; Rankine, *Landownership,* 4th ed., 720.
[7] *Chaplins' Trs.* v. *Hoile* (1890) 18 R. 27. But as to the effect of a trust-disposition for behoof of creditors where the irritancy in the will was restricted to " selling " and " mortgaging," see *Chaplin's Tr.* v. *Hoile* (1891) 19 R. 237.
[8] *Veitch's Trs.* v. *Rutherford,* 1914 S.C. 182; *Ironside's Exor.* v. *Ironside's Exor.,* 1933 S.C. 116; *Ford's Trs.* v. *Ford,* 1940 S.C. 426; *Parlane's Exrx.* v. *Dunlop,* 1948 S.L.T.(Notes) 21.
[9] *Lyon* v. *Lyon* (1888) 15 R. 394; *Rae's Trs.* v. *Rae* (1893) 20 R. 826; *Mitchell* v. *General Assembly of the Church of Scotland* (1895) 2 S.L.T. 629; *Young's Trs.* v. *Young* (1899) 7 S.L.T. 266; *Reid* v. *Dobie,* 1921 S.C. 662; *Duncan* v. *Edinburgh Royal Infirmary,* 1936 S.C. 811; *Turner's Trs.* v. *Turner,* 1961 S.L.T. 319.
[10] *Clark and Others* (1871) 9 M. 435; *Johnstone* v. *Mackenzie's Trs.,* 1912 S.C.(H.L.) 106 (the prior cases are conveniently tabulated in the Lord Ordinary's opinion, 1911 S.C. 324); *Montgomerie-Fleming's Trs.* v. *Carre,* 1913 S.C. 1018; *Milne's Tr.* v. *Milne,* 1920 S.C. 456; *Countess of Lauderdale,* 1962 S.C. 302.
[11] *Sanderson's Exor.* v. *Kerr* (1860) 23 D. 227; *Anderson* v. *Thomson* (1877) 4 R. 1101; *Lawson's Trs.* v. *Lawson* (1890) 17 R. 1167.

RESTRICTIONS ON CREATION

There are restrictions on the creation of liferents.

Deeds executed before November 25, 1968

The Entail Amendment Act 1848, s. 48, provided that a liferent of heritage could competently be granted in favour only of a party who was in life at the date of the grant and where land was held in liferent by virtue of a deed dated after August 1, 1848, by a party of full age born after the date of the deed the party was to be deemed to be fee simple proprietor and could obtain a Court of Session decree declaring him to be fee simple proprietor.[12] The words " the date of the deed " must be given their literal meaning of the date of execution of the deed and cannot be construed to mean the date of the granter's death.[13] Where the liferent is constituted by a codicil, the relevant date is the date of execution of the codicil.[13] The Act applies to estate which is heritable property at the date when the application is presented to the court even although it was acquired by the trustees during the administration of the trust.[13] The provision cannot be extended to allow a pupil to petition.[14] It has been suggested that the section applies only to direct liferents by constitution and not to trust liferents which fall to be dealt with under section 47 of the 1848 Act.[15]

The Entail (Scotland) Act 1914[16] applied section 48 of the 1848 Act to deeds dated before August 1, 1848, the date of the deed being deemed to be August 10, 1914, in the application of section 48 to the deed and to the right of any party thereunder.

The Trusts (Scotland) Act 1921 provided[17]:

" It shall be competent to constitute or reserve by means of a trust or otherwise a liferent interest in moveable and personal estate in Scotland in favour only of a person in life at the date of the deed constituting or reserving such liferent, and, where any moveable or personal estate in Scotland shall, by virtue of any deed dated after the thirty-first day of July, eighteen hundred and sixty-eight, (the date of any testamentary or mortis causa deed being taken to be the date of the death of the granter, and the date of any contract of marriage being taken to be the date of the dissolution of the marriage) be held in liferent by or for behoof of a person of full age born after the date of such deed, such moveable or personal estate shall belong absolutely to such person, and, where such estate stands invested in the name of any

---

[12] A special case cannot be used in place of the statutory petition: *Harvey's Trs.* v. *Harvey*, 1942 S.C. 582.

[13] *Earl of Moray*, 1950 S.C. 281.

[14] *Crichton-Stuart's Tutrix*, 1921 S.C. 840.

[15] Dobie, *Liferent and Fee*, 259. See *Middleton*, 1929 S.C. 394. In *Davie* v. *Davie's Trs.* (1900) 8 S.L.T. 28, the section seems to have been applied to heritage held in trust.

[16] 4 & 5 Geo. 5, c. 43, s. 8.

[17] s. 9. The section is an almost verbatim re-enactment of s. 17 of the Entail Amendment (Scotland) Act 1868 (31 & 32 Vict. c. 84); see *Reid's Trs.* v. *Dashwood*, 1929 S.C. 748, 751, *per* L.P. Clyde.

trustees, such trustees shall be bound to deliver, make over, or convey such estate to such person: Provided always that, where more persons than one are interested in the moveable or personal estate held by trustees as hereinbefore mentioned, all the expenses connected with the transference of a portion of such estate to any of the beneficiaries in terms of this section shall be borne by the beneficiary in whose favour the transference is made."

The Conveyancing (Scotland) Act 1924 [18] extended the provisions of section 9 of the 1921 Act to deeds dated on or prior to July 31, 1868, the date of such deeds being deemed to be August 1, 1924, in the application of section 9 to the deed and to the right of any party thereunder.

The division of the section into a general or declaratory part and an operative part has caused difficulty in interpretation and in particular has raised the following questions:

(1) Is there an inconsistency between the first part which appears to render it incompetent to create some liferents and the second part which converts the liferents to fees only on the liferenter attaining majority?

(2) Does the expression " in life " in the first part have the same meaning as " born " in the second part?

(3) Is the definition in parenthesis of the date of the deed in the second part applicable to the expression " date of the deed " in the first part?

It would appear that under both section 48 of the 1848 Act and section 9 of the 1921 Act, a liferent created in favour of a person not in life at the relevant date is valid during the person's minority and if he dies during the minority the fee passes as directed by the deed.[19]

Under both sections, a child *in utero* at the date of the grant is entitled to the fee because he was " born after " the grant.[20]

It has been held that a liferent created by the exercise of a special or limited power of appointment is struck at if the person to whom the liferent was granted was not in life at the date of the original settlement which granted the power although he was alive at the date of the exercise of the power.[21] The same principle was applied where the granter of an *inter vivos* trust subsequently exercised a reserved special power to limit to a liferent the interest of a grandson who was born after the date of the original trust deed.[22] Where supplementary funds were conveyed to trustees after the beneficiary was born, to be held for the purposes contained in the

---

[18] s. 45.

[19] *Reid's Trs.* v. *Dashwood*, 1929 S.C. 748, 752, *per* L.P. Clyde; *Muir's Trs.* v. *Williams*, 1943 S.C.(H.L.) 47, 52, *per* Lord Thankerton.

[20] *Reid's Trs.* v. *Dashwood, supra*—opinions were reserved as to whether the words " in life " in the first part of the section mean the same as the word " born " in the second part.

[21] *Muir's Trs.* v. *Williams*, 1943 S.C.(H.L.) 47.

[22] *Malcolm's Trs.* v. *Malcolm*, 1950 S.C.(H.L.) 17. See, as to the distinction between special and general powers, *Muir's Trs.* v. *Williams, supra*, at p. 59, *per* Lord Romer; *Malcolm's Trs.* v. *Malcolm, supra*, at p. 30, *per* Lord MacDermott.

original *inter vivos* deed dated before his birth, it was held that the statute did not affect the supplementary funds.[23]

There are two significant differences between the two provisions.[24] Under the 1921 Act the person in whose favour the liferent was created becomes entitled to the fee on attaining majority but under the 1848 Act the liferenter on attaining majority must obtain a decree establishing his right and it seems that if he does not do so the liferent of the heritage continues.[25] Secondly, under the 1848 Act the *punctum temporis* is the date of execution of the deed, whereas under the 1921 Act it is the date of the granter's death or the date of dissolution of the marriage in the case of a marriage contract.

Deeds executed on or after November 25, 1968

Because of these differences and certain other anomalies, the law was altered by section 18 of the Law Reform (Miscellaneous Provisions) (Scotland) Act 1968, which applies to deeds executed on or after November 25, 1968.[26] Where, by such a deed, there is created a liferent interest in any property, heritable or moveable, and a person who was not living or *in utero* at the date of the coming into operation of the deed becomes entitled to that interest, then if he is of full age at the date on which he becomes entitled to the interest, the property belongs absolutely to him as from that date, and, if it is vested in trustees, they are bound to convey it, deliver it or make it over to him at his expense. If he is not of full age at the date on which he becomes entitled to the interest, the property belongs to him and he is entitled to a conveyance thereof as from the date on which, being still entitled to the liferent interest, he becomes of full age. The fact that any property has come to belong absolutely to any person is not to affect the rights of the superior of the property in the case of heritage or of any person holding a security over the property, or any rights in the property created independently of the deed by which the liferent was created.[27]

A testamentary or other *mortis causa* deed comes into operation at the date of the granter's death and a marriage contract comes into operation at the date of the dissolution of the marriage. The date of execution, or of coming into operation, of any deed made in the exercise of a special power of appointment is to be taken to be the date of execution or, as the case may be, of the coming into operation, of the deed creating the power.[28]

---

[23] *Malcolm's Trs.* v. *Malcolm*, 1948 S.C. 616 (there was no appeal against the finding on this point).

[24] For discussions of the differences between the provisions, see *Reid's Trs.* v. *Dashwood, supra*, at p. 752, *per* L.P. Clyde; *Harvey's Trs.* v. *Harvey*, 1942 S.C. 582, 585, *per* L.J.-C. Cooper.

[25] *Crichton-Stuart's Tutrix*, 1921 S.C. 840.

[26] s. 48 of the 1848 Act and s. 9 of the 1921 Act do not have effect in relation to any such deed.

[27] s. 18 (2).

[28] s. 18 (5).

Full age

After January 1, 1970, a person becomes of full age on attaining the age of eighteen. A person who had attained the age of eighteen but not the age of twenty-one before that date attained full age on that date.[29]

What is a liferent?

Difficult questions have arisen as to whether a particular right is a " liferent interest " within the meaning of the statute.

In *McCulloch's Trs*. v. *Macculloch*,[30] the testator had directed his trustees to hold the residue of his estate for behoof of his four children *nominatim* equally in alimentary liferent and their issue in fee; if a child died leaving issue, the income of the child was to belong to the issue; if a child died without issue, the income was to form part of the income for division among the survivors and issue of predeceasers; on the death of all the children the fee was to be divided among his children's children *per stirpes*. One child died without issue and another died leaving a son who was born after the testator's death and, on attaining majority, claimed one-third of the trust estate in fee. In the Court of Session this claim was rejected on the ground that, although the claimant was vested in one-third of the fund, as two of the testator's children were still alive, the period of payment fixed by the testator had not arrived and, moreover, if payment were made before the period fixed, the other beneficiaries might be pre-judiced because of an alteration in the value of the fund. In an unsuccessful appeal to the House of Lords the claimant attempted to found on the 1868 Act.[31] The Lord Chancellor (Halsbury) opined that the Act did not apply. Lord Davey expressed the same view and said [32]:

> " The statute apparently (I express no opinion upon what may be the construction of it) converts a person with a limited interest into one holding a larger interest, and says that the trustees, notwithstanding any directions to the contrary in the will, are to transfer his share to him; but it says nothing at all as to the time when it is to be transferred, nor is there anything in the statute which in the least degree overrides any apt and competent provisions in a will for the purpose of fixing the period."

In *Shiell's Trs*. v. *Shiell's Trs*.,[33] the income of the trust estate was to be divided among the testator's four children, the issue of any who pre-deceased the last survivor taking their parent's share of income, and on the death of the last surviving child the fee was to be divided among the grandchildren and the issue of predeceasing grandchildren *per stirpes*. The testator was survived by four children one of whom died leaving three sons. One of the three sons, who was born after the testator's death, died

[29] Age of Majority (Scotland) Act 1969.
[30] (1900) 2 F. 749; (1903) 6 F.(H.L.) 3.
[31] The ancestor of s. 9 of the 1921 Act.
[32] p. 6.
[33] (1906) 8 F. 848.

after attaining majority but before the death of the last surviving child and his representatives claimed a share of the capital of the estate under the 1868 Act. It was conceded that there was no vesting before the death of the last surviving child. The Second Division held that the right of the deceased grandchild was not a liferent within the sense of the Act but a contingent fee coupled with a right to enjoy the income of the estate until the right to the fee became absolute.

In *Baxter* v. *Baxter*,[34] specified proportions of the estate were to be held for behoof of the testator's children but were not to vest in the children or in the grandchildren. The income of the shares was to be paid to the children, the issue of any who died taking the income of their parent's share. On the death of each grandchild, his issue was to be paid the capital of his parent's share. The whole estate was to be managed as a common fund. Two grandchildren who had been born after the testator's death and who had attained majority claimed immediate payment of a proportion of the capital of their deceased parent's share. It was held that the statute applied and they were therefore entitled to payment. Lord Dunedin distinguished *McCulloch's Trs.* and *Shiell's Trs.* on the ground that,

> " In both these cases the testator had himself fixed a period of division at which the interests of certain persons, *inter se*, were to be fixed, and therefore, of course, if you took away a share before that period came, you frustrated the possibility of certain beneficiaries getting the shares which they would otherwise get." [35]

He went on to say: " Here there is nothing of that sort, because the shares vesting in each family are not affected by any survivorship clause in favour of anyone."

This distinction is not easy to follow [36] because, in the first place, the claimant in *McCulloch's Trs.* had a vested right and the potential prejudice to the other beneficiaries could not arise from the operation of the survivorship clause. The prejudice which was contemplated was that caused by a decrease in the value of the estate and precisely the same prejudice could have arisen in *Baxter* because the trust estate was being administered *in globo*.

In *Mackenzie's Trs.* v. *Mackenzie*,[37] a proportion of the income of the trust estate corresponding to a capital sum of £80,000 was to be paid, on the death of the testator's son, to the son's children equally; on the marriage of a child the trustees could settle the capital of the child's share of the £80,000 in his marriage contract or otherwise in such a way that the fee would be destined to the child's issue who survived him; if a child died before such a settlement was made in respect of his share, or died without issue, his share was to accrue to those of the other children; if all the

---

[34] 1909 S.C. 1027.
[35] p. 1031.
[6] As was noted by Lord Ormidale in *Mackenzie's Trs.* v. *Mackenzie*, 1922 S.C. 404, 412.
[7] 1922 S.C. 404.

children died before such settlements were made, or died without issue, the whole £80,000 was to revert to the testator's general estate. The youngest of the son's four children, who had been born after the testator's death, and who had attained majority, claimed the fee of one-quarter of the £80,000 fund under section 9 of the 1921 Act. Two children had already had a sum settled in their marriage contracts. The Second Division, reversing the Lord Ordinary, held that the claimant's right was a liferent within the meaning of the statute and that, as the gifts were several, *McCulloch's Trs.* was not in point.

It is not easy to reconcile all that was said in these cases but some propositions can be advanced. If the claimant's right is something more than a right to income and includes a contingent right to the fee the statute does not apply.[38] A claimant is not entitled to immediate payment of the fee by virtue of the statute if the result might be to prejudice beneficiaries other than postponed liferenters and ultimate fiars [39] (" the purpose of the statute could not possibly be carried out without prejudicing someone " [40]). Prejudice of this kind will normally arise where there is a gift of the fee to a class and the amount of the share falling to each member of the class cannot be determined until a date prescribed by the testator. It will not occur " where the testator directs an immediate severance of the shares of his children, and trusts are declared of the severed aliquot portions of the estate." [41] An annuity is not a liferent within the meaning of the Act.[42] An implied right to income can be a liferent.[43] A right may be a liferent notwithstanding that it may terminate before the beneficiary's death.[44]

Where a share of an estate has to be paid to the beneficiary in terms of the statutory provisions, the estate has to be valued at the date of payment and not at the date of the testator's death or the date when the liferent opened.[45]

ALIMENTARY LIFERENTS

To protect the beneficiary against his own improvidence, his interest may be declared to be alimentary.

> " Where a right conferred upon a party has been declared to be alimentary, and where it is protected by a trust, the liferenter or annuitant is given the privilege of security for the alimentary provision, not excessive in amount, so that it is not subject to the diligence of creditors, but the counterpart of this privilege is a conventional incapacity of the liferenter or annuitant to assign or discharge the right or to revoke the trust by which it is safeguarded." [46]

[38] *Shiell's Trs.* v. *Shiell's Trs., supra.*
[39] Menzies, 179; Candlish Henderson, *Vesting*, 2nd ed., 322. *Cf.* Dobie, *Liferent and Fee*, 262.
[40] *Mackenzie's Trs.* v. *Mackenzie, supra,* at p. 410, *per* L.J.-C. Scott Dickson.
[41] *Macculloch* v. *McCulloch's Trs.* (1903) 6 F.(H.L.) 3, 6, *per* Lord Davey.
[42] *Drybrough's Tr.* v. *Drybrough's Tr.*, 1912 S.C. 939.
[43] *Davie* v. *Davie's Trs.* (1900) 8 S.L.T. 28.
[44] Dobie, *Liferent and Fee*, 262, and the decisions there cited.
[45] *Baxter* v. *Baxter, supra.*
[46] *Per* Lord Guthrie, *Douglas-Hamilton* v. *Duke and Duchess of Hamilton's Trs.*, 1961 S.C. 205, 225.

An alimentary fee is a legal impossibility [47]—" You cannot give a fee to a man and say to his creditors ' Do not attach it.' " [48] Trustees may have a discretion to withhold part of the income of the alimentary liferent and add it to the capital. [49]

A continuing trust

To make an alimentary liferent effective, there must be a continuing trust. [50] Trustees cannot without an express or implied direction from the testator constitute a special trust to make the alimentary liferent effectual. [51] Where the testator bequeathed certain alimentary annuities but directed that the trust should be wound up on the death of his widow, it was held that the trustees were not obliged to keep up the trust purely to protect the annuities. [52]

If a general power of appointment is not limited expressly or impliedly to the apportionment of shares of fee, the donee of the power can competently appoint an alimentary liferent. [53] It seems that express authority to adject limitations or restrictions is not necessary. But the donee of a power to give an annuity cannot impress on the annuity an alimentary character without express power to do so. [54]

The granter

A person cannot convey his own property so as to create a liferent thereof for himself which will not be subject to the diligence of his own creditors. [55] There may be a question as to the provenance of the funds [56] and evidence extraneous to the trust deed can be used to determine from whom the funds were derived. [57] There is an exception in that a woman can in her antenuptial marriage contract create an alimentary liferent of funds provided by herself [58] in favour of herself.

The wording

In the ordinary form the gift is first of all declared to be an alimentary

---

[47] *Wilkie's Trs.* v. *Wight's Trs.* (1893) 21 R. 199; *Watson's Trs.* v. *Watson*, 1913 S.C. 1133.
[48] *Per* Lord Kinnear, 1913 S.C. 1140.
[49] *White's Tr.* v. *White's Trs.*, 1917, 1 S.L.T. 272.
[50] *Murray* v. *Macfarlane's Trs.* (1895) 22 R. 927; *Kennedy's Trs.* v. *Warren* (1901) 3 F. 1087; *Brown's Trs.* v. *Thom*, 1916 S.C. 32; *Dempster's Trs.* v. *Dempster*, 1921 S.C. 332; *Forbes's Trs.* v. *Tennant*, 1926 S.C. 294. *Cf. Dunsmure's Trs.* v. *Dunsmure*, 1920 S.C. 147, 153, *per* Lord Skerrington.
[51] *Branford's Trs.* v. *Powell*, 1924 S.C. 439.
[52] *Ewing's Trs.* v. *Mathieson* (1901) 9 S.L.T. 367.
[53] *Angus's Trs.* v. *Monies*, 1939 S.C. 509.
[54] *Gavin's Trs.* v. *Johnston*, 1926 S.L.T. 187.
[55] *Wood* v. *Begbie* (1850) 12 D. 963; *Ker's Tr.* v. *Justice* (1866) 5 M. 4; *Harvey* v. *Ligertwood* (1872) 10 M.(H.L.) 33; *White's Trs.* v. *Whyte* (1877) 4 R. 786, 789, *per* L.P. Inglis; *Robertson* v. *Moore* (1878) 16 S.L.R. 13; *Hamilton's Trs.* v. *Hamilton* (1879) 6 R. 1216; *Leslie* v. *Leslie*, 1910, 2 S.L.T. 254.
[56] *Lord Ruthven* v. *Drummond*, 1908 S.C. 1154.
[57] *Corbet* v. *Waddell* (1879) 7 R. 200. If funds from several sources have been inextricably mingled, so that the liferenter's contribution cannot be distinguished, there is no alimentary liferent (*Wilson*, 1968 S.L.T.(Notes) 83).
[58] *Christie's Factor* v. *Hardie* (1899) 1 F. 703, 709, *per* Lord McLaren.

provision for the subsistence of the grantee and there follows a declaration that the subject of the gift shall not be assignable or subject to the diligence of creditors. It seems that the word " alimentary " by itself is sufficient but no *voces signatae* are necessary to achieve the result.[59] Declarations that the provision is neither assignable nor subject to the diligence of creditors are probably sufficient without a further indication that the gift is for an alimentary purpose but they will not be effectual when the purpose of the gift is clearly not alimentary.[60] It is not sufficient that the rights of creditors are excluded; there must also be an exclusion of the beneficiary's right to deal with the money so as to put it beyond his use.[61] " If the beneficiary is in such a position that the fund can be sold or assigned, then the exclusion of creditors will not be effectual." [62] Similarly, a provision against anticipation without an exclusion of the rights of creditors is not enough.[63] The word " alimentary " need not be used.[64]

The following expressions have been held to be sufficient to constitute an alimentary liferent:

" for their maintenance and entertainment;" [65]

" for her maintenance and support during her life;" [66]

" for his support and maintenance;" [67]

" for the maintenance of." [68]

Where the stated purpose was " for his own use and for the maintenance and education of the issue " it was decided that, as the issue had all attained majority, the liferent could no longer be alimentary.[69]

Where the testator's son was given a power to grant an alimentary liferent of a fund to his widow, and the son in his will, after reciting the power under his father's settlement, granted his widow a life interest without using the word " alimentary," it was held that an alimentary liferent had been intended and the power had been validly exercised.[70]

Effect: renunciation

Apart from the provisions of section 1 of the Trusts (Scotland) Act 1961, an alimentary liferent cannot be renounced by the liferenter once he

[59] *Chambers' Trs.* v. *Smiths* (1878) 5 R.(H.L.) 151, 156, *per* Lord Hatherley, p. 163, *per* Lord Blackburn.

[60] *Dewar's Trs.* v. *Dewar*, 1910 S.C. 730; McLaren, I, 619. *Cf. Rogerson* v. *Rogerson's Tr.* (1885) 13 R. 154, 156, *per* Lord McLaren.

[61] *Douglas Gardiner and Mill* v. *Mackintosh's Trs.*, 1916 S.C. 125.

[62] *Per* L.J.-C. Scott Dickson, at p. 127.

[63] *Mackie's J.F., Petr.*, 1920, 2 S.L.T. 95.

[64] *Chambers' Trs.* v. *Smiths* (1878) 5 R.(H.L.) 151; *Douglas' Trs.* (1902) 5 F. 69, 74, *per* Lord McLaren.

[65] *West-Nisbet* v. *Moriston* (1627) Mor. 10368.

[66] *Douglas' Trs., supra; Thomson's Trs.* (1893) 1 S.L.T. 56.

[67] *Arnold's Trs.* v. *Graham*, 1927 S.C. 353.

[68] *Bailey* v. *McLetchie's Trs.*, 1935 S.C. 95; *Miller* v. *Miller's Trs.*, 1953 S.L.T. 225.

[69] *McMurdo's Trs.* v. *McMurdo* (1897) 24 R. 458.

[70] *Cook* v. *Cook's Trs.*, 1911, 2 S.L.T. 64.

has entered into possession thereof.[71] This is so even where the liferenter is also the beneficial fiar [72] and even where the truster consents.[73]

But if the beneficiary is not yet enjoying the gift he can renounce the liferent.[74] In *Gray* v. *Gray's Trs.*,[75] in exceptional circumstances trustees were authorised to convey estate, with the consent of alimentary annuitants to the trustees of a newly constituted trust under which the alimentary interests continued to receive protection.

An alimentary liferenter cannot homologate the actings of the trustees in making an unauthorised investment.[76]

Effect: assignation

An alimentary liferent cannot be assigned by the liferenter.[77] It is, however, assignable in so far as it is in excess of the amount required for a reasonable alimentary provision.[78] The court has refused to determine *ab ante* the amount of the excess; the excess must be decided on the position in each year and in a question with creditors.[79] Each term's payment of an alimentary liferent, when reduced into possession, is at the absolute disposal of the recipient and if payments are made under an assignation of the liferent the liferenter may be held to have acceded to them term by term and cannot claim repetition of them.

Effect: arrestment

An alimentary liferent cannot be arrested [80] except (a) as to arrears,[81] (b) *quoad excessum*,[82] (c) for alimentary debts.[82]

An alimentary payment is excessive and can be arrested to the extent that it is more than a reasonable provision, regard being had to the station and circumstances of the beneficiary.[83] Alimentary debts are

" all articles of annual expenditure required for the comfort, or suitable to the situation of the party; and in regard to articles in which

---

[71] *Smith and Campbell* (1873) 11 M. 639; *Cosens* v. *Stevenson* (1873) 11 M. 761; *White's Trs.* v. *Whyte* (1877) 4 R. 786; *Hughes* v. *Edwardes* (1892) 19 R.(H.L.) 33; *Thomson's Trs.* (1893) 1 S.L.T. 56. *Cf. Bailey* v. *McLetchie's Trs.*, 1935 S.C. 95.

[72] *Duthie's Trs.* v. *Kinloch* (1878) 5 R. 858; *Barron* v. *Dewar* (1887) 24 S.L.R. 735; *Eliott's Tr.* v. *Eliott* (1894) 21 R. 975; *Howat's Trs.* v. *Howat*, 1922 S.C. 506; *Anderson's Trs.*, 1932 S.C. 226.

[73] *Main's Trs.* v. *Main*, 1917 S.C. 660.

[74] *Ford* v. *Ford's Trs.*, 1961 S.C. 122; *Douglas-Hamilton* v. *Duke and Duchess of Hamilton's Trs.*, 1961 S.C. 205.

[75] (1877) 4 R. 378. See also *Stillie's Trs.* v. *Stillie's Trs.* (1901) 3 F. 1054.

[76] *Sanders* v. *Sanders' Trs.* (1879) 7 R. 157.

[77] *Rennie* v. *Ritchie* (1845) 4 Bell's App.Cas. 221. See also *Balls* v. *J. & W. Macdonald*, 1909, 2 S.L.T. 310.

[78] *Claremont's Trs.* v. *Claremont* (1896) 4 S.L.T. 144.

[79] *Cuthbert* v. *Cuthbert's Trs.*, 1908 S.C. 967; *Coles*, 1951 S.C. 608.

[80] *Bell* v. *Innes* (1855) 17 D. 778.

[81] *Drew* v. *Drew* (1870) 9 M. 163.

[82] *Lewis* v. *Anstruther* (1852) 14 D. 857; 15 D. 260; *Livingstone* v. *Livingstone* (1886) 14 R. 43; *Dick* v. *Russell* (1887) 15 R. 261; *Haydon* v. *Forrest's Trs.* (1895) 3 S.L.T. 182; *Thomson* v. *Thomson* (1905) 13 S.L.T. 245; *Craig* v. *Pearson's Trs.*, 1915, 2 S.L.T. 183.

[83] *Livingstone* v. *Livingstone* (1886) 14 R. 43. See also *Dick* v. *Russell* (1887) 15 R. 261; *Haydon* v. *Forrest's Trs.* (1895) 3 S.L.T. 182; *Thomson* v. *Thomson* (1905) 42 S.L.R. 711; *Maitland* v. *Maitland*, 1912, 1 S.L.T. 350.

ready-money dealing is unusual and inconvenient, and in which an absolute disability to contract debt would operate to his advantage, that disability has been departed from." [84]

What is alimentary depends on the party's station in life.[85] A creditor who had made an advance for alimentary purposes is an alimentary creditor.[86] Interest on an alimentary debt is not itself an alimentary debt.[87] The beneficiary's wife holding an alimentary decree is an alimentary creditor,[88] as are his children.[89]

" The order is that the alimentary fund is to be drawn on, in the first place, for the current alimentary debts; secondly, for arrears of alimentary debts; and thirdly (though I do not think this point has ever arisen), if there is any balance over I suppose that it would go to the ordinary creditors." [90]

Accordingly, if there is no creditor suing for current debt, alimentary creditors who have supplied goods in previous years are entitled to attach the fund, subject, perhaps, to the beneficiary's claim to a sum for current expenses.[91] A trustee in bankruptcy does not represent alimentary creditors.[91]

Where the liferent is to cohabiting spouses jointly the whole fund is subject to arrestment for alimentary debts incurred by the husband.[92]

If no action of furthcoming has been raised, the question of whether the fund is subject to arrestment can be determined in a petition for recall of the arrestment.[93]

Retention

The trustees cannot retain the liferenter's share of income in satisfaction of a debt due by the beneficiary to the trust in respect of advances made to him by the testator.[94]

ANNUITIES

An annuity is a right to a yearly payment of money. It is an annual charge payable out of income preferably to the liferenter of the income of residue and it is a special annual legacy payable out of capital if the income runs short and immune from abatement in a question with residuary or reversionary interests in the capital.[95] *Prima facie* it is presumed to be only for

[84] *Greig* v. *Christie* (1837) 16 S. 242, 244, *per* Lord Fullerton.
[85] *Earl of Buchan* v. *His Creditors* (1835) 13 S. 1112.
[86] *Waddell* v. *Waddell* (1836) 15 S. 151.
[87] *Ruthven* v. *Pulford*, 1909 S.C. 951, 955.
[88] *Baird* v. *Baird*, 1910, 1 S.L.T. 95; *cf. Maitland* v. *Maitland*, 1912, 1 S.L.T. 350.
[89] *Fitzgerald* [1903] 1 Ch. 933, 935 (an opinion of Lord Dunedin when Lord Advocate).
[90] *Ruthven* v. *Pulford*, 1909 S.C. 951, 954, *per* Lord McLaren.
[91] *Ibid.*
[92] *Corbet* v. *Waddell* (1879) 7 R. 200.
[93] *Lord Ruthven* v. *Drummond*, 1908 S.C. 1154.
[94] *Hardie* v. *Macfarlan's J.F.*, 1912 S.C. 502; *Cook* v. *Cook's Trs.*, 1911, 2 S.L.T. 64. *Cf. Kidstons, Watson, Turnbull & Co.* v. *McFarlane's Trs.* (1905) 12 S.L.T. 722 (surplus income).
[95] *Colquhoun's Trs.* v. *Colquhoun*, 1922 S.C. 32. The presumption is that it is to be paid under deduction of tax (*Hunter's Trs.* v. *Mitchell*, 1930 S.C. 978).

the life of the annuitant but the language of the deed creating it may indicate that it is to be payable during the life of the granter [96] or the life of a third party [97] in which cases it can transmit to the representatives of the original annuitant.

If an annuity has to be provided for, the trustees must set aside and invest a sum of money which will fully secure the annuity and thus set free the rest of the estate for disposal to the beneficiaries entitled to it. The trustees are not entitled to retain the whole estate on deposit receipt at low interest and charge the annuity to the whole revenue.[98] The amount retained is a matter for the trustees' discretion.[99] The annuitant is not entitled to have the annuity created a real burden upon the heritable estate unless the testator directed expressly or by clear implication that this should be done.[1] When the testator directed payment of an annuity to his widow and of the balance of income to his children among whom the capital was to be divided on the widow's death, it was held that, as the capital had vested in the children *a morte testatoris* they were entitled to immediate payment thereof subject to the retention of sufficient to provide for the annuity.[2]

Where capital is held to provide an annuity, the surplus revenue can be divided as it arises among the beneficiaries entitled to the residue.[3]

The purchase of an annuity from capital in order to allow immediate distribution of the trust fund is not an ordinary act of trust administration and requires the consent of all the beneficiaries in right of the capital.[4] Where the trustees were directed to hold a sum for the liferent use allenarly of the testator's son with power to pay the whole or part of the principal to him, a judicial factor on the trust estate was authorised, with the consent of those presumptively entitled to succeed the son, to invest a part of the sum in the purchase of an annuity for him.[5] In the absence of express direction the trustees are not entitled to convey the residue to the beneficiary entitled thereto on condition that he makes payment of an annuity to another beneficiary.[6] It is, of course, different if the annuity can be made a real burden on the heritable estate.[7] If, of course, the annuitant is

---

[96] *Reid's Exrx.* v. *Reid*, 1944 S.C.(H.L.) 25. See also *Fleming* v. *Reuther's Exors.*, 1921 S.C. 593.

[97] *Young's Trs.* v. *Shelton's Exors.*, 1937 S.C. 28; *McDonald's Trs.* v. *McDonald's Exrx.*, 1940 S.C. 433.

[98] *Clarke* v. *Clarke's Trs.*, 1925 S.C. 693.

[99] *Chivas' Trs.* v. *Stewart*, 1907 S.C. 701.

[1] *Buchanan* v. *Eaton*, 1911 S.C.(H.L.) 40.

[2] *Coats' Trs.* v. *Coats* (1903) 5 F. 401.

[3] *Henderson's Factor* (1874) 11 S.L.R. 507.

[4] *Graham's Trs.* v. *Graham's Trs.* (1898) 1 F. 357; *Parlane's Trs.* v. *Parlane* (1902) 4 F. 805. But see *Isaacs' J.F.* v. *Isaacs*, 1935 S.C. 243, where abatement was necessary and the annuitants were held entitled to immediate payment of the capitalised value as abated.

[5] *Simson* (1883) 20 S.L.R. 359.

[6] *Colt* v. *Colt's Trs.* (1868) 5 S.L.R. 660. But see *Lucas' Trs.* v. *Trustees and Patrons of " The Lucas Trust "* (1881) 8 R. 502; 16 S.L.R. 363.

[7] *Munro* v. *Macarthur* (1878) 16 S.L.R. 126. See also *Sinclair's Trs.* v. *Sinclair*, 1913 S.C. 178, where there was a question as to the security of alimentary annuities but the conveyance seems to have been contemplated by the testator.

sui juris and agrees with the beneficiary to accept satisfactory security, the estate can be divided.[8]

Alimentary annuities

An annuity can be made alimentary if the testator uses appropriate language.[9] An alimentary annuity cannot be discharged or assigned by the beneficiary and it cannot be attached by his creditors except for alimentary debts, *quoad excessum* or as to arrears.[10]

If the trustees are directed to purchase an annuity in their own names and make payment to the beneficiary the alimentary character is protected.[11] This is so even although the trustees have a discretion to authorise for a period direct payment by the insurance company to the beneficiary.[12] Mackenzie Stuart suggests [13] that such an arrangement would not prevent creditors from doing diligence against that part of the annuity which represents capital.

In *Hutchinson's Trs.* v. *Young*,[14] the testatrix directed her trustees to purchase Government annuities for certain beneficiaries. The annuities were to be payable to the annuitants on their own receipt and were not to be " assignable or affectable by creditors." There was no provision for a continuing trust. By statute, Government annuities were not assignable except on insolvency or bankruptcy. It was held that the trustees were bound to invest in annuities in accordance with the directions and the beneficiaries were not entitled to immediate payment of capital sums to purchase the annuities.[15] The directions were express and specific and had to be carried out even although there could not be complete protection against creditors in the absence of a continuing trust.

In *Turner's Trs.* v. *Fernie*,[16] the annuities were to be purchased either from the British Government or a reputable insurance company. It was not stated that they were to be alimentary. *Hutchinson's Trs.* was distinguished on the ground that there the direction was more specific and the annuities were to be alimentary. The beneficiaries were held to be entitled to the capital.

In *Brown's Trs.* v. *Thom*,[17] the annuity was to be alimentary and was to be purchased from " some well established Insurance Company." *Hutch-*

---

[8] *Mackay's Trs.* (1878) 16 S.L.R. 197.

[9] See *supra*, p. 95; *West-Nisbet* v. *Moriston* (1627) Mor. 10368; *Arnold's Trs.* v. *Graham*, 1927 S.C. 353. The donee of a power to create annuities cannot make the annuities alimentary (*Gavin's Trs.* v. *Johnston*, 1926 S.L.T. 187).

[10] *Smith and Campbell* (1873) 11 M. 639; *Cosens* v. *Stevenson* (1873) 11 M. 761; *Thomson's Trs.* (1893) 1 S.L.T. 56. The fact that the amount is excessive does not affect the obligation of the granter of the bond of annuity (*Weir* v. *Weir*, 1968 S.C. 241).

[11] *Graham's Trs.* v. *Graham's Trs.* (1898) 1 F. 357; *Arnold's Trs.* v. *Graham*, 1927 S.C. 353; *Anderson's Trs.*, 1932 S.C. 226.

[12] *Branford's Trs.* v. *Powell*, 1924 S.C. 439.

[13] p. 347.

[14] (1903) 6 F. 26.

[15] The contention that they were so entitled being based on the principle explained on pp. 83–84 *supra*.

[16] 1908 S.C. 883.

[17] 1916 S.C. 32.

inson's Trs. was again distinguished as " a very special case " on the ground that the purchase of a non-assignable Government annuity would give some degree of protection although it might not be exhaustive. The same result was reached in *Dempster's Trs.* v. *Dempster*.[18]

[18] 1921 S.C. 332.

CHAPTER 8

ACCUMULATION OF INCOME

THE Accumulations Act 1800,[1] commonly called the Thellusson Act or Lord Loughborough's Act,[2] made it illegal to accumulate income under a trust except during one of a number of specified periods. The statute originally applied in Scotland only to moveable estate but was extended to heritage by the Entail Amendment Act 1848.[3] Section 2, which created exceptions for provisions for payment of the grantor's debts,[4] and for raising portions for his children [5] and in relation to the produce of timber, was repealed so far as Scotland was concerned by the Entail (Scotland) Act 1914.[6]

The 1800 Act was repealed and substantially re-enacted so far as England was concerned by the Law of Property Act 1925,[7] which together with sections 13 and 14 of the Perpetuities and Accumulations Act 1964 [8] contains the present English legislation.[9] Section 5 of the Trusts (Scotland) Act 1961 [10] repealed and substantially re-enacted section 1 of the 1800 Act in relation to Scotland and further provisions are contained in section 6 of the Law Reform (Miscellaneous Provisions) (Scotland) Act 1966.[11]

---

[1] 39 & 40 Geo. 3, c. 98. There seems to have been an initial doubt as to whether the Act applied to Scotland—See Bell, *Commentaries*, 5th ed. 1826, I, 38, n. 4; *cf.* Hume, *Lect.* V, 193; *Strathmore* v. *Strathmore's Trs.* (1831) 5 W. & S. 170, 192, *per* Lord Brougham L.C. See also Holdsworth, *History of English Law*, Vol. VII, 228; Keeton, *Social Change in the Law of Trusts* (1958) Chap. IV; *Re Burns* (1960) 25 D.L.R. (2d) 427. " An Act which has hardly ever been discussed, in Courts either of law or equity, without the Judge having occasion to observe upon the inartificial, and, in several respects, ill-defined language, in which its provisions are expressed " (*per* Lord Brougham L.C., *Shaw* v. *Rhodes* (1835) 1 My. & Cr. 135, 141. Appvd. by L.J.-C. Alness, *Union Bank* v. *Campbell*, 1929 S.C. 143, 149).

[2] See *Thellusson* v. *Woodford* (1805) 11 Ves. 112.

[3] 11 & 12 Vict. c. 36, s. 41. See *Ogilvie's Trs.* v. *Kirk-Session of Dundee* (1846) 8 D. 1229; *Keith's Trs.* v. *Keith* (1857) 19 D. 1040; *McLarty's Trs.* v. *McLaverty* (1864) 2 M. 489; *Cathcart's Trs.* v. *Heneage's Trs.* (1883) 10 R. 1205.

[4] See *Smyth's Trs.* v. *Kinloch* (1880) 7 R. 1176.

[5] See *Moon's Trs.* v. *Moon* (1899) 2 F. 201; *Colquhoun's Trs.* v. *Colquhoun*, 1907 S.C. 346; *Mackay's Trs.* v. *Mackay*, 1909 S.C. 139.

[6] 4 & 5 Geo. 5, c. 43, s. 9.

[7] ss. 164, 165, 207 and Sched. 7. See *Henderson's Trs.* v. *Anderson*, 1930 S.L.T. 346; *Chisholm's Tr.* v. *Menzies*, 1931 S.N. 41; *Smith's Trs.* v. *Gaydon*, 1931 S.C. 533; *Lindsay's Trs.* v. *Lindsay*, 1931 S.C. 586.

[8] 1964, c. 55.

[9] The English legislation differs from the Scots in the following respects: (1) The exceptions for payment of debt, raising portions for children, and produce of timber are retained in England (Law of Property Act, 1925, s. 164 (2)). (2) A period of accumulation during a minority under any statutory power (*e.g.* Trustee Act 1925, s. 31) or under the general law is not to be taken into account in determining the permitted periods (Law of Property Act 1925 s. 165. See *Re Maber* [1928] 1 Ch. 88). (3) There is a presumption as to future parenthood (Perpetuities and Accumulations Act 1964, ss. 2, 14).

[10] 9 & 10 Eliz. 2, c. 57.

[11] 1966, c. 19.

101

It is still permissible to look at the 1800 Act to see the mischief it was intended to restrain.[12] " The mischief at which the Act is aimed is a direction or power to accumulate income which is excessive in duration and unduly penalises the present generation of potential beneficiaries in order to amass capital for the benefit of a generation to come." [13]

Section 5 of the Trusts (Scotland) Act 1961 provides that no person may by any will, settlement or other disposition dispose of any property in such manner that the income thereof shall be wholly or partially accumulated for any longer period than one of six specified periods.

Accumulation

As McLaren points out,[14] an aid to the interpretation of " accumulate " can be found in the preamble of the 1800 Act which refers to " dispositions . . . whereby the profits and produce thereof are directed to be accumulated, and the beneficial enjoyment thereof is postponed. . . ."

> " I doubt if the word ' accumulation ' signifies more than a simple aggregation of instalments of income to create a single fund, but the reference to accumulation for a *period* clearly implies, in my judgment, a mounting fund which reaches a climax at the end of the period. The mere fact that the testator has authorised interim payments out of the accumulating fund would not in itself exclude the operation of the section, but unless the effect of the disposition is the building up of a fund which is to become available for some specific object at the end of a period, the case is *prima facie* not within the mischief of the statute at all." [15]

A trust to invest income is a trust for accumulation.[16] The statutory prohibition applies to a power to accumulate whether or not the power extends to income produced by the investment of income previously accumulated.[17]

Provision for future deficiencies

The retention of income as an administrative precaution against future deficiencies in the amount available to service annuities is not struck at.[18] The Act does not apply wherever the reason for the postponement of beneficial enjoyment is that in the due course of administration the relevant facts relating to the assets of the estate are not yet sufficiently ascertained.[19]

---

[12] *Re Berkeley, decd.* [1968] Ch. 744, 771, *per* Harman L.J.
[13] *Ibid.* p. 780, *per* Widgery L.J.
[14] I, 310. See *Vine* v. *Raleigh* [1891] 2 Ch. 13; *Re Berkeley, decd.* [1968] Ch. 744.
[15] *Re Berkeley, decd.* [1968] Ch. 744, 780, *per* Widgery L.J.
[16] *Mathews* v. *Keble* (1868) 3 Ch.App. 691.
[17] Law Reform (Miscellaneous Provisions) (Scotland) Act 1966, s. 6 (2) (in instruments taking effect on or after August 3, 1966). This is derived from the Perpetuities and Accumulations Act 1964, s. 13 (2), which resulted from a recommendation of the Law Reform Committee (Fourth Report, 1956 Cmnd. 18, para. 60). The law was said to be in doubt as a result of *Re Garside* [1919] 1 Ch. 132 and *Union Bank* v. *Campbell*, 1929 S.C. 143.
[18] *Re Berkeley, decd.* [1968] Ch. 744. See also *Re Clothier* [1971] N.Z.L.R. 745.
[19] *Ibid.* p. 776, *per* Russell L.J.

Insurance premiums

Where trustees, in the exercise of a discretion conferred on them by the will, had applied income for more than twenty-one years in paying the premiums on a policy of insurance on the life of the testator's nephew, the proceeds of which were to be applied for the purposes of the trust, it was held that the Thellusson Act did not apply.[20] It is difficult to understand this decision. The policy became an asset of the trust estate and was the form in which the trustees chose to invest the income which they were accumulating. There was accumulation in that the beneficial enjoyment of the income was postponed.[21] As the Lord Ordinary, whose decision was reversed, pointed out, there is a distinction between a policy of this kind, and the case where the testator has insured the life of his debtor and has directed his trustees to continue payment of the premiums and in the latter case there is no " settling or disposing."

In England, accumulations for the improvement and repair of land and houses are outwith the effect of the Act.[22] On the same principle, the application of rents from leaseholds to keep up an insurance policy to secure the replacement at the end of the term of capital that would be lost through not selling the leaseholds does not fall within the Act.[23] The effect of these decisions is that " a provision for accumulating income which goes no further than a prudent owner would go in the management of the property in question is not within the Act." [24]

Savings

In *Lindsay's Trs.*,[25] the trustees were directed to hold the residue of the estate and apply the income to maintain a library. The balance of the income was to be accumulated to erect a suitable building to house the library but no power was given to use the capital for this purpose. It was held that the direction to accumulate ceased to have effect after twenty-one years but " the Thellusson Act does not prevent trustees or anyone else from saving out of income " and the trustees could continue to " save " from their income until a fund accrued. The distinction between saving and accumulation is not easy to see. The decision may be affected so far as regards deeds taking effect on or after August 3, 1966 by section 6 (2) of the Law Reform (Miscellaneous Provisions) (Scotland) Act 1966 which provides that the statutory restrictions shall apply, not only in relation to directions to accumulate, but also in relation to a power to accumulate, whether or not there is a duty to exercise that power.

[20] *Cathcart's Trs.* v. *Heneage's Trs.* (1883) 10 R. 1205. See *Bassil* v. *Lister* (1851) 9 Hare 177; *Halford* v. *Close* (1883) W.N. 89; *Re Gardiner* [1901] 1 Ch. 697.
[21] Lord McLaren, whose decision as Lord Ordinary in *Cathcart's Trs.* was reversed, suggests (I, 312) that the decision of the Inner House is wrong. He points out that of the five judges who considered the case only two were convinced that the statute could be defeated in this way. *Cf.* Menzies, 530.
[22] *Vine* v. *Raleigh* [1891] 2 Ch. 13; *Mason* v. *Mason* [1891] 3 Ch. 467.
[23] *Re Gardiner* [1901] 1 Ch. 697.
[24] *Re Rochford's Settlement Trusts* [1965] Ch. 111, 124, *per* Cross J. See also *Inland Revenue* v. *Gammell's Trs.*, 1949 S.L.T. (Notes) 29.
[25] 1911 S.C. 584.

Section 6 (2) has curious antecedents. In *Re Robb*,[26] Danckwerts J. held that a power to accumulate was affected by the statutory prohibition. The Law Reform Committee recommended in three sentences of their Fourth Report [27] that " the opportunity might with advantage be taken of stating in terms that the restrictions on accumulation apply to powers to accumulate as well as to directions to accumulate." This was duly implemented by the Perpetuities and Accumulations Act 1964, s. 13 (2). When the Law Reform (Miscellaneous Provisions) (Scotland) Bill was introduced, a provision in rather different wording was criticised in the debate in the House of Lords [28] on the ground that its effect would be to force charitable trusts to spend all of their income in each year. The Bill was then amended to the wording of the 1964 Act and passed into law.[29]

It would seem that any lawful act of trustees must be either in compliance with a duty or in the exercise of a power and therefore any act of accumulation, including " saving," is subject to the statutory prohibition. On the other hand, it may be possible to argue that the distinction between saving and accumulation is a matter of accounting. If unspent income is carried forward for a limited period without being added to capital, it might not be regarded as an accumulation.[30]

Conditional payments

In *Mitchell's Trs.* v. *Fraser*,[31] the trustees were given a discretion to make payments out of the free residue of the estate to such of the testator's children and grandchildren as in the opinion of the trustees satisfied certain conditions. There was no further disposal of the residue. For twenty-one years after the testator's death the income of the residue was accumulated as the trustees had not been satisfied that the conditions had applied in respect of any child. It was held that further accumulation was not struck at by the Act because the testator had neither directed nor contemplated accumulation and accumulation was not a necessary consequence of the directions given. The accumulation was due to something extraneous to the deed, the accident that there had been no objects on which the testator's bounty could have been bestowed. Lord Guthrie thought the case was one of savings from income as in *Lindsay's Trs.*[32] Lord Salvesen compared it to the case of a direction to pay income to a beneficiary whom the trustees could not find with the result that the income accumulated in their hands for more than twenty-one years.

In *Innes's Trs.* v. *Bowen*,[33] it was indicated that the decision in *Mit-*

26 [1953] Ch. 459.
27 1956 Cmnd. 18, para. 60.
28 270 H.L.Deb. 1390.
29 276 H.L.Deb. 77.
30 The effect of s. 2 (1) (*b*) (iv) of the Finance Act 1894 (as substituted by Finance Act 1969 s. 36) is that there is a passing of property for estate duty purposes where a *power* to accumulate ceases on death.
31 1915 S.C. 350.
32 *Supra*, p. 103.
33 1920 S.C. 133, 141, 145. Lord Salvesen reiterated his opinion that the accumulation was lawful because it was due to an extraneous circumstance.

chell's Trs. was largely based on the fact that the residue had vested in the testator's issue.

In *Watson's Trs.* v. *Brown*,[34] the trustees were directed to hold a legacy, for the testator's elder son in liferent, and for the son's children in fee, the fee being payable only on their attaining the age of twenty-five, with a destination-over. The residue of the estate and the accumulations thereon were to be held to provide certain legacies, payable only when the necessary sums were provided, and thereafter the residue was to be divided between the testator's two sons and, if a son predeceased the date of payment his issue on attaining twenty-five were to take their parent's share, with a destination-over. The trustees were empowered to apply the income of a minor beneficiary's share towards the maintenance and education of such beneficiary. The elder son died before acquiring a vested interest in the residue and his issue did not attain twenty-five until more than twenty-one years after the testator's death. After the son's death, part of the income of the legacy in each year was applied to the maintenance of the issue and the remainder was accumulated. It was held that the accumulation after the twenty-one years was illegal because there was an implied direction to accumulate so much of the income as was not applied to the maintenance of the minor beneficiaries. Lord Skerrington [35] distinguished *Mitchell's Trs.* on the ground that there the testator's issue had a vested right to have a fund applied for their benefit at the trustees' discretion " from which it followed that any savings of income effected by the trustees belonged to the trust and did not fall into intestacy." Lord Cullen said [36]:

> " In *Mitchell's Trs.* v. *Fraser* the Court were able, in the circumstances of that case, to reach the conclusion that the *de facto* accumulation resulted not from any direction by the testator but from extraneous causes operating adversely to his intentions. In the circumstances of the present case I do not think there is any room for such a view."

It is obvious that *Mitchell's Trs.* has not been regarded with enthusiasm and its effect must be restricted to the rather unusual terms of the particular settlement. In any event, it would seem that a testator who restricted the payment of income to beneficiaries who satisfied certain conditions must have contemplated that at some time there might not be in existence any qualified beneficiaries and therefore must have contemplated that accumulation would result.

Capital

The fixed rents paid for coal-mines opened after the testator's death are capital and not income and are accordingly not affected by the statutory prohibition even while the mines are not being worked.[37] The same

---

[34] 1923 S.C. 228.
[35] p. 240.
[36] p. 243.
[37] *Ranken's Trs.* v. *Ranken*, 1908 S.C. 3.

rule could presumably apply to the proceeds of timber or other produce of the estate.[38]

Implied directions to accumulate

The prohibition applies whether the direction to accumulate is express or implied.[39]

> " If a truster directs that to be done which as a consequence leads to indefinite accumulation, he must, within the meaning of the statute, be taken to have directed accumulation." [40]

> " If a testator directs his property to go in such a course, that upon certain contingencies there must be an accumulation beyond twenty-one years, he does direct that upon those contingencies, the accumulation shall take place beyond that time." [41]

The fact that the testator did not intend accumulation to take place is of no consequence. " It is not the intention of the truster which determines the question of the application of the Thellusson Act. If *de facto* the accumulations extend beyond twenty-one years they are struck at by the Act." [42] " The Thellusson Act was passed to destroy intention." [43]

It was held that there was an implied direction to accumulate where the will only directed that the capital was to be paid to beneficiaries who could not be ascertained until a future date [44]; where the will made no disposal of the income on the failure of certain beneficiaries [45]; where there was no disposal of the surplus income after payment of annuities [46]; where there was no disposal of the income in so far as it was not applied at the trustees' discretion for the maintenance of minor beneficiaries [47]; where there was no disposal of the income of part of the estate in the period between the testator's death and the death of his widow.[48] Where there was a direction to accumulate the income of a share of the estate for a beneficiary and a provision that another share of the estate would accrue to that beneficiary, it was held, on accretion occurring, that the direction to accumulate impliedly applied to the accrescing share.[49] Where there was a direction to pay, on the expiry of a liferent, a specified sum to a kirk session to be applied by them in erecting a spire on the church and furnishing a church hall, it was held that there was an implied direction to accumulate the income of the fund until these purposes could be carried out.[50]

[38] Dobie, *Liferent and Fee*, 270.
[39] *Lord* v. *Colvin* (1860) 23 D. 111, appvd. in *Moss's Trs.* v. *Bramwell*, 1936 S.C.(H.L.) 1, 6, *per* Lord Thankerton, p. 10, *per* Lord Macmillan.
[40] *Per* Lord McLaren, *Logan's Trs.* v. *Logan* (1896) 23 R. 848, 852.
[41] *Tench* v. *Cheese* (1855) 6 De G.M. & G. 453, 462, *per* Lord Cranworth.
[42] *Mackenzie* v. *Mackenzie's Trs.* (1877) 4 R. 962, 970, *per* Lord Shand.
[43] *Per* Kekewich J., *Re Errington* (1897) 76 L.T. 616.
[44] *Gollan's Trs.* v. *Dallas* (1906) 13 S.L.T. 720; *Carey's Trs.* v. *Rose*, 1957 S.C. 252.
[45] *Lord* v. *Colvin, supra.*
[46] *Logan's Trs.* v. *Logan, supra.*
[47] *Watson's Trs.* v. *Brown*, 1923 S.C. 228.
[48] *Campbell's Trs.* v. *Clarke* (1871) 10 M. 227.
[49] *Paris' Trs.* v. *Gow* (1870) 8 S.L.R. 184.
[50] *Barbour* v. *Budge*, 1947 S.N. 100.

In two cases,[51] it was held that accumulation carried out to effect equitable compensation was affected by the Act. Both cases were later distinguished by the House of Lords on the ground that there had been implied directions to accumulate because the trusters must have contemplated that, if legal rights were claimed, the doctrine of equitable compensation would be applied and accumulation would therefore occur. In *Moss's Trs.* v. *Bramwell*,[52] there was an express clause of forfeiture and a direction as to the disposal of the forfeited provisions. Questions arose as to the application of the forfeited provisions and the court remitted to an actuary to consider the method by which equitable compensation was to be effected. The trustees thereafter carried out a scheme framed by the actuary and approved by the court which involved accumulation for a period of more than twenty-one years. The House of Lords held that this accumulation was not affected by the Act because it was not directed by the testator. " The author of the scheme was Mr. Lidstone (the actuary), not the testator, and it was the Lord Ordinary, not the testator, who put it into operation." [53]

The specified periods

(a) *The life of the grantor.*

If there has been a direction by *inter vivos* deed to accumulate during the grantor's life, accumulation must cease at his death [54] unless period (d), (e) or (f) can be invoked. As the periods are alternative and not cumulative it is not permissible, after period (a) has run, to add the period (b) of twenty-one years from the grantor's death. If the direction by *inter vivos* deed is to accumulate during the life of someone other than the grantor accumulation is valid only during the joint lives of the grantor and that person.[55]

(b) *A term of twenty-one years from the grantor's death.*

This period cannot apply if accumulation began before the grantor's death.[56] In computing the period the day of death is excluded so that dividends falling due on the twenty-first anniversary of the testator's death can lawfully be accumulated.[57] The Act does not permit accumulation in a period of twenty-one years commencing at a point after the testator's death.[58]

---

[51] *Hutchison* v. *Grant's Trs.*, 1913 S.C. 1211; *Innes's Trs.* v. *Bowen*, 1920 S.C. 133. See also *Reid's Trs.* v. *Adam*, 1938 S.N. 124.

[52] 1936 S.C.(H.L.) 1.

[53] *Per* Lord Macmillan, at p. 11.

[54] *Stewart's Trs.* v. *Stewart*, 1927 S.C. 350; *Union Bank* v. *Campbell*, 1929 S.C. 143; *Jagger* v. *Jagger* (1883) 25 Ch.D. 729; *McIver's Trs.* v. *Inland Revenue*, 1974 S.L.T. 202.

[55] *Re Lady Rosslyn's Trust* (1848) 16 Sim. 391.

[56] *Jagger* v. *Jagger* (1883) 25 Ch.D. 729.

[57] *Gorst* v. *Lowndes* (1841) 11 Sim. 434; *Menzies*, 538; *McLaren*, I, 312.

[58] *Campbell's Trs.* v. *Campbell* (1891) 18 R. 992; *Att.-Gen.* v. *Poulden* (1844) 3 Hare 555. The question seems to have been overlooked in *Maxwell's Trs.* v. *Maxwell* (1877) 5 R. 248.

(c) *The duration of the minority or respective minorities of any person or persons living or in utero at the grantor's death.*

This applies to testamentary deeds or *inter vivos* deeds directing accumulation from the date of the grantor's death.[59] It cannot apply if accumulation was directed to begin prior to the grantor's death.[60]

As " minority " is defined as ending with the attainment of the age of twenty-one years [61] the Age of Majority (Scotland) Act 1969 has no effect.

The Act does however apply in the absence of a definition or of any indication of a contrary intention for the construction of certain expressions in deeds executed on or after January 1, 1970, other than deeds made in the exercise of a special power of appointment where the deed creating the power was executed before that date.[62] A testamentary instrument or codicil executed before that date is not to be treated for this purpose as made on or after that date by reason only that it is confirmed by a codicil executed on or after that date.[63] The expressions concerned are " majority," " full age," " perfect age," " complete age," " lawful age," " minor," " minority," " under age," " less age," and similar expressions. It will be observed that such wording as " the age of twenty-one years " is not affected.

(d) *The duration of the minority or respective minorities of any person or persons who, under the terms of the will, or other deed directing the accumulation, would for the time being, if of full age, be entitled to the income directed to be accumulated.*

Period (d) is designed to deal with the situation in which the testator provides for the income of a fund being enjoyed by a liferent or other intervening interest and directs that, on the death of the liferenter or the termination of that intervening interest, the income is to be accumulated for a beneficiary who on attaining majority is to be entitled to the accumulated funds.[64] The period can therefore start at a point of time after the grantor's death and can run beyond the expiry of the twenty-one years from the grantor's death. But if accumulation is directed *a morte testatoris*, period (b) applies and the accumulation cannot be continued after the twenty-one years from the testator's death even although there is then in existence a minor beneficiary who would be entitled to the income on attaining majority. Where, in these circumstances, accumulation in fact took place for a period exceeding twenty-one years, it was held that the unlawfully accumulated income was that of the years after the expiry of twenty-one years from the testator's death and not that of the years between the testator's death and the birth of the minor beneficiary.[65]

---

[59] *Union Bank* v. *Campbell,* 1929 S.C. 143, 152, *per* L.J.-C. Alness.
[60] *Jagger* v. *Jagger, supra.*
[61] 1961 Act, s. 5 (6).
[62] 1969 Act, s. 1 (2) (*b*).
[63] 1969 Act, s. 1 (6).
[64] *Carey's Trs.* v. *Rose,* 1957 S.C. 252, 257, *per* L.P. Clyde.
[65] *Carey's Trs.* v. *Rose, supra; Ellis* v. *Maxwell* (1841) 3 Beav. 587.

The minors referred to are minors who would if of full age be entitled to the income directed to be accumulated and not only those who, if no accumulation had been directed, would be entitled to the income.[66] Children who become entitled to the income on attaining twenty-three are not persons who would if of full age be entitled to the income.[67] Where payment of the income is subject to trustees' discretion, the children do not satisfy the condition.[67]

In the case of a settlement *inter vivos* a direction to accumulate during period (d) is not void and the accumulation is not contrary to the Act solely by reason of the fact that the period begins during the life of the grantor and ends after his death.[68]

The Age of Majority (Scotland) Act 1969, has already been discussed.[69] " Full age " is not defined in the 1961 Act but it must presumably bear a meaning corresponding to that of minority.

There can be successive accumulations if, for example, the bequest is to the children, born and to be born, of the testator's sons, and the income is to be accumulated during their respective minorities. At the testator's death there is one such child and accumulation of the whole income takes place. After that child attains majority there is born another child who will be entitled to half of the estate and the income of that half can then be accumulated during this child's minority, although it has already been accumulated during the other minority.[70]

(e) *A term of twenty-one years from the date of the making of the settlement or other disposition.*[71]

(f) *The duration of the minority* [72] *or respective minorities of any person or persons living or in utero at the date of the making of the settlement or other disposition.*[71]

Where period (a) is used, the property passes on the death of the settlor and estate duty is payable.[73] Periods (e) and (f) were added to avoid this difficulty.[74] They are permissible only under instruments taking effect on or after August 3, 1966 and, in the case of a special power of

---

[66] *Re Cattell* [1914] 1 Ch. 177.

[67] *Re Bourne's Settlement* [1946] 1 All E.R. 411.

[68] 1961 Act, s. 5 (4). This provision was presumably intended to alter the law impliedly established by *Stewart's Trs.* v. *Stewart*, 1927 S.C. 350, although period (d) did not arise in that case. See *Russell's Trs.* v. *Russell*, 1959 S.C. 148; Halliday, " Trusts (Scotland) Act 1961," 3 *Conveyancing Review*, 57.

[69] See *supra*, p. 108.

[70] *Re Cattell* [1914] 1 Ch. 177; Megarry and Wade, *Law of Real Property*, 3rd ed., 279. In *Re Cattell* [1907] 1 Ch. 567, it was argued that " respective minorities " did not mean " successive minorities " but minorities of different persons entitled to different funds.

[71] Law Reform (Miscellaneous Provisions) (Scotland) Act 1966, s. 6 (1).

[72] As to the definition of " minority," see *supra*, p. 108.

[73] *Re Bourne's Settlement* [1946] 1 All E.R. 411; *Lord Advocate* v. *Smith's Trs.*, 1949 S.C. 618; Law Reform Committee's Fourth Report (1956 Cmnd. 18) paras. 56, 57; J. G. Monroe " Notes on the Perpetuities and Accumulations Act 1964 " [1964] *British Tax Review*, 218; V. G. H. Hallett, " Some Notes on Income Tax, Estate Duty and Stamp Duty for the Draftsman of *Inter Vivos* Settlements," [1965] *British Tax Review*, 15.

[74] They were introduced in England by the Perpetuities and Accumulations Act 1964, s. 13.

appointment, only where the instrument creating the power takes effect after that date.[75]

Accumulation is permissible in these periods even although the period begins during the life of the grantor and ends after his death.[76]

Date of settlement

Where the court approves an arrangement to vary an *inter vivos* trust under section 1 of the Trusts (Scotland) Act 1961, the date of the interlocutor may be treated as the date of the making of the settlement if the arrangement fundamentally and almost—completely supersedes the original trust provisions and in effect makes a new settlement.[77]

Who is the grantor ?

" Grantor " includes settlor and, in relation to a will, the testator.[78]

Where under the trust deed the income of the residue was to be accumulated and paid with the residue to the testator's son's children on attaining twenty-five and the trustees subsequently entered into an agreement with, *inter alios*, the son, to pay half of the income to the son and accumulate the other half in accordance with the provisions of the trust deed, it was argued that the son and not the testator was the settlor in the sense of the Thellusson Act. The argument was rejected on the ground that the agreement was not a settlement by the son more than by the other parties to the deed and the trust deed retained its full efficacy in so far as the agreement did not alter it and never ceased to be the deed by which the estate was settled.[79]

The opinion has been expressed,[80] that, where the accumulation is directed in the exercise of a special power of appointment, the donee of the power, and not the donor, is to be treated as the " grantor or settlor " under the Act but this may not be consistent with the reasoning of the House of Lords on the analogous question of the constitution of liferents in the exercise of a power of appointment.[81]

Choice of period

It has been suggested that the court should try to determine which period the testator had in mind but this is a difficult and artificial test because, as a rule, the testator does not have the rule against accumulation in mind at all.[82]

The logical starting point is to ascertain the point of time at which accumulation is to begin. If it falls within the period between the date o the deed and the date of the testator's death, the choice is restricted to

75 1966 Act, s. 6 (3).
76 1966 Act, s. 6 (1).
77 *John Sutherland Aikman*, 1968 S.L.T. 137.
78 1961 Act, s. 5 (6).
79 *Muir's Trs.* v. *Jameson* (1903) 10 S.L.T. 701.
80 *Stewart's Trs.* v. *Whitelaw*, 1926 S.C. 701, 716, *per* L.P. Clyde, p. 721, *per* Lord Sands.
81 *Muir's Trs.* v. *Williams*, 1943 S.C.(H.L.) 47—see p. 89, *supra*.
82 *Re Watts Will Trusts* [1936] 2 All E.R. 1555; *Re Ransome decd.* [1957] Ch. 348.

periods (a), (d), (e) and (f); if it falls within the period after death the choice is confined to (b), (c) and (d). The application of periods (c), (d) or (f) presumably requires some reference by the grantor to the minor beneficiaries. Period (e) will presumably now apply in most *inter vivos* trusts unless the deed refers to the period of the grantor's life.

Scope of the prohibition

Where, under the trust deed, the trustees of a unit trust had to add the balance of undistributed income to the capital of the fund, it was held that the statutory prohibition had no effect because the prescribed periods were inapplicable to a unit trust and the deed did not fall within the mischief which the statute was designed to prevent.[83]

Personal bar cannot be pleaded to defeat the provisions of the Act.

" No private arrangement or consent to defeat the provisions of the Thellusson Act, which, as is well known, was dictated by public policy, and has for its object the repression of public evils, can be entertained and given effect to by the Court. Were it otherwise, I can readily understand that the Act might, without much difficulty, be so entirely defeated as to render it of no more effect that if it had been repealed." [84]

The Act does affect public trusts.[85] There is an exemption of trusts for accumulation to be applied in reduction of the National Debt.[86]

Disposal of accumulations

If accumulation is directed for a period which is necessarily longer than any of the permitted periods, the direction must be given effect so far as possible and only after this has been done can the question of the disposal of the subsequent income be considered.[87]

Where accumulation is directed in contravention of the statute, the direction is void and the income directed to be accumulated, so long as it is directed to be accumulated contrary to the statute, is " to go to and be received by the person or persons who would have been entitled thereto if such accumulation had not been directed." [88] The application of this statutory provision has been a matter of considerable difficulty. The approach adopted by the courts is to re-write the deed in conformity with the statute.

" Although the trust for accumulation is cut down and reduced to a limited period, the whole of the rest of the will remains in point of disposition, in point of the meaning, effect and true interpretation of

[83] *Re A.E.G. Unit Trusts (Managers) Ltd.'s Deed* [1957] Ch. 415.
[84] *Maxwell's Trs.* v. *Maxwell* (1877) 5 R. 248, 254, *per* Lord Ormidale. (There is an error in the punctuation of the Rettie report—see 15 S.L.R. 155, 158.)
[85] *Ogilvie's Trs.* v. *Kirk-session of Dundee* (1846) 8 D. 1229; *Donaldson's Trs* v. *H.M. Advocate*, 1938 S.L.T. 106; *Re Bradwell* [1952] Ch. 575.
[86] Superannuation and Other Trust Funds (Validation) Act 1927, s. 9.
[87] *Edward's Trs.* v. *Edward* (1891) 18 R. 535.
[88] 1961 Act, s. 5 (3).

its language, precisely as if there had been no such operation performed by the statute." [89]

" The deed is to be read as if it had expressly declared that the accumulation directed should stop at the end of twenty-one years; and for the rest the deed is to be read and receive effect exactly as it stands." [90]

" You must take the will as it stands, but suppose that, for the direction which is there, this direction were substituted, *viz.*, ' I direct my trustees to accumulate income for the period of twenty-one years after my death ... and twenty-one years after my death, I direct such accumulations to cease,' and then (taking the will as it stands) see where the accumulations go." [91]

Present gift

If there is an absolute or present gift of the fund the income of which was being accumulated, the income which cannot lawfully be accumulated falls to the beneficiary of the gift.

" If there is an absolute gift, and then a series of limitations modifying that gift, so far as the limitations do not extend, the absolute gift remains. If, on the other hand, there is no absolute gift, but only a series of limitations, then, so far as the limitations do not take effect, the property is undisposed of." [92]

" If the fund directed to be accumulated is not the subject of any present gift, then the right of the eventual beneficiary will not be accelerated or arise at the term of twenty-one years, but the heir-at-law *in mobilibus* will take it as intestate succession. But if there be a present gift of the fund itself, and the direction to accumulate be only a burden on the gift, then the burden will terminate at the expiration of twenty-one years, and the gift will become absolute in the person of the donee." [93]

The fact that the beneficiary has a vested right does not necessarily mean that there is a present gift.[94] It is a question of intention, depending on the express or implied directions of the testator, whether such a beneficiary is entitled to claim the fruits accruing prior to the date fixed for payment of the legacy. There cannot be a present gift to a beneficiary in whom there is vesting subject to defeasance.[95]

An initial direction that " I leave all I have at the time of my death to

[89] *Per* Lord Westbury L.C., *Green* v. *Gascoyne* (1865) 4 De G.J. & S. 565, 570.

[90] *Elder's Trs.* v. *Treasurer of Free Church of Scotland* (1892) 20 R. 2, 6, *per* Lord Kyllachy.

[91] *Smith* v. *Glasgow Royal Infirmary*, 1909 S.C. 1231, 1236, *per* L.P. Dunedin. The direction in the deed may still be referred to for purposes of interpretation of other provisions of the deed—*Stewart's Trs.* v. *Whitelaw*, 1926 S.C. 701, 720, *per* Lord Sands.

[92] *Combe* v. *Hughes* (1865) 2 De G.J. & S. 657, 663, *per* Turner L.J.

[93] *Maxwell's Trs.* v. *Maxwell* (1877) 5 R. 248, 250, *per* L.J.-C. Moncreiff.

[94] *Wilson's Trs.* v. *Glasgow Royal Infirmary*, 1917 S.C. 527, 532, *per* Lord Skerrington.

[95] *Russell's Trs.* v. *Russell*, 1959 S.C. 148, 154, *per* L.P. Clyde, p. 156, *per* Lord Russell.

establish a fund to be called ' The Humble Heroes Fund ' " was said to be apt and habile to denote the intention to make a present gift.[96]

If the term for payment of the capital is postponed solely for the purpose of effecting accumulation, and further accumulation becomes unlawful, the capital is then payable even although the sum specified by the testator has not been raised.[97]

The following are cases in which it was held that there was a present gift:

(1) Where the residue of the truster's estate was to be paid to a kirk session and invested in Government stock and the dividends accumulated for one hundred years when the sum was to be used to build a hospital for poor boys, it was held that, when accumulation became unlawful, the kirk session were entitled to apply the fund for purposes of the bequest free from any obligation to accumulate.[98] " Here the party to whom this bequest would go, if there had been no such illegal directions as to accumulation, is the very same party to whom it was directed to go, *viz.*, the kirk session of Dundee." [99]

(2) Where the residue of the trust fund was to be used to purchase land which was to be entailed on the heir in possession of an estate previously entailed by the truster, and until a purchase was made three-fourths of the trust income was to be paid to the heir in possession and the other fourth was to be accumulated " to increase the amount of the disposable funds," it was held that when the accumulation became illegal, the income fell to the heir in possession.[1]

(3) Where after the lapse of certain annuities, a sum was to be invested as a fund for payment of bequests to charities, three-fourths of the income being paid to charities each year and the other fourth being accumulated with the fund, it was held that when accumulation became unlawful the one-fourth of the income fell to the charities because " the capital or *corpus* of the fund was bestowed on the trustees for behoof of these charities, and . . . the direction to accumulate was a mere burden or a limitation of the bequest." [2] As Lord Ormidale demonstrated,[3] this decision did not altogether accord with the theory that the will should be read with the direction to accumulate deleted—" I doubt very much whether anything more can be held to have been bequeathed to the religious and charitable institutions than the revenue or interest arising on three-fourths of the £4,000."

(4) In *Stewart's Trs.* v. *Whitelaw*,[4] a provision was to be held for the

---

[96] *Donaldson's Trs.* v. *H.M. Advocate*, 1938 S.L.T. 106.
[97] *Colquhoun* v. *Colquhoun's Trs.* (1892) 19 R. 946.
[98] *Ogilvie's Trs.* v. *Kirk-session of Dundee* (1846) 8 D. 1229. See also *Donaldson's Trs.* v. *H.M. Advocate*, 1938 S.L.T. 106; *Fisher's Trs.* v. *Barnard's Court Mission*, 1948 S.L.T. (Notes) 16.
[99] *Per* Lord Jeffrey, at p. 1243.
[1] *Mackenzie* v. *Mackenzie's Trs.* (1877) 4 R. 962. The decision proceeded very largely on prior decisions in the law of entail.
[2] *Maxwell's Trs.* v. *Maxwell* (1877) 5 R. 248.
[3] p. 253.
[4] 1926 S.C. 701.

testator's daughter in liferent and for her issue in fee subject to such conditions as the daughter might appoint. The daughter directed that the
provision was to be held for her issue in liferent and their issue in fee and
that if a child was in pupillarity at the time of its succession the income of
its share, except for such part as the trustees thought proper to expend on
its behoof, was to be accumulated until it reached the age of twenty-five.
The daughter was survived by a child five days old and it was held that,
when accumulation became unlawful, the income fell to be paid to the
child because the child had a present gift of the whole liferent, subject only
to the trustees' discretion to retain and accumulate part of it.

In the following instances, it was held that there was no present gift:

(1) Where there was a direction to pay annuities, or liferents, an
implied direction to accumulate the surplus income, and a direction to pay
to a residuary legatee on the death of the last annuitant or liferenter.[5]

(2) Where the income had to be accumulated for behoof of minors
and paid to them on their attaining a certain age.[6]

(3) Where the residuary legatees could not be ascertained until the
death of an annuitant or other date of division appointed by the testator.[7]

The first of these examples has to be contrasted with *Dowden's Trs.*[8]
In that case the testator in his trust disposition and settlement directed his
trustees to convey and make over the residue to a school on the death of
the last surviving liferenter. By a codicil he provided for payment from
the residue of certain annuities and directed that on the death of the last
surviving annuitant the capital of the residue, together with any free revenue
which had accrued after meeting the annuities, was to be paid to the
school. Accumulation became illegal twenty-one years after the testator's
death and, on the subsequent death of the last surviving liferenter, the
heir *in mobilibus* claimed the free revenue accruing after payment of the
annuities. It was held, on a construction of the testamentary writings, that
there was an absolute and unqualified initial gift of the residue as at the
death of the last surviving liferenter and the codicil merely postponed
payment of the part of the capital required to secure payment of the
annuities. The balance of the capital, on the authority of *Miller's Trs.* v.
Miller,[9] was immediately payable to the residuary legatees who had an
unqualified and indefeasible right of fee, there being no trust purpose
which could not be secured without retention of the fee.

---

[5] *Burgh of Ayr* v. *Shaw* (1904) 12 S.L.T. 126. See also *Pursell* v. *Elder* (1865) 3 M. (H.L.) 59;
Smyth's Trs. v. *Kinloch* (1880) 7 R. 1176; *Smith* v. *Glasgow Royal Infirmary*, 1909 S.C.
1231; *Wilson's Trs.* v. *Glasgow Royal Infirmary*, 1917 S.C. 527; *Pyper's Trs.* v. *Leighton*,
1946 S.L.T. 255; *Young's Trs.* v. *Chapelle*, 1971 S.L.T. 147.

[6] *Gillies' Trs.* v. *Bain* (1893) 30 S.L.R. 651; *Mackay's Trs.* v. *Mackay*, 1909 S.C. 139.

[7] *Lord* v. *Colvin* (1860) 23 D. 111; *Cathcart's Trs.* v. *Heneage's Trs.* (1883) 10 R. 1205;
Campbell's Trs. v. *Campbell* (1891) 18 R. 992; *Elder's Trs.* v. *Treasurer of Free Church of
Scotland* (1892) 20 R. 2; *Logan's Trs.* v. *Logan* (1896) 23 R. 848; *Moon's Trs.* v. *Moon*
(1899) 2 F. 201; *Russell's Trs.* v. *Russell*, 1959 S.C. 148; *Thomson's Trs.* v. *Keddie*, 1969
S.C. 220.

[8] 1965 S.L.T. 88.

[9] (1890) 18 R. 301. See p. 141, *infra*.

The residue clause

Where there is no present gift, the income which cannot be accumulated may fall into residue if the residue clause is in appropriate terms, otherwise it falls into intestacy. If the estate which the residuary legatee is to take is defined by reference to the position of the funds in the trustees' hands at a specific date, that is what is given to the residuary legatee and nothing more. On the other hand, the residuary clause may be in such terms that it embraces everything which has not been otherwise disposed of.[10]

The following residue clause was said to be " conceived in ample and comprehensive terms, which are habile to include all parts of the estate not otherwise effectively disposed of "—" the residue of my means and estate, including therein all accumulations of profit, mineral rents or lordships, and other revenue in so far as not required for the purposes of the Trust." [11]

The normal wording of a testamentary disposition—" my whole means and estate heritable and moveable, real and personal, of every kind and description and wherever situated which shall belong to me at the time of my death or over which I may have power of disposal by will or otherwise " was said to form a clause " expressed in the widest possible terms " and could include income ineffectually directed to be accumulated.[12]

Accumulating residue

Where the accumulation of the income of a legacy fund became unlawful and the residue clause was wide enough to catch the subsequent income but the residue itself was to be retained for beneficiaries who were not entitled to payment, it was held that the subsequent income fell into intestacy.[13] On the other hand, in *Union Bank* v. *Campbell*,[14] the surplus income of an *inter vivos* trust was caught by the residue clause of a *mortis causa* deed and it was held that the income could be retained and added to the capital of the testamentary trust. Lord Alness said [15]:

" I am not satisfied that the taint of illegality which no doubt attaches to the accumulations directed to be made under the *inter vivos* deed of trust continues to attach to the surplus funds when they come to be dealt with under the provisions of the trust-disposition and settlement."

Watson's Trs. was distinguished on the ground that there the residue had not vested, there was no liferent of the residue, and there was only one deed.

In *Gibson's Trs.*[16] it was agreed that accumulation under an *inter vivos* trust became unlawful on the death of the truster and that the income

10 *Smith* v. *Glasgow Royal Infirmary*, 1909 S.C. 1231. See also *Burgh of Ayr* v. *Shaw* (1904) 12 S.L.T. 126.
11 *Watson's Trs.* v. *Brown*, 1923 S.C. 228.
12 *Union Bank* v. *Campbell*, 1929 S.C. 143.
13 *Watson's Trs.* v. *Brown*, 1923 S.C. 228.
14 1929 S.C. 143.
15 p. 153.   16 1963 S.L.T. 373.

thereafter fell into the truster's estate. The truster, however, had left a will in which she directed that the residue of her estate (which was defined in terms wide enough to include the income falling to the estate) should be paid to the trustees of the *inter vivos* trust and added to the capital thereof. It was argued that once the income fell into the truster's testamentary estate it had to be dealt with under the will and that, as the will was a *mortis causa* deed, the Thellusson Act permitted accumulation after the grantor's death. This contention was rejected. The court held that it was not possible to do by the two deeds what could not have been done by one and the income fell into intestacy. Lord Sorn [17] distinguished *Union Bank* v. *Campbell* in respect that, firstly, there the sums were held by the testamentary trustees and administered by them independently of the *inter vivos* trust and for a different purpose, and, secondly, there was no direction to accumulate the sums because they were to be added to the capital and the income was to be paid to a liferentrix. The latter point of distinction is not altogether clear as, although there was no accumulation of the income of the income paid into the testamentary trust, the effect of the arrangement was to accumulate the income of the *inter vivos* trust.

Intestacy

Where income falls into intestacy, the heirs *in mobilibus* are ascertained as at the date of the testator's death.[18] " The pail may, at the date of the testator's death, seem to be quite empty (just as may a residue pail), but the pail, such as it is, passed to the heir *in mobilibus*, and anything that may subsequently drop into it, however unexpectedly, belongs to him." [19] Under the law prior to the Succession (Scotland) Act 1964, it was held that, where the income comprised rents of heritage, each termly payment as it accrued vested in the person holding at that time the character of heir-at-law of the truster.[20] For tax purposes, the payments to the heir were treated as income and not as capital.[21] The heir in heritage had to collate before he could claim a share of the income falling into intestacy.[22]

Where the accruing revenue of a mixed estate falls to be divided as intestate succession, the funds are treated as heritable or moveable according to their source as existing at the date of the testator's death without regard to any conversion authorised or directed by the settlement.[23]

---

[17] p. 376.
[18] *Lord* v. *Colvin* (1860) 23 D. 111; *Logan's Trs.* v. *Logan* (1896) 23 R. 848.
[19] *Mair's C.B.* v. *Inland Revenue*, 1932 S.C. 151, 156, *per* Lord Sands.
[20] *Campbell's Trs.* v. *Campbell* (1891) 18 R. 992; *Logan's Trs.* v. *Logan, supra.* These decisions were approved by Lord Trayner in *Moon's Trs.* v. *Moon* (1899) 2 F. 201, 209. The rule was followed in *Hunter's Trs.* v. *Edinburgh Chamber of Commerce*, 1911, 2 S.L.T. 287. See also *Mair's C.B.* v. *Inland Revenue*, 1932 S.C. 151, 156, *per* Lord Sands; *Robertson's Trs.* v. *Robertson's Trs.*, 1933 S.C. 639, 646, *per* Lord Sands.
[21] *Mair's C.B.* v. *Inland Revenue*, 1932 S.C. 151.
[22] *Moon's Trs.* v. *Moon, supra*; *Hunter's Trs.* v. *Edinburgh Chamber of Commerce, supra*; *Watson's Trs.* v. *Brown*, 1923 S.C. 228.
[23] *Moon's Trs.* v. *Moon* (1899) 2 F. 201.

The income arising from the rents of heritage which have been lawfully accumulated is moveable estate.[24]

Legal rights

There is an apparent conflict of decisions as to whether a widow can claim *jus relictae* out of income falling into intestacy. In *Moon's Trs.* v. *Moon*[25] and *McGregor's Trs.* v. *Kimbell*[26] it was held that she could. In *Wilson's Trs.* v. *Glasgow Royal Infirmary*,[27] the First Division decided that she could not on the ground that *jus relictae* could not extend to a fund which had no existence at the date of the testator's death. *Moon's Trs.* was cited in argument but is not referred to on this point in the opinions. In *Lindsay's Trs.* v. *Lindsay*,[28] the Second Division followed *Wilson's Trs.* but commented upon the difficulty of reconciling the prior decisions.

The solution seems to be this. The estate in *Moon's Trs.* was partly heritable and partly moveable and the question of the income accruing from the lawfully accumulated rents of heritage was not raised. In *Wilson's Trs.* the estate comprised heritage and the invested accumulated income of heritage. By virtue of *Logan's Trs.*[24] the heirs *in mobilibus* were entitled to claim the income derived from the accumulated income but it did not follow that the widow was entitled to *jus relictae* from income from this particular source. This appears from the opinion of Lord Skerrington[29]:

> " Further, assuming it to be the law, as was decided in the case of *Logan's Trs.* v. *Logan*, that surplus income arising from rents lawfully accumulated by and in the hands of trustees is moveable estate and falls to the heir *in mobilibus* as at the testator's death, it does not in the least follow that the widow can claim *jus relictae* out of a fund which had no existence at the date of the testator's death."

He later referred to the fund as " money, the right to which formed no part of the moveable *hereditas jacens*, but was an indirect, though undisposed of, fruit of the heritable estate." Moreover, one of the arguments against the widow's claim set forth in one report[30] of the case is that she was not entitled to *jus relictae* out of something which was not *moveable* estate at the death of the testator. It would, therefore, seem that *Lindsay's Trs.* was wrongly decided as part of the income there was derived from moveable estate.[31] Lord Alness to some extent relied on a statement by the First Division in *Russel* v. *Att.-Gen.*[32] that "*jus relicti* is a certain

---

[24] *Logan's Trs.* v. *Logan* (1896) 23 R. 848; *Watson's Trs.* v. *Brown*, 1923 S.C. 228. But see *Wilson's Trs.* v. *Glasgow Royal Infirmary*, 1917 S.C. 527, 533, *per* Lord Skerrington.
[25] (1899) 2 F. 201.
[26] 1911 S.C. 1196. See also *Mackay's Trs.* v. *Mackay*, 1909 S.C. 139.
[27] 1917 S.C. 527.
[28] 1931 S.C. 586. In *Campbell's Trs.* v. *Campbell's Trs.*, 1950 S.C. 48, Lord Cooper reserved his opinion as to the conflict.
[29] p. 532.
[30] 1917, 1 S.L.T. 328, 329 (*sub nom. Wilson's Trs.* v. *Wilson*).
[31] An argument of this kind seems to have been advanced but is ignored in the judgments.
[32] 1917 S.C. 28, 34. This was a petition under the British Law Ascertainment Act 1859, and no opinions were delivered.

share of the wife's estate fixed, so far as regards value, as at the date of the
wife's death." This case was, however, concerned with the date at which
the estate was to be valued and not with the extent of the estate subject to
jus relicti.

There would therefore seem to be no rule that a surviving spouse, in
cases where the Succession (Scotland) Act 1964 applies, is not entitled
to prior and legal rights out of income which cannot lawfully be
accumulated.

Other disposal

Surplus income accruing to a married woman after accumulation has
become illegal does not fall under a general assignation contained in an
antenuptial marriage contract.[33]

Where trustees were authorised by the court to make advances out of
accumulated income for the education of minor beneficiaries, it was held
that such payments could lawfully be made after the accumulation had
become illegal under the Thellusson Act.[34]

Accumulations Act 1892

The Accumulations Act 1892,[35] provides that no person shall settle
property in such a manner that the rents or income thereof shall be wholly
or partially accumulated for the purchase of land only, for any longer
period than during the minority or respective minorities of any person or
persons who under the uses or trusts of the instrument directing accumulation would for the time being, if of full age, be entitled to receive the
rents or income so directed to be accumulated.

Despite its wording, which differs from that of the Thellusson Act, the
effect of the statute is not to render the settlement wholly null and void; it
merely annuls the direction to accumulate.[36] The principles governing the
disposal of the revenue which cannot be accumulated are those which are
applied under the Thellusson Act.[37]

---

[33] *Murdoch's Trs.* v. *Stock*, 1923 S.C. 906.
[34] *Muir's Trs.* v. *Jameson* (1903) 10 S.L.T. 701.
[35] 55 & 56 Vict. c. 58. Now re-enacted in altered form for England by Law of Property Act
1925, s. 166. As to the policy of the Act, see *Re Baroness Llanover* [1903] 2 Ch. 330.
[36] *Robertson's Trs.* v. *Robertson's Trs.*, 1933 S.C. 639.
[37] *Ibid.*

CHAPTER 9

THE BENEFICIARY'S RIGHT

THE beneficiary's right has often been described as a *jus crediti* [1] and this term is to some extent appropriate in that the right is a right of action and not a *jus in re* or right of property. *Jus crediti*, however, is frequently applied to a mere contractual right and the beneficiary's right is higher than this. He can vindicate the trust property on the sequestration of the trustee and he can procure the recovery of property from a third party who has received it gratuitously or in the knowledge that the conveyance is in breach of trust. McLaren favours the expression *jus ad rem* but the meaning of this term is not precise. [2] He suggests in the alternative " a personal right of property " but the passage in which the expression occurs was subsequently criticised in *Inland Revenue* v. *Clark's Trs.* [3]

That decision established that the beneficiary's interest consists of the following rights of action: (i) a right by personal action, usually of declarator or accounting, to compel the trustees to administer the trust according to its terms; (ii) a right to interdict the trustees from breach of trust; (iii) a right to recover damages from the trustees for breach of trust; (iv) a right to petition the court to change the administration of the trust by replacing the trustees by new trustees or a judicial factor. [4]

The beneficiary has no right of action by which he can vindicate for himself any of the trust property but he can either compel the trustees to give the use of their names in an action or sue a third party and call the trustees as defenders.

Rights against trustees

The beneficiary's rights of action against the trustees are treated elsewhere. [5] So long as a trust subject remains entire in the hands of the trustee, no lapse of time will bar a claim for it by the beneficiary. [6]

The one other point which requires mention here is the beneficiary's use of diligence against assets forming part of the trust estate. A beneficiary cannot, by arresting funds due to the estate, or by means of an inhibition, prevent the trustees or executors from ingathering the estate. [7]

---

[1] Bell, *Prin.* s. 1996; Forsyth, 329; McLaren, II, 832; *Speirs* v. *Speirs* (1850) 13 D. 81.
[2] *Edmond* v. *Gordon* (1858) 3 Macq. 116, 122, *per* Lord Cranworth, p. 129, *per* Lord Wensleydale.
[3] 1939 S.C. 11, 26, *per* Lord Moncrieff, p. 22, *per* L.P. Normand.
[4] *Inland Revenue* v. *Clark's Trs., supra.*
[5] See Chaps. 24 and 25.
[6] *University of Aberdeen* v. *Irvine* (1866) 4 M. 392, 401, *per* Lord Kinloch, 6 M.(H.L.) 29, 37, *per* Lord Cairns L.C.; *Cooper Scott* v. *Gill Scott*, 1924 S.C. 309; *Bertram Gardner & Co's Tr.* v. *King's and Lord Treasurer's Remembrancer*, 1920 S.C. 555, 565, *per* Lord Mackenzie; *United Collieries* v. *Lord Advocate*, 1950 S.C. 458. See Prescription and Limitation (Scotland) Act 1973, Sched. 3 (*e*).
[7] *Young* v. *Ramage* (1838) 16 S. 572; *Hay* v. *Morrison* (1838) 16 S. 1273.

" I venture to lay down as a general—though it may not be a universal—proposition, that a beneficiary, when raising an action against his trustee to compel payment of money to which he is entitled under the trust, is not entitled to use arrestments on the dependence of that action, so as to prevent the trust-funds coming into the hands of the trustee. The object of these arrestments must be either to obtain a preference, or to get a security. If the object be to secure to one beneficiary a preference over another in the distribution of a trust-fund, then I think that is incompetent. The right of a beneficiary, whether to a *pari passu* preference with others, or to a preference over other beneficiaries, must depend on the terms of the trust, and not on any diligence whatever. If, again, the object is to secure a preference over the creditors of the trust, that is just as plainly out of the question. No beneficiary is entitled to preference over the creditors of a trust; but, on the contrary, must submit to the creditors having a preference over him." [8]

The trustee's creditors

The trust property is not subject to the diligence of the trustee's creditors. " The creditors cannot attach or take in execution any estate of which the bankrupt is a trustee. They can attach such interest only as the bankrupt is beneficially entitled to." [9]

Property held in trust by the bankrupt does not pass to the trustee in his sequestration.[10] Property held in trust by a limited company which goes into liquidation must be surrendered by the liquidator.[11]

It must be possible to identify the property. Bell states the rule, so far as an agent in a fiduciary position is concerned, thus:

" In all cases of factory, where the property remitted by the principal, or acquired for him by his order, is found distinguishable in the hands of the factor, capable of being traced by a clear and connected chain of identity, in no one link of it degenerating from a specific trust into a general debt; the creditors of the factor, who has become a bankrupt, have no right to the specific property." [12]

Property which is shown to have been directly acquired by conversion of trust property can be claimed by the beneficiaries.

" If the property in its original state and form was covered with a trust in favour of the principal, no change of that state and form can divest it of such trust, or give the factor, or those who represent him in right, any other more valid claim in respect to it, than they respectively

---

[8] *Mags. of Dundee* v. *Taylor and Grant* (1863) 1 M. 701, 703, *per* L.J.-C. Inglis.
[9] *Fleeming* v. *Howden* (1868) 6 M.(H.L.) 113, 121, *per* Lord Westbury.
[10] *Heritable Reversionary Co. Ltd.* v. *Millar* (1892) 19 R.(H.L.) 43; *Forbes's Trs.* v. *Macleod* (1898) 25 R. 1012. See also *Fleeming* v. *Howden* (1868) 6 M.(H.L.) 113; *Watson* v. *Duncan* (1879) 6 R. 1247.
[11] *Turnbull* v. *Liqr. of Scottish County Investment Co.*, 1939 S.C. 5.
[12] *Comm.* I, 287.

had before such change. An abuse of trust can confer no rights on the party abusing it, nor on those who claim in privity with him." [13]

Money

Where the trustee has paid a sum of money forming part of the trust fund into his own bank account which was in credit, the beneficiary can recover it from the trustee in the sequestration.[14] If the money becomes inmixed in the account with the trustee's own money, the court will disentangle the account and may treat any withdrawals made by the trustee as having been made from his own funds and not from the trust funds.[15] Subsequent payments into the account cannot be appropriated to replace trust money withdrawn.[16] On the other hand, if the balance remaining in the account is less than the trust fund, the beneficiary can recover the property acquired with the money withdrawn by the trustee.[17] In England, once the trustee's own money is exhausted and there is more than one trust fund involved, the rule in *Clayton's* case is applied and the earliest drawings are attributed to the earliest deposits.[18]

If the trustee's account was overdrawn when the trust funds were deposited the beneficiary cannot recover if the bank acted in good faith.[19] If it is proved that the bank knew that the funds did not belong to the trustee and that he had no authority to pay them into his account, there will be liability to repay.[20] If the fund is paid into an account in credit and the bank does not choose to set off the account against another which is in debit prior to the bankruptcy or liquidation, the fund can be recovered.[21]

Shares which are pledged to a bank along with other securities under a general letter of hypothecation do not lose their identity.[22]

Rights against third parties

It is clear that the beneficiary cannot recover trust property from a third party who has acquired it in good faith and for value.[23] If the third party took *in mala fide* or gratuitously the property can be recovered.[24]

---

[13] *Taylor* v. *Plumer* (1815) 3 M. & S. 562, 574, *per* Lord Ellenborough C.J. See also *Mags. of Edinburgh* v. *McLaren* (1881) 8 R.(H.L.) 140.

[14] *Macadam* v. *Martin's Tr.* (1872) 11 M. 33.

[15] *Jopp* v. *Johnston's Tr.* (1904) 6 F. 1028; *Pennell* v. *Deffell* (1853) 4 De G.M. & G. 372; *Knatchbull* v. *Hallett* (1879) 13 Ch.D. 696. See also *Sinclair* v. *Brougham* [1914] A.C. 398.

[16] *James Roscoe (Bolton) Ltd.* v. *Winder* [1915] 1 Ch. 62.

[17] *Re Oatway* [1903] 2 Ch. 356; *Re Tilley's Will Trusts* [1967] Ch. 1179.

[18] Lewin, 652.

[19] *Thomson* v. *Clydesdale Bank Ltd.* (1893) 20 R.(H.L.) 59; *Hofford* v. *Gowans*, 1909, 1 S.L.T. 153.

[20] *Taylor* v. *Forbes* (1830) 4 W. & S. 444.

[21] *Smith* v. *Liqr. of James Birrell Ltd.*, 1968 S.L.T. 174.

[22] *Newton's Exrx.* v. *Meiklejohn's J.F.*, 1959 S.L.T. 71.

[23] *Redfearn* v. *Somervail* (1813) 1 Dow's App. 50; *Burns* v. *Lawrie's Trs.* (1840) 2 D. 1348; *Thomson* v. *Clydesdale Bank Ltd.* (1893) 20 R.(H.L.) 59. See Chapter 1. The case-law on this topic is surprisingly sparse. See, as to reduction of a null transfer, *Adair's J.F.* v. *Connell's Trs.* (1894) 22 R. 116; *Kidd* v. *Paton's Trs.*, 1912, 2 S.L.T. 363. A limited company is not concerned with the fact that the transfer of its shares is in breach of trust (*Elliot* v. *Mackie & Son*, 1935 S.C. 81).

[24] *Taylor* v. *Forbes* (1830) 4 W. & S. 444; *Macgowan* v. *Robb* (1864) 2 M. 943; *Bertram Gardner & Co.'s Tr.* v. *King's Remembrancer*, 1920 S.C. 555. See also *Banque Belge pour*

If the third party has innocently inmixed the property with his own funds, the beneficiary and the third party rank *pari passu* on the mixed fund.[25] If the trustees refuse to sue to recover, they can be forced to lend their names to the beneficiaries to enable them to raise an action.[26] The residuary legatee or heir *ab intestato* can pursue an action for repetition of a sum paid by the trustees to a third party in error, provided that the action is brought against the trustees as well as the third party.[27] A special legatee can bring an action directly against the holder of a subject specially bequeathed provided that he calls the trustee or executor as a party to the action.[28]

The fact that trustees have acted negligently does not bar them from recovering the assets concerned on behalf of the beneficiaries unless the negligence would have been an effectual obstacle to an action at the instance of a judicial factor on the trust estate.[29]

The right of the beneficiary to proceed against a gratuitous disponee is not subject to prescription.[30]

If a partner who is a trustee improperly employs trust property in the business or on the account of the partnership, no other partner is liable for the property to the beneficiaries.[31] This does not prevent trust money being followed and recovered from the firm if still in its possession or under its control.

Transmission on death

If the beneficiary's right is vested it is transmitted by testate or intestate succession. In this connection, and in relation to diligence by the beneficiary's creditors, the question of whether the interest is heritable or moveable may still be of importance. If the estate is wholly heritable and there is a direction to convey it *in specie* to the beneficiary at some point of time, his interest is heritable. Similarly, if the estate is wholly moveable, unless there is a direction to convert it to heritage, the interest is moveable. Difficulties arise where there is a direction, express or implied, to convert the estate into another form. Certain actings before the date of death may affect the nature of the beneficiary's right.

Actings of the truster

The nature of the estate may be affected by the actings of the truster. Where, at the time of his death intestate, the deceased had entered into a

---

l'Etranger v. *Hambrouck* [1921] 1 K.B. 321; *Nelson* v. *Larholt* [1948] 1 K.B. 339. The basis of the claim in Scotland may well be unjustifiable enrichment (see Smith, *Studies Critical and Comparative*, 224).

[25] *Re Diplock, Diplock* v. *Wintle* [1948] 1 Ch. 465.

[26] *Blair* v. *Stirling* (1894) 1 S.L.T. 599; *Brown's Trs.* v. *Brown* (1888) 15 R. 581.

[27] *Armour* v. *Glasgow Royal Infirmary*, 1909 S.C. 916. But as to overpayment of income, see p. 376, *infra*.

[28] *Innerarity* v. *Gilmore* (1840) 2 D. 813.

[29] *Kidd* v. *Paton's Trs.*, 1912, 2 S.L.T. 363.

[30] *Thain* v. *Thain* (1891) 18 R. 1196, 1201, *per* Lord Kinnear. See Prescription and Limitation (Scotland) Act 1973, Sched. 3 (*f*).

[31] Partnership Act 1890, s. 13. See J. Bennett Miller, *Law of Partnership in Scotland*, Ch. 8.

contract for the purchase of heritage and had almost completed negotiations for its re-sale, it was held that the price was a debt of the moveable estate but the heritage fell to the heir-at-law.[32] Where the deceased was engaged in the erection of buildings at his death, the portion of the moveable estate required for their completion was held to be heritable *destinatione*.[33]

Where the trustees of an *inter vivos* trust for administration invested the proceeds of an insurance policy, with the truster's knowledge, on heritable security, the sum did not form part of his moveable estate on the truster's death.[34]

Curatory administration

The succession cannot be affected by any act of ordinary administration on the part of a curator *bonis* or factor [35] unless it was a proper and necessary act on the part of the curator and would have been a necessary and unavoidable act on the part of the ward if *sui juris*.[36] The test is whether the purpose for which the curator thought it necessary to sell is one which the law recognises as a sufficient justification for converting land into money. There is a presumption in favour of honest administration and if the curator when applying for the requisite authority represented to the court that the sale was an act of necessity, the *onus* is on the other party to show the contrary.

Where a husband and wife were both under curatory and the curator sold the house of which they were *pro indiviso* proprietors, it was held that when, on the husband's death, his share of the proceeds passed as heritage to the wife under his will, that share became moveable in her succession.[37]

Principle of conversion

" The mode in which trustees actually deal with property left in trust by a testator, is admitted in many cases to be of no relevancy whatever. If the deed contain directions to sell, it shall be of no consequence that the trustees make over to the parties interested, the residue of the estate, without sale and *in forma specifica* as they received it; and the same shall be the result, where the direction to sell has not been express, but inferred from the combined consideration of a power of sale on the one hand, with the purposes of the trust on the other." [38]

---

[32] *Ramsay* v. *Ramsay* (1887) 15 R. 25.
[33] *Malloch* v. *McLean* (1867) 5 M. 335; *Bank of Scotland* v. *White's Trs.* (1891) 28 S.L.R. 891. But see *Fairlie's Trs.* v. *Fairlie's C.B.*, 1932 S.C. 216, 223, *per* Lord Clyde.
[34] *Pringle's Trs.* v. *Hamilton* (1872) 10 M. 621. Heritable securities were then heritable estate.
[35] *Kennedy* v. *Kennedy* (1843) 6 D. 40; *Moncrieff* v. *Miln* (1856) 18 D. 1286; *Laurie's Trs.* v. *Stewart*, 1952 S.L.T. (Notes) 19.
[36] *McAdam's Exor.* v. *Souters* (1904) 7 F. 179; *Dick* v. *Dick*, 1925 S.L.T. 337.
[37] *McLellan* v. *McLellan*, 1960 S.C. 348.
[38] *Advocate-General* v. *Smith* (1852) 14 D. 585, 589.

Express direction

An express direction by the testator to alter the nature of the estate operates conversion even although the direction has not been implemented.

" There is no doubt as to what is the principle of the law of conversion. The question arises as to a man's will. It is whether the testator directed his money to be turned into land by buying land, or it may be his land to be turned into money by selling land. The estate is to be considered as of that character, land or money, to which he intended it to be converted." [39]

If there is an express direction to convert the whole estate into cash, the interest of the beneficiaries is moveable.[40] But a direction will not affect the rights of the persons entitled to succeed on intestacy if the estate is not given to some other person.[41] If there is an unqualified direction to sell, and the bequest to which it is attached does not fail, conversion operates although the circumstances which presumably suggested the direction to sell do not obtain, e.g., if the direction is to sell the house and divide the proceeds among A, B and C and the survivors and A and B die before the date of vesting.[42]

Implied direction

An implied direction to sell has to be distinguished from a mere power of sale.

" The principle or doctrine of conversion appears to be the same both in England and in Scotland. Conversion is a question of intention, and depends on the nature and effect of the directions given in any settlement or will. If real or heritable property be vested in trustees upon an absolute and unconditional trust for sale, either declared or necessarily implied, and the proceeds of such sale are disposed of, there is (in the quaint phrase of the English law) an out and out conversion for the purposes of that disposition; and the interest of every beneficiary taking under the disposition is of the nature of personal or moveable property. But if, instead of an absolute and unqualified trust or direction for sale, the right to sell is made to depend on the discretion or will of the trustees; or is to arise only in case of necessity; or is limited to particular purposes, as, for example, to pay debts; or is not, in the appropriate language of Lord Fullerton in the case of Blackburn ' indispensable to the execution of the trust '; then in any of these cases, until the discretion is exercised, or the necessity arises and is acted on, or after the particular purposes

[39] Brown's Trs. v. Brown (1890) 18 R. 185, 188, per Lord Young.
[40] McGilchrist's Trs. v. McGilchrist (1870) 8 M. 689; Neilson v. Stewart (1860) 22 D. 646, 656, per L.P. McNeill; Smith v. Wighton's Trs. (1874) 1 R. 358.
[41] Cowan v. Cowan (1887) 14 R. 670; Logan's Trs. v. Logan (1896) 23 R. 848; Brown's Trs. v. McIntosh (1905) 13 S.L.T. 72.
[42] Bryson's Tr. v. Bryson, 1919, 2 S.L.T. 303.

are answered, or if the sale is not indispensable, there is no change in the quality of the property; and the heritable estate must continue to be held and transmitted as heritable." [43]

The dictum of Lord Fullerton to which reference is made is:

" The question always is solved by determining whether, on a sound construction of the deed, the heritable property is necessarily to be converted into money, or is to be divided unconverted, among the parties taking benefit; whether, in short, there is a mere power or option to sell and convert, or a direction, expressed or implied, that such conversion shall take place. And the implication does receive effect when, combined with the power, there are such directions for the disposal of the property, as render the exercise of it imperative on the trustees." [44]

The exercise of a power of sale is not " indispensable to the execution of the trust " if the direction to divide the estate can be implemented by conveying the heritage to the beneficiaries in *pro indiviso* shares. [45] This is so even if the number of beneficiaries is large. [46] But where shares have to be paid to beneficiaries at different times it is impracticable for the trustees to grant a succession of conveyances of the heritage *pro indiviso* to themselves and to each beneficiary. [47]

If the alternatives mentioned in the will are sale and allocation *in specie* a *pro indiviso* conveyance is impliedly excluded. [48] Where there was an express power either to sell the heritage or to convey it to the beneficiaries with a declaration that the trustees should not sell if a majority of the beneficiaries requested them not to, it was held that there was no conversion. [49]

An implied direction to sell effects conversion only in so far as it is necessary to sell to carry out the operative trust purposes. [50]

Wording

" Pay " used alone indicates conversion; it can be used in the sense of " transfer " [51] ; but in most of the cases in which this meaning has been

---

[43] *Buchanan* v. *Angus* (1862) 4 Macq. 374, 379, *per* Lord Westbury L.C.   See also *Williamson* v. *Advocate-General* (1843) 2 Bell's App. 89.

[44] *Advocate-General* v. *Blackburn's Trs.* (1847) 10 D. 166, 189.

[45] *Buchanan* v. *Angus* (1862) 4 Macq. 374; *Auld* v. *Anderson* (1876) 4 R. 211; *Aitken* v. *Munro* (1883) 10 R. 1097; *Sheppard's Tr.* v. *Sheppard* (1885) 12 R. 1193 (there is a strong dissenting opinion by Lord Young, *cf. Fotheringham's Trs.* v. *Hay* (1873) 11 M. 848; *Nairn's Trs.* v. *Melville* (1877) 5 R. 128; *Baird* v. *Watson* (1880) 8 R. 233.

[46] *Duncan's Trs.* v. *Thomas* (1882) 9 R. 731; *Bank of Scotland* v. *White's Trs.* (1891) 28 S.L.R. 891. In any event, the testator would not know the number at the date of division (*McCall's Trs.* v. *Murray* (1901) 3 F. 380, 386, *per* Lord Moncreiff) but the number presumably in contemplation of the testator is not to be disregarded (*Smith* v. *Wighton's Trs.* (1874) 1 R. 358; *Campbell's Tr.* v. *Dick*, 1915 S.C. 100).

[47] *Playfair's Trs.* v. *Playfair* (1894) 21 R. 836; *Galloway's Trs.* v. *Galloway* (1897) 25 R. 28; *Watson's Trs.* v. *Watson* (1902) 4 F. 798; *Steel's Trs.* v. *Steedman* (1902) 5 F. 239.

[48] *Henderson's Trs.* v. *Henderson*, 1907 S.C. 43.

[49] *Seton's Tr.* v. *Seton* (1886) 13 R. 1047.

[50] *Advocate-General* v. *Smith* (1852) 14 D. 585; (1854) 1 Macq. 760; *McConochie's Trs.* v. *McConochie*, 1912 S.C. 653; *Swain* v. *Benzie's Trs.*, 1960 S.C. 357.

[51] *Advocate-General* v. *Smith* (1854) 1 Macq. 760, 763, *per* Lord St. Leonards.

adopted it has been coupled with " convey." [52] Where " pay " is used in relation to " free proceeds " it is almost conclusively in favour of conversion.[53]

The following have been held to indicate an intention that there should be conversion of heritage: the use of the expression " free proceeds " [54]; a direction to pay by equal instalments [55]; that the bequest is of residue [56]; that shares might have to be divided into fractions [57]; that the power of sale is described as requisite [56]; that the destination-over was to issue and not to heirs in heritage [56]; that the heritage was held only as an investment [56]; that the trustees are given power to lay out a share in the purchase of heritage for a beneficiary.[57]

An express power to allocate heritage in satisfaction of a share is not conclusive.[58]

The following have been taken to indicate that there should not be conversion: the use of " dispone " [59] or " denude " [60] or " convey " [61] in the direction to transfer to the beneficiaries; the use of the words " share and share alike " which are applicable to a *pro indiviso* conveyance of the heritage [62]; power to use uninvested funds to purchase additional heritage; the use of the alternative " or the price thereof." [63]

Powers of sale

A power of sale will be implied if the purposes of the trust cannot be fulfilled without a sale and the beneficiaries' share will be moveable.[64] If trustees sell heritage by virtue of powers granted by the court under section 5 of the 1921 Act, the sale does not operate conversion.[65] A judicial sale following upon an action for the division and sale of common property does operate conversion.[66]

Reconversion

Even if there is a direction in the deed which effects constructive conversion, the beneficiaries may nevertheless elect to take the property in its existing state. This is known as reconversion. " In order to effect reconversion there must be either an overt act by the party in right of the succession or such lapse of time as, coupled with surrounding circum-

---

52 *Brown's Trs.* v. *Brown* (1890) 18 R. 185, 188, *per* L.J.-C. Macdonald; *Watson's Trs.* v. *Watson* (1902) 4 F. 798, 804, *per* Lord McLaren.
53 *Campbell's Tr.* v. *Dick*, 1915 S.C. 100.
54 *Campbell's Tr.* v. *Dick*, *supra*.
55 *Brown's Trs.* v. *Brown* (1890) 18 R. 185.
56 *Baird* v. *Watson* (1880) 8 R. 233.
57 *McCall's Trs.* v. *Murray* (1901) 3 F. 380.
58 *Watson's Trs.* v. *Watson* (1902) 4 F. 798.
59 *Sheppard's Tr.* v. *Sheppard* (1885) 12 R. 1193.
60 *Duncan's Trs.* v. *Thomas* (1882) 9 R. 731.
61 *Leggat's Trs.* v. *Leggat's Trs.*, 1957 S.L.T. (Notes) 28.
62 *Buchanan* v. *Angus* (1862) 4 Macq. 374.
63 *Buchanan* v. *Angus*, *supra*.
64 *Boag* v. *Walkinshaw* (1872) 10 M. 872.
65 *Taylor's Trs.* v. *Tailyour*, 1927 S.C. 288.
66 *Macfarlane* v. *Greig* (1895) 22 R. 405.

stances, imports unequivocally a determination to take the property as realty." [67]

Where there was a direction to sell the heritage but the beneficiary as a trustee let it on a long lease and referred to it by implication as her heritable property in a trust-settlement it was held that the beneficiary's actings had made her beneficial interest heritable.[68] Where the beneficiary consented to the application of moveable funds to buildings on the heritable estate, his interest was held to have become heritable.[69]

Reconversion may be operated by an agreement between the trustees and the beneficiary.[70] A mere delay in enforcing the sale is not enough to operate as an election to take the subject *in forma specifica*.[71]

Assignation

The interest of the beneficiary can be transferred to a third party by assignation. This is so even if his right is a mere non-vested *spes successionis*.[72] If an alimentary liferent is assigned the court will fix a reasonable alimentary allowance so that any excess can be paid by the trustees to the assignee.[73] If a legacy is declared to be alimentary and not assignable, the legatee can borrow from the trustees as individuals and authorise them to repay themselves from the legacy when it becomes payable.[74]

To complete the assignee's right, the assignation must be intimated to the trustees. If this is not done the trustee in the beneficiary's sequestration will be preferred to the assignee.[75] Intimation to the solicitors of the trust may be sufficient.[76] Intimation to the one of two trustees who held the whole trust fund and in practice administered the trust was sufficient.[77] If the sole trustee is the granter of the assignation intimation is unnecessary.[76]

An assignee is not affected by the actings of the cedent after the date of intimation of the assignation. So where a beneficiary who was also a trustee assigned his interest and subsequently drew sums from the trust estate exceeding his share, the assignees were entitled to rank on the trust estate for the full amount of the interest as at the date of intimation of the assignation.[78]

But this applies only to actings *qua* beneficiary. Where marriage-contract trustees had power to alter investments with the consent of the

---

[67] *Bryson's Tr.* v. *Bryson*, 1919, 2 S.L.T. 303, 305, *per* Lord Sands.
[68] *Grindlay* v. *Grindlay's Trs.* (1853) 16 D. 27. See also *Williamson* v. *Paul* (1849) 12 D. 372; *Hogg* v. *Hamilton* (1877) 4 R. 845, 847, *per* Lord Adam, p. 854, *per* Lord Shand.
[69] *Bank of Scotland* v. *White's Trs.* (1891) 28 S.L.R. 891.
[70] *Wingate's Trs.* v. *Wingate*, 1917, 1 S.L.T. 75.
[71] *Macgregor* (1876) 13 S.L.R. 450; *Bryson's Tr.* v. *Bryson*, 1919, 2 S.L.T. 303; *Mackintosh* v. *Mackintosh*, 1925 S.L.T. 674.
[72] *Trappes* v. *Meredith* (1871) 10 M. 38. But see Chap. 5 as to policies under the Married Women's Policies of Assurance (Scotland) Act 1880.
[73] *Craig* v. *Pearson's Trs.*, 1915, 2 S.L.T. 183. But see p. 96 *supra*.
[74] *Rothwell* v. *Stuart's Trs.* (1898) 1 F. 81.
[75] *Tod's Trs.* v. *Wilson* (1869) 7 M. 1100; *Moncreiff's Tr.* v. *Balfour*, 1928 S.N. 64, 139.
[76] *Browne's Tr.* v. *Anderson* (1901) 4 F. 305.
[77] *Jameson* v. *Sharp* (1887) 14 R. 643.
[78] *Macpherson's J.F.* v. *Mackay*, 1915 S.C. 1011.

spouses, it was held that the husband's assignation of his interest in the trust did not deprive him of the power to give such consent.[79] It was said that such a power was not alienable or in any way transmissible.

An assignation by the testator's widow of her interest under his will is an intimation that she intends to accept her conventional provisions and she is thereafter barred from claiming her legal rights.[80]

An assignee has a right to inspect the trust accounts even if his right is a mere *spes successionis* and even if the assignation is partial but if additional expense is thereby occasioned he must indemnify the trust.[81] The trustees are not obliged to give information to an assignee which the beneficiary himself could not demand.[82]

Diligence attaching interest

The creditor of a beneficiary can attach his debtor's interest in the trust. The appropriate diligence depends upon the nature of the beneficiary's interest at the time at which the diligence is executed.[83] A non-vested and future *spes successionis* is not arrestable,[84] but an interest vested subject to defeasance is.[85] A diligence which would prevent the trustees from realising the estate and thus injure the interests of all the beneficiaries will normally be recalled.[86]

If the interest of the beneficiary is exclusively a right to heritage as to which no power of sale or direction to sell was given by the truster, arrestment is not competent[87] and inhibition and adjudication are the appropriate forms.[88] If the interest is moveable it may be arrested even although the trust estate consists of heritage not yet realised.

Arrestment in the hands of two out of six trustees, a majority of trustees being a quorum, was invalid.[89] " The ideal way of arresting in the hands of trustees is to find them present at a trustees' meeting and there and then arrest in their joint hands. That is rarely practicable, and therefore an equivalent must be found by arresting in the hands of the individual trustees what is due by them jointly. But to make such arrestment complete it must be laid on in the hands of the whole trustees, or at least of a quorum."[90] Arrestment can be made in the hands of a factor to the trust.[91]

The arrestment should be served on the trustees as trustees.[92] The

79 *Duke of Devonshire* v. *Fletcher* (1874) 1 R. 1056.
80 *Robinson* v. *Robinson's Trs.*, 1934 S.L.T. 183.
81 *Salamon* v. *Morrison's Trs.*, 1912, 2 S.L.T. 499.
82 *Low* v. *Bouverie* [1891] 3 Ch. 82, 99, per Lindley L.J.; *Salamon* v. *Morrison's Trs.*, 1912, 2 S.L.T. 499.
83 *Wilson* v. *Smart*, May 31, 1809, F.C.
84 *Trappes* v. *Meredith* (1871) 10 M. 38; *Waddell* v. *Waddell's Trs.*, 1932 S.L.T. 201.
85 *Chambers' Trs.* v. *Smiths* (1878) 5 R.(H.L.) 151.
86 McLaren, II, 851.
87 *Douglas* v. *Mason* (1796) Mor. 16, 213; *Learmonts* v. *Shearer* (1866) 4 M. 540.
88 *Broughton* v. *Fraser* (1832) 10 S. 418; *Speirs* v. *Speirs* (1850) 13 D. 81; *Watson* v. *Wilson* (1868) 6 M. 258.
89 *Black* v. *Scott* (1830) 8 S. 367.
90 *Gracie* v. *Gracie*, 1910 S.C. 899, 905, per Lord Johnston.
91 *Dunlop* v. *Weir* (1823) 2 S. 167.
92 *Gracie* v. *Gracie*, supra.

debt should be sufficiently identified. A reference in schedules served on each of the two trustees to a sum of £350 " due and addebted by you as trustee foresaid " to a named person was held sufficient identification of a legacy due to that person.[92]

The trustees are not obliged to do something which they would not have done in the ordinary course of trust administration in order to fortify the position of a creditor who has adjudged the interest of a beneficiary. So trustees were not bound to retain the security writs of the trust funds in Scotland merely because if the writs were, in the proper course of administration, deposited in the United States, the beneficiary might be in a position to defeat the creditor's title when his interest became payable.[93]

The trustees do not stand in a fiduciary relationship to an assignee but it has been suggested that they may have a duty to protect the beneficiary by challenging the amount of the claim of an assignee in security.[94]

An arrestment of legitim is effectual notwithstanding that the child subsequently discharges his right to legitim.[95]

If the beneficiary dies, his interest can be attached by an executor-creditor.[96]

Sequestration of beneficiary

A vested interest is, of course, transferred to the trustee in the beneficiary's sequestration. A *spes successionis, i.e.,* a non-vested contingent right, is transferred to the trustee in the sequestration to the same effect as if an assignation thereof had been executed by the bankrupt and intimated at the date of sequestration.[97]

---

[93] *Brower's Exor.* v. *Ramsay's Trs.,* 1912 S.C. 1374.
[94] *Briggs' Trs.* v. *Briggs,* 1923 S.L.T. 755.
[95] *Waddell* v. *Waddell's Trs.,* 1932 S.L.T. 201.
[96] *Maxwell* v. *Wylie* (1837) 15 S. 1005.
[97] Bankruptcy (Scotland) Act 1913, s. 97 (4).

CHAPTER 10

REVOCATION OF TRUSTS

IN the absence of some contractual restraint, a testamentary trust is revocable until it takes effect on the granter's death.

A question may arise, however, as to whether an *inter vivos* trust can be revoked by the granter.[1] If it can be revoked by the granter it can be revoked at the instance of his creditors in the event of his insolvency.[2] Another form in which the question may arise is whether, on the granter's death, the trust funds are subject to the claims for legal rights of the surviving spouse [3] or children [4] or subject to the provisions of his *mortis causa* settlement.[5] Prior to the Succession (Scotland) Act 1964, the creation of an *inter vivos* trust was used by a husband in contemplation of an expected action of divorce as a method of defeating his wife's claim to her legal rights.[6] Now such a settlement could be reduced under section 27 of the 1964 Act.

A trust is irrevocable if the following conditions are satisfied [7]:

(1) the granter must have been solvent at the date of the divestiture and must not have been made insolvent by the divestiture.[8] Provided that this condition is satisfied, the alienation can be gratuitous. If the granter was insolvent, a gratuitous alienation may be reduced at the instance of his creditors but not at the instance of his wife and children.[9]

(2) the trust-deed must have been delivered to the trustees and the estate conveyed to them. The conveyance must be absolute and unqualified by any back bond or other similar reservation.[8] A provision that the truster was to be a necessary consenting party to acts of trust administration was held not to affect the divestiture.[10] The fact that the truster is one of the trustees does not prevent irrevocability.[11]

---

[1] *Byres' Trs.* v. *Gemmell* (1895) 23 R. 332; *Lyon* v. *Lyon's Trs.* (1901) 3 F. 653; *Middleton's Trs.* v. *Middleton*, 1909 S.C. 67; *Bertram's Trs.* v. *Bertram*, 1909 S.C. 1238; *Torrance* v. *Torrance's Trs.*, 1950 S.C. 78.

[2] In *Lawson's Tr.* v. *Lawson*, 1938 S.C. 632, the question—raised by a method of doubtful competency—was whether the trust funds were available for payment of the truster's debts.

[3] *Walker* v. *Amey* (1906) 8 F. 376.

[4] *Drysdale's Trs.* v. *Drysdale*, 1940 S.C. 85.

[5] *Murray* v. *Macfarlane's Trs.* (1895) 22 R. 927. The funds of a revocable trust may be liable to estate duty. See *Christie's Trs.* v. *Christie's Trs.*, 1943 S.C. 97.

[6] *Scott* v. *Scott*, 1930 S.C. 903.

[7] *Scott* v. *Scott*, 1930 S.C. 903.

[8] *Corbidge* v. *Somerville's Trs.*, 1911 S.C. 1326; *Scott* v. *Scott*, supra, p. 914, *per* L.P. Clyde.

[9] Goudy, *Bankruptcy*, 4th ed., 292. As to a trust deed for creditors see *Salaman* v. *Rosslyn's Trs.* (1900) 3 F. 298.

[10] *Rowley* v. *Rowley*, 1915, 2 S.L.T. 66; 1917, 1 S.L.T. 16.

[11] *Ross* v. *Ross's Trs.*, 1967 S.L.T. 12; *Campbell* v. *Campbell's Trs.*, 1967 S.L.T. (Notes) 30.

(3) there must be in existence an ascertained beneficiary. There is an exception in the case of an antenuptial marriage-contract trust.

(4) the beneficiary must have a *jus quaesitum*—an immediate beneficial interest—and not merely a *spes successionis* under a testamentary provision. The beneficial interest may be vested or contingent. If it is contingent, it does not matter that emergence of the maturity of the interest can occur only on the granter's death.

The first condition does not require further discussion. The second is treated elsewhere.[12]

The Beneficiary

Where the granter has constituted the trust purely for the management of his affairs it is clear that the trust, which is known as a " trust for administration," is revocable.

" It is a very well-settled rule of law that a trust for the administration of the granter's affairs in his lifetime, including the payment of his debts, does not divest the granter. Notwithstanding the execution of such a deed, he retains the radical beneficial interest in his estate. He may revoke the deed at pleasure, or may even without noticing the trust make an effectual destination of his property to heirs or legatees." [13]

" A man may think it prudent to protect himself against his own facility or improvidence, and for that object may convey his estate to trustees, but if he changes his mind he is entitled to revoke the deed and to call on the trustees to denude." [14]

It follows that a trust of this type does not place the trust estate beyond the reach of the granter's creditors.

" I know of no authority or precedent either here or in England for holding that a man of full age and *sui juris* can put his property out of his power, and beyond the reach of his creditors, without constituting at the same time some right, direct or contingent, in regard to that property in another." [15]

The trust may be one for administration and thus revocable *quoad* a part of, or an interest in, the estate.[16] This may occur, for example, where the divestiture is subject to a liferent reserved to the granter, or where the granter has a contingent reversion.

Where the trust estate is to be held for persons other than the granter but such persons are not in existence or are not ascertained, the trust is

---

12 See Chap. 3.
13 *Byres' Trs.* v. *Gemmell* (1895) 23 R. 332, 337, *per* Lord McLaren. See also *Walker* v. *Amey* (1906) 8 F. 376, 379, *per* Lord Dundas (L.O.).
14 *Bertram's Trs.* v. *Bertram*, 1909 S.C. 1238, 1241, *per* Lord Low.
15 *Hamilton's Trs.* v. *Hamilton* (1879) 6 R. 1216, 1221, *per* L.J.-C. Moncreiff. See also *Globe Insurance Co.* v. *Murray* (1854) 17 D. 216; *Forrest* v. *Robertson's Trs.* (1876) 4 R. 22; *Corbet* v. *Waddell* (1879) 7 R. 200, 209, *per* L.P. Inglis; *Eliott* v. *Eliott's Tr.* (1894) 21 R. 955; *Smith* v. *Davidson* (1901) 8 S.L.T. 354.
16 *Scott* v. *Scott, supra*, p. 914, *per* L.P. Clyde.

still a trust for administration and is revocable. So, where the trustees are
to hold for the granter and any future wife he may marry in liferent, and
for the children *nascituri* of his future marriage with her in fee, the trust is
revocable until the granter marries and has children.[17] Similarly, where a
woman, in contemplation of marriage, set up a trust by a unilateral deed
under which the income of the trust funds was to be paid to the granter
during her life and to her intended husband if he survived her, and the fee
was to be held for the children of the marriage, it was held that the granter
could revoke the trust with her husband's consent while there were no
children of the marriage.[18] The majority of the court drew a distinction
between a trust contained in an antenuptial marriage-contract, which
would not have been revocable even if there were no children in existence,
and a trust constituted by a unilateral deed executed without reference to
any contract of marriage. As it was put in an earlier case, it is not the law
that a woman " could reduce herself directly to the state of an alimentary
liferenter, merely of her own property, in favour of parties not existing,
who never might exist, and whose possible existence was not yet the subject of any contract with any existing party." [19]

On the other hand, where there are beneficiaries in existence, the trust
cannot be revoked.[20] It follows from what has been said that a revocable
trust may become irrevocable when beneficiaries come into existence [21]
and an irrevocable trust may become revocable because of failure of the
trust purposes.[22] A more complex situation arose in *Drysdale's Trs.* v.
Drysdale. The trust funds were to be held for the granter's wife in liferent
and for the children of the marriage in fee. There was to be no vesting
until the termination of the liferent and on the children attaining the age of
thirty years. Subject to these provisions, the funds were to be paid as they
became available to the granter whom failing to his assignees, whom failing
to his heirs *in mobilibus.* The granter was survived by his wife and children
but they subsequently renounced their rights under the trust deed. It was
held that although the deed was irrevocable *quoad* the benefits to the wife
and children, the granter had retained a radical right in the trust funds
subject to the burden of the purposes in favour of the wife and children
and the funds were therefore *in bonis* of him at the date of his death and
formed part of the legitim fund.

[17] *Ibid.; Steel's Trs.* v. *Cassels,* 1939 S.C. 502.
[18] *Watt* v. *Watson* (1897) 24 R. 330. See also *Murison* v. *Dick* (1854) 16 D. 529; *Mackenzie* v.
  Mackenzie's Trs. (1878) 5 R. 1027; *Stevenson* v. *Currie* (1905) 13 S.L.T. 457; *McGregor* v.
  Sohn (1908) 15 S.L.T. 926.
[19] *Murison* v. *Dick, supra,* p. 532, *per* Lord Rutherfurd.
[20] *Smitton* v. *Tod* (1839) 2 D. 225; *Lyon* v. *Lyon's Trs.* (1901) 3 F. 653.
[21] *Middleton's Trs.* v. *Middleton,* 1909 S.C. 67; *Bertram's Trs.* v. *Bertram,* 1909 S.C. 1238;
  Torrance v. *Torrance's Trs.,* 1950 S.C. 78, 99, *per* Lord Patrick.
[22] *Montgomery's Trs.* v. *Montgomery* (1895) 22 R. 824; *Smith* v. *Davidson* (1901) 8 S.L.T.
  354; *Drysdale's Trs.* v. *Drysdale,* 1940 S.C. 85.

(4) the jus quaesitum

Obviously, if the beneficiaries take immediately a vested interest in the trust fund, the trust is irrevocable.[23] " When a man conveys to trustees it is the same as if he conveyed to the beneficiaries themselves." [24] But even if the interest is contingent revocation is not possible [25]; the test is *jus quaesitum*, not *jus crediti*.[26]

> " The argument really comes to this, that it is impossible to pro-
> tect a contingent interest by means of a trust, and that is an absolutely
> untenable proposition. The fee could not be vested during the gran-
> ter's life in all or any of the persons whom the granter intended to
> benefit, because it could not be known till her death which of them,
> if any, would survive to take. But it was vested in trustees for the pro-
> tection of contingent interests, and so long as it was possible that
> beneficiaries might survive to exclude the heirs and assignees of the
> granter the trustees were bound to hold against the granter herself." [27]

So the trust may be irrevocable even although there is no vesting in the beneficiaries until the death of the granter.[28]

On the other hand, if the provision in favour of the beneficiaries does not confer a beneficial interest but is merely testamentary in effect, the trust can be revoked by the granter.[29] The distinction is between a *jus quaesitum* on the one hand, and a mere *spes successionis* on the other.[30] Whether there is a present gift of a beneficial interest or merely a testamentary provision depends on the intention of the truster.

> " Is he saying to the *mortis causa* beneficiaries, ' I am here and
> now setting apart and appropriating a fund which will be unaffected
> by my future circumstances and which will at my death, if you survive
> me, be available intact for distribution to you ' ? Or is he merely
> saying to his trustees, ' I am setting up a trust for the administration
> of my affairs and for my own liferent and it is fitting that I should give
> instruction to the trustees as to what I want done with it on my death
> if I leave it in their hands till then. If I do nothing more, the bene-
> ficiaries are the parties who will take if they survive me, but whether

---

[23] *Mackie* v. *Gloag's Trs.* (1884) 11 R.(H.L.) 10; *Laurence* v. *Murray* (1901) 9 S.L.T. 165; *Lawson's Tr.* v. *Lawson,* 1938 S.C. 632.

[24] *Spalding* v. *Spalding's Trs.* (1874) 2 R. 237, 245, *per* L.P. Inglis.

[25] *Turnbull* v. *Tawse* (1825) 1 W. & S. 80; *Smitton* v. *Tod* (1839) 2 D. 225; *Robertson* v. *Robertson's Trs.* (1892) 19 R. 849; *Murray* v. *Macfarlane's Trs.,* (1895) 22 R. 927; *Lyon* v. *Lyon's Trs.* (1901) 3 F. 653.

[26] *Lawson's Tr.* v. *Lawson, supra,* p. 649, *per* Lord Wark.

[27] *Murray* v. *Macfarlane's Trs., supra,* p. 939, *per* Lord Kinnear.

[28] *Robertson* v. *Robertson's Trs., supra*; *Lyon* v. *Lyon's Trs., supra*; *Walker* v. *Amey* (1906) 8 F. 376.

[29] *Byres' Trs.* v. *Gemmell* (1895) 23 R. 332; *Bertram's Trs.* v. *Bertram,* 1909 S.C. 1238; *Corbidge* v. *Somerville's Trs.,* 1911 S.C. 1326. Any testamentary disposition may, of course, be irrevocable because of a prior contractual obligation. (*Paterson* v. *Paterson* (1893) 20 R. 484.)

[30] *Spes successionis* is an ambiguous expression—" It may mean that A hopes to benefit by the will of B, who is still alive, or it may mean, as here, that A has a right under the will of B, who is dead, subject to a certain contingency " (*Salaman* v. *Tod,* 1911 S.C. 1214, 1223, *per* Lord Johnston). See also *Parker* v. *Lord Advocate,* 1958 S.C. 426, 437, *per* Lord Mackintosh.

any funds are left in the trust at the time of my death depends on me ' ? " [31]

"The question must always be one of intention, whether, on the one hand, the granter intended the trust to be one merely for the administration of his affairs, he retaining the radical and beneficial interest in the estate conveyed, and being entitled to revoke the deed at pleasure; or whether, on the other hand, he must be held to have truly divested himself of the estate, so as to enable the trustees to hold it against him." [32]

In this context, intention means intention *tota re circumspecta* that the gift is to take effect irrevocably no matter how circumstances may alter. "Many an elderly testator, I daresay, thinks the will he makes will be his last word. He has no intention to alter it. But something more than this frame of mind must be evidenced by a deed such as the present if it is to be held to be irrevocable." [33]

The question of intention is to be determined upon a construction of the trust deed in relation to the surrounding circumstances.[34] "In all such cases it is held to be a question of fair construction, depending on the different clauses of the deed, and principally on the considerations which led to its execution, and the chief object which the truster had in view, how far he is to be considered as divested of all right and power over his property, and to what extent, whether absolutely or only sub modo, a *jus quaesitum* can be insisted on by those who are favoured in the deed." [35] In construing one deed in this way very little assistance is to be derived from the construction put upon other deeds conceived in different language.[36]

In the construction of the deed, the most important element for consideration is whether or not there is an express declaration of irrevocability. Such a declaration is not conclusive and would not prevail where the truster has said expressly or by clear implication that his directions are to have only testamentary effect; but there is no case in which an *inter vivos* divestiture has been found revocable in spite of a declaration of irrevocability contained in the deed.[37] "As it appears to me, it is futile to

---

[31] *Per* L.J.-C. Thomson, *Torrance* v. *Torrance's Trs.*, 1950 S.C. 78, 90.

[32] *Per* Lord Dundas, *Walker* v. *Amey* (1906) 8 F. 376, 379, cited with approval by Lord Low in *Bertram's Trs.* v. *Bertram*, 1909 S.C. 1238, 1241, but see the comment in *Nelson* v. *Nelson's Trs.*, 1921, 1 S.L.T. 82, 83, *per* Lord Sands.

[33] *Per* Lord Sands, *Nelson* v. *Nelson's Trs.*, 1921, 1 S.L.T. 82, 83.

[34] *Mackie* v. *Gloag's Trs.* (1884) 11 R.(H.L.) 10, 12, *per* Earl Selborne L.C., p. 17, *per* Lord Watson; *Byres' Trs.* v. *Gemmell* (1895) 23 R. 332; *Scott* v. *Scott*, 1930 S.C. 903, 920, *per* Lord Sands.

[35] A passage from the respondent's case in *Turnbull* v. *Tawse* (1825) 1 W. & S. 80, quoted with approval by Lord Gifford at 99.

[36] *Per* Lord Kinnear, *Byres' Trs.* v. *Gemmell, supra*, p. 339.

[37] *Byres' Trs.* v. *Gemmell, supra*; *Laurence* v. *Murray* (1901) 9 S.L.T. 165; *Walker* v. *Amey, supra*; *Scott* v. *Scott*, 1930 S.C. 903; *Lawson's Tr.* v. *Lawson*, 1938 S.C. 632; *Torrance* v. *Torrance's Trs., supra*. There are, of course, cases in which a trust was held to be revocable because there was no existing beneficiary although the deed did contain a declaration of irrevocability—*Mackenzie* v. *Mackenzie's Trs.* (1878) 5 R. 1027 and *McGregor* v. *Sohn* (1908) 15 S.L.T. 926.

piece this and that together in order to warrant an inference as to whether a truster intended a gift to be revocable, if the truster has unambiguously stated that it shall be irrevocable." [38]

The other matter of cardinal importance in the ascertainment of the truster's intention is the form in which the provisions are expressed. A direction to the trustees to hold for the beneficiaries subject to the truster's life interest favours the view that a beneficial interest has been created; on the other hand, a direction to divide the trust estate in a certain manner at the truster's death indicates a testamentary intention.[39] However, as Lord Stormonth-Darling pointed out in *Smith* v. *Davidson*,[40] if a liferent is reserved the fee can *never* be paid till the granter's death and there is therefore little difference between the direction " my trustees are to hold for myself in liferent and AB in fee " and the direction " my trustees are to pay the annual proceeds to me, and at my death they are to pay the capital to AB." The form in which any reference to vesting is expressed may also be important—" It appears to me that there is a testamentary sound and atmosphere about this provision. If this clause were excised and laid before any practitioner and he were asked what he took it to be, I have no doubt that he would reply, ' A clause in a will.' " [41]

Other relevant factors are:

(1) The truster's motive

Obviously the inducing cause of the execution of the deed is cogent evidence of the truster's intention. Where the sole object of the deed was to put the truster's estate beyond the reach of his wife's claim for legal rights on divorce, it was said that, as this object could be achieved only by irrevocable divestiture, it could be inferred that the intention was to make the provision irrevocable.[42] On the other hand, if the primary purpose of the trust is administration for the truster's benefit, or to make provision for a future wife and for children *nascituri*, any subsidiary provisions may be held to have merely testamentary effect.[43] The absence of motive, if anything, points to complete divestiture.[44]

(2) The nature of the subjects conveyed

A conveyance of a specific fund or of specific subjects supports the inference that the deed is irrevocable,[45] particularly if a *mortis causa*

[38] *Per* Lord Sands, *Scott* v. *Scott, supra,* p. 921.
[39] *Byres' Trs.* v. *Gemmell, supra,* p. 337, *per* Lord McLaren; *Scott* v. *Scott, supra,* p. 915, *per* L.P. Clyde; *Torrance* v. *Torrance's Trs., supra,* p. 91, *per* L.J.-C. Thomson.
[40] (1901) 8 S.L.T. 354.
[41] *Nelson* v. *Nelson's Trs.,* 1921, 1 S.L.T. 82, 84, *per* Lord Sands.
[42] *Scott* v. *Scott, supra.* See also *Smitton* v. *Tod* (1839) 2 D. 225; *Wright* v. *Harley* (1847) 9 D. 1151.
[43] *Byres' Trs.* v. *Gemmell* (1895) 23 R. 332; *Bertram's Trs.* v. *Bertram,* 1909 S.C. 1238; *Campbell* v. *Campbell's Trs.,* 1967 S.L.T.(Notes) 30.
[44] *Torrance* v. *Torrance's Trs., supra.*
[45] *Robertson* v. *Robertson's Trs.* (1892) 19 R. 849, 851, *per* Lord Kyllachy; *Murray* v. *Macfarlane's Trs.* (1895) 22 R. 927, 934, *per* Lord Kyllachy; *Foucart* v. *Foucart's Trs.* (1896) 4 S.L.T. 211; *Laurence* v. *Murray* (1901) 9 S.L.T. 165; *Walker* v. *Amey, supra,* p. 379, *per* Lord Dundas; *De Pitchford* v. *Robertson,* 1918, 2 S.L.T. 276; *Torrance* v. *Torrance's Trs., supra,* p. 91, *per* L.J.-C. Thomson.

settlement of the remainder of the truster's property is executed on the same day.[46] A conveyance of the *universitas* of the truster's estate and, *a fortiori*, such a conveyance including *acquirenda* or the whole property belonging to the truster at his death, will be more readily held to be testamentary.[47] It has been said that the only cases in which a transfer of the whole estate including *acquirenda* was held to be irrevocable were cases in which the truster was a woman who was about to marry.[48]

(3) The language of the deed

It favours the view that the deed is testamentary if reference is made to " legacies " rather than to " provisions," [49] if the deed bears to be a " settlement " [50] and if the deed revokes prior settlements.[51]

(4) The powers of the trustees

A power to the trustees to make advances at their discretion from the trust funds for the maintenance of the truster indicates irrevocability. It cannot be said that this amounts to a power to revoke because the trustees must exercise the power in their discretion and in accordance with the conditions of the trust.[52] If the truster reserves a power to require repayment of a specified part of the funds conveyed, this tends to indicate that the conveyance is irrevocable so far as the remainder of the funds is concerned.[53] On the other hand, where the truster or his spouse could at any time demand whatever sums they desired for maintenance, it was said that this provision militated against irrevocability because the truster might have thought it desirable that he should be able to obtain such payments without upsetting the whole trust which had presumably been created for some good reason and at some expense.[54]

(5) The nature of the right conferred [55]

A testamentary intention is inferred where the right of the beneficiaries is stated to be subject to the provisions of any *mortis causa* settlement which the truster might execute.[56] The reservation by the truster of a power of appointment among the beneficiaries is inconsistent with any idea of revocability.[57] The fact that the beneficiaries are the truster's children as a class favours irrevocability.[58]

---

[46] *Walker* v. *Amey, supra.*
[47] *Smitton* v. *Tod* (1839) 2 D. 225, 231, *per* Lord Mackenzie; *Scott* v. *Scott, supra,* p. 917, *per* L.P. Clyde; *Ross* v. *Ross's Trs.,* 1967 S.L.T. 12.
[48] *Ross* v. *Ross's Trs., supra. Middleton's Trs.* v. *Middleton,* 1909 S.C. 67 is an example.
[49] *Foucart* v. *Foucart's Trs., supra; Scott* v. *Scott, supra,* p. 917, *per* L.P. Clyde.
[50] *Smitton* v. *Tod, supra,* p. 231, *per* Lord Mackenzie. See also *Sommerville* v. *Sommerville,* May 18, 1819 F.C.
[51] *Byres' Trs.* v. *Gemmell, supra,* p. 340, *per* Lord Adam.
[52] *Murray* v. *Macfarlane's Trs., supra.,* p. 938, *per* Lord Kinnear; *Shedden* v. *Shedden's Trs.* (1895) 23 R. 228; *Walker* v. *Amey, supra,* p. 379, *per* Lord Dundas.
[53] *Lawson's Tr.* v. *Lawson,* 1938 S.C. 632.
[54] *Nelson* v. *Nelson's Trs.,* 1921, 1 S.L.T. 82.
[55] *Ross* v. *Ross's Trs.,* 1967 S.L.T. 12.
[56] *Lockhart* v. *Martin* (1904) 12 S.L.T. 142.
[57] *Mackie* v. *Gloag's Trs.,* 11 R.(H.L.) 10; *Lawson's Tr.* v. *Lawson, supra.*
[58] *Nelson* v. *Nelson's Trs., supra.*

The court will regard the argument for revocability more favourably where it is advanced by the truster himself than where it is put forward by a third party after the truster's death.[59]

In view of what has been said earlier it is hardly necessary to state that a deed is not revocable merely because it is gratuitous.[60]

A deed can, of course, be revocable as to one provision and irrevocable as to another.[61]

[59] *Walker* v. *Amey, supra,* p. 380, *per* Lord Dundas (L.O.).
[60] *Robertson* v. *Robertson's Trs., supra,* p. 852, *per* Lord Adam.
[61] *Leckie* v. *Leckies* (1776) Mor. 11581; *Spalding* v. *Spalding's Trs.* (1874) 2 R. 237, 240, *per* L.P. Inglis; *Bertram's Trs.* v. *Bertram,* 1909 S.C. 1238; *Scott* v. *Scott, supra,* p. 922, *per* Lord Sands.

CHAPTER 11

TERMINATION BY THE BENEFICIARIES

IN certain circumstances trustees may be required to denude in favour of the beneficiaries before the time contemplated in the trust deed.

Agreement

If all interests in the trust have vested in beneficiaries who are of full age and *sui juris*, the trust can be terminated with the consent of all of the beneficiaries.[1] There is an important exception in the case of an alimentary provision, which cannot be effectually renounced by the person entitled to it.[2]

> " When, in a private trust, every possible beneficiary desires and consents to a particular course being adopted—all the beneficiaries being of full age and *sui juris*—and none of them being placed under any restraint or disability by the trust deed itself—then no one has any right or interest to object, and the Court will not interfere to prevent the sole and unlimited proprietors doing what they like with their own." [3]

Renunciation of liferent

When a liferent is renounced,[4] a question arises as to whether vesting of the fee is accelerated so that the fiars are entitled to immediate payment. The principle is that if the testator has chosen a time for the selection of beneficiaries, the court will not interfere with this, and will not intervene to make a new will for the testator by giving the fee to persons selected at an earlier time and who may be different from those who would take at the later time.

> " In my opinion it is impossible to hold as a matter of principle that the act of any person outside of and hostile to the trust can *per se* effect an alteration of the truster's dispositions with regard to the vesting of interests in his estate. Such an act may be of material importance if the testator has either expressly or by implication signified his intention that upon its occurrence the period of vesting shall shift." [5]

---

[1] See Chap. 12 as to the power of the court to consent on behalf of beneficiaries who are unborn, unascertained or subject to disability.

[2] See Chap. 7.

[3] *Gray* v. *Gray's Trs.* (1877) 4 R. 378, 383, *per* Lord Gifford; *Earl of Lindsay* v. *Shaw*, 1959 S.L.T. (Notes) 13.

[4] An alimentary liferent cannot be renounced if the beneficiary has begun to enjoy the gift— see Chap. 7.

[5] *Muirhead* v. *Muirhead* (1890) 17 R.(H.L.) 45, 50, *per* Lord Watson. See also *Rose's Trs.* v. *Rose*, 1916 S.C. 827; *Paton's Trs.* v. *Rowan*, 1947 S.L.T. 199.

The testator's intention as to vesting must therefore be found by construction of the deed.[6] It has been held, on such construction, that " expiry " and " termination " of the liferent were equivalent to the death of the liferenter and that payment of the fee was not accelerated by renunciation.[7] In such circumstances the income liberated by the renunciation of the liferent may have to be accumulated.[8] On the other hand, where " termination " was mentioned as an alternative to death, it was held that a forfeiture of the liferent involved its " termination." [9]

If it is clear that the time of payment is postponed only to secure payment of an annuity or liferent, an immediate division can be made if the fee is indefeasibly vested or if the entire class of persons to whom, or to one or more of whom, the beneficial interest must eventually belong, concurs in seeking payment.[10] It is easier to presume this result in the case of an annuity than in that of a liferent.[11]

In *Hamilton's Trs.* v. *Hamilton*,[12] the granter of an *inter vivos* trust renounced his liferent and executed a deed of apportionment directing an immediate division of part of the capital among his children. In terms of the trust, the capital was to be held after the granter's death for behoof of his whole lawful children and was to be paid to them on attaining majority. It was held that the deed of apportionment should receive immediate effect. The possibility that the granter would have further issue was accepted, it being pointed out, firstly, that the granter could have excluded such issue by the apportionment in any event, and, secondly, that sufficient of the capital remained in the trustees' hands to equalise all possible claims in the end of the day.

When, on the expiry of the widow's liferent of the residue, specified sums were to be paid to the testator's son and daughters, and the widow agreed to discharge her liferent over the sum provided for the son, it was held that the trustees were not bound to pay the sum to the son because it was possible that on the expiry of the liferent there might be insufficient funds to provide the daughters' provisions in full.[13]

Vested provisions

A beneficiary in whom the residue has vested is entitled to payment thereof if the trustees retain sufficient funds to make payment of any legacies which have not vested or are not yet payable.[14] A direction to

---

[6] *Jacks's Trs.* v. *Jacks*, 1913 S.C. 815; *A.* v. *B's Trs.*, 1941 S.L.T. 193; *Gray's Trs.* v. *Neilson*, 1946 S.N. 81.
[7] *Middleton's Trs.* v. *Middleton*, 1955 S.C. 51; *Chrystal's Trs.* v. *Haldane*, 1960 S.C. 27.
[8] *Ross's Trs.* v. *Ross* (1894) 21 R. 927; *Middleton's Trs.* v. *Middleton, supra.*
[9] *Hurll's Trs.* v. *Hurll*, 1964 S.C. 12. Note in forfeiture cases the odd result of *Gillies* v. *Gillies' Trs.* (1881) 8 R. 505, and *Hannah's Trs.* v. *Hannah*, 1924 S.C. 494.
[10] *Per* Lord Watson, *Muirhead* v. *Muirhead, supra,* at p. 48. See also *Hughes* v. *Edwardes* (1892) 19 R.(H.L.) 33, 34, *per* Lord Watson; *Mackie's J.F.*, 1920, 2 S.L.T. 95.
[11] *Alexander's Trs.* (1870) 8 M. 414, 418, *per* L.J.-C. Moncreiff.
[12] (1879) 6 R. 1216. See also *Lawson* v. *Cormack's Trs.*, 1940 S.L.T. 202 (renunciation of power of appointment).
[13] *Haldane's Trs.* v. *Haldane* (1895) 23 R. 276. See also *Souter Robertson* v. *Robertson's Trs.* (1900) 8 S.L.T. 50; *White* v. *White's Trs.*, 1916 S.C. 435.
[14] *Scott* v. *Scott's Trs.* (1876) 4 R. 229.

" pay one-third part of the annual income or produce of the residue " to the testator's widow was interpreted as a direction to pay the income of a third of the residue so that the capital of the two-thirds of the residue could be paid to the beneficiaries in whom it had vested.[15]

Where the testator directed that the residue of his estate was to be paid to beneficiaries on the expiry of the lease of a mill held by him, " but not sooner," it was held that as there were no liferents or destinations-over vesting took place *a morte testatoris* and the trustees were entitled to pay over the residue at once if they retained the money invested in the mill and a sufficient sum for administration of the trust.[16]

In *Elder's Trs.* v. *Treasurer of the Free Church of Scotland*,[17] the residue was to be held and the income accumulated until the death of the testator's widow who was to receive a small annuity, and then, after payment of a specified sum to A, the remainder was to be paid to B. The trustees proposed to pay the sum to A during the widow's life, with her consent, but the court refused to allow this to be done as B might be prejudiced.

Where the residue was to be divided between the testator's two sons when the younger attained twenty-five, and the younger died in minority when the elder was aged twenty-one, it was held that the elder was entitled to immediate payment of the whole residue as the suspensive condition had become inoperative.[18]

Where the testator bequeathed his business to A subject to payment of a legacy of £2,000 to B which was to be payable twenty years after the testator's death to prevent an undue burden in the conduct of the business, and the business was discontinued when A died nine years after the testator, it was held that as the legacy vested *a morte testatoris* and there was no longer any interest to be served by the postponement of the period of payment B was entitled to immediate payment subject to a discount.[19]

In *Smith's Trs.* v. *Dinwoodie*,[20] A was given a liferent of a one-half share of the residue but the trustees had power to pay up to £1000 a year of the capital thereof to B. On A's death one half of the one-half share was to be held for the alimentary use of B for five years during which period no vesting was to take place. At the expiry of the five year period the capital of the quarter share was to be paid to B or his issue, whom failing to certain legatees with a survivorship clause. B predeceased A without leaving issue. On A's death, it was held that the trustees were bound to retain the fund until the expiry of the five year period as there was no vesting until that time.

Miller's Trs. v. Miller

Where a beneficiary has right to the fee of the trust estate, he is en-

[15] *Robertson's Trs.* v. *Black*, 1910 S.C. 1132.
[16] *Archibald's Trs.* v. *Archibald* (1882) 9 R. 942.
[17] (1881) 8 R. 593.
[18] *Mackie* v. *Gladstone* (1876) 13 S.L.R. 368.
[19] *Finlay's Trs.* v. *Finlay* (1886) 13 R. 1052.   [20] 1958 S.L.T. 305.

titled to demand payment from the trustees. In the leading case on this subject, *Miller's Trs.* v. *Miller*,[21] the testator directed his trustees to hold heritable property for behoof of his son until he attained the age of twenty-five when they were to denude in his favour. It was declared that there was to be no vesting in the son until he attained twenty-five or married with the consent of the trustees after attaining the age of twenty-one. The son was also given a share in the residue of the moveable estate with a vesting clause in similar terms but with no direction to the trustees to hold the share. However, the trustees were given a discretion as to the application of the annual interest of the shares of residue and the son was to be entitled to any accumulation of interest at the age of twenty-five. The son married with the consent of the trustees after attaining the age of twenty-one but before attaining the age of twenty-five and called upon the trustees to denude in his favour. A majority of seven judges held that he was entitled to immediate payment. Lord President Inglis said [22]:

> " There is, in my opinion, a general rule, the result of a comparison of a long series of decisions of this Court, that where by the operation of a testamentary instrument the fee of an estate or parts of an estate, whether heritable or moveable, has vested in a beneficiary, the Court will always, if possible, relieve him of any trust management that is cumbrous, unnecessary, or expensive. Where there are trust purposes to be served which cannot be secured without the retention of the vested estate or interest of the beneficiary in the hands of the trustees, the rule cannot be applied, and the right of the beneficiary must be subordinated to the will of the testator. But I am not aware of any case in which the mere maintenance of a trust management without any ulterior object or purpose has been held to be a trust purpose in the sense in which I have used that term."

Lord McLaren said [23]:

> " Ever since I knew anything of the law of trusts I have considered it to be a settled and indeed an elementary proposition that where trustees hold property for a person in fee, that is a simple trust which the Court will execute by divesting the trustees at the suit of the person interested. It seems to me that a beneficiary who has an estate in fee has by the very terms of the gift the same right of divesting the trustees, and so putting an end to the trust, which the truster himself possessed, because under a gift in fee the grantee acquires all the right in the property which the truster had to give. It seems to me to be not only an unsound proposition in law, but a logical impossibility, that a person should have an estate in fee, and that some other person should at the same time have the power of withholding it."

---

[21] (1890) 18 R. 301. Approved by the whole court in *Yuill's Trs.* v. *Thomson* (1902) 4 F. 815 and by Lord Davey in *Macculloch* v. *McCulloch's Trs.* (1903) 6 F.(H.L.) 3, 6. See also *Cochrane's Exrx.* v. *Cochrane*, 1947 S.C. 134, 138, *per* Lords Cooper and Jamieson.
[22] p. 305.
[23] p. 310.

The trust purposes for which the trustees are entitled to retain the fee must be connected with other objects and persons than the beneficiary whose share is in question.[24]

Liferent and fee

On the principle of *Miller's Trs.* v. *Miller*, if the liferenter acquires right to the fee, he is entitled to demand a denuding.

> " If an estate or a sum of money be given to an individual, who is *sui juris*, without words of limitation, or a declaration as to the extent of his ownership, but with words indicative of the intention of the testator that he should have the absolute *jus disponendi*, then, in any cases, those words are to be taken as indicating an intention that he should be the absolute owner. Thus, if I give an estate to AB to do therewith as he pleases, to give to such persons as he shall think fit, and to deal with it at his will and pleasure, all those expressions are nothing more than a form of denoting absolute ownership, and the intention to give absolute ownership." [25]

Before this rule operates, however, both the liferent right and the right to the fee must be absolute and unlimited.

> " No doubt when the liferent of an estate and the absolute *jus disponendi* concur in the person of one individual, it may not be an unfair inference that that person is the full proprietor of the estate, because it is difficult to see what other right a proprietor can have than the full right of enjoyment, and the full right of disposal. But no deed will give that right which confers anything short of the full right of liferent, and the absolute *jus disponendi*." [26]

Lord President Dunedin [27] criticised this doctrine and suggested that it should, on a suitable occasion, be reviewed by a higher court but in a recent case [28] the House of Lords refused to reopen the question. " Property has been enjoyed by persons whose right depended on the validity of the rule, which has now become part of the accepted law of succession." [29]

In conformity with this principle, it is established that the beneficiary cannot demand a denuding where his liferent interest is alimentary.[30] Similarly, it has been said that the protected life interest of a married woman can never be expanded into a right of fee [31] but as the basis of this

---

24 *Miller Richard's Trs.* v. *Miller Richard* (1903) 5 F. 909, 913, *per* Lord Moncreiff.
25 *Per* Lord Westbury L.C., *Pursell* v. *Elder* (1865) 3 M.(H.L.) 59, 68. See *Whitehead's Trs.* v. *Whitehead* (1897) 24 R. 1032; *Veitch's Trs.* v. *Rutherford*, 1914 S.C. 182; *Graham* v. *Graham's Trs.*, 1927 S.C. 388.
26 *Per* L.J.-C. Inglis, *Alves* v. *Alves* (1861) 23 D. 712, 717.
27 *Mackenzie's Trs.* v. *Kilmarnock's Trs.*, 1909 S.C. 472, 477.
28 *Baird* v. *Baird's Trs.*, 1956 S.C.(H.L.) 93.
29 *Per* Lord Normand, at p. 108.
30 *Millar* v. *Millar's Trs.* (1907) 45 S.L.R. 6; *Ewing's Trs.* v. *Ewing*, 1909 S.C. 409. See also *Douglas' Trs.* (1902) 5 F. 69, 74, *per* Lord McLaren; and p. 95, *supra*.
31 *Pursell* v. *Elder* (1865) 3 M.(H.L.) 59; *Mackenzie's Trs.* v. *Kilmarnock's Trs.*, *supra*.

dictum was that a married woman is not *sui juris*, it must be reconsidered in the light of the reasoning in *Beith* v. *Beith*.[32]

It is also established that where there is a power of disposal followed by a destination-over in the event of failure to exercise the power, the beneficiary's right cannot be construed as a right of fee in any event as long as the conditional destination is in force.[33] A destination to the liferenter's " nearest heirs " may be a destination-over in this connection.[34] Even where there is no destination-over, however, a power of disposal may not amount to an absolute *jus disponendi*. " But a liferent with a power to test is not a fee." [35] The power may be " only a power to affect the succession to the estate, and not a power to disturb the trustees in the possession of it during the grantees' lives." [36] The question depends on the testator's intention as deduced from the construction of the deed and the decisions turn on rather narrow distinctions. The right was held to be limited where the trustees were directed to hold the funds for the beneficiaries [37]; where the power was to be exercised by " will or other testamentary writing " [38] or by " any revocable deed " [39]; where the testator directed that the beneficiaries " shall have no power to obtain payment " [40]; and where the gift was to the testator's sister " for her sole and separate use in liferent, and at her own option as to destination in the event of her death." [41]

Where the testator directed the trustees to pay, at the beneficiary's death, his share to his " heirs or assignees " it was held that this amounted to a right of fee [42]; but in a later case, in which there were other *indicia* of the testator's intention, the view was taken that " ' heirs and assignees ' mean that if the daughter dies without leaving a settlement, then the fund is to go to her heirs, but if she dies leaving a settlement, then to her assignees under that settlement." [43] Where the trustees were directed to pay on the liferenter's death to his " testamentary trustees or executors the trust estate which shall thereafter form part of his estate and be administered by such trustees and executors in accordance with any will or other deed which may be executed by (the liferenter)," the House of Lords held that this conferred a complete proprietary right.[44]

---

[32] 1950 S.C. 66. See p. 31, *supra*.
[33] *Per* Lord St. Leonards, *Morris* v. *Tennant* (1855) 27 Sc.Jur. 546; *Tait's Trs.* v. *Neill* (1903) 6 F. 138; *Rattray's Trs.* v. *Rattray* (1899) 1 F. 510. *Cf. Steward* v. *Vanner* (1894) 1 S.L.T. 549. In *Forrest's Trs.* v. *Reid* (1904) 7 F. 142, Lord McLaren suggested (at p. 145) that the observations of Lord Westbury L.C. in *Pursell* v. *Elder*, *supra*, did not fully accord with the speech of Lord St. Leonards. But this doubt seems to have little substance. As to other trust purposes, see *Brown* v. *Brown's Trs.*, 1911, 2 S.L.T. 513; 1912, 1 S.L.T. 474.
[34] *Forrest's Trs.* v. *Reid, supra*.
[35] *Peden's Trs.* v. *Peden* (1903) 5 F. 1014, 1015, *per* Lord Trayner.
[36] *Per* Lord McLaren, *Forrest's Trs.* v. *Reid, supra*, p. 146.
[37] *Douglas' Trs., supra*; *Forrest's Trs.* v. *Reid, supra*.
[38] *Mackenzie's Trs.* v. *Kilmarnock's Trs., supra*.
[39] *Forrest's Trs.* v. *Reid, supra*.
[40] *Peden's Trs.* v. *Peden, supra*.
[41] *Reid* v. *Reid's Trs.* (1899) 1 F. 969.
[42] *Rattray's Trs.* v. *Rattray, supra*.
[43] *Douglas' Trs., supra*, p. 73, *per* Lord Adam.
[44] *Baird* v. *Baird's Trs.*, 1956 S.C. (H.L.) 93.

In some decisions attention has been directed to the question of whether the beneficiary has a saleable interest. In *Mackenzie's Trs.* v. *Kilmarnock's Trs.*,[45] Lord Dunedin suggested that the beneficiary could assign the life-rent (which was not alimentary) and bind himself by contract to execute a testamentary disposition in favour of the assignee who would then have everything: " And it is almost a travesty of trust law to think that a trust has to be kept up merely to postpone that other individual entering into possession of the money." The device of the contract was based on *Paterson* v. *Paterson* [46] and was designed to meet the point made by Lord McLaren in *Mackenzie's Trs.* that any irrevocable deed of appointment in favour of a purchaser might be held not to be a testamentary writing and therefore not a good exercise of the power. In *Baird* v. *Baird's Trs.*, how-ever, Lord Normand [47] suggested that an obligation to exercise a power in a certain way is not an exercise of the power but a limitation upon it and that a sum received under a writing executed in implement of such an obligation has not " the character of a free and voluntary benefaction." In any event, the existence of a saleable interest does not mean that immediate payment must be made; the purchaser may have to wait until the liferenter's death.[48]

Repugnancy

The principle of *Miller's Trs.* v. *Miller* has also been applied to cases in which the beneficiary has been given a right of fee followed by some restriction or qualification of his right. So a beneficiary on whom the fee had been conferred was entitled to immediate payment where there was a direction to the trustees to hold the fund for administration [49]; and where the trustees were directed to withhold payment of the capital until the death of a third party [50] or the expiry of a fixed period of time.[51] The beneficiary was denied payment where there was a direction to retain the fund for his behoof and make the interest available for his aliment [52]; where the carrying out of other trust purposes might involve encroachment on the capital [53]; and where there were ultimate interests to be protected.[54]

---

[45] 1909 S.C. 477.

[46] (1893) 20 R. 484.

[47] p. 108. Reference was made to Stair, III, 8, 33, and Ersk. III, 9, 6.

[48] *Per* Lord McLaren, *Douglas' Trs., supra*, p. 74.

[49] *Jamieson* v. *Lesslie's Trs.* (1889) 16 R. 807; *Duthie's Trs.* v. *Forlong* (1889) 16 R. 1002; *Wilkie's Trs.* v. *Wight's Trs.* (1893) 21 R. 199; *Greenlees' Trs.* v. *Greenlees* (1894) 22 R. 136; *Brown* v. *Brown's Trs.* (1890) 17 R. 517; *Lawson's Trs.* v. *Lawson* (1890) 17 R. 1167; *Veitch's Trs.* v. *Rutherford*, 1914 S.C. 182; *Graham* v. *Graham's Trs.*, 1927 S.C. 388. Cf. *Russell* v. *Bell's Trs.* (1897) 24 R. 666.

[50] *Hargrave's Trs.* v. *Schofield* (1900) 3 F. 14; *Bate's Trs.* v. *Bate* (1906) 8 F. 861.

[51] *Stewart's Trs.* v. *Stewart* (1897) 25 R. 302; *Ballantyne's Trs.* v. *Kidd* (1898) 25 R. 621. Cf. *Bryson's Trs.* v. *Clark* (1880) 8 R. 142, where there was a direction to convey on the expiry of a period but no other words of gift.

[52] *Campbell's Trs.* v. *Campbell* (1889) 16 R. 1007.

[53] *Graham's Trs.* v. *Graham* (1899) 2 F. 232.

[54] *Cuningham* v. *Cuningham* (1896) 4 S.L.T. 132; *Mackay's Trs.* v. *Mackay's Trs.* (1897) 24 R. 904; *Macculloch* v. *McCulloch's Trs.* (1903) 6 F.(H.L.) 3; *Brown* v. *Brown's Trs.*, 1911, 2 S.L.T. 513; 1912, 1 S.L.T. 474.

The decisions on this topic turn on nice questions of construction. " A very small difference of expression determines the point whether a direction intended for the benefit of the proprietor shall be disregarded as repugnant to the truster's intention, or whether it is operative and may be carried out." [55] " It is quite certain that you cannot give money or anything else upon the condition that it is not to be spent, or that only so much be spent and the remainder saved. That is a repugnancy. If you make a person proprietor he must act as proprietor." [56] On the other hand, if the initial gift is contained in the will and the subsequent directions in a codicil it may be possible to hold that the bequest of the fee in the will has been revoked by the codicil.

> " No proper question of repugnancy arises, as might perhaps have occurred if these limitations had been inserted in the original will. A condition or modification inserted in a codicil executed after a lapse of time is not quite in pari casu with a condition superadded in the same deed to an apparently absolute gift of fee; it records a deliberate change of testamentary intention." [57]

Alternatively, it may be possible to regard the subsequent directions, whether in a codicil or not, as consistent with the terms of the initial gift: " A testator, having given a right of fee to certain beneficiaries, may nevertheless go on to divest them of that right, if he does so in clear and sufficiently effectual terms." [58] Or it may be held that the initial gift was not one of fee.[59]

There is, however, a further difficulty which is not merely one of construction. In Christie's Trs. v. Murray's Trs.[60] the testator left a share of his estate to his son and added " his share to remain in the hands of my trustees for his behoof. In the event of his demise, his share to return to his nearest of kin." It was held that although the share vested a morte testatoris, the trustees were bound to retain it. Lord Young said,[61]

> " The shares are the property of the donees, but they are in the hands of the trustees, to be managed by them, and withheld from the donees for their protection. The trustees are not limited to giving the donees the interest merely. They may deal with the shares in the course of their administration and management as trustees—capital and interest—as they may think best for the interest of the donees as proprietors. Their interest as proprietors is, I think, committed to the charge of the trustees by these words, although we are determining no more at this moment except that it is according to the true

[55] Per Lord Young, Duthie's Trs. v. Forlong (1889) 16 R. 1002, 1003.
[56] Per Lord Young, Christie's Trs. v. Murray's Trs. (1889) 16 R. 913, 916.
[57] Miller Richard's Trs. v. Miller Richard (1903) 5 F. 909, 914, per Lord Moncreiff.
[58] Watson's Trs. v. Watson, 1913 S.C. 1133, 1138, per Lord Kinnear.
[59] Muir's Trs. v. Muir's Trs. (1895) 22 R. 553.
[60] (1889) 16 R. 913.
[61] p. 916. Lords Rutherfurd Clark and Lee concurred. L.J.-C. Macdonald had had " great difficulty " in the matter " which I understand some of your Lordships have shared."

meaning of the deed, and the duty of the trustees under it, to retain
these shares, and not allow either to pass into the hands of the
proprietors."

In the immediately preceding passage in his opinion, however, Lord
Young had said:

> " We are merely determining that it is their duty to retain these
> shares in their own hands, and not to allow them to go into the hands
> of the beneficiaries. And I think that, in that way, very substantial
> protection may be given to the beneficiaries, just such as the testator
> thought was required. I do not speak of creditors, or what may be
> done, possibly, in order to frustrate the testator's view, but I think it
> desirable that the protection contemplated by the testator should at
> least be started, and, for my part, I should think that the law would be
> efficacious, if appealed to, to prevent the testator's will being
> frustrated."

This states a curious and confusing position. In cases decided shortly
afterwards, Lord Young referred to *Christie's Trs.* as an example of a case
" where the giver may constitute a protection by keeping the fund out of
the hands of the object of his bounty, and putting it under the care of
managers of his own appointment," [62] and Lord Justice-Clerk Macdonald
remarked that it decided that " there may be a fee in a person, although the
sum may remain in the hands of trustees who can only pay him over the
interest annually." [63]

If it is assumed that the right to income is not alimentary, it is not
possible to reconcile these statements with the *Miller's Trs.* principle. It is
to be observed that Lord Young dissented from, and continued to
disapprove of, the decision in *Miller's Trs.*[64]

Discretionary powers

There is another difficulty arising from the situation in which the
trustees are given a discretionary power over the beneficiary's provision.
In *Smith* v. *Chambers' Trs.*[65] the House of Lords upheld, in a question
with creditors, the validity of a discretionary power of the trustees to
postpone payment of capital or to restrict the beneficiary's interest to a
liferent and settle the fee on his issue. The beneficiary was given a vested
right to the fund in an earlier part of the deed but it was held that the right
thus conferred was controlled by the later provisions. It seems, however,
that a discretion to postpone payment unaccompanied by a power to
restrict to a liferent and resettle the fee is not effectual.[66]

---

[62] *Duthie's Trs.* v. *Forlong* (1889) 16 R. 1002, 1003.

[63] *Campbell's Trs.* v. *Campbell* (1889) 16 R. 1007, 1013. See *Brown* v. *Brown's Trs.* (1890) 17
R. 517, 519, *per* L.J.-C. Macdonald.

[64] See 18 R. 305; *Stewart's Trs.* v. *Stewart* (1897) 25 R. 302, 309. *Cf. Ritchie's Trs.* v. *Ritchie*
(1894) 21 R. 679, 682.

[65] (1878) 5 R.(H.L.) 151. See also *White's Trs.* v. *White* (1896) 23 R. 836; *Walker* v. *Buchanan*
(1905) 8 F. 201.

[66] *Mackinnon's Trs.* v. *Official Receiver in Bankruptcy* (1892) 19 R. 1051; *Ritchie's Trs.* v.
Ritchie (1894) 21 R. 679; *Watson's Trs.* v. *Watson*, 1913 S.C. 1133, 1139, *per* Lord Kinnear

In *Smith's Tr.* v. *Michael*,[67] under an *inter vivos* trust deed, the beneficiary's share vested when he attained the age of twenty-one years but
there was a proviso that " the trustees are not, however, obliged to comply
with the beneficiary's request to make over any capital even after the
beneficiary attains the age of twenty-one unless the trustees are satisfied
that there is good reason for so doing." It was held that the principle of
Miller's Trs. applied to *inter vivos* deeds and that the proviso was accordingly ineffectual. *Chambers' Trs.* was distinguished on the ground that
there an alternative disposal of the fee had been made.

Payment of debts

In a number of cases the trustees were directed to accumulate revenue
until debts affecting the estate were paid off and then convey it to a person
satisfying a description at that date. A question has arisen where the person who would be entitled to a conveyance if the debts were paid has
offered to pay off the debts and called upon the trustees to denude in his
favour. The trustees were held bound to refuse when the testator clearly
contemplated that the debts were to be paid by accumulation of revenue
and no other means and that the selection of the favoured heir was to be
postponed until this had been done; there were other purposes rendering it
necessary for the trust administration to continue.[68] On the other hand,
where the will did not restrict the trustees expressly or by necessary implication to accumulated revenue as the source from which the debts were to
be paid, and there was nothing to indicate that the testator intended the
disponee to be selected when the debts were paid off by accumulation of
revenue only, the trustees were bound to accept the offer.[69] It is material
that the conveyance in the first case was to be to the person in right of a
certain peerage at the relevant date; in one of the other two cases, the conveyance was to A and his heirs, while in the other the trustees were
directed to execute a deed of entail in favour of a named series of heirs.

In *Sinclair's Trs.* v. *Sinclair*,[70] the trustees were to accumulate to free
the heritable estate from debt " in so far as this may reasonably be attained." After thirty-six years of prudent administration there was no
prospect of paying the debts within any period which could be specified,
and the court in the circumstances authorised the trustees to denude in
favour of the person who, if the period of distribution had arrived, was
entitled to the fee.

Child-bearing age

There is a *praesumptio juris* that a woman who has attained the age of
fifty-three years is past the age of child-bearing and cannot have issue.[71]
Before the presumption was established, there were cases in which the

---

[67] 1972 S.L.T. 89.
[68] *Scarlett* v. *Lord Abinger's Trs.*, 1907 S.C. 811.
[69] *Home's Trs.* v. *Fergusson's Exrx.*, 1921 S.C. 474; *White's Trs.* v. *Nicol*, 1923 S.C. 859.
[70] 1913 S.C. 178.
[71] *G.'s Trs.* v. *G.*, 1936 S.C. 837; *A.* v. *B.'s Trs.*, 1941 S.L.T. 193.

court allowed trust funds to be distributed on the ground that there was no practical possibility of the birth of children.

Where the fund was destined to the testator's daughter in liferent, and her issue whom failing the testator's heir (who was in fact the daughter) in fee, the court authorised payment of the capital to the daughter, who was aged fifty-five and had no issue.[72] The Lord Ordinary (McLaren) assumed that there was no possibility of issue but there was a stronger alternative ground of judgment founded on the rule in *Frog's Creditors*.[73] In *De la Chaumette's Trs.* v. *De la Chaumette*,[74] it was held " without laying down any general rule " that a woman of seventy was past child-bearing; and in other cases distribution of the estate has been authorised on caution being found to protect the trustees.[75] More recently the expedient has been used in the cases of bachelors aged eighty-one and seventy-six.[76] The statutory provisions for the variation of trusts may now provide a partial solution.[77]

Trustees may be able to resist the claim of a beneficiary to denude in his favour on the ground that they have entered into some administrative arrangement which cannot be prematurely terminated without loss to the whole estate.[78]

---

[72] *Williamson* v. *Williamson's Trs.* (1881) 19 S.L.R. 276.
[73] (1735) Mor. 4262. See p. 62, *supra*.
[74] (1902) 4 F. 745; *McPherson's Trs.* v. *Hill* (1902) 4 F. 921.
[75] *Turnbull* v. *Turnbull's Tr.* (1907) 44 S.L.R. 843.
[76] *Munro's Trs.* v. *Monson*, 1965 S.C. 84.
[77] See Chap. 12.
[78] *De Robeck* v. *Inland Revenue*, 1928 S.C.(H.L.) 34.

CHAPTER 12

THE JUDICIAL VARIATION OF TRUSTS

Introduction

The jurisdiction to vary trusts is principally a statutory one introduced by the Trusts (Scotland) Act 1961. In order, however, to understand the effects of the statute it is necessary to consider the pre-existing methods of varying trusts both under Scots and English law. The 1961 Act was based on a similar English Act of 1958 [1] which in turn was passed to circumvent the effect of the decision of the House of Lords in *Chapman* v. *Chapman*.[2] The 1961 Act cannot be fully understood without also comprehending the termination or variation of trusts by concerted action of all the beneficiaries dealt with in the previous chapter. In one sense the new jurisdiction may be regarded as merely an extension of the beneficiaries' power to terminate or vary the trust purposes—if all interests concur.

The detailed techniques for varying trusts under the 1961 Act are mainly concerned with avoiding the pitfalls of revenue law and are not the concern of the present volume. It is intended in this chapter to concentrate more upon the principles of trust variation. As the law is stated as at 1st June, 1973 many of the references to revenue law may have since become superseded by subsequent legislation.

The common law jurisdiction prior to 1961

(a) Public trusts

Under the *nobile officium* the court has jurisdiction to vary the trust purposes of public trusts where these purposes have failed. This jurisdiction is exercised under the *cy-près* doctrine in accordance with which the court can substitute new trust purposes as nearly as possible akin to the original. The court can also alter the trust administration where this is necessary for the carrying on of the trust.[3]

(b) Private trusts

There is only a limited jurisdiction under the *nobile officium* to vary the trust purposes or administration of private trusts. In practice the jurisdiction has become limited to cases where it is necessary to prevent hardship such as where it is required to make advances for the maintenance of minor beneficiaries or even of adults. The narrow extent of the jurisdiction was indicated in *Coles* [4] where it was observed by Lord Justice-Clerk Thomson :

---

[1] Variation of Trusts Act 1958.   [2] [1954] A.C. 429.
[3] For a fuller consideration of the *cy-près* jurisdiction and the court's powers in regard to the administration of public trusts, see Chap. 14.
[4] 1951 S.C. 608, 617.

" I would be slow to think that it would be a proper exercise of the *nobile officium* to interfere with the trust purposes at any rate in cases where the interference is not required to prevent the trust from becoming unworkable or to protect the trust estate from loss or the beneficiary from hardship."

There is however a limited jurisdiction—somewhat akin to the modern trust variation jurisdiction yet entirely the product of the common law—to sanction the distribution of trust funds where the only impediment to such distribution is the existence of contingent rights in unborn issue most unlikely ever to be born.[5] Sanction however is only granted on a proper indemnity to the trustees protecting the unborn children's interests. The interlocutor pronounces that the trustees are " entitled " and not " bound " to denude.[6]

The statutory jurisdiction prior to 1961

Under section 5 of the Trusts (Scotland) Act 1921 it is competent for the court on the petition of the trustees under any trust to grant authority to them to do any of the acts mentioned in section 4 of the Act—notwithstanding that such act is at variance with the terms or purposes of the trust. The court can only do so, however, on being satisfied that such acts are in all the circumstances expedient for the execution of the trust. The general powers granted to trustees under section 4 are mainly of an administrative character but it is necessary to mention section 4 (i) which grants power *inter alia* to compromise all claims connected with the trust estate. This power however (which may be authorised by the court under section 5 even if at variance with the trust purposes) is confined to the compromise of an actual litigation in court.[7]

Section 16 of the Trusts (Scotland) Act 1921 also gives the court power to authorise trustees to advance any part of the capital of a trust fund destined either absolutely or contingently to beneficiaries who at the date of the application are not of full age. Such an advance can be authorised if the income of the trust fund is insufficient or not applicable to, and such advance is necessary for the maintenance or education of such beneficiaries and is not expressly prohibited by the trust deed; and also if the rights of the beneficiaries, if contingent, are contingent only on their survivance.[8]

All these powers both at common law and under statute are related to keeping private trusts in being by making good defects in the trust machinery. They do not enable the court in any way to innovate upon the basic trust purposes. Most important of all they do not enable the court under the changed circumstances of revenue legislation to improve the position of beneficiaries by varying the trust so as to avoid part of the burden of estate duty or income tax.

---

[5] Mackenzie Stuart, 349. See p. 148, *supra*.   [6] *Munro's Trs.* v. *Monson,* 1965 S.C. 85.
[7] *Tennent's J.F.* v. *Tennent,* 1954 S.C. 215, 226, *per* L.P. Cooper.
[8] Mackenzie Stuart, 244. See pp. 331–332, *infra*.

Variation by consent of all the beneficiaries

A trust basically involves a trust fund the legal title to which is vested in trustees who hold the fund under trust purposes stated in the trust deed on behalf of all the beneficiaries. The beneficiaries' rights against the trustees are rights *in personam*. If all the beneficiaries being *sui juris* agree among themselves on how the trust fund should be disposed of—and there are no remoter beneficiaries who might acquire a vested interest— then the trustees are bound to comply with their agreement.

The principle is thus stated in Mackenzie Stuart [9]: " If all those who are beneficially interested in the trust estate concur in asking the trustees to denude and if they are legally capable of giving their consent, the trustees must terminate the trust on being exonered and discharged." In *Gray* v. *Gray's Trs.*[10] Lord Gifford said:

> " When in a private trust every possible beneficiary desires and consents to a particular course being adopted—all the beneficiaries being of full age and *sui juris* and none of them being placed under any restraint or disability by the trust deed itself—then no-one has any right or interest to object and the court will not interfere to prevent the sole and unlimited proprietors doing what they like with their own."

All interests must therefore be indefeasibly vested and the consenting beneficiaries must be capax and over eighteen years of age.[11]

Under a private trust there is usually a liferent and any agreement to terminate the trust will then entail the renunciation of his or her liferent by the current liferenter. It follows therefore that the trustees cannot denude unless the liferenter agrees to renounce his or her liferent interest which cannot be done if the liferent is alimentary. Furthermore in many trust deeds the interests in the capital have not yet vested and for this reason also the trustees cannot denude in accordance with an agreement reached among certain of the principal beneficiaries—for other interests may later arise.

The question of whether a liferent can be renounced or whether vesting can be accelerated by the exercise of a special power of appointment is therefore often crucial to whether the existing trust purposes can be terminated or varied by mutual agreement. It also has an important bearing on applications under the new trust variation jurisdiction. The arrangement which the court is then asked to authorise or approve can be simplified by prior agreement or prior action on the part of one or more of the trust beneficiaries.

In general an alimentary liferent cannot be renounced once it has become an interest in possession.[12] In theory it may be renounced *quoad*

---

[9] p. 346.
[10] (1877) 4 R. 378, 383.
[11] Age of Majority (Scotland) Act 1969, Schedule 1, Part I.
[12] See also Chap. 7.

excessum but in practice the court has only a limited jurisdiction to decide what is excessive.[13]

But an alimentary liferent may be renounced under a will before it has come to be enjoyed [14] or before it has become an interest in possession.[15]

The effect of the trustees' denuding without the consent of all the beneficiaries

This is an unlikely occurrence since the passing of the Trusts (Scotland) Act 1961 but occasionally happened before the introduction of the new variation jurisdiction where the interests of minor or unborn beneficiaries were very remote. The trustees were then sometimes persuaded to denude in breach of trust on being granted a suitable indemnity or insurance cover. As already mentioned the courts too, in certain cases, were prepared to grant an interlocutor stating that trustees were " entitled " to denude on being granted a suitable indemnity. The position of the Inland Revenue in such cases is ambiguous and has, as yet, never been properly tested. It is submitted that under Scots law, as the various rights of the beneficiaries are rights *in personam* against the trustees, the Inland Revenue could not successfully contend that trust funds which had in fact been dispersed with the principal beneficiaries' agreement still remained in trust and therefore notionally passed for the purposes of estate duty upon the death of a liferenter—at least where the remote interests of non-consenting parties never in fact materialised by the date of the relevant death. The position however may be different where the interests did materialise and also where there is an alimentary liferent. The alimentary liferenter has no inherent power to renounce his or her liferent; and the renunciation itself would therefore be void. In such a case the Revenue would at least be in a stronger position to contend that the trust was still in being at the liferenter's death and therefore amenable to an estate duty claim. It might for instance be contended that the income on such invalid renunciation being unpayable to the liferenter simply reverted to the settlor's estate and on his death the capital passed under the trust deed. But, as already stated, the better view appears to be that under Scots law where trustees have denuded in breach of trust there can only remain a right *in personam* on the relevant death to claim damages; and that there is no passing of a notional trust estate for estate duty purposes.

As the Revenue's position is not entirely clear however it is obviously unwise for trustees to act upon a resettlement where any of the interests are unvested or any of the parties (however remote) do not concur in the resettlement. The proper course is nowadays an application under the Trusts (Scotland) Act 1961—hence the importance of the new trust variation jurisdiction.

---

13 *Coles,* 1951 S.C. 608.
14 *Ford's Trs.* v. *Ford,* 1961 S.C. 122.
15 *Douglas-Hamilton* v. *Duke and Duchess of Hamilton's Trs.,* 1961 S.C. 205.

The development of the English trust variation jurisdiction

The Chancery Division has somewhat wider powers both at common law and under statute. In relation to private trusts it exercised wide curatorial powers enabling maintenance to be made to infants or adults. Statutory powers analogous to the Trusts (Scotland) Act 1921 are to be found in sections 32 and 57 of the Trustee Act 1925 and section 64 of the Settled Land Act 1925. The Chancery courts could however also authorise some transactions by way of " salvage " and do what was to become by a judicial fiction the basis of the new trust variation jurisdiction. It could sanction the compromise of suits on behalf of infants. Despite the presence of sections 5 and 4 (i) of the Trusts (Scotland) Act 1921 the Scottish courts have never exercised such a wide jurisdiction. Indeed in a recent case, *Lord Glentanar's Trs.*,[16] which involved the compromise of a legal dispute relating to a Scottish trust (but without any action being in court) a trust variation petition had to be brought under section 1 (1) of the Trusts (Scotland) Act 1961 to enable the court to approve an arrangement embodying a compromise on behalf of certain minor and unborn beneficiaries. The Chancery Division was able simply at common law to authorise English executors to agree to the same compromise, the English executors being also beneficiaries under the Scottish trust.

The inroads which taxation has made in recent years on private trust funds duly began to tax the ingenuity of English Chancery lawyers who endeavoured to build on the common law jurisdiction just mentioned.

The Chancery Division's curatorial power to sanction compromises on behalf of infants was originally exercised in regard to genuine litigations. The extension of the jurisdiction at first was merely through " compromises " of genuine lawsuits which came to include rearrangements without very much relation to the matter in dispute. The court then gave its approval to the compromise on behalf of all persons incapable of consenting. This was what Lord Asquith in *Chapman* [17] described as " doing beneficent violence to the terms of the trust though it is perhaps inappropriate to speak of violence to terms to which different persons attribute different meanings." It became apparent how advantageous it was to have badly drafted trusts containing some litigious matter which could be brought before the court for " interpretation." The litigation was then " torpedoed " before it had really started with a general compromise involving wholesale trust variations. Provided a lawsuit had been raised the Chancery judges sitting in chambers in exercise of their curatorial jurisdiction (or supposed jurisdiction) were prepared to grant orders on behalf of incapable or unborn beneficiaries approving the new arrangement. The court in the exercise of this jurisdiction was not actually authorising the new arrangement in the manner of a *cy-près* scheme; but merely providing missing links, so to speak, in the chain of consents in order to enable the trustees to denude.

---

[16] Unreported, July 24, 1970.
[17] [1954] A.C. 469.

The " litigation " which preceded some of these compromised lawsuits eventually became so thin that it was decided to drop the veil altogether and without any litigation at all merely to seek an order on behalf of incapable beneficiaries for approval of new arrangements. Some Chancery judges were again ready to oblige and there are reported cases of the court making orders approving trust arrangements on behalf of children without any lawsuit being before the court. Most applications however were heard in chambers and there was never a contradictor to argue against the jurisdiction. This practice however did not last long for in 1952 the matter was put boldly (and perhaps indiscreetly) to the test when orders were sought on behalf of certain infants approving three large trust arrangements designed to avoid estate duty: *Re Downshire Settled Estates*; *Re Blackwell Settlement Trusts*; and *Re Chapman Settlement Trusts*.[18] That there was no settled jurisdiction was emphasised by the initial refusal of all three applications as incompetent because there was no litigation before the court. On appeal, the Attorney-General instructed counsel to appear as *amicus curiae* and for the first time a contradictor was heard. The Court of Appeal refused to grant the order sought in the case of *Chapman* but did so in the other two cases—Lord Denning in particular favouring the new jurisdiction. The applicants appealed in the case of *Chapman* but the House of Lords refused the appeal and stated that the orders in the other two cases had been wrongly granted—despite counsel informing the House that the Lord Chancellor had himself made an order of the type sought when once sitting as a judge of first instance. The House of Lords unequivocally stated that whatever the departure from proper practice had once been, the Chancery Division did not have jurisdiction to sanction compromises on behalf of incapable or potential beneficiaries, except where there was a proper legal dispute in court. Lord Morton of Henryton even went so far as to say [19]:

> " If the court had power to approve and did approve schemes such as the present scheme, the way would be open to a most undignified game of chess between the Chancery Division and the legislature. The alteration of one settlement for the purpose of avoiding taxation already imposed might well be followed by scores of successful applications for a similar purpose by beneficiaries under other settlements. The legislature might then counter this move by imposing fresh taxation on the settlements thus altered. The beneficiaries would then troop back to the Chancery Division and say—' Please alter the trust again—you have the power, the adults desire it, and it is for the benefit of the infants to avoid this fresh taxation. The legislature may not move again.' So the game might go on if the judges of the Chancery Division had the power which the appellants claim for them and if they thought it right to make the first move."

18 [1953] Ch. 218.
19 *Chapman, supra,* p. 468.

The actual common law powers of the English court in this matter were fully set forth by Lord Simonds as follows [20]:

" The major proposition I state in the words of one of the great masters of equity: ' I decline,' said Farwell J., in *Re Walker*,[21] ' to accept any suggestion that the court has an inherent jurisdiction to alter a man's will because it thinks it beneficial. It seems to me that is quite impossible.' It should then be asked, what are the exceptions to this rule ? They seem to me to be reasonably clearly defined. There is no doubt that the Chancellor (whether by virtue of paternal power or in the exercise of a trust, it matters not) had and exercised the jurisdiction to change the nature of an infant's property from real to personal estate and vice versa, though his jurisdiction was generally so exercised as to preserve the rights of testamentary disposition and of succession. Equally, there is no doubt that from an early date the court assumed the power, sometimes for that purpose ignoring the direction of a settlor, to provide maintenance for an infant, and, rarely, for an adult, beneficiary. So too the court had power in the administration of trust property to direct that by way of salvage some transaction unauthorised by the trust instrument should be carried out. Nothing is more significant than the repeated assertions by the court that mere expediency was not enough to found the jurisdiction. Lastly, and I can find no other than these four categories, the court had power to sanction the compromise by an infant in a suit to which that infant was a party by next friend or guardian ad litem."

The new jurisdiction under the Trusts (Scotland) Act 1961

The powers which some English Chancery judges wrongly exercised for several years and which were disapproved in *Chapman* have now however been granted both in England and in Scotland by the legislature. The Trusts Act 1958 gave the Chancery Division express power to consent to arrangements varying English trusts on behalf of unborn or minor beneficiaries where this would be for their benefit. A similar Scottish Act followed three years later in almost identical terms where the proposed arrangement would not be prejudicial to the persons on whose behalf approval was sought. Special provisions also had to be included to authorise the renunciation of Scottish alimentary liferents. This apart, however, the jurisdiction is thought to be basically the same.

It has been necessary in this chapter to consider the practice of the English Chancery Division which terminated in *Chapman*, to understand the basis of the jurisdiction introduced under the 1958 and 1961 Acts. It remains essentially a curatorial function under which the court is acting in place of minor, incapable or unborn beneficiaries in granting consents on their behalf which might have been granted by themselves if they had been in existence or *sui juris*. By providing the necessary consents the court

---

[20] *Ibid.* p. 445. [21] [1901] 1 Ch. 879, 885.

enables an effective trust variation to occur. It is submitted that the new jurisdiction of the court is correctly stated by Stamp J. in *Re Cohen's Settlement Trusts* [22] as follows:

" Apart from the Act of 1958, the trusts of a settlement can only be effectively varied as against those who consent to the variation and what I think the Act of 1958 envisages is the court supplying the consent of those whose consents will in the event be necessary but whose actual consent by reason of their disability, or because they have not appeared on the scene, cannot be obtained. The consents which are contemplated to be given by the court are, in my judgment, precisely those consents which under a deed of family arrangement or variation would have to be obtained before the trustees could safely act upon it, but at present cannot be obtained. In order to ascertain what those consents are one must, in my judgment, consider all possible events and all persons who would or might become entitled on the happening of those events. Only if all the latter have consented could the trust fund safely be distributed in accordance with the deed of family arrangement."

Section 1 (1).   The court's approval

The Court of Session is now given power under section 1 (1) of the Trusts (Scotland) Act 1961 to approve [23] on behalf of three classes of persons any arrangement varying or revoking all or any of the trust purposes of the trust, or enlarging the powers of the trustees of managing or administering the trust estate—if in their opinion the carrying out thereof would not be prejudicial to any of those persons. [24]

The persons on whose behalf the court's approval may be granted are:

(a) " Any of the beneficiaries who by reason of non-age or other incapacity is incapable of assenting."

It is to be noted from section 1 (6) that the beneficiaries' interests need not be vested and indeed may be indirect. [25] It is also provided under section 1 (2) that a person who is over the age of pupillarity but has not attained the age of twenty-one years shall be deemed to be incapable of assenting; but before approving an arrangement on behalf of such a person the court has to take into account as it thinks appropriate his attitude to the arrangement. In practice, the court appears to leave this to instructing solicitors concerned to inform the minor beneficiary as to the details of the arrangement and such minors are of course represented by a *curator ad litem* on

---

22   [1965] 1 W.L.R. 1229, 1234. See also *Callender* v. *Callender,* 19th September, 1974 (so far unreported).

23   As to the difference between approval under s. 1 (1) and authorisation under s. 1 (4), see *Young's Trs.,* 1962 S.C. 293.

24   See *Young's Trs., supra; Pollok-Morris,* 1969 S.L.T. (Notes) 60.

25   Where Y died having acquired a vested right in the fee of an estate under X's trust, and left a trust disposition and settlement under which Z was to have the fee of the estate, Z was said to have an indirect interest in X's trust (*Countess of Lauderdale, Petitioner,* 1962 S.C. 302).

whose behalf a minute of consent is lodged. Section 1 (3) provides that an arrangement cannot subsequently be reduced during the *quadriennium utile* on grounds of minority and lesion. Since the coming into force of the Age of Majority (Scotland) Act 1969 [26] the age of eighteen has to be substituted for twenty-one. Now therefore the court requires to approve on behalf of any person under the age of eighteen. If over eighteen, the beneficiary's own minute of consent requires to be lodged.

> (b) " Any person (whether ascertained or not) who may become one of the beneficiaries as being at a future date or on the happening of a future event a person of any specified description or a member of any specified class of persons, so however that this paragraph shall not include any person who is capable of assenting and would be of that description or a member of that class as the case may be if the said date had fallen or the said event had happened at the date of the presentation of the petition to the court."

This provision covers the situation of a destination over to a person's heirs in which case the court can approve on behalf of future heirs but one has to obtain the actual consent of anyone who is capable of consenting and would be the heir had the inheritance opened at the date of the hearing for the petition.[27]

> (c) " Any person unborn."

This provision requires no further comment.

It will be noted that the court's approval can be obtained on behalf of incapable and other persons, not only to wholesale alterations of trust purposes but also to schemes of a minor nature for enlarging the powers of the trustees for managing or administering the estate. Thus in England under the 1958 Act the court granted approval to schemes enlarging the trustees' powers of investment. But since the passing of the Trustee Investments Act 1961 [28] both the English and Scottish courts have held that the discretionary jurisdiction to alter investment powers will only be exercised where there are special circumstances such as where alteration is necessary to clear up ambiguities in the investment powers.[29] Minor applications sometimes made are to vary the period of accumulation provided in the original deed to take account of changes in revenue legislation.

On whose behalf approval or consent is necessary

There is a distinction between the primary question of whether certain approvals are necessary on behalf of minor or unborn beneficiaries before there is an effective trust variation; and the secondary question whether the court should exercise its discretion to approve an arrangement on

[26] Age of Majority (Scotland) Act 1969, Schedule 1, Part I.
[27] *Buchan, Petitioner*, 1964 S.L.T. 51.
[28] 9 & 10 Eliz. 2, c. 62.
[29] See *Re Cooper's Settlement* [1962] Ch. 826; *Re Clarke's Will Trusts* [1961] 1 W.L.R. 1471; *Inglis and others, Petitioners*, 1965 S.L.T. 326.

their behalf or refuse its consent because they are materially prejudiced thereby. The secondary question goes only to *quantum*. In illustration of the secondary question, there have been arrangements approved by the court on behalf of beneficiaries whose interests were unlikely ever to materialise or which were of minimal value under which these beneficiaries received small capital sums; or alternatively, there was merely a personal undertaking by the liferenter binding upon his estate to pay them a certain sum of money in certain events. It is of course for the court to judge in each case whether the persons on whose behalf its approval is sought are or are not prejudiced by the arrangement. All possible eventualities must be taken into account but the test, in the end of the day, will be whether on a balance of probabilities, the arrangement will not be prejudicial in the circumstances most likely to occur. This is how an adult would judge the situation if asked to give his own consent to the arrangement: and this is normally the attitude adopted by the court. As Danckwerts J. said in *Re Cohen's Will Trusts* [30] " . . . if people ask the court to sanction this sort of scheme they must be prepared to have some sort of risk and if it is a risk that an adult would be prepared to take, the court is prepared to take it on behalf of the infant."

Provided the court's approval is given, and the consents of all beneficiaries who are *sui juris* are also obtained, there will always be an effective trust variation binding upon the trustees. If the court's approval is not given on behalf of remoter beneficiaries or the consent of remote adult beneficiaries is not obtained then the trust will not be effectively varied *quoad* those other beneficiaries. The trustees will be open to an action of damages at their instance—however small the value of their interest at the time of the trust variation—should the circumstances under which they inherit unexpectedly materialise. [31]

The point is illustrated by the case of *Re Suffert's Settlement* [32] where the court was prepared to give its consent *quantum valeat* on behalf of proximate beneficiaries leaving it to the trustees to protect themselves against the claims of certain remoter relatives by obtaining their formal consents. Nothing however has ever been said in any of the English cases to indicate that the court can bind persons who are not parties to the arrangement.

In the case of *Phillips* [33] however, a contrary indication was given by the Court of Session. It is respectfully submitted that this case was wrongly decided. In effect the court approved an arrangement on behalf of proximate beneficiaries but encouraged the trustees to remain completely at risk in relation to the remoter beneficiaries in regard to whom the trust was not effectively varied, but whose interests were stated to be too remote. The facts of the case were that the capital of the trust fund was destined on the death of the testator's last surviving child to the issue of his children then

---

[30] [1959] 3 All E.R. 523. See also *Buchanan, Petitioner*, 1964 S.C. 26.
[31] For a discussion of the position of the Revenue see *supra* p. 152.
[32] [1961] Ch. 1.   [33] 1964 S.C. 141, *cf.*, however, *Buchanan, supra*.

alive with destinations over in favour of certain remote collateral relatives and charitable organisations. The latter were very numerous and the task of obtaining all their consents would have been difficult. The court decided that service upon and the consents of the very remote beneficiaries were unnecessary; and further that insurance cover provided for them under the arrangement should be deleted although this could be provided by the trustees outwith the scheme if they so desired.

This is, of course, a decision of convenience to parties in trust variation petitions. Indeed, one can contemplate situations where a scheme could not be presented at all due to the presence of remote beneficiaries spread throughout the world, unless the court was prepared to consent *quantum valeat* on behalf of the more proximate unborn and incapable beneficiaries. But the court's consent, like an adult's, cannot override the interests of non-consenting parties nor can a refusal of approval " as unnecessary " constitute a finding that is *res judicata* in a question with non-compearing parties or persons unborn.

It has to be mentioned, however, that there is a contrary theory namely, that the court's approval of a new trust arrangement operates in the same manner as its approval of a *cy-près* scheme to elide all beneficial interests under the old trust being varied. But this is certainly not the view taken south of the border of the equivalent English statute and it is difficult to think that when Parliament passed the 1961 Act— based on that of 1958—it intended to achieve a different result.

As mentioned at the beginning of this chapter a clue to the correct interpretation may be found in a reading of the decision of the House of Lords in *Chapman* v. *Chapman, supra*. The judicial variation or termination of trusts is merely a statutory extension of their variation or termination by deeds of family arrangement entered into with the concurrence of all interested parties.

It is thought that no special significance is to be derived from the contrast in section 1 between the phrase " approve an arrangement " and the corresponding assent of individuals mentioned in the same section. The wording of the Variation of Trusts Act 1958 is identical and the word " assent " also derives from the English statute. That the Scottish Parliamentary draftsman should have found it necessary to provide specifically that an arrangement approved on behalf of a minor beneficiary should not thereafter be reducible on grounds of minority and lesion—is also an indication that approval was regarded as merely equivalent to his consent.

Under section 1 (4) which has no counterpart in the English Act the Court of Session may certainly authorise the arrangement but in the normal style of the interlocutor this is only " in so far as it varies or revokes the alimentary liferent and makes new provisions in lieu thereof." As it is illegal to renounce an alimentary liferent such validation is of course required. But again, it is not a blanket authorisation serving to operate even against non-consenting parties.

The court's approval of an arrangement or its authorisation of the removal of an alimentary qualification is not therefore the equivalent of the approval of a *cy-près* scheme. Approval in terms of section 1 (1) can only be granted on behalf of certain specified persons and merely constitutes a contractual consent on their behalf.[34]

If this be the correct interpretation then certain important consequences appear to ensue. It follows that an approval on behalf of some beneficiaries cannot bind other non-consenting beneficiaries—however remote their interests. This must be so even where the actuarial value of their interests as at the date of the hearing are purely nominal. Such nominal value may justify an adult remote beneficiary granting his consent without compensation; and perhaps even the court itself so doing on behalf of incapable or unborn beneficiaries on the ground that there appears to be no real prejudice. But without such consent the trust will not be effectively varied *quoad* all the beneficiaries. If their interests unexpectedly materialised they would still have an action *in personam* against the trustees and could call them to account.

It is thought therefore that a clear distinction should be drawn in practice between a mere *spes* which only arises through the exercise of a power of appointment and an existing contingent interest which can be defeated by appointment in another direction.

An example of the former is a power given to a liferenter under a trust to confer some benefit on a future spouse. Approval of a new arrangement on behalf of the future spouse is unnecessary although the trustees for their additional protection may sometimes prefer to have such approval, " refused as unnecessary." In general, however, objects of a power of appointment who have no interest in default of an appointment in their favour do not require to be made consenting parties to an arrangement—whether as individuals or through the court. The power itself can simply be released as part of the arrangement. But it is usual to include express provisions to this effect rather than to leave the matter to implication. Contradictory views have been expressed on this matter in England: see *in re Courtauld's Settlement* and *in re Bell's Settlement Trusts*.[35] But it is difficult to see how the mere possibility of benefit under a power which has since been expressly released by the appointor as party to an arrangement—could ever give rise to any subsequent right of action.

In contrast, however, the parties to an arrangement and, in particular, the trustees acting under the Trust being varied cannot disregard the contingent interests of any beneficiaries entitled to succeed in default of the exercise of a power whose interests have not in fact been excluded by exercise of that power prior to the hearing of the petition. This is because the arrangement—by removing the power and the possibility of defeasance —will bring the contingency of succession nearer. And if that contingency unexpectedly materialised it would be no answer for the trustees

---

[34] *Callender* v. *Callender*, 19th Sept., 1974 (so far unreported).
[35] [1965] 1 W.L.R. 1385; [1968] 1 W.L.R. 899.

then to contend that, as at the date of the hearing, the interests of non-consenting beneficiaries were of purely nominal value because they might have been defeated by other appointment. That is merely an argument which goes to the secondary question of *quantum* of compensation. It has properly led to restricted insurance cover or purely nominal provisions in certain beneficiaries' favour. Nevertheless, for the trustees' full protection, the appropriate consents must be obtained from all beneficiaries who are *sui juris* and the court's approval on behalf of those who are minor, incapax or unborn. The trust is then effectively varied notwithstanding the fact that certain of the consenting parties may have opted to receive no benefit whatsoever under the arrangement.

In some cases, it is possible, however, by prior exercise of a power of appointment effectively to exclude the interests of remoter beneficiaries by accelerating vesting of the trust capital in favour of the proximate beneficiaries. As already mentioned this should be done by an actual exercise of the power rather than by moving the court to refuse consent on their behalf as unnecessary because their interests could have been readily defeated.

Whether a special power of appointment can be used to accelerate vesting depends upon the wording of the relevant trust deed and, in particular, whether the settlor intended the donee of the special power to be able to fix a vesting date in advance of the death of the liferenter. Sometimes, however, it is clear that only survivors of the liferenter are intended to be objects of the power.

Care has to be taken where a special power of appointment is exercised as a precursor to a new trust arrangement in order to exclude remoter beneficiaries whose consents are not sought (whether individually or through the court) to ensure that the exercise of the power is not fraudulent. This is because those entitled in default would otherwise have a continuing interest and right to sue the trustees.

Fraud in this context does not involve any moral turpitude. It merely means that the power has not been exercised as it should be for the benefit of the trust beneficiaries in whose favour it was created. If the power is exercised principally to benefit the appointor as part of a general arrangement the exercise would be fraudulent. It is not however a fraudulent exercise of a power if it is exercised as a precursor to a new arrangement under which the appointor takes a capital sum equivalent to the actuarial value of his or her liferent interest and no more. In *Pelham Burn* [36] the liferentrix received a capital sum equivalent to the actuarial value of her liferent interest but did not take any of the prospective estate duty saving under the new trust arrangement. Lord President Clyde referred with approval to a dictum by Lord Romilly M.R. in *Re Huish's Charity*.[37]

> " The meaning and good sense of the rule appears to be that if the appointor either directly or indirectly obtains any exclusive advantage

[36] 1964 S.C. 3.   [37] (1870) L.R. 10 Eq. 5.

to himself and that to obtain this advantage is the object and the reason of its being made then the appointment is bad; but if the whole transaction taken together shows no such object but only shows an intention to improve the whole subject matter of the appointment for the benefit of all the objects of the power then the exercise of the power is not fraudulent or void although by the force of circumstances such improvement cannot be bestowed on the property in the subject of the appointment without the appointor to some extent participating therein."

The Lord President then went on to say that in the case before him it appeared there was accordingly no fraud on the power. The whole transaction taken together showed the real object and intention was to benefit the objects of the power who would secure a much larger sum of money from the trust as a result of the possible estate duty saving; and any advantage which the liferenter was securing was merely incidental to the primary purpose of the whole scheme. This decision was in contrast to *Wyndham* [38] where the liferentrix who had exercised a special power of appointment was intended under a proposed arrangement to take part of the prospective estate duty saving as well as the actuarial value of her liferent interest. Approval of the arrangement was refused at the first hearing and the arrangement required to be amended. There have been a number of conflicting decisions in England upon this topic. [39]

Section 1 (4): variation of an alimentary liferent

As previously mentioned [40] the presence of an alimentary liferent has always been the greatest barrier of all to a trust variation by consent because it cannot be effectively renounced by the liferenter.

The analogous power in England to impose restraints on the anticipation of income had been abolished before the passing of the Trusts Act 1958. The new jurisdiction to vary or revoke an alimentary liferent is therefore peculiar to Scotland and a vital part of the new variation jurisdiction.

Under section 1 (4) of the Trusts (Scotland) Act 1961 the court may now authorise an arrangement varying or revoking the trust purposes under which a beneficiary is entitled to an alimentary liferent and making new provision in lieu thereof, including if the court thinks fit, new provision for the disposal of the fee or, as the case may be, of such part thereof as was burdened with the liferent. This authorisation, however, may not be granted by the court unless:

" (a) it considers that the carrying out of the arrangement would be reasonable having regard to the income of the alimentary beneficiary from all sources and to such other factors, if any, as the court considers material ", and

---

[38] 1964 S.L.T. 290.
[39] See *Re Wallace's Settlements* [1968] 1 W.L.R. 711; *Re Bell's Settlement Trusts* [1968] 1 W.L.R. 899; and *Re Brook's Settlement* [1968] 1 W.L.R. 1661. It is thought, however, that the Scottish courts would not follow the latter decision.   [40] *Supra*, p. 151.

" (b) The arrangement is approved by the alimentary beneficiary or (where incapable) is approved by the court on his or her behalf."

In practice this means that the alimentary beneficiary must be left with an income adequate for all foreseeable needs according to his or her station. In exceptional cases where an alimentary liferenter has a substantial income of his own independently of the trust being varied, the court has sanctioned arrangements under which he takes no capital at all. In such a case, all the capital is transferred to his children so effecting a saving in estate duty if he survives the statutory period. In the more normal case where the liferenter takes some capital, it is often possible to demonstrate to the court that he can use some of the capital transferred to him under the arrangement to purchase an annuity and so maintain his nett income position. This is due to the " capital element " of the annuity which avoids income tax under existing income tax provisions.

If it is possible for the alimentary beneficiary to renounce his or her alimentary liferent before it has fallen into possession, then the renunciation is merely effected by his or her consent to the arrangement and the court's authorisation is not required.[41]

Procedure

Petitions under the Trusts (Scotland) Act 1961 are presented to the Inner House of the Court of Session.[42] The petition requires to be served on all interested parties and a *curator ad litem* thereafter appointed to all minor and incapax beneficiaries. The trustees represent the interest of unborn beneficiaries and where there is any conflict between existing beneficiaries it is necessary to have separate counsel although the same solicitors may act for all. The petition proceeds upon an agreed narrative of facts and the terms of the draft arrangement are usually negotiated beforehand among the principal beneficiaries. The proposed arrangement is printed as an appendix to the petition and any new trusts embodied therein are usually printed as a schedule thereto.[43] Before a diet of hearing can be fixed, minutes of consent require to be lodged on behalf of all beneficiaries who are *sui juris, i.e. capax* and over the age of eighteen.[43] Minutes also have to be lodged on behalf of the *curators ad litem* to the minor and incapax beneficiaries indicating to the court whether consent should be granted on behalf of their wards and whether there are any particular points for the court's consideration. A minute of consent also requires to be lodged on behalf of the trustees. Should any adult beneficiary refuse his or her consent to the proposed arrangement the trust will not be effectively varied.

In addition to the narrative of facts stated in the petition, certain documentary evidence is normally required. This usually comprises an up-to-

---

[41] *Findlays Petitioners*, 1962 S.C. 210; *Smillie and Another, Petitioners*, 1966 S.L.T. 41; Age of Majority (Scotland) Act 1969, Schedule 1, Part I.

[42] R.C. 190. As to whether the English or the Scottish court is the appropriate forum see *Clarke's Trustees, Petitioners*, 1966 S.L.T. 249.

[43] *Colville, Petitioner*, 1962 S.C. 185.

date valuation of the trust fund certified by stockbrokers; a statement of the estate duty calculated to be payable in the event of the liferenter's immediate death certified by solicitors. In many cases an actuary's report certified by the actuary is lodged in order to demonstrate that beneficiaries have not been prejudiced and have received full value in return for their consent to the petition. In the simpler type of case, such a report usually contains a valuation of the liferenter's and fiar's interests under the trust being varied, and also of the Inland Revenue's interest for tax purposes—all expressed as percentages of the trust fund. The actuary then suggests a fair apportionment of the prospective estate duty saving bringing out final figures which are again expressed as percentages of the trust fund. This is normally done by apportioning the estate duty saving in proportion to the value of the various interests or simply by dividing it equally. The actuary's first set of figures is usually referred to in court as indicating the " nett actuarial value " of the various interests concerned; and the second set of figures as indicating the " full actuarial value." However these are both really misnomers as only the former is strictly an actuarial calculation. As mentioned below, an actuary's report is not always required. If the arrangement contains insurance provisions, copies of the relevant insurance policies require to be lodged and a letter from the insurance company stating that, subject to payment of the premium, they are prepared to undertake the risk.

Where the court's authorisation is sought under section 1 (4) in respect of the revocation of an alimentary liferent, a full statement of the alimentary beneficiary's income from all sources both gross and nett is required. This statement should contain a calculation of the diminution in nett income which will result if the arrangement is approved; also, where appropriate, what the nett income would be if an annuity were to be purchased using part of the capital reserved under the arrangement. The purpose of this production is to demonstrate that the alimentary beneficiary is left with an adequate income.

The petitioners are usually the principal beneficiaries and it is inadvisable for the trustees (whose primary duty is to maintain the existing trust purposes) to present a trust variation petition unless it is an administrative application or there is no other appropriate person to do so. They are, however, empowered to present a petition under section 1 (1) of the 1961 Act. After counsel for the petitioners have addressed the court, counsel for the trustees, for the adult beneficiaries and for the *curator ad litem* to any minor beneficiaries then address the court under reference to the various minutes of consent which have been lodged. At the conclusion of the hearing—if there are no unresolved difficulties—the court indicates that it is prepared to approve the arrangement on behalf of the minor and unborn beneficiaries on whose behalf its consent has been sought and, where appropriate, is also prepared to authorise the arrangement in so far as it varies or revokes an alimentary liferent and makes new provisions in lieu thereof. The signed interlocutor of the court then gives effect to this decision. After signing this interlocutor the court is *functus* and the interlocutor cannot be changed even with the consent of all parties.[44]

The arrangement

No two arrangements follow exactly the same form because the trust purposes of the original trust deed and the present circumstances of the various beneficiaries are never alike. Each arrangement has therefore to be tailor made. Furthermore, revenue law has changed considerably since the Trusts (Scotland) Act 1961 was first enacted and major new changes are proposed at the time of publication. This has in itself affected the form of arrangements approved or authorised by the court.

Only a most general sketch of the usual type of arrangement is therefore given along with some of the tax considerations which at the current date have to be borne in mind.

Arrangements always commence with a definitive clause which *inter alia* defines the principal parties to the arrangement, the trust fund and the operative date of the arrangement. The latter is either the date of the court's interlocutor approving or authorising the arrangement; or, where there are insurance policies involved, the date of the last insurance policy to be effected. There then follow the provisions, if any, for insurance cover. These may include an estate duty cover policy protecting the capital transferred to beneficiaries other than the liferenter and also contingency or issue risks insurance policies to protect remoter beneficiaries.

The arrangement then usually proceeds to provide for division of the trust capital between the liferenter and principal beneficiaries. The liferenter often receives a capital sum as his or her own absolute property and the remainder of the trust capital is often transferred to his or her children equally between them if they are *sui juris*, and it is desired that they receive capital immediately.

As already mentioned the division of the trust capital between the liferenter and fiars is normally based upon an actuary's report of the various interests concerned. Such a report provides the most appropriate basis for an arm's length bargain and is moreover essential where it is necessary to prove that full value has been received.

If the fiar's interests in the capital of the trust being varied have not yet vested then the interest of remoter beneficiaries (whether born or unborn) must be protected. It may, however, be possible to preclude their interests by a prior exercise of a special power of appointment if this can be exercised so as to confer vested indefeasible interests on existing adult beneficiaries. The circumstances under which this can be done without constituting a fraud on the power have already been considered above. It must be borne in mind that if a power is exercised as a precursor to an arrangement the appointer may not take under the arrangement more

---

[44] *Bailey and Another, Petitioners,* 1969 S.L.T. (Notes) 70.

than the " nett actuarial value " of his liferent interest *i.e.* he may take no part of the prospective estate duty saving.[45]

If the remoter beneficiaries' interests cannot be so excluded their interests may be catered for under a new trust incorporated in the schedule to the arrangement. The court will, of course, be concerned to see that they are not prejudiced by the substituted trust interests. As an alternative their interests may be protected by insurance. This may take the form of a contingency policy providing a sum insured in the event of a person or persons failing to survive a certain event; or an issue risks policy with a sum assured payable upon the death of a certain person survived by issue. The court will usually consent on behalf of minor or unborn beneficiaries if the insurance policies are designed to provide a sum assured payable in the event on which (apart from the variation) they would have succeeded to the trust capital and equal to the present value of their nett expectancy, *i.e.* after deduction of estate duty at the appropriate rate. Care has to be taken in regard to the payment of premiums to ensure that the policy proceeds are not subject to estate duty or surtax.

The most common reason for presenting a trust variation petition has in the past been to save estate duty on the death of an existing liferenter. If no variation occurs there will, of course, be a levy to duty upon the whole trust estate. By varying the trust this danger can often be removed; but there will, nevertheless, be a levy to duty on the capital which is transferred by the arrangement to persons other than the liferenter if the liferenter dies within a period of seven years from the operative date of the arrangement. This levy is now made under section 2 (1) (*b*) of the Finance Act 1894, as amended by section 36 (2) (*b*) of the Finance Act 1969. Section 36 (2) (*b*) (1) provides that

" if at any time during the period of seven years ending with the date of the deceased's death, the property was comprised in a settlement and the deceased was entitled to a beneficial interest in possession in that property as, or as successor to an interest of, a beneficiary under the settlement "

the property is deemed to pass at his death for estate duty purposes. For this reason the capital transferred to the children is often protected against the risk of diminution by means of a policy of assurance under which the sum assured is the estate duty calculated to be due. On the other hand, there is no estate duty levy in respect of capital transferred to the liferenter under the arrangement unless it forms part of his free estate on his death. This is due to the savings provisions of the Finance Act 1969 Sched. 17, Part II, Para. 2 (1).

On calculating the tax advantages of proceeding with an arrangement it should be kept in mind that the arrangement itself constitutes a " deemed disposal " for the purposes of Capital Gains Tax, and hence such tax is payable upon any increase in value of the trust funds since April 1965.[46]

---

45 *Pelham Burn Petitioners*, 1964 S.C. 3.   46 Finance Act 1965, s. 25.

The normal arrangement also contains clauses providing that there will be no apportionment of incomings or outgoings as at the operative date; and also preserving the trustees' lien under section 44 (4) of the Finance Act 1950 (as amended) over the capital to be transferred to the fiars unless they have obtained a certificate from the Inland Revenue that no duty is leviable.

The arrangement also contains provisions governing expenses. These and any tax exigible as a result of the coming into effect of the arrangement are normally stated to be payable out of the trust fund prior to its distribution.

Where the schedule to the arrangement incorporates a new trust for the benefit of minor children, grandchildren or remoter issue, its precise form will of course vary with the particular circumstances and the various ages concerned. Flexible trusts have in some cases been approved by the court where the trust being varied itself contains flexible powers.[47] The introduction of wide powers of resettlement however or discretionary powers to benefit persons who were not among the original class of discretionary beneficiaries is not generally allowed. Thus in *Pollok-Morris* [48] it was held that the introduction of adopted children among the class of beneficiaries who were not within the scope of the trust deed could not be sanctioned.

If the accumulation of income is desired under the new trust, a useful new permitted period of accumulation has been introduced by section 6 (1) (*a*) of the Law Reform (Miscellaneous Provisions) (Scotland) Act 1966, namely a period of twenty-one years from " the making of the settlement or other disposition." It was decided in *John Sutherland Aikman* [47] that as the new arrangement in that case involved a new settlement it was competent to incorporate a new period of twenty-one years running from the operative date of the arrangement.

Where a new trust is instituted by the arrangement, it has to be a Scottish trust. Only in very exceptional circumstances will the court authorise the transfer of funds into a foreign trust.[49]

---

[47] *John Sutherland Aikman, Petitioner*, 1968 S.L.T. 137.
[48] 1969 S.L.T. (Notes) 60.
[49] *Baroness Lloyd and others, Petitioners*, 1963 S.C. 37.

CHAPTER 13

PUBLIC TRUSTS

THERE can be no divestiture of a man's heirs unless his testamentary directions confer a patrimonial benefit on a third party or a benefit upon the public or any section thereof.[1] If the benefit is conferred on a third party, the trust is a private trust; if the benefit is conferred on the public the trust is a public trust. In Scotland, the Court of Session exercises "plenary jurisdiction over the administration of all trusts, whether public or private, irrespective of the particular purposes to which the estate or income of the trust may be appropriated."[2]

Charitable trusts

It is convenient to summarise much of the subsequent argument of this chapter at this point in order to show the relationship between public trusts and charitable trusts. In Scotland, if a trust is for the public benefit it is valid. In England, on the other hand, a trust for the public benefit is valid only if it is a charitable trust.[3] "Charitable" in this context has a technical meaning developed by the Court of Chancery and extends not merely to the relief of poverty, but also to certain purposes of general public utility. Except in revenue and rating statutes, this technical meaning has no place in the law of Scotland. In Scotland, "charitable" has a sense wider than the relief of poverty but unrestricted by the technicalities of the English sense. The effect of the use of the words "charity" and "charitable" is quite different in Scotland. Firstly, a bequest which is stamped as charitable is entitled to a benignant construction. The second effect is where the testator gives his trustees a power of selection; if a testator directs his trustees to distribute his estate among a class of objects the bequest is valid only if the class is sufficiently defined; the words "charity" and "charitable" are sufficiently precise for this purpose. Certain other words are of sufficient precision; some of these other expressions connote objects which can also be described as charitable. Charitable trusts, therefore, are merely a species of public trusts and there are some public trusts which are not charitable.[4] The prominence of

---

[1] *Ross* v. *Ross* (1770) M. 5019; *Gardner* v. *Ogilvie* (1857) 20 D. 105, 109, *per* Lord Curriehill; *Neilson* v. *Stewart* (1860) 22 D. 646, 650, *per* Lord Neaves; *Cowan* v. *Cowan* (1887) 14 R. 670. The principle applied equally to heritable and moveable estate (*Aitken's Trs.* v. *Aitken,* 1927 S.C. 374, 380, *per* Lord Sands).

[2] *Per* Lord Watson, *Commissioners for Special Purposes of Income Tax* v. *Pemsel* [1891] A.C. 531, 560. See also *Ross* v. *Governors of Heriot's Hospital* (1843) 5 D. 589, 609, *per* Lord Cuninghame; *Blair* v. *Duncan* (1901) 4 F.(H.L.) 1, 6, *per* Lord Robertson.

[3] See *Bowman* v. *Secular Society Ltd.* [1917] A.C. 406, 441, *per* Lord Parker.

[4] McLaren, II, 917; *Blair* v. *Duncan* (1901) 4 F.(H.L.) 1, 6, *per* Lord Robertson; *Trustees for the Roll of Voluntary Workers* v. *Inland Revenue,* 1942 S.C. 47. *Cf. Dundas* (1869) 7 M. 670, 675, *per* L.P. Inglis; Gloag and Henderson, 656. In *Robertson's Trs.,* 1948 S.C. 1,

charitable trusts in legal decisions results from nothing more than their being the most numerous class of public trusts.

Enforcement of the trust

Public trusts can be enforced in several ways. The testator's heirs, although they have no right to interfere in the proper and ordinary administration of the trust, have a title to challenge any positive abuse of the trust or any diversion of funds to purposes other than those for which it was instituted.[5] Then anyone possessing an interest, existing or contingent, in the objects of the trust has a good title to enforce it.[6] An action at the instance of such a party has sometimes been called an *actio popularis*[7] but it has been said that " What is known under the denomination of a popular action forms no part of the law of Scotland." [8] Thirdly, the Lord Advocate can intervene in the public interest.[9]

Certainty

A valid public trust will be constituted even if the testator's directions are not specific. A direction to expend a fund for " the maintenance of a school for boys for reading and writing and arithmetic " was held to be sufficiently certain.[10] A direction to establish a " hospital " in Dundee for a hundred boys was held to be sufficient, the administrative machinery being supplied by the court.[11]

Examples of Public Trusts

A bequest for the erection and maintenance in the City of Dundee of a popular astronomical and scientific institution was said to be valid as the

---

L.P. Cooper carefully referred to a " public charitable bequest " and a " public charitable trust." R.C. 189 refers to charitable trusts. A further illustration of confusion on this point is found in *Mitchell's Trs.* v. *Fraser,* 1915 S.C. 350, where the testator directed payments " to such of my children or children's children as they may think most deserving, with special instructions to relieve any of them who may appear to be in want, provided always that they have not brought themselves into such circumstances by their own misconduct." The opinion was expressed that the trust was charitable. Lord Guthrie said at p. 359: " I do not see why the mere fact that the charity not only begins but ends at home should prevent the trust being a charitable one."

[5] *Christie* v. *Magistrates of Stirling,* July 5, 1774, F.C.; *Campbell* v. *McIntyre* (1824) 3 S. 126; *Hill* v. *Burns* (1826) 2 W. & S. 80, 91, *per* Lord Gifford; *McLeish's Trs.* v. *McLeish* (1841) 3 D. 914; *Trs. of Mackintosh Fund* v. *Mackintosh* (1852) 14 D. 928.

[6] *Bow* v. *Patrons of Cowan's Hospital* (1825) 4 S. 276; *Miller* v. *Black's Trs.* (1837) 2 W. & S. 866, 893, *per* Lord Brougham; *Ross* v. *Governors of Heriot's Hospital* (1843) 5 D. 589, 609, *per* Lord Cuninghame; *Andrews* v. *Ewart's Trs.* (1886) 13 R.(H.L.) 69, 73, *per* Lord Watson. But see *Addison* v. *Whyte* (1870) 8 M. 909; *Mackie* v. *Presbytery of Edinburgh* (1896) 23 R. 668.

[7] McLaren, II, 917; *per* Lord Watson *loc. cit.*

[8] *Ewing* v. *Glasgow Commissioners of Police* (1839) McL. & Rob. 847, 860, *per* Lord Cottenham L.C. See also, Ersk. IV, 1, 17; *Robertson* v. *Eskdale Road Trustees* (1886) 24 S.L.R. 24. *Cf. Grahame* v. *Magistrates of Kirkcaldy* (1882) 9 R.(H.L.) 91, 93, *per* Lord Watson.

[9] *Mitchell* v. *Burness* (1878) 5 R. 954, 959, *per* Lord Deas; *Cobb* v. *Cobb's Trs.* (1894) 21 R. 638, 640, *per* Lord Stormonth-Darling; *McCaig* v. *University of Glasgow,* 1907 S.C. 231, 244, *per* Lord Kyllachy; *Aitken's Trs.* v. *Aitken,* 1927 S.C. 374, 387, *per* Lord Ashmore. But see *Camille and Henry Dreyfus Foundation Incorporated* v. *Inland Revenue,* 1955 S.L.T. 335, 337, *per* Lord Normand.

[10] *Murdoch* v. *Mags. of Glasgow* (1827) 6 S. 186.

[11] *Magistrates of Dundee* v. *Morris* (1858) 3 Macq. 134; 20 D.(H.L.) 9; (1861) 23 D. 493. For a criticism, see McLaren, II, 920.

purpose was " an intelligible and tangible object of public utility." [12] A direction to trustees to devote the income of a fund to the education of orphans was held to convey the fee not to the beneficiaries but to the trustees. There is nothing incompetent in the creation of a perpetual trust of this kind.[13] Bequests to provide and maintain a public park or a library or the like are valid even although no individual or defined class of individuals can qualify an enforceable interest.[14] So is one to re-build the Old Bridge of Ayr,[15] or to establish a " Humble Heroes Fund." [16] Where a testator directed his trustees to hold a property to be used as a sanatorium for the treatment by methods of " natural therapeutics " of persons in ill-health who were to pay maintenance charges, two judges doubted whether the purposes were public and the third (Lord Mackay) opined that the trust was private.[17]

In *Glentanar* v. *Scottish Industrial Musical Association* [18] a silver shield was given to an association to be held in trust by them for the purpose of presentation in each year to the winner of a competition. There was a diversity of judicial opinion as to the nature of the trust. Lord Ormidale thought that it did not fall precisely into the category of a public trust. Lord Hunter thought it partook " to some extent, at all events, of the nature of a public trust." Lord Anderson considered it to be " more akin to a private trust than to a public trust in the proper sense of that term "; he said:

> " There are no funds which have to be administered for public ends. In such a case the matter of the personnel of the trustees is of importance. Here the only patrimonial interest involved is the annual possession of a corporeal moveable which does not produce any revenue. The only interest which the beneficiaries—the juvenile brass bands—have is to be assured that the contests for the shield will be conducted under fair conditions."

It is not easy to follow this argument. The trust would clearly appear to be a public one. The court was probably influenced by its desire to overcome a procedural difficulty in a matter of small value.

Public benefit

An object is for the public benefit if it is one, not immoral or contrary to public order, which a certain section of opinion may regard as of public benefit.[19] The opinion of the community affected by the proposals is

---

[12] *Ness* v. *Mills's Trs.*, 1923 S.C. 344.
[13] *Craig's Trs.* v. *Hunter*, 1956 S.L.T. (Notes) 15.
[14] *Per* Lord Patrick, *Davidson's Trs.* v. *Arnott*, 1951 S.C. 42, 61.
[15] *Burgh of Ayr* v. *Shaw* (1904) 12 S.L.T. 126.
[16] *Donaldson's Trs.* v. *H.M. Advocate*, 1938 S.L.T. 106. See also *Jowett's Trs.* v. *Jowett's Heirs*, 1952 S.L.T. 131 (" Homes for men totally disabled by war service.").
[17] *Tait's J.F.* v. *Lillie*, 1940 S.C. 534.
[18] 1925 S.C. 226.
[19] *Sutherland's Tr.* v. *Verschoyle*, 1968 S.L.T. 43.

relevant.[20] It is not sufficient that there is an indirect benefit conferred upon a section of the public—

" Every trust which is created for the purpose of spending money upon anything—irrespective altogether of the nature of the purpose—must incidentally benefit somebody, such as servants, workmen, professional men, and the like, and none the less that they give value for the money which they receive—value, that is to say, in the shape of services rendered or skill employed. But in the ordinary use of language such persons are not described as beneficiaries of the trust, or as persons for whom the heritage is held by the trustees." [21]

Public policy

An object can be contrary to public policy without being illegal in the sense of being contrary to any express rule of the common law or contrary to any statute. A direction is against public policy if it involves a complete waste of money or has as its only motive the gratifying of the testator's vanity.[22] Directions to lay the testator's estate waste and keep it so, or to throw money into the sea or to hold monthly funeral services in the testator's memory would be clearly contrary to public policy.[23]

The McCaig cases

The case-law on public benefit is confused. Some cases have been decided on the ground that there was no divestiture of the testator's heirs; in others the trust has been held invalid because it was contrary to public policy. It seems that a purpose can benefit a section of the public but nevertheless be contrary to public policy. The first approach was adopted in the first *McCaig* case,[24] where the trustees were directed to use the income of the trust estate in perpetuity for the erection of statues and artistic towers to commemorate the testator and his relatives. It was held that, as no public benefit would result, and as the trustees could not go on building for ever, the testator's heir had not been excluded from her rights and could demand an immediate conveyance of the estate. The other approach was used in the second *McCaig* case [25] where the testatrix directed her trustees to convert a large circular tower into a private enclosure and erect therein bronze statues of her parents and their nine children. It was held that as the bequest would create no benefit for the public, and, as it was of an unreasonable, extravagant and useless character, it was contrary to public policy and thus invalid. In a later case,[26] Lord Sands said:

---

[20] *Aitken's Trs.* v. *Aitken*, 1927 S.C. 374.
[21] *Per* Lord Stormonth-Darling, *McCaig* v. *University of Glasgow*, 1907 S.C. 231, 245. See also p. 240, *per* L.J.-C. Macdonald, p. 243, *per* Lord Kyllachy.
[22] *McCaig's Trs.* v. *Kirk-Session of U.F. Church of Lismore*, 1915 S.C. 426, 434, *per* Lord Salvesen, p. 438, *per* Lord Guthrie.
[23] *McCaig* v. *University of Glasgow*, 1907 S.C. 231, 242, *per* Lord Kyllachy.
[24] *McCaig* v. *University of Glasgow*, 1907 S.C. 231.
[25] *McCaig's Trs.* v. *Kirk-Session of U.F. Church of Lismore*, 1915 S.C. 426.
[26] *Aitken's Trs.* v. *Aitken*, 1927 S.C. 374, 381, *per* Lord Sands.

" The difference between the rules applied in the two *McCaig* cases is dialectical, and, in my view, devoid of substance. In the first case the Court affirmed: ' This bequest confers no benefit upon anybody, therefore it is ineffectual to oust the heir.' In the second case they affirmed: ' This bequest confers no benefit upon anybody, accordingly it is unreasonable and wasteful, and therefore it fails as being contrary to public policy.' There might be substance in the discrimination between the two cases if it were possible to figure a bequest which could confer no conceivable benefit, direct or indirect, upon any person or class of persons, but which was nevertheless reasonable and not wasteful. Counsel were unable, however, to suggest any such testamentary direction except one, to erect a suitable sepulchral memorial to the deceased; but that is a special case, and the direction would be just as good against the heir as against any other party. I ventured to suggest a bequest for the benefit of certain animals; but it has been held that such a provision may be beneficial to the community as encouraging kindness. Accordingly, I take the law applicable to the present case as based upon the *McCaig* cases to be that, if testamentary directions are unreasonable as conferring neither a patrimonial benefit upon anybody nor a benefit upon the public or any section thereof, the directions are invalid."

Lord Russell conveniently summarised the results of the cases on this subject as follows:

" Invalidity was held to arise in respect of: I. The dedication of testamentary estate to an object which either (a) created no beneficial interest in any person sufficient to exclude heirs and executors, or (b) had no utility, public or private, or (c) gave to no one a title to enforce it.

II. The dedication of testamentary estate to an object where the means provided for effecting the object were demonstrably ineffective for that purpose.

III. The dedication of testamentary estate to an object which was manifestly extravagant, wasteful, or irrational to a degree which brings it within the concept of ' contrary to public policy '—as, for example, a purpose whose only use was to perpetuate at great cost and in an absurd manner the idiosyncrasies of an eccentric testator." [27]

Memorials

Monuments to commemorate historical events and memorials to historical personages or even local celebrities may have an educational value and therefore are of public benefit [28] but elaborate monuments to which the public do not have access are not.[29] It is, however, accepted

---

[27] *Campbell Smith's Trs.* v. *Scott*, 1944 S.L.T. 198, 200.
[28] *Campbell Smith's Trs.* v. *Scott*, 1944 S.L.T. 198.
[29] *McCaig, supra*, p. 244, *McCaig's Trs., supra*, p. 432.

that a direction to provide and maintain " on a customary and rational scale," a burial place for a testator or a monument in memory of the testator or his relatives is valid.[30]

" The law has always made a concession to the natural and human sentiments of ordinary people who desire that there should be some memorial of themselves, or who desire that some act of piety which they have performed during their lives should be continued after their death. That is a concession or indulgence shown by the law, but it is conditioned by the consideration that the bequest should not be extravagant to the point of caprice." [31]

What is " rational " is a question of circumstances and degree and depends on, *inter alia*, any other provision made for commemoration, the place selected in relation to the persons commemorated, the method of commemoration and the possible extent of the cost.[32] A direction to apply the income of a fund of £1,000 in perpetuity for the purpose of putting flowers on the grave of the testatrix and her mother was held to be so extravagant that no effect could be given to it.[33] A bequest by the same testatrix for providing a bi-weekly mass for the testatrix and her mother was held valid but the ground of judgment was that the bequest was a general charitable gift for a religious purpose.[34]

The provision of sepulchral memorials may be regarded as an exception to the general rule grounded on public sentiment or custom [35] or it can be argued that it is of public benefit that the reasonable wishes of the testator should not be disregarded even though it may be impossible to qualify any other interest in the carrying out of his wishes—" To discourage regard to such pious sentiments towards the dead may perhaps be considered as detrimental to the moral interests of the living." [36] It becomes clear, however, that such provisions are true exceptions to the general principle if a third approach to the problem is adopted—that of the enforcement of the performance of the trust purposes. The general principle is that the test of the efficacy of a trust is to inquire whether there is anyone who can enforce its performance.[37]

Anyone interested in the carrying out of the directions is entitled to

---

[30] *McCaig, supra,* p. 244, *per* Lord Kyllachy; *McCaig's Trs.,* p. 433, *per* Lord Salvesen, p. 436, *per* Lord Guthrie. See also *Moncrief* v. *Monipenny* (1713) Mor. 3945; *MacKintosh's J.F.* v. *Lord Advocate,* 1935 S.C. 406.

[31] *Lindsay's Exor.* v. *Forsyth,* 1940 S.C. 568, 571, *per* L.J.-C. Aitchison.

[32] *McCaig's Trs., supra,* p. 436, *per* Lord Guthrie. See also *MacKintosh's J.F.* v. *Lord Advocate,* 1935 S.C. 406.

[33] *Lindsay's Exor.* v. *Forsyth,* 1940 S.C. 568.

[34] See *Att.-Gen.* v. *Delaney* (1875) I.R. 10 C.L. 104; *O'Hanlon* v. *Logue* [1906] 1 I.R. 247; *Re Caus, Lindeboom* v. *Camille* [1934] Ch. 162.

[35] *Per* Lord Salvesen *loc. cit.,* Lord Guthrie *loc. cit.; Lindsay's Exor.* v. *Forsyth, supra,* p. 576, *per* Lord Wark. As to trusts for animals, see Lewin, 18; Underhill, 119; *Flockhart's Trs.* v. *Bourlet,* 1934 S.N. 23.

[36] *Aitken's Trs.* v. *Aitken, supra,* p. 381, *per* Lord Sands.

[37] *McCaig* v. *University of Glasgow,* 1907 S.C. 231, 244, *per* Lord Kyllachy, p. 246, *per* Lord Stormonth-Darling, p. 247, *per* Lord Low; *McCaig's Trs., supra,* p. 432, *per* Lord Salvesen; *Aitken's Trs.* v. *Aitken, supra,* p. 387, *per* Lord Ashmore. But see *Davidson's Trs.* v. *Arnott,* 1951 S.C. 42, 61, *per* Lord Patrick.

enforce due fulfilment of the trust and when the trust is for purposes of public benefit the Lord Advocate can intervene. It would seem that in the case of a trust to establish sepulchral memorials there is no one who could enforce it but it is nevertheless a valid trust.[38]

Selection of objects

Most of the difficulties relating to public trusts have arisen where the testator has not specified the objects of the trust with precision and has merely designated a class of objects among which a selection has to be made by his trustees or executors.

> " By the law of Scotland, as by that of England, a testator can defeat the claim of those entitled by law in the absence of a valid will to succeed to the beneficial interest in his estate only if he has made a complete disposition of that beneficial interest. He cannot leave it to another person to make such a disposition for him unless he has passed the beneficial interest to that person to dispose of as his own." [39]

There is, however, a relaxation of this fundamental principle. If the testator designates with sufficient precision a class of persons or objects to be benefited he may delegate to his trustees, or to other persons,[40] the selection of individual persons or objects within the defined class.

The classical statement of the law is the dictum of Lord Chancellor Lyndhurst in *Crichton* v. *Grierson* [41]:

> " A party may, in the disposition of his property, select particular classes of individuals and objects, and then give to some particular individual a power, after his death, of appropriating the property, or applying any part of his property, to any particular individuals among that class whom that person may select and describe in his will."

The testator must point out some class of objects. A bequest of residue to be disposed of as the trustees shall think proper or at the discretion of the trustees is ineffectual.[42]

There are three conditions which must be satisfied for a bequest of this kind to be valid. These conditions relate to the appointment

---

[38] This seems to be the position in England—*Re Dean* (1889) 41 Ch.D. 552, 557, *per* North J.; Underhill, 118–119.

[39] *Turnbull's Trs.* v. *Lord Advocate*, 1918 S.C.(H.L.) 88, 91, *per* Viscount Haldane. See also *Chichester Diocesan Fund and Board of Finance (Incorp.)* v. *Simpson* [1944] A.C. 341, 349, *per* Lord Macmillan; *Denny's Trs.* v. *Dumbarton Magistrates*, 1945 S.C. 147, 152, *per* L.J.-C. Cooper.

[40] *Laurie* v. *Brown*, 1911, 1 S.L.T. 84; *Bannerman's Trs.* v. *Bannerman*, 1915 S.C. 398 (Lord Skerrington discusses in his opinion the distinction between fiduciary and proprietary powers of appointment); *Paterson's Trs.* v. *Finlay*, 1918 S.C. 713.

[41] (1828) 3 W. & S. 329, 338.

[42] *Sutherland's Trs.* v. *Sutherland's Tr.* (1893) 20 R. 925; *Shaw's Trs.* (1893) 1 S.L.T. 308; *Wilson's Trs.* (1894) 1 S.L.T. 548; *McGregor's Trs.* v. *Bosomworth* (1896) 33 S.L.R. 364; *Anderson* v. *Smoke* (1898) 25 R. 493; *Dodds* v. *McBain*, 1933 S.N. 16; *Dunlop's Trs.* v. *Farquharson*, 1955 S.L.T. (Notes) 79.

of trustees, the powers of the trustees and the description of the class of objects.

The appointment of trustees

The first condition is that there is an appointment of trustees or executors [43] who have to make the selection. If there is no such appointment the bequest falls.

In the first case [44] in which this question arose, *Robbie's J.F.* v. *Macrae*,[45] two executors-nominate had been given a discretionary power of selection but had died before the fund was distributed. It was held that the selection could not be made by a judicial factor because the exercise of the power through a factor was not within the powers and duties of the court. A distinction was drawn between a discretion to select objects of the bequest and a discretion to vary the income of a named beneficiary.[46] Lord McLaren, who delivered the opinion of the court, said [47]:

" If it appears plainly that a testator did not mean to confine the selection of objects to persons nominated by himself, but only to take measures for ensuring that the selection of objects of his charity should be entrusted to competent persons, possessed of the necessary local knowledge, I do not say that it would not be within the powers of the Court to supply a vacancy in such a trust."

His lordship then pointed to the distinction between trustees appointed by the court, who administer the trust on their own responsibility and who are liable to be called to account by the heirs, and a judicial factor who is the agent of the court and responsible only for carrying out the instructions of the court.

This observation, which appears to be at variance with the earlier part of the opinion, was explained in a later decision to be a reference to cases in which the bequest was not to charitable purposes generally but to charities of a particular nature and in a particular locality or in which the testator had defined the objects of his bounty but the appointment of trustees and the approval of a scheme of administration had become necessary to give effect to his wishes.[48] On this principle, it was held in another case that, where the nominated trustees had predeceased the testatrix, trustees appointed by the court could exercise a power of allocation among specified charities.[49]

---

[43] As to executors, see *Allan's Exor.* v. *Allan*, 1908 S.C. 807, 812, *per* Lord Kinnear.
[44] In *Low's Exors.* (1873) 11 M. 744, a bequest to " charities in Glasgow " unaccompanied by an appointment was held void from uncertainty but neither the report of the argument nor the opinion of the court discloses the *ratio* of the decision.
[45] (1893) 20 R. 358. Followed in *Goudie* v. *Forbes* (1904) 12 S.L.T. 377.
[46] As in *Allan* v. *Mackay* (1869) 8 M. 139; *Simson* (1883) 10 R. 540. See *Leith's J.F.* v. *Leith*, 1957 S.C. 307.
[47] p. 362.
[48] *Angus's Exrx.* v. *Batchan's Trs.*, 1949 S.C. 335, 364, *per* Lord Jamieson. See also the qualification made by L.P. Cooper in the second last sentence of his observation quoted on p. 176, *infra*.
[49] *Grieve's Trs.* v. *Wilson* (1904) 12 S.L.T. 347. See also *Hill's Trs.* v. *Thomson* (1874) 2 R. 68, 69, *per* L.J.-C. Moncreiff.

An attempt to distinguish *Robbie's J.F.* v. *Macrae* was made in *Woodard's J.F.* v. *Woodard's Exrx.*,[50] where on a construction of the will it was held that there was no *delectus personae* by the testator and a judicial factor could therefore distribute the estate to charities. Reliance was placed upon the provisions of the Trusts (Scotland) Act 1921, by virtue of which a judicial factor is a trustee within the meaning of the Act.

The general question arose sharply again in *Angus's Exrx.* v. *Batchan's Trs.*[51] where the will directed: " All money after paying, please give to charities." There were no instructions as to the selection of the charities and no trustee or executor was appointed. A majority of a Court of Seven Judges overruled *Woodard's Judicial Factor* and held that the bequest was void from uncertainty.

> " A bequest to charities in the abstract is only capable of being given effect to at the hands of one or more persons empowered, expressly or by implication, to select the particular objects to be benefited. It is from the power of selection so given that ' charities ' have come to be regarded as a sufficiently designated class and such a bequest derives its validity." [52] " No encroachment has ever yet been tolerated on the basic requirement that a testator must make his own will, and that, when he makes it by designating a class and a person to choose within that class, the designation of both must be his own act, express or plainly implied. To allow a testator to confine himself to designating the class, while deliberately leaving the choice of the individual beneficiaries to anyone who may anyhow acquire a title to administer the estate, is, in my opinion, to authorise that testator to delegate the power to test—at least in a case such as the present in which the class is so vast and amorphous as to include every institution and object capable of being covered by the comprehensive term ' charity.' A *mortis causa* declaration of charitable benevolence is not a will." [53]

Assumed trustees

In *Robbie's Judicial Factor*, Lord McLaren stated [54] that where there was a power of assumption in the will the assumed trustees could exercise the power of selection because " in principle their position is not distinguishable from that of the original trustees." In *Shedden's Trustee* v. *Dykes* [55] it was decided that trustees assumed under the statutory power of assumption [56] could exercise the wide discretionary power of selection of objects contained in a settlement which was silent on the subject of assumption. The terms of the settlement indicated that there was no

---

[50] 1926 S.C. 534. Followed in *Macrae's J.F.* v. *Martin*, 1937 S.L.T. 209.
[51] 1949 S.C. 335.
[52] *Per* Lord Jamieson, p. 365.
[53] *Per* L.P. Cooper, p. 367.
[54] p. 362.
[55] 1914 S.C. 106.
[56] Trusts (Scotland) Act 1861, s. 1, now Trusts (Scotland) Act 1921, s. 3.

delectus personae. It was said that the testatrix must be presumed to have known of the statutory power of assumption.

" The precise effect of the statute is equivalent to an inscription in the deed of a power of assumption of new trustees. The trustee thus assumed derives his authority from the testatrix, and from the moment of his appointment is, I think, clothed with all the powers, discretionary and otherwise, confided to the original trustee, unless the testatrix has clearly indicated a contrary intention." [57]

Shedden's Tr. was followed in the Outer House in *McCredie's Trs.* v. *McCredie*.[58] In *Miln's Trs.* v. *Drachenhauer*,[59] Lord Blackburn further extended the doctrine by holding that trustees appointed by the court could exercise a power to select beneficiaries under a bequest for " charitable or benevolent purposes." The ground of the decision was that there was no indication of *delectus personae* and it was difficult to draw a line between trustees assumed under a statutory power and trustees nominated by the court.

In *Angus's Exrx.*, Lord Jamieson thought that *Shedden's Tr.* could be supported on the ground stated by Lord McLaren in *Robbie's Judicial Factor*, namely, that an assumed trustee derives authority from the testator. Lord Jamieson thought it immaterial that the will contained no express power of assumption because the testator must be presumed to have been aware of the statutory power to assume and also aware that, especially where the trust purposes could not be fully carried out until the lapse of a considerable period, it might become necessary to exercise the power. The assumed trustees could therefore exercise a power of selection unless the power is expressly or by implication conferred on the nominated trustees personally. There is still in such circumstances *delectus personae* because " the testator must be taken as assuming that, if necessity arises, the trustees whom he has nominated will assume persons on whom reliance may be placed to carry out his wishes." Lord Cooper also was prepared to let *Shedden's Tr.* stand. Lord Mackay would have been prepared to overrule it " to keep the doctrine pure " and he opined that the decision could not validate, *inter alia*, a case where no discretion is specially conveyed to the trustees. This limitation was not made by Lord Jamieson or Lord Cooper and it is difficult to reconcile it with *Wordie's Trs.* v. *Wordie* [60] in which the House of Lords held that a power of selection could be impliedly conferred.

From *Shedden's Tr.* and *Woodard's J.F.* can be gathered the following factors which indicate the absence of *delectus personae*—(a) that the testator had referred to the nominated trustees as " my said trustees " but when referring to his trustees generally had used " my trustees "; (b) that as the testator had given the nominated trustees all the immunities and

[57] *Per* L.P. Strathclyde, p. 110.
[58] 1915, 1 S.L.T. 410.
[59] 1921, 1 S.L.T. 152.
[60] 1916 S.C.(H.L.) 126.

privileges of gratuitous trustees, he must have contemplated that they might resign; (c) that, because the bequest to charities was in a destination-over, the testator must have regarded as remote the probability of the charities taking any benefit at all; (d) that the trust was likely be of long duration and there might be no distribution to charities during the lives of the nominated trustees [61]; (e) that there was no indication in the will that the testator had communicated to the nominated trustees any wishes he had as to the charities to be selected; (f) that none of the nominated trustees was a *sine quo non*. The width of the powers of selection was not regarded as an indication that only the nominated trustees could act. Lord President Strathclyde opined that in the absence of contrary indications in the will it was to be assumed that there was no *delectus personae*.[62] In *Laurie* v. *Brown* [63] there was a *delectus personae*. The selection was to be made by the testator's brothers who, it seems, were not expressly appointed trustees or executors.

Executor-dative

Lord Mackintosh, whose decision as Lord Ordinary in *Angus's Exrx*. was reversed, held that although the discretionary power could in his view be exercised by a judicial factor it could not be exercised by an executor-dative because his duties were purely executorial and he was not a trustee within the meaning of the Trusts (Scotland) Act 1921. By virtue of section 20 of the Succession (Scotland) Act 1964, an executor-dative has now been placed substantially in the position of a trustee under the 1921 Act, but, with respect to the exercise of a discretionary power of selection, he cannot be in a better position than a trustee appointed by the court. He lacks, as do the trustees appointed by the court and the judicial factor, the link with the testator desiderated by Lords Jamieson and Mackay in *Angus's Exrx*.[64]

Summary

The effect of the decisions can be summarised as follows:

(1) Where the testator has not created a trust, and has not nominated executors, the bequest is void.[65]

(2) Where a trust created by the testator has lapsed, the power of selection cannot be exercised by a judicial factor.[66]

(3) Where a trust created by the testator has lapsed, trustees appointed by the court cannot exercise a power to make a selection from charitable purposes generally but they may be able to exercise a power to select from

---

[61] In *Robbie's J.F.*, on the other hand, the will contemplated immediate distribution of the estate and the administration was executorial in character.

[62] *Shedden's Tr.*, p. 111.

[63] 1911, 1 S.L.T. 84. See also *Landale's Tr.* v. *Nicol*, 1918, 2 S.L.T. 10; *Paterson's Trs.* v. *Finlay*, 1918 S.C. 713.

[64] p. 366; p. 359.

[65] *Angus's Exrx*. v. *Batchan*; *Shedden's Tr.* and *Woodard's J.F.* were cases of lapsed trusts and, as Lord Cooper emphasised in his opinion in *Angus's Exrx.*, the wills left by the testators were good wills. Power of appointment cases, of course, stand apart. (See p. 174, n. 40, *supra*.)

[66] *Angus's Exrx.* v. *Batchan*; *Vollar's J.F.* v. *Boyd*, 1952 S.L.T. (Notes) 84.

among objects more specifically described by reference to their nature or locality.[67]

(4) An executor-dative is in this respect in the same position as a trustee appointed by the court.

(5) If the power of selection is not made personal to the nominated trustees, it may be exercised by trustees assumed either under an express power in the will or under the statutory power of assumption.[68]

The merit of *Angus's Exrx.* is that it draws a clear line. It is arguable, however, that the line has not been drawn at the right point. Lord McLaren in *Robbie's J.F.* and the judges of the majority in *Angus's Exrx.* justified their decision by the principle of *delectus personae*. It is difficult enough to reconcile this with the acceptance of *ex officio* trustees. It is even more difficult to reconcile it with the extension to assumed trustees— " the delegation to persons named to choose other persons to choose the objects of the testator's testamentary intention." [69]   Lord Cooper [70] recognised that the line was not being drawn at the logical point but argued that it was better that it should be drawn somewhere than that the whole doctrine should be abrogated. The answer to this was given with his usual felicity of expression by Lord Justice-Clerk Thomson in his dissenting opinion [71]: " We were pressed with the metaphor of the *facilis descensus*. Why should one be less happy in Avernus than clinging unhappily to the edges of the pit ? But why not change the metaphor and let us rejoice that another Everest has been conquered ? " Lord Thomson also argued cogently [72]:

> " Why should a testator who does not desire to make a selection from a class himself, either because he has not the time or the knowledge or the confidence in his own judgment, not be content to leave the selection to someone appointed by the Supreme Court of the country to which he belongs ? "

Yet another consideration is that in most cases one would agree with the sentiment of Lord Justice-Clerk Alness; " I feel certain that the testator would have preferred that the intention should be carried out by successors to his trustees rather than that his charitable designs should be frustrated, and that the residue of his estate should fall into intestacy." [73]

Power of selection

The second condition is that the trustees are given a power of selection. The power can be conferred by implication. It is enough if the testator has appointed trustees to carry out all the purposes of his will with all the powers which are necessary to enable them to do so. This was estab-

---

[67] *Angus's Exrx.* v. *Batchan*, p. 364, *per* Lord Jamieson.
[68] *Shedden's Tr., supra; Angus's Exrx. supra*, p. 366, *per* Lord Jamieson.
[69] *Shedden's Tr.*, p. 112, *per* Lord Johnston.
[70] *Angus's Exrx., supra*, p. 368.
[71] 1949 S.C., 350.
[72] *Ibid.* p. 344.
[73] *Woodard's J.F., supra*, p. 537.

lished at an early date in *Dundas* v. *Dundas* [74] and was later affirmed by the House of Lords. [75]

The omission of a time limit within which the estate must be distributed does not affect the validity of the bequest. [76]

Where the trustees were to apply to charitable purposes so much of the revenue of the estate " as they may deem expedient " it was held that, as there was no uncertainty as to the objects of the testatrix's bounty, the direction was valid and the question of the disposal of any undistributed income could be dealt with when it arose. [77]

Description of the class: " charity "

It is essential that the class to be benefited should be defined with sufficient precision and not described in terms so vague and indeterminate that the trustees are afforded no effective guidance as to the ambit of their power of selection. The degree of precision required is a question of considerable difficulty which in the present century has given rise to a " long and lengthening series of decisions." [78]

From an early date it was established that if the class of objects to be benefited is described as " charitable " then it is described with sufficient precision. " In the eye of the law charity has this saving grace, that it is held to be by itself denominative of a distinct class." [79] " Unhappily it is only too easy to recognise the aged and the poor, who are always with us." [80] Where the testamentary instruction was " Any money left after paying all expenses, I wish may be laid out on charities. I leave and bequeath to A.B. the sum of £200 sterling with power to see this will executed," it was held that the provision was valid and imported a discretionary power to make a selection *secundum arbitrium boni viri*. [81] Lord President Hope justified the decision thus:

> " Nothing is more common than to see one person place a sum of money at another's discretion, merely directing him to apply it to charitable purposes. A man, for instance, sends a donation to the minister of a parish to be distributed by him. And if this be frequently done, *inter vivos*, I cannot see why it may not equally be done, by the intervention of a Will."

The meaning of " charity "

English law has attached a wide and somewhat artificial meaning to the words " charity " and " charitable " derived from the enumeration of objects in the Statute of Elizabeth I [82]; it extends to purposes of general

---

[74] (1837) 15 S. 427.
[75] *Wordie's Trs.* v. *Wordie*, 1916 S.C.(H.L.) 126. See also *Flockhart's Trs.* v. *Bourlet*, 1934 S.N. 23.
[76] *Dick's Trs.* v. *Dick*, 1907 S.C. 953; 1908 S.C.(H.L.) 27.
[77] *Macduff* v. *Spence's Trs.*, 1909 S.C. 178.
[78] *Per* L.J.-C. Cooper, *Denny's Trs.* v. *Dumbarton Mags.*, 1945 S.C. 147, 152.
[79] *Turnbull's Trs.* v. *Lord Advocate*, 1918 S.C.(H.L.) 88, 95, *per* Lord Shaw of Dunfermline.
[80] *Per* Lord Macnaghten, *Weir* v. *Crum Brown*, 1908 S.C.(H.L.) 3, 5.
[81] *Dundas* v. *Dundas* (1837) 15 S. 427.
[82] 43 Eliz. 1, c. 4.

benevolence and public utility and covers, as it has been put, everything from the Royal Society to a Home for Lost Dogs.

"'Charity' in its legal sense comprises four principal divisions: trusts for the relief of poverty; trusts for the advancement of education; trusts for the advancement of religion; and trusts for other purposes beneficial to the community, not falling under any of the preceding heads. The trusts last referred to are not the less charitable in the eye of the law, because incidentally they benefit the rich as well as the poor, as indeed, every charity that deserves the name must do either directly or indirectly." [83]

It was declared at an early stage that this technical sense had no application in Scotland.[84] In *Baird's Trs.* v. *Lord Advocate* [85] the Court of Session, in interpreting "charitable purposes" in the Income Tax Act 1842, declared that the ordinary familiar and popular meaning of charity was the relief of poverty—the giving of alms or providing for the relief of persons from physical privations or suffering arising from poverty—and that it did not extend to the wider activities embraced by the English meaning.[86]

This decision was disapproved by the House of Lords in *Commissioners for Special Purposes of Income Tax* v. *Pemsel* [87] in interpreting the same words in the same statute. It was held that in a United Kingdom taxing statute "charity" and "charitable" must be construed according to the technical meaning given to them in English law—"The necessary effect of *Pemsel's* case . . . is that the English law of charity has, for income tax purposes and for them alone, to be regarded as part of the law of Scotland and not as a foreign law." [88]

Lord Watson opined that at least in the legislative language of Scotland —for example, in the Act 1633, c. 6. Against "the inverting of pious donations"— "charitable" had a comprehensive meaning almost co-extensive with that given to it by the English Courts of Chancery. He added that the reported decisions of the Court of Session threw little light on the question because

"ever since its institution the Court has exercised plenary juris-

---

[83] *Per* Lord Macnaghten, *Commissioners for Special Purposes of Income Tax* v. *Pemsel* [1891] A.C. 531, 583. Lord Macnaghten's fourth division is misleading because not every object of public general utility is charitable; a purpose beneficial to the community must also be within the spirit and intendment of the preamble to the Statute of Elizabeth before it is a charity (*Williams' Trs.* v. *Inland Revenue* [1947] A.C. 447, and the authorities there cited).

[84] *Miller* v. *Black's Trs.* (1837) 2 S. & McL. 866, 891, *per* Lord Brougham.

[85] (1888) 15 R. 682.

[86] This decision was not altogether consistent with the prior case-law. In *McLean* v. *Henderson's Trs.* (1880) 7 R. 601, L.J.-C. Moncreiff referred to a bequest for the advancement of the science of phrenology as a charitable bequest. [87] [1891] A.C. 531.

[88] *Inland Revenue* v. *Glasgow Police Athletic Association*, 1953 S.C.(H.L.) 13, 21, *per* Lord Normand. As to taxing statutes, see also *Jackson's Trs.* v. *Inland Revenue*, 1926 S.C. 579; *Scottish Flying Club* v. *Inland Revenue*, 1935 S.C. 817; *Trustees for the Roll of Voluntary Workers* v. *Inland Revenue*, 1942 S.C. 47. An error seems to have been made in the Race Relations Act 1968, s. 9.

diction over the administration of all trusts, whether public or private, irrespective of the particular purposes to which the estate or income of the trust may be appropriated, and there has consequently been no room for those numerous questions, as to a trust being charitable or not, which have arisen in England under the statute of Elizabeth." [89]

In *Blair* v. *Duncan* [90] Lord Halsbury said *obiter* that *Baird's Trs.* was still an authoritative exposition of the meaning of " charitable " where it occurs in a Scottish deed. This *dictum* was quoted by Lord Moncreiff in his dissenting opinion in *Grimond* [91] which was expressly approved by the House of Lords,[92] although, again, the meaning of " charitable " was not necessary for the decision of the case. This " partial and surely inadvertent exhumation " [93] of *Baird's Trs.* was not well received in the Scottish courts. In *Allan's Exor.* v. *Allan* [94] Lord Kinnear, with the concurrence of Lords Dunedin and McLaren, expressed disapproval of *Baird's Trs.* and a similar view was contained in the opinion of the court in *Anderson's Trs.* v. *Scott*.[95] Although Lord Mackay later accepted the authority of *Baird's Trs.*[96] with some fervour, in *Wink's Exors.* v. *Tallent* [97] Lord President Cooper and Lord Keith rejected the interpretation in strong terms. Lord Cooper ventured the hope " that *Baird's Trustees* will in all time coming be allowed to repose undisturbed in the grave to which it has so often been consigned." [98] It was made equally clear in the same case that " charity " in Scots law, except for the limited purpose of United Kingdom taxing statutes, does not bear the technical meaning ascribed to it by English law; this opinion was reinforced by *Inland Revenue* v. *Glasgow Police Athletic Association*.[99]

It seems, therefore, that in the general law of Scotland, " charity " bears a meaning wider than the relief of poverty and extends to certain purposes of general public utility but this connotation is not circumscribed by the technicalities of the English law.[1]

" *Pemsel's* case is an authority in income tax law on the meaning of ' charitable ' in an income tax statute, but it has never been held to apply to the construction or administration of a Scottish testamentary trust. Nor can I hold that the narrow interpretation put on the word ' charitable ' in the case of *Baird's Trustees* has ever been adopted into the law of charitable trusts." [2]

[89] p. 560.
[90] (1901) 4 F.(H.L.) 1, 2.
[91] *Macintyre* v. *Grimond's Trs.* (1904) 6 F. 285, 294.
[92] (1905) 7 F.(H.L.) 90.
[93] *Per* L.P. Cooper, *Wink's Exrs.* v. *Tallent,* 1947 S.C. 470, 478.
[94] 1908 S.C. 807.
[95] 1914 S.C. 942, 954.
[96] *Reid's Trs.* v. *Cattanach's Trs.,* 1929 S.C. 727, 730.
[97] *Supra.*
[98] p. 478.
[99] 1952 S.C. 102; 1953 S.C.(H.L.) 13.
[1] *Anderson's Trs.* v. *Scott,* 1914 S.C. 942, 954.
[2] *Wink's Exors.* v. *Tallent, supra,* p. 482, *per* Lord Keith.

Educational purposes and religious purposes provided that they are sufficiently specified are charitable purposes.[3] The question of whether the Scottish sense of " charitable " is wider than the English one has not been fully explored. Lord Low thought that the English sense was wider than the Scottish [4]; Lord McLaren thought the two meanings were substantially the same.[5]

The benignant construction

It has often been said that the law of Scotland is more liberal in the interpretation of bequests for charitable purposes than other bequests.[6] " Now, there is no better rule than that a benignant construction will be placed upon charitable bequests." [7] " The Courts have, I think, as matter of historical fact, reflected more or less, consciously or unconsciously, the bias which disposes everyone favourably towards charity." [8] There is, however, a considerable divergence of judicial view as to the form in which this benevolence is expressed.

In the first place, there is obviously a distinction between the favour to be shown in determining whether a class of objects is sufficiently defined and the favour shown by providing machinery to effectuate a paramount charitable intention which is imperfectly described or unworkable or has failed.[9] The distinction has, however, not always been observed.[10]

Lord Cooper took a narrow view of the favour shown to charities— " That favour receives full and sufficient effect in the acceptance of a bare reference to charity or charities as a sufficient identification of a definite class." [11]

Most judges have adopted a more liberal approach. If the purposes are charitable

> " the Courts will disregard a merely subordinate deficiency in particular expression of intention to dispose of the entire beneficial interest to a class, and will even themselves, by making a scheme of some kind, give effect to the general intention that the estate should be disposed of for charitable purposes." [12]

For example, if the bequest is to benefit a particular class of poor persons then, as the relief of poverty is undoubtedly charitable, the court should

---

[3] *Allan's Exor.* v. *Allan,* 1908 S.C. 807, 814, *per* Lord Kinnear; *Chalmers' Trs.* v. *Turriff School Board,* 1917 S.C. 676; *Craig's Trs.* v. *Hunter,* 1956 S.L.T. (Notes) 15.
[4] *Macintyre* v. *Grimond's Trs.* (1904) 6 F. 285, 288.
[5] *Hay's Trs.* v. *Baillie,* 1908 S.C. 1224, 1232. See also *Inland Revenue* v. *Glasgow Musical Festival Association,* 1926 S.C. 920, 928, *per* Lord Sands.
[6] *Per* Lord Gifford, *Hill* v. *Burns* (1826) 2 W. & S. 80, 86; *Magistrates of Dundee* v. *Morris* (1858) 3 Macq. 134, 155, *per* L.C. Chelmsford; *McLeish's Trs.* v. *McLeish* (1841) 3 D. 914, 924, *per* Lord Moncreiff.
[7] *Per* Lord Loreburn L.C., *Weir* v. *Crum Brown,* 1908 S.C.(H.L.) 3, 4.
[8] *Per* Lord Robertson, *Blair* v. *Duncan* (1901) 4 F.(H.L.) 1, 6. See also p. 2, *per* Lord Shand.
[9] *Angus's Exrx.* v. *Batchan's Trs.,* 1949 S.C. 335, 367; *Magistrates of Dundee* v. *Morris* (1858) 3 Macq. 134, 166, *per* Lord Cranworth; *Macduff* v. *Spence's Trs.,* 1909 S.C. 178, 180, *per* Lord Johnston.
[10] See *Allan's Exor.* v. *Allan,* 1908 S.C. 807, 817.
[11] *Angus's Exrx.* v. *Batchan, supra,* p. 367.
[12] *Turnbull's Trs.* v. *Lord Advocate,* 1918 S.C.(H.L.) 88, 92, *per* Viscount Haldane.

take a benignant view in considering whether the particular class within
the general category of the poor is sufficiently definite.[13]

The most liberal view of all is that of Lord Chelmsford: " When it is
said that charitable bequests must receive a benignant construction, the
meaning is, that when the bequest is capable of two constructions, one
which would make it void, and the other which would render it effectual,
the latter must be adopted." [14]

This dictum cannot be taken literally, and must be considered in its
context. The bequest under consideration was in these words: " The
whole of the balance of my property I leave to poor of this presbytery to be
divided—I mean the interest—by the sessions of the several churches, but
to be paid to all Christians, except Roman Catholics." It was thus clearly
stamped as charitable.

In another decision of the same type where the expression was " institutions of a benevolent or charitable nature " it was said that a construction which called in aid the " almost impossible " case of a class of
benevolent institutions which were not charitable to render the bequest
invalid was not the benignant construction which was appropriate to
charitable bequests.[15] If the question is whether the bequest is charitable,
the argument that because it is charitable it should be given a benignant
construction involves a *petitio principii*.[16]

It has been suggested in England that there is no reason to give a
benignant construction to a bequest of a legacy to charity if the residue
itself is given to charity because this would be to favour one charity
against another.[17]

Words other than " charity "

The bulk of the case-law has been concerned with words other than
" charity " and " charitable." Usually, the question posed has been
whether the words used are sufficiently definite and precise to describe one
of the " particular classes " referred to in Lord Lyndhurst's dictum.[18]
Some judges, however, have created confusion by treating the issue as
whether the purposes expressed by the testator are " charitable purposes." [19] This is wrong. Lord Lyndhurst's proposition is not restricted
to charitable trusts.[20]

---

[13] *Murdoch's Trs.* v. *Weir*, 1907 S.C. 185; *sub nom. Weir* v.*Crum Brown*, 1908 S.C.(H.L.) 3.
[14] *Bruce* v. *Presbytery of Deer* (1867) 5 M.(H.L.) 20.
[15] *Hay's Trs.* v. *Baillie*, 1908 S.C. 1224, 1233, *per* Lord McLaren.
[16] *Caldwell's Trs.* v. *Caldwell*, 1920 S.C. 700, 701, *per* Lord Skerrington. See also *Mackin-
      non's Trs.* v. *Mackinnon*, 1909 S.C. 1041, 1043, *per* Lord Johnston.
[17] *Re Goldschmidt decd.* [1957] 1 W.L.R. 524.
[18] Cited at p. 174, *supra*.
[19] *McLean* v. *Henderson's Trs.* (1880) 7 R. 601, 611, L.J.-C. Moncreiff; *Harper's Trs.* v.
      Jacobs, 1929 S.C. 345; *Rintoul's Trs.* v. *Rintoul*, 1949 S.C. 297, 300, *per* L.J.-C. Thomson.
      It has, of course, to be remembered that " charity " means more than the relief of poverty
      and that educational or religious purposes can be charitable (see p. 191 and *Renouf's Trs.*
      v. *Haining*, 1919 S.C. 497, 509, *per* Lord Guthrie).
[20] *Allan's Exor.* v. *Allan*, 1908 S.C. 807, 814, *per* Lord Kinnear; *Turnbull's Trs.* v. *Lord
      Advocate*, 1917 S.C. 591, 598, *per* Lord Dundas; *Renouf's Trs.* v. *Haining*, 1919 S.C. 497,
      505, *per* Lord Dundas.

Principles of construction

The width of the general purpose does not matter so long as it is possible to say in a reasonable sense what lies within it.[21] There are bound to be borderline cases: " The fact is that whenever any one wishes to describe a class of people otherwise than by referring to their age, sex, birthplace, or similar facts capable of precise ascertainment, the language used must of necessity be general, and there must always be numerous cases on the border line." [22] It is no answer to an objection on the ground of vagueness to aver that the trustees would have no difficulty in applying the bequest to purposes which answer the description and which would have met with the truster's approval.[23] Where the trust has been administered for a long period before its validity is challenged, there is a greater onus on the heirs to demonstrate the invalidity beyond doubt [24]; but on the other hand, the interpretation adopted by the testator's original trustees is not conclusive.[25] It has been said that the proper approach is to try, if possible, to avoid intestacy and to construe the will *ut res valeat potius quam pereat*.[26] The principles governing the construction of provisions of a charitable or quasi-charitable character in *mortis causa* deeds do not apply to the interpretation of contractual obligations.[27]

Authority

Previous decisions are of value only in so far as they show the principle which determines the validity of the bequest. The true meaning of the testator must be ascertained in each case by reading the language of the will and giving it its natural meaning without reference to what prior judgments have held to be the meaning of other testators using different language.[28]

It has been said that the laws of Scotland and of England with respect to charities are not dissimilar.[29] English authorities are relevant [30] and are frequently cited but the different historical and doctrinal background of the English law of charitable trusts must be kept in view.[31] In particular, the Mortmain Act, the rule against perpetuities and the Statute of Elizabeth with the technical meaning of " charity " stemming therefrom operate to produce markedly different results. The Scottish courts have reached conclusions differing from earlier English decisions with regard to the

---

21 *Harper's Trs.* v. *Jacobs*, 1929 S.C. 345, 350, *per* Lord Sands.
22 *Per* Lord Loreburn, L.C., *Weir* v. *Crum Brown, supra*, p. 4.
23 *Macintyre* v. *Grimond's Trs.* (1904) 6 F. 285, 294, *per* Lord Moncreiff.
24 *Brough* v. *Brough's Trs.*, 1950 S.L.T. 117.
25 *Macrae's J.F.* v. *Martin*, 1937 S.L.T. 209.
26 *Edgar's Trs.* v. *Cassells*, 1922 S.C. 395.
27 *Denny's Trs.* v. *Dumbarton Mags.*, 1945 S.C. 147.
28 *Hay's Trs.* v. *Baillie*, 1908 S.C. 1224, 1234, *per* Lord Kinnear.
29 *Magistrates of Dundee* v. *Morris* (1858) 19 D. 918; 3 Macq. 134, 154, *per* Lord Chelmsford L.C. In *Crichton* v. *Grierson* (1828) 3 W. & S. 329, 343, Lord Lyndhurst L.C., suggested that the law of England was more strict than Scots law as to charitable purposes.
30 *Hay's Trs.* v. *Baillie*, 1908 S.C. 1224; *Rintoul's Trs.* v. *Rintoul*, 1949 S.C. 297, 302, *per* Lord Mackay. Cf. *Reid's Trs.* v. *Cattanach's Trs.*, 1929 S.C. 727, 743, *per* L.J.-C. Alness.
31 *Hay's Trs.* v. *Baillie*, 1908 S.C. 1224, 1236, *per* Lord Dundas; *Wink's Exrs.* v. *Tallent*, 1947 S.C. 470, 476, *per* L.P. Cooper. Cf. *Williams' Trs.* v. *Inland Revenue* [1947] A.C. 447, 456, *per* Lord Simonds.

validity of bequests for religious purposes [32] and with regard to the exegetical construction of " or." [33]

Lord Loreburn's test

A test of the validity of a trust which was applied in a number of cases was propounded by Lord Chancellor Loreburn: " All that can be required is that the description of the class to be benefited shall be sufficiently certain to enable men of common sense to carry out the expressed wishes of the testator." [34]

In later decisions, this dictum was subjected to some criticism. It was said that it was not an absolute rule for the solution of all doubts in the construction of wills in such cases [35]; and Lord Dundas, who delivered a number of illuminating opinions on this branch of law, said:

" I do not think it is enough to say that a sensible body of trustees might be able to administer this trust in a sensible fashion. I apprehend that we must go further and say that the testator has sufficiently indicated or described the class of objects or institutions from which the trustees are to select beneficiaries." [36]

It was also pointed out that it did not accord with the pronouncement of Sir William Grant M.R. in *Morice* v. *Bishop of Durham* [37]: " The question is, not, whether he (the trustee) may not apply it (the bequest) upon purposes strictly charitable, but whether he is bound so to apply it."

As Lord Atkinson demonstrated by a careful analysis in his speech in *Turnbull's Trs.* v. *Lord Advocate*,[38] Lord Chancellor Loreburn's dictum cannot be divorced from its context. In *Weir* v. *Crum Brown* the bequest was in favour of indigents and was therefore clearly charitable. The *dictum* was delivered with reference to a further condition that the recipients must have " shewn practical sympathy in the pursuits of science." The effect of a qualification placed upon a gift which is already clearly charitable is obviously different from the question of whether a gift is charitable.

The relief of poverty

Even if the word " charity " is not used, a bequest for the relief of

---

[32] *Grimond* v. *Grimond's Trs.* (1905) 7 F.(H.L.) 90; *White* v. *White* [1893] 2 Ch. 41, C.A.

[33] *Wink's Exrs.* v. *Tallent, supra; Chichester Diocesan Fund and Board of Finance (Incorp.)* v. *Simpson* [1944] A.C. 341.

[34] *Weir* v. *Crum Brown*, 1908 S.C.(H.L.) 3, 4. Applied in *Allan's Exor.* v. *Allan*, 1908 S.C. 807; *McPhee's Trs.* v. *McPhee*, 1912 S.C. 75; *Wordie's Trs.* v. *Wordie*, 1915 S.C. 310; *Bannerman's Trs.* v. *Bannerman*, 1915 S.C. 398, 403, *per* Lord Ormidale; *Craig's Trs.* v. *Hunter*, 1956 S.L.T. (Notes) 15. Approved by Lord Kinnear in *Wordie's Trs.* v. *Wordie*, 1916 S.C.(H.L.) 126, 129.

[35] *Turnbull's Trs.* v. *Lord Advocate*, 1918 S.C.(H.L.) 88, 95, *per* Lord Atkinson.

[36] *Symmers's Trs.* v. *Symmers*, 1918 S.C. 337, 342. See also *Salvesen's Trs.* v. *Wye*, 1954 S.L.T. 299, 303, *per* L.P. Cooper.

[37] (1804) 9 Ves. 399. See also *Mackinnon's Trs.* v. *Mackinnon*, 1909 S.C. 1041, 1044, *per* Lord Johnston.

[38] 1918 S.C.(H.L.) 88, 94. *Cf. Reid's Trs.* v. *Cattanach's Trs.*, 1929 S.C. 727, 744, *per* L.J.-C. Alness.

poverty in some form will be valid. Thus, the " reclamation, maintenance, education, and upbringing of destitute children " is the object of a charitable bequest [39] as is " a female society for the relief of indigent widows or those who have made an unfortunate marriage." [40] A bequest " to the Bursary Fund of the University of Aberdeen to help in the education of poor and struggling youths of merit " was held to be valid,[41] and a bequest " to poor of this presbytery to be divided—I mean the interest—by the sessions of the several churches, but to be paid to all Christians, except Roman Catholics " was held not to be void from uncertainty.[42]

The use of the adjective " poor " is not always sufficient. Where the class was " any poor relations, friends or acquaintances of mine," it was held that, while " relations " and " friends " were sufficiently definite, " acquaintances " was not.[43] Lord President Cooper said [44] it was a private trust because the " dominant determining factor " was that the beneficiaries were connected with the testator and not that they were a section of the poor.

Formerly, a question of construction could arise as to whether a bequest for " the poor of the parish " was limited in its application to persons who were in receipt of parochial relief.[45]

Further qualifications

If the objects of the bequest as a whole are described as charitable the vagueness of any further description of objects within the class does not affect the validity of the bequest. So where the bequest was for " charitable institutions or societies which exist for the benefit of women and children requiring aid or assistance of whatever nature, but said institutions and societies to be under the management of Protestants," it was accepted that the actual selection might be a matter of difficulty but this did not affect the validity of the provision.[46]

Similarly, a direction to institute " a scheme for the relief of indigent bachelors and widowers, of whatever religious denomination or belief they may be, who have shewn practical sympathy, either as amateurs or professionals, in the pursuits of science in any of its branches, whose lives have been characterised by sobriety, morality, and industry, and who are not less than fifty-five years of age, or of aiding any scheme which now exists or may be instituted by others for that purpose " was held valid.[47]

The vagueness introduced by a local restriction did not affect the

[39] *Forrest's Trs.* v. *Alexander*, 1925 S.N. 80.
[40] *Emslie's Trs.* v. *Aberdeen Female Society for the Relief of Aged and Indigent Women*, 1949 S.L.T.(Notes) 61.
[41] *Milne's Exors.* v. *Aberdeen University Court* (1905) 7 F. 642.
[42] *Bruce* v. *Presbytery of Deer* (1867) 5 M.(H.L.) 20.
[43] *Salvesen's Trs.* v. *Wye*, 1954 S.C. 440.
[44] p. 447.
[45] See, for example, *Parish Council of Kinloss* v. *Morgan*, 1908 S.C. 192, and the decisions there cited.
[46] *Wordie's Trs.* v. *Wordie*, 1916 S.C.(H.L.) 126.
[47] *Weir* v. *Crum Brown*, 1908 S.C.(H.L.) 3. In any event, the House of Lords thought that the qualifications were not too uncertain.

validity of a bequest to " charitable institutions connected with the county of Lanark." [48] Where the expression was " various charities, Nursing Associations, Infirmaries, etc.," it was held that *et cetera* must be construed on the *ejusdem generis* principle and therefore referred only to charitable objects.[49] " The words were *et cetera* not *et alia quaecunque*." [50]

The addition of the words " or for any similar purpose " to a list of specified objects which were clearly charitable did not render the bequest void.[51] Similarly, where the bequest was for " the maintenance of a nurse available for the sick poor of Galston or for some analogous purpose in such manner as my trustees may decide and direct " it was held that the words " or for some analogous purpose " merely provided for an alternative method of helping the sick poor of Galston and the whole bequest was valid.[52]

The provision of a fund as " a permanent source of charity " was held to be a valid charitable bequest.[53]

A charity must be distinguished from a friendly society or mutual association in which the members contribute money for the purpose of distributing it among present and future members or their wives or children. Even if the right to benefit is contingent upon need it still rests on contract and the association is not a charity. The court has no power to give directions as to the application of the funds of a friendly society.[54]

Synonyms of "charitable ": " philanthropic "

" Philanthropic " so far resembles " charitable " that it can easily be understood as exegetical of " charitable " so a bequest to " charitable or philanthropic institutions " is valid.[55] Lord Dunedin opined that the words were not synonymous and, as he also said that " philanthropic " was close to " benevolent " (" the only difference between the two words seems to be that the one is derived from the Latin and the other from the Greek, and that while the one rather directs your attention to a state of mind in general, the other directs your attention to a state of mind with regard to your fellow-men "), it appears that " philanthropic " standing alone would not be sufficient for validity. In the same case, the Lord Ordinary (Johnston) thought that it was a word of wider and more indefinite meaning than " charitable." [56]

" Benevolent "

" Benevolent " is probably too uncertain.[57] It has been suggested that

---

[48]　*Cleland's Trs.* v. *Cleland*, 1907 S.C. 591.

[49]　*Milne's Trs.* v. *Davidson*, 1956 S.L.T. 34.　　　　　　[50]　*Per* Lord Patrick, p. 35.

[51]　*Forrest's Trs.* v. *Alexander*, 1925 S.N. 80. *Cf. Campbell's Trs.* v. *Edinburgh Royal Infirmary*, 1932 S.N. 10.

[52]　*Forrest's Trs.* v. *Forrest's Trs.*, 1959 S.L.T.(Notes) 24.

[53]　*Anderson* v. *Gow* (1901) 9 S.L.T. 174.

[54]　*Mitchell* v. *Burness* (1878) 5 R. 954; *Smith* v. *Lord Advocate* (1899) 1 F. 741; *Lord Provost of Edinburgh*, 1956 S.L.T. (Notes) 31. (See *infra*, p. 218.)

[55]　*Mackinnon's Trs.* v. *Mackinnon*, 1909 S.C. 1041.

[56]　p. 1042. See also *Re Macduff* [1896] 2 Ch. 451, and *Re Eades* [1920] 2 Ch. 353.

[57]　*Hay's Trs.* v. *Baillie*, 1908 S.C. 1224.

although all charitable institutions are benevolent, it might be possible to conceive of a benevolent institution which was not charitable. In *Caldwell's Trs.* v. *Caldwell*,[58] Lord Skerrington opined that " benevolent " in its natural and primary sense had not the same meaning as " charitable " and was too vague and indefinite. " To increase the virtue and happiness of persons who are already virtuous and happy is essentially benevolent, but is not necessarily charitable." He thought that, although there was English authority to the contrary,[59] anything which is charitable is also benevolent. " Christian and benevolent " has been upheld in the Outer House on the view that it fell within Lord Watson's description of " pious and godly " uses.[60]

" Useful "

In *Cobb* v. *Cobb's Trs.*[61] opinions were reserved as to whether " useful " was too vague.

" Deserving "

" Deserving institutions " [62] and " deserving agencies " [63] have been held to be too vague:

> " If such a disposition was tolerated, it would enable a testator to appoint another, not, indeed, in a broad sense, to make his will for him, but, according to his individual vagary and idiosyncrasy, to make pecuniary benefactions to such an infinite variety of institutions that it would be impossible to conceive a greater breach of the doctrine which has been laid down in so many familiar cases, that the objects of testamentary bounty must be indicated with a reasonable degree of certainty and precision. " [64]

On the other hand, Lord President Dunedin, sitting in the Outer House, held that " the deserving working people in the parish of Annan " was sufficiently specific.[65]

" Public "

" Public " is too vague. " Public purposes " is much wider than charitable purposes and might cover such non-charitable objects as a payment to the election fund of a political party or a subscription towards

---

[58] 1920 S.C. 700, 702.
[59] *Re Best* [1904] 2 Ch. 354. The English court was clearly referring to " charity " in the wide sense because the example given was a trust for the propagation of the sacred writings of Joanna Southcote.
[60] *Macray* v. *Macray*, 1910, 2 S.L.T. 74. See also *Pomphrey's Trs.* v. *Royal Naval Benevolent Trust*, 1967 S.L.T. 61.
[61] (1894) 21 R. 638.
[62] *Campbell's Trs.* v. *Campbell*, 1921 S.C.(H.L.) 12.
[63] *Symmers's Trs.* v. *Symmers*, 1918 S.C. 337. See also *Fraser's Trs.*, 1947 S.L.T.(Notes) 56 (" any deserving Schemes which my Trustees may consider necessary "—invalid).
[64] *Campbell's Trs.* v. *Campbell*, *supra*, p. 13, *per* Lord Birkenhead L.C.
[65] *Laurie* v. *Brown*, 1911, 1 S.L.T. 84. But see *Brown's Trs.* v. *McIntosh* (1905) 13 S.L.T. 72 (" deserving individuals of good character ").

raising a Yeomanry regiment.[66] " Public institution " is also too vague.[67]

" Public " is a word of " singular ambiguity." [68] " Does ' public ' mean (a) open to the public, or (b) supported by the public, or (c) beneficial to the public ? " [69]

> " The foundation of political clubs, schools of art, a zoological garden, or an astronomical observatory in Lesmahagow, along with a thousand other things in connexion with that parish or its neighbourhood, might, in the trustees' opinion, be excellent, but the bequest is void by reason of the uncertainty as to which of them, or which class of them, the truster meant to favour." [70]

" Social "
" Social " is too wide—

> " I have no doubt at all that the word ' social ' is a word of very wide connotation indeed, and its use raises much the same sort of problems as the use of the word ' public.' A bequest to social institutions seems to me to leave the trustees with practically a free choice of institution." [71]

However, the promotion of any local plan for " the social or ethical amelioration " of the people of Kilsyth that commended itself to the kirk session was held to be sufficiently certain in view of the restriction as to locality and the constitution of the administering body.[72]

" Patriotic purposes " is too vague.[73]

Religious purposes
Although " religious purposes " may be more restricted than " public purposes " and are regarded as charitable purposes in English law, the words have been held in Scotland to be too vague because they do not impose a limit as to locality or creed.[74] However, a bequest for a specified purpose can be valid even although it falls within the general category of religious purposes. So a bequest to " foreign missions in India, China, Africa, and South America, or any other in the foreign field suitable " was effectual because in the mouth of a Scottish testator the expression has the clear meaning of " enterprises conducted by some Church or association in this country for the propagation of the Gospel in foreign parts." [75]

---

[66] *Blair* v. *Duncan* (1901) 4 F.(H.L.) 1, 6, *per* Lord Robertson.
[67] *Reid's Trs.* v. *Cattanach's Trs.*, 1929 S.C. 727.
[68] *Reid's Trs.* v. *Cattanach's Trs.*, 1929 S.C. 727, 738, *per* Lord Ormidale.
[69] *Ibid.* p. 742, *per* Lord Anderson.
[70] *Turnbull's Trs.* v. *Lord Advocate, supra,* p. 96, *per* Lord Shaw of Dunfermline.
[71] *Rintoul's Trs.* v. *Rintoul,* 1949 S.C. 297, 300, *per* L.J.-C. Thomson.
[72] *Lord Advocate* v. *Anton,* 1909, 2 S.L.T. 326.
[73] *Att.-Gen.* v. *National Provincial Bank* [1924] A.C. 262.
[74] *Grimond* v. *Grimond's Trs.* (1905) 7 F.(H.L.) 90. The opinion of Lord Moncreiff in the Court of Session (*Macintyre* v. *Grimond's Trs.* (1904) 6 F. 285, 291) was adopted by the House of Lords. See also *Shaw's Trs.* v. *Esson's Trs.* (1905) 8 F. 52; *Brown's Trs.* v. *McIntosh* (1905) 13 S.L.T. 72; *McConochie's Trs.* v. *McConochie,* 1909 S.C. 1046; *Shaw's Trs.* v. *Weir,* 1927 S.L.T. 641; *Macrae's J.F.* v. *Martin,* 1937 S.L.T. 209.
[75] *Allan's Exor.* v. *Allan,* 1908 S.C. 807.

" Missionary operations " is sufficiently definite although it would include home and Jewish missions and is thus wider than foreign missions.[76] Similarly, " for such missionary purposes as they in their sole discretion may determine, keeping in view specially missions in Africa " was upheld in the Outer House.[77] " The most needful Schemes of the Church of Scotland (now United), Edinburgh " was considered to be sufficient identification.[78]

In *Bannerman's Trs.* v. *Bannerman* [79] " religious or charitable Institutions conducted according to Protestant principles " was held not to be too uncertain because the qualifying words made the class sufficiently precise and definite to enable a selection to be made. A direction to pay " the salaries of two native missionaries chosen of them, for preaching the Gospel of Jesus Christ my Lord among the heathen " was held valid.[80]

In *Brough* v. *Brough's Trs.*,[81] Lord Strachan decided with some hesitation that " other religious work " was sufficiently precise in its context in that the earlier provisions of the will included specific bequests to the deacons' court of a Free Church and to the National Bible Society, the establishment of bursaries expressly limited to Protestants and the appointment as *ex officio* trustees of ministers of the principal Scottish Churches and it could therefore be inferred that by " religious " the testator referred to the Protestant branch of the Christian religion.

A bequest for the promotion of free thought is void from uncertainty.[82]

Educational purposes

Educational purposes are favoured by the court.[83] " Educational " is sufficiently precise.[84] An " educational scheme for the poor " was held valid.[85] The " upbringing, training and educating orphans of Scottish parentage exclusively with the object of dissociating them from their surroundings which would throw them back a generation (as happened in our own case) and making them worthy citizens or eminent citizens if further help can effect it " was held to be a valid purpose.[86] Where the

---

[76] *Brough* v. *Brough's Trs.*, 1950 S.L.T. 117.
[77] *Adam's Trs.* v. *Adam* (1908) 16 S.L.T. 144.
[78] *Fraser's Trs.*, 1947 S.L.T.(Notes) 56. See also *National Bible Society of Scotland* v. *Church of Scotland*, 1946 S.L.T.(Notes) 26 (" Protestant evangelistic work in British South Africa Rhodesia ").
[79] 1915 S.C. 398 (a power of disposal case). See also *Macray* v. *Macray*, 1910, 2 S.L.T. 74 (" Christian and benevolent purposes ").
[80] *Renouf's Trs.* v. *Haining*, 1919 S.C. 497. [81] 1950 S.L.T. 117.
[82] *Hardie* v. *Morison* (1899) 7 S.L.T. 42.
[83] As Dykes (p. 231) points out, eleemosynary and educational elements tend to be merged and confused but a purely educational purpose is nevertheless favoured.
[84] *Brough* v. *Brough's Trs.*, 1950 S.L.T. 117. See also *Robbie's J.F.* v. *Macrae* (1893) 20 R. 358, 361, *per* Lord McLaren; *Commissioners for Special Purposes of Income Tax* v. *Pemsel* [1891] A.C. 531, 561, *per* Lord Watson; *Brown's Trs.* v. *Young* (1898) 6 S.L.T. 32; *Harper's Trs.* v. *Jacobs*, 1929 S.C. 345, 348, *per* L.P. Clyde, p. 350, *per* Lord Blackburn; *Reid's Trs.* v. *Cattanach's Trs.*, 1929 S.C. 727, 737, *per* Lord Ormidale, p. 744, *per* L.J.-C. Alness. Cf. *McConochie's Trs.* v. *McConochie*, 1909 S.C. 1046, 1049, *per* Lord Ardwall; *Reid's Trs.* v. *Cattanach's Trs.*, *supra*, p. 730, *per* Lord Mackay.
[85] *Chalmers' Trs.* v. *Turriff School Board*, 1917 S.C. 676.
[86] *Craig's Trs.* v. *Hunter*, 1956 S.L.T.(Notes) 15.

trustees were directed to erect statues and artistic towers and the testator declared that his wish was to encourage young artists by the offering of prizes for the best plans of the proposed statues and towers, it was held that the bequest was not educational.[87]

In *Harper's Trs.* v. *Jacobs*,[88] it was held that while a bequest for the advancement of a specified art or science was valid a direction to trustees to apply the residue of a small estate " for the advancement of art, science, or literature in the burgh of Castle-Douglas " was too vague.

> " I think myself that a general bequest for the advancement of science is too vague to receive effect. Science covers any and every branch of knowledge systematised or formulated with reference to general laws or principles. A bequest for the advancement of objects so general as art and literature would seem to me to be at least as vague and uncertain as a bequest for the advancement of science." [89]

Lord Sands thought that the result might have been different if the trust had been well-endowed. The decision with regard to " science " is surprising in view of the remarks of Lords Macnaghten and Robertson in *Weir* v. *Crum Brown*. The latter said [90]: " The word ' science ' embraces a wide but perfectly ascertainable range of subjects." In an earlier case, " the advancement and diffusion of the science of phrenology " was held to be sufficiently precise.[91]

A bequest for the benefit of " Gaelic-speaking persons " was upheld, presumably because there was a later reference in the will to bursaries, schools and lodgings.[92]

The noun

In the decisions, some significance has been attached to the nouns used in the testator's direction. A direction to give to certain " purposes " is much more vague than one to give to " institutions " of a certain character.[93] " Agencies " is perhaps more vague than " institutions." [94] " Work " is wider than " institutions " but not wider than " purposes " or " objects." [95] " Objects " is more vague than " societies or institutions." [96] The use of " schemes " does not introduce such an element of vagueness as to make a bequest void.[97]

[87] *McCaig* v. *University of Glasgow*, 1907 S.C. 231.
[88] 1929 S.C. 345.
[89] *Per* L.P. Clyde, p. 348.
[90] 1908 S.C.(H.L.) 3, p. 5.
[91] *McLean* v. *Henderson's Trs.*, (1880) 7 R. 601.
[92] *Macdonell's Trs.* v. *Macdonell's Trs.*, 1911, 2 S.L.T. 170.
[93] *McConochie's Trs.* v. *McConochie*, 1909 S.C. 1046; *Edgar's Trs.* v. *Cassells*, 1922 S.C. 395, 401, *per* Lord Salvesen; *Reid's Trs.* v. *Cattanach's Trs.*, 1929 S.C. 727. *Cf. Macrae's J.F.* v. *Martin*, 1937 S.L.T. 209.
[94] *Campbell's Trs.* v. *Campbell*, 1920 S.C. 297, 300, *per* Lord Dundas. *Cf.* Lord Birkenhead L.C., 1921 S.C.(H.L.) 12, 13.
[95] *Brough* v. *Brough's Trs.*, 1950 S.L.T. 117.
[96] *Wink's Exors.* v. *Tallent*, 1947 S.C. 470, 478, *per* L.P. Cooper.
[97] *Brough* v. *Brough's Trs.*, *supra.* See also *Dick's Trs.* v. *Dick*, 1907 S.C. 953; *Chalmers' Trs.* v. *Turriff School Board*, 1917 S.C. 676.

Where the trustees were directed to distribute the residue " amongst such charitable institutions, persons, or objects, as they may think desirable " it was held that " charitable persons " fell to be construed as meaning persons in need of charity and the bequest was, in the particular circumstances, valid.[98]

Qualifications

If the terms of the initial gift are sufficiently precise, the validity of the bequest is not as a rule affected by directions subsequently added.

Where the codicil to a will contained a bequest for " charitable or benevolent purposes " and in a subsequent testamentary writing there was a wish expressed that a portion of the fund should go to missionary associations and a recommendation that a certain association should be included in the selection, it was argued that this showed that the testator interpreted " benevolent " as including " religious purposes " which made the bequest void from uncertainty. This contention was rejected on the ground that a bequest for " religious purposes " was void because of its vagueness and the terms of the subsequent writing here did not mention religion and made the original bequest more specific and not less.[99]

Locality

A question frequently arises as to whether the vagueness of a purpose is cured by the addition of some kind of geographical limitation. For example, in *Turnbull's Trs.* v. *Lord Advocate*,[1] it was argued that a bequest " for such public, benevolent, or charitable purposes in connection with the parish of Lesmahagow or the neighbourhood " was saved by the local limitation. The general principle is that " the vagueness of the purpose is not cured by the specification of the locality to be benefited." [2]

However, in *Shaw's Trs.* v. *Esson's Trs.*,[3] Lord Salvesen, in an opinion later approved in the House of Lords as a " lucid and valuable judgment," [4] propounded the doctrine that if the bequest is to *existing* organisations in a relatively small area the class becomes identified and ascertainable but the local limit cannot save the bequest where the trustees have power to " institute " objects or purposes. In *McGrouther's Trs.* v. *Lord Advocate*,[5] Lord Mackenzie held that a bequest for " religious or charitable purposes in connection with Rio Janeiro " was ineffectual because it could not be construed as confined to existing organisations within a defined area.

[98] *Cameron's Trs.* v. *Mackenzie*, 1915 S.C. 313.
[99] *Miln's Trs.* v. *Drachenhauer*, 1921, 1 S.L.T. 152.
[1] 1918 S.C.(H.L.) 88.
[2] *Ibid.* p. 90, *per* Lord Finlay L.C. See also *Symmers's Trs.* v. *Symmers*, 1918 S.C. 337; *Campbell's Trs.* v. *Campbell*, 1920 S.C. 297, 301, *per* Lord Dundas (whose dissenting opinion was approved by the House of Lords (1921 S.C.(H.L.) 12)); *Harper's Trs.* v. *Jacobs*, 1929 S.C. 345; *Shaw's Trs.* v. *Weir*, 1927 S.L.T. 641.
[3] (1905) 8 F. 52. See also *Smellie's Trs.* v. *Glasgow Royal Infirmary* (1905) 13 S.L.T. 450; *Lord Advocate* v. *Anton*, 1909, 2 S.L.T. 326.
[4] Lord Finlay, L.C., *Turnbull's Trs.* v. *Lord Advocate*, 1918 S.C.(H.L.) 88, 90.
[5] (1908) 15 S.L.T. 652.

The doctrine was eventually approved by the House of Lords in *Turnbull's Trs.* v. *Lord Advocate* [6] in which Lord Chancellor Finlay said: " The addition of a local limit might well make a difference in favour of a bequest if the bequest was in favour of institutions within a certain area, the particular institution to be selected by the trustee." Lord Shaw of Dunfermline said:

"Local limitations do come into play and make the bequest effective if and when they provide the means of identifying the particular objects or institutions which the testator has meant to benefit. I am of opinion that the local connexion cannot limit the area of selection of purpose, unless the reference of the testator is to persons, societies, agencies, or institutions actually existing or projected to be established in a particular district." [7]

The doctrine must be taken to be established and has been applied on several occasions.[8]

" Secret trusts "

Words which are too vague are not saved by a subsequent reference to verbal communications made by the truster to the trustees, which might be said to constitute a " secret trust." A bequest " for behoof of sundry religious or benevolent institutions to be selected by him (the trustee), and regarding which he knows my mind, and therefore may be assured of my absolute approval thereof " was held void.[9]

Collocations of adjectives

Most of the substantial volume of twentieth-century case-law relates to the effect of collocations of adjectives. Most of the problems have arisen where the adjectives are connected by " or."

The primary function of the word " or " is to co-ordinate two or more words between which there is an alternative; that is the disjunctive meaning. The word has, however, a secondary use in which it connects, not distinct and contrasted classes of objects, but convertible and equivalent synonyms and is equivalent to " alias " or " otherwise called." " The House of Lords or the House of Commons " is an illustration of the disjunctive meaning; " the House of Lords or the Upper Chamber " of the exegetical or explanatory meaning.[10]

---

[6] *Supra*, p. 90. See also *McPhee's Trs.* v. *McPhee*, 1912 S.C. 75. [7] p. 96.
[8] *Caldwell's Trs.* v. *Caldwell*, 1920 S.C. 700, 703, *per* Lord Skerrington (the House of Lords decided the case on a different ground); *Edgar's Trs.* v. *Cassells*, 1922 S.C. 395—" benevolent, charitable and religious institutions in Glasgow and Greenock " (Lord Ormidale dissented on the ground that in no prior case where effect had been given to a local limitation was " religious " the sole qualification of the object); *Reid's Trs.* v. *Cattanach's Trs.*, 1929 S.C. 727 (Lords Ormidale (p. 738) and Anderson (p. 742) opined that Scotland might not be too wide an area for " public institutions." This does seem to be an extension of the doctrine.)
[9] *Shaw's Trs.* v. *Greenock Medical Aid Society*, 1930 S.L.T. 39. See also *Campbell's Trs.* v. *Edinburgh Royal Infirmary*, 1932 S.N. 10.
[10] *Chichester Diocesan Fund and Board of Finance (Incorp.)* v. *Simpson* [1944] A.C. 341, 349, *per* Viscount Simon L.C.

Where the disjunctive meaning is assigned to " or " and at least one of the adjectives is too vague the whole bequest falls. So where it was held that the phrase " for public, benevolent, or charitable purposes " was to be read as if it had been expressed as " for public purposes, or benevolent purposes, or charitable purposes " and that " public purposes " was too indefinite, the whole bequest was void.[11] The result is the same where the adjectives qualify different nouns connected by " or "—for example, " charitable institutions or deserving agencies." [12]

The authority for the proposition that if one alternative is vague the whole bequest falls seems to rest on *Blair* v. *Duncan*.[13] In the Court of Session, Lord Young said [14]:

> " Nor can I hold that a direction, to apply money to ' charitable purposes ' chosen by the trustee can be sustained if followed by words which extend his powers so that he may decline ' charitable purposes ' altogether, and choose any other he thinks proper, whether ' public ' or ' private '—or either exclusive of the other. To hold otherwise would be to hold that a testamentary trustee may be validly empowered to apply the testamentary funds to any purpose he thinks proper, charitable or not, provided only that it is public or private, and of course lawful."

Observations to a similar effect were made in the House of Lords.

The exegetical construction

On the other hand if " or " can be construed so that the other adjectives are exegetical of " charitable " the whole bequest is valid. So far as Scots law is concerned, the exegetical construction stems from *Hay's Trs.* v. *Baillie*.[15] There the bequest was to " societies or institutions of a benevolent or charitable nature," and it was held, on a construction of the will, that the testator had intended to use " benevolent " as exegetical of " charitable " and that the bequest was accordingly valid. There was some suggestion that, although all charitable institutions were benevolent, it might be possible to conceive of a benevolent institution which was not charitable. The decision was followed where the words were " charities or benevolent or beneficent institutions "; it was inferred that the testatrix had in mind only one class of objects which she had described by the three

---

11 *Turnbull's Trs.* v. *Lord Advocate*, 1918 S.C.(H.L.) 88. See also *Blair* v. *Duncan* (1901) 4 F.(H.L.) 1 (" charitable or public purposes "); *Shaw's Trs.* v. *Esson's Trs.* (1905) 8 F. 52 (" charitable, benevolent, or religious objects or purposes "); *Grimond* v. *Grimond's Trs.* (1905) 7 F.(H.L.) 90 (" charitable or religious institutions and societies "); *McGrouther's Trs.* v. *Lord Advocate* (1908) 15 S.L.T. 652 (" religious or charitable purposes "); *Campbell's Trs.* v. *Campbell*, 1921 S.C.(H.L.) 12 (" charitable or other deserving institutions "); *Rintoul's Trs.* v. *Rintoul*, 1949 S.C. 297 (" charitable or social institutions "); *Brown's Trs.* v. *McIntosh* (1905) 13 S.L.T. 72 (" religious, charitable, or educational institutions ").
12 *Reid's Trs.* v. *Cattanach's Trs.*, 1929 S.C. 727 (" Charitable, Educational or Benevolent Societies or public institutions "). See also *Symmers's Trs.* v. *Symmers*, 1918 S.C. 337.
13 (1900) 3 F. 274; (1901) 4 F.(H.L.) 1. *Playfair's Trs.* v. *Playfair* (1900) 2 F. 686, established the rule for private trusts.
14 p. 277.
15 1908 S.C. 1224.

epithets—charitable, benevolent and beneficent.[16] It was said that the use
of two substantives rather than one substantive qualified by two adjectives
did not distinguish the case from *Hay's Trs.* It was again emphasised that
each will must be interpreted by its own terms. The principle was again
applied where the words were " charitable or philanthropic institutions." [17]

The House of Lords, in the *Chichester* case,[18] rejected the exegetical
construction and held that " charitable or benevolent objects " was void
for uncertainty, because " charitable " had a technical meaning in English
law and " benevolent " could not be exegetical of that meaning. Lord
Macmillan seemed to regard with doubt the Scottish decisions based on
the exegetical interpretation.

The *Chichester* case and the doubt expressed by Lord Macmillan therein were used to challenge the authority of *Hay's Trs.* v. *Baillie* in *Wink's
Executors* v. *Tallent*,[19] where the expression used was " such Societies or
Institutions of a benevolent or charitable nature." The First Division
emphatically refused to reconsider the decision—" If there is one rule in
this branch of Scots law which can fairly be described as settled, it is the
rule in *Hay's Trustees*." [20] It was pointed out that the rule had been
formulated by judges of great eminence, had been adopted unquestioningly
by textbook writers and had regulated the disposal of many bequests in
settlements which had never come before the courts. Lord President
Cooper emphasised the difference between the English and the Scottish
law of charitable trusts and said:

> " With such a fundamentally distinct historical and doctrinal
> background it is impossible for a Scots lawyer and an English lawyer
> to approach the present problem of construction without entirely
> different predilections, and I have failed to understand why it should
> be supposed to be remarkable that the rule in *Hay's Trustees* should
> be good law in Scotland and not in England—still less why it should
> be supposed that the English solution is preferable to the Scottish, or
> that it is desirable that in this respect Scots law should now sink its
> identity in English law. It would be much more remarkable if two
> streams of thought, originating so far apart and travelling by such
> diverse channels, happened to coalesce."

Before " or " can be read as exegetical there must be substantial
identity between the two words which are in juxtaposition.[21] The use
cannot be exegetical if " or " is followed by " other " as in " charitable or
other deserving institutions." [22] Where the bequest was " for such public,

---

[16] *Paterson's Trs.* v. *Paterson*, 1909 S.C. 485.
[17] *Mackinnon's Trs.* v. *Mackinnon*, 1909 S.C. 1041. See also *Jackson's Trs.* v. *Inland Revenue*,
1926 S.C. 579.
[18] *Chichester Diocesan Fund and Board of Finance (Incorp.)* v. *Simpson* [1944] A.C. 341.
[19] 1947 S.C. 470.
[20] *Per* L.P. Cooper, p. 475.
[21] *Rintoul's Trs.* v. *Rintoul*, 1949 S.C. 297.
[22] *Campbell's Trs.* v. *Campbell*, 1921 S.C.(H.L.) 12. The judges of the majority in the Court

benevolent, or charitable purposes . . ." it was said that the commas after " public " and " benevolent " supported the disjunctive construction.[23] It is more open to adopt the exegetical construction where the vaguer word is followed by the word of more precise meaning—e.g. " benevolent or charitable." [24] It is permissible to use the will as its own lexicon to discover how the testator used the word " or " and the exegetical construction is supported if the will contains such expressions as " legacy or other bequest." [25]

Conjunctive " or "

It has been said that " or " can be given a third meaning in which it can be read as " and " but this can be done only where the testator has given some very clear indication in the will that he intended it to be used in that unusual sense.[26]

" And "

Where the adjectives are connected by " and " there are again two possible constructions—the conjunctive (or copulative) and the disjunctive (or distributive). The primary signification of " and " is the conjunctive—the expression refers to one class of objects to each member of which each of the adjectives applies. If the meaning is disjunctive, the expression refers to two or more classes to each of which only one of the adjectives applies.

> " Such a construction . . . is sometimes referred to as a disjunctive construction, and as involving the change of the word ' and ' into ' or.' This is a short and compendious way of expressing the result of the construction, but I doubt whether it indicates accurately the mental conception by which the result is reached. That conception is one, I think, which regards the word ' and ' as used conjunctively and by way of addition, for the purpose of enlarging the number of objects within the area of selection; and it does not appear to be a false mental conception, or one really at variance with the ordinary use of language, merely because it involves in the result that the qualifications for selection are alternative or disjunctive." [27]

of Session (1920 S.C. 297), whose decision was reversed, thought that the use of " other " favoured the validity of the bequest because the *ejusdem generis* principle could be applied. If, however, there is only one item specified, no *genus* is defined (*United Towns Electric Co. Ltd.* v. *Att.-Gen. for Newfoundland* [1939] 1 All E.R. 423, 428, *per* Lord Thankerton). In *Re Bennett* [1920] 1 Ch. 305, to which Lord Guthrie referred, there was a list of items. *A fortiori* a bequest in favour of " charitable or other institutions " failed (*Jaffrey's Trs.* v. *Lord Advocate* (1903) 11 S.L.T. 119).

[23] *Turnbull's Trs.* v. *Lord Advocate*, 1918 S.C.(H.L.) 88.
[24] *Chichester Diocesan Fund and Board of Finance* (*Incorp.*) v. *Simpson* [1944] A.C. 341.
[25] *Wink's Exors.* v. *Tallent*, 1947 S.C. 470, 478, *per* L.P. Cooper.
[26] *Rintoul's Trs.* v. *Rintoul*, 1949 S.C. 297, 300, *per* L.J.-C. Thomson. *Cf. Hay's Trs.* v. *Baillie*, 1908 S.C. 1224, 1225, *per* Lord Johnston; *Symmers's Trs.* v. *Symmers*, 1918 S.C. 337.
[27] *Re Eades* [1920] 2 Ch. 353, 356, *per* Sargant J. Adopted in *Edgar's Trs.* v. *Cassells*, 1922 S.C. 395.

The distinction is between " epithets creating conjunctive or cumulative classes of objects " and " epithets creating conjunctive or cumulative
qualifications for each object." The greater the number of qualifications,
the more probable is the construction multiplying the classes within the
area of selection and the less probable is the construction multiplying the
number of qualifications to be complied with and so diminishing the
number of objects within the area of selection.

In two early cases, bequests to " institutions for charitable and benevolent purposes " were held valid although the point does not appear to
have been discussed at length.[28] Where the expression was " useful,
benevolent, and charitable institutions " it was argued that the " and "
was disjunctive and not copulative and that " useful " was too vague. The
court held that the words " benevolent " and " charitable " were exegetical
of each other and " useful " qualified both.[29]

Where the testator directed his trustee to divide the residue of his
estate " amongst such educational, charitable, and religious purposes
within the city of Aberdeen as he shall select to be the recipients thereof "
it was held that the bequest was to three different classes and as one of
these was religious purposes the bequest was void because of uncertainty.[30] The use of the word " purposes " was taken to indicate that there
were three different classes of objects because, apparently, an institution
could be at the same time educational, charitable and religious, but a
purpose could not possess the three characteristics. Reliance was also
placed upon the words " divide " and " amongst " as indicating that the
trustee had to give a part of the fund to selected objects within each of the
three classes.

In *McPhee's Trs.* v. *McPhee*,[31] the words " religious and charitable
institutions " were held to refer *prima facie* to institutions of a religious and
charitable character. The argument that the use of " divide " compelled a
disjunctive interpretation of " and " was rejected.

In *Caldwell* v. *Caldwell*[32] the House of Lords declared that the conjunctive was the primary meaning.

" The judgments appealed from are based upon the view that
' charitable and benevolent ' really mean such charitable gifts as are
benevolent, and there is considerable authority, both in Scotland and
in England, to show, not only that such a construction is possible, but
also that, in the absence of words to the contrary, it is the one that

28 *Hill* v. *Burns* (1826) 2 W. & S. 80; *Miller* v. *Black's Trs.* (1837) 2 S. & M. 866.
29 *Cobb* v. *Cobb's Trs.* (1894) 21 R. 638 (" the authority of *Cobb* does not stand high in this
    department of the law "—Dykes, 228). See also *Re Sutton* (1885) 28 Ch.D. 464.
30 *McConochie's Trs.* v. *McConochie*, 1909 S.C. 1046. The *ratio* is discussed by Lord Dundas
    in *McPhee's Trs.* v. *McPhee*, 1912 S.C. 75, 78.
31 1912 S.C. 75. See also *Blair* v. *Duncan* (1901) 4 F.(H.L.) 1, 3, *per* Lord Davey; *Macintyre*
    v. *Grimond's Trs.* (1904) 6 F. 285, 291, *per* Lord Trayner; *Brown's Trs.* v. *Young* (1898) 6
    S.L.T. 32 (" charitable, religious, educational, and public institutions "); *Macray* v.
    Macray, 1910, 2 S.L.T. 74 (" Christian and benevolent purposes ").
32 1921 S.C.(H.L.) 82.

ought to be adopted." [33] "I see no reason why a word which has a perfectly plain meaning, and should ordinarily be read as signifying something conjoined with what has gone before, should have its meaning altered in order that a gift, which upon the face of it would be good, should be made bad by severing two things which the testator had himself joined together." [34]

In the Court of Session, it was argued that as " benevolent " has a wider meaning than " charitable," and as the testator must not be taken to have used mere verbiage, tautology must be avoided by reading " charitable and benevolent " disjunctively. [35] It was also suggested that as the bequest was to institutions " in Glasgow and Paisley " the fact that it was not argued that that " and " should be read conjunctively, indicated that the " and " between " charitable " and " benevolent " should be read disjunctively.

Where there were legacies to specified institutions in Glasgow and Greenock, of which most were charitable in character but some were religious, and the residue was to be divided among " other Benevolent, Charitable and Religious institutions in Glasgow and Greenock," it was held that the use of " other," when taken with the different types of specified institutions, compelled the court to give a distributive meaning to " and." [36]

Interpretation of directions

Once the validity of the trust has been established, a question may arise as to whether a particular object falls within the class specified by the testator. A payment to the trustees of a church for behoof of the " Minister's Salary Fund " was held to be within the scope of the expression " charitable uses." [37] The National Trust for Scotland was held to be a " charitable institution " but it is to be noted that the National Trust was mentioned in notes addressed by the testator to his trustees. [38]

There may be a question as to the identity of the beneficiary. It was held that funds given for behoof of the Free Church of Scotland could not be used for purposes of the United Free Church—a body formed by a union between a majority of the Free Church and the United Presbyterian Church, and holding principles differing from those of the original Free Church. [39]

---

[33] *Per* Lord Buckmaster, p. 83. Reference was made to *Re Best* [1904] 2 Ch. 354.
[34] *Ibid.* p. 84.
[35] *Caldwell's Trs.* v. *Caldwell,* 1920 S.C. 700, 702, *per* Lord Skerrington.
[36] *Edgar's Trs.* v. *Cassells,* 1922 S.C. 395.
[37] *Roberts* v. *Smith's J.F.,* 1929 S.L.T. 71.
[38] *Highgate's Trs.* v. *National Trust for Scotland,* 1957 S.L.T.(Notes) 37. See also *Bogie's Trs.* v. *Swanston* (1878) 5 R. 634 (" Ragged Schools in Dundee "); *Magistrates of Irvine* v. *Muir* (1888) 15 R. 396 (" natives of Irvine "); *Anderson's Bursary Trs.* v. *Sutherland* (1889) 16 R. 574 (" residenters in the parish of Alves, or in the parish and burgh of Elgin "); *Jowett's Trs.* v. *Jowett's Heirs,* 1952 S.L.T. 131; *University of Strathclyde* v. *Carnegie Trs.,* 1968 S.C.(H.L.) 27 (" the Universities of Scotland ").
[39] *Free Church of Scotland* v. *Lord Overtoun* (1904) 7 F.(H.L.) 1.

Administration of public trusts

It can be said that in general the administration of a public trust does not differ greatly from that of a private trust. A public trust is a trust within the meaning of the Trusts Acts and the trustees can avail themselves of their provisions.[40] Apart from the *cy-près* jurisdiction, which is dealt with in the next chapter, a few specialties require notice.

Petitions relating to charitable trusts (which presumably means public trusts) have to be presented to the Inner House of the Court of Session.[41] A trust is nonetheless charitable although some of its purposes are not charitable.[42]

New trustees are frequently appointed as part of a *cy-près* scheme [43] but a petition under section 22 of the 1921 Act can be used in appropriate circumstances.[44] New *ex officio* trustees can be appointed by a petition to the *nobile officium*.[45]

Section 24 of the 1921 Act, which allows a person entitled to the possession " for his own absolute use " of property held in a lapsed trust to apply to the court for authority to complete title to it in his own name, cannot be used by the trustees of a charitable trust who are entitled to an immediate conveyance of property held in the lapsed trust for the purpose of administering it in terms of their own trust. Such trustees are not entitled to possession for their own absolute use.[46]

Any person possessing an interest, existing or contingent, under the trust purposes has a title to enforce the due execution of the trust.[47] A person having an interest in the trust has a right of access to the deeds and accounts of the trust. He is not however entitled to a copy of the accounts unless on payment of the expense occasioned by his demand.[48]

The liability of trustees of a public trust in respect of an *ultra vires* act differs from that of trustees in a private trust. If the trustees of a public trust have in good faith expended the funds in excess of their powers under a deed which is difficult to construe, they do not incur personal liability.[49]

Where the trustees of a public trust were directed by the testator to make payments to the ministers of two parishes which were to be expended for charitable purposes at the discretion of the ministers, it was held that the ministers were not obliged to render accounts to the trustees showing how the money had been expended.[50] The trustees were exonerated if the money was paid over and duly vouched for by the ministers.

---

[40] Special statutory provisions may give trustees in certain trusts access to the court on questions of construction or administration. See, *e.g. Nimmo's Trs.*, 1941 S.C. 58.

[41] R.C. 190; *Myles*, 1951 S.C. 31.

[42] *Ossington's Trs.*, 1966 S.L.T. 19.

[43] See pp. 216, 272, *infra*. and *Lindsay's Trs.* v. *Lindsay*, 1938 S.C. 44.

[44] *Myles*, *supra*.   [45] *Mackay*, 1955 S.C. 361.

[46] *McClymont Trs.*, 1922 S.C. 503.

[47] *Ross* v. *Governors of Heriot's Hospital* (1843) 5 D. 589; *Liddle* v. *Kirk Session of Bathgate* (1854) 16 D. 1075; *Carmont* v. *Mitchell's Trs.* (1883) 10 R. 829; *Murray* v. *Cameron*, 1969 S.L.T.(Notes) 76.   [48] *Murray* v. *Cameron*, *supra*.

[49] *Andrews* v. *Ewart's Trs.* (1886) 13 R.(H.L.) 69; *Free Church of Scotland* v. *MacKnight's Trs.*, 1914, 2 S.L.T. 236.

[50] *Trs. of Buchanan Bequest* v. *Dunnett* (1895) 22 R. 602.

CHAPTER 14

THE NOBILE OFFICIUM AND
THE CY-PRÈS JURISDICTION

THE Court of Session has an extraordinary equitable jurisdiction known as the *nobile officium* which can be exercised in the administration of public trusts in the following situations [1]:

(a) where there is undoubtedly a gift for a public purpose but the testator has not specified the means by which the purpose is to be effected;

(b) where the truster's directions cannot be carried out but it is possible to find in the settlement a general charitable intention;

(c) where there is a bequest to a particular public object and that object has failed after the bequest has taken effect.

(a) Provision of machinery

The first application of the jurisdiction is that where the testator has evinced a charitable intention which is particularised but is imperfectly expressed in that he has not specified the machinery by which it is to be effected, the court will supply the omission and will provide the means for carrying out the directions—" where there undoubtedly is a gift for a charitable purpose, but where the means are not indicated, and where the Court will supply the means owing to the favour that the Court has always shown to charitable bequests." [2] This is done in the exercise of the *nobile officium* but it is not an application of the doctrine of *cy-près* or approximation.[3] The leading case on this subject is *Magistrates of Dundee* v. *Morris* [4] in which the testator expressed a wish to establish in Dundee a hospital for a hundred boys drawn from certain towns. The House of Lords held that this bequest was not void from uncertainty and that the Court of Session should frame a scheme to enable the intention to be carried out. " There has always been a latitude allowed to charitable bequests, so that when the general intention is indicated, the Court will find the means of carrying the details into operation." [5]

" The testator may indicate his intention that his estate is to go for

---

[1] *Gibson's Trs.*, 1933 S.C. 190. See also *University of Aberdeen* v. *Irvine* (1869) 7 M. 1087, 1094, *per* Lord Deas; *Grigor Medical Bursary Fund Trs.* (1903) 5 F. 1143, 1145, *per* Lord McLaren.

[2] *Burgess's Trs.* v. *Crawford*, 1912 S.C. 387, 395, *per* L.P. Dunedin, approving the judgment of Lord Herschell L.C. in *Re Rymer* [1895] 1 Ch. 19, 27. See also *Campbell* v. *Campbell's Trs.* (1752) Mor. 7440.

[3] *Gibson's Trs.* 1933 S.C. 190, 200, *per* L.P. Clyde; *Re Robinson* [1931] 2 Ch. 122, 128, *per* Maugham J. *Cf.* Gloag and Henderson, 658.

[4] (1858) 3 Macq. 134. For a criticism of the decision see McLaren, II, 920.

[5] *Per* Lord Cranworth, p. 166.

> charitable purposes. If these purposes are of the kinds which the law recognises . . . as charitable, the Courts will disregard a merely subordinate deficiency in particular expression of intention to dispose of the entire beneficial interest to a class, and will even themselves, by making a scheme of some kind, give effect to the general intention that the estate should be disposed of for charitable purposes." [6]

Where the bequest was in favour of " blind soldiers who have lost their sight in the present war," the court supplied what was lacking in the matter of machinery.[7]

(b) Initial failure

The second field of application of the jurisdiction is where the intentions of the truster cannot be carried into effect by obedience to his explicit instructions and it is possible to find in the settlement an overriding charitable purpose of which the truster's explicit instructions are only the machinery. The court will authorise a variation of the objects of the trust, by approving a scheme under the doctrine of *cy-près* or approximation.[8]

> " It is a general principle of charity law and administration that, where it is not possible to carry out the intentions of a testator in the precise manner directed by him, either from a failure in the objects of the charity, or from an increase in the trust-funds beyond the sum required for the prescribed purpose, it is within the power of the Court to direct that the funds shall be applied to other purposes as near as possible to those prescribed by the testator." [9]

> " If the testator has manifested a general intention to give to charity, the failure of the particular mode, in which the charity is to be effectuated, shall not destroy the charity: but, if the substantial intention is charity, the law will substitute another mode of devoting the property to charitable purposes, though the formal intention as to the mode cannot be accomplished." [10]

The word " charity " is used, not as denoting any beneficent purpose, but some definite general object—" By charity I mean . . . not charitable purposes generally, but some charitable purpose in the concrete, definitely, however generally, defined." [11] " Charity " and " charitable " are to be taken in the wider sense and so include public purposes.[12]

---

[6] *Turnbull's Trs.* v. *Lord Advocate*, 1918 S.C.(H.L.) 88, 91, *per* Viscount Haldane.
[7] *Sanderson's Tr.* v. *Royal Blind Asylum*, 1919, 1 S.L.T. 39. See also *Caird* (1874) 1 R. 529; *Lindsay's Trs.* v. *Lindsay*, 1938 S.C. 44.
[8] *Galloway* v. *Elgin Magistrates*, 1946 S.C. 353, 364, *per* L.J.-C. Cooper. See also *Re Wilson* [1913] 1 Ch. 314. In *Bowman* v. *Secular Society Ltd.* [1917] A.C. 406, 442, Lord Parker of Waddington remarked that the doctrine of the general charitable intention " however admirable in the interest of the public, has, I think, gone further than any other rule or canon of construction in defeating the real intention of testators."
[9] *Trs. of Carnegie Park Orphanage* (1892) 19 R. 605, 608, *per* Lord McLaren.
[10] *Moggridge* v. *Thackwell* (1802) 7 Ves.Jun. 36, 69, *per* Lord Eldon L.C.   See also *Re Packe* [1918] 1 Ch. 437; *Re Willis* [1921] 1 Ch. 44; *Att.-Gen.* (*N.S.W.*) v. *Perpetual Trustee Co.* (*Ltd.*) [1940] 63 C.L.R. 209, 225, *per* Dixon and Evatt JJ.
[11] *Burgess's Trs.* v. *Crawford*, 1912 S.C. 387, 396, *per* Lord Johnston. Appvd. by L.P. Cooper in *Angus's Exrx.* v. *Batchan's Trs.*, 1949 S.C. 335, 367. See also *Re Lysaght* [1966] 1 Ch. 191.
[12] *Davidson's Trs.* v. *Arnott*, 1951 S.C. 42, 60, *per* Lord Patrick.

The following tests have been formulated:

(1) " Was the testator's object here to establish a charity for the benefit of a certain class, with a particular mode of doing it ? or was the mode of application such an essential part of the gift that it is not possible to distinguish any general purpose of charity ? " [13]

(2) whether " it is possible, taking the will as a whole, to say that, notwithstanding the form of the gift, the paramount intention, according to the true construction of the will, is to give the property in the first instance for a general charitable purpose rather than a particular charitable purpose, and to graft on to the general gift a direction as to the desires or intentions of the testator as to the manner in which the general gift is to be carried into effect." [14]

(3) " Unless there be an absolute dedication of the fund to the purposes of charity generally, or unless it can be affirmed that the truster has preferred the general object of charity to his residuary legatees, there is no room for the application of the principle of cy-près or approximation." [15]

(4) whether " it is possible to find in the settlement an overriding charitable purpose of which the truster's explicit instructions are only the machinery." [16]

The recognised principles of the construction of wills apply and the testator's intention must be found in his words and not in speculation as to what he would have done, or intended, in emerging circumstances which he did not and could not foresee.[17]

If the testator has specifically defined the mode in which his charity is to be applied and has expressly contemplated the failure of that particular mode and has in that event given over the money to another party, there is no room for the application of the cy-près doctrine because the court must not contravene the declared intentions of the testator, and the doctrine cannot be applied to defeat a right expressly given to another.[18]

The indication of a motive is not the same thing as the expression of a purpose.[19] It favours the existence of a general charitable purpose that the testator authorised his trustees to select one of several purposes.[20] It is not permissible to infer that, as the testator's intention in making the particular gift must have been to benefit the persons who would benefit if the direction were carried out, there must have been a general and paramount intention to benefit those persons.[21]

---

[13] *Burgess's Trs.* v. *Crawford*, 1912 S.C. 387, 398, *per* Lord Mackenzie. Appvd. by L.J.-C. Aitchison in *Tait's J.F.* v. *Lillie*, 1940 S.C. 534, 539.

[14] *Re Wilson* [1913] 1 Ch. 314, 320, *per* Parker J.

[15] *Young's Tr.* v. *Deacons of the Eight Incorporated Trades of Perth* (1893) 20 R. 778, 786, *per* Lord McLaren.

[16] *Galloway* v. *Elgin Magistrates*, 1946 S.C. 353, 364, *per* L.J.-C. Cooper.

[17] *Burgess's Trs.* v. *Crawford, supra,* p. 396, *per* Lord Johnston.

[18] *Young's Tr.* v. *Deacons of the Eight Incorporated Trades of Perth* (1893) 20 R. 778.

[19] *Young's Tr.* v. *Deacons of the Eight Incorporated Trades of Perth* (1893) 20 R. 778, 786, *per* Lord McLaren.

[20] *Hay's J.F.* v. *Hay's Trs.*, 1952 S.C.(H.L.) 29.

[21] *Re Wilson* [1913] 1 Ch. 314.

" I do not think it is a right way of treating the authorities to argue that because in one decided case there was what appears to be very little indication out of which a general charitable intention has been spelled, therefore one is necessarily bound in every case to spell a general charitable intention out of very little. I think one is bound to consider each case by itself." [22]

Locality

A reference to a particular town or district does not exclude the idea of a general charitable intention albeit referable to a named locality. It is different if there are restrictions limiting the scope of the benefaction to a particular building or to the activity of a particular institution.[23] Where " locality " is of the essence of the bequest and the purpose specified by the testator cannot be effected in the locality, there is no room for the application of a *cy-près* scheme.[24]

Illustrations

It was held that there was no general charitable intention where the testatrix's house was to be used as a memorial hospital [25]; where the testator's house was to be used as a sanatorium [26]; where a private ward was to be provided in a named hospital [27]; where the bequest was to a named hospital " for payment of nurses' pensions " [28]; where the trust income was to be paid to ministers of certain specified charges.[29] A general charitable intention was found to exist where the direction was to augment funds already bequeathed for the building of a cottage hospital for a named town [30]; where the bequest was to be applied " towards the maintenance of a nurse available for the sick poor of Galston or for some analogous purpose in such manner as my trustees may decide and direct." [31]

Types of Initial Failure

The following cases can be distinguished:

(i) where there is a bequest to a particular institution and that institution has ceased to exist before the bequest has taken effect;

(ii) where there is a bequest to a society or institution which does not exist and never has existed;

(iii) where there is a bequest with a direction that it is to be used to establish a particular type of institution and it is not possible to carry out the direction.

---

[22] *Burgess's Trs.* v. *Crawford, supra,* p. 395, *per* L.P. Dunedin.
[23] *Macrae's Trs.,* 1955 S.L.T.(Notes) 33.
[24] *Pennie's Trs.* v. *Royal National Lifeboat Institution,* 1924 S.L.T. 520.
[25] *Hay's J.F.* v. *Hay's Trs.,* 1952 S.C.(H.L.) 29.
[26] *Tait's J.F.* v. *Lillie,* 1940 S.C. 534.
[27] *McRobert's Trs.* v. *Cameron,* 1961 S.L.T.(Notes) 66.
[28] *Paterson* v. *Aberdeen Sailors' Mission Institute,* 1953 S.L.T.(Notes) 33.
[29] *Galloway* v. *Elgin Magistrates,* 1946 S.C. 353.
[30] *Macrae's Trs.,* 1955 S.L.T.(Notes) 33.
[31] *Forrest's Trs.* v. *Forrest's Trs.,* 1959 S.L.T.(Notes) 24.

(i) Defunct Institutions

Where there is a bequest to a particular charitable institution and that institution has ceased to exist [32] at the testator's death the bequest lapses and falls into residue or intestacy unless the testator has evinced a general charitable intention, in which case the fund may be applied to charity *cy-près*.

> ·" Now there is a distinction well settled by the authorities. There is one class of cases in which there is a gift to charity generally, indicative of a general charitable purpose, and pointing out the mode of carrying it into effect; if that mode fails, the Court says the general purpose of charity shall be carried out. There is another class in which the testator shews an intention, not of general charity, but to give to some particular institution; and then if it fails, because there is no such institution, the gift does not go to charity generally: that distinction is clearly recognised; and it cannot be said that, wherever a gift for any charitable purpose fails, it is nevertheless to go to charity." [33]

So, where the testatrix directed that the residue of her estate was to be divided equally among four institutions, one of which was " the Speygate Free Night Shelter, Perth " which had closed some years prior to the testatrix's death, it was held that, as no general charitable intention could be discerned, one quarter of the bequest lapsed.[34] It was argued that, as the three other institutions were carrying on charitable work in Perth, there was a general charitable intention to benefit the inhabitants of that city, but Lord Carmont took the view that the charitable intention had to be spelled out of the particular bequest of one quarter of the residue. This narrow approach makes it extremely difficult for the court to find a general charitable intention. Lord Carmont relied on a statement in Lord Dunedin's opinion in *Burgess's Trs.* v. *Crawford* [35]:

> " When you come to the concrete, the application, no doubt, in some cases may be difficult, and when one goes through the very large number of decided cases on this subject, no doubt there are some of them in which, speaking for oneself, perhaps one might not have found it easy to spell out of the particular bequest the general charitable intention."

It would seem that in this context " the particular bequest " does not

---

[32] See, as to whether a hospital ceased to exist on the institution of the National Health Service, *McClement's Trs.* v. *Campbell*, 1951 S.C. 167; *Thomson's Tr.* v. *Leith Hospital*, 1951 S.C. 533. As to the substitution of public for private control of a school, see *Pope's Trs.* v. *Scott*, 1927 S.N. 122. See also *Playfair* v. *Kelso Ragged Industrial School* (1905) 13 S.L.T. 105. In *Re Servers of the Blind League* [1960] 2 All E.R. 298, Pennycuick J. refused to make an order under s. 352 of the Companies Act 1948, declaring the dissolution of a charitable company void, the effect of which would have been to enable the company to claim a bequest.

[33] *Clark* v. *Taylor* (1853) 1 Drew. 642, 644, *per* Vice-Chancellor Kindersley, approved by Lord Herschell L.C. in *Re Rymer* [1895] 1 Ch. 19, 34, and by L.P. Dunedin in *Burgess's Trs.* v. *Crawford*, 1912 S.C. 387, 395.

[34] *Laing's Trs.* v. *Perth Model Lodging House*, 1954 S.L.T.(Notes) 13.

[35] 1912 S.C. 387, 395.

mean a particular part of the will but the particular case examined out of the large number of decided cases. In any event, *Burgess's Trs.* was not a case of a bequest to a particular institution which had been in existence; it was a bequest for a particular purpose and in such a case there would be more material in the particular clause from which to spell out the intention.

In *Davidson's Trs.* v. *Arnott*,[36] where the bequest was to a named hospital founded by the testator it was held that there was no general charitable intention because, in the words of Lord Chancellor Herschell in a leading English authority, the bequest was as " localised and connected with that institution as distinctly . . . as a bequest could be." [37]

In England, it has been recognised that in this type of case there is great difficulty in finding a general charitable intention.[38] In most of the cases dealing with particular institutions which had ceased to exist, the court addressed itself to the question of whether the gift was to a particular institution carried on in a particular place and for no other purpose or whether it was a gift in augmentation of existing funds which were still devoted to the work of the charity for which the institution was founded.[39] This approach is not, however, in accordance with the law of Scotland.[40]

(ii) Non-existent institutions

Where the bequest is to a particular institution which has never existed it is permissible to impute to the testator a general charitable intention if the words used in describing the non-existent institution are sufficiently definite to prevent the expression of intention failing from uncertainty.[41] The charitable intention is spelled out from the mere fact of the non-existence of the institution. This distinction between an institution which has existed and then ceased to exist and an institution which has never existed at all does not seem to have been given effect in a reported case prior to *Tod's Trs.*[41] but it is recognised in Lord Herschell's dictum[42] which was adopted as the law of Scotland by Lord President Dunedin in *Burgess's Trs.* v. *Crawford*.[43]

Lord Sorn thought that the distinction was not altogether logical but he justified it thus:

" To me the most satisfying way of looking at the distinction is to

---

[36] 1951 S.C. 42.
[37] *Re Rymer* [1895] 1 Ch. 19, 28.
[38] *Re Harwood* [1936] Ch. 285. See *Re Finger's Will Trusts* [1971] 3 W.L.R. 775.
[39] *Re Faraker* [1912] 2 Ch. 488; *Re Withall* [1932] 2 Ch. 236; *Re Goldney decd.* (1946) 62 T.L.R. 587; *Re Lucas* [1948] Ch. 424; *Re Hutchinson's Will Trusts* [1953] Ch. 387; *Re Bagshaw* [1954] 1 All E.R. 227; *Re Roberts decd.* [1963] 1 W.L.R. 406; *Re Slatter's Will Trusts* [1964] Ch. 512. See also *Re Wedgwood* [1914] 2 Ch. 245; Hutton, " The Lapse of Charitable Bequests " (1969) 32 M.L.R. 283.
[40] *Fergusson's Trs.* v. *Buchanan*, 1973 S.L.T. 41. See J.M. Thomson, " A Question of Identity —The Problem of Bequests to Non-Existent Institutions in Scots Law " (1973) J.R. 281.
[41] *Tod's Trs.* v. *The Sailors' and Firemen's Orphans' and Widows' Society*, 1953 S.L.T.(Notes) 72. See also *Cumming's Exors.* v. *Cumming*, 1967 S.L.T. 68.
[42] *Re Rymer* [1895] 1 Ch. 19.
[43] 1912 S.C. 387, 395.

think that, in all cases where the institution cannot be found at the date of death, the Court, from favour to charity, leans towards recognising a general charitable intention but that, where the named institution actually existed at the date of the will, this course is excluded on the view that the testator's particularity of intention must be treated as a certainty." [44]

The doctrine can be applied even although the testator clearly intended to benefit a definite body or institution.[45] It can be applied where there are in existence two or more institutions with names closely resembling the expression used by the testator, but the court decides that he did not have in mind either or any of these institutions.[46]

The situation in which the court concludes that the testator intended to benefit one of two institutions of similar name but is unable to determine which has not arisen in Scotland. In *Re Goldschmidt decd.*[47] Harman J. held that no general charitable intent could be found in these circumstances but in *Re Songest decd.*[48] the Court of Appeal applied the *cy-près* doctrine and divided the fund equally between the two institutions.

In *Pomphrey's Trs.*,[45] Lord Fraser opined that it was possible to find a general charitable intention where the testator had a particular beneficiary in mind but had failed to name it correctly. The English decision to which his lordship referred [49] does not, however, support this view because both Harman and Russell L.JJ. concluded that the testatrix did not intend to benefit the organisation which once had borne the designation used in the will.

Inferences as to the testator's intention can be drawn from the nature of any other institutions named in the will but the appearance of the name of the non-existing body in a list of existing and undoubted charitable societies is not enough.[50] It has been said that the name must be such that it is possible to infer the charitable intention from it; so that " the Merchant Navy Fishing Fleet " was rejected.[51]

A charitable intention was inferred from the following: " The Society for Old and Infirm Officers of the Mercantile Marine " [52]; " the Royal Navy Benevolent Fund " [53] (general charitable intention towards members of the Royal Navy of all ranks); " the Aged Peoples Home, Glasgow " [54] (" a charitable desire to aid elderly people in need of a home or shelter "); " the School for Blind Children, Glasgow " [54] (" a general benevolent

---

[44] *Tod's Trs.* v. *The Sailors' and Firemen's Orphans' and Widows' Society, supra.*
[45] *Pomphrey's Trs.* v. *Royal Naval Benevolent Trust*, 1967 S.L.T. 61. See also *Re Knox* [1937] Ch. 109.
[46] *Pomphrey's Trs., supra* (bequest to " Royal Navy Benevolent Fund " claimed by the " Royal Naval Benevolent Trust " and " the Royal Naval Benevolent Society "). See also *Re Songest* [1956] 1 W.L.R. 897.
[47] [1957] 1 W.L.R. 524.
[48] *Supra.*
[49] *Re Satterthwaite's Will Trusts* [1966] 1 W.L.R. 277.
[50] *Pomphrey's Trs., supra.*
[51] *Mactavish's Trs.* v. *St. Columba High Church*, 1967 S.L.T.(Notes) 50.
[52] *Tod's Trs.* v. *The Sailors' and Firemen's Orphans' and Widows' Society, supra.*
[53] *Pomphrey's Trs. supra.*   [54] *Cumming's Exors.* v. *Cumming, supra.*

effect in favour of blind children requiring special schooling "); " The Scottish Convalescent Home for Children." [55] In England, a charitable intention has been inferred from: " The Clergy Society " [56]; " Church Pastoral Aid Society in Ireland " [57]; " The Home for the Homeless " [58]; " Protestant Church Bible Society " [59]; " Peace Society of Belfast " [60]; " The Newcastle-upon-Tyne Nursing Home." [61] It was, in the circumstances, not inferred from " The Oxford Group." [62]

Where there is a bequest to a named institution which does not exist but the name can be taken to refer to charitable activities carried on by the testator in his own lifetime, the bequest will be treated as one for the purpose of these activities and a *cy-près* scheme will, if necessary, be made.[63]

The general principle is applied where the institution is not named but is given a definite description—*e.g.* " the fund for the relief of the widows and orphans of the clergy in the diocese of Worcester." [64]

(iii) Failure of purpose

Where the will directs the establishment of a particular type of institution and it is not possible to carry out the direction, the bequest lapses unless a general charitable intention is disclosed.

In *Burgess's Trs.* v. *Crawford,*[65] the testator directed his trustees to found, erect and endow in Paisley an industrial school for females. At the time when the direction fell to be implemented, it was not possible to give effect to the testator's wishes and, as no general charitable intention could be detected, it was held that the bequest failed. Lord President Dunedin said [66]:

> " The bequest seems to me therefore to be in precisely the same situation as if the money had been given to a particular existing institution, and that institution had disappeared before the time when the will came into operation. This seems to me to be giving the money to an existent institution in potentiality, and when the will comes into operation there is no longer an existent institution in potentiality."

The *onus* is on the parties asserting that the bequest has failed to establish this.[67] If the trust deed prescribes an object in general terms and does not prescribe the methods to be employed, it is more difficult to demonstrate that the trust has failed.[68] It is usual to determine the question of

---

[55] *Mactavish's Trs.* v. *St. Columba High Church, supra.*
[56] *Re The Clergy Society* (1856) 2 K. & J. 615.
[57] *Re Maguire* (1870) L.R. 9 Eq. 632.
[58] *Re Davis* [1902] 1 Ch. 876.
[59] *Re Parkes* (1909) 25 T.L.R. 523.
[60] *Re Harwood* [1936] Ch. 285.
[61] *Re Knox* [1937] Ch. 109.
[62] *Re Thackrah* [1939] 2 All E.R. 4. See also *Re Thorp* [1942] 2 All E.R. 358.
[63] *Re Mann* [1903] 1 Ch. 232; *Re Webster* [1912] 1 Ch. 106; *Re Cunningham* [1914] 1 Ch. 427.
[64] *Re Kilvert's Trusts* (1871) L.R. 12 Eq. 183.
[65] 1912 S.C. 387.
[66] p. 395.
[67] *Tait's J.F.* v. *Lillie,* 1940 S.C. 534, 542, *per* Lord Mackay.
[68] *Scotstown Moor Children's Camp,* 1948 S.C. 630.

practicability at the opening of the bequest on the evidence then available [69] but in exceptional cases it has been held that the practicability of the testator's directions should be put to the test of experience.[70] Where the bequest is not an immediate gift, the question is not merely whether at the testator's death it was immediately practicable but also whether it could at that date be said that it would at any relevant date be practicable.[71] Where the bequest was for the rebuilding of a bridge " when such a thing may be required " and the bridge was restored with other funds before the bequest became available, so that there was no need for immediate rebuilding, it was held that the trust had not lapsed merely because the rebuilding had been postponed to an indefinite date.[72]

Adequacy of fund

The bequest fails if the testator has failed to provide proper and sufficient means or machinery to give effect to his purpose. A mere deficiency in administrative directions is not sufficient but there will be a failure if there is a deficiency which arises from insufficient resources to carry out the gift and which is not such as might be predicted with certainty could be repaired within a reasonable time.[73] Where the trustees were directed to accumulate the income of the estate with the capital for the twenty-one years following the testator's death, it was held that the date at which the question of adequacy fell to be determined was the expiry of the period of accumulation.[74] Where the testator's direction to accumulate the trust income could not be carried out for more than twenty-one years because of the operation of the Thellusson Act, it was held that the fact that the accumulated fund was inadequate to effect the trust purpose did not operate to defeat the testator's intention.[75]

In *Marquess of Bute's Trs.* v. *Marquess of Bute*,[76] the testator's trustees were directed to erect two churches which were to be conveyed on certain conditions to trustees appointed by the church authorities. The church authorities stated that they were unable to accept the bequests under the conditions specified because there were no endowments which could be used to fulfil the conditions. The testamentary trustees then proposed that they should accumulate the income of the trust fund until they were in a position to provide an endowment. The court held that this course could not be followed because the testator clearly did not intend to provide an endowment. The bequest accordingly failed.

---

[69] *Edinburgh Corporation* v. *Cranston's Trs.*, 1960 S.C. 244.

[70] As in *Cuthbert's Trs.* v. *Cuthbert*, 1958 S.C. 629.

[71] *Re Moon's Will Trusts* [1948] 1 All E.R. 300; *Re Wright* [1954] Ch. 347; *Re White's Will Trusts* [1955] Ch. 188; *Re Tacon* [1958] Ch. 447.

[72] *Templeton* v. *Burgh of Ayr*, 1910, 2 S.L.T. 12.

[73] *Tait's J.F.* v. *Lillie*, 1940 S.C. 534.

[74] *Ness* v. *Mills's Trs.*, 1923 S.C. 344.

[75] *Ogilvie's Trs.* v. *Kirk-Session of Dundee* (1846) 8 D. 1229. The decision should be regarded *cum nota* as the question of failure does not appear to have been fully explored. A different result seems to have been reached by the Lord Ordinary in *Barbour* v. *Budge*, 1947 S.N. 100. *Donaldson's Trs.* v. *H.M. Advocate*, 1938 S.L.T. 106, was decided on the ground that the inadequacy of the fund had not been established.   [76] (1904) 7 F. 49.

In considering the adequacy of the fund, a distinction can be made between the testator's main and essential purpose and those things which are not *sine quibus non* but merely qualifications and incidents of the main object, however desirable in themselves.[77]

Impracticable conditions

Where a bequest is made subject to a condition, the condition may be " so wrought into the substance of the bequest, that, unless it can be carried out, the bequest fails." [78] So a bequest of a sum to purchase a lifeboat to be stationed on or near the Island of Bressay lapsed when the Lifeboat Institution stated that it was not practicable to station a lifeboat at Bressay or elsewhere in the Shetlands.[79]

Surplus funds

In England, a variant of this branch of the doctrine has been developed in that where there has been a residuary bequest for a defined charitable purpose and there remains a surplus of the fund after the purpose has been carried out, the surplus must be applied *cy-près* if the testator manifested an intention to part with the whole subject-matter of the bequest for the defined purpose, although there was not indicated any general charitable intention in the wider sense.[80]

(c) Subsequent failure

The third application of the doctrine is where there is a bequest to a particular charitable object and that object has failed after the bequest has taken effect. On the theory that there is a perpetual destination of the fund to charitable purposes the court will devise a *cy-près* scheme, even although no general charitable intention was evinced by the testator. This branch of the doctrine seems to have been recognised for the first time in Scotland in a short passage in the opinion of the court delivered by Lord Skerrington in *Anderson's Trs.* v. *Scott*.[81] Its existence was the subject of a concession in *Davidson's Trs.* v. *Arnott* [82] and a majority of the court readily accepted that once the bequest had taken effect a general charitable intention was not a requisite for the exercise of the *cy-près* jurisdiction. It was, however, strongly attacked by Lord Mackay in his opinion on the grounds that there was no substantial Scottish authority to support it, it was not in accordance with English law and it was not recognised in two important Scottish decisions—*Tait's Judicial Factor* v. *Lillie* [83] and

---

[77] *Ness* v. *Mills's Trs.*, 1923 S.C. 344.
[78] *Dunbar* v. *Scott's Trs.* (1872) 10 M. 982, 983, *per* Lord Cowan.
[79] *Pennie's Trs.* v. *Royal National Lifeboat Institution*, 1924 S.L.T. 520. *Cf. Re Richardson's Will* (1887) 58 L.T. 45.
[80] *Re King* [1923] 1 Ch. 243; *Re Royce* [1940] 1 Ch. 514; *Re Raine* [1956] 1 Ch. 417. See Keeton and Sheridan, *The Modern Law of Charities*, 2nd ed., 1971, 159.
[81] 1914 S.C. 942, 952. In *Grant* v. *Macqueen* (1877) 4 R. 734, the court seems to have discerned a general object of promoting education.
[82] 1951 S.C. 42.
[83] 1940 S.C. 534.

Galloway v. *Elgin Magistrates* (*The Pringle Trust*) [84] In *Tait's Judicial Factor* the bequest had not taken effect and the decision is therefore not in point. In *The Pringle Trust* Lord Cooper said that " in a case of this class " it was a pre-requisite of the exercise of the *nobile officium* that an over-riding charitable purpose could be found in the settlement. It is therefore material to consider what class of case this was. The trust had come into operation in 1941 and had been administered in a certain manner for two years. Thereafter, there was a dispute between the trustees and certain beneficiaries as to the interpretation of the trust deed. As a result of the court's decision on that dispute the trustees presented a *cy-près* petition to alter the method of administration. Strictly, therefore, the trust had taken effect but it may be that because of the delay in ascertaining the effect of the trust deed Lord Cooper regarded it as a case of initial failure. In any event, the *cy-près* petition was dismissed on the ground that there was no failure of the trust purpose, so Lord Cooper's statement was *obiter*.

The subsequent failure doctrine is accepted as established law. [85] It is qualified in this respect, that if the will has a destination-over in the event of the failure of the particular mode prescribed, there is no room for the application of *cy-près*. [86]

It is clearly established in England that once money is dedicated absolutely to charity the testator's next-of-kin or residuary legatees are forever excluded unless the testator expressly contemplated failure of the purpose. This is so where the fund has been paid over to an institution or body which subsequently ceases to exist [87]; where the institution ceases to exist after the testator's death but before payment has been made [88]; and where the fund has to be applied at a time after the testator's death by his own trustees for a particular purpose which ceases to be practicable. [89]

The test of failure

The question of subsequent failure involves some considerations different from those relevant to the question of initial failure. It is not sufficient that the duties of the trustees, owing to changed circumstances, have become more arduous to perform and discouraging in their results.

" The principle of approximation properly applies only to cases in which the object of a charitable foundation can—owing to changed circumstances—no longer be carried into practical effect in the particular form or by the particular means prescribed by the founder. In such cases the Court has power to vary the means, and to substitute

---

84 1946 S.C. 353.
85 Mackenzie Stuart, 127; *Walls's Trs.* v. *Scottish Council for Women's Trades and Careers*, 1941 S.L.T. 197.
86 *Young's Tr.* v. *Deacons of the Eight Incorporated Trades of Perth* (1893) 20 R. 778.
87 *Re Wokingham Fire Brigade Trusts* [1951] Ch. 373; *Re Peel's Release* [1921] 2 Ch. 218.
88 *Re Slevin* [1891] 2 Ch. 236. In *Walls's Trs.* v. *Scottish Council for Women's Trades and Careers, supra,* the institution was dissolved three hours after the testator's death.
89 *Re Wright* [1954] Ch. 347.

for a particular form of charity another form approximating as closely as may be to the old one." [90]

The fact that, because of financial stringency, the trust has had to reduce the scale of its operations does not mean that it has failed.[91] Nor does the fact that the number of applicants for the benefits of the trust fund is substantially less than the number envisaged by the testator.[92] It is different if great difficulty in obtaining objects of the charity has been proved by long experience.[93]

Where the bequest was for a medical bursary for young men, natives of Nairnshire, and the trustees stated that they experienced difficulty in finding suitable candidates, the court refused to approve a scheme extending the bursary to women. It was pointed out that the bequest had not become practically unworkable and that, if in any year no suitable candidate came forward, the income could be accumulated.[94]

There is, of course, in this respect, a distinction between a trust for paying a bursary and a trust to carry on a school in that a school cannot be carried on intermittently.[95]

" Taking effect "

Where there was a direction to trustees to apply the income of the residue of the estate for the benefit of a hospital which the testator had established during his lifetime but which ceased to exist some twenty years after his death, it was held that the bequest had " taken effect " *quoad* the funds still in the trustees' hands.[96] It is sufficient if, firstly, the whole funds have vested in the trustees for the particular charitable purpose which has failed and, secondly, the particular purpose has survived the date from which the trustees were directed to hold the funds for the use of the purpose. There is no distinction between the case where the funds are held by the testamentary trustees and the case where the funds are made over to and held by the trustees administering the charity.

Davidson's Trs. was distinguished where a bequest to Edinburgh Corporation for the purpose of establishing a maternity and child welfare hostel was insufficient for the purpose.[97] It was argued that the bequest had taken effect as there was vesting *a morte testatoris* in the Corporation but the court held that in *Davidson's Trs.* the existence of the hospital at the date of vesting was an essential point in the decision.

If an attempt is made over a period of years to give practical effect to the testator's directions but the experiment fails and it is shown that they

---

[90] *Glasgow Domestic Training School*, 1923 S.C. 892, 895, *per* L.P. Clyde.
[91] *Scotstown Moor Children's Camp*, 1948 S.C. 630. See also *Watt* (1895) 23 R. 33.
[92] *Edinburgh Corporation* v. *Cranston's Trs.*, 1960 S.C. 244.
[93] *Governors of Mitchell's Hospital* (1902) 4 F. 582. *Cf. Anderson* v. *Gow* (1901) 9 S.L.T. 174.
[94] *Grigor Medical Bursary Fund Trs.* (1903) 5 F. 1143; *Duart Bursary Fund Trs.*, 1911 S.C. 9. But see *Kirk-Session of Dunbar*, 1908 S.C. 852.
[95] *Trs. of the Anderson Female School*, 1911 S.C. 1035.
[96] *Davidson's Trs.* v. *Arnott*, 1951 S.C. 42.
[97] *Cameron's Trs.* v. *Edinburgh Corporation*, 1959 S.L.T.(Notes) 32.

are impossible of fulfilment, the bequest is not treated as having " taken effect." [98]

Where income was still being accumulated to found a hospital at the date of commencement of the National Health Service, it was held that the trust had never taken effect and as there was no general charitable intent there was no room for a *cy-près* scheme.[99]

Operation of cy-près

The operation of the *cy-près* doctrine was described by Lord Westbury as follows:

> " You look to the charity which is intended to be created—that is to say, the benefit of the beneficiary—and you distinguish between the charity and the means which are directed to the attainment of that charity. Now, the means of necessity vary from age to age. Take a charity consisting, as it does here, of the relief of the poor. The condition of the country or the condition of the town at the time when that charity was created, may have dictated what were at that time very convenient means for the application of the particular charity. In the progress of society, and with the greater diffusion of wealth and the growth of population, the means originally indicated may become inadequate to the end. And the Courts of Equity have always exercised the power of varying the means of carrying out the charity from time to time, according as by that variation they can secure more effectually the great object of the charity, namely, the benefit of the beneficiary. Now, it is perfectly true that you cannot substitute one charity for another. You may substitute for a particular charity, which has been defined and which has failed, another charity *ejusdem generis*, or which approaches it in its nature and character; but it is quite true that you cannot take a charity which was intended for one purpose, and apply it altogether to a different purpose." [1]

> " The jurisdiction which this Court exercises in relation to charitable trusts is not a general discretionary jurisdiction to divert the funds of charities from one object to another as we may think appropriate. We are not a charitable endowments commission clothed with subordinate legislative powers." [2]

Nor is the jurisdiction " a sort of cornucopia of judicial favours for distribution as may seem expedient among deserving applicants." [3]

The cardinal principle is that the court must select the scheme " most nearly in accordance with the original purpose for which the fund was established." [4]

---

[98] *Cuthbert's Trs.* v. *Cuthbert*, 1958 S.L.T. 315.
[99] *Lindsay's Trs.* v. *Lindsay*, 1948 S.L.T.(Notes) 81.
[1] *Clephane* v. *Magistrates of Edinburgh* (1869) 7 M.(H.L.) 7, 15.
[2] *Scotstown Moor Children's Camp*, 1948 S.C. 630, 634, *per* L.P. Cooper.
[3] *Gibson's Trs.*, 1933 S.C. 190, 202, *per* L.P. Clyde.
[4] *Kirk-Session of Prestonpans* v. *School Board of Prestonpans* (1891) 19 R. 193; *Trs. of Carnegie Park Orphanage* (1892) 19 R. 605, 608, *per* Lord McLaren. " You can deviate

" I entirely concur with your Lordship in thinking that, in exercising a power or jurisdiction of that kind, it is our duty to keep as nearly as may be to the will of the founder, and that the only thing that justifies us in making any variance on that which he has done is, that if we did not do that, we would not only not be carrying out his purpose, but we would probably be defeating his purpose." [5]

Each case obviously depends on its particular circumstances but some general principles have been laid down.

(1) The court will not approve the application of charitable funds in such a way that the expenditure will relieve the burden on local rates or general taxation.[6] This principle, however, applies only to expenditure which is obligatory on the local authority by statute; it does not apply to purposes to which the local authority has a discretion to contribute.[7] The rule is increasingly difficult of application because of the expansion of the activities of central and local government. Payments made by other bodies, the Church of Scotland, for example, are not necessarily to be regarded in the same way as expenditure financed from rates and taxes.[8]

(2) A local connection should be maintained. The court was reluctant to transfer the entire assets of two district nursing associations of the Queen's Institute of District Nursing to the Pension Fund of the Queen Victoria Nursing Institute because that fund had no connection with the two local areas concerned and only an indirect connection with the future care of the sick poor there.[9] Similarly the court will not sanction a proposal to apply the funds of a local nursing association to centralised institutions for the benefit of ex-Service men unless there is a marked connection between the locality in which the nursing association operated and the institution.[10]

(3) Scottish funds should be retained in Scotland. If a Scottish testator names only Scottish institutions in the will, a scheme should not provide for payment of the funds to English institutions.[11] Where a scheme related to the regimental funds of various army units in Scotland which had become defunct it was said that the funds should continue to be held in Scotland under Scottish administration and under the jurisdiction of the Scottish courts.[12]

---

from the letter of the testator's intention so long as you have kept within its spirit " (*Att.-Gen.* v. *National Provincial Bank* [1924] A.C. 262, 266, *per* Viscount Haldane).
[5] *University of Aberdeen* v. *Irvine* (1869) 7 M. 1087, 1094, *per* Lord Deas.
[6] *Governors of Jonathan Anderson Trust* (1896) 23 R. 592. See also *Allan* v. *Stiell's Trs.* (1876) 4 R. 162; *Kirk-Session of Prestonpans* v. *School Board of Prestonpans* (1891) 19 R. 193; *Gerard Trs.* v. *Mags. of Monifieth* (1901) 3 F. 800; *Arbroath Female Home Mission,* 1966 S.C. 1.
[7] *Campbell Endowment Trust,* 1928 S.C. 171.
[8] *Per* Lord Cooper, *Galloway* v. *Elgin Magistrates,* 1946 S.C. 353, 366.
[9] *Milngavie District Nursing Association,* 1950 S.L.T.(Notes) 45. See also *Connell's Trs.* v. *Milngavie District Nursing Association,* 1953 S.C. 230.
[10] *Pencaitland, Saltoun and Humbie District Nursing Association,* 1954 S.L.T.(Notes) 28.
[11] *Glasgow Society for Prevention of Cruelty to Animals* v. *National Anti-Vivisection Society,* 1915 S.C. 757.
[12] *Goodman and Others, Petitioners,* 1959 S.L.T. 254.

(4) The peculiar ideas or whims of testators are not to be disregarded.[13]

(5) The court must be careful to avoid any assumption that a certain detail was not intertwined with the main purpose in the view of the testator.[14]

The court varies the trust by virtue of its *cy-près* jurisdiction, the law on this matter being the same in Scotland and England.[15] The *cy-près* doctrine can be used in relation to any public trust and not only in relation to charitable trusts.[16] It can be applied to bequests for religious purposes.[17] It has no application to a private trust.[18] Where a bequest is void from uncertainty it cannot be saved by a *cy-près* scheme.[19]

Examples

In the exercise of the *cy-près* jurisdiction the court has approved the extension of the class of persons entitled to benefit from men only to persons of both sexes [20]; from natives of a specified area to natives of a wider area [21]; from children over eight to children over five.[22]

The court approved the removal of a condition of the grant of a bursary that bursars had to study prescribed religious books in the library of the testator's house for one hour on each lawful day of one month in the summer.[23] A trust to provide a bursary for a divinity student at Edinburgh University was varied to permit payment to divinity students at other Scottish universities.[24] A trust constituted in an infirmary for " a fever convalescent home when erected " was altered into a trust " towards payment of the cost of a nurses' home," the local authority having erected a fever hospital in implement of their statutory duty.[25]

Where two regiments had been amalgamated, it was held that the regimental trust funds of the two regiments could be amalgamated into one fund for the new regiment, even although there were in existence retired members of the two regiments who could be benefited by the two trusts.

---

[13] *Gibson's Trs.*, 1933 S.C. 190, 212, *per* Lord Sands.

[14] *Gibson's Trs.*, *supra*, p. 212, *per* Lord Sands.

[15] *University of Aberdeen* v. *Irvine* (1868) 6 M.(H.L.) 29, 41, *per* Lord Westbury; *Clephane* v. *Mags. of Edinburgh* (1869) 7 M.(H.L.) 7, 15, *per* Lord Westbury. Forsyth (p. 385) seems to have thought that the Scottish courts enjoyed less power in relation to charities than the English.

[16] *Anderson's Trs.* v. *Scott*, 1914 S.C. 942. See, however, the doubt expressed by Lord Mackay in *Tait's J.F.* v. *Lillie*, 1940 S.C. 534, 545.

[17] *National Bible Society of Scotland* v. *Church of Scotland*, 1946 S.L.T.(Notes) 26.

[18] *Hedderwick's Trs.* v. *Hedderwick's Exor.*, 1910 S.C. 333; *Tait's J.F.* v. *Lillie*, *supra*, p. 544, *per* Lord Mackay.

[19] *Vollar's J.F.* v. *Boyd*, 1952 S.L.T.(Notes) 84.

[20] *Clark Bursary Fund (Mile-end) Trs.* (1903) 5 F. 433. *Cf. Duart Bursary Fund Trs.*, 1911 S.C. 9.

[21] *Kirk-Session of Dunbar*, 1908 S.C. 852. As to the effect of the disjunction of parishes, see *St. Nicholas Kirk-Session* v. *St. George's-in-the-West Kirk-Session*, 1915 S.C. 834. *Cf. Mailler's Trs.* v. *Allan* (1904) 7 F. 326.

[22] *Trs. of Carnegie Park Orphanage* (1892) 19 R. 605.

[23] *McCrie's Trs.*, 1927 S.C. 556. *Cf. Mailler's Trs.* v. *Allan* (1904) 7 F. 326. See also *Re Robinson* [1923] 2 Ch. 332; *Re Dominion Students' Hall Trust* [1947] Ch. 183 (removal of " colour bar "); *Re Lysaght* [1966] 1 Ch. 191 (removal of religious discrimination).

[24] *Pollock Ptnrs.*, 1948 S.L.T.(Notes) 11.

[25] *Glasgow Royal Infirmary* (1887) 14 R. 680. *Cf. Glasgow Royal Infirmary* v. *Mags. of Glasgow* (1888) 15 R. 264.

It was said that the underlying charitable purpose of each trust was to promote the welfare and *esprit de corps* of the existing and past members of each regiment and this purpose was rendered impossible by the amalgamation.[26]

Changes in administration: the trustees

It has been said [27] that the powers of the court do not extend beyond what is necessary (a) to put the testator's general charitable intention in a practicable shape at the beginning (including the setting up of a body of managers or trustees), or (b) to adapt the testator's trust directions with regard to the particular mode of administering his bequest to circumstances which have altered in the course of time; but the court will act not only in cases of necessity but also in circumstances of strong expediency.[28]

If the testator's intention to make a bequest is clear, the court will appoint trustees to administer it.[29] The court will not normally set up a new body to administer the trust unless the trustees appointed by the testator are unable, or are not a suitable body, to do so.[30] It may find that the trustees of an existing trust are the most suitable body to administer the bequest.[31] .The court will not normally approve a scheme involving the transfer of the trust from *ex officio* trustees to another body,[32] but a transference from private individuals to a permanent body of some kind may be permitted.[33] Similarly, there can be a transfer to the trustees of another trust.[34] Where the institution named as trustee by the testatrix was unable to devote the fund to the purposes set forth in the will, a transfer of the fund to other bodies was authorised.[35]

Although it is doubtful if the court will appoint *ex officio* trustees on a lapsed trust, where the local and official character of the trust body was intimately bound up with the practical execution of the trust, approval was given to a scheme substituting new *ex officio* trustees in place of those who were named by the testator and whose offices had been abolished by statute. It was recognised that this lay near the borderline of the court's equitable jurisdiction.[36]

Where the trustees were directed to use the income of the fund for certain purposes, they were not allowed to alienate part of the capital to an independent body to be expended on the same purpose.[37]

---

26 *Clutterbuck and Another, Petitioners,* 1961 S.L.T. 427.
27 *Thomson's Trs.,* 1930 S.C. 767, 770, *per* L.P. Clyde.
28 *Gibson's Trs.,* 1933 S.C. 190.
29 *Lindsay's Trs.* v. *Lindsay,* 1938 S.C. 44.
30 *Lipton's Trs.,* 1943 S.C. 521.
31 *Murray* (1891) 29 S.L.R. 173.
32 *McLean* v. *Alloa School Board* (1898) 1 F. 48.
33 *McGrouther's Trs.,* 1911 S.C. 315; 1910, 2 S.L.T. 257. See also *Aberdeen Servants' Benevolent Fund,* 1914 S.C. 8; *Clyde Industrial Training Ship Association,* 1925 S.C. 676.
34 *Rosyth Canadian Fund Trs.,* 1924 S.C. 352.
35 *Glasgow Society for Prevention of Cruelty to Animals* v. *National Anti-Vivisection Society,* 1915 S.C. 757.
36 *Thomson's Trs.,* 1930 S.C. 767, but see *Mackay,* 1955 S.C. 361.
37 *Philp's Trs.* (1893) 20 R. 900.

Alteration of powers

The court can approve a scheme providing for the sale of trust heritage in the exercise of the *nobile officium* without having regard to the powers conferred by the 1921 Act.[38] But this will be done only where the whole scheme would be abortive if the power of sale was not granted and, in general, the trustees under the new scheme must petition for powers of sale under the 1921 Act.[39]

In *Scott's Hospital Trs.*,[40] the court held that it did not have powers in the exercise of the *nobile officium* to authorise an alteration of the testator's express directions as to investment of the trust estate. However, in *McCrie's Trs.*,[41] it was held that, where the court is asked to approve a new scheme of administration, and the practicability of the scheme depends upon the removal of restrictions in investment imposed by the trust deed, the court can competently approve of the removal of the restrictions. Lord President Clyde said:

" It seems to me that the *nobile officium*, which is rightly appealed to for the purpose of making the charity effective by means of a new scheme, must be held to cover an enlargement of the powers of investment when that is a necessary part of the new scheme."

As Lord Sands pointed out, it is not easy to see the distinction between a situation of this type and a situation of the *Scott's Hospital* type in which, owing to changed circumstances, investments of the kind prescribed by the testator have become unsuitable. A further erosion of the decision in *Scott's Hospital* occurred in *Gibson's Trs.*[42] where a majority of a Court of Seven Judges decided that enlarged powers of investment could be granted not only in cases of necessity but also in a case of strong expediency. " To save a charitable trust from wreckage it is not necessary for the Court to hesitate until the trust is actually upon the rocks." [43]

Power to invest in securities outwith the classes authorised by the general legislation relating to trusts will not be granted.[44]

In considering *cy-près* schemes, the court is not entitled in matters which have been made the subject of specific regulation by statute to disregard the express injunctions of the statute.[45]

Procedure: the petition

The petition is presented to the Inner House.[46] It should be presented

---

[38] *McCrie's Trs.*, 1927 S.C. 556.
[39] *Stranraer Original Secession Congregation*, 1923 S.C. 722. See *Chalmers Hospital (Banff) Trs.*, 1923 S.C. 220.
[40] 1913 S.C. 289.
[41] 1927 S.C. 556.   [42] 1933 S.C. 190.
[43] *Glasgow Young Men's Christian Association*, 1934 S.C. 452, 458, *per* Lord Blackburn.
[44] *Mitchell Bequest Trs.*, 1959 S.C. 395. But the powers of the court are saved by the Trustee Investments Act 1961, s. 15.
[45] *Mitchell Bequest Trs.*, 1959 S.C. 395. See also *Tennents' J.F.* v. *Tennent*, 1954 S.C. 215, 225, *per* L.P. Cooper.
[46] R.C. 190. See *Myles*, 1951 S.C. 31; *Viscountess Ossington's Trs.*, 1965 S.C. 410. A single petition can be presented for the approval of a scheme for a number of separate trusts (*Provost, etc. of Kirkcaldy*, 1973 S.L.T.(Notes) 11).

by the trustees who were appointed to administer the bequest and not by the testator's general testamentary trustees if these are different.[47] The court will not approve a scheme put forward by trustees who have not accepted office.[48] Opinion has been reserved on whether the *cy-près* doctrine could be applied in the absence of any person (including the Lord Advocate) asking that it should be applied.[49]

Jurisdiction

It is not usual for the Court of Session to exercise its *cy-près* jurisdiction in the case of a body incorporated by Royal Charter, particularly where the Crown has reserved right to vary or modify the provisions of the charter, but where the Privy Council indicated that it did not propose to modify the terms of the charter and had no objection to the proceedings in the Court of Session, the court did accept jurisdiction.[50] The court has no power to give directions as to the application of the funds of a friendly society.[51]

Where it is contended that the trust purposes have failed, it is desirable that there should be some declaratory process to establish this before the *cy-près* petition is presented.[52] If the trustees prepare a scheme which conforms to the testator's directions and is within their powers under the trust deed, there is no need to seek the court's approval and a petition will be refused as unnecessary.[53] There may be an exception where there is a difference of opinion on the merits of the proposals between the trustees and persons having a title to contest the administration, such as the local authorities in the district in which the charity is to be founded.[54] In a few cases, the court has granted petitions for additional powers which in substance produce the same effect as the approval of a scheme.[55]

If the testator's residuary legatees or heirs *ab intestato* contend that there is no room for a *cy-près* scheme because of the uncertainty of the gift or the absence of a general charitable intention, the question at issue cannot be determined in the petition for approval of the *cy-près* scheme. No operative order for payment of the trust funds could be pronounced. The petition has to be sisted to allow the claimants to take other proceedings.[56] The question of whether an institution is the beneficiary designated by the testator cannot be determined within the *cy-près* jurisdiction.[57]

---

[47] *Lindsay's Trs.* v. *Lindsay*, 1938 S.C. 44.
[48] *Watt* (1895) 23 R. 33.
[49] *Tait's J.F.* v. *Lillie*, 1940 S.C. 534, 548, *per* Lord Wark.
[50] *The Glasgow Magdalene Institution, Petitioners*, 1964 S.L.T.(Notes) 53. See *Re Whitworth Art Gallery Trusts* [1958] Ch. 461.
[51] *Mitchell* v. *Burness* (1878) 5 R. 954; *Smith* v. *Lord Advocate* (1899) 1 F. 741; *Lord Provost of Edinburgh*, 1956 S.L.T.(Notes) 31.
[52] *Grigor Medical Bursary Fund Trs.* (1903) 5 F. 1143, 1145, *per* Lord McLaren; *Robertson's Trs.*, 1948 S.C. 1.   [53] *Robertson's Trs.*, 1948 S.C. 1.
[54] *Gerard Trs.* v. *Magistrates of Monifieth* (1901) 3 F. 800.
[55] *Trs. of Carnegie Park Orphanage* (1892) 19 R. 605; *Guardian of Thomson's Mortification*, 1908 S.C. 1078.
[56] *Church of Scotland Trust* v. *O'Donoghue*, 1951 S.C. 85.
[57] *McLevy's Trs.*, 1947 S.N. 119.

It is not in accordance with practice for the parties to submit written answers to the report made by the reporter appointed by the court.[58]

The scheme

The court will not sanction a scheme in a form which implies retro-spective validation of acts of administration by trustees which might prove to have been *ultra vires* [59] and, indeed, will normally require information as to any distribution of the funds made before presentation of the petition.[60] Where the scheme involves a transfer of the trusteeship from one body to another, the trusts of the settlement must be declared *in gremio* of the scheme.[61]

Multiplepoindings

If it appears in the course of a multiplepoinding in the Outer House that trustees will have to submit a *cy-près* scheme there are two possible procedures. The " usual and least complicated " approach is for the multiplepoinding to be sisted to allow the trustees to present a *cy-près* petition to the Inner House.[62] The alternative is to proceed under section 26 of the 1921 Act which provides that when, in the exercise of the court's powers of appointing trustees and regulating trusts, it is necessary to settle a scheme for the administration of any charitable or other per-manent endowment, the Lord Ordinary shall, after preparing such scheme, report to the Inner House, by whom the scheme will be finally adjusted and settled, intimation having been made to the Lord Advocate who is entitled to appear and intervene for the interests of the charity or any object of the trust or the public interest. The Lord Ordinary's function under this pro-vision is confined to remitting to a reporter to prepare the scheme and then reporting the scheme to the Inner House; he should not himself approve the scheme. The Inner House orders intimation to the Lord Advocate and any interested parties and may remit the scheme to a reporter in the light of any objections lodged.

Foreign elements

Where a Scottish testator directs his executors to constitute a charitable trust in England, the executors should present a scheme to the Court of Session which will consider whether the proposals are expedient in the circumstances and in accordance with the law of the domicile and the intention of the testator.[63] Thereafter, authority is granted to the executors to make application to the English courts for settlement of the scheme. The general approval granted by the Court of Session is not intended to

[58] *Scotstown Moor Children's Camp*, 1948 S.C. 630.
[59] *East Kilbride District Nursing Association, Ptnrs.*, 1951 S.L.T.73.
[60] *Armadale and District Nursing Association, Ptnrs.*, 1954 S.L.T.(Notes) 37.
[61] *McGrouther's Trs.*, 1911 S.C. 315.
[62] *Forrest's Trs.* v. *Forrest*, 1960 S.L.T. 88. The first alternative was adopted in *Pomphrey's Trs.* v. *Royal Naval Benevolent Trust*, 1967 S.L.T. 61, the second in *Cumming's Exrs.* v. *Cumming*, 1967 S.L.T. 68.
[63] *Neech's Exrs.*, 1947 S.C. 119.

fetter the discretion of the English courts to adjust the scheme in the light of English law, local conditions and any representations made before it.

Where a testator domiciled in England directs the establishment of a charitable trust in Scotland, the trustees apply in the first instance to the English courts for approval of a scheme which is thereafter submitted to the Court of Session for final approval.[64] The Court of Session is merely exercising an auxiliary jurisdiction and it must be satisfied that the English court regards the scheme as expedient in the circumstances and in conformity with English law.

Where the testatrix made a trust disposition in the Scottish form but at the time of her death was domiciled and resident in England, where probate was granted, and had directed her trustees to pay over funds to the trustees of a regimental association to be applied towards educational bursaries, it was held that as the regiment was Scottish with a depot in Scotland and the bursaries were tenable at Scottish schools and the deed was in Scottish form, the court had jurisdiction to consider a *cy-près* scheme.[65]

EDUCATIONAL ENDOWMENTS

An " educational endowment " is any property, heritable or moveable, dedicated to charitable purposes (other than funds of certain incorporations or societies contributed by members by way of entry moneys or fixed payments or burgess or guildry fines or certain funds bequeathed or given to such incorporations or societies) which has been applied or is applicable, in whole or in part, whether by the declared intention of the founder, or by consent of the managers, governors or trustees, or in pursuance of any scheme approved under any Act or of a Provisional Order or by custom or otherwise, to educational purposes, including the payment of professional training and apprenticeship fees, the provision of maintenance, clothing and payment of grants for travel.[66]

The governing body of an educational endowment (other than the Carnegie Trust and certain theological and university endowments [67]) must, within twelve months of the date when the deed creating the endowment came into operation, furnish the Registrar of Educational Endowments with prescribed information.[68] The Secretary of State has power to prepare draft schemes for the future government and management of educational endowments with other than " new endowments," *i.e.* where the deed has been in operation for less than twenty years.[69] Such schemes may provide for altering the purposes of the endowment, for the appli-

---

[64] *Lipton's Trs.*, 1943 S.C. 521. See *Re Fraser* (1883) 22 Ch.D. 827; *Re Robinson* [1931] 2 Ch. 122; *Re Marr's Will Trusts* [1936] Ch. 671; *Bateman*, 1972 S.L.T.(Notes) 78.

[65] *Martin Drummond Vesey Holt*, 1952 S.L.T.(Notes) 22. See also *Betts Brown Trust Fund Trustees*, 1968 S.C. 170.   [66] Education (Scotland) Act 1962, s. 135 (1).

[67] There are other exemptions in the Regulations cited in Note 68 *infra*.

[68] s. 117 (2); Educational Endowments (Prescription of Information) (Scotland) Regulations, 1951 (S.I. 1951 No. 548).

[69] s. 135 (2). The Carnegie Trust, and university and theological endowments are also excepted unless the governing body consents. (s. 118 (4)).

cation of its funds to such educational purposes as the Secretary of State thinks fit having regard to the public interest and to existing social and educational conditions, for the amalgamation of endowments, for altering the constitutions of governing bodies and for altering the powers of investment. The Secretary of State must, however, have special regard to the interest of the locality to which the endowment belongs, to the possibility of effecting economy of administration by amalgamations, to the need for continuing the provision from endowments for competitive bursaries at universities and similar institutions and to " the spirit of the intention of the founders " [70] as embodied in the original deed or in a statutory scheme. The Secretary of State, in a scheme which abolishes or modifies any privileges or educational advantages to which a particular class of persons is entitled, whether as inhabitants of a particular area or as belonging to a particular class in life or otherwise, must also have regard to the educational interests of such class but if the deed or existing scheme expressly provides for the education of children of the poorer classes, the endowment must continue to be applied for their benefit.[71]

A scheme must provide first that in making a selection from amongst those eligible for benefits due regard shall be paid to diligence, attainment and promise as ascertained in such manner as the Secretary of State shall determine and, secondly that, so far as can be equitably arranged and as the circumstances of each particular locality require, the benefit of the endowment shall be extended to both sexes.[72] Every scheme must provide for the dismissal at pleasure of every officer in the employment of the governing body and of every teacher and officer in any endowed school to which the scheme relates.[73] A scheme may provide for the removal of any religious test or qualification applicable to teachers.[74]

Procedure

The Secretary of State prepares a draft scheme, sends copies thereof to the governing body and causes it to be published in such manner as he thinks sufficient for giving information to all persons interested in it.[75] There must be prefixed to the draft a memorandum setting out the reasons why, in the Secretary of State's view, the reorganisation is necessary, the respects in which the scheme involves any substantial alteration of the purposes of the endowment and the reasons for any such alteration.[76] The governing body or any other person interested may within one month from the first publication of the draft send in writing to the Secretary of State objections to the draft or proposed amendments or both. If no objections or amendments are received the Secretary of State can make the scheme by statutory instrument.[77]

---

[70] As to these words, see *Knudsen's Trs.* v. *Secretary of State for Scotland*, 1962 S.L.T. 40.
[71] s. 118 (3).
[72] s. 123 (1).
[73] s. 123 (2).   [74] s. 123 (3).
[75] s. 125 (1), as amended by the Education (Scotland) Act 1969, s. 19.
[76] s. 125 (9).   [77] s. 125 (2).

If there are objections or amendments the Secretary of State must consider them and may thereafter, if he thinks fit, frame a scheme in such form as he thinks expedient.[78] As soon as practicable thereafter he must give the persons who made objections or proposed amendments written notice of his decision thereon together with the reasons for his decision. He must also send to the governing body copies of the scheme and cause it to be published in such manner as he thinks sufficient for giving information to all persons interested in the scheme. Along with the scheme there must be published a notice stating that he proposes to make the scheme unless within one month a petition or appeal is presented to the Court of Session and drawing to the attention of all persons concerned their right to petition praying that the scheme be laid before Parliament.[79]

If no petition or appeal to the Court of Session is presented within the period of one month, or if any petition or appeal is refused, the Secretary of State may make the scheme by statutory instrument in the terms in which it was published.[80] However, if within the one month period from the date of publication, the governing body, any education authority or town council of a burgh directly affected by the scheme, or twenty or more ratepayers of a burgh, parish or place directly affected or any person having a vested interest in the endowment, presents to the Secretary of State a petition praying that the scheme be laid before Parliament, he must lay the statutory instrument before Parliament and it will be subject to annulment in pursuance of a resolution of either House.[81]

If within the one month period, the governing body petitions the Court of Session to amend the scheme or substitute a new one, the court may make an amended or a new scheme and for those purposes has the powers conferred on the Secretary of State regarding schemes for the future government and management of educational endowments.[82] In exercising this jurisdiction the court is not restricted to considering whether the Secretary of State has made an administrative decision which is unreasonable; its function is to consider the issue *de novo* in the light of the scheme and the representations made in the petition and answers.[83]

If within the one month period the governing body or any other person directly affected by the scheme appeals to the Court of Session on the ground that the scheme is not within the scope of, or is not made in conformity with, the Act or any person holding any office or employment or receiving any payment under or arising out of the endowment appeals to the Court of Session on the ground that the scheme does not comply with the Act as to saving or making due compensation for his vested interests, and the court decides that the scheme is contrary to law, the Secretary of

[78] s. 125 (3).
[79] s. 125 (4).
[80] s. 125 (5).
[81] s. 125 (6).
[82] s. 125 (7).
[83] *Madras College Trs.* v. *Secretary of State for Scotland*, 1959 S.C. 335; *Knudsen's Trs.* v. *Secretary of State for Scotland*, 1962 S.L.T. 40.

State cannot make the scheme but he may frame an amended scheme in such form as he thinks expedient. The procedure for publication of an amended draft and dealing with objections thereto is then repeated.[84]

A scheme comes into operation on the date of the making of the statutory or other instrument or, if the statutory instrument has been laid before Parliament, on the date specified in the instrument. The scheme has effect as if it had been enacted in the Act and from the date it comes into operation any enactment, letters patent, deed, instrument, trust or direction relating to the subject matter of the scheme so far as inconsistent with the scheme's provisions, ceases to have effect. The statutory or other instrument containing the scheme shall be conclusive evidence that the scheme is within the scope of, and was made in conformity with, the Act and its validity " shall not be questioned in any legal proceedings whatever." [85]

There are special provisions relating to endowments of less annual value than five hundred pounds.[86] There is a special procedure for university endowments.[87]

If a governing body fails to give effect to a scheme, the Secretary of State may send a requisition to the governing body, requiring them to give effect to it and if the body fails to comply with the requisition within such time as may be specified in the requisition it may be summarily compelled to do so by the Court of Session on the application of the Lord Advocate.[88]

Duties of governing bodies

The governing body of an endowment administered under a scheme must send audited accounts annually to the Secretary of State.[89] Every governing body must make such returns and reports and give such information to the Secretary of State as he may from time to time require.[90] The majority of members of a governing body who are present at a duly constituted meeting has power to do anything that may be required to be done by a body for the purposes of the Act.

Education authorities

An education authority is at liberty to accept bequests or gifts of property or funds for behoof of any school or educational establishment under their management, whether generally or for the promotion of any particular branches of education or instruction, or for increasing a teacher's income. The authority has a duty to administer the property or funds according to the wishes and intentions of the donors and in such manner as

[84] s. 125 (8).
[85] s. 127 (Education (Scotland) Act 1969, s. 19).
[86] s. 128 as amended by Education (Scotland) Act 1969, s. 20.
[87] s. 126 (Education (Scotland) Act 1969, s. 19).
[88] s. 133. See Grubb v. Perth Educational Trust (1907) 15 S.L.T. 492.
[89] s. 124; Educational Endowments (Statement of Accounts) (Scotland) Order 1957 (1957 No. 1646) s. 81.
[90] s. 131.

to raise the standard of education and otherwise increase the efficiency of the school or establishment.[91]

Where property or money is vested in any persons as trustees for behoof of a public school or other educational establishment under the management of an education authority or for the promotion of any branch of education in such school or educational establishment, or to increase the income of any teacher therein, the free income of the property or money must be accounted for and paid to the education authority and must be applied and administered by the education authority according to the trusts attaching thereto.[92]

However, the authority, with the approval of the Secretary of State, can vary or depart from the trusts with a view to increasing the efficiency of the school or establishment by raising the standard of education therein or by other means.[93]

Non-educational endowments

There is an odd provision [94] of the Education (Scotland) Act 1962 dealing with non-educational endowments—that is, endowments dedicated to charitable purposes other than educational purposes. The governing body of such an endowment may intimate in writing to the Secretary of State their consent to the endowment being dealt with under the Act as if it were an educational endowment if the governing body are of opinion that it is expedient that this should be done on the ground that (a) there are no persons entitled to benefit out of the endowment; or (b) the purposes have failed altogether or become obsolete or useless or prejudicial to the public welfare or are otherwise sufficiently provided for, or are insignificant in comparison with the magnitude of the endowment or are not substantially beneficial to the class of persons for whom the endowment was originally intended; or (c) it is impossible owing to the inadequacy of the endowment or to the impracticable character of the founder's intentions to carry these intentions into effect.

Alternatively, the Lord Advocate, if he is of opinion on any of these grounds that a scheme should be found for the future government and management of any non-educational endowment or any new endowment, may, without the consent of the governing body, present a petition to the Court of Session for such a scheme. The Court of Session may then form such a scheme for the future management and government of the endowment and for the application of the capital or income " to any purposes, as nearly as may be analogous to those contained in the governing instrument, as the Court shall think fit."

[91] 1962 Act, s. 92. See also Local Government (Scotland) Act 1973, s. 128.
[92] Education (Scotland) Act, 1962, s. 93 (1).
[93] s. 93 (2).
[94] s. 121.

PART II TRUSTEES

CHAPTER 15

THE ORIGINAL TRUSTEES

(a) WHO MAY BE A TRUSTEE ?

THIS question can most conveniently be considered from the point of view of trusteeship in the sense in which that term is most commonly used, that is to say, the trustee appointed under some settlement or deed of trust *mortis causa* or *inter vivos*. The qualifications for the other offices falling within the statutory definition of " trustee," [1] that is to say, executors, tutors, curators and judicial factors, in so far as they differ from those applicable to trusteeships generally are covered in the separate treatment of these offices. [2] Again, such special considerations as apply when new as opposed to original trustees are being appointed judicially or otherwise are discussed under the heading of new trustees. [3]

The creator of a trust it has been said " can select as his trustee any person he chooses of whatever character." That statement made by an English judge [4] many years ago accords with the views of Scottish writers on the subject that anyone who has legal capacity for holding property and dealing with it may act as trustee in a trust regulated by the law of Scotland. [5]

Certain qualifications of this rule are considered later [6] but in the first place it is necessary to examine in some detail the question of capacity as applied to trusteeship.

Incapacities and disqualifications of natural persons

The textbook writers have drawn a distinction, not always easy to apply, between limitations of capacity which are natural to or inherent in the person of the prospective trustee and limitations (in this context designated " conventional ") which are imposed by some rule of law. [7] On this basis states or conditions of insanity and pupillarity are treated as natural incapacities while minority, bankruptcy or insolvency, alien status and criminal guilt are termed conventional limitations of capacity. Statutory changes removing the disabilities of married women have eliminated an example of conventional incapacity which occupied the attention

---

[1] Trusts (Scotland Act) 1921, s. 2 as in effect extended by the Trusts (Scotland) Act 1961, s. 3 (in relation to the definition of " judicial factor "), and by the Succession (Scotland) Act 1964, s. 20 covering executors-dative.

[2] See *infra* pp. 424 and 432 (*re* executors) and *Judicial Factors*, Chapter XI. In the case of tutors and curators at law as opposed to factors judicially appointed to act in such capacities reference should be made to the standard works such as Fraser, *Parent and Child*.

[3] *Infra*, Chaps. 16, 17 and 18.

[4] Chitty J. in *Tempest* v. *Camoys*, 1888 58 L.T.N.S. 221, 223.

[5] Menzies, 49; McLaren, II, 880; Mackenzie Stuart, 51.

[6] *Infra*, pp. 236 *et seq.*

[7] Menzies, 49.

of the earlier writers on this subject.[8] The practical result of the distinction is that while a natural incapacity forms an absolute disqualification for trusteeship, the truster may, in effect, disregard conventional limitations on the capacity of his nominee and, " clothe him with a power to deal with property as a trustee untramelled by these limitations." [9]

Insanity

Obviously an insane person cannot accept office as a trustee,[10] although in practice insanity will more often emerge as a ground for removal of a trustee from office [11] than as a nullification of his appointment because normally the condition of insanity, even if existing *de facto* at the time of taking office will not then have been legally established.

Nonage

A pupil being, like an insane person, devoid of legal capacity cannot accept trust office but a minor being regarded as affected only by a conventional restriction on capacity may do so.[12] In any event there is authority for a minor being nominated and accepting office in a private trust [13] although the courts will not appoint a minor either as trustee or as judicial factor.[14] Trusters or existing trustees appointing minors must be regarded as accepting, as they are entitled to do, the potential immaturity of judgment which in most cases will form an obvious practical objection to the appointment. The appointment of a minor can, however, give rise to legal problems. If the minor has a curator or curators there is a question, apparently unresolved by authority, whether the curator, whose consent to the minor's acceptance of office is apparently essential, can interfere with or control the actings of the minor as a trustee, thus preventing the free exercise of personal discretion impliedly involved in the proper performance of a trustee's duties, and indeed resulting that the minor cannot effectively take any action in relation to the trust without the curator's concurrence.[15] If, in relation to trusteeship, minority is properly regarded as a conventional as opposed to a natural incapacity it would seem that a truster should be able in conferring on a minor powers which the latter

---

[8] *e.g. ibid.* 51. McLaren, II, 881 *et seq.*

[9] Menzies, 49.

[10] McLaren, II, 882.

[11] As to Removal see *infra* pp. 293 *et seq.*

[12] Looking to the somewhat arbitrary line of demarcation between pupillarity and minority in the case of males and females respectively, the treatment of the former as a natural state and the latter as a conventional incapacity may not be entirely satisfactory; *cf.* Fraser, *Parent and Child*, 2nd ed., pp. 342–345 where the author seems to regard minority as a natural incapacity disqualifying a party for any public office or for trusteeship in a public trust but not from trusteeship in a private trust.

[13] *Hill* v. *City of Glasgow Bank* (1879) 7 R. 68; see particularly the observations of L.P. Inglis at p. 74.

[14] McLaren, II, 882; *Threshie, Petitioner*, May 30, 1815, F.C. (appointment of minor as trustee in sequestration rejected—a minor may apparently be decerned executor-dative; *Johnstone* v. *Lowden* (1838) 16 S. 541 but as to difficulties arising see Currie 120–123).

[15] McLaren, II, 882; indicating that the guardian can interfere: the opposite view is expressed by Menzies 51 by Mackenzie Stuart 51 (founding on *Hill* v. *City of Glasgow Bank supra*) and by the learned author (J. R. Dickson) of the relevant article in Green's *Encyclopaedia of the Laws of Scotland* Vol. 15 para. 428.

does not have in relation to his own affairs, by implication to empower the minor to act as trustee without the concurrence of a curator who may be regarded as *functus* in this matter once he has authorised the acceptance of office. This would at least be consistent with the view taken by the court in relation to the now obsolete disabilities of married women.[16]

Whether or not the minor has curators, a serious difficulty will arise if his actings as a trustee are to be affected by the normal rule permitting reduction of contractual obligations on grounds of minority and lesion. Loss or detriment to the trust estate and those beneficially interested therein does not constitute lesion to the minor unless either he is himself beneficially interested or his actings are to be regarded as rendering him liable to the beneficiaries for breach of his duties as a trustee. If neither of these contingencies applies the minor's right of reduction on grounds of minority and lesion will not operate unless it can be shown that by his acceptance of office or by some action taken in his capacity as a trustee he has incurred a personal liability otherwise than to the beneficiaries. That situation arose in what appears to be the only reported case on the matter,[17] the trustees as registered shareholders in an unlimited company being liable personally for calls made in the liquidation but the party whose trusteeship and membership of the company originated in his minority failing to take the opportunity of withdrawing from office or repudiating membership during his *quadriennium utile*. Where the minor is neither beneficially interested nor personally liable to the other parties to the transaction in question his right to reduce the transaction will depend on whether or not it involves him in a liability to the beneficiaries for breach of trust. It seems to be unsettled how far a minor who becomes a trustee incurs the normal liabilities of the office. Breach of trust, it would appear, is a breach of duty *sui generis* and not exactly equivalent either to a breach of contract or to a delict [18]; if and in so far as it is a form of delict the difficulty remains unresolved as there appears to be no authority on the liability of a minor in reparation.[19] The absence of liability for breach of trust would be satisfactory to third parties contracting with the minor in his capacity as a trustee in resulting that the transaction would not be reducible provided it did not affect the minor personally, but it would be unfortunate for the beneficiaries and likewise for any co-trustees concerned in the transaction in question, the beneficiaries having no remedy against the minor trustee and his co-trustees being liable to the beneficiaries without contribution from the minor. This assumes, of course, that the act or acts constituting the breach of trust involve the trustees as a body and are not those of the minor alone. In the latter event the gratuitous trustees' privilege of being liable for their own actings only [20] would afford relief to

[16] See Menzies, 51–52 and the case of *Stoddart* v. *Rutherford*, June 30, 1812 F.C.
[17] *Hill* v. *City of Glasgow Bank*, *supra*.   [18] See *Allen* v. *McCombie's Trs.*, 1909 S.C. 710.
[19] Glegg, *The Law of Reparation in Scotland*, 4th ed., p. 98. *Cf.* Walker, *The Law of Delict in Scotland*, p. 94.
[20] See Trusts (Scotland) Act 1921, s. 3 (*a*), the provisions of which are frequently embodied in and amplified by documents constituting trusts.

the minor's co-trustees. On the other hand if the minor is liable, like a person of full age, for breach of trust, parties dealing with him as trustee would appear, irrespective of any personal loss or liability on the minor's part, and, it is thought, even in cases affected by the statutory provision protecting the normal transactions of trustees from challenge,[21] to take the risk of reduction on grounds of minority and lesion, whether or not they knew they were dealing with a minor. Such a situation, while leaving the beneficiaries protected, creates difficulties for parties transacting with the trust. Again, reduction on any ground connected with the minority of a trustee can entail serious inconvenience for his co-trustees.[22]

Whatever view may be taken of the undecided questions of law to which reference has just been made it seems clear that in practice a minor should not be nominated as a trustee except on the basis that his appointment is conditional on his being of age when the trust takes effect or alternatively does not become effective until he comes of age. Nominations in such terms are not uncommon in the testamentary settlements made by parents while their children are under age.[23]

Insolvency

Bankruptcy or insolvency even when it has resulted in sequestration is covered by the general rule enabling the truster to give his nominee, affected by a conventional incapacity, power of dealing with the trust estate as he could not deal with his own property.[24]

Criminal guilt

Under the heading of criminal guilt it appears that only a conviction for high treason now forms a definite disqualification for trusteeship.[25] It has been suggested, however, that there may be other infamous crimes which would disqualify and again that acceptance of office by a party undergoing punishment for crime would be void.[26] This last proposition, if based on the inability of a prisoner while incarcerated to perform the duties of a trustee, might not hold good unless it could be shown that his current incarceration was likely to impede or prejudice the administration of the trust at its inception. In practice criminal guilt seems more likely to be founded on as a ground for removal of a trustee than as disqualification for the office.[27]

Alien status

An alien as such is not disqualified from being a trustee unless he be an

---

[21] Trusts (Scotland) Act 1961, s. 2.
[22] McLaren, II, 883 and Dykes, 215.
[23] For examples, see Elder, *Forms of Wills*, 11, 12.
[24] Menzies, 49, 53.
[25] McLaren, II, 884 and Forsyth, 93. Outlawry or fugitation which in the past apparently disqualified the offender was abolished by the Criminal Justice (Scotland) Act 1949, s. 15 (3). The statement made by Menzies, 50 to the effect that a criminal is disqualified seems too general and is unsupported by authority.
[26] McLaren, *ibid.*
[27] As to " Removal of Trustees," see *infra*, pp. 293 *et seq.*

alien enemy.[28] Statutory provisions [29] have revoked the common law rule whereby an alien could not have a right or title to heritable property in Scotland or real property in England but it remains the law that an alien cannot be owner of a British ship [30] either beneficially or in trust.

Residence abroad

In itself, residence abroad is no bar to trusteeship, although by statute it is made a ground on which, in certain circumstances, the court may remove a trustee.[31] With modern facilities for travel and communication such residence must cause less inconvenience than in former times.[32] Trustees, however, like beneficial owners, are subject to the current rules of exchange control [33] restricting dealings in securities and other forms of property by or with persons resident outwith the " Scheduled Territories " (which as specified in the statute correspond roughly with the Sterling Area), and so making it, in some cases, impracticable, if not impossible, for persons resident in certain foreign parts to have the trust assets vested in them and to perform their duties as trustees.

Juristic persons as trustees

Thus far the question of capacity for trusteeship has been examined with reference to the position of natural persons. The office may, however, be held by juristic persons such as political entities or corporate bodies.

The Crown

It is established that the Crown [34] may be nominated and, if so, act as trustee even in trusts created by private individuals. In practice this will happen only where the trust purposes are of a public or quasi-public nature. Common examples are college and university chairs endowed by some private individual who has entrusted to the Crown the appointment of governors or professors. Writers on the subject of trusts [35] have commented on the absence of control by ordinary legal process affecting the Crown's administration in any trust in which it acts. In this respect the difficulties of beneficiaries or other interested parties would seem to have been reduced, if not entirely removed, by the statutory provisions [36] now in force whereby the courts have the same powers in proceedings involving

---

[28] McLaren, II, 883; Menzies, 53.
[29] Status of Aliens Act 1914, s. 17 (as amended by British Nationality Act 1948, Sched. 4, Part II).
[30] *Ibid.* proviso (3).
[31] Trusts (Scotland) Act 1921, s. 23, *infra*, p. 295.
[32] *Cf.* Forsyth, 99–101. The practice of the English courts appears to be to require a non-resident trustee to give an undertaking to implement the purposes of the trust before any trust assets are made over to him (see Maugham J. in *Re Robinson* [1931] 2 Ch. 122, 129–130). *Cf.* the attitude of the Scottish court in relation to the appointment of parties abroad to replace resigning trustees; see pp. 277–278, *infra*.
[33] Exchange Control Act 1947—see generally Halsbury's *Laws of England*, 3rd ed., Vol. 27, 108–147.
[34] Presumably as a corporation sole—see *infra*, p. 234, n. 49.
[35] Menzies, 50; Mackenzie Stewart, 51.
[36] Crown Proceedings Act 1947, ss. 21 and 43.

the Crown as in proceedings between subject litigants except that the Crown cannot be interdicted or ordered to make specific performance.

Foreign governments

It has been held in England that a British truster may effectively appoint a foreign government, which is not at the time of the trust's inception that of any enemy country, as trustee to hold and administer funds for charitable purposes within its own territory.[37]

Other public bodies

It was for long customary for the creators of trusts intended to benefit the inhabitants of some particular district to confer the trusteeship on local authorities or other public bodies operating within that district. With the development of the welfare state, trusts of this kind seem less likely to be created but many remain in existence. The capacity of local authorities or similar bodies to hold trusteeships for purposes concerning their own area or sphere of operations has never been doubted; indeed, there are cases in which such trusteeships have been held to arise in the absence of express appointment by necessary implication from the objects of the trusts.[38] In the past, at least, the practice of trusters seems to have been to vest the trust office and the trust property in the personnel or office bearers for the time being of the public body rather than in the public body as an entity.[39] Whether this practice represented a recognition of the fact that the actual administration of the trust must be done by natural persons or arose from doubts as to the corporate nature of the body and its capacity to take a title to property, particularly Scottish heritage, is not entirely clear.[40] Various statutory provisions passed to regulate the exercise by local authorities of their functions and those of their members as trustees in such trusts are now embodied in consolidating legislation.[41]

Private corporations

In modern practice trusteeships are frequently held by corporate bodies formed as a result of private enterprise. The capacity of such bodies to hold trust office depends on whether or not it is *intra vires* in terms of their constitution. Some writers [42] have equated this application of the doctrine of *ultra vires* in incorporated bodies to a natural, as opposed to a conventional, limitation of capacity in the case of private individual, and it is certainly true that where the holding of trust office would be *ultra vires* a corporate body in terms of its constitution its nomination by a truster cannot extend its powers to the effect of enabling it to accept office and act

---

[37] *Re Robinson, supra.*
[38] McLaren, II, 881, and cases therein cited.
[39] McLaren, *ibid.*, and cases therein cited, particularly *Incorporated Trades of Edinburgh* v. *George Heriot's Hospital* (1836) 14 S. 873 and *Governors of Gordon's Hospital* v. *Ministers of Aberdeen* (1831) 9 S. 909.
[40] *Cf. Gardner* v. *Trinity House of Leith* (1845) 7 D. 286.
[41] Local Government (Scotland) Act 1947, ss. 357–360.
[42] *e.g.* Menzies, 50.

in the trust. In this, as in many other matters, however, it is necessary to distinguish between different types of incorporation. The category generally termed companies contains three classes namely, chartered, statutory and registered. Of chartered companies, otherwise termed common law corporations, it is sometimes said that they are unaffected by the doctrine of *ultra vires* and have the powers of private individuals. If that is so they could be nominated and act as trustees in any matter irrespective of the terms of their constitution. That result, while supported by English authority,[43] would seem to be of doubtful validity in Scotland, where the better view may be that a chartered company could not act as trustee in any trust having purposes wholly unrelated to those for which the company was incorporated.[44]

In the case of companies of either of the other two classes which are purely statutory creations the doctrine of *ultra vires* will, of course, apply in determining whether or not they can act as trustees in any trust, their activities being restricted to those actually authorised by their constitutions or such others as are truly incidental thereto. It may be that in certain circumstances the Memorandum of Association of an ordinary trading company registered under the Companies Acts authorising it in terms of the standard formula to engage in any business which can conveniently and advantageously be carried on in conjunction with any of its stated objects and to do all things conducive to the attainment of these objects would be construed as rendering certain trusteeships *intra vires*. In practice, however, trading companies will rarely, if ever, act as trustees and this form of corporate activity tends to be confined to concerns such as banking or insurance companies whose constitutions will make specific provision for it, or companies formed, sometimes independently and sometimes as subsidiaries of other concerns, with the holding of trusteeships as a main object.[45] In modern times the advantages of the corporate trustee in holding property continuously unaffected by contingencies such as death, disappearance or insolvency have come to be more and more appreciated. In the provision of long-term finance for large industrial concerns, as, for example, by debenture issue, corporate trustees are almost always appointed to take care of the interest of the investors and hold any security subjects. Again in the matter of unit trusts, an important feature of present-day investment facilities, the appointment of a corporate trustee with substantial capital reserves is a statutory requirement.[46] In private and family trusts too the corporate trustee, often a bank, is frequently to be found, trusters and especially testators apparently considering, rightly or wrongly, that the assurance of continuity and financial stability more than offsets

---

[43] See Menzies, 50 and cases therein cited; *cf.* McLaren (and Dykes), II, 880, 881.

[44] See *Gloag on Contract*, 2nd ed., 102 and 103, and the decisions there cited, which, while concerning matters of contract, might be applicable, in principle at least, to the question of the capacity of a corporation for trusteeship.

[45] A typical example of an objects clause for a " trust " company will be found in Palmer's *Company Precedents*, 17th ed., Part I (General Forms), p. 367, No. 180.

[46] Prevention of Frauds (Investments) Act 1958, s. 17.

the disadvantages of somewhat impersonal administration and lack of true *delectus personae*.[47] As a general rule it is large concerns that are appointed corporate trustees whatsoever the nature of the trust and accordingly the absence of personal responsibility involved in limited liability is not of practical moment. In the less common case where a small private company is formed by some person or group of persons such as a professional firm with a view to offering clients certain advantages of corporate trusteeship the element of personal liability can be preserved by forming the company with unlimited liability or as a limited company with a substantial capital largely uncalled or again as a guarantee company with the members liable up to a substantial amount.

Trust corporations and similar entities operating in England

In connection with the holding of trust office by juristic persons such as corporate bodies it seems appropriate to mention briefly certain developments in England which have no real counterparts in Scotland.

In England the term " trust corporation " is applied to bodies specially constituted to act as corporate trustees and is for some purposes the subject of statutory definition.[48] In the case of public trusts (termed " charitable " in England) the Official Trustee of Charity Lands as a corporation sole [49] and the Official Trustees of Charitable Funds as a corporation aggregate, both operating under the Charitable Trusts Acts 1853–1939, have important functions holding and safeguarding the trust estate without superseding the nominated or duly appointed trustees in the discretionary administration of the trust. This is one example of the distinction which has grown up in English law between the ordinary or managing trustee on the one hand and the custodian trustee on the other.[50] There seems no reason why this division of functions, which secures the stability and continuity of the corporate trustee side by side with the personal discretion of selected individuals, should not be adopted in the constitution and administration of Scottish trusts but in fact Scottish law and practice have not developed to the same extent on these

---

[47] But see the observations of the court in *Ommanney, Petitioner*, 1966 S.L.T.(Notes) 13: " An impersonal body such as a bank or a trust corporation is not a suitable party to exercise . . . a discretion involving personal and family considerations for its proper exercise."

[48] *e.g.* by the Settled Land Act 1925, s. 117 (1) (xxx), it means the Public Trustee (a corporation sole) or a corporation appointed to act under the Public Trustee (Custodian Trustee) Rules 1926, which rules permit the appointment of *inter alia* any incorporated company with an issued capital of not less than £250,000 paid up in cash to the extent of at least £100,000; see also Supreme Court of Judicature (Consolidation) Act 1925, s. 175 (1), and Law of Property (Amendment) Act 1926, s. 3. See generally Halsbury's *Laws of England*, 3rd ed., Vol. 38, pp. 905–909.

[49] The corporation sole as opposed to the corporation aggregate is an institution seldom encountered in but not entirely unknown to Scots law; in Bell's *Principles* (s. 2176) it is indicated that the only examples recognised in Scotland are the Crown and the minister of a parish. Post-war legislation for nationalised undertakings provided some examples functioning in both countries, *e.g.* the Minister of Fuel and Power under the Ministry of Fuel and Power Act 1945, s. 5 (1) (now repealed by the Ministry of Technology Order, S.I. 1969 No. 1498) and the Postmaster-General under the Post Office Act 1953, s. 46 (the office of Postmaster-General being abolished in terms of the Post Office Act 1969, s. 1).   [50] See Halsbury, *loc. cit.*, at pp. 902–905.

lines. The relationship of trustees holding the property of unincorporated bodies such as associations or clubs to the committee or managing body is, however, very similar to that of the custodian trustee to the managing trustee. Again in Scotland as in England assets such as stock exchange securities are frequently held by or registered in the names of nominees for the true owners whose identity is thus concealed. Such nominees are in effect custodian trustees functioning under the directions of the true owners or of the management trustees if a trust in the true sense exists.[51]

For the administration of private trusts there is in England the Public Trustee,[52] a statutory corporation sole empowered to act alone or with other trustees on an original or subsequent appointment and either as ordinary managing trustee or as custodian trustee. While the conception of a single official corporate trustee or body of trustees to hold and/or administer trust funds settled by different trusters for varying purposes has not found any general acceptance in Scotland there is, within the specialised sphere of Established Church administration, an example of a statutory creation of this kind in the Church of Scotland General Trustees [53] set up for the purpose of holding properties formerly held by various bodies of trustees on behalf of different committees of the Church.

Bodies disqualified

While the more specialised forms of incorporation such as building societies and societies incorporated under the Industrial and Provident Societies Acts have by reason of their incorporation the necessary juristic personality to hold trust office they will, as a general rule, be precluded from doing so by the restricted terms of their constitutions which are determined to a large extent by statutory provisions. On the other hand the lack of juristic personality disqualifies unincorporated bodies such as clubs or associations from holding trust office. The separate *persona* which in Scotland, but not in England, belongs to a firm or partnership must result that, theoretically at least, a firm could hold trust office. For obvious reasons, such as the difficulties arising from changes in personnel and the effect of such changes on the identity of the firm, such an appointment is seldom if ever made in practice.[54] As already mentioned, however, professional firms wishing to offer clients their services as trustees may adopt the course of incorporating a private company for that particular purpose.[55]

---

[51] See Companies Act 1967 s. 28 (8), treating " a simple trustee " (apparently not a *nomen juris* of Scots law) as the equivalent of the English " custodian trustee."

[52] Under the Public Trustee Act 1906—see Halsbury, *loc. cit.* pp. 894–902.

[53] Incorporated by the Church of Scotland (General Trustees) Order 1921, their powers and functions being greatly extended by the Church of Scotland (Property and Endowments) Act 1925; see generally Black and Christie, *Parochial Ecclesiastical Law of Scotland* (1928), Chap. XIII.

[54] The difficulties which an appointment of a Scottish firm as a trustee would create are in some respects not unlike those which have led to the proposals for the prohibition of their appointment as company directors (see Report of the (Jenkins) Company Law Committee, Cmnd. 1749, paras. 84 and 85 (d)).

[55] *Supra*, p. 234.

Objections other than incapacity or disqualification

Having dealt with the question of capacity for trusteeship as affecting parties and bodies in various circumstances we have now to consider certain special cases in which, apart from any lack of capacity or actual disqualification on the part of the prospective trustee, his appointment may be objectionable by reason of his interest in or connection with the purposes of the trust or some of them.

Trusters and interested parties

Prima facie the truster himself is not ineligible for trusteeship even as a sole trustee [56] although he could not effectively use the creation of the trust simply as a means of putting his assets beyond the reach of his creditors. While the trust will be extinguished *confusione* if the same person become sole trustee and sole beneficiary, there is, generally speaking, no bar to the appointment of a beneficiary as trustee. It appears, however, that an exception to this rule may have to be recognised in the special case of the alimentary liferent. The effectiveness of such a liferent is dependent on the existence of a continuing trust and the balance of authoritative opinion appears to be that some at least of the trustees in such a trust must be independent of the liferenter.[57] The case usually cited in support of this view concerned a marriage contract trust in which the wife's liferent, although declared alimentary, was held in questions with a creditor to whom the spouses had assigned their interests in the trust funds, to be unprotected because the trustees, of whom the spouses were the majority, were empowered to lend or advance trust funds to the husband.[58] Lord McLaren [59] went so far as to say that it was essential to the constitution of an effectual marriage-contract trust that at least one of the trustees should be a neutral person, a trust in which the spouses were sole trustees giving no protection to beneficiaries against the voluntary acts of the spouses and therefore being ineffective against creditors. This dictum has been criticised [60] and would appear to be open to the comment that the protection would not be fully effective if the neutral trustee or trustees

---

[56] Menzies, 30; and see *Allan's Trs.* v. *Inland Revenue*, 1971 S.L.T. 62, where it was confirmed that a person can make himself a trustee of his own property provided there is a bona fide physical act equivalent to conveyance, transfer or delivery of the subject of the trust. In the circumstances of the case, which concerned an endowment policy taken out to cover death duties, intimation to one of a number of parties beneficially interested in the deceased's estate was held sufficient for this purpose.

[57] See Dobie, *Liferent and Fee* 232; and Encyc. Vol. 1, para. 753 (*sub voce* " Alimentary Interest " by J. R. Dickson).

[58] *McCallum* v. *McCulloch's Trs.* (1904) 7 F. 337; it seems probable that in the context of this contract the word " advance " was synonymous with and merely explicatory of the word " lend " (*cf.* Lord Macmillan in *Lincolnshire Sugar Co. Ltd.* v. *Smart* [1937] A.C. 697, 703–705, " a polite euphemism for loans ") and not meaning a prepayment of what was to become due; another meaning sometimes borne by the word is an encroachment on capital to supplement a liferent; a power to that effect has been held ineffective as inconsistent with an alimentary liferent of contractual origin, the position as regards a similar provision in a testamentary deed being expressly reserved (*Arnot* v. *Arnot's Trustees*, 1945 S.L.T. 240). In such a case the neutral or independent status of the trustees or a majority of them *vis-à-vis* the liferenter might be a significant factor.

[59] At p. 344.   [60] See Menzies, 49.

were in a minority. Logically, however, there seems much to be said for a requirement of some neutral or disinterested trustees among the personnel of the trust necessary for the constitution of an alimentary liferent. Even if they are in a minority they should be in a position to prevent such a breach of trust as an advance to the liferenter. It has been suggested on the basis of the decision in *McCallum's* case [61] that the fact of the husband being the sole trustee of the policy may prejudice the effectiveness of a trust set up under the Married Women's Policies of Assurance (Scotland) Act 1880.[62]

Apart from the possibility of nullifying or rendering inoperative any of the provisions of a trust there are cases where the uninhibited exercise of a truster's freedom in the selection of his trustees may be unwise. Obviously, a truster should be advised against placing himself or anyone else in a position where personal interest and duty as a trustee are likely to conflict, as, for instance, where trustees have discretionary power affecting the disposal of the trust funds among a certain class or group of beneficiaries and include in their number a member or members of that class or group. Intending trusters may not always be prepared to accept such advice and may in their knowledge of the parties and circumstances decide to accept the risk of the administration being prejudiced by such conflicts.[63] In the modern practice whereby family trusts with discretionary provisions are widely used for tax avoidance the question of the selection of trustees has acquired a new significance of which a trustee and his advisors must take cognisance if the intended fiscal results of the trust are not to be imperilled.[64] Most of the questions on this topic seem to arise out of the truster's appointment of himself as a trustee. Even if the customary wide investment powers are given, such an appointment does not in itself result that for death duty purposes the trust estate is treated as passing on the trustee's death or as having remained in his possession or being affected by a benefit reserved to him. If, however, the deed conferred on the trustees such discretionary powers as the advancement of capital to beneficiaries whose rights have not vested, or, as in the standard discretionary trust, the appointment or apportionment of certain funds among a class or group of beneficiaries, the truster's death within seven years [65] of his having been concerned in the exercise of such a discretion in favour of some relative of his may give rise to a claim for estate duty in respect of a gift.[66] Again, unless the deed is so worded as to exclude completely the possibility of the truster-trustee deriving any personal benefit, the inclusion of the customary professional charging clause

---

[61] *Supra*, n. 58.

[62] Burns, *Conveyancing Practice*, 4th ed., 684; and see *infra*, p. 238 as to estate duty aspect.

[63] *Cf.* Menzies, 54–55, where the matter is considered in relation to the appointment of new trustees.

[64] For a full discussion of this matter, see Potter and Monroe, *Tax Planning with Precedents*, 7th ed., pp. 58 *et seq.*

[65] Finance Act 1968, s. 35 and Sched. 14.

[66] Finance Act 1940, s. 44 (1), as amended by Finance Act 1950, s. 46.

may be regarded for estate duty purposes as a benefit reserved,[67] resulting
in the trust funds being deemed to pass on the truster's death and/or for
income tax purposes as a power of diminution causing the whole income
to be treated as the truster's own.[68]

The appointment of the truster as a trustee would appear to be particularly unwise where the trust estate includes, or is likely at any time to
include, holdings in family companies. In construing the provisions of the
taxing statutes concerning the control of such companies the courts have
more than once held that a fiduciary interest in shares or debentures is no
less relevant than a beneficial one.[69]

From the taxation point of view the grounds of objection to the
appointment of a beneficiary as a trustee are much more limited in scope
than those applicable to the appointment of the truster himself. In discretionary trusts, however, it should be kept in view that if a party who is
appointed as or subsequently becomes sole trustee is himself one of the
class or group of beneficiaries among whom there is a discretionary power
to divide or apportion trust funds, he may be regarded for estate duty
purposes as competent to dispose of the trust property as a whole, with the
result that it would be deemed to pass on his death.[70]

(b) NOMINATION OR APPOINTMENT

The nomination of a trustee may take any one of a number of different
forms and in the main is a matter unaffected by formal rules or conveyancing technicalities. " Trustees," it has been said,

" may be appointed not only by name but by any such description
or reference as shall be sufficient to point out the person or persons
intended whether by official situation or as the legal successors of a
party nominated or as party to be nominated by a particular person,
public body or private society." [71]

---

[67] The only decision bearing on this point appears to be *Oakes* v. *Commissioners of Stamp
Duties of New South Wales* [1954] A.C. 57, where a provision expressly entitling a truster-
trustee to remuneration for acting as trustee was held to be a benefit reserved in terms of a
provision resembling s. 43 (2) (*a*) of the Finance Act 1940, now repealed by the Finance
Act 1969. (See Potter and Monroe, *op. cit.*, 61 re this matter under current legislation.)

[68] Finance Act 1958, ss. 21 (2) and 22 (1) (*b*) (now replaced by ss. 446 and 448 respectively of
the Income and Corporation Taxes Act 1970 (c. 10)). These provisions may have to be considered even where it is the truster's wife and not the truster himself who is to be a trustee
(see Potter and Monroe, *op. cit.*, 62–63).

[69] *e.g. I.R.C.* v. *Bibby & Sons Ltd.* [1945] 1 All E.R. 667 (excess profits tax under Finance
Act (No. 2) 1939, s. 13 (2) (*b*), (3) and (9) and Sched. VII, Part I, para. 10 (2)); *Barclays
Bank Ltd.* v. *I.R.C.* [1961] A.C. 509 (estate duty—" assets valuation "—Finance Act
1940, ss. 55 and 58, as amended by Finance Act 1946, s. 47 and Sched. II), but as to the
construction of " control " as defined in the Income Tax Act 1952, s. 333 (1) (now replaced
by s. 534 of the Income and Corporation Taxes Act 1970 (c. 10), see the decision of the
Court of Session in *Inland Revenue* v. *Lithgows Ltd.*, 1960 S.C. 405, in which the question at
issue was the position of a first-named trustee who in terms of the company's articles had
the power to exercise the voting rights in respect of the holding.

[70] Finance Act 1894, ss. 5 (2) and 22 (2) (*a*); and see Potter and Monroe, *op. cit.*, 146–147, as
to means of avoiding this result.

[71] Forsyth, 102.

Reported cases exemplify the nomination of the holder of an office (generally termed an *ex officio* trustee) and show that his acceptance and actings in no way involve the body or trust of which he is already a member.[72] There are also decisions illustrating the nomination of the proprietor of an estate [73] and that of the trustees of a settlement made by another truster [74] (which may include persons not being original trustees [75]). Again a nomination which is not of trustees as such may be construed as a nomination of the parties in question as trustees, as when executors are nominated in a settlement containing trust purposes of a continuing nature.[76] Apart from certain cases concerning executors [77] the reported instances of delegation by the truster of the power of appointment appear all to be cases concerning new trustees.[78] Delegation of the nomination or appointment of an original trustee although apparently competent seems unlikely to occur in practice.

In modern practice the majority of appointments appear to fall into one or other of two categories, *i.e.* that of named persons (natural or corporate) as commonly found in private trusts and that of *ex officio* trustees as frequently occurring in trusts having charitable or public purposes.

The rule epitomised in the maxim *falsa demonstratio non nocet* will normally be applied by the courts in dealing with errors, inaccuracies or omissions affecting the nomination of trustees. This is consistent with the principle whereby, particularly in testamentary cases, effect is given if at all possible to bequests or other trust purposes although defective in form.[79] The reports of the English Probate Court contain a number of examples concerning trusts of a private nature [80] while Scottish decisions [81] illustrate the same approach in nominations of *ex officio* trustees in public or charitable trusts where, of course, the benignant construction applicable to deeds constituting such trusts is also a relevant factor.

Ex officio appointments

A difficulty may arise out of the nomination of *ex officio* trustees where some change takes place affecting the body in which the nominee holds office, *e.g.* its reconstitution or its amalgamation with or replacement by

---

[72] *e.g. Ministers of Edinburgh* v. *Mags. of Edinburgh* (1849) 6 Bell's App. 509.
[73] *e.g. Wylie* (1850) 12 D. 1110 (the difficulties arising in this case should not occur under modern settlements where the normal provisions for survivorship and quorum apply).
[74] *Martin* v. *Ferguson's Trs.* (1892) 19 R. 474, 478, *per* L.P. Robertson.
[75] *Re Waidanis* [1908] 1 Ch. 123.
[76] *Ainslie* v. *Ainslie* (1886) 14 R. 209 (the question raised as to the executor's power of assumption could not now arise with executors-nominate who now have the powers of gratuitous trustees; see Executors (Scotland) Act 1900, s. 2).
[77] *Vide* Currie, 68–69.
[78] *Infra*, pp. 253–254; see *e.g. Bowman* v. *Bowman*, 1910, 1 S.L.T. 381.
[79] *Cf. Crawford's Trs.* v. *Fleck*, 1910 S.C. 998, in which reference is made to various English decisions including *Re Redfern* (1877) 6 Ch.D. 133 and *Mellor* v. *Waintree* (1886) 33 Ch.D. 198.
[80] *e.g. De Rosaz* (1877) 2 P.D. 66; *Cooper* [1899] P. 193; *cf. Hubbuck* [1905] P. 129 (for a Scottish instance, see *Robertson* v. *Ogilvie's Trs.* (1844) 7 D. 236).
[81] *e.g. Murdoch* v. *Magistrates and Ministers of Glasgow* (1827) 6 S. 186; *Bruce* v. *Presbytery of Deer* (1867) 5 M.(H.L.) 20.

some other body. While the appointment of an *ex officio* trustee does not as a rule imply the individual *delectus personae* involved in the selection of a named person the effect of a change in the body in which the nominee holds office is a question of circumstances and if the *ex officio* appointment is to remain effective, despite the change, this must be not inconsistent with the apparent intention of the truster. Where the constitution of an ecclesiastical body was changed so that the vestrymen who were *ex officio* trustees came to be replaced by election and not by assumption the elected vestrymen were held entitled to act as trustees.[82] A union of churches which left virtually unaltered the official duties and functions of certain ministers was held not to affect their trusteeship in a bursary fund [83] but the opposite result was reached in a case where a statutory change involved the replacement of one local government body by another although the trust purposes had no connection with the functions of either body.[84] The cases cited in this connection relate to changes taking place after the inception of the trust but it is thought that a similar approach would be appropriate if the change occurred between the granting of the trust deed and such inception although the point is apparently not covered by direct authority. In the case of an individual nominated descriptively, however, the view has been expressed under reference to an English decision concerning a testamentary gift of real property to the eldest son of a certain party, that where a person who is in existence at the date of the deed constituting the trust answers the description of the trustee nominated therein but predeceases the truster, the nomination lapses.[85]

Single and plural appointments

The nomination in any trust may be of a single person or of a number of persons and again may provide for alternative trustees or substitute trustees.[86] Except where the nominee is an *ex officio* trustee, or a corporate trustee unaffected by normal contingencies such as death, the nomination of a single party simpliciter is undesirable unless the trust purposes are taking immediate effect and likely to be completed within a very limited time.

Broadly speaking plural nominations of trustees may be classified as simple and joint.[87] It appears that in *inter vivos* trusts as well as in testamentary trusts simple nominations of several trustees imply a destination to acceptors and survivors, although such destination is commonly ex-

---

[82] *Vestry of St. Silas Church* v. *Trs. of St. Silas Church*, 1945 S.C. 110.
[83] *Mailler's Trs.* v. *Allan* (1904) 7 F. 326.
[84] *Parish Council of Kilmarnock* v. *Ossington's Trs.* (1896) 23 R. 833. Nationalisation statutes in various spheres have of course included express provision for the transfer of trust duties as well as trust property to newly constituted authorities, *e.g.* National Health Service (Scotland) Act 1947.
[85] Menzies, 28; Mackenzie Stuart, 53, both referring to *Amyot* v. *Dwarris* [1904] A.C. 268, where it was held that a younger son who was the eldest son alive at the testator's death did not take the bequest to the eldest son.
[86] For examples of alternative or substitutional nominations, see Elder, *Forms of Wills*, 11, 12.
[87] As to the various forms plural nominations may take, see McLaren, II, 892.

pressed in deeds and settlements.[88] Such a nomination is thus in effect joint and several, the appointment of each nominee being unaffected by the failure of another or others by death or declinature.[89] In the now rare cases where the nomination is in terms a joint one it will be ineffective unless all the nominees survive and accept office and the trust will lapse on the death of one trustee before completion of the administration.[90] A simple nomination in a deed which does not express the usual destination may become in effect a joint one by reason of the provisions of the deed re quorum [91] but by statutory implication a majority of accepting and surviving trustees constitute a quorum [92] and the relative provisions in trust deeds usually follow this rule.[93] The failure to take office of one of several nominees designated as a *sine quo non* trustee does not affect the nomination of the other or others or the existence of the trust, the right of veto conferred on a *sine quo non* trustee being a personal privilege arising only on his acceptance of office.[94] While a simple nomination of guardians vests the office in the acceptor or acceptors [95] the appointment of testamentary trustees as guardians to beneficiaries under age is by implication a joint one [96] although in practice this construction is commonly elided by appointing the accepting and surviving trustees.[97]

(c) ACCEPTANCE OF OFFICE

Whatever form the nomination of a trustee may take the appointment is not effective and the status of trustee is not attained until there has been acceptance on the part of the nominee. Only then does the relationship of trustee and beneficiary come into being and the nominee become vested in the rights and affected by the liabilities of the office.

Acceptance as a voluntary act

As a general rule acceptance is a voluntary act, no one being obliged to undertake trusteeship.[98] This applies to *ex officio* as well as to personal nominees [99] although it is conceivable that in the case of an *ex officio* nominee the acceptance of the trusteeship might be made a condition of his office or employment.[1] On the other hand an undertaking by a nominee

---

[88] For a discussion of this matter and examination of the authorities, see McLaren, II, 892.

[89] *Halley* v. *Gowans* (1840) 2 D. 623; *Adam* v. *Grieve* (1867) 5 M. 284.

[90] *Dawson* v. *Stirton* (1863) 2 M. 196; a case in which joint nomination although not so expressed was held to be implied in a trust deed for creditors, a doubtful interpretation even at common law (see McLaren, II, 896 and Menzies, 87, s. 158 (Note 2)).

[91] McLaren, II, 895; as to the matter of quorum generally, see *infra*, pp. 303 *et seq*.

[92] Trusts (Scotland) Act, 1921 s. 3 (c).

[93] See Elder, *Forms of Wills*, 14, 15.

[94] McLaren, II, 896; *Forbes* v. *Earl of Galloway's Trs.*, May 31, 1808, F.C.; *sub nom. Forbes* v. *Honeyman* (1808) 5 Pat. 226: see Currie, 88, referring to the article " Non-acceptance of *sine quo non* executor," (1935) S.L.R. Vol. 51, p. 178; as to the *sine quo non* trustee generally, see, *infra*, p. 301.

[95] McLaren, II, 896 and authorities there cited.

[96] *Johnston* v. *Johnston's Trs.* (1892) 20 R. 46.

[97] See Elder, *Forms of Wills*, 176–177.

[98] Ersk., *Principles*, III XA5.

[99] *Vestry of St. Silas Church* v. *Trs. of St. Silas Church*, 1945 S.C. 110.

[1] *Shepherd* v. *Hutton's Trs.* (1855) 17 D. 516, 520; see also Mackenzie Stuart, 153.

to accept trusteeship given in advance and before the trust comes into
operation would seem to be valid and effective, the granting of the undertaking having been a voluntary act and the acceptance which follows
merely the fulfilment of the obligation so incurred.[2] Unless, however, its
terms clearly preclude such a construction any form of acceptance given
before the trust takes effect may be regarded as a mere statement of intention or at highest an honourable understanding and not as a legally
binding obligation.[3] In any event it seems doubtful if an undertaking to
accept office as trustee would be enforceable by specific implement and
moreover the statutory power of resignation now enjoyed by all gratuitous
trustees other than sole trustees [4] would normally make such enforcement
of limited practical value, the nominee being under no obligation to retain
office after his acceptance.

In the case of testamentary trustees the rule that acceptance is voluntary
may be said to require qualification by the proviso that in certain circumstances a nominee who is entitled to legacy or bequest in terms of the
settlement is not entitled to receive that benefit unless he accepts office as
trustee. The practice fairly commonly adopted of framing bequests in
favour of accepting trustees so described [5] resolves any question that may
arise under this head but in any event there appears to be a presumption [6]
that bequests in favour of parties nominated as trustees or executors or
for other fiduciary offices are conditional on acceptance of office [7] although
a number of decisions have turned on the terms of the particular settlements as determining whether or not the benefit was given to the recipient
in his fiduciary capacity.[8]

Time for acceptance

There is no rule of law imposing a time limit within which a nominee
must accept the office of trustee. While as explained later [9] the continued
failure of all nominees or a sole nominee to accept office may affect the
existence of the trust it is clear that where one or more of a group of
nominees have accepted at the appropriate time others who have not done
so but have not expressly disclaimed may do so at any time subsequently,
subject to their confirming the actings of the trustees already in office.[10]

Scope and effect of acceptance

Acceptance of trusteeship to be effective must be general and not
partial. A truster who contemplates partial acceptance by the persons he

---

2 Menzies, 63.
3 McLaren, II, 1177.
4 1921 Act, s. 3 (a) and proviso (1).
5 Vide e.g. Elder, Forms of Wills, 120.
6 Menzies, 511 distinguishing in this respect between specific and residuary bequests.
7 Scrimzeour v. Wedderburn (1675) Mor. 6357; Leckie v. Renny (1748) Mor. 6347.
8 Henderson v. Stuart (1825) 4 S. 309; Mellis's Trs. v. Legge's Exor. (1898) 25 R. 954;
   Michie's Exors. v. Michie (1905) 7 F. 509.
9 Infra, pp. 247–248.
10 Darling v. Watson (1823) 2 S. 519; affd (1825) 1 W. & S. 188.

nominates as trustees should make separate trust provisions perhaps embodied in different documents [11] and this course is frequently adopted where assets to be administered are located in or trust purposes fall to be executed in different jurisdictions. Where a single document (*e.g.* a marriage contract dealing separately with the respective funds of husband and wife) nominates the same parties as trustees in different trusts there is no necessary inference that acceptance of one trusteeship must involve acceptance of the other or others. It is questionable whether one acceptance will be implied from another as seems sometimes to occur in England,[12] but *ob majorem cautelam* the terms of acceptance should perhaps be qualified if only one office is to be accepted.

Again where one document nominates the same parties for other offices as well as trusteeship, *e.g.* executorship or guardianship, acceptance of trusteeship will not necessarily involve or be conditional upon acceptance of the other office or offices [13] but where, as frequently happens, the other offices are conferred on the trustees as such, it may be advisable, if acceptance of the other office or offices is not intended, that the terms of the acceptance of trusteeship should elide any implication which might otherwise be inferred from actings.[14] In practice the advisability of this course seems clearest in the case where parties accepting trusteeship do not desire to act as guardians [15]; in the case of executorship where confirmation is the only valid title to intromit with the estate it seems less likely that acceptance of office by a party who did not apply or concur in applying for confirmation would be inferred from his acceptance of the office of trustee, despite the practice of appointing testamentary trustees as executors [16] and the statutory rule whereby they can confirm as executors nominate where no other appointment to that office is made.[17]

Form of acceptance

Acceptance of trusteeship may be express or implied and there are no rules prescribing the form which an express acceptance must take.[18] Improbative and even verbal acceptances may be effective but where nothing has followed upon the acceptance it appears that there may be *locus poenitentiae* entitling the nominee to decline unless the acceptance is in probative writing.[19]

The approved practice is to obtain the signatures of all accepting trustees to an attested minute which is often indorsed on the settlement and registered with it for preservation. Such a document should embody any

---

[11] *Re Lord Fullerton's Contract* [1896] 1 Ch. 228; see also *Cumming* v. *Hay* (1834) 12 S. 508 and Mackenzie Stuart, 156.

[12] See McLaren, II, 1113.

[13] Menzies, 64.

[14] *Mollison* v. *Murray* (1833) 12 S. 237; *Hill* v. *City of Glasgow Bank* (1879) 7 R. 68, 76, *per* L.P. Inglis.

[15] See *Mollison* v. *Murray*, *supra*.

[16] See Elder, *op. cit.*, 11, 12.

[17] Executors (Scotland) Act 1900, s. 3.

[18] Ersk., *Principles*, III XA5.

[19] McLaren, II, 1110; *Bannerman* v. *Bannerman* (1842) 5 D. 229.

necessary consents, a matter which was important when an acceptance by a married woman required her husband's consent but will not normally arise now except in the case of a minor becoming a trustee.[20] A letter from a nominee to the trust agents or to his co-nominees, if holograph of the nominee, would be equally effective unless its terms were such that it could be construed as a statement of intention to accept and not an actual acceptance.[21]

Implied acceptance

The actings of a nominee for trusteeship may be significant in either of two ways in establishing his acceptance of office. In the first place they may constitute the ratification or homologation necessary to make effective an informal or improbative expression of acceptance. A nominee who has taken part in or given directions for the management of the trust will not be permitted to resile from an informal acceptance.[22] Secondly where there is no express acceptance in any form the conduct or actings of a nominee may preclude him from denying that he has accepted office, but failure to give any definite indication of declinature by a nominee aware of his nomination does not in itself imply acceptance and the nominee's actings may be such that no inference of acceptance can arise.[23] Again consistently with the fact already mentioned [24] that there is in general no time limit for acceptance of trust office, lapse of time is a neutral element whether it is sought to establish acceptance or declinature.[25] Knowledge of the nomination is of course a prerequisite of implied acceptance and such knowledge being established may result in certain actings which might have been done in another capacity being regarded as done *qua* trustee and so inferring acceptance.[26] Likewise such knowledge may result in an inference of acceptance by a nominee who although himself taking no active steps permits matters to proceed on the footing that he has accepted office, *e.g.* the inclusion of his name in the trust title as completed or in proceedings concerning the trust.[27] No such inference would arise however if the nominee could show that the steps founded upon had been taken without authority from him and that he had repudiated them immediately on their coming to his knowledge.[28] Cases of this kind can arise where agents on their own initiative have recorded a heritable title in

---

[20] *Supra*, p. 228.

[21] *Bannerman* v. *Bannerman, supra.*

[22] *Davidson* v. *Mackenzie* (1875) 13 S. 1082.

[23] *Mitchell* v. *Davidson* (1855) 18 D. 284.

[24] See p. 242, *supra.*

[25] See Menzies, 66, referring to certain English decisions in which more significance was attached to lapse of time, the suggestion being that, as there is a presumption of acceptance, complete inactivity by the nominee will normally imply acceptance: see, however, *Re Clout and Frewer's Contract* [1924] 2 Ch. 230, where a delay of 30 years in a testamentary trust was held to have the opposite effect.

[26] *Conyngham* v. *Conyngham* (1750) 1 Ves. 522.

[27] McLaren, II, 1111 and authorities there cited, including *Cumming* v. *Hay* (1834) 12 S. 508.

[28] *Ibid.*; and see *Paul* v. *Boyd* (1833) 11 S. 292.

name of the trustees or registered the trustees in respect of shareholdings in companies.[29]

As a general rule any positive act done alone or with another or others in relation to the administration of a trust will infer acceptance by a nominee who knows of his nomination.[30] Examples of such acts are concurring in the appointment of a factor or participating, even passively, in court proceedings, or intromitting with trust funds.[31] The same will apply to completion of title to heritable or moveable assets where that has been done with the proper authority of the nominee or has involved his co-operation in the signing of necessary documents or otherwise,[32] the signature of a nominee given in error as to the true purport of the document having however no such effect.[33]

Reference has already been made to the question whether acceptance of trusteeship involves acceptance of other offices to which the acceptor may have been nominated by the same document.[34] The converse question arising here is whether acceptance of such other offices implies acceptance of trusteeship. While there appears to be no direct authority in Scotland, the view has been expressed that a nominee's acceptance of the office of executor will infer his acceptance of the office of trustee for which he is nominated in the same document.[35] It would appear however that the inference thus arising should be fairly readily elided by actings indicating an intention to confine the acceptance to the executorship. There is between the respective offices of executor and trustee a fundamental distinction [36] which has not really been eliminated by statutory developments such as the extension to executors of the powers of gratuitous trustees.[37] In Scottish practice, however, the question is unlikely to arise as it is customary for testamentary trustees in that capacity to be appointed executors [38] and there is in any event a statutory implication to that effect if no other appointment to the executorship is made.[39] Where the parties nominated in a trust settlement decline office both as trustees and executors it has been held that a party confirmed as executor-dative becomes a trustee for all concerned in the succession but is not obliged to

---

29 Compare *Ker* v. *City of Glasgow Bank* (1879) 6 R. 575; affd. 6 R.(H.L.) 52 and *Gillespie* v. *City of Glasgow Bank* (1879) 6 R. 813; the Stock Transfer Act of 1963, dispensing with transferees' signatures to transfers of fully paid shares, may be said to have made such registration without the trustees' express consent more likely but most disputes in the past arose out of the now rare case of shares which were not fully paid.

30 *Logan* v. *Meiklejohn* (1843) 5 D. 1066 (see the opinion of the Lord Ordinary at pp. 10–11: the question at issue in the case was actually one of resignation).

31 *Watson* v. *Crawcour* (1843) 5 D. 1182; (1844) 6 D. 688; *Ker* v. *City of Glasgow Bank*, *supra*.

32 Cf. *Paul* v. *Boyd*, *supra*; *Cumming* v. *Hay*, *supra*; and *Ker* v. *City of Glasgow Bank*, *supra*.

33 *Gillespie* v. *City of Glasgow Bank*, *supra* (a case concerning a party alleged to have been assumed as a trustee).

34 *Supra*, p. 243.

35 Menzies, 67, and authorities therein cited. See also *Re Sharman's Will Trusts, Public Trustee* v. *Sharman* [1942] Ch. 311; and Underhill, 251.

36 See Menzies, 849–854, " Note on the offices of Executor and of Trustee " and Ch. 28, *infra*.

37 Executors (Scotland) Act 1900, s. 2; Succession (Scotland) Act 1964, s. 20.

38 See *e.g.* Elder, *op. cit.*, 11, 12.

39 Executors (Scotland) Act 1900, s. 3.

carry on the administration of the trust.[40] This recognises the basic difference between the two offices as referred to above and it would appear that the position in such circumstances will not have been altered as a result of the statutory provisions whereby executors now confirm to heritable as well as moveable estate [41] and executors-dative have, like executors-nominate, in general, the powers of gratuitous trustees.[42] The inclusion of heritage in the confirmation of executors, however, seems effectively to negative any possible argument that the inference of acceptance of trusteeship arising from acceptance of executorship is limited in its application to the moveable property affected by the trust.

To the rule that actings and intromissions by a nominee can or will infer acceptance of trust office an exception exists in the cases where to enable a trust to function it is necessary for a party, who without any concurrence on his part has been put in the position of a trustee, to take some action such as assuming other trustees or granting conveyances to denude himself of trust property. Thus when a title to a trust estate had been made up by mistake in name of a nominee who had not accepted trusteeship he was required to take the necessary steps to denude himself on being relieved of or indemnified against all resulting liability and expense.[43] In such cases the act of denuding or other action requiring to be taken is not to be regarded as inferring even partial acceptance of office but rather as constituting an act of disclaimer or declinature, the nominee incurring no liability except in so far as he has intromitted with trust property.[44] Likewise a nominee for trusteeship who had declined office but after the death of one of the acting trustees joining in granting a deed of assumption because of a doubt as to the competency of its being granted by a sole trustee did not incur liability as an intromitter.[45]

(d) DECLINATURE OR DISCLAIMER OF OFFICE

As in the case of acceptance declinature or disclaimer of trusteeship may be express or implied and if express does not require to be evidenced by writing probative or otherwise.

Express declinature

The power of voluntary resignation which since 1861 has by statute belonged to all gratuitous trustees other than sole trustees [46] has reduced the importance of this matter from the point of view of the nominee who does not desire to hold the responsibilities of trusteeship; but since, as has

---

[40] McLaren, II, 1116; cf. *Kirkpatrick* v. *Innes* (1830) 4 W. & S. 48.
[41] Succession (Scotland) Act 1964, s. 14.
[42] *Ibid.* s. 20.
[43] *Dallas* v. *Leishman* (1710) Mor. 16191; cf. *Royal Infirmary* v. *Lord Advocate* (1861) 23 D. 1213, 1221, per Lord Ivory; see also Bell, *Prin.* s. 1993, 3.
[44] Menzies, 71; cf. McLaren, II, 1118.
[45] *Blair* v. *Paterson* (1836) 14 S. 361; cf. *Miller* v. *Black's Trs.* (1837) 2 S. & McL. 866, 899, per Lord Brougham.
[46] Trusts (Scotland) Act 1921, s. 3 (a) and proviso (1).

been mentioned,[47] there is no precise time limit within which acceptance is competent it is desirable that declinature, when intended, should be irrevocable in effect and satisfactorily evidenced, the matter being of importance to third parties such as purchasers of trust property. The approved practice is to embody the declinature in an attested minute similar to that used for acceptance [48] and, where some nominees are accepting and some declining office, the same minute may serve both purposes. As in the case of acceptance it appears that anything less than a probative document of declinature may, where nothing has followed upon it, leave the nominee free subsequently to withdraw the declinature and accept office.[49]

Implied declinature

Declinature by actings may be rather difficult to establish. As has been seen, lapse of time may not in itself give rise to any inference either of acceptance or declinature.[50] An inference of declinature may, however, arise from conduct inconsistent with the acceptance of trusteeship as when a nominee refuses to allow his name to be included in the trust title as completed to assets such as heritable property or again knowingly permits such titles to be completed with his name excluded.[51]

Effect and results of declinature

In general the effect of declinature is to deprive or relieve the nominee of all concern or connection with the trust and the trust estate; he becomes, as it has been said, a stranger to the trust.[52] In the case of *ex officio* nominees however, their declinature or failure to act does not preclude their successors in office from accepting and acting as trustees.[53]

A question arises as to the position at the inception of a trust when every trustee nominated has failed or declined to accept office. In general this situation is not fatal to the existence and operation of a duly constituted trust.[54] In the case of an *inter vivos* trust the truster has an inherent right of appointment which will enable him to make good the deficiency.[55] In a testamentary trust or in any other case where the truster is not available to supply the deficiency the necessary action will be taken by the court in appointing a new trustee or trustees.[56] Two special

---

[47] *Supra*, p. 242.
[49] *Young* (1901) 9 S.L.T. 20.
[48] *Supra*, pp. 234–244.
[50] *Supra*, p. 244.
[51] Bell, *Comm.* I, 31, and see generally Menzies, 72.
[52] Menzies, 72, 73; and see the English case of *Dove* v. *Everard* (1830) 1 R. & M. 231, where the subsequent actings of a trustee who had declined office were held not to be trust intromissions but acts done in an agency capacity. In Scotland the court has refused to appoint as judicial factor on the trust estate a trustee who has declined: *Pennycuik* (1851) 14 D. 311.
[53] *Mags. of Edinburgh* v. *McLaren* (1881) 8 R.(H.L.) 140.
[54] *Gill* v. *Arizona Coffee Company* (1900) 2 F. 843, 860, *per* Lord McLaren; *Miller* v. *Black's Trs.* (1837) 2 S. & McL. 866, 890, *per* Lord Brougham; *Earl of Mansfield* v. *Lord Scone's Tutor*, 1908 S.C. 459, 471–472, *per* Lord Kinnear.
[55] *Infra*, p. 262.
[56] Trusts (Scotland) Act 1921, s. 22; alternatively a judicial factor may be appointed should the circumstances make this the more suitable course.

or exceptional cases should, however, be mentioned in this connection. Firstly in an *inter vivos* trust where the trustee himself is to be the sole trustee the act of acceptance may be the act constituting the delivery or its equivalent without which the trust is not effectively constituted.[57] Secondly it is possible to conceive of cases in which failure in acceptance will defeat the trust because the discretionary powers to be exercised are inseparably connected with the person nominated.[58] Normally, however, the failure of trustees to act will not have the effect of defeating the interests of the beneficiaries who, although they cannot compel trustees nominated to take up office or even, perhaps, compel the truster, if alive, to nominate new trustees, can seek relief by applying to the court for an appointment of trustees or a judicial factor. Only if the beneficiaries take no action and the trust remains inoperative for the period of the long negative prescription may the trust purpose be nullified and the beneficial rights extinguished.[59]

(e) COMPLETION OF TITLE

By accepting office trustees become vested in a personal right to the trust estate. Except in cases where early disposal is intended and the expense of completion of the trustees' title can and should be avoided [60] they have a duty to complete their title *habili modo* [61] to the various assets or categories of assets comprised in the estate in so far as it is within their power to do so.[62] Apart from the cases of bearer securities, cash or corporeal moveables in which simple delivery suffices, some form of documentation will be required for completion of the trustees' title and it is important that such documentation should, where possible, disclose the fiduciary nature of the title, thus preserving the rights of the beneficiaries in questions with personal creditors of the trustees.

Heritable property

In the case of heritable property this matter creates no problem where the trust is made a condition of the conveyance, *i.e.* the purposes of the

---

[57] *Cameron's Trs.* v. *Cameron*, 1907 S.C. 407, 415, *per* Lord Kyllachy.

[58] Bell, Comm. I, 38; *Dick* v. *Ferguson* (1758) Mor. 7446, 16206; *cf. Hepburn* (1692) Fount. 60 and *Hill* v. *Burns* (1826) 2 W. & S. 80, 89. *Per contra* see *Fraser* v. *Fraser* (1810) Hume 885 and Menzies, 73.

[59] *Earl of Mansfield* v. *Lord Scone's Tutor*, 1908 S.C. 459, 465, *per* Lord President Dunedin. Extinction of the beneficial rights by prescription involves regarding these rights as being of a personal as opposed to a proprietary nature.

[60] For example the realisation of heritable property may be carried out by using the facilities given by s. 3 of the Conveyancing (Scotland) Act 1924 for dispositions by uninfeft parties without title having been completed in terms of s. 4 of that Act: again shares in a company may be transferred by testamentary trustees as personal representatives of a deceased shareholder without the trustees having themselves been registered: Companies Act 1948, s. 76. See in this connection *Wishart* v. *City of Glasgow Bank* (1879) 6 R. 1341, 1349–1350, *per* Lord Shand.

[61] Where the trust estate includes items of property situated outwith Scotland professional advice from the appropriate jurisdiction should be sought by trustees for the completion of their title.

[62] There may be cases where actual completion of title is impossible, *e.g.* where directors of a company exercise powers to refuse registration of transferees or of personal representatives of deceased shareholders.

trust and the transfer of assets to the trustees are contained in the one document. Where, however, the conveyance of the property is in itself unqualified, a separate document such as a declaration of trust embodying the trust purposes will be effective to qualify the title of the trustees while that title remains personal but will not do so in questions with third parties when the trustees take infeftment on the unqualified conveyance unless by the recording of the deed of trust or in some other way the trust purposes as affecting the property are caused to appear in the Sasine Register.[63]

In the cases of *ex officio* trustees and trustees for religious or educational bodies the due completion of the original trustee's title to such heritable property as is comprised in the trust estate has a special significance because of certain statutory provisions affecting the title of the successors to such trustees.[64] Prima facie there may be a difficulty in the completion of title in such cases by reason of the trustees being descriptive disponees not actually named in the relative documents but it appears that even where title is being completed by the recording of the trust deed *de plano* in the Sasine Register this difficulty can be overcome by the incorporation of the requisite details in the warrant of registration.[65]

Incorporeal moveable property

In the case of incorporeal moveable rights generally the disclosure of the fiduciary character of the title as completed presents no difficulties. The difficulties in this respect formerly affecting government securities registered in the Books of the Bank of England have been removed [66] but it is still the case that trusts cannot be recognised in relation to the stocks or shares of companies registered in England under the Companies Acts with the result that the trustees can only be registered as individuals in respect of such securities.[67]

In examining in more detail the procedure and documentation applicable in the completion of title of trustees it is necessary to deal separately with *inter vivos* trusts on the one hand and *mortis causa* trusts on the other.

Inter vivos trusts

While testamentary trusts frequently embrace the whole corpus of a deceased party's estate and are commonly constituted by deeds dealing

---

[63] McLaren, II, 909.

[64] Conveyancing (Scotland) Act 1874, s. 45; Titles to Land Consolidation (Scotland) Act 1868, s. 26; see *infra*, pp. 268–269.

[65] McLaren, II, 913; Menzies, 75.

[66] By the Government Stock Regulations made under s. 47 of the Finance Act 1942 (S.I. 1965 No. 1420, reg. 12 (1)) stockholders may be described as trustees of a specified trust or as trustees without specification of a trust.

[67] Companies Act 1948, s. 117, which does not apply to companies registered in Scotland; but Scottish companies may in terms of their Articles be precluded from registering trusts and will be in this position if they adopt or allow to apply without modification the Form of Articles contained in Table A of Sched. 1 to the Act (see reg. 7). For an example of a Scottish company unable to register trustees as such, see *Elliot* v. *Whyte*, 1935 S.C. 81.

with the truster's whole estate, *inter vivos* trusts will normally affect only certain particular funds or assets. To vest these in the trustees and put the latter in a position to complete titles thereto *habili modo* it is necessary that the deed defining the trust purposes or some other deed emanating from the truster should identify the assets comprised in the trust estate and effectively convey these to the trustees. Heritable property will not normally be described by trust deeds or settlements in such terms as to permit of completion of title thereto being effected by *de plano* recording of the trust deed or settlement in the Register of Sasines. More often the deed or settlement will, *quoad* any heritage affected by the trust, constitute a general disposition through which the trustees' title can be completed by the expeding and recording of a notarial instrument or its modern equivalent a notice of title.[68] On the analogy of certain cases concerning testamentary trusts [69] it may be possible to regard a deed constituting a trust affecting certain assets as implying a conveyance of these assets to the trustees although it does not in terms so convey them. Normally, however, the truster being alive will be willing and able to put matters beyond doubt by granting a conveyance or other supplementary deed.[70]

The above-mentioned facilities for completion of title through a general disposition or conveyance apply only to heritable property. There are no corresponding facilities for incorporeal moveables of any kind which accordingly require not merely identification in the trust deed but also conveyance in the form and manner appropriate to the type of asset involved. The necessary special conveyances such as transfers of stocks or shares or assignations of policies of assurance may be embodied in the trust deed but are more frequently comprised in separate documents.

Testamentary trusts

As has been indicated testamentary trusts generally comprise the whole corpus of the deceased truster's estate and are normally constituted by a document dealing with that estate as a whole. In any event however completion of a title by testamentary trustees is governed in the first place by the statutory rule that every part of the estate of a deceased person (whether consisting of moveable property or heritable property) falling to be administered under the law of Scotland vests, for the purposes of administration, by virtue of confirmation thereto in the executor thereby confirmed, to be administered and disposed of by him according to law.[71]

---

[68] Titles to Land Consolidation (Scotland) Act 1868, s. 19; Conveyancing (Scotland) Act 1924, ss. 4, 5 and 6; but as to circumstances in which completion of the trustees' title may be unnecessary, see *supra*, p. 248 and n. 60.

[69] *e.g. McLeod's Trs.* v. *McLuckie* (1883) 10 R. 1056.

[70] This would appear to be the reason why the provisions of the Conveyancing Act 1874, s. 46 (now repealed by Succession (Scotland) Act 1964, s. 34 and Sched. 3), whereby testamentary trustees or executors could complete title to heritage although there was no conveyance in their favour did not extend to *inter vivos* trusts.

[71] Succession (Scotland) Act 1964, s. 14 (1), applying to deaths on or after Sept. 10, 1964 (see s. 38 (3)).

The personal title thus acquired by confirmation is an executry title and not a trust title but where, as frequently happens under Scottish testamentary settlements, the parties confirming as executors-nominate are the trustees named in the settlement, the one title is regarded as merging into the other so that when the executry administration is completed the assets will be regarded as held by the trustees as owners in trust.[72] Apart from cases in which its fiduciary character cannot be reflected [73] the title as completed through the confirmation will bear to be that of executors but in practice at least it is considered unnecessary for the holders in that capacity to convey to themselves as trustees the assets which are to be retained in a continuing trust. Conveyance by executors will, however, be requisite where separate trusts are created by the same testator whether or not by a single document and again in the case where the trustees who are to act in a continuing trust are not identical with the executors-nominate even, it would appear, if the settlement purports to convey the property in question direct to the trustees.[74] In such circumstances the statutory facilities available in the case of certain assets make it unnecessary for executors to complete title to these assets in their own names before granting conveyances.[75]

The provisions of the Succession (Scotland) Act 1964 for the inclusion of heritable property in the confirmation of executors,[76] have given rise to the question whether trustees or executors-nominate seeking to complete title in their own names or intending to dispone as uninfeft proprietors are now obliged to proceed in the manner prescribed by the Act, using the confirmation as the link of title. The view has been expressed that it is still competent for them to proceed as they did before the passing of the Act and use the will or settlement as the link of title but that it is preferable that the provisions of the Act should be followed and confirmation used as the link.[77]

---

[72] See Menzies, s. 131, n. 4, s. 557, n. 1, and appendix, pp. 849–852: see also McLaren, II, 1127.

[73] See *supra*, p. 249 and n. 67.

[74] See the Memorial and Opinion referred to in n. 77, *infra*, indicating doubts about the completion of title under a direct bequest.

[75] *Cf. supra*, p. 248 and n. 60.

[76] ss. 14, 15, 22 and Sched. 1. See also Act of Sederunt (Confirmation of Executors) 1964, as amended by Act of Sederunt (Confirmation of Executors Amendment) 1966, prescribing that the inventory embodied in or appended to the confirmation of an executor is to include in respect of heritable property only such description as will be sufficient to identify the property as a separate item of the estate.

[77] See Memorial and Opinion of the Professors of Conveyancing on " Completion of Title after the Succession (Scotland) Act 1964," 1965 J.L.S. Vol. 10, p. 153: support for the view that the former procedure is no longer available would seem to be derived from the repeal by the Succession (Scotland) Act (s. 34 and Sched. 3) of s. 19 of the Titles to Land Consolidation (Scotland) Act 1868 (except in relation to general disposition by conveyance *inter vivos* as to which see *supra*, p. 250 and n. 68) and s. 46 of the Conveyancing Act 1874, which enabled testamentary trustees or executors to complete title through a will or settlement containing no conveyance to them; *cf.* (1965) 10 J.L.S. 189–190 and 215–216.

CHAPTER 16

THE ASSUMPTION OF TRUSTEES

THE assumption of trustees although nowhere authoritatively defined or interpreted is generally understood as signifying their appointment by existing holders of trust office and is dealt with first here because it is the usual and much the commonest way in which new trustees are introduced in a subsisting trust.

The power of assumption and its exercise

At common law trustees had no power of assumption unless such power was conferred on them by the trust deed. Since 1861, however, there has been statutory provision for assumption in all trusts affected by the Trusts Acts and it is now provided that except where the contrary is expressed, such trusts shall be held to include power to the trustee if there be only one or to the trustees if there be more than one, or to a quorum of the trustees if there be more than two, to assume new trustees.[1] This power extends to assumed trustees [2] and to trustees appointed by the court unless excluded by the terms of the appointment,[3] and is operative whether the trustees are acting gratuitously or being remunerated. Doubts have however been expressed as to the competency of an assumption by *ex officio* trustees.[4]

Executors-nominate being trustees within the statutory meaning [5] and as such having the powers of trustees [6] may assume new executors and likewise tutors or curators appointed by deed,[7] but not tutors or curators at law,[8] may assume new or additional parties to act in their respective offices.

The statutory power of assumption is operative " unless the contrary be expressed "[9] and it was held in a case dealing with the corresponding provisions of the Trusts (Scotland) Act 1861 but relating to a deed made before that Act that the inclusion in the trust deed of a limited power of

---

[1] Trusts (Scotland) Act 1921, s. 3 (*b*).
[2] Although the terms of the trust deed might be such as to confine the power to the original trustees.
[3] Trusts (Scotland) Act 1921, s. 22, and the same would presumably apply where the appointment was made in exercise of the *nobile officium*.
[4] *Vestry of St. Silas Church* v. *Trs. of St. Silas Church*, 1945 S.C. 110, 121, *per* L.J.-C. Cooper.
[5] Trusts (Scotland) Act 1921, s. 2.
[6] Executors (Scotland) Act 1900, s. 2.
[7] S. 2 of the Trusts (Scotland) Act 1921 defines " trust " as meaning and including *inter alia* the appointment of any tutor, curator or judicial factor by deed, decree or otherwise but by s. 3 (3) the Act excludes the power of assumption in the case of judicial factors: see in this connection the definition of " judicial factor " in s. 2 of the Act as extended by s. 3 of the Trusts (Scotland) Act 1961.
[8] Their " trust " does not fall within the statutory definition: Trusts (Scotland) Act 1921, s. 2. [9] 1921 Act, s. 3 (*b*).

assumption did not by inference exclude the statutory power.[10] In the case of trusts created with the statutory power in existence, however, the opinion has been expressed, on the analogy of certain decisions concerning the power of the court to authorise trustees to make advances of capital to beneficiaries as affected by the existence of express powers to that effect,[11] that a provision that new trustees may be assumed under certain conditions or in certain circumstances should be construed as an unequivocal direction that they are not to be assumed except as thus provided.[12] In the most recent case concerning the statutory provision for assumption a direction that the truster's widow and others whom she might select to act along with her should be trustees and executors was held to be an expression of contrary intention excluding the statutory power so long as the widow remained a trustee.[13] While the earlier practice of including in trust deeds express provisions for assumption of new trustees [14] continued even after the introduction of the statutory power of assumption, the tendency now appears to be not to include such provisions unless some restriction of or innovation on the statutory powers is intended. Such provisions, where they exist, are more likely to be found in *inter vivos* trusts than in testamentary settlements. In cases such as marriage settlement trusts the statutory power will be regarded as excluded if that appears to be the intention of the contracting parties; and this construction was applied where, as commonly happens, a marriage contract reserved to the spouses the power to appoint new trustees in the case of the death, resignation or incapacity of the original trustees.[15] Again, where the trustees appointed by a marriage-contract were expressly authorised to assume new trustees with the consent of the spouses, the statutory power was held to be excluded; the wife having become insane, the court in the exercise of their *nobile officium*, authorised the assumption of new trustees and conferred on the trustees the power to assume trustees without the consent of the wife while her mental incapacity continued.[16]

It appears that the statutory power of assumption must be exercised so as to take effect immediately and unconditionally. A truster may empower a trustee to appoint someone to take that trustee's place after the latter's death but such an appointment is not regarded as made in exercise

---

10 *Allan's Trs.* v. *Hairstens* (1878) 5 R. 576; *cf. Maxwell's Trs.* v. *Maxwell* (1874) 2 R. 71 concerning resignation.

11 The statutory power as now contained in 1921 Act, s. 16; in cases not covered by these provisions the *nobile officium* may be invoked.

12 Mackenzie Stuart, 293, referring to *Thomson* v. *Miller's Trs.* (1883) 11 R. 401 and *Anderson's Trs.*, 1932 S.C. 226, 231, *per* L.P. Clyde: but see *per contra* Menzies, 39, referring particularly to the opinion of Lord Gifford in *Allan's Trs.* v. *Hairstens, supra*, p. 580, as approved by L.J.-C. Moncreiff in *Munro's Trs.* v. *Young* (1887) 14 R. 574, 577: and *cf.* McLaren, II, 1125.

13 *Thomson's Trs.*, 1948 S.L.T.(Notes) 27.

14 See McLaren, II, 1124.

15 *Munro's Trs.* v. *Young* (1887) 14 R. 574. Emphasis was placed on the fact that the power of assumption was to be regarded as *reserved* by rather than *granted* to the spouses, a feature distinguishing the case from *Allan's Trs., supra*, n. 10.

16 *Adamson's Trs.*, 1917 S.C. 440.

of the statutory power and a power to that effect derived from the trust deed will be construed strictly in accordance with its terms.[17]

The power of assumption has been held to subsist even when the trust estate has been sequestrated [18] and placed under the control of a judicial factor but an assumption made in these circumstances did not operate to vest the new trustees in their powers until recall of the sequestration and factory.[19]

In the matter of personal qualifications or disqualifications the position of the new trustee who is to be introduced by assumption or otherwise is in no way different from that of a nominee for original trusteeship.[20] The statutory power of assumption is a discretionary power of the existing trustees in effect deemed to be written into the trust deed.[21] As however the exercise of the power is an act of administration in which the existing trustees must conform to the usual duties of care and suchlike it is subject to certain considerations and limitations not affecting the truster in his selection of original trustees.[22] Ideally trustees in exercising their power of assumption should put themselves in the position adopted by the court when petitioned for an appointment of new trustees [23] but the fact that the court would not in the circumstances have appointed the party or parties assumed will not per se be regarded as rendering the exercise of the power of assumption culpable and certainly not as justifying interference by the court. Except perhaps in the special case of a change in the personnel of the trust in effect putting the administration in the sole control of parties outwith the court's jurisdiction [24] the court will not normally intervene in these matters unless on specific allegations of corruption or extreme impropriety.[25] Where an insolvent trustee, who was leaving the country with a large part of the trust funds unaccounted for, assumed as trustees parties whom he at the same time appointed his mandatories and attorneys the court on the petition of a beneficiary and in respect of the adverse interest of the appointees sequestrated the estate and appointed a judicial factor.[26] Again where a trust was involved in a litigation and certain of the trustees, having a competing interest, had refrained from participating in the administration quoad the question at issue, the court sustained an objection

---

[17] Bowman v. Bowman, 1910, 1 S.L.T. 381.

[18] Re sequestration see Judicial Factors, pp. 4, 5, 31 and 32.

[19] Shedden (1867) 5 M. 955, a case in which the assumption of additional trustees was held to justify the recall of a sequestration and factory imposed when a sole trustee who was notour bankrupt was neglecting the administration of the trust and would not assume new trustees.

[20] See supra, pp. 227 et seq.

[21] Trusts (Scotland) Act 1921, s. 3, under which trusts are " held to include " certain powers and provisions (cf. Roughead v. Hunter (1833) 11 S. 516, in which the assumed trustee was treated as if he were nominated by the truster himself).

[22] Menzies, 54.

[23] Infra, pp. 276 et seq.

[24] See the case of Simpson's Trs., 1907 S.C. 87 (infra, p. 277), indicating that resigning trustees should seek judicial authority before assuming foreigners to replace themselves in the trust administration.

[25] Neilson v. Neilson's Trs. (1885) 12 R. 670.

[26] Foggo (1893) 20 R. 273: the new trustees were not removed by the court but it was indicated that it would be appropriate for them to resign (per the Lord President, p. 275).

to the assumption *pendente lite* of a party who appeared to be a nominee of these trustees but on the termination of the litigation held that an objection on this ground was no longer maintainable.[27] Assumption of a trustee or trustees is an obvious method of resolving a deadlock among the existing trustees and in such a case is not objectionable merely because the party to be assumed has been proposed by certain of the existing trustees and so might be expected to support the viewpoint of his sponsors.[28] A petition to the court for an appointment of trustees in the exercise of the *nobile officium* is apparently the only available course if such a deadlock cannot be resolved by an assumption.[29]

Reference has been made to various considerations which may as matters of policy if not as matters of law have to be regarded as restricting a truster's freedom of choice in nominating trustees.[30] Such considerations will apply with equal, if not greater, force to the nomination or assumption of new trustees by existing trustees. In practice it is generally recognised that parties whose beneficial interests in the trust may conflict or be at variance with that of other beneficiaries, or persons such as solicitors acting for such parties, should not be assumed or appointed, at least in circumstances where they would have a position of control or predominant influence in the administration. There appears, however, to be no case reported in Scotland in which the court has intervened to prevent or nullify such an appointment, nor any case in which an appointment made in circumstances of this kind has resulted in the trustees responsible for making it being held personally liable on that account.[31] Yet the fact that the court will not, in the circumstances, intervene to prevent the appointment or assumption taking effect does not in itself eliminate the question of culpability and consequent personal liability on the part of a trustee exercising a power of appointment or assumption. Once again the only authorities on the matter appear to be English decisions,[32] indicating that such liability will not arise except where the trustees responsible for the appointment, having themselves resigned, have left the appointees in control in circumstances in which it was reasonably obvious that a breach of trust by the latter was likely and a breach of the kind which should have been anticipated actually occurs. For example a trustee who, having resisted pressure to make unauthorised advances out of the trust estate,

---

[27] *Neilson* v. *Neilson's Trs., supra.*
[28] *Ibid.*
[29] *Aikman* (1881) 9 R. 213; *Taylor,* 1932 S.C. 1 (both being cases of petitions by beneficiaries where the court appointed additional trustees, the existing trustees concurring or at least not objecting).
[30] *Supra,* pp. 236 *et seq.*
[31] For a discussion of the English authorities on the matter, see Menzies, 54; see also the more recent case of *Briggs* v. *Parsloe* [1937] 3 All E.R. 831, 838, *per* Farwell J., confirming that a lifetenant may be appointed (*i.e.* assumed) as a trustee even in circumstances where the court might refuse to appoint him: *cf. Forster* v. *Abraham* (1874) L.R. 17 Eq. 351, 354 and 355 *per* Jarman M.R.
[32] For discussion of these authorities, see Menzies, 54–55. (*Cf.* Mackenzie Stuart, 297–298.) The statement of the law most commonly referred to is to be found in the opinion of Lord Westbury in the case of *Webster* v. *Le Hunt* (1860) 8 W.R. 534; (1861) 9 W.R. 918, but its application has been considerably restricted in terms of the decisions noted below.

resigns and appoints parties who may be expected to accede to the impor-
tunities of the beneficiaries may himself be liable for his successors' breach
of trust.[33] The liability arising in such circumstances has been attributed
in some cases to an implied agency on the part of the new trustees for
their predecessors but in others, and more appropriately as it would seem,
to failure by the latter in their duty of care.[34]

The power of assumption as a discretionary power of trustees can be
exercised or not as the trustees see fit and likewise there is no general rule
of law determining the number of trustees to be assumed at any particular
time, although it has been suggested that for the avoidance of expense and
delay in trust administration, the personnel of the trust should not, unless
in exceptional circumstances, be increased so as to exceed the number
originally nominated by the truster.[35] The trust deed may however circum-
scribe the trustees' discretion in these matters, for example by directing
that a certain party or parties will be assumed in certain circumstances,
e.g. on their attainment of majority, or again by prescribing a maximum or
minimum number of trustees to hold office, the requirement of a minimum
most commonly arising from provisions as to quorum.[36] Normally the
power of assumption will be exercised when by reason of non-acceptance,
death, resignation or other cause the personnel of the trust has been
reduced to a single trustee or at least to a smaller number than can conveniently and effectively carry on the administration. In practice it is
recognised that a person finding himself in the position of sole remaining
trustee should, where possible, avoid the danger of the trust lapsing on his
death or incapacity, by exercising his power of assumption without
delay, unless the outstanding purposes of the trust are merely ministerial
ones which can be implemented within a short period as, for example,
where all that remains to be done is to transfer the assets to the ultimate
beneficiaries who are ascertained and have vested rights.[37] A sole trustee
(and presumably the existing trustees as a body) cannot resign until at
least two new trustees have been assumed and accepted office or the court
has appointed new trustees or a judicial factor.[38] There is, however, no
objection to an arrangement whereby a sole trustee (or all the existing
trustees) resign in terms of the deed whereby the new trustees are assumed
and accept office.[39]

The statutory provisions make it clear that, apart from any contrary
provision in the trust deed, the power of assumption may be exercised by a

---

[33] *Head* v. *Gould* [1898] 2 Ch. 250 (a case of advances to beneficiaries who had themselves
been assumed); *Palairet* v. *Carew* (1863) 32 Beav. 564 (opinion of Lord Romilly M.R.);
and *Clark* v. *Hoskins* (1867) 36 L.J.Ch. 689; (1868) 37 L.J.Ch. 561 (opinion of Wood L.J.).
[34] *Per* Kekewich J. in *Head* v. *Gould*, *supra*, pp. 268–269.
[35] Menzies, 60.
[36] See McLaren, II, 1125, explaining the difficulties to which such provisions which are not
common in modern practice can give rise.
[37] Menzies, 60.
[38] Trusts (Scotland) Act 1921, s. 3, proviso (1): it appears that in such circumstances the
assumption of one trustee alone would not be competent; see Burns, *Conveyancing
Practice*, 4th ed., 837.
[39] See Burns, *op. cit.*, 844–845.

sole trustee or by a quorum, that is to say a majority of the existing trustees if more than two.[40] A provision in the trust deed prescribing a certain number of trustees as a quorum will normally be construed as operative only while not less than the prescribed number are acting and accordingly as not preventing the only surviving trustees or trustee from exercising powers such as that of assumption of additional trustees. On this view the court dismissed an application by beneficiaries for appointment of additional trustees when the only existing trustee was able and willing to make an assumption.[41]

As indicated in the discussion of declinature [42] a nominee of the truster who does not intend to accept the office of trustee may assume or, for the purpose of making up a prescribed quorum, concur with other nominees in the assumption of a trustee or trustees without prejudicing the freedom from responsibility secured by his declinature, such a course being considered particularly appropriate where the declinature would otherwise result in an application to the court being necessary because there were no trustees acting.[43]

The importance of the power of assumption has been recognised by the courts in their insistence that in the exercise of the power the utmost fairness must be observed among the trustees with a complete absence of concealment or deception in any form.[44] Hence if a quorum of trustees are to make an assumption without consulting with or referring to the other trustees or trustee there must be some good reason for their proceeding in this way,[45] such as the absence of a trustee abroad.[46]

The deed of assumption and conveyance

The statutory provision for the assumption of trustees [47] which contemplates the assumption being effected by a Deed of Assumption and Conveyance in a form prescribed [48] authorises the remaining trustees to execute the deed where any trustee is incapable of acting by reason of mental or physical disability or by continuous absence from the United Kingdom for a period of six months or upwards. If it is clear that a trustee who has gone abroad is likely to be abroad for at least six months it appears that his co-trustees may execute the deed without waiting for that period to elapse from the date of his departure, although unless there is some urgency it may be prudent to delay for the prescribed time.[49] The statutory provision in question has been held not to result that a trustee

---

[40] Trusts (Scotland) Act 1921, s. 3 (b) and (c): as to quorum generally, see Chap. 20 *infra*, pp. 303 *et seq.*
[41] *Scott* v. *Lunn* (1908) 15 S.L.T. 1045.
[42] *Supra*, pp. 246–248.
[43] *Blair* v. *Paterson* (1836) 14 S. 361; *Miller* v. *Black's Trs.* (1837) 2 S. & McL. 866, 889, *per* Lord Brougham.
[44] *Reid* v. *Maxwell* (1852) 14 D. 449.
[45] *Wyse* v. *Abbott* (1881) 8 R. 983.
[46] *Malcolm* v. *Goldie* (1895) 22 R. 968.
[47] Trusts (Scotland) Act 1921 s. 21.
[48] *Ibid.* Sched. B.
[49] *Malcolm* v. *Goldie supra*, *per* Lord Kinnear, p. 973.

who is abroad continuously for six months or more *ipso facto* demits office.[50]

Provision is made for the Deed of Assumption and Conveyance being executed with the consent of the court, granted on the application of the acting trustee or trustees or that of one or more of the beneficiaries, where the signatures of a quorum of the trustees cannot be obtained.[51] In a case where the sole surviving and acting trustee had died suddenly just after executing a Deed of Assumption in which it was narrated that the only other surviving trustee was resident in China consent was granted on the petition of a residuary legatee.[52] This facility, however, is not available where the obstacle to the normal execution of the deed is a disagreement or deadlock among the trustees,[53] nor again where the trustee whose signature is unobtainable has, in terms of the trust deed, the exclusive power of selecting new trustees.[54] In such circumstances an application to the court under the *nobile officium* for a judicial appointment appears to be the only available course.[55]

In addition to the appointment or assumption of the new trustees the statutory form of Deed of Assumption and Conveyance [56] embodies a conveyance of the trust estate in general and comprehensive terms to the existing trustees (with the exception, it would appear, of any who may be resigning contemporaneously with the assumption of the new trustees [57]) and the new trustees.

Where the power of assumption is being exercised by a quorum of trustees the schedule provides for the deed running in names of the trustees by whom it is to be signed and not in the names of the whole body of trustees.[58] If the schedule were followed literally the conveyance would vest the estate in the new trustees and the granters with the other existing trustees excluded, but in practice it is always adapted to include the last-mentioned trustees in the title to the trust estate.[59]

The statutory schedule provides optionally for the incorporation of special conveyances of items of heritable or moveable property.[60] In practice special conveyances are rarely incorporated in Deeds of Assumption and Conveyance, the general conveyance being normally found

---

[50] *Thomson's Trs., Petitioners*, 1948 S.L.T.(Notes) 28.

[51] Trusts (Scotland) Act 1921, s. 21.

[52] *Lewis* (1895) 3 S.L.T. 29.

[53] *Aikman* (1881) 9 R. 213; *Taylor*, 1932 S.C. 1.

[54] *Thomson's Trs., Petitioners, supra.*

[55] See *Adamson's Trs.*, 1917 S.C. 440; *Aikman, supra: Taylor, supra.*

[56] Trusts (Scotland) Act 1921, Sched. B.

[57] See *Encyclopaedia of Scottish Legal Styles*, Vol. 9, p. 153, Form 131, adapting the statutory schedule in this respect to the case where one or more of the existing trustees are resigning: *cf.* Burns, *op. cit.* 844.

[58] s. 7 of the Trusts (Scotland) Act 1921 permitting deeds granted by trustees to be executed by a majority and quorum would not apply here as it excepts *inter alia* deeds in favour of co-trustees.

[59] *Encyclopaedia of Scottish Legal Styles*, Vol. 9, p. 151, Form No. 126: and see the comments in Burns, *op. cit.* 837.

[60] Trusts (Scotland) Act 1921, Sched. B; *cf.* s. 21 referring specifically to the special conveyance of heritage as provided for in the Schedule.

sufficient for all purposes. Indeed there are cases in which even the general conveyance may be unnecessary as for example where the trust estate consists entirely of assets such as corporeal moveables, cash, or bank balances or bearer securities which require no documentary transmission or again securities standing in names of the trustees *ex facie* as individuals.[61]

The conveyance in the statutory schedule is in customary terms as regards destination and quorum, provision being however made for effect being given to any specialities of the trust deed in these matters.[62] Looking to the effect of the Succession (Scotland) Act 1964 it would appear that the destination to the heir of the last surviving trustee as appearing in the schedule, and in the past, at least, in most trust deeds, may no longer serve any useful purpose.[63]

In some cases Deeds of Assumption and Conveyance relating to testamentary trusts bear to be granted by and in favour of trustees and executors, thus confirming that the parties concerned are acting in both capacities. This would seem to be unnecessary, particularly if the will or settlement adopts the usual formula appointing the trustees to be executors and defining the term " trustees " so as to include new as well as original trustees.[64]

Where two or more separate trusts in the person of the same parties are constituted by one deed the statutory form of assumption should be adapted to disclose expressly whether the assumption affects all or only one or more of the trusts involved.[65]

Acceptance of office

Although theoretically the rules and considerations affecting the question of acceptance of office by original trustees [66] would apply to new or assumed trustees, such a question is in practice unlikely to arise in this context as the intention of the trustee designate to accept office and act will almost always have been confirmed before his name is included in a Deed of Assumption or similar document. It is customary, however, to put the matter entirely beyond doubt by incorporating in the deed an express acceptance of office by the new trustee(s).[67] Alternatively but less commonly the acceptance may be evidenced by a docquet on the deed or by a separate minute or other document. As indicated below express

---

[61] See *Encyclopaedia of Scottish Legal Styles*, Vol. 9, p. 150, Form No. 125: In practice the general conveyance is seldom omitted whatever the content of the trust estate although its exclusion reduces the stamp duty on the deed from £1 to 50p.

[62] *e.g. ibid.* p. 151, Form No. 127 incorporating a provision *re* a *sine quo non* trustee: see also Burns, *op. cit.* 838 " Destination and Quorum."

[63] See *infra*, pp. 283–284.

[64] See Elder, *Forms of Wills*, 11, 12 and 18. The practice of referring to both capacities in a deed of assumption may be attributable to the fact that, while s. 3 of the Executors (Scotland) Act 1900 enables testamentary trustees original or assumed to be confirmed as executors, there is no statutory provision corresponding exactly with s. 28 of the Trusts (Scotland) Act 1921 which provides for resignation as testamentary trustee inferring, unless the contrary intention appear, resignation as executor.
See Burns, *op. cit.* 838 and 843.

[66] See *supra*, pp. 241 *et seq.*

[67] See *Encyclopaedia of Scottish Legal Styles*, Vol. 9, pp. 149 *et seq.*

acceptance in some form is necessary to meet the requirements of the
Government Stock Regulations.[68] It is also requisite where a sole trustee
or all the remaining trustees are resigning at the same time as the assumption of new trustees takes place.[69] Such specialities apart, the actings of the
assumed trustees would normally make it unnecessary to have written
evidence of their acceptance of office.

The question of declinature [70] of an assumed trustee does not appear
to have arisen in any reported case and seems unlikely to occur in practice.

Completion of title

The rules governing the completion of title of original trustees in *inter
vivos* trusts [71] may be said to apply generally to the completion of title of
assumed trustees whether in *inter vivos* or in *mortis causa* trusts, but in the
latter case it may be advantageous to have any executor trustees who have
been assumed before confirmation is expede, included in that confirmation.[72] In all cases the general conveyance of the estate provided for in
the statutory form of Deed of Assumption and Conveyance [73] is equivalent for the purposes of the conveyancing statutes to a general disposition
of any heritable property comprised in the trust estate,[74] and likewise the
deed is effectual as an assignation in favour of the existing and assumed
trustees of the whole personal property belonging to the trust estate.
With moveable property as with heritable property the option to include
special conveyances in the Deed of Assumption and Conveyance is in
practice seldom exercised. In the matter of personal or moveable property,
however, a practical distinction exists between securities in respect of
which trustees are registered in their fiduciary capacity and those in which
their title or registration is *ex facie* as individuals. In the former case, as
applying generally in companies registered in Scotland, presentation of the
Deed of Assumption and Conveyance (or a duly authenticated extract
thereof) is regarded as sufficient warrant for alteration of the register of
members to give effect to the change in trust personnel. Companies
registered in England, however, are precluded from recognising trusts
affecting their stocks or shares.[75] Accordingly trustees have to be registered

---

[68] See *infra*, p. 261 and n. 79.   [69] See *supra*, p. 256 and n. 38; also *infra*, pp. 286–287.
[70] See *supra*, pp. 246–248 as to declinature of original trustees: *mutatis mutandis* the same rules
would no doubt apply to assumed trustees.
[71] *Supra*, pp. 248–250: the Succession (Scotland) Act 1964 does not affect assumed trustees in
mortis causa trusts.
[72] It appears that only the executors in whose favour confirmation is expede can use the
facilities provided by s. 15 of and Sched. 1 to the Succession (Scotland) Act 1964 for
denuding by means of a docquet endorsed on the confirmation.
[73] Trusts (Scotland) Act 1921, s. 21 and Sched. B.
[74] Titles to Land Consolidation Act 1868, ss. 18 and 19; Conveyancing (Scotland) Act 1924,
ss. 3, 4 and 5.
[75] Companies Act 1948, s. 117, *supra*, p. 249, n. 67. But in a testamentary trust cognisance
of the change of personnel resulting from a deed of assumption may be taken by an English
company if the shareholding affected has remained registered in name of a truster, *i.e.* the
original trustees or executors have elected not to be registered themselves but merely to
have their title to the holding noted in the company's books (Companies Act 1948, s. 76
refers). See in this connection the pamphlet published in 1966 by the Chartered Institute of
Secretaries entitled " Representative Capacity—the Registration of Documents by
Scottish and English Companies."

ex facie as individuals in respect of the stocks or shares of such companies comprised in the trust estate. This results that a Deed of Assumption and Conveyance is not accepted by such companies as a warrant for altering their register to reflect the change in trust personnel, and separate transfers in the appropriate form have to be executed.[76] Formerly a similar position obtained as regards government securities registered in the books of the Bank of England, but now, provided the statutory facilities for designating stockholders as trustees have been used,[77] the Bank, subject to receiving a statutory declaration that a particular holding of stock forms part of a trust the execution of which is governed by the law of Scotland, will accept as sufficient evidence of transmission to the new trustees (whether or not in conjunction with any trustee remaining in office) a Deed of Assumption executed in pursuance of the relative statutory provisions [78] with a Minute of Acceptance by the assumed trustee(s) or a duly authenticated extract of such deed and minute.[79]

---

[76] In the normal case of fully paid securities of registered companies limited by shares the form of transfer is now that prescribed by the Stock Transfer Act 1963.

[77] See *supra*, p. 249 and n. 66.

[78] Trusts (Scotland) Act 1921, s. 21 and Sched. B.

[79] The Government Stock Regulations 1965 (S.I. 1965 No. 1420), reg. 15 (2) (*b*) (1); a form of statutory declaration for the purpose will be found in the section dealing with Government Stock Regulations in the Memorandum Book issued annually by the Scottish Law Agents Society to their members.

CHAPTER 17

NOMINATION OF TRUSTEES

UNDER this head there fall to be considered cases in which parties may become trustees in an existing trust not by their assumption by a party or parties already in office but by the exercise of powers of nomination or appointment vested in some person not himself a trustee or at least not exercising the power of nomination in that capacity.

The truster's power of nomination

At common law there is by implication reserved to the creator of any trust as the holder of the original or radical right to the assets placed in trust a right to nominate new trustees on the failure for any reason of these originally or subsequently appointed.[1] In practice this results that in *inter vivos* trusts the contingency of a lapse by failure of trustees will not normally arise while the truster survives. The rule is, however, operative only in private trusts. The failure or lapse from any cause whatsoever of a trust of a public nature which has once taken effect is the exclusive concern of the court in the exercise of its *nobile officium* and in such a case the appointment of new trustees, like other matters affecting the future administration of the trust, must be dealt with judicially.[2]

Most of the reported cases concerning the implied reservation to the creator of a private trust of a power of appointment relate to marriage settlements where the power belongs to the husband and wife in that capacity.[3] The view generally accepted appears to be that in such settlements involving, as commonly happens, separate funds for husband and wife respectively, each spouse and the surviving spouse have a power of appointment but only as regards their own respective funds.[4] Within these limits the rule is so well established that it is now unnecessary to seek a declarator or other form of authority from the court for the exercise of the power,[5] although it appears that it was at one time the practice to obtain judicial sanction.[6] The existence of the power was in one case

[1] Menzies, 36; *Newlands* v. *Miller* (1882) 9 R. 1104, 1113–1114, *per* Lord Shand.
[2] *Glentanar* v. *Scottish Industrial Musical Association*, 1925 S.C. 226, where the trust involving the presentation of a shield for brass band competition was held not to be a public one, but the court accepted the proposition that as a general rule judicial appointment of new trustees is necessary where there is a failure of trustees in a trust involving the public interest (see particularly L.J.-C. Alness at p. 230; *cf.* Lord Hunter at p. 233 reserving his opinion on the universality of the rule in practice).
[3] *Lindsay* v. *Lindsay* (1847) 9 D. 1297; *Tovey* v. *Tennent* (1854) 16 D. 866 (a case of declinature by a *sine quo non* trustee); *Newlands* v. *Miller, supra*.
[4] Burns, *Conveyancing Practice*, 4th ed., 839–840, founding on *Newlands* v. *Miller, supra* and *Glentanar* v. *Scottish Industrial Musical Association, supra*: this accords with the principles applied in cases of mutual testamentary settlements *infra*, p. 263.
[5] *Newlands* v. *Miller, supra*.
[6] See *Lindsay* v. *Lindsay, supra*; *Tovey* v. *Tennent, supra*.

regarded as justifying the refusal of an application for an appointment by the court, but this occurred before there were any statutory provisions for the court appointing trustees.[7]

The implied power of appointment operates in private trusts on the failure of existing trustees during the subsistence of the trust. It does not extend to the making of changes or additions to the personnel of the trust in which there are trustees acting. In this respect the express reservations of power of appointment or nomination not infrequently found in public trusts as well as in private trusts will often go beyond the limits governing the power implied by law in private trusts.[8] While in any trust the existence of such a power operative on the complete failure of trustees has obvious advantages, its extension to cover the filling of vacancies and/or the appointment of additional trustees may be said to be less desirable as it can lead to disharmony within the trust by the introduction of persons who are unacceptable to or incompatible with the existing trustees.[9] As a general rule express reservations of the power to nominate trustees will be construed strictly in accordance with their terms, as has been shown by cases concerning mutual testamentary settlements, which when made by spouses may in effect be post-nuptial marriage contracts. Thus where a settlement conveyed the estate of the spouses to trustees with power reserved to the testators during their joint lives and to the survivor of them to innovate upon or revoke the settlement, the wife, as survivor, was held not entitled *quoad* her husband's estate to make changes in the personnel of the trustees and it was pointed out that there is in any event a significant distinction between a power to nominate additional trustees and a power to revoke the appointment of trustees already in office.[10] On the other hand, on the basis that the penal effects of divorce extended only to financial benefits enuring to the benefit of the innocent spouse and not to rights such as faculties and powers, a divorced wife who survived her former husband was held entitled, despite the fact that the whole trust funds were derived from the husband's father, to exercise a power in the marriage settlement authorising the spouses and the survivor of them to appoint new trustees in place of any dying, resigning or becoming incapacitated.[11]

Powers vested in parties other than the truster

Instead of having the power of appointment of new trustees reserved to themselves, trusters may confer it on parties other than the existing trustees

---

[7] *Lindsay* v. *Lindsay, supra* as commented on in Burns, *Conveyancing Practice, ut sup.*

[8] Menzies, 36. The rule referred to above (see p. 262 and n. 2) whereby the power to appoint new trustees in a public trust belongs to the court is apparently not regarded as preventing extrajudicial appointments made in terms of powers expressly reserved.

[9] Burns, *Conveyancing Practice*, 4th ed., 839, and see the comments in the English case of *Re Stamford* [1896] 1 Ch. 288, 295, *per* Stirling J.

[10] *Welsh's Trs.* v. *Welsh* (1871) 10 M. 16, 20, *vide* L.P. Inglis; *cf. Malcolm* v. *Goldie* (1894) 22 R. 968 where an appointment of trustees in a codicil made by a husband to the mutual settlement of his wife and himself was held wholly invalid because it purported to affect the estates of both parties, it being admitted that it could not validly affect the wife's estate.

[11] *McGrady's Trs.* v. *McGrady's Trs.* 1932 S.C. 191; but see the opinion of Lord Hunter who dissented partly at least on the ground that the funds came from the husband's side and the comments on the decision in Dykes, 260.

whether or not these parties are interested beneficially in the trust. Such an arrangement is unusual in private trusts but in trusts of a public nature and permanent character it is sometimes used as means of securing the continuity of trust administration otherwise obtainable only by the appointment of a corporate trustee or of *ex officio* trustees. Thus where property is to be held in trust for the use of a religious association or the endowment of a charitable fund the nomination of trustees may be entrusted to the members or office bearers of the association or charitable institution and it appears that such provisions will be liberally construed by the court.[12]

While an appointment of new trustees made by existing trustees must normally be effected *inter vivos* in the recognised form of an assumption, it is possible although not usual for a trustee to empower a trustee nominated by him to nominate a trustee or trustees who will succeed that trustee on his death. Such an exceptional provision will be strictly construed, however, and can only be exercised *modo et forma*. Thus where a truster had provided for the sole trustee whom he nominated being succeeded on his death by such person as that trustee should by last will and testament nominate, a nomination of two trustees by the sole trustee, who died intestate *quoad* his own estate, was held invalid.[13]

Acceptance of office

The rules governing acceptance of office by original trustees [14] will operate so far as applicable in the circumstances of the case. The question of acceptance may seldom arise with trustees appointed in this way but it will sometimes at least be possible and may be useful to have their acceptance incorporated in the document comprising their nomination or appointment.[15]

There appears to be no reported case of declinature [16] on the part of a

---

[12] McLaren, II, 1130: in the case of *Morison* (1834) 12 S. 307 and 547, decided before the statutory power of assumption was introduced, the court refused an application by a sole trustee for appointment of additional trustees in respect that the trust, which was for the erection of a church, contained a provision for the election of new trustees by the male members of the congregation although it might have been said that the circumstances were not exactly those contemplated in the power as conferred. Following upon the election the courts confirmed the appointment and granted warrant to the existing trustee to execute all necessary deeds to vest the new trustees in the funds. On the other hand in the case of *Robertson* v. *Harper* (1833) 11 S. 365, where the trust was conferred on certain parties, whom failing anyone appointed by the Court of Session, the court, on the failure of the trustees, granted a petition by the trustees themselves for the appointment of a factor but refused a crave for special powers, including the power to complete title, presumably because the petitioners were regarded as being in a position to give the factor a title.

[13] *Bowman* v. *Bowman*, 1910, 1 S.L.T. 381. The actual *ratio* of the decision was the appointment of two trustees instead of one, but *obiter* the Lord Ordinary (Salvesen) indicated that he would have difficulty in accepting the documents containing the purported nomination as complying with the power when they did not properly constitute a last will and testament of their grantor.

[14] *Supra*, pp. 241 *et seq.*

[15] *Cf.* acceptance of office by assumed trustees *supra*, pp. 259–266. But the style of deed commonly used for an appointment of new trustees by the spouse under a marriage contract contains no provision for acceptance of office: *Encyclopaedia of Scottish Legal Styles*, Vol. 9, p. 153, Form 130.

[16] As to declinature of original trustee, see *supra*, pp. 246–248; presumably the same rules would apply *mutatis mutandis* to new trustees.

trustee thus nominated or appointed and the situation seems unlikely to arise in practice.

Completion of title

When new trustees are brought into a trust otherwise than by their assumption by the existing trustees, problems of title may arise, because the parties nominating the new trustees are not normally in a position to vest the new trustees in the assets of the trust as is done by the existing trustees granting a Deed of Assumption and Conveyance in statutory form. When the case is one of adding to or replacing existing and surviving trustees the latter will of course be able to give the new trustees any necessary conveyance of the assets, but a different situation arises where the appointment is being made on the total failure of trustees by death or incapacity. In relation to moveable property the Deed of Nomination or Appointment although containing no conveyance will, if accompanied by suitable evidence of the death or other cause of the cessation of office of the former trustees, normally be regarded as sufficient warrant for the registration or other completion of the title of the new trustees to assets such as bank balances, insurance policies and securities of Scottish companies where the account books, registers or other records disclose the existence of the trust. In cases, however, of securities of companies which are precluded from recognising trusts,[17] and again perhaps with government securities registered with the Bank of England,[18] difficulties can arise from the fact that the parties nominating the new trustees will not be in a position to grant the necessary transfer or other conveyance which existing trustees would normally grant. In such cases it may be found necessary to invoke the aid of personal representatives of deceased trustees or guardians of trustees who have become incapable or in the last resort to seek from the court the necessary warrant.

The completion of title to heritage by new trustees extrajudicially appointed as opposed to being assumed is a matter on which views have tended to differ. On the one hand it is maintained that parties competently appointed to a trust whether created *inter vivos* or *mortis causa* in which the trusteeship carries a right to heritage do not require an actual or express conveyance to enable them to complete their title in the Register of Sasines; on this view a conveyance is to be regarded as implied in the deed of appointment by virtue of statutory provisions interpreting the words " deed " and " conveyance " in wide general terms and providing that such writs as deeds of nomination shall be regarded as part of the conveyances to which they relate or have reference and that any writing whereby a right to land or to an estate in land is vested in or transmitted to any

---

[17] Companies Act 1948, s. 117, applying to all companies registered in England—see *supra*, p. 249.

[18] As to Government Stock Regulations 1965 (S.I. 1965 No. 1420), see *supra*, p. 261: there appears to be no provision in the Regulations for the acceptance of a deed of appointment as opposed to a deed of assumption.

person can form a link of title.[19] Carried to its logical conclusion this argument would result that *quoad* heritable property there is no need to incorporate a conveyance in a deed of assumption of trustees although it appears to be accepted that the form prescribed by statute [20] should in practice be adopted.[21] The argument for conveyance by implication seeks to equate the position of the new trustee when appointed or nominated with that of a trustee nominated as a substitute in the deed creating or constituting the trust. It is admitted, however, that the practice where trustees are called in succession as substitutes to original trustee(s) (which, incidentally, is not a common form in modern usage) has been to complete their title by service as heirs of provision, and again that service has sometimes been used where new trustees are appointed by trusters such as spouses under a marriage settlement or by someone other than a trustee on whom the truster has conferred the power of appointment.[22] It appears too that even if the relevant statutory provisions be construed as validating completion of a new trustee's title on a warrant such as a Deed of Nomination or Appointment without any conveyance, this will apply only where the truster has been infeft in the heritable property in question and the former trustee's title to that property has flowed from him.[23] In the case of property acquired in the course of the trust administration the notional substitution of the appointed trustee in the original conveyance comprised in the trust deed [24] would be of no effect as that conveyance would not form part of the title to the property.

The view that service or some equivalent is essential in all cases where a new trustee is appointed without an express conveyance in his favour derives support from a dissenting judgment of high authority [25] and is adopted by certain writers and editors.[26] On this view the new trustee like any substitute in a heritable destination must derive his title to the assets

[19] *Encyc.* Vol. 4, paras. 547, 553 and 554 founding *inter alia* upon Titles to Land Consolidation (Scotland) Act 1868, s. 3 and Conveyancing (Scotland) Act 1924, s. 5 (1) and on *Kerr's Trs.* v. *Yeaman's Trs.* (1888) 15 R. 520.

[20] Trusts (Scotland) Act 1921, Sched. B, containing the form of deed of assumption incorporating a conveyance or conveyances of the trust estate.

[21] *Encyc. ut sup.,* para. 553.

[22] *Ibid.* paras. 553 and 554.

[23] Such was the position in the case founded upon, namely, *Kerr's Trs.* v. *Yeaman's Trs. supra.*

[24] Regarded as resulting from s. 3 of the Titles to Land Consolidation (Scotland) Act 1868.

[25] Lord Rutherfurd Clark in *Kerr's Trs.* v. *Yeaman's Trs., supra.*

[26] See Burns, *Conveyancing Practice,* 4th ed., 148, 718; *Encyclopaedia of Scottish Legal Styles,* Vol. 9, p. 153, footnote to Form No 130 (in striking contrast with the *Encyclopaedia of the Laws of Scotland* as cited above). See also the article entitled " Completion of Title by Appointed Trustees " (1939 S.L.T.(News.) 88) discussing *Kerr's Trs.* v. *Yeaman's Trs., supra* and referring also to the case of *Royal Bank of Scotland* (1893) 20 R. 741 (which like *Kerr's* case concerned a trust deed for creditors) where the truster concurred in the principal creditors' application to the court for appointment of a trustee to replace the original one who had died in office, although as truster in an *inter vivos* trust he could have made the appointment and on the view adopted in *Kerr's* case given the necessary title himself. The writer of the article argues somewhat cogently that the statutory enfranchisement of documents not comprising or constituting conveyances in the normal sense (*e.g.* minutes of meeting under Conveyancing (Scotland) Act 1924, s. 5) should be regarded as creating specific exceptions to but not derogating in general from the basic principles applicable.

of the trust from or through his predecessors. In an *inter vivos* trust the theory of the persistence of a radical right in the truster would mean that he, while he survives, could grant the necessary conveyance to new trustees when appointed [27] but it appears that this course is not often adopted.[28]

It may thus be said, in the case of heritage at least on one view, and in the case of certain moveable assets on any view, that the extrajudicial appointment as opposed to the assumption of new trustees while obviating the lapsing of the trust may leave problems to be solved in the completion of the title of the new trustees. In the past, as has been indicated, completion of title to heritage was achieved by way of service. On the view that the newly appointed trustee was simply a substitute he could be served as heir of provision in trust of his predecessor in office.[29] Alternatively resort could be had to the statutory provisions whereby an heir of a last surviving trustee could be served as heir in trust and thereafter and convey the trust property to the appointed trustee(s).[30] Service of heirs has been abolished by the Succession (Scotland) Act 1964 [31] as regards deaths occurring after September 10, 1964; but the assimilation of heritable and moveable succession brought about by that Act results that in the case of deaths after that date the facilities of the Executors (Scotland) Act 1900 for obtaining a title to moveable assets standing in name of a trustee or executor who has died, by having the deceased's executor confirm to the trust assets for the purpose of making them over to the appropriate party, are now adapted to cover heritable estate also.[32]

Application of the confirmation procedure as means of obtaining a title for new trustees, depending as it does on the availability and co-operation of an executor of a deceased trustee, the question arises what alternative courses are available as regards moveable assets requiring actual conveyance and again as regards heritable property if and in so far as a Deed of Appointment or Nomination without a conveyance is not regarded as an effective warrant or link of title. In cases where service

---

[27] See the observations of Lord Rutherfurd Clark in *Kerr's Trs.* v. *Yeaman's Trs., supra,* 532–533.

[28] It is not mentioned as a possible course either in Burns, *Conveyancing Practice, ut sup.* or in the *Encyclopaedia of Scottish Legal Styles, ut sup.*

[29] See Burns, *Conveyancing Practice,* 4th ed., 720.

[30] Conveyancing (Scotland) Act 1874, s. 43; alternatively the service could be as heir of provision in trust if the destination in the deed of trust expressly included the heir of the last surviving trustee. Burns, *op. cit.,* 720–721.

[31] s. 34 and Sched. 3.

[32] Executors (Scotland) Act 1900, s. 6, as amended by Succession (Scotland) Act 1964, Sched. 2, para. 13, procedure and documentation being regulated by the Act of Sederunt (Confirmation of Executors) 1964: See further Chap. 28 *infra*: reference may also be made to Currie, Chap. 16 " Transmission of Trust Property ": Two limited alternatives to this procedure would appear to exist—(a) in testamentary trusts confirmation *ad non executa*: by the deceased trustee's executor under the Executors (Scotland) Act 1900, s. 7, as amended by the Succession (Scotland) Act 1964, Sched. 2, para. 14 (see Currie, *ibid.* 219–220) could cover assets which had belonged to the truster but not assets acquired during the trust administration; and (b) under s. 18 (2) of the Succession (Scotland) Act 1964 the executor of an institute in a destination which had not been evacuated can confirm to heritable property affected by the destination in order to grant any necessary conveyance to the substitute. Presumably this provision could be used to obtain a title for a substitute trustee or for a newly appointed trustee as a constructive substitute but in practice it seems likely that its application will be restricted to property held beneficially.

procedure was for any reason impossible declaratory adjudication was generally regarded as the competent and appropriate procedure. Likewise adjudication was used to obtain a title for judicially appointed trustees before statutory facilities for that purpose existed. Adjudication in any form is normally regarded as a form of diligence special to heritable property but it appears that where no other form of diligence is available it may be applied to moveables.[33]

Such statutory provisions as deal with completion of title of trustees appear to apply only to trustees appointed by the court.[34] There are no statutory provisions for the granting of warrants for completion of title to trustees otherwise appointed. It is thought however, that if it could be shown in any particular case that the newly appointed trustees had not available any practicable means of vesting themselves in the trust assets the court in the exercise of its *nobile officium* would make the requisite order.[35] There appear to be no direct precedents here but in such circumstances the discretion of the court is not infrequently exercised to resolve procedural difficulties for trustees.[36]

Ex officio nominations

The case of *ex officio* trustees may be said to represent a somewhat special instance of the introduction of new trustees into a trust otherwise than by judicial appointment or assumption by existing trustees. *Ex officio* trustees as already indicated may not have the power of assumption of new trustees enjoyed by trustees generally [37] and indeed their position normally involves that the power of nomination of new trustees is vested in parties other than the existing trustees, *i.e.* in the parties or body entitled to elect or appoint the holder of the office which carries with it the trusteeship. In normal course this would involve that the successors to the original *ex officio* trustees would have to derive their title to the assets of the trust estate independently of their nomination, by conveyance from someone *in titulo* to convey such as their predecessors or the representatives of the latter if deceased, or from other trustees continuing in office. So far as heritage is concerned however these difficulties are overcome by a

---

[33] Graham Stewart, *Law of Diligence*, 607 and authorities there cited. See also Parker, *Notes on the Diligence of Adjudication* (1850) pp. 16 and 17 and again pp. 85, 86, where reference is made to the use of adjudication by assumed trustees without a conveyance: it is indicated at p. 87 that the heirs of line of the former trustee or trustees should be called as defenders in the process: perhaps the appropriate defenders would now be the executors of such trustees in view of the changes made by the Succession (Scotland) Act 1964.

[34] *e.g.* Trusts (Scotland) Act 1921, ss. 19 and 22: Conveyancing (Scotland) Act 1874, s. 44 as amended by Conveyancing (Scotland) Act 1924, s. 5 (3), but as result of s. 1 of the Conveyancing Amendment (Scotland) Act 1938 warrants as provided for in these sections are not now necessary in the case of heritage and will not normally be granted. See *Boazam*, 1938 S.N. 103.

[35] Query whether declaratory adjudication as referred to above would be regarded as a possible course which the trustees must first attempt or at least explore.

[36] The case of *Morison* (1834) 12 S. 307 and 547 referred to *supra*, p. 264, n. 12 may be said to exemplify a disposition on the part of the court to facilitate the actings of trustees in such matters as completion of title.

[37] *Vestry of St. Silas Church* v. *Trs. of St. Silas Church*, 1945 S.C. 110, 121, *per* L.J.-C. Cooper, and see *supra*, p. 252.

statutory provision [38] which applies where, by the tenor of the title to an estate in land held in trust duly completed by infeftment in favour of a trustee or trustees therein named, the office of trustee is conferred on the holder of a place or office or the proprietor of an estate and his successors therein. In that case anyone becoming a trustee by appointment or succession to the place or office or estate in question is deemed to have taken a valid and complete title to the heritable property thus held in trust without the necessity for any conveyance or other procedure. Thus when the office of trustee is in terms annexed to another office each successive incumbent of the latter office automatically takes the right and title of his predecessor as trustee.

A similar statutory provision [39] covers the case of heritable property held in trust whether feudally or on lease for bodies of persons associated for religious or educational purposes; but here *ex officio* trusteeship in the proper sense of that term is not essential, the provisions extending to successors of the original trustees appointed as indicated in the title or according to the rules of the religious or educational body.[40]

While the foregoing provisions where applicable render unnecessary the normal requirements for completion of title to heritage such as the production and specification of links of title or warrants, they do not eliminate the necessity for documentary evidence of the identity of the successors in the trusteeship.[41]

The abovementioned provisions apply to heritable property only. There are no corresponding facilities for dealing with items of moveable property. So far as these are located in Scotland and registered or otherwise evidenced or recorded as being held in trust, as for example in the case of securities of Scottish companies, there should be no difficulty in having effect given to changes in the personnel of the trust on production of the appropriate evidence. Again in the case of government securities the provisions for registration of trusts and for entry of the official description of holders [42] would appear to make transfers unnecessary for such changes. With securities of companies registered in England, however, transfers will be required as they are in other cases of changes in trust personnel.[43]

---

[38] Conveyancing (Scotland) Act 1874, s. 45.

[39] Titles to Land Consolidation (Scotland) Act 1868, s. 26.

[40] For a comparison between the two statutory provisions see Burns, *Conveyancing Practice*, 4th ed., 258–259 and *Conveyancing Review*, Vol. 2, 24–25: somewhat similar facilities exist for trustees holding property of any kind for Friendly Societies in terms of ss. 49 and 50 of the Friendly Societies Act 1896 but here there is no provision for automatic infeftment of succeeding trustees in heritable subjects and accordingly while they will not require any form of conveyance as a warrant or link of title they must complete title to heritage in the normal way or deduce title appropriately if conveying without having completed title.

[41] *Cf. Mitchell* v. *St. Mungo Lodge of Ancient Shepherds*, 1916 S.C. 689, a case concerning summary diligence on a bond which had vested in successors of the original creditor-trustees by virtue of s. 50 of the Friendly Societies Act 1896. Presumably a certified copy of or extract from the minutes of the meeting at which the appointment took place would be acceptable and adequate evidence: *cf.* Conveyancing (Scotland) Act 1924, s. 5 (1).

[42] The Government Stock Regulations (S.I. 1965 No. 1420) regs. 12 (1) and (2).

[43] *Supra*, pp. 260–261.

CHAPTER 18

TRUSTEES APPOINTED BY THE COURT

The court's power at common law and by statute

In a Scottish trust the Court of Session has power to appoint trustees whenever that appears to be necessary. The court, however, will not make an appointment in an English or foreign trust even where the trust estate includes heritable property in Scotland [1] but when the English court had appointed trustees to replace a sole trustee who had become an incapax the Court of Session, in the exercise of its *nobile officium*, granted the necessary authority for the new trustees to register in respect of certain investments in Scotland in place of the incapax.[2]

As it existed and still exists at common law the power to appoint trustees has been regarded as inherent in the court as part of its general jurisdiction over the administration of Scottish trusts.[3] Since 1867, however, there has been statutory provision [4] covering most, but not all of the cases in which the judicial appointment of trustees is found necessary. These provisions have been held to apply to non-gratuitous as well as to gratuitous trusteeship [5] and their existence displaced a presumption earlier prevalent that the exercise of judicial power of appointment should be confined to trusts of a public or charitable nature.[6]

The current general statutory provision [7] applies when trustees cannot be assumed under any trust deed or when any sole trustee has become insane or incapable of acting by physical or mental inability or by continuous absence from the United Kingdom or disappearance for as long as six months. In any of these circumstances the court is empowered, upon the application of anyone interested in the trust estate, after such intimation and inquiry as appears necessary to appoint a trustee or trustees under the trust deed with all the powers incident to the office.

The statutory wording " when trustees cannot be assumed " has been

---

[1] *Hall* (1869) 7 M. 667; *Brockie* (1875) 2 R. 923; *cf. Cripps's Trs.* v. *Cripps*, 1926 S.C. 188 (a case concerning the special provisions of s. 8 (2) of the Trusts (Scotland) Act 1921. See *infra* n. 7).

[2] *Evans-Freke's Trs.*, 1945 S.C. 382.

[3] Menzies, 42.

[4] The original provision was s. 12 of the Trusts (Scotland) Act 1867, subsequently extended in scope by the enlargement of the definition of " trust " made by s. 2 of the Trusts (Scotland) Amendment Act 1884; *vide Royal Bank of Scotland* (1893) 20 R. 741.

[5] *Royal Bank of Scotland, supra,* applying s. 12 of the 1867 Act as extended in terms of the 1884 Act to a trust deed for creditors; *cf. Mitchell,* 1937 S.L.T. 474.

[6] *Royal Bank of Scotland, supra,* 743, *per* Lord McLaren.

[7] Trusts (Scotland) Act 1921, s. 22; it follows closely the terms of s. 12 of the 1867 Act, *supra,* but adds as alternative grounds for appointment the prolonged absence from the United Kingdom or disappearance of a sole trustee. The 1921 Act makes separate provision in s. 8 (2) for the judicial appointment of trustees in the special case of conveyances of property to non-existing or unidentifiable persons—See under " Fiduciary Fee " Chap. 5, *supra,* p. 69.

construed as " intended to comprehend every case where the trust cannot
be kept up by means of powers within the deed." [8] In particular it covers
the case of a lapsed trust resulting from the death of all trustees whether
before or after the trust has taken effect.[9] Likewise, although there seems
to be no direct authority on the point, it would appear to cover the situation arising out of the declinature of all nominated trustees but here it has
been indicated that declining nominees should when possible prevent the
lapsing of the trust by assuming others to take their places.[10] The statutory
provision, however, does not cover the situation where disagreement
among the existing trustees is preventing the assumption of one or more
additional trustees to resolve a deadlock in the administration. Here the
application must be made at common law to the *nobile officium* of the
court.[11] While an appointment by virtue of the statutory provision is
competent where a trust has been created expressly or by implication but
without any nomination of trustees or provision for their appointment [12]
it may be stated as a general rule that neither under the Trusts Acts passed
as they have been to provide machinery for carrying out a truster's intentions, nor at common law will the court make an appointment of
trustees for the administration of any property or assets in the absence of
some clear indication of the intention to create a trust affecting the
property or assets in question.[13]

The statutory provisions covering, as they do, most of the cases where
judicial appointments of trustees are required, applications at common law

[8] *Graham* (1868) 6 M. 958, 959, *per* L.P. Inglis.

[9] *Zoller* (1868) 6 M. 577; *Graham, supra*: in each of these cases, arising as they did shortly
after the passing of the 1867 Act, the Lord Ordinary, before making the appointment,
reported to the Inner House who confirmed its competency: see also *Milroy* v. *Tawse*
(1905) 12 S.L.T. 777; s. 18 of the Judicial Factors Act 1899 referred to in that case is now
replaced by s. 17 of the Trusts (Scotland) Act 1921.

[10] *Supra*, p. 246 and cases cited in n. 45.

[11] See *infra*, p. 272 and cases in nn. 15 and 16.

[12] *Pattullo* (1908) 16 S.L.T. 637; see n. 9 above as to replacement of s. 18 of the Judicial
Factors Act 1889.

[13] *Miller* v. *Black's Trs*. (1837) 2 S. & McL. 866, 890, *per* Lord Brougham; *Murray* v. *Macfarlane's Trs*. (1895) 22 R. 927, 941, *per* Lord McLaren: *cf*. Menzies 43 and 45 where
reference is made also to certain cases where it was sought to continue the administration
of trustees against the wishes of the beneficiaries who were claiming the trust funds fell
to be made over to them. The general rule thus formulated does not, of course, prevent the
setting up by the court of a trust in certain circumstances where that is regarded as necessary
in connection with proceedings. In the past it was the practice of the court *ex proprio motu*
to appoint a trustee or trustees to administer sums for which a decree was being granted in
favour of litigants who were incapax by reason of nonage or otherwise and the course was
frequently taken when damages were awarded to pupils or minors without legal guardians
or whose guardians were not regarded as suitable to be entrusted with substantial funds
(see *e.g. Sharp* v. *Pathhead Spinny Co*. (1885) 12 R. 574; *Cooper* v. *Fife Coal Co*., 1907
S.C. 564) [The Workmen's Compensation Act 1897, under which damages were there
awarded, appears to contemplate an arrangement of this kind—see First Sched. paras. 4
and 6]. In such circumstances, however, the course now followed is the appointment of a
judicial factor to take the place of or supersede the legal guardian: see *Taylor* v. *Hunter*,
1922 S.C. 80 and Rules of the Court of Session 1965 (as enacted by Act of Sederunt of
Nov. 10, 1964): 131–134 " Minors' and Pupils' Damages."

A statutory specialty of diminishing importance is to be found in the Entail (Scotland)
Act 1882, s. 23 (4) whereby the court, on the motion of a party to the process before it,
may constitute a trust and appoint trustees to administer securities representing the proceeds of sale of entailed estate: by s. 23 (5) the Act authorises the appointment by the
court of new or additional trustees as occasion arises.

for such appointments have tended to be infrequent in modern practice. Yet the court's common law jurisdiction in this matter, now generally exercised as part of its *nobile officium*, has always extended to every case where an appointment is necessary for the administration of a trust [14] and so remains available to be invoked in any case of necessity where the statutory provisions are inapplicable. Thus appointments have been made at common law where disagreements among existing trustees have prevented the assumption of an additional trustee or trustees to resolve a deadlock in the administration [15] this not being regarded as a case in which " trustees cannot be assumed " within the meaning of the statutory provision.[16] Likewise an appointment of new trustees was made at common law where a sole trustee whose conduct had been unsatisfactory was at the same time removed from office [17] and again where the offices held by *ex officio* trustees of an employees' welfare organisation had ceased to exist as a result of the industry being nationalised.[18] In many cases of public or charitable trusts the appointment of new trustees at common law is made by the court incidentally to their authorisation of a general scheme for the future administration of the trust.[19]

Procedure for and terms of appointment—the alternative of a judicial factor

Petitions for the appointment of new trustees under the above mentioned statutory provision [20] as applications to the court under the authority of the Trusts (Scotland) Act 1921 are initiated in the Outer House of the Court of Session.[21] While in the past, in most of the reported instances, common law appointments have been made in the Inner House presumably because they involved an exercise of the *nobile officium*, it appears that under the Rules of Court now in force they too will be dealt with in the Outer House.[22] Where, however, the trust includes any purposes

---

[14] *Melville* v. *Preston* (1838) 16 S. 457, 471, *per* Lord Mackenzie; *Miller* v. *Black's Trs.*, *supra*, 889–891, *per* Lord Brougham: the authorities are reviewed in McLaren, II, 1132–1137.

[15] *Aikman* (1881) 9 R. 213; *Dick* (1899) 2 F. 316; *Taylor*, 1932 S.C. 1.

[16] *Taylor*, *supra*, where it was accepted that s. 22 of the 1921 Act did not apply.

[17] *Lamont* v. *Lamont*, 1908 S.C. 1033.

[18] *Coal Industry Social Welfare Organisation*, 1959 S.L.T.(Notes) 3.

[19] See p. 216 *supra*: cases exemplifying this practice include *McGrouther* v. *McGrouther's Trs.*, 1911 S.C. 315 (where transfer of the assets to a permanent body of trustees was sanctioned after a proposed transfer to a more temporary body had been rejected)—*per contra* see *McLean* v. *Alloa School Board* (1898) 1 F. 48 (where *ex officio* trustees in administrative difficulties were refused authority to transfer the assets to another body whose office bearers would have replaced them as trustees). See also *Clyde Industrial Training Ship Association*, 1925 S.C. 676 (where the appointment of the nominees of certain bodies was sanctioned as securing sufficient permanency of administration) and *Lindsay's Trs.* v. *Lindsay*, 1938 S.C. 44 (where although declining to deal then with the scheme submitted the court appointed trustees to carry out certain purposes of a testator's settlement signed by him under the erroneous impression that a Declaration of Trust by representatives of the hospital to be benefited had been simultaneously executed; the circumstances here may be said to be not unlike those existing in the cases of *Pattullo* (1908) 16 S.L.T. 637 and *Auld*, 1925 S.L.T. 83 dealt with under the statutory provision but the charitable nature of the trust presumably brought the matter within the privative jurisdiction of the Inner House).

[20] Trusts (Scotland) Act 1921, s. 22.

[21] *Ibid.* s. 26.

[22] Rules of the Court of Session 1965, 189 (a) (iii), (iv) and 190 (vii).

of a charitable nature the petition for appointment, whether at common law or under statute, must be presented in the Inner House.[23]

The statutory provision [24] permits the petition to be presented by anyone having an interest in the trust estate; normally the petitioners, whether proceeding at common law or under statutory provision, will be beneficiaries or parties representing beneficiaries: and as a first step intimation will be ordered with service on all persons known to have beneficial interests, but not themselves petitioners or consentors, as well as on any existing trustees who are not in either of these positions.[25] In special circumstances interim appointments may be made without awaiting the expiry of the *induciae* on such intimation and service [26] but these are rarely found necessary. In the normal unopposed case appointment of the parties nominated by the petitioners will be made on the expiry of the *induciae* on the basis of the facts stated in the petition and without enquiry. Irrespective of whether the application be made at common law or under statutory provision, however, the court, even in unopposed cases, may or may not make the appointment of the parties nominated or any other parties and if making an appointment may do so conditionally or unconditionally.[27]

The statutory provision [28] contemplates the trustee or trustees appointed thereunder having " all the powers incident to the office " and it is customary for appointments, whether at common law or under statutory provision, to be made expressly on this basis. In any event, however, a trustee appointed by the court, being a trustee within the meaning of the statutory definition,[29] has all the powers belonging to trustees generally, including the power of assumption of new or additional trustees [30] unless the contrary be expressed in or implied from the terms of the trust deed [31] or prescribed by court in making the appointment.[32]

When a petition for the appointment of new trustees is opposed the question which the court are most likely to be called upon to decide is whether the case is suitable for the appointment of a trustee or trustees who

---

[23] *Ibid.* 189 (a) (iii); and see *Myles*, 1951 S.C. 31, as explained in *Viscount Ossington's Trs.*, 1966 S.L.T. 19: for this purpose s. 26 of the Trusts (Scotland) Act 1921 is to be regarded as modified by the Rules of Court 1965 in terms of the Administration of Justice (Scotland) Act 1933, s. 16 (*a*) and (1).

[24] Trusts (Scotland) Act 1921, s. 22.

[25] The section refers to " such intimation and enquiry as may be thought necessary "; for standard forms of petition see *Encyclopaedia of Scottish Legal Styles*, Vol. 9, pp. 202–205, Forms Nos. 191 and 192.

[26] *Mitchell*, 1937 S.L.T. 474, concerning a trust deed for creditors.

[27] *Graham* (1868) 6 M. 958, 959, *per* L.P. Inglis.

[28] Trusts (Scotland) Act 1921, s. 22.

[29] *Ibid.* s. 2.   [30] *Ibid.* ss. 3 and 4.

[31] In *Angus's Exors.* v. *Batchan's Trs.*, 1949 S.C. 335 the majority of the consulted judges took the view that a discretionary power involving selection of beneficiaries would not be exercisable by trustees judicially appointed.

[32] As an example of the case, unusual in practice, where the court made the appointment with restricted powers see *Glasgow Lock Hospital*, 1949 S.L.T.(Notes) 26; pending settlement of a *cy-près* scheme the appointment made was not to imply the usual powers of realisation. It is not permissible for the petition for appointment to include a crave for special powers outwith or beyond those implied by law. If it is considered necessary to obtain such powers the trustees when appointed should apply to the court under s. 5 of the Trusts (Scotland) Act 1921. See *Gibson Petitioner*, 1967 S.C. 161, a case under s. 8 (2) in which, however, it was indicated that the same would apply under s. 22.

in the absence of any special restriction will take the place of their predecessors in office with all the usual discretionary powers or is one calling for the appointment of a judicial factor [33] who, as an officer of the court, has to act under its directions, is subject to the supervision of its Accountant and must find caution for his intromissions. The appointment of a factor while it will normally increase the expense of administering the trust [34] is the inevitable course when there is no suitable person prepared to act as trustee but even where there are eligible nominees for trusteeship it has obvious advantages in cases involving personal disputes, conflicts of interest or similar difficulties. Before statutory provisions for the judicial appointment of new trustees existed there appears to have been a tendency on the part of the courts to appoint factors in all cases unless the express concurrence of everyone in any way interested had been signified. [35] It has been suggested too that while the statutory provisions for the judicial appointment of new trustees make it clear that in cases which they cover the court is always entitled to appoint a trustee or trustees if it sees fit to do so, there is an implication from these provisions that in cases outwith their scope the court should not exercise its discretion to appoint trustees at common law except with the concurrence of all interested parties. [36] It appears to be true that in the more recent of the reported cases of judicial appointments of trustees made at common law the petitions have been unopposed or at least any compearing respondents have not ultimately maintained their objections. [37] The fact, however, that in one such case the court appointed new trustees despite the contention of a respondent that a judicial factor should be appointed would seem to indicate the assumption of unfettered judicial discretion in this matter. [38]

In certain cases in which they have appointed new trustees with the usual powers the court have imposed conditions designed to provide some of the safeguards involved in the appointment of a judicial factor. In an early case [39] the appointment of trustees in a lapsed trust although approved by all parties beneficially interested, was made subject to those trustees finding caution for their intromissions. In a similar case [40] in

---

[33] See *Judicial Factors*, pp. 30, 31.

[34] See *Yuill* v. *Ross* (1900) 3 F. 97, 98–99.

[35] See *Moir* (1826) 4 S. 801, where the appointment of new trustees was refused and a factor appointed although all interested parties except some beneficiaries who were abroad and not available to be consulted, had approved the former course; but Bell, *Comm.* I, 31, Note 4 cites various cases decided before the passing of the 1867 Act as an indication that the court sometimes took a broader view of its discretion than in *Moir, supra*; see *e.g. Melville* v. *Preston* (1838) 16 S. 457, 472, *per* L.P. Hope.

[36] Menzies, 46 and authorities there cited: For the fullest review of the authorities see McLaren, II, 1132.

[37] *e.g. Aikman, supra, Dick, supra* and *Taylor, supra*.

[38] *Lamont* v. *Lamont*, 1908 S.C. 1033. While no opinions were delivered the report discloses that it had been argued that as the petition was being opposed the appointment of trustees was incompetent.

[39] *Glasgow* (1844) 7 D. 178.

[40] *Milroy* v. *Tawse* (1905) 12 S.L.T. 777, McLaren, *op. cit.* being quoted as indicating that the course taken was that normally appropriate with judicially appointed trustees. See opinion of the Lord Ordinary (Low) at p. 778. While his Lordship does not specify an actual passage in the work it would appear he was referring to the latter part of para. 2106 in Vol. II.

which, on account of the smallness of the trust estate the court elected to appoint trustees under the relative statutory provisions despite the contention of a respondent that a judicial factor should be appointed, the appointment was made conditionally upon the trust being placed under the superintendence of the Accountant of Court.[41] The same condition was attached to the unopposed appointment made under the statutory provisions in a testamentary trust lacking a nomination of trustees.[42] There however, some of the beneficiaries were in minority. In a similar case not involving that speciality it was considered unnecessary to impose such a condition [43] and in no reported case of recent date have the superintendence provisions been invoked on the occasion of a judicial appointment of trustees.

A case in which the legislature has specifically contemplated the alternatives of new trustees on the one hand and a judicial factor on the other arises under the provision whereby a sole trustee desiring to resign office may petition for the appointment of new trustees or of a judicial factor.[44] This facility originated as part of a statutory provision [45] which inter alia required a sole trustee who was resigning to obtain the consent of the beneficiaries to the assumption of certain parties as new trustees; and the view was expressed that under that provision the judicial appointment procedure should be invoked only where the assumption procedure was unavailable as it would be if the consent of the beneficiaries was not forthcoming.[46] A fortiori this view would seem justified under the current statutory provisions which, while requiring the application for the judicial appointment of a trustee or a factor to be intimated to beneficiaries [47] attach no requirement of consent to the sole trustee's assumption of new trustees.[48] Indeed it would appear that the current provision [49] for a judicial appointment being made on the application of a sole trustee is unlikely to be invoked except when there are no suitable parties willing to be assumed (when the application must almost inevitably be for the appointment of a judicial factor) or perhaps where it is proposed to place the administration of the trust entirely in the hands of foreigners or non residents.[50] In the only reported case under that provision, however, it was confirmed that irrespective of the terms of the application the court has a discretion as to the form of appointment to be made.[51] There certain of the

---

[41] Under s. 18 of the Judicial Factors (Scotland) Act 1889, now replaced by s. 17 of the Trusts (Scotland) Act 1921; see Chap. 20, infra, p. 316.
[42] Pattullo (1908) 16 S.L.T. 637.
[43] Auld, 1925 S.L.T. 83.
[44] Trusts (Scotland) Act 1921, s. 19 (2); by proviso (1) to s. 3 a sole trustee cannot resign unless he has assumed new trustees who have accepted office or the court has made an appointment under s. 19 (2): see under " Resignation " infra, p. 287.
[45] Trusts (Scotland) Act 1867, s. 10.
[46] Menzies, 46 and 553 where it is suggested that a trustee applying to the court in disregard of this matter might incur personal liability for the expenses of the unsuccessful application.
[47] Trusts (Scotland) Act 1921, s. 19 (2).
[48] Ibid. s. 3 (a) and proviso (1).
[49] Ibid. s. 19 (2).
[50] See infra, pp. 277–278.   [51] Walker v. Downie, 1933 S.L.T. 30.

beneficiaries who had opposed the sole trustee's application for the appointment of a judicial factor were themselves appointed trustees.[52]

Eligibility for appointment

The proposition that anyone who has legal capacity for holding property and dealing with it may act as a trustee [53] applies basically to the judicial appointment of trustees just as it does to their appointment by the truster or their nomination or assumption by existing trustees or other parties entitled to nominate them. In practice, however, the court in appointing trustees, particularly in opposed applications [54] will tend to have regard to some considerations by which trusters in selecting original trustees and even existing trustees or others entitled to select new trustees may in law, at least, be unaffected.[55] There is here a lack of direct authority in Scotland but the following statement of the position as existing in England may, it is thought, be taken as indicative of the attitude the Scottish court might be expected to adopt on such questions arising:

> " In all cases of appointment by the court of a new trustee the court has regard to the wishes of the creator of the trust if expressed in or to be inferred from the instrument creating the trust and to the question whether the appointment will promote or impede the execution of the trust and will not appoint a trustee with a view to the interests of some of the *cestuis que trust* in opposition to those of others." [56]

English decisions have exemplified the reluctance on the part of the court, except where no other suitable nominee is available, to appoint as trustees beneficiaries, either in liferent or in fee [57] or again representatives of beneficiaries such as their solicitors.[58] The cases in which this objection has arisen however, have involved separate and potentially conflicting beneficial interests in the trust estate. There can obviously be no such objection to the appointment of parties having the sole or together the whole beneficial interest in the estate.[59]

---

[52] The question of expenses referred to in n. 46 *supra* does not appear to have arisen, possibly because the position was complicated by a dispute and litigation involving the sole trustee and certain beneficiaries.

[53] *Supra*, pp. 227 *et seq.* where the question of capacity for trusteeship and certain qualifications of this general rule are discussed at some length.

[54] The question is less likely to arise in unopposed applications in which the court normally proceeds on the customary averment that petitioners believe their nominees " fit and proper persons " to be appointed (*vide Encyclopaedia of Scottish Legal Styles*, Vol. 9 pp. 202–203, Form No. 199); but in cases such as foreign nominees referred to *infra*, pp. 277 *et seq.*, the court may be expected to raise objections or at least questions *ex proprio motu*.

[55] *Supra*, pp. 236 *et seq.* as affecting the nomination of original trustees and pp. 255–256 as affecting the assumption of new trustees.

[56] Halsbury's *Laws of England*, 3rd ed., Vol. 38 p. 929 where the matter is dealt with in paras. 1593 *et seq.* under reference to relevant English authorities; *cf.* the discussion in Menzies, ss. 86–88 where all the authorities cited are English.

[57] *Ex p. Clutton* (1853) 17 Jur. 988.

[58] *Kemp's Settled Estate* (1883) 24 Ch.D. 485.

[59] Such a case is exemplified in *Encyclopaedia of Scottish Legal Styles*, Vol. 9 pp. 203–204, Form No. 192.

Foreign nationality or residence

In Scotland the question of eligibility for judicial appointment as a trustee has been canvassed mainly in relation to foreigners or parties resident abroad. Where the trust estate consisted entirely of debenture stock of an English company, the court, on the application of whole parties interested, all being resident in England, considered it competent and eminently convenient to appoint English residents on the Scottish trust which had lapsed.[60] Reference was made to certain earlier authorities[61] as establishing the proposition that in a trust constituted in Scotland and falling to be executed in Scotland the trustees, wherever they might be resident, remained subject to the jurisdiction of the Scottish court in all matters concerning the trust. In more recent decisions however, the court appear to have been concerned about the practical difficulties of exercising effective control over trustees resident abroad. In a case concerning a marriage-contract trust[62] where the spouses, who by reason of the possibility of issue being remote were in effect the sole beneficiaries, had taken up residence in Canada, the existing trustees who were resident in Scotland were desirous of resigning to make way for the spouses' nominees who were also resident in Canada. They were, however, advised that they could not properly assume non-residents to replace themselves but their petition for the appointment of the spouses' nominees, presented at the request of the spouses, was granted on the appointees giving a written undertaking to submit to the jurisdiction of the Court of Session and obey its orders in all matters concerning the trust. The justification for this decision was doubted in a later case[63] where the spouses who were resident in Canada, along with two persons resident in England, being the trustees acting under a Scottish marriage-contract trust and at the same time under an English marriage settlement between the spouses, were refused authority to resign and make over the trust estate to a Canadian trust company, which was to be appointed sole trustee. Even apart from the existence of a connected trust affected by English law and subject to the jurisdiction of the English court, which was one factor influencing the decision, there were features which were regarded as distinguishing this case from the earlier one just mentioned and which enabled it to be distinguished in another case referred to below[64]; certain of the beneficiaries were in minority and although the trust corporation as the prospective trustee was prepared to give a suitable undertaking to submit to the jurisdiction and orders of the Scottish court, it was considered that such an undertaking was of questionable effect coming from a corporate body absolutely beyond the power of the court and unlike an individual having no possibility of coming within the court's jurisdiction.

[60] *Allardice* (1900) 8 S.L.T. 6.
[61] *Kennedy* v. *Kennedy* (1884) 12 R. 275, 282, *per* Lord McLaren; *cf. Ashburton* v. *Escombe* 20 R. 187, 196, *per* Lord Kinnear.
[62] *Simpson's Trs.*, 1907 S.C. 87.
[63] *Stewart's Trs.*, 1912 S.C. 647.
[64] *Coats's Trs.*, 1925 S.C. 104.

In a more recent case [64] where all the beneficiaries under a trust set up in Scotland were of full age and had gone to reside in America the authority of the earlier case [62] was affirmed and it was held competent and expedient to grant the application of the existing trustees, made with the consent of all the beneficiaries, for the appointment of three American citizens to whom the existing trustees were to transfer the trust estate before themselves resigning; the appointees gave an undertaking to submit to the jurisdiction and orders of the Scottish court but the necessity for such an undertaking and its practical value was questioned.[65] The course authorised in this case was described by one of the judges [66] as the conversion of a Scottish trust into an American trust, a step which at first sight at least seems at variance with the proposition that a Scottish trust irrespective of changes in personnel or otherwise, remains subject to the jurisdiction of the Scottish court.[67] As a result of the decisions just discussed the matter of the judicial appointment (and perhaps also that of the assumption or nomination) of foreigners or non-residents as new trustees may be said to be in a somewhat indefinite and unsatisfactory position.[68] It appears, however, to be clear that the court is prepared to sanction appointments which will result in a transfer of the effective control of the trust administration to another jurisdiction if the expediency of this course is established and the concurrence of all parties having interests in the trust estate can be obtained.

Corporate bodies

While, as has been indicated there are possible objections to the judicial appointment of a foreign corporate body there is in general no objection to the appointment of a corporate body with suitable objects and powers registered and domiciled in Scotland [69] and such an appointment was regarded as competent and expedient in one case [70] of a charitable trust which had lapsed, ensuring, as it did, the continuity of the administration. It would appear, however, that the court would be unwilling to appoint a corporate trustee in a trust of a discretionary nature involving personal and family considerations at least unless the terms of the trust clearly contemplated such a body holding office.[71]

---

[65] *Ibid. per* Lords Hunter and Anderson at pp. 108, 109: *cf.* Mackenzie Stuart, 305 expressing the view that such an undertaking is now inappropriate: on this view it might at least be argued that a foreign corporate body is no more objectionable as a trustee than a natural person resident or domiciled abroad.

[66] *Ibid, per* Lord Hunter at p. 108; *cf.* L.J.-C. Alness at p. 106 referring to a change in the domicile of the trust.

[67] See the cases of *Kennedy* v. *Kennedy* and *Ashburton* v. *Escombe* referred to *supra*, p. 277 and n. 61.

[68] *Cf.* here the views expressed by Mackenzie Stuart, 303–305 and Dykes, 261–262.

[69] Looking to the fact that the existence of a place of business in Scotland makes a company subject to the jurisdiction of all courts a company having its registered office in some other part of the United Kingdom might be considered eligible.

[70] *Leith's Exor.*, 1937 S.L.T. 208 (the petition was presented under s. 22 of the 1921 Act).

[71] See the case of *Ommanney*, 1966 S.L.T.(Notes) 13 where the inclusion in a scheme for variation of a trust of a clause entitling the trustees to assume any bank or trust corporation was disapproved.

Single or plural appointment

In dealing with an application for appointment of trustees the court may find it necessary to exercise its discretion as to the number of trustees to be appointed. As a general rule of practice the court should not be asked to appoint a single trustee, not being a corporate body, in a case such as that of a lapsed trust, as the situation necessitating the judicial appointment will then be liable to recur unless the appointee exercises his power of assumption. Again where there have been or are likely to be differences or disputes in the administration of a trust and it is difficult to find disinterested parties to take office, the court, in making an appointment, may insist on a plurality of trustees chosen so as to represent and balance the conflicting interests.[72] On the other hand in one case where application was made for the appointment of a plurality of trustees the appointees were restricted in number in the interests of facility and economy in administration.[73]

Acceptance of office

The rules and practice affecting acceptance of office by original trustees [74] would appear to apply *mutatis mutandis* where new trustees are judicially appointed. In practice, however, the matter of acceptance appears to be ignored in relation to judicially appointed trustees where acceptance is normally left to be inferred from their actings. While the petitioners seeking the appointment usually aver that their nominees are fit and proper persons for the office, neither in the petition [75] nor in the court's interlocutor following thereon is there to be found any reference to the willingness of the nominees to act.

The question of declinature [76] by a judicially appointed trustee does not appear to have arisen in any reported case and seems unlikely to arise in practice.

Completion of title

It has been customary for the court in appointing trustees, whether at common law or under statutory provision, to grant, in response to the appropriate crave, a warrant enabling the appointees to complete their title to the assets other than items such as corporeal moveables or cash comprised in the trust estate. The statutory provisions for the judicial appointment of trustees [77] contemplate such warrants being applied for and granted with an appropriate description of any heritable property and a specification (which may be by reference to an inventory annexed) of any moveable or personal property and being equivalent to a conveyance of the heritable property and an assignation or transfer of the moveable or

---

[72] *Milroy* v. *Tawse* (1905) 12 S.L.T. 777, where the court, while rejecting the contention that a judicial factor should be appointed, made an appointment of two trustees instead of one as the petitioners had craved.

[73] *Glasgow Lock Hospital*, 1949 S.L.T.(Notes) 26. [74] *Supra*, pp. 241 *et seq.*

[75] See *Encyclopaedia of Scottish Legal Styles*, Vol. 9 pp. 202–203, Form No. 191.

[76] See *supra*, pp. 246–248 as to declinature by original trustees. *Mutatis mutandis* the same rules would seem to apply to judicially appointed trustees should the question ever arise.

[77] Trusts (Scotland) Act 1921, ss. 22 and 19 (2).

personal property as the case may be.[78] Since 1938,[79] however, trustees appointed by the court have been in the position of parties having right to any lands, heritable securities, registered leases or securities over such leases comprised in the trust estate within the meaning of the statutory provisions for completion of title and for conveyance or transfer without such completion [80] and warrants for completion of title to assets in any of these categories are now regarded as unnecessary and will not be granted.[81] It remains, however, competent and indeed appropriate for decrees appointing new trustees to embody warrants for completion of title to certain items of moveable or personal property.[82] Such a warrant should always be applied for if the trust estate includes items such as securities of companies registered in England whose registers will not disclose the existence of the trust.[83] In this case, the extract decree, if containing a warrant in appropriate terms will normally be accepted for registration of the new trustees but in any case where such a warrant is not acceptable in respect of property or assets outwith Scotland application will require to be made to the court in whose jurisdiction the property in question is located for the necessary vesting order or similar authority.[84] With assets such as the securities of companies registered in Scotland where the existence of a trust is disclosed in the relevant books or registers, production of the extract decree of appointment or its equivalent, even if not containing a special warrant, will generally be accepted as sufficient for registration of the new trustees and provision has been made for government securities registered with the Bank of England being dealt with similarly.[85]

[78] *Ibid.*, s. 22.

[79] Conveyancing (Amendment) (Scotland) Act 1938, s. 1. For the position as it existed before this Act see *Leslie*, 1925 S.C. 464.

[80] Conveyancing (Scotland) Act 1924, ss. 3 and 4 dealing with lands and heritable securities and s. 24 dealing with registered leases. All such provisions will now extend to the new form of heritable security, the standard security, created by the Conveyancing and Feudal Reform (Scotland) Act 1970 (see s. 9 (5)).

[81] *Boazman*, 1938 S.L.T. 582 and see *Encyclopaedia of Scottish Legal Styles*, Vol. 9, pp. 202–205, Forms 191 and 192 and footnotes thereto; *cf. McMurtrie*, 1939 S.N. 48 giving a similar ruling for a judicial factor.

[82] *Boazman, supra.* The Lord Ordinary (Lord Robertson) held that s. 13 of the Judicial Factors (Scotland) Act 1889, giving the effect of an assignment and transfer to extracts of appointments of judicial factors and others " subject to the provisions of that Act," did not apply to an appointment under s. 22 of the Trusts (Scotland) Act 1921 in a lapsed testamentary trust.

[83] As shown by the case of *Brower's Exor.*, 1938 S.C. 451, the practice with decrees appointing judicial factors which constitute warrants to complete title but do not specify the assets of the trust estate, has been for a certificate of the assets to be given by the Accountant of Court in terms of s. 60 of the Finance Act 1916.

[84] *Cf. Evans-Freke's Trs.*, 1945 S.C. 382. It is indicated in the pamphlet " Representative Capacity—The Registration of English and Scottish documents by Companies " (Chartered Institute of Secretaries 1966) (pp. 34–35) that appointments of new trustees made by the Scottish court are not recognised by English companies but it would appear that this may refer to cases in which the decree of appointment does not embody an appropriate warrant for completion of title.

[85] Government Stock Regulations 1965 (S.I. 1965 No. 1420) reg. 15 (2) (*b*) (ii) making a certified copy interlocutor acceptable. See also the more general provisions affecting government stocks in the Finance Act 1916, s. 66 (as amended in respect of the definition of " Government Stock " by the National Debt Act 1958, s. 15). Under this provision any order or decree of a United Kingdom court whereby the right to transfer or call for transfers of any government stock is expressed to be vested in anyone is sufficient authority to the Bank of England or Ireland, the National Debt Commissioners, the Post Office or any Savings Bank authority to allow transfers or pay dividends conform to the order.

CHAPTER 19

CESSATION OF TRUSTEESHIP

THERE would appear to be three ways in which the office of trustee is terminated *ipso facto* before the trust which he is administering has come to an end: *viz.* Death, Resignation or Removal. Supervening incapacity, *e.g.* in the form of insanity, does not *per se* terminate the office of trustee nor does absence abroad for an extended period.[1]

DEATH

Whereas Resignation and Removal, both discussed below, involve a divestment of office by a trustee who continues to exist, death (of which the equivalent in the case of a corporate trustee is its dissolution by liquidation or otherwise) is regarded as the extinction of the *persona* to which the office of the trustee is attached.[2] As such it ranks as a public fact and is not dependent for its effect on the giving of any form of intimation or notification.[3]

Survivorship as operating in plural trusteeships

In every trust there is, in the absence of express provision or clear indication to the contrary, an implication of survivorship whereby the title, interest and powers of one of a number of trustees who dies, devolve automatically upon his co-trustees or co-trustee instead of passing to a personal representative or heir of the deceased trustee. In this respect the right and title of trustees is regarded as one and indivisible and not as being a *pro indiviso* holding. Deeds setting up trusts frequently contain express provisions for survivorship among trustees but the rule to which reference has just been made results that such provisions are unnecessary and merely declaratory of the position in law.[4] It is implicit in certain of statutory provisions relating to trusts [5] that this presumption or rule is operative and applies to all trusts whether constituted *inter vivos* or *mortis causa* and whether gratuitous or non-gratuitous on the part of the trustees.[6] If, as rarely happens in modern practice, the appointment or nomination of the trustees is in terms expressly a joint one the death of any one of the trustees will bring the administration to an end.[7]

---

[1] Such circumstances may, however, constitute statutory grounds of removal: see Trusts (Scotland) Act 1921, ss. 22, 23 *infra*, pp. 295–296; again the *curator bonis* of an insane trustee may with judicial sanction resign on his behalf: *Laidlaw* (1882) 10 R. 130, *infra*, p. 289.

[2] Menzies, 544.

[3] *Oswald's Trs.* v. *City of Glasgow Bank* (1879) 6 R. 461.

[4] Menzies, 81–83; *Gordon's Trs.* v. *Eglinton* (1851) 13 D. 1381; *Findlay* (1855) 17 D. 1014; *Oswald's Trs.* v. *City of Glasgow Bank, supra.*

[5] Trusts (Scotland) Act 1921, s. 3 (c) read along with the definitions of " Trusts," " Trust Deed " and " Trustee " in s. 2.

[6] *Clark's Trs.* v. *M'Rostie*, 1908 S.C. 196; *cf.* Menzies, 83 and Mackenzie Stuart, 59.

[7] McLaren, II, 896; Menzies, 86 and see also *supra*, p. 241 and n. 90.

The operation of the survivorship rule results that on the death of one trustee there is automatically vested in any surviving trustees a complete and valid title to the assets comprised in the trust.[8] In the case of company securities the death has the effect of a transfer of the deceased's interest to the surviving trustees relieving the deceased's executors and his estate of any contributory liabilities arising after the date of death, even if, by reason of the absence of intimation of the death, the deceased's name has remained on the company's register of members.[9] For the rule to operate in this way it is not necessary that the registration should disclose the existence of the trust [10] but if the trust is not so disclosed proof that the registered holders are in fact trustees may be required.[11]

Death of a sole trustee—the lapsed trust

Thus far we have been considering the consequences of the death of one of a number of acting trustees. A very different situation arises on the death of a sole trustee. Unlike the co-trustee he is not, by reason of his death, " blotted out " of the title to the trust assets but such title remains with him and has to be taken out of his name by a process of conveyancing.[12] In the absence of a surviving co-trustee there is no one in whom the title to the trust assets can vest automatically; accordingly the automatic exclusion of future liabilities which takes place on the death of a co-trustee cannot operate here. Thus the executors of a sole trustee who was registered in respect of shares in an unlimited company were held to be rightly put on the list of contributories when the company defaulted six years after the trustee's death although the death had been known to the company while the executors had themselves been unaware of the holding in question.[13]

Apart from the exceptional case mentioned earlier in which there is a substitution in the trusteeship,[14] there arises on the death of a sole trustee who is not an *ex officio* trustee [15] the problem of the lapsed trust involving the question how the title to the trust assets is to be vested in some person or persons who will carry on the administration of the trust. To some

---

[8] *Gordon's Trs.* v. *Eglinton* (1851) 13 D. 1381; *Findlay* (1855) 17 D. 1014.

[9] *Oswald's Trs.* v. *City of Glasgow Bank* (1879) 6 R. 461.

[10] s. 117 of the Companies Act 1948 precludes such disclosure in the case of companies registered in England but does not affect companies registered in Scotland.

[11] *Oswald's Trs., supra.* In Scotland joint beneficial holders are presumed to have separate individual interests which will pass on their deaths to their respective personal representatives with contributory liabilities continuing to affect the estates of deceased holders unless and until a transferee or successor is registered; *vide* Companies Act 1948, s. 215; *cf. Palmer's Company Law*, 21st ed., p. 447, and *Re Agricultural Cattle Insurance Company*, (*Baird's* case) 1870 L.R. 5 Ch.App. 725. In England, on the other hand, there is a presumption of survivorship in joint holdings generally which in practice may render proof of trust unnecessary; *Re Maria Anna and Steinback Coal and Coke Company* (*Hill's* case) (1875) L.R. 20 Eq. 585; and see Companies Act 1948, Sched. I, Table A, Part I, Reg. 29.

[12] Menzies, 83.

[13] *Low's Exors.* v. *City of Glasgow Bank* (1879) 6 R. 830.

[14] There is in effect a substitution where someone outwith the personnel of the trust has a power of appointment but even in that case there can be problems of completion of title. See generally *supra*, pp. 262–268.

[15] As to completion of title of successors to *ex officio* trustees see *supra*, pp. 268–269.

extent the choice of a solution may be affected by the stage reached in the administration of the trust and in the execution of its purposes. Where it appears that the administration will require to continue for some considerable time, *e.g.* during the subsistence of one or more liferents, the most appropriate course is likely to be an application by the beneficiaries to the court for the appointment of new trustees or for the appointment of a judicial factor.[16] Where, however, the trust funds are of a limited amount or where the execution of the trust purposes is nearing completion, *e.g.* where it only remains to make over the estate to the beneficiaries in fee, some course involving less expense than an application to the court may be desirable and feasible. In the case of deaths occurring before the Succession (Scotland) Act 1964 came into force on September 10, 1964,[17] there remains available the procedure by way of service of the heir of the last surviving trustee as heir of provision in trust. If, as often happens, the deed constituting the trust contains a destination to the heir of the last surviving trustee in such terms as to make him a trustee for all purposes such heir may, if prepared to co-operate, be served as heir of provision in trust and so enabled to administer the trust estate both heritable and moveable with all the powers of his predecessors in office.[18] Again there is statutory provision [19] for the heir at law of a last surviving trustee, independently of any provisions in the trust deed, obtaining a title to any heritable property comprised in the trust by serving as heir in trust. To invoke this provision the heir must be major and subject to no legal incapacity and there must be no contrary provision in the deed and no contrary order made by the court.[20] Except under order of the court or with the consent of all beneficiaries (being all of full age and *capax*) the heir cannot administer the trust but is required forthwith to make over the property to any trustee or factor appointed by the court or to any trustee appointed by a person having power under the trust deed to appoint trustees (*e.g.* the spouses in a marriage-contract trust) or to any person whom the beneficiaries may have concurred in appointing to execute the remaining purposes of the trust or to the beneficiaries themselves if the stage for a denuding by the trustees in their favour has been reached.[21] The heir at law unless acting as trustee under order or with consent and approval as provided for in the section incurs no responsibilities.[22] In practice the absence of administrative powers of a party serving as heir in trust under these provisions has resulted that the facilities have been little used except in cases where immediate divestiture on the part of the trustee

---

[16] *Supra*, pp. 270 *et seq.*: the appointment of a judicial factor will not normally be sought unless circumstances such as the absence of suitable nominees for trusteeship or difficulties or disputes affecting the administration are present: see *supra*, pp. 273–274.

[17] 1964 Act, s. 38 (3).

[18] *Glasgow Western Infirmary* v. *Cairns*, 1944 S.C. 488; but see the earlier cases of *White* v. *Anderson* (1904) 12 S.L.T. 493 and *Brown* v. *Hastie*, 1912 S.C. 304 showing how the power of the heir as trustee may be limited by the form and terms of the destination.

[19] Conveyancing (Scotland) Act 1874, s. 43 repealed *quoad* deaths occurring on or after Sept. 10, 1964, by the Succession (Scotland) Act 1964, s. 34 and Sched. 3.   [20] *Ibid.*

[21] *Ibid.*   [22] *Ibid.*

is appropriate. Their utility has also been limited by the fact that their application is restricted to heritage whereas the heir of provision may as indicated above be able to intromit with moveable as well as heritable estate.[23]

The terms of the corresponding statutory provisions for moveable property [24] resulted that where any sole or last surviving trustee or executor-nominate died having any funds in Scotland standing or invested in his name as trustee or executor, his executor-nominate, by virtue of confirmation if he died domiciled in Scotland, and his executors by virtue of probate resealed in Scotland if he died domiciled in England or Ireland may by adopting a prescribed procedure obtain, through their confirmation or probate as the case might be, a title to ingather such funds and convey them to the person or persons legally authorised to continue the administration of the trust or to the beneficiaries or their nominees or assignees.

Service, whether as heir of provision in trust or heir in trust, is incompetent in respect of deaths occurring on or after September 10, 1964,[25] but with effect from that date the above-mentioned provisions relating to moveable property have been adapted to cover heritable property as well as moveable property vested in a sole trustee who has died, and extended to be available to executors-dative as well as to executors-nominate of the deceased trustee.[26] They have also been affected by statutory changes making grants of representation in Scotland, England and Wales, and Northern Ireland effective as regards property or assets situated in the other countries without the necessity for resealing there.[27] These provisions, referring as they do to " *any* sole or last surviving trustee or executor," would seem to apply to *inter vivos* trusts as well as to testamentary trusts; but the restrictions which they impose on the power of the executor to intromit with or administer the trust property must in practice limit the utility of the procedure to cases in which the administration of the trust estate is virtually at an end.[28] With the procedure for serving as heir of provision in trust no longer available there is now no means apart from the judicial appointment of new trustees or a factor [29] whereby the gap usually created by the death of a sole trustee can be filled in such a way as to allow the administration of a continuing trust to be carried on under normal conditions.[30]

---

[23] *Glasgow Western Infirmary* v. *Cairns, supra.*   [24] Executors (Scotland) Act 1900, s. 6.

[25] Succession (Scotland) Act 1964, s. 34 (2) and Sched. 3 repealing all provisions for service of heirs.

[26] *Ibid.* ss. 14 (1), 34 (1) and Sched. 2, para. 13 amending Executors (Scotland) Act 1900, s. 6. As to the scope and application of that section as originally framed and as now enlarged see Currie, 248 *et seq.* and Chap. 28, *infra*, p. 415.

[27] Administration of Estates Act 1971: see Sched. 1, para. 2 for the amendment of s. 6 of the Executors Act of 1900 replacing the reference to Ireland with a reference to Northern Ireland and eliminating the reference to the resealing of probates.

[28] *Cf.* heir in trust served under Conveyancing (Scotland) Act 1874, s. 43, *supra.*

[29] *Supra*, pp. 270 *et seq.* See also *Judicial Factors,* Chap. VI.

[30] In a testamentary trust confirmation *ad non executa* might be obtained in terms of s. 7 of the Executors (Scotland) Act 1900 as amended by the Succession (Scotland) Act 1964, ss. 15 (1) and 34 (1) and Sched. 2 para. 14; these provisions apply where confirmation has

It remains to notice briefly the statutory provisions [31] for completion of title by beneficiaries in lapsed trusts whereby a person entitled to possession for his own absolute use of any property heritable or moveable, the title to which is in name of a trustee who has died or become incapable of acting or anyone deriving right immediately or otherwise from such a person, may by petitioning the court in appropriate terms [32] obtain a warrant to complete title in his own name, effective as a conveyance or assignation as the case may be, of the property in question.[33] Clearly this procedure is appropriate only when the trust administration is at an end and nothing remains to be done but to vest the estate in the beneficiaries. Even in these circumstances it may be found less expensive for the beneficiaries to obtain their title through the medium of the deceased trustee's executor if that course is available.[34] The words " for his own absolute use " as used in the statutory provisions for completion of title by beneficiaries [35] have been construed as restricting their application to parties having a beneficial right or persons whether beneficially or fiduciarily interested deriving right from such parties and excluding the case where the interest of the party directly entitled to the trust estate is a fiduciary one.[36]

RESIGNATION

Resignation as applied to trustees may be defined as the voluntary divestment of office during the subsistence of a trust and before the completion of its administration. In modern practice it is almost invariably effected in accordance with statutory provisions [37] which have the effect of reversing, in principle, a rule of the common law by giving every trustee power to resign " unless the contrary is expressed " in the terms of the trust.[38] At common law, apart from some enabling provision in the deed of trust, a

become inoperative by death or incapacity of all the executors in whose favour confirmation was issued and as now amended cover heritable property as well as moveable but their application remains restricted to property included in the original confirmation and to the death of an executor in whose favour that confirmation was issued. The executor holding confirmation *ad non executa* has all the powers of his predecessors in office. See further under Executors, *infra*, Chap. 29, p. 435.

[31] 1921 Act, s. 24.

[32] See *Encyclopaedia of Scottish Legal Styles*, Vol. 9, pp. 214–215, Form No. 197.

[33] It appears that English companies, unless precluded by their constitution or regulations, will register as members beneficiaries of trust on production of a warrant in terms of this section: " Representative Capacity—The Registration of Documents of Scottish and English Companies " (Chartered Institute of Secretaries 1966) p. 35.

[34] 1900 Act s. 6—see *supra*, p. 284.

[35] 1921 Act s. 24.

[36] *M'Clymont Trs.*, 1922 S.C. 503: *cf. Scott's Trs.*, 1957 S.L.T.(Notes) 45: See also " Some thoughts on Section 24 of the Trusts (Scotland) Act 1921 " (S. O. Kermack) *Conveyancing Review*, Vol. II, pp. 244 *et seq.* where these cases and certain unreported decisions on the section are discussed.

[37] Trusts (Scotland) Act 1921, ss. 3, 19, 20.

[38] While the point does not appear to have been judicially tested in Scotland it seems likely that if the question arose for decision the Scottish courts would follow the English courts in holding that a resignation intended to facilitate a breach of trust will not relieve the resigning trustee of liability if the breach in question subsequently occurs. See Menzies, 54 and authorities there cited. See also under Assumption of Trustees, *supra*, pp. 255–256.

trustee had as a general rule no power to resign at his own hand.[39] There are, however, authorities which would seem to indicate that in certain circumstances such as conflict of personal and fiduciary interests or physical debility the resignation of a trustee without judicial sanction, if it has the approval of all co-trustees and beneficiaries, may be valid and effective at common law.[40] With the statutory power of resignation now available this question may be said to have become largely academic, although it may still be of practical significance in a case where the statutory provisions would necessitate judicial consent for the resignation to be valid.[41] In practice, however, it should never be assumed that a resignation made without judicial consent, when that is necessary for the exercise of the statutory power, will be sustained on common law grounds or otherwise in exercise of judicial discretion. The court will not normally confirm or ratify *ex post facto* a resignation for which judicial consent should have been sought before it was made.[42]

The statutory power of resignation

Like other powers derived by trustees from the Trusts Acts, the statutory power of resignation is operative " unless the contrary is expressed in the terms of the trust," [43] and will not be regarded as excluded by inference or implication. Thus the fact that certain of the discretionary powers in a trust were conferred in terms which might result in them not being exercisable by a judicial factor was held not to deprive an original and sole trustee of his right to resign on the appointment of the factor.[44] Again the existence of a qualified power of resignation in a trust set up before there was statutory provision for resignation was not regarded as eliding the power subsequently derived from the Trusts Acts.[45] It has however been suggested, on the analogy of certain dicta affecting other statutory powers of trustees, that an express power of resignation conferred in qualified terms in a trust originating after the introduction of the statutory power of resignation might be regarded as equivalent to an express exclusion of that power.[46]

Expressly disqualified from exercising the general statutory power of

---

[39] Menzies, 545; *Carstairs* (1776) Hailes 678; *Logan* v. *Meiklejohn* (1843) 5 D. 1066 (see the Lord Ordinary's note at p. 1072).

[40] *Hill* v. *Mitchell* (1846) 9 D. 239; *Maclean* (1895) 22 R. 872; and see comments in McLaren, II, 1138 and Mackenzie Stuart, 306.

[41] See *infra*, pp. 287–290.

[42] Menzies, 548; in *Hill* v. *Mitchell, supra,* an extrajudicial resignation was subsequently sanctioned but only on the basis of the very special circumstances (*vide* Lord Jeffrey at p. 243); *per contra* in *Maclean, supra* confirmation of a resignation for which sanction had not been sought was held incompetent.

[43] Trusts (Scotland) Act 1921, s. 3.

[44] *McConnell's Trs.* (1897) 25 R. 330.

[45] *Maxwell's Trs.* v. *Maxwell* (1874) 2 R. 71.

[46] Mackenzie Stuart, 307, founding on *Thomson* v. *Miller's Trs.* (1883) 11 R. 401 (a case concerning advances to beneficiaries) and *Anderson's Trs.*, 1932 S.C. 226 (a case in which power was sought to purchase an annuity to augment the income of an alimentary life-renter).

resignation are (a) sole trustees unless they have first assumed new trustees who have accepted office or new trustees or a judicial factor have been appointed by the court [47]; (b) trustees who in terms of the trust have received some benefit such as a legacy given on condition of acceptance of office or have been appointed on the basis of receiving remuneration for their services as trustees [48] and (c) judicial factors.[49]

The statutory provision contains no specific restriction affecting the resignation of a *sine quo non* trustee nor that of a trustee appointed to act jointly with another or others. It seems questionable whether the appointment of someone as a *sine quo non* trustee could be construed as an expression of intention [50] depriving him of the statutory power of resignation; but the effect of his resignation on the continuance of the administration may be a matter for consideration.[51]

While the statutory provisions for resignation prescribe conditions for the resignation of a sole trustee they do not, in terms, place any restriction on the simultaneous resignation of all acting trustees where there is more than one person holding office. Such a course of action has, however, been judicially characterised as " extremely improper " and the view has been expressed that unless at the time of their resignation the acting trustees are able to assume new trustees who accept office, the existing trustees, if all desirous of resigning, should first apply to the court for the appointment of new trustees or a judicial factor.[52]

Position of non-gratuitous trustees

The specialties affecting the resignation of non-gratuitous trustees [53]

---

[47] Trusts (Scotland) Act 1921, s. 3 proviso (1). It appears to be the practice for sole trustees who petition the court for the appointment of new trustees or of a judicial factor with a view to their own resignation to crave at the same time authority for that resignation but such authority is not normally included in the court's deliverance. See *Encyclopaedia of Scottish Legal Styles*, Vol. 9, Form 190, pp. 199–201 and n. on p. 201.

[48] *Ibid.* proviso (2). [49] *Ibid.* proviso (3) and see *Judicial Factors*, pp. 32,33.

[50] *Ibid.* preamble.

[51] See *Encyclopaedia of Scottish Legal Styles*, Vol. 9, Form No. 137, p. 156 referring to Bell, *Prin.* s. 1993: if as indicated *sub voce* Nomination or Appointment *supra*, p. 241, the right of veto of a *sine quo non* trustee is to be regarded as a personal privilege conferred on the trustee in the event of his accepting office leaving a quorum of the other trustees competent to administer the trust should he decline office (see McLaren, II, 896) it seems reasonable to infer that the resignation should not prejudice the continuance of the trust administration. Bell, however, in the passage cited (see particularly para. 5 and authorities therein mentioned) takes the view that the declinature, death or incapacity of a joint or *sine quo non* trustee defeats the nomination of trustees entirely leaving radical rights or beneficial interests to be made effective by judicial process but it would appear that he may be contemplating the situation arising at the inception of the trust rather than the case in which a *sine quo non* trustee who has accepted office subsequently purports to resign. In any event the question can and should be put beyond doubt in any deed nominating a *sine quo non* trustee. (See *e.g.* Burns, *Conveyancing Practice*, 4th ed., p. 802, Form (c) and Elder, *Forms of Wills*, 11, Form (f).)

[52] *Maxwell's Trs.* v. *Maxwell* (1874) 2R. 71, 74, *per* L.P. Inglis; instances of this procedure being adopted are to be found in *McConnell's Trs.* (1897) 25 R. 330 and *Erentz's Trs.* v. *Erentz's J.F.* (1897) 25 R. 53. Where it is proposed that existing trustees should resign on the appointment as trustees of parties outwith the jurisdiction of the Scottish courts the practice appears to be for the existing trustees in petitioning for the appointment of the new trustees to seek the court's authority for their own resignations: see in this connection *Coats's Trs.*, 1925 S.C. 104 and other authorities discussed under Appointment of Trustees by the Court, *supra*, pp. 277–278.

[53] Trusts (Scotland) Act 1921, s. 3 (*a*) proviso (2).

are encountered most frequently in testamentary trusts containing legacies or bequests to parties nominated as trustees. There is a presumption that a legacy or other benefit, however small, bequeathed to someone nominated as trustee, is given conditionally upon his accepting office.[54] The statutory provision affecting resignation is, however, restricted in its application to legacies or bequests expressly given on that condition although a specific declaration of such intent is probably unnecessary.[55] Where the condition applies it results that the trustee will not be entitled to resign at his own hand unless expressly empowered to do so under the terms of the trust.[56] It appears to be unsettled whether a beneficiary-trustee can preserve for himself the privileges of gratuitous trusteeship, including the right of voluntary resignation, by declining the legacy or other bequest.[57] It is, however, customary for wills and other testamentary settlements to authorise, in terms, the voluntary resignation of beneficiary-trustees[58]; but the statutory requirement of an express declaration has been held to be met by a provision whereby trustees resigning office and accounting for their intromissions should be entitled to a discharge from their co-trustees[59] and again by a declaration that the legacies were bequeathed without prejudice to the position of the recipients as gratuitous trustees.[60]

There appears to be no reported case in Scotland concerning the resignation of a trustee appointed on the basis of receiving remuneration for his services. It is the practice of concerns such as banks who undertake trusteeships on a basis of payment for services rendered to insist that the terms of any trust in which they accept office should permit their voluntary resignation to take place at any time. Here the wording of the statutory provision[61] may be said to result that nothing other than an express and specific authority for resignation will be effective.[62]

The statutory provisions empower the court to authorise the resignation of an non-gratuitous trustee subject to such conditions (if any) with respect to repayment or otherwise of his legacy as may be thought just.[63]

---

[54] See under Acceptance of Office, *supra*, p. 242.
[55] Menzies, 550.
[56] 1921 Act, s. 3 (*a*) proviso (2).
[57] Menzies, 549. *Cf. Maclean* (1895) 22 R. 872 (where the fact that the legacy had still not been accepted some years after the inception of the trust was held irrelevant in an unsuccessful application for confirmation of a resignation made shortly after the trust took effect). See also Mackenzie Stuart, 308, suggesting that in some cases the desired result may be achieved with the co-operation of the other trustees if the beneficiary-trustee declines office but is subsequently assumed.
[58] *Vide e.g.*, Elder, *Forms of Wills*, 120, Form 160 and Burns, *Conveyancing Practice*, 4th ed., 841 indicating that if a legacy is not to be forfeited or repayable on resignation this should be made clear in the settlement.
[59] *Bunten* v. *Muir* (1894) 21 R. 370.
[60] *Assets Co. Ltd.* v. *Shirness* (1896) 4 S.L.T. 120.
[61] 1921 Act, s. 3 (*a*) proviso (2).
[62] *Cf.* the wording of the same proviso as affecting the authority for resignation of a beneficiary-trustee as referred to *supra*, nn. 59, 60, but see *per contra* Mackenzie Stuart, 308 where the verbal difference is attributed to careless drafting and considered insignificant.
[63] 1921 Act, s. 3 (*a*) proviso (2).

This power has been exercised in cases where a conflict of personal and fiduciary interests has arisen.[64] Such a conflict of interests, however, may not be regarded as justifying the exercise of the judicial discretion if it appears that the probability of its emergence has been within the contemplation of the truster.[65]

Authority to resign has been granted where personal circumstances of health or otherwise have made it impossible for the trustee to give proper attention to his fiduciary duties.[66] Authority was, however, refused despite the trustee's offer to repay his legacy where the trustee having found his fiduciary duties unexpectedly onerous was maintaining that his retention of office would be prejudicial to his personal affairs but was unable to show that circumstances beyond his control would prevent him giving due attention to the administration of the trust.[67]

The legal guardian of a trustee who has become incapax may be authorised to resign on behalf of his ward.[68]

As already mentioned the court is empowered in authorising the resignation of a trustee who has accepted a legacy or bequest or annuity expressly given on condition of acceptance of office to impose conditions " with respect to repayment or otherwise of his legacy." [69] Despite the apparent discrepancy between the wording at the commencement of the proviso (" legacy or bequest or annuity ") and the foregoing phraseology affecting the imposition of conditions, it has been suggested,[70] that here the word " legacy " is being used in a sense wide enough to cover the requirement of repayment of some benefit other than a simple legacy, e.g. an annuity. If, however, the terms of the annuity are such that it continues only during the trustee's retention of office there may be said to be no case for ordering repayment on resignation.[71]

The statutory provision under discussion [72] does not, in terms, contemplate any condition such as repayment being imposed when the resignation of a trustee remunerated for his services is authorised and here

---

[64] *Johnston*, 1932 S.L.T. 261; repayment of the legacy was not required but no award of expenses of the trustee's petition out of the trust estate was made as circumstances indicated he should have anticipated the situation when accepting office; *cf. Guthrie* (1895) 22 R. 879, where, however the report makes no reference to the matters of expenses or repayment of the legacy; presumably expenses were allowed and repayment not required.

[65] *McLean* (1895) 22 R. 872, 875, per Lord McLaren.

[66] *Orphoot* (1887) 24 R. 871 (judicial duties as sheriff substitute—an offer to repay the legacy was noted and made a condition of the authorisation). *Cf. Alison* (1886) 23 S.L.R. 362 (military duties involving absence abroad in the case of one petitioning trustee and age (74) in the case of another: expenses were allowed out of the trust estate and no condition as to repayment of the annuities which the trustees had been receiving was imposed, these being payable so long as they continued to act). In both these cases the petition was unopposed and the resigning trustees did not ask for exoneration. On matters of health reference is sometimes made (see *e.g.* Mackenzie Stuart, 309) to the case of *Dick's Trs.* v. *Pridie* (1855) 17 D. 835, a contested case in which the trustee seeking to resign was not a beneficiary but required judicial authority, no statutory power of resignation then existing. The court on consideration of certain medical evidence decided that the trustee should be relieved of his office and exonerated and discharged him accordingly.

[67] *Scott* v. *Muir's Trs.* (1894) 22 R. 78.

[68] *Laidlaw, Petitioner* (1882) 10 R. 130.

[69] 1921 Act, s. 3 (*a*) proviso (2).

[70] Mackenzie Stuart, 309.

[71] See *Alison, supra*, n. 66.

[72] 1921 Act, s. 3 (*a*) proviso (2)

again the view may be taken that if, as will usually happen, payment becomes due as and when services are rendered, a refund on resignation would be inappropriate.

While certain of the earlier cases in which resignation of non-gratuitous trustees was judicially authorised were dealt by the court at common law in exercise of the *nobile officium* [73] the practice now is for all such applications to proceed in terms of the relevant statutory provisions [74] and be dealt with in ordinary course in the Outer House, service being effected on all beneficiaries who have not previously indicated their consent or concurrence. [75]

Documentation

The statutory provisions [76] for resignation by trustees contemplate documentation in one of two forms. The first of these forms, infrequently adopted in practice, is a Minute, which does not require to be probative, entered in the Sederunt Book of the trust and signed by the resigning trustee and all other trustees acting at the time. [77] It appears that a resignation in this form can be competently incorporated in a Minute of Meeting of the Trustees dealing also with other matters. [78] The reference to the trustees " acting at the time," *i.e.* at the time of the meeting at which it is apparently contemplated the minute will be signed, means, in effect, that the signatures of a *quorum* of the remaining trustees are sufficient. This is consistent with the intent of the statutory provision [79] making a resignation in this form immediately operative while as explained below the alternative form does not take effect until it has been intimated to all co-trustees who can be traced.

In practice, however, most resignations are effected in the form last mentioned, that is to say by attested Minute of Resignation. [80] The relative statutory schedule provides for reference being made to the trust deed or other origin of the trust and for resigning trustees who are not original trustees referring also to the source of their appointments such as Deeds of Assumption or orders of the court. [81]

The Minute of Resignation in this form does not take effect unless and until it has been intimated to the other acting trustees. [82] Provision is made

[73] *Orphoot, supra*; *Alison, supra*.
[74] 1921 Act, s. 3 (*a*) proviso (2): *e.g. Johnston*, 1932 S.L.T. 261.
[75] See *Encyclopaedia of Scottish Legal Styles*, Vol. 9, Form No. 189, pp. 196 *et seq*.
[76] Trusts (Scotland) Act 1921, s. 19.
[77] See Burns, *Conveyancing Practice*, 4th ed. 841, 842; the Act does not provide or prescribe any form of minute for this case but the practice appears to be to adopt or at least follow the form provided in Schedule A to the Act for resignation by deed of the trustee. For exemplification see *Encyclopaedia of Scottish Legal Styles*, Vol. 9, Form No. 134, p. 155.
[78] Burns, *ut sup*.
[79] See Menzies, 556 (note 3 to para. 883).
[80] Trusts (Scotland) Act 1921, s. 19 (1) and Sched. A.
[81] For exemplification see *Encyclopaedia of Scottish Legal Styles*, Vol. 9, Forms 131–133 and 135–138, pp. 153–156 and Burns, *op. cit.*, pp. 845–846 where it is indicated that if resignation is taking place with judicial authority (*e.g.* under Trusts (Scotland) Act 1921, s. 3 (*a*), proviso (2)) the order of court should be specified in the deed.
[82] Trusts (Scotland) Act 1921, s. 19 (1).

for edictal intimation to any trustee where residence cannot be traced after inquiry.[83] In practice intimation, which must apparently be to all the remaining trustees and not merely to a *quorum* of them, is frequently effected by obtaining their signatures to the Minute of Resignation having incorporated therein an acceptance of intimation [84] and the same procedure can be conveniently adopted when, as often happens, there is a composite deed covering the assumption of a new trustee or trustees and the resignation of an existing trustee or trustees.[85] The resignation when duly intimated becomes irrevocable.[86]

These statutory provisions for documentation of resignation being in permissive or enabling terms do not exclude the possibility of some other form of documentation being effective [87] but writing in some form appears to be essential, there being no authority for the effectiveness of a verbal resignation or one inferred from actings.

Effects—termination of office and disposition of assets

The resignation of a testamentary trustee who in that capacity is also an executor is by statute made to infer his resignation as executor unless otherwise expressly declared.[88]

In terms of the relevant statutory provision [89] the resignation of a trustee, duly effected, divests him of all his interest in trust property which then automatically accrues to and devolves upon the remaining trustees continuing in office. It is clear that in a question with beneficiaries the resignation absolves the resigning trustee of liability for future actings of the trustees as a body.[90] To be completely effective, however, the resignation which unlike the trustee's death is not regarded as a public fact, must, in addition to being intimated to co-trustees as already explained, be brought to the notice of other interested parties. Formal written intimation may not be essential provided it can in some way be established that the resignation has come to the knowledge of the party concerned.[91] This matter is of particular significance when, as seldom happens in modern practice, company shares with uncalled liabilities, or shares in an unlimited company form part of a trust estate. The name of the resigning trustee

---

[83] *Ibid.*

[84] Burns, *op. cit.*, pp. 845–846: *Encyclopaedia of Scottish Legal Styles*, Vol. 9, Form 135, p. 155.

[85] Burns, *op. cit.* p. 845: *Encyclopaedia of Scottish Legal Styles*, Vol. 9, Form 131, pp. 153–154.

[86] *Fullarton's Trs.* v. *James* (1895) 23 R. 105. This case arose under s. 10 of the Trusts (Scotland) Act 1867 whereby the effect of the resignation was deferred until a month after its intimation. The question of revocation seems less likely to arise under the provision now in force (Trusts (Scotland) Act 1921, s. 19) whereby intimation makes the resignation immediately effective.

[87] *Encyl.* 15, para. 453: *cf.* Trusts (Scotland) Act 1921, s. 20, referring to a resignation " in either of the modes provided by the immediately preceding section *or otherwise* " and see *Kerr* v. *City of Glasgow Bank* (1879) 6 R.(H.L.) 52 where there are indications that a letter written by a trustee to his co-trustees or to the agent acting in the trust might in certain circumstances be effective as a resignation.

[88] Trusts (Scotland) Act 1921, s. 28.

[89] *Ibid.*, s. 20.

[90] See Menzies, 558. As to the right of a resigning trustee to a discharge in respect of his intromissions (Trusts (Scotland) Act 1921, s. 18 refers) see Chap. 24 *infra*, p. 376.

[91] *Tochetti* v. *City of Glasgow Bank* (1879) 6 R. 789, 793, 794, *per* Lords Deas and Shand.

remains on the register and accordingly his liability as a member or contributory subsists until there is produced to the company the document evidencing the cessation of his trusteeship.[92] In cases where the company is permitted to recognise trusts and the holders of the shares have been registered accordingly, the trustee is entitled, on production of the document effecting his resignation, to have his name removed from the Company's register of members so long as the company is not in liquidation. He is so entitled despite any regulations of the particular company making a transfer necessary for alteration of the register or (as is usual in the articles of private companies) giving the directors discretionary powers to decline to register transferees.[93] This assumes, of course, that at least one other trustee is on the company's register in respect of the shareholding in question and is continuing in office. Where a sole trustee resigns or a whole body of trustees are resigning and there is a new trustee or trustees being assumed or judicially appointed the trustees assumed or appointed will require to be registered before the name of the resigning trustee or trustees can be removed from the register.[94]

When the fiduciary nature of the title is not disclosed on the register, as it will not be in the case of companies registered in England,[95] a document of transfer or its equivalent will be necessary to divest a resigning trustee[96]; and this would appear to be contemplated in the relative statutory provision[97] declaring the automatic vesting of the resigning trustee's rights to the trust assets in the continuing trustee or trustees for which it provides, to be without prejudice to the right of the latter to require the resigning trustee to grant, at the expense of the trust, any conveyance or transfer considered expedient.

In the case of British Government securities registered with the Bank of England provision has been made[98] whereby the bank, if given a statutory declaration or other acceptable evidence of the securities in question forming part of a trust governed by the law of Scotland, will accept as sufficient evidence of the divestiture of a resigning trustee a Minute of Resignation in statutory form[99] with an acceptance of intimation of resignation by the remaining trustees (or an official or duly authenticated extract of such Minute and Acceptance).

[92] *Kerr* v. *City of Glasgow Bank* (1879) 6 R.(H.L.) 52; *Sinclair* v. *City of Glasgow Bank* (1879) 6 R. 571; *cf. Oswald's Trs.* v. *City of Glasgow Bank* (1879) 6 R. 461 (showing that intimation is unnecessary on the death of a trustee).

[93] *Dalgleish* v. *Land Feuing Company* (1895) 13 R. 223.

[94] There will be no practical problem in this respect where as often happens the resignation and the assumption are contained in one document: see *supra*, n. 85.

[95] Companies Act 1948, s. 117, whereby no notice of any trust can be registered by a company registered in England.

[96] See the pamphlet " Representative Capacity—The Registration of English and Scottish Documents by Companies " (Chartered Institute of Secretaries 1966), p. 30.

[97] Trusts (Scotland) Act 1921, s. 20.

[98] Government Stock Regulations. (S.I. 1965 No. 1420), para. 15 (2) (c).

[99] See Trusts (Scotland) 1921, s. 19 and Sched. A discussed *supra*, pp. 290–291.

REMOVAL

Judicial intervention to deal with a situation in which the actings or conduct or the condition, physical or mental, of a trustee appear to render his continuance in office prejudicial to the interests of the trust may take different forms. Often such cases are dealt with by the appointment of a judicial factor either permanently and in replacement of the trustee or trustees concerned or again, as in cases of irregularities or mismanagement not appearing to justify removal, as a temporary expedient to supersede the trustee or trustees in the administration without actually terminating their tenure of trust office.[1] Considerations such as the saving of expense in administration [2] and sometimes also the wider measure of discretion he enjoys [3] will often render the appointment of a trustee preferable to that of a factor, but in cases of conflict of interest or other special difficulty the appointment of an officer of court in the person of a judicial factor may be more appropriate.[4] Such cases are considered in another context. Here we are concerned only with cases of removal of trustees in which either the administration is left to be carried on by the remaining trustees without a judicial appointment being made, or the appointment made is that of a trustee and not a judicial factor.

The court's power at common law

The common law power of the Court of Session to remove a trustee in the exercise of its *nobile officium* though well established as a discretionary jurisdiction of wide scope has always been sparingly and somewhat reluctantly applied. The fact that its exercise in modern practice is extremely rare may be accounted for partly by the existence of the statutory facilities for resignation and assumption, which in the absence of quite unreasonable attitudes afford an easier and less unpleasant mode of resolving disagreements among trustees, and partly by the availability of statutory provisions [5] which cover most, if not all cases, in which the necessity for removal of a trustee is likely to arise. It has been the practice of the court before exercising their common law jurisdiction in this matter to insist on being satisfied that the continuance in office of the trustee concerned would be likely to prejudice or obstruct the due execution of the trust purposes. Breaches of trust in the form of minor irregularities or technical illegalities will not generally be regarded as sufficient justification, some decided malversation of office having to be established.[6] As has been said in an English case,[7] something must be found " which induces the court to think either that the trust property will not be safe or that the trust will not be properly executed in the interests of the beneficiaries." While

---

[1] See *Judicial Factors*, pp. 33 *et seq.*
[2] *Lamont* v. *Lamont*, 1908 S.C. 1033; *cf. Whittle* v. *Carruthers* (1896) 23 R. 775.
[3] See *Dryburgh* v. *Walker's Trs.* (1873) 1 R. 31.
[4] See *Thomson* v. *Dalrymple* (1865) 3 M. 336.
[5] 1921 Act, s. 23, *infra*, pp. 295 *et seq.*
[6] *Gilchrist's Trs.* v. *Dick* (1883) 11 R. 22, 24, *per* L.P. Inglis.
[7] *Wrightson* v. *Cooke* [1908] 1 Ch. 789, 803, *per* Warrington J.

moral turpitude need not be established some degree of slight or even stigma in respect of his being held unfit to retain office will almost inevitably affect the trustee removed; but removal will not be ordered simply as a means of punishing a trustee for some past misdemeanour connected with his actings in the trust where a recurrence to the prejudice of the trust seems unlikely.[8] Persistent and obstructive refusal by a trustee to discharge his legal responsibilities may however be regarded as equivalent to or as serious as some positive action constituting malversation of office.[9] Thus in a case where four trustees were holding office the court ordered the removal of one of them who having been recently assumed was found to be behaving in complete and persistent disregard of his duties to the prejudice of the trust administration,[10] and likewise with four trustees acting the removal was ordered of two of these trustees who having been sequestrated and gone abroad were ignoring correspondence.[11] Again the court ordered the removal of one of two trustees, a solicitor who was preventing investment of trust funds by withholding his concurrence therein, but refusing to resign or co-operate in assuming a third trustee pending settlement of his claim to share, quite improperly as it happened, in legal fees payable for professional services rendered to the trust by his co-trustee.[12] On the other hand disharmony among trustees not resulting in actual deadlock will not normally be regarded as justifying the removal of one of more of the trustees.[13] The case for removal will, however, be fairly clear when there exists or emerges a conflict between the personal interests of a trustee and his fiduciary duty,[14] unless such a conflict of interest affects an original trustee and appears to have been within the knowledge or contemplation of the truster who appointed him.[15]

A petition for the removal of a trustee may be presented by all or some of his co-trustees and/or by all or some of the beneficiaries interested in the trust. The fact that all or a substantial majority of the parties concerned are either petitioning or concurring in the petition may be of significance,

---

[8] *Hay* v. *Binny* (1861) 23 D. 594 (appointment of judicial factor to replace trustees refused where funds improperly lent by trustees had been replaced by them out of their own funds: this, however, was a decision of the Lord Ordinary, the matter not being tested in the Inner House because the trustees resigned before a hearing on the reclaiming motion could take place).

[9] *MacGilchrist's Trs.* v. *MacGilchrist*, 1930 S.C. 635, 638, *per* L.P. Clyde.

[10] *MacGilchrist's Trs., supra*; perhaps the court will be more disposed to remove an assumed trustee than an original trustee selected by the truster himself—see McLaren, II, 1278 referring to *Christy* v. *Paul* (1834) 12 S. 916 in which, however, the assumed trustee who was removed had not acted or intromitted at all.

[11] *Walker* (1868) 6 M. 973.

[12] *Stewart* v. *Chalmers* (1904) 7 F. 163.

[13] *Hope* v. *Hope* (1884) 12 R. 27. *Yuill* v. *Ross* (1900) 3 F. 96: and see Dykes, 295 suggesting that in such cases a petition by beneficiaries may have better prospects of success than one by trustees; but in *Taylor*, 1932 S.C. 1, where there was a deadlock owing to the two trustees disagreeing, the court appointed an additional trustee.

[14] *Cherry* v. *Palmer*, 1910 S.C. 32 (action raised by testamentary trustee against trust estate in respect of alleged fraud by testator), *cf. Whittle* v. *Carruthers* (1896) 23 R. 775 (claim by trust against a trustee who had himself been sequestrated). But see *Yuill* v. *Ross, supra*, showing that an adverse intent is not always to be regarded as a ground for removal.

[15] See *Dryburgh* v. *Walker's Trs.* (1873) 1 R. 31 (where the claim by the trust against a trustee was represented by a loan given to him by his father, the testator).

but in any event some grounds of the kind referred to above must always be established, and the court will not exercise its powers simply with a view to providing the beneficiaries with administrative arrangements more acceptable to them.[16]

As a general rule the court will not exercise their power of removal so as to leave a sole trustee acting in the trust. Thus where two trustees were removed the petition was continued pending the lodging of a Deed of Assumption by the remaining trustee introducing two new trustees,[17] and it seems clear that where a sole trustee is removed the court, if they are to make an appointment, will insist on appointing more than one trustee to take his place unless the continuance of the administration is being provided for by the appointment of a judicial factor.[18]

The court's statutory power

The statutory power of the court to remove trustees as now constituted [19] (affecting all trustees including *ex officio* trustees and trustees judicially appointed [20]) is available where a trustee is or becomes insane or incapable of acting by reason of physical or mental disability, or is absent from the United Kingdom continuously for at least six months, or has disappeared for a like period. Application can be made by any co-trustee, any beneficiary or any other person interested in the trust. It is usual and where possible desirable that all acting trustees other than the trustee whose removal is sought and all beneficiaries (including particularly in the case of marriage contract trusts the spouses) should be petitioners or concur in the petition.[21] Again, wherever possible, personal service should be made on the trustee whose removal is sought even if the ground of removal be his incapacity unless, in that case, medical reasons accepted by the court make such a course undesirable.[22] The Court of Session has jurisdiction in all such petitions and they are presented in the Outer House [23] but alternatively, in the case of a testamentary trust, the petition may be presented in the Sheriff Court in which the original confirmation of the trustees as executors was granted,[24] and in the case of a marriage trust in the Sheriff Court of the district in which the spouses or the surviving spouse are domiciled. In cases of incapacity, mental or physical, the terms of the Act result that the court, on the facts being established, must make the order for removal,[25] but where the ground of application is absence or

[16] *McWhirter* v. *Latta* (1889) 17 R. 68, 70, *per* Lord Lee.
[17] *Stewart* v. *Chalmers supra.*
[18] In such circumstances the appointment of a judicial factor may be considered the more appropriate course, particularly if the sole trustee has been insolvent or financially embarrassed. See Dykes, 293.
[19] Trusts (Scotland) Act 1921, s. 23.
[20] See *ibid.* s. 2 for definition of " trustee."
[21] *Walker* (1868) 6 M. 973; *Lees* (1893) 1 S.L.T. 42; *Dickson's Trs.* (1894) 2 S.L.T. 61.
[22] See *Encyclopaedia of Scottish Legal Styles*, Vol. 9, p. 206 (footnote).
[23] *Reid* (1897) 5 S.L.T. 124; *Johnston* v. *Johnston* (1900) 2 F. 467.
[24] Trusts (Scotland) Act 1921, s. 23; presumably the reference to confirmation means the confirmation of the original executor-trustees: see Menzies, 565.
[25] *Tod* v. *Marshall* (1895) 23 R. 36 dealing with the corresponding provisions of s. 8 of the Act of 1891.

disappearance the jurisdiction is discretionary.[26] Whatever the ground of application the court has a discretion as to the evidence necessary in support of the Petitioners' averments.[27] In case of mental incapacity medical certificates in the form used in petitions for the appointment of curators *bonis*[28] are normally regarded as sufficient evidence of the trustee's state,[29] but if the petition is opposed a proof, or at least a remit, may be required for investigation of the circumstances.[30] In a case arising out of the disappearance of a trustee the fact that a factor *loco absentis* had been appointed on the private estate of the trustee whose removal was sought was not regarded as in itself sufficient proof of the position, and affidavits were taken from a brother of the absent trustee and from his co-trustee.[31]

The statutory provisions referred to above cover satisfactorily the case where it is sought to have removed one of a number of trustees acting or holding office. Where, however, removal of a sole trustee or of all acting trustees is sought provision must obviously be made for the administration of the trust, being continued without hiatus. This may, of course, be achieved by the appointment of a judicial factor,[32] but in some cases, at least, it is preferable to have the removed trustee or trustees replaced by other gratuitous trustees appointed by the court on the nomination of some interested party. The statutory provisions for the appointment of new trustees by the court[33] are so framed as to cover the case of a sole trustee[34] being or having become insane or incapable of acting by reason of physical or mental disability or by being absent continuously from the United Kingdom for a period of at least six months or by having disappeared for a like period (*i.e.* the same contingencies as are covered by the statutory provisions for removal *simpliciter*[35]) and provide in such cases for the trustee in question ceasing to hold office on the appointment of the new trustee or trustees being made.

Transfer and vesting of assets

Where the court, either at common law or in terms of their statutory powers, removes one of a number of trustees the practice is for the interlocutor or decree to include a declaration that the right to transfer or call for a transfer of the securities comprised in the trust estate, or to receive dividends or interest thereon, has vested in the remaining trustees for all

[26] *Walker, supra, Dickson's Trs., supra,* p. 295 n. 21.

[27] *Dickson's Trs., supra.*

[28] See *Judicial Factors,* pp. 24, 25.

[29] *Lees* (1893) 1 S.L.T. 42.

[30] *A* (1896) 6 S.L.T. 149.

[31] *Dickson's Trs., supra.*

[32] See *Judicial Factors,* pp. 33 *et seq.*

[33] Trusts (Scotland) Act 1921, s. 22; see *supra,* pp. 270 *et seq.*

[34] The section does not in terms contemplate a situation in which there are a number of trustees in office all of them being subject to removal on statutory grounds. In such circumstances it might not be possible to achieve the substitution of new trustees for the existing trustees in the course of a single process.

[35] Trusts (Scotland) Act 1921, s. 23; *supra,* p. 295.

purposes.[36] Production of an extract of the decree or order of removal containing a specification of the security in question, or accompanied by a letter from some authorised person such as a solicitor acting in the trust, will be sufficient warrant for effect to be given to the removal and divestiture in the register of members of a company registered in Scotland.[37]

In the case of a company registered in England, however, it would appear that such an order of the Scottish court will not normally be recognised and it may be necessary to seek a vesting order from the English court unless a transfer can be obtained from the trustee removed.[38]

---

[36] See *Encyclopaedia of Scottish Legal Styles*, Vol. 9, Form 194, pp. 205–206 and Dobie, *Sheriff Court Styles*, p. 544. In relation to Government Stocks these forms refer to s. 66 of the Finance Act 1916 (now amended in respect of the definition of " Government Stock " by s. 15 of the National Debt Act 1958) which provides that any order or decree of a United Kingdom court whereby the right to transfer or call for transfer of any Government Stock is expressed to be vested in anyone is sufficient authority to the Banks of England and Ireland, the National Debt Commissioners, the Post Office or any Savings Bank authority to allow transfers or pay dividends conform to the order. These provisions although still in force appear to be largely superseded as regards securities registered with the Bank of England or with the Bank of Ireland by the Government Stock Regulations 1965 (S.I. 1965 No. 1420) made under s. 47 of the Finance Act 1942 (as amended by various subsequent enactments) Reg. 15 (2) (a) providing that in relation to stock held in a Scottish trust the bank, in the event of the removal of a trustee, will accept as sufficient evidence of removal and divestiture a certified copy of the court's interlocutor.

[37] See the Pamphlet " Representative Capacity—The Registration of English and Scottish Documents by Companies " (Chartered Institute of Secretaries 1966) p. 34.

[38] *Ibid.*, indicating that such orders are not recognised by English companies; *cf.* " Secretarial Practice," Manual of the Chartered Institute of Secretaries, 6th ed. Revised 1964, p. 100.

CHAPTER 20

ADMINISTRATION OF THE TRUST

ADMINISTRATIVE DUTIES

TRUSTEES have a duty to meet together to administer the trust. " No two trustees can do a trust act without consultation with their co-trustee. It is of the essence of the duty of a body of trustees that they should meet and exchange views on the trust affairs." [1]

Trustees must take reasonable steps to ascertain the trust estate and the purposes of the trust. There is a duty to give intimation to the beneficiaries of the provisions in their favour. [2]

Control of estate

Trustees have a primary duty to keep the estate under their own control. [3] Trust moneys should be kept in a separate bank account for behoof of the trust. They should not be held in an account in the name of the trust solicitor except for a temporary purpose. [3] The trustees should not authorise an arrangement under which one of their number or the solicitor can alone operate the trust account.

Titles to heritage and securities can be held by one trustee or the solicitor [4] but they should be inspected at intervals either by the trustees themselves or in the course of audit of the trust accounts. Bearer securities should be deposited in joint names. [5] Although the truster is of Scottish domicile, the estate need not be invested, and the writs need not be held, in Scotland. [6] Where the trust holds shares in a company, the trustees can decide in what order their names will appear as joint holders in the company register. [7] If the trustee first named in the register acts in defiance of a majority of his co-trustees he can be interdicted from so doing. [8]

Accounts

Trustees are under a duty to keep proper accounts of their intromissions with the trust estate. [9] The accounts should show the amount spent,

---

[1] *Wyse* v. *Abbott* (1881) 8 R. 983, 984, *per* L.P. Inglis: *Darling* v. *Darling* (1898) 25 R. 747. See p. 301, *infra*.

[2] *Rodger's Trs.* v. *Allfrey*, 1910 S.C. 1015.

[3] *Ferguson* v. *Paterson* (1898) 25 R. 697.

[4] *Re Sisson's Settlement* [1903] 1 Ch. 262.

[5] *Lewis* v. *Nobbs* (1878) 8 Ch.D. 591. This is in any event affected by Exchange Control legislation.

[6] *Orr Ewing's Trs.* v. *Orr Ewing* (1885) 13 R.(H.L.) 1; *Brower's Exor.* v. *Ramsay's Trs.*, 1912 S.C. 1374.

[7] *Inland Revenue* v. *Lithgows Ltd.*, 1960 S.C. 405; *Re T. H. Saunders & Co. Ltd.* [1908] 1 Ch. 415.

[8] *Wolfe* v. *Richardson*, 1927 S.C. 305; 1927 S.L.T. 220; 1927 S.L.T. 490.

[9] *Ross* v. *Ross* (1896) 23 R.(H.L.) 67. See also *Polland* v. *Sturrock's Exors.*, 1955 S.L.T. (Notes) 76.

the person to whom payment was made and the nature of the payment. *In dubio* the presumption must be against a trustee who has failed to keep accounts but, in a case involving a tutrix and curatrix, the House of Lords allowed the accounting to proceed on the basis of estimates and inference.[9]

Trustees who have failed to keep accounts will probably be held personally liable in the expenses of an action for an accounting brought by a beneficiary.[10] Trustees who kept no books were found guilty of gross neglect.[11] Sometimes the inference may be drawn that the truster did not intend accounts to be kept.[12]

The accounts should be audited at reasonable intervals as a matter of prudent administration. In England, once in every three years is the standard set by statute unless the nature of the trust or any special dealings with the trust property make a more frequent audit reasonable.[13]

If the funds are administered by a factor, the trustees must require him to present periodical accounts and they have a duty to check the accounts and vouchers.[14] A multiplepoinding relating to the funds does not absolve them from this duty.[15] Failure to obey the truster's directions as to audit of the factor's accounts is not an omission covered by the usual form of indemnity clause.[16]

The beneficiary and his assignee have a right to see the trust accounts even although the interest is contingent, and, in the case of the assignee, even although the assignation is partial.[17] They are entitled to see that the trust has been duly and legally administered. The trust solicitor is entitled to a suitable fee. It is for the benefit of the trustees themselves that any breach of trust committed should be pointed out at a time when it can possibly be rectified easily and cheaply.

> " Now, we apprehend it to be a rule in the law of trusts, which it would require the most positive and unmistakeable provision to exclude—that the parties beneficially interested in them, shall at all times have full and unrestrained access to the accounts and vouchers of the trust-estate. In substance and reality the estate is their estate; they have the natural interest to check mistakes, and even to give suggestions and aid to the trustees, presuming the latter have right views and intentions." [18]

A residuary legatee has a right to receive a copy of the accounts at the expense of the estate; a special legatee has only a right to inspect.[19]

---

[10] Underhill, 465.
[11] *Wilson* v. *Guthrie Smith* (1894) 2 S.L.T. 338.
[12] *Leitch* v. *Leitch*, 1927 S.C. 823.
[13] Trustee Act 1925, s. 22 (4).
[14] *Sym* v. *Charles* (1830) 8 S. 741.
[15] *Gordon's Trs.* v. *Gordon* (1882) 19 S.L.R. 549.
[16] *Carruthers* v. *Carruthers* (1896) 23 R.(H.L.) 55.
[17] *Salamon* v. *Morrison's Trs.*, 1912, 2 S.L.T. 499. As to the right to see other documents, see *Re Londonderry's Settlement* [1965] Ch. 918.
[18] *Tod* v. *Tod's Trs.* (1842) 4 D. 1275, 1287, *per* Lords Cuninghame and Ivory.
[19] Menzies, 596. See *Murray* v. *Cameron*, 1969 S.L.T.(Notes) 76.

An arresting creditor cannot object to the accounts as stated by the trustees to the date of arrestment.[20]

Letting

Where heritage is held as a mere investment for the purpose of profit, the trustees have a duty to administer it to the best advantage and this will normally involve letting it.[21]

Maintenance and protection

The trustees have a duty to manage the estate on reasonable business principles. This can include a duty to keep the estate in repair and carry out amelioration and extension of the heritable property. Rebuilding of heritable subjects may be carried out. The extent of the operations and the amount to be expended are matters in the discretion of the trustees, who must have regard to the advantage of the estate and in particular to the possibly conflicting interests of the liferenter and the fiar.[22]

Trustees who had rebuilt heritable subjects which twenty-one years after the rebuilding had realised less than the sum expended on them were held not to have acted imprudently or negligently because they had acted in the honest belief, reached on reasonable grounds, that they were enhancing the value of the estate.[23]

Although English law may be different,[24] trustees in Scotland have a duty to insure against normal risks to the estate.[25] Heritage which the trust holds in security should be insured.[26]

The trustees have a duty to protect the estate from injury by interdict or other proceedings.[27]

MAJORITY DECISION

The strong element of *delectus personae* involved in the appointment of trustees and the obvious applicability of the maxim *delegatus non potest delegare* to the office of trustee result that basically trustees must perform their duties personally and where they are more than one in number act as a body with individual responsibility for every step taken in the administration of the trust.[28] Practical difficulties and considerations of business expediency have brought about some considerable relaxation of the rigour of these principles, sometimes, but not always, in the form of statutory provisions. Such departure from basic principle can conveniently be discussed under two general heads: firstly the extent to which, where there

---

[20] *Muir's Tr.* v. *Hamilton's Trs.* (1908) 24 Sh.Ct.Rep. 260.
[21] *Noble's Trs.*, 1912 S.C. 1230.
[22] *Noble's Trs.*, 1912 S.C. 1230. As to the apportionment of expenditure between liferenter and fiar see *Shaw's Trs.* v. *Bruce*, 1917 S.C. 169.
[23] *Armstrong* v. *Wilson's Trs.* (1904) 7 F. 353.
[24] Lewin, 224; Underhill, 378.
[25] *Glover's Trs.* v. *Glover*, 1913 S.C. 115; McLaren, II, 1156; Menzies, 182; *Encyc.* Vol. XV para. 561, p. 267; Mackenzie Stuart, 212.
[26] *Thomson* v. *Christie* (1852) 1 Macq. 236, *per* Lord St. Leonards L.C.
[27] Mackenzie Stuart, 212.
[28] Menzies, 85.

is more than one trustee holding office, decisions or actions in the administration of the trust can be taken without every trustee participating or
concurring and, secondly, the circumstances in which and conditions
under which the duties of trustees may be delegated as in the employment
of agents or other representatives.

On the first of these matters there is a notable divergence between
Scots law and English law. In a private trust governed by English law a
majority of the trustees cannot bind either a dissenting minority or the
trust estate; if the trust estate is to be bound the act must be the act of all
trustees.[29] In Scottish trusts, however, as explained below, the decision of
a majority of the trustees will normally prevail, but a situation similar to
that existing in English law can arise if the appointment of a number of
trustees is made on a basis of joint tenure, or again if one or more of a
number of trustees are designated *sine quo non*. Where the appointment of
two or more trustees is expressed to be a joint one each and all of the
appointees must accept office for the trust to come into operation, and
thereafter must participate, or at least concur, in all acts of administration,
each individual being in effect a *sine quo non* trustee.[30] It appears, however, that non-acceptance of office by an individual trustee or trustees
designated a *sine quo non* may not effect the operation of the trust at its
inception, but in the administration of the trust the *sine quo non* trustee is in
the same position as a trustee under a joint appointment.[31] The administrative inconvenience of either arrangement is obvious. In the absence of
express provision, or very clear indication in the terms of the trust, joint
appointments or *sine quo non* appointments will not be implied and are, in
fact, seldom found in modern Scottish practice.[32] Such special cases
apart, Scots law while requiring that unless circumstances render it impossible every one of a number of trustees should be consulted about and
give consideration to each step to be taken in the administration of the
trust, allows the decision of the majority to determine the course of action
to be taken.[33] The requirement of consultation with co-trustees, which
affects even *sine quo non* trustees,[34] involves that whenever possible
questions arising in the trust administration will be considered at meetings
of which fair notice and a reasonable opportunity to attend is given to all
trustees.[35] Circumstances may, of course, render meetings impracticable
if not impossible and in such cases consultation by written or telephonic
communication would usually be acceptable.

[29] Underhill, 380; *cf.* Menzies, 99.
[30] McLaren II, 896.
[31] McLaren, II, 896, 897, and see under " Appointment of Trustees," *supra*, p. 241.
[32] But where banks are appointed other than as sole trustees in testamentary or other family
trusts it will normally be a condition of their acceptance of office that the deed designates
the bank a *sine quo non* trustee.
[33] *McCulloch* v. *Wallace* (1846) 9 D. 32, 34, *per* Lord Jeffery.
[34] Menzies, s. 162 particularly note 1 distinguishing the position of a *sine quo non* trustee from
that of a sole trustee.
[35] Menzies, s. 173 and authorities there cited particularly *Freen* v. *Beveridge* (1832) 10 S. 727;
Wyse v. *Abbott* (1881) 8 R. 983 and *Malcolm* v. *Goldie* (1895) 23 R. 968, 971–972, *per* Lord
Kinnear.

While a majority of trustees are, as a general rule, entitled to determine the course of action to be followed in the administration of a Scottish trust it is clear that normally no action or decision can be taken except by or with the concurrence of a majority.[36] Where there is an equal division of opinion the difficulty may be overcome by the resignation of one or more of the trustees or again by the trustees as a body agreeing to assume additional trustees,[37] but in cases of real disharmony among trustees it may be found that neither of these solutions is available. While the statutory provision for the appointment of new trustees by the court where trustees cannot be assumed has been regarded as inapplicable to cases of disagreement or even deadlock among trustees,[38] the court, in exercise of its *nobile officium*, has on occasions made appointments to meet such a case.[39] It can in any event appoint a judicial factor if the administration of the trust can be said to be being obstructed or brought to a standstill.[40]

Having regard to the powers vested in the majority the question arises what action can or should be taken by a trustee or trustees forming a minority who dissent from, or disagree with, the course of action adopted by the majority. Assuming that it is not maintainable that the course of action in question involves anything in the nature of a breach of trust it appears that the remaining trustees must abide by the majority decision. A different situation, however, exists if it is contended that the action proposed to be taken, or the refusal of the majority to take certain action, constitutes a breach of trust or a failure to fulfil the obligations of the trustees, or again that the action or decision involves some element of *mala fides* or is for some reason clearly detrimental to the interests of the trust and the beneficiaries therein. Then in the interests of the trust, and probably also for their own protection, the dissenting trustee or trustees should take whatever steps may be appropriate to deal with the situation. In such circumstances an exception is made to the normal rule whereby an individual trustee, or a number of trustees constituting a minority of those acting, are not entitled to take action on behalf of or in name of the trust,[41] and the competency of an action raised by one or more individual trustees cannot be challenged.[42]

---

[36] *Wolfe* v. *Richardson*, 1927 S.L.T. 490.

[37] But changes in the personnel of trustees by way of resignation and/or assumption which can be said to have taken place in anticipation of or to facilitate a breach of trust would involve the trustees concerned in these changes in personal liability for the breach of trust in question if and when it occurred whether or not these trustees were then still holding office; see under Assumption of Trustees *supra*, pp. 255–256 and Resignation *supra*, p. 285 n. 38.

[38] 1921 Act, s. 22 as construed in *Taylor*, 1932 S.C. 1.

[39] *Taylor, supra*; see also *Aikman* (1881) 9 R. 213 and *Dick* (1899) 2 F. 316.

[40] See Judicial Factors, pp. 35, 36. The appointment of a judicial factor will normally involve the removal of the trustees as a body or at least a suspension of their powers during the subsistence of the factory. Apart from cases in which the appointment of factor is made the court have been reluctant to exercise their common law power of removal of trustees as a means of resolving disputes or disagreements: see under Removal of Trustees *supra*, pp. 293–295.

[41] As to the operation of this rule see *Coulter* v. *Forrester* (1823) 2 S. 387; and *Duncan* (1899) 20 R. 200.

[42] *Ross* v. *Allen* (1880) 13 D. 44; *Reid* v. *Maxwell* (1852) 14 D. 449.

QUORUM

Where several trustees are acting in a trust there will normally be applicable some provision whereby a number of the trustees less than the whole body constitutes a quorum. The word " quorum " in its ordinary signification has reference to the existence of a complete body of persons of whom a certain specified number are competent to transact the business of the whole.[43] As appears below that statement of the concept requires some qualification in its application to trustees but in general the existence of a quorum, whether by virtue of express provision or by legal implication, constitutes another relaxation of the rule requiring the participation of every trustee in every act of administration. An express provision for a quorum may, however, be so framed so as to make the inception of the trust and the continuance by the trustees of its administration conditional on the acceptance and continued tenure of office a minimum number of trustees,[44] although normally a provision prescribing a certain number of trustees as a quorum will be treated as inoperative when the number of trustees holding office falls below the number prescribed.[45] There are, however, cases in which in the event of death or other cause having reduced the number acting, the remaining trustee or trustees will be regarded as obliged to exercise the power of assumption in order to bring the number of the trustees up to the number prescribed as a quorum.[46]

The more usual application of a quorum is as a facility enabling part at least of the trust administration to be carried on without the active concurrence or participation of some of the trustees for the time being in office. Under the relevant statutory provision [47] the terms of the trust, in the absence of express contrary provision, are regarded as including a provision that the majority of the trustees accepting and surviving shall be a quorum. It is customary, however, to include in deeds constituting trusts express provisions as regards quorum which normally reproduce, and in some cases extend, the statutory implication, for example, by providing that the majority of trustees for the time being in Great Britain will be a quorum.[48] While it is usual for such express provisions for quorum to follow the statutory implication in making the majority a quorum it is competent to specify as the quorum a number of trustees which may be more or less than the majority for the time being in office.[49] Again where by virtue of the terms of the trust (or it would appear under

---

[43] Hawkins J. in *Faure Electric Accumulator Co. Ltd.* v. *Phillipart* (1888) 58 L.T. 525, 527.
[44] The case of *Ireland* v. *Glass* (1833) 11 S. 626 exemplifies such a situation. There a trust involving special discretionary powers prescribed a quorum of three. A petition by the two remaining trustees for the appointment of new trustees to replace the petitioners was refused and a judicial factor was appointed. The case, of course, arose before the Trusts (Scotland) Act 1861 introducing powers of assumption and resignation.
[45] McLaren, II, 1655.
[46] See Mackenzie Stuart, 294–295.
[47] Trusts (Scotland) Act 1921 s. 3.
[48] See *e.g.* Elder, *Form of Wills*, 14–15.
[49] *Cambuslang West Church* v. *Bryce* (1897) 25 R. 322; s. 7 of the 1921 Act discussed *infra*, p. 304 in defining " quorum " for its own purposes inferentially contemplates such an arrangement.

the statutory implication) the quorum is to be a majority of the trustees holding office, or a certain number of trustees, a minority, or a number less than that prescribed, may become a quorum for some particular purpose by reason of an adverse interest disqualifying certain trustees from acting in relation to the matter at issue.[50]

The rights of persons dealing *bona fide* and onerously with the trust are protected by a statutory provision [51] whereby deeds other than those in favour of beneficiaries or co-trustees, bearing to be granted by the trustees as a body and in fact executed by a quorum, are not to be rendered void or to be challenged on the ground of irregularities in administration such as failure to inform or consult with other trustees. The provision, however, is made expressly without prejudice to questions between the trustees themselves or with beneficiaries. It is well established that the actings of a quorum regularly performed are binding on all concerned including beneficiaries and co-trustees, but while there are matters of routine management which can properly be dealt with by a quorum without reference to the remaining trustees, consultation of all trustees for the time being available should always precede any important step in the trust administration. Thus, despite a statutory provision [52] contemplating the assumption of new trustees by a quorum of the existing trustees it is thought that the rule followed in certain earlier cases [53] would still apply, and that an assumption would be open to objection if done without the concurrence, or at least without the knowledge, of all acting trustees who were available for consultation. Again the exercise of a discretionary power such as the postponement of settlement of a legacy or bequest is a matter which should be considered by all the trustees [54] and the same would appear to apply to the decision affecting the taking or defending of proceedings in name of the trust.[55] On the other hand, there may be circumstances such as the continuing inaccessibility of a trustee or trustees which would entitle a quorum to proceed without consulting those trustees even in matters such as the assumption of new trustees [56] and it is established that where the remaining trustees are aware that the transaction of certain business is under consideration their absence from the meeting at which the decision relating to that business is taken, will not, in itself, invalidate the actings of the quorum in the matter.[57]

In many cases the appropriate function of a quorum will be to carry through the operative or executive steps implementing some decision reached by the trustees as a body. In such cases no distinction in the

[50] *Shaw* v. *Aitken* (1830) 8 S. 639; *Nelson* v. *Mossend Iron Co.* (1885) 12 R. 419.
[51] Trusts (Scotland) Act 1921 s. 7.
[52] *Ibid.* s. 3 (3).
[53] *Reid* v. *Maxwell* (1852) 14 D. 449; *Kelland* v. *Douglas* (1863) 2 M. 150; *Wyse* v. *Abbott* (1881) 8 R. 983. As to the conveyancing difficulties affecting a Deed of Assumption in name of a quorum see Burns, *Conveyancing Practice*, 4th ed., 837.
[54] *Stewart* v. *Stewart's Trs.*, 1915, 2 S.L.T. 19.
[55] *Stewart* v. *Dobie's Trs.* (1899) 1 F. 1183.
[56] *Kelland* v. *Douglas, supra.*
[57] *Darling* v. *Darling* (1898) 25 R. 7

matter of liability or responsibility will be drawn between the members of the quorum who take the operative step, for example by signing a deed, and the remaining trustees who are not thus involved.[58] This rule applies whether or not the actings of the quorum are such as to render the remaining trustees liable in questions with third parties dealing with the trust. Thus although the name of one of a number of trustees did not appear in a bond granted by the trust, his co-trustees in whose names the document was drawn up would have a right of relief or contribution from him if themselves found personally liable for the obligations thus constituted, provided, always, that the trustees entering into the obligation had taken such steps as might be open to them to avoid personal liability on the part of themselves and their co-trustees and limit the claims to the extent of the trust estate.[59] Where personal liability on the part of the trustees or some of them is unavoidable, trustees incurring such a liability, if entitled to act in the matter on behalf of the trustees as a body, will have a right of relief against co-trustees whose non-participation in the transaction, for example by not signing the bond or other document results that they are not directly liable to the other party to the transaction in question. On the other hand, where the actings of a quorum have involved the trustees as a whole unnecessarily or unwarrantably in liabilities connected with the trust a right of relief against the trustees constituting the quorum will be available to the remaining trustees. Again where for any reason, valid or otherwise, a quorum of trustees have seen fit to take some action without reference to their co-trustees, it appears that the latter will be free from personal liability, provided that, if and when the matter comes to their notice, they take prompt and effective steps to disclaim responsibility, as for example by lodging a minute in court proceedings in which the quorum have involved the trust [60] or by having their names removed from the register of the company in whose shares the quorum have taken the decision to invest.

Where the actings of a quorum are taking place in accordance with express provision in the trust deed or under the statutory implication it is clear that a number of trustees sufficient to constitute a quorum must in fact be parties to the action taken.[61] Apart from the circumstances already mentioned of action taken to combat breach of trust or default in fulfil-

---

[58] *Cunningham* v. *City of Glasgow Bank* (1879) 6 R.(H.L.) 98; *Roberts* v. *City of Glasgow Bank* (1879) 6 R. 805.

[59] See *e.g. Gordon* v. *Campbell* (1842) 1 Bell's App. 428 where a heritable bond in name of trustees as such was held not to involve them in personal liability and *Lyon* v. *Sibbald* (1823) 2 S. 591, where the same result was reached in respect of an account incurred *qua* trustees only. *Per contra* see *Horsburgh's Trs.* v. *Welch* (1886) 14 R. 67 indicating that it may not be possible to qualify or limit the obligations statutorily implied from the warrandice clause in a heritable bond. Again although the register of members of a Scottish company may disclose, as that of an English company cannot do, the existence of a trust the personal liabilities of trustees registered in that capacity are the same as those of any other members: *Muir* v. *City of Glasgow Bank* (1879) 6 R.(H.L.) 21.

[60] *Cambuslang West Church* v. *Bryce, supra*: and see the interlocutor pronounced in the case of *Bon Accord Marine Assurance Co.* v. *Souter* (1859) 13 D. 295, 302–303.

[61] *Lynedoch* v. *Ouchterlony* (1821) 5 S. 538.

ment of trust purposes, it appears that an individual trustee, or a number of trustees less than a quorum, cannot act by themselves in name of the trust unless by virtue of a delegation of powers to them from the trustees as a body.[62] Thus if one of a body of trustees proceed with the defence of an action without the concurrence of his co-trustees where that concurrence could in the circumstances have been sought, he will not be entitled to indemnification out of the trust estate for the liabilities and expenses he incurs unless he can show that his interference has resulted in actual benefit to the trust estate. In such cases it appears that the individual trustee acting on his own initiative does not have the rights normally pertaining to a *negotiorum gestor*.[63]

DELEGATION TO AGENTS

By statutory provisions operative when not at variance with the terms or purposes of the trust, trustees are empowered to appoint factors and law agents and to pay them suitable remuneration.[64] Apart, however, from statutory power and from any enabling provisions in the terms of the trust, trustees have by implication a general power to employ agents which properly exercised is not regarded as a delegation of functions the trustees should perform personally.[65] Indeed it appears that the employment of an agent, competent and suitably qualified to perform the duties entrusted to him, is permissible in any circumstances in which a person of reasonable prudence dealing with his own affairs would consider such employment appropriate.[66] The qualifications or skills possessed by the trustees themselves may to some extent affect their right and duty to employ agents. It would appear to be their duty to employ suitable agents such as solicitors for any matter which they themselves do not have the required skills or qualifications,[67] but it is questionable whether a trustee who is acting gratuitously could be required to make such professional qualifications as he may possess available to the trust free of charge.[68] In the matter of personal performance of their duties, however, more may be required of trustees who are being remunerated for their services.[69] The corporate trustee, which must of necessity function through some human agency, might be thought to be in an exceptional position in this matter of employment of agents but in theory, at least, functions undertaken by responsible

---

[62] As to delegation by trustees see *infra*, pp. 309–310.

[63] *Stewart* v. *Dobie's Trs.* (1899) 1 F. 1183.

[64] 1921 Act, s. 4 (*f*).

[65] See *Hay* v. *Binnie* (1865) 23 D. 594, where a contention that the trustees were bound to perform the whole duties of their office personally was expressly refuted: in England the same ruling was given in the case of *Speight* (1883) 9 App.Cas. 1 for long the leading authority but there the matter is now covered in wide general terms by s. 23 of the Trustee Act 1925.

[66] *Hay* v. *Binnie*, *supra*.

[67] Walker, 1624.

[68] As to the right of trustees to charge for services rendered to the trust see *infra*. p. 309,

[69] *Wilson's Trs.* v. *Wilson's Creditors* (1863) 2 M. 9, where a trustee in bankruptcy entitled to commission on his intromissions was held not entitled to charge against the trust funds fees incurred to a law agent for work the trustee could himself have performed.

executives of such a body will normally be regarded as performed by the trustee personally.[70]

In most trusts the employment of law agents or solicitors as contemplated in the statutory provisions will be found necessary for some purpose at least. A distinction, however, falls to be drawn between cases in which solicitors are employed to act in some particular matter such as a property transaction or a litigation, and cases in which a solicitor or a legal firm are appointed solicitors to the trust, when the solicitor or solicitors then appointed will be confidential advisers in all matters within the sphere of their profession. The term " factor," however, in the context of the statutory provision seems to imply a range of activities extending beyond the exclusive province of solicitors. In practice, although the term " factor " is now less commonly used than formerly in relation to trusts, there is a tendency for trustees, particularly where they are empowered to employ solicitors of their own number, to leave the conduct of the trust business generally in the hands of those solicitors who in effect become factors although they may not have been formally appointed as such.[71] In certain circumstances, however, the distinction of capacity between solicitor or law agent on the one hand and factor on the other may be significant.[72] Yet despite the broad generality of the term " factor " it has been held that the power to employ a factor does not entitle trustees to engage a manager for the conduct of a business belonging to the trust.[73]

While the majority of cases in which trustees find it expedient to use the services of agents will be covered by their common law rights if not by their statutory powers, it is the practice for trusts to embody certain express provisions for this matter. In some cases [74] the powers thus conferred go no further as regards the permissible categories of agents than the statutory powers [75]; in other instances they go as far or even further than the common law implication.[76] It would appear to be desirable that if such powers are to be expressed they should be in terms wide enough to cover all contingencies in which, in the circumstances of the particular trust, the employment of agents is likely to be necessary and not be confined, as is often the case, to expressing the statutory right to appoint factors or law agents.[77]

---

[70] In many cases corporate trustees such as banks acting on the basis of remuneration for their services make it a condition of acceptance of office that the terms of the trust empower them to employ and remunerate agents such as solicitors in circumstances where gratuitous trustees would be entitled to do so.

[71] See the comments in Menzies, 119–120. At one time it was customary to appoint factors as such whenever the business of the trust was so extensive as to require the continuous attention of someone authorised to represent the trustees but in modern practice the person or firm appointed as solicitors will often fill this role.

[72] *Mayne* v. *McKeand* (1835) 13 S. 870, 872, *per* Lord Cockburn (Ordinary).

[73] *Miller* v. *Brown's Trs.* (1900) 2 F. 1037.

[74] See *e.g.* Elder, *Forms of Wills*, 73, and *Encyclopaedia of Scottish Legal Styles*, Vol. 9, p. 267.

[75] Although they will normally entitle the trustees to employ a solicitor or factor of their own number which as indicated, *infra*, p. 309 is essential if such trustees/agents are to be remunerated for their services.   [76] See *e.g.* Burns, *Conveyancing Practice*, 4th ed., 803.

[77] This is especially the case where administration of the trust is to involve responsibilities such as carrying on and managing a business (see *Miller* v. *Brown's Trs.*, *supra*, n. 73). Without the appropriate provisions a trustee who performs such services for the trust will not be entitled to claim remuneration therefor: see *infra*, p. 309.

Normally the selection of agents will be a matter in the discretion of the trustees but exceptionally the trust may contain directions for the employment by the trustees of a certain person or firm in some particular capacity. Such a direction will not by implication deprive the trustees of the right to terminate the employment as and when they consider it necessary to do so.[78] If, however, the person nominated by the trusters for some particular function is one of the trustees the direction may be construed as conferring on that trustee additional powers of which his co-trustees are not entitled to deprive him.[79]

Where, as will usually be the case, the selection of agents is within their discretion it is the duty of the trustees to exercise due care in selecting agents of standing or repute qualified and competent to perform the functions entrusted to them.[80] As a general rule trustees will be free of liability for losses resulting from the defaults of the agents nominated in terms of the trust, or justifiably selected by the trustees themselves, in so far as the losses could not have been prevented by the trustees exercising such supervision of the activities of the agent as would have been reasonable and appropriate in the particular circumstances.[81] If, however, an agent is entrusted by trustees with duties outwith his proper sphere, or with duties which he could not be regarded as qualified to undertake, the trustees will be personally liable for any loss to the trust resulting from his default.[82] It is customary for trusts to contain provisions purporting to give trustees a general immunity from liability for the actings or defaults of the agents employed by them [83] but it is established that the protection derived from such provisions extends only to the actings of agents legitimately appointed and acting within the scope of their agency.[84] Yet such provisions may be useful in practice in so far as the application and extent of the indemnity

---

78 Cormack v. Keith & Murray (1893) 24 R. 977. Menzies comments on the matter at 116–117 and cites certain English decisions to the same effect. In Nairn's Trs. v. R. Stewart & Son, 1910, 2 S.L.T. 433, it was decided that when the appointee is a firm termination results from the retiral of a partner.

79 Fulton v. McAlister (1831) 9 S. 442, an unusual case about the decision in which Menzies, loc. cit., expresses some doubts.

80 As an indication of what the legislature may be said to expect of trustees in this matter, s. 30 of the Trusts (Scotland) Act 1921 concerning valuations of property offered as security for a loan from the trust may be significant in referring to " a person whom the trustees reasonably believe to be an able practical valuator."

81 Most of the leading decisions on this topic come from the 19th century, e.g. Thomson v. Campbell (1838) 16 S. 560; Seton v. Dawson (1841) 4 D. 310. In present-day circumstances developments such as guarantee funds and professional indemnity insurance make litigation arising out of the defaults of professional persons acting as agents less likely and again the private banks as operating in former times have virtually disappeared.

82 Ferguson v. Paterson (1900) 2 F.(H.L.) 40, 41, per Lord Macnaghten, indicating that a solicitor or law agent cannot be treated as a banker in whose hands uninvested moneys may be left for an indefinite time; per contra see Buchanan v. Eaton, 1911 S.C.(H.L.) 70, where trustees were held not responsible for the default of a law agent to whom funds had been entrusted for the specific purpose of paying Estate Duty.

83 See e.g. Encyclopaedia of Scottish Legal Styles, Vol. 10, p. 267; Elder, Forms of Wills, 174; Burns, op. cit., 803.

84 Ferguson v. Paterson, supra; Wynne v. Paterson (1900) 2 F.(H.L.) 37, 40, per Lord Halsbury.

available to trustees at common law is not absolutely clear and there are in Scotland no statutory provisions directly bearing on this matter.[85]

There are no rules of law prescribing the manner or form in which trustees should appoint their agents but at least in cases of continuing or permanent agency such as law agents or factors it is advisable that the appointment should be made at a meeting of trustees and duly minuted. This course is especially desirable where the appointee is one of the trustees or a firm of which a trustee is a member.[86]

Where their number includes persons with professional qualifications such as a solicitor it is customary for trustees to appoint such a person or his firm to act for the trust in that capacity. Such an arrangement will normally be sanctioned, at least in the case of solicitors, by an express provision in the trust deed coupled with an authority for payment of the normal professional charges to the person thus employed or his firm [87] but it is settled that power to employ agents of their own number implies power to remunerate these agents appropriately.[88] In the absence of any such provision for the employment of trustees, however, the fiduciary position of a trustee results that any claim he or his firm may have against the trust will be restricted to recovery of outlays and disbursements. He will be precluded from making a profit out of his office by receiving payment for the services which he or his firm may render to the trust except with the knowledge and consent of all the beneficiaries affected whose consent when not expressly given will not be readily inferred.[89] Provisions in a trust enabling trustees or their firms to receive payment for services rendered to the trust are regarded as conferring a beneficial interest on the trustees concerned which in the case of a solicitor will disqualify him or any member of his firm from acting in a notarial capacity under the relevant statutory provisions [90] in executing a settlement or other deed of trust for a party unable to write.[91]

---

[85] See Menzies, 115. In England the matter is now specifically provided for in s. 23 of the Trustee Act 1925. In Scotland a trustee might claim relief under s. 3 (a) of the Trusts (Scotland) Act 1921 covering omissions or apply to the court for relief under s. 32 of the Act: it seems doubtful if either course would succeed in a case where relief was not available at common law.

[86] See Menzies, 118–122, dealing particularly with appointees such as solicitors: see also the opinion of the court in *Lewis's Trs.* v. *Pirie*, 1912 S.C. 574.

[87] Examples contained in the Style Books are referred to in nn. 74, 76, *supra*. Such provisions will normally be construed as covering as appointors and appointees not only the original trustees but also any trustees appointed by the court (*Allan's Trs.* v. *McDougall* (1899) 7 S.L.T. 26) and presumably any trustees who may be assumed.

[88] *Lewis's Trs.* v. *Pirie, supra*; presumably the same would apply where the appointment of a certain person or firm arose from a direction in the trust. Again a general power enabling trustees as individuals to contract with the trust would seem to cover the point although the practice appears to be to make express provision for the employment and remuneration of solicitor/trustees even where contracting is authorised: Burns, *op. cit.*, 803–804.

[89] *Scott* v. *Handyside's Trs.* (1868) 6 M. 253; *Munro's Trs.* v. *Murray & Ferrier* (1871) 9 S.L.R. 174.

[90] Conveyancing (Scotland) Act 1924, s. 18.

[91] *Finlay* v. *Finlay's Trs.*, 1948 S.C. 16; *Gorrie's Trs.* v. *Steven's Exor.*, 1952 S.C. 1. As these cases show, a deed affected by this objection is rendered null and void, but the objection does not arise where the signatory is an employee of the solicitor or firm concerned and possibly not where he is a salaried partner: see *Fraser's Exor.*, 1955 S.L.T.(Sh.Ct.) 35 and *obiter dicta* in *Hynd's Exor.* v. *Hynd's Trs.*, 1955 S.C.(H.L.) 1: *per contra* it was held in

The appointment by trustees of one of their number to act for the trust in a capacity such as solicitor, law agent, or factor makes the appointee an agent for each and all of the trustees. They are accordingly liable for the results of any culpable neglect in their dealings with him in his agency capacity and cannot disclaim responsibility for his actings on the basis on which they might do so for the actings of a co-trustee.[92] In this matter indemnity clauses [93] sometimes purport to equate the position of agents, whether or not themselves trustees, with that of co-trustees [94] but such provisions will not relieve the trustees of liability for the consequences of failure to exercise a measure of supervision reasonable in the circumstances over the actings of a trustee who is conducting the business of the trust in an agency capacity.[95]

TRUST LITIGATION

Petition for directions

Trustees under any trust deed, or a majority and quorum of them, can apply to the court for direction on questions relating to the investment, distribution, management or administration of the trust estate, or as to the exercise of any power vested in, or as to the performance of any duty imposed on, them notwithstanding that such direction may affect contingent interests in the trust estate whether of persons in existence at, or of persons who may be born after, the date of such direction.[96] The application is by petition signed by counsel and presented to the Inner House. The petition, after such narrative as may be necessary, sets forth clearly and succinctly the questions upon which directions are asked and may include in an appendix any relevant documents. The court may order intimation to creditors, beneficiaries or other persons interested and such parties wishing to appear to support or oppose the petition may lodge a minute setting forth their position. The petition is disposed of in the summar roll. The court disposes of all questions of expenses and any direction pronounced on the petition is in the form of an interlocutor extractable in common form. It has been indicated that there can be an appeal to the House of Lords.[97] If an interested party through excusable error has not been represented, the court has an inherent power to give

---

Hadden v. Hadden's Trs. (Outer House, Nov. 4, 1953, unreported) that the notarial execution by a solicitor of a Will appointing his clerk as trustee was invalid. As demonstrated in the case of Irving v. Snow, 1956 S.C. 256, different rules operate in England. Legislative effect has not yet been given to the proposals in the Halliday Report (Cmnd. 3118 (1966), para. 23) whereby the court in Scotland would have power to uphold the validity of the deed on being satisfied that it represented the true intent of the granter with a discretion to deprive the notarial signatory or anyone whose relationship with him had created the disqualifying interest, of any benefit derived from the deed.

[92] Home v. Pringle (1841) 2 Robinson's Appeals 384.
[93] See e.g. Burns, op. cit., p. 803.
[94] See Trusts (Scotland) Act 1921, s. 3 (b).
[95] See the comments in Menzies, 121, and the cases of Thomson v. Campbell and Seton v. Dawson, supra, p. 308 n. 81.
[96] Administration of Justice (Scotland) Act 1933, s. 17 (vi); R.C. 232–233.
[97] Grant's Trs. v. Hunter, 1938 S.C. 501, 504, per L.P. Normand.

him an opportunity of being heard and, if necessary, to alter its inter-locutor.[98]

The question must require an immediate decision by the trustees subject to the directions which they seek from the court.[99] When the petition comes before the court for debate there must be representation of all the parties who would have had to be represented if the question had been submitted in a competent special case.[1] Simple questions as to investment, distribution, administration or as to the powers and duties of the trustees can be dealt with even although only the trustees are repre-sented at the bar.[2] A question of vesting would not be decided in the absence of parties other than the trustees.

It is not necessary that the petition proceed only on agreed facts or the terms of the trust-deed.[3] There can be inquiry by proof before an Inner House judge, or by remit to a reporter or by affidavit, as may be con-sidered necessary. But the nature of the facts to be inquired into, or the unsuitability of the pleadings, may indicate that some other form of process is appropriate. Regard must be had to convenience as well as competency.[4]

It is not an objection that the question could be raised in a special case or multiplepoinding[5] but Lord President Normand deprecated the view that a petition could be resorted to at will in preference to a special case. He declared that the use of a petition had to be justified " as, for example, by some emergency or specialty which renders more formal procedure inefficacious or by circumstances which render other procedure incom-petent." [6] " A summary remedy has its place and its uses, but a formal question deserves form." [7] It is understood, however, that in modern practice the stringency of these requirements has been somewhat relaxed and the court is prepared to entertain petitions presented by trustees who are confronted with a live problem provided that the question is not hypo-thetical.

The following have been considered appropriate questions: whether a sum is to be treated as capital or income[8]; whether a beneficiary was entitled to receive immediately a portion of the trust fund[9]; whether the testator's direction to apply the whole estate to the erection of a funeral vault was contrary to public policy and therefore invalid.[10]

Questions as to the following have been entertained: the meaning of

[98] *Milne's Tr.*, 1936 S.C. 487.
[99] *Andrew's Trs.* v. *Maddeford*, 1935 S.C. 857.
[1] *Peel's Trs.* v. *Drummond*, 1936 S.C. 786.
[2] *Peel's Trs.* v. *Drummond, supra.*
[3] *Andrew's Trs.* v. *Maddeford, supra.*
[4] *Grant's Trs.* v. *Hunter*, 1938 S.C. 501.
[5] *Andrew's Trs.* v. *Maddeford, supra.*
[6] *Henderson's Trs.* v. *Henderson*, 1938 S.C. 461, 464.
[7] *Grant's Trs.* v. *Hunter, supra*, p. 505, *per* Lord Moncrieff.
[8] *Lord Hamilton's Trs.*, 1935 S.C. 705.
[9] *Peel's Trs.* v. *Drummond, supra.*
[10] *MacKintosh's J.F.* v. *Lord Advocate*, 1935 S.C. 406.

the word " wife " in a will [11]; construction of a power of investment [12]; construction of a clause authorising advances of capital to beneficiaries [13]; whether the trust deed contained an implied direction to appropriate particular investments to each legacy [14]; whether a bequest failed because of impossibility [15]; the disposal of income which could no longer be accumulated [16]; whether a tax repayment effeired to the liferenter or the trust capital [17]; whether the Scottish or the English court was the appropriate forum for a petition to vary trust purposes under the Trusts (Scotland) Act 1961.[18]

"Questions of vesting or conflicting claims, raising complex considerations depending on the construction of the trust-deed or partly on construction and partly on facts " are not suitable.[19] The procedure should not be used when there is no real question to be solved.[20]

If the pleadings do not afford a satisfactory basis for answering the question put, the court may refuse to entertain the petition and may direct proceedings in another form.[21] The court is unwilling to dismiss a petition on or near the borderline although it may be that the only direction which can be given is that the trustees continue to hold the estate until a claim to denude is established in another process.[22] A petition cannot be brought by trustees who are not acting under a trust deed.[23]

Special case

If there is agreement between all interested parties on the facts of a dispute, a special case can be submitted to the Inner House setting forth the facts which are agreed and the question of law thence arising upon which the opinion of the court is desired.[24] The contentions of the parties must be stated.[25] If the parties wish to have a judgment which can be extracted and appealed to the House of Lords they must ask for " the opinion and judgment of the court " and not merely an opinion.[26]

The special case is not appropriate where a special statutory procedure is available.[27] The court will not answer questions which are not argued.[28]

[11] *Burns's Trs.*, 1960 S.C. 17.
[12] *Thomson's Trs.* v. *Davidson*, 1947 S.C. 654; *Merchant Company's Widows' Fund Trs.*, 1948 S.L.T.(Notes) 69.
[13] *Moss's Trs.* v. *King*, 1952 S.C. 523.
[14] *Duncan's Trs.*, 1951 S.C. 557.
[15] *Tait's J.F.* v. *Lillie*, 1940 S.C. 534 (but see Lord Mackay's criticism at 542).
[16] *Dowden's Trs.* v. *Governors of Merchiston Castle School*, 1965 S.C. 56.
[17] *Menzies's Trs.* v. *Lindsay*, 1957 S.C. 44.
[18] *Clarke's Trs.*, 1966 S.L.T. 249.
[19] *Andrew's Trs.* v. *Maddeford*, *supra*, p. 864, *per* L.P. Normand.
[20] *Henderson's Trs.* v. *Henderson*, 1938 S.C. 461.
[21] *Peel's Trs.* v. *Drummond*, *supra*.
[22] *Andrew's Trs.* v. *Maddeford*, *supra*.
[23] *Leven Penny Savings Bank*, 1948 S.C. 147; *Territorial Auxiliary and Volunteer Reserve Association for the Lowlands of Scotland*, 1971 S.L.T. 297.
[24] Court of Session Act 1868, s. 63. See, as to the questions of law, *Davidson's Trs.*, 1912 S.C. 693.
[25] *Stewart's Trs.* v. *Stewart* (1895) 23 R. 93.
[26] *Macdougall* (1869) 7 M. 976.
[27] *Harvey's Trs.* v. *Harvey*, 1942 S.C. 582.
[28] *Mackinnon's Trs.* v. *MacNeill* (1897) 24 R. 981; *Turner's Trs.* v. *Turner*, 1943 S.C. 389.

Trustees should not state contentions unless they have a duty to represent and protect the interests of parties or possible parties who cannot state their own contentions, for example, to protect the interests of children who may yet be born or unless the trustees have a duty to maintain their right to hold the trust estate contrary to the claims of some or all of the parties to the case.[29] An agreement between the parties that one of them by entering into the case is not to be deemed to have made an election between a testamentary provision and legal rights does not render the case incompetent.[30]

If a will is to be construed it should be printed in an appendix to the case and the body of the case should not contain long excerpts from it but should merely specify the clauses most material to the question at issue.[31]

The procedure has been used to determine *inter alia*, whether a codicil revoked a legacy [32]; a question of vesting [33]; the validity of a bequest [34]; the disposal of income which could no longer be accumulated [35]; the validity of a liferent [36]; the validity of an exercise of a power of appointment [37]; the revocability of a trust [38]; the existence of a radical right in trust funds [39]; whether a sum received by the trustees was income or capital [40]; the amount payable in respect of an annuity [41]; the effect of forfeiture of an alimentary liferent [42]; whether a widow's executors could claim *jus relictae* from part of her husband's estate [43]; whether a destination could be evacuated [44]; whether conditions attached to legacies were void from uncertainty.[45]

The procedure may be regarded as incompetent if the question raised is hypothetical [46] or premature [47] or if there is not complete agreement on the facts [48] or if all interested parties are not represented.[49]

Multiplepoinding

Multiplepoinding is a form of action appropriate where two or more

---

[29] *Bell's Trs.* v. *Skeil*, 1944 S.C. 153.
[30] *Turner's Trs.* v. *Turner*, 1943 S.C. 389.
[31] *Murray's Trs.* v. *Wilson's Exors.*, 1945 S.C. 51.
[32] *Lawrie's Trs.* v. *Church of Scotland*, 1963 S.C. 497.
[33] *Smith's Trs.* v. *Dinwoodie*, 1958 S.L.T. 305; *Munro's Trs.* v. *Monson*, 1962 S.C. 414.
[34] *Pirie's Trs.* v. *Pirie*, 1962 S.C. 43; *Dewar's Trs.* v. *Board of Management for Glasgow and District Children's Hospitals*, 1962 S.C. 100.
[35] *Russell's Trs.* v. *Russell*, 1959 S.C. 148.
[36] *Muir's Trs.* v. *Williams*, 1943 S.C.(H.L.) 47; *Malcolm's Trs.* v. *Malcolm*, 1950 S.C.(H.L.) 17.
[37] *Coats's Trs.* v. *Tillinghast*, 1944 S.C. 466.
[38] *Steel's Trs.* v. *Cassels*, 1939 S.C. 502.
[39] *Drysdale's Trs.* v. *Drysdale*, 1940 S.C. 85.
[40] *Forgie's Trs.* v. *Forgie*, 1941 S.C. 188; *Thomson's Trs.* v. *Thomson*, 1955 S.C. 476.
[41] *Turner's Trs.* v. *Turner*, 1943 S.C. 389.
[42] *Hurll's Trs.* v. *Hurll*, 1964 S.C. 12.
[43] *Melville's Trs.* v. *Melville's Trs.*, 1964 S.C. 105; *Mill's Trs.* v. *Mill's Trs.*, 1965 S.C. 384.
[44] *Shand's Trs.* v. *Shand's Trs.*, 1966 S.C. 178.
[45] *Gore-Browne-Henderson's Trs.* v. *Grenfell*, 1968 S.C. 73.
[46] *Scott's Trs.* v. *Aiton* (1891) 28 S.L.R. 673. See also *Bailey's Trs.* v. *Bailey*, 1954 S.L.T. 282.
[47] *Cuthbert* v. *Cuthbert's Trs.*, 1908 S.C. 967; *Robson Scott's Trs.* v. *Robson Scott*, 1945 S.C. 52.
[48] *Lawson's Trs.* v. *Lawson* (1883) 10 R. 1278; but see *Macnaughton* v. *Macnaughton's Trs.*, 1953 S.C. 387.   [49] *Lawson's Tr.* v. *Lawson*, 1938 S.C. 632.

persons have competing claims to the same fund or property. It has been held competent

(a) where a trust fund is claimed by an arrester and another party [50];
(b) where an estate is claimed by a beneficiary and by the assignees of the beneficiary [51];
(c) where trustees are unable to obtain a discharge from the beneficiaries. [52]

It is not necessary that competing claims should have been presented to the trustees before the action was raised. " The process of multiple-poinding is the common mode by which trustees seek to obtain judicial exoneration. They do not require to allege actual double distress to entitle them to bring that process." [53] If there is doubt as to the persons entitled to the estate but competing claims have not been advanced, the trustees, on being advised by counsel as to which of the parties has the better right, should communicate with the other party and ask him whether he wishes to make a claim. If he makes no claim, the trustees can safely pay in accordance with counsel's opinion. If he does make a claim, the trustees are justified in raising a multiplepoinding. [54]

The trustees can " throw the estate into court " only where there are competitions of right under the trust-deed between legatees and creditors, or between different persons claiming as beneficiaries under the trust or there is so much difficulty and embarrassment in the distribution of the estate that the trustees would not be in safety to act on their own judgment. [55] If the trustees resist the claim of a legatee or creditor, his remedy is to sue the trustees by petitory action for payment. If the dispute is a competition of right between several persons in relation to one item of the estate, only that item should be placed *in manibus curiae.* Similarly testamentary provisions other than the one in dispute should not be submitted for adjudication.

Trustees cannot raise a multiplepoinding merely to obtain advice from the court, [56] nor can they resort to this form of action because a beneficiary objects to a creditor's claim being met. [57] The fact that a creditor raises an action against the trustees is not a sufficient ground. [58] It may be different if the creditor will neither abandon his claim nor constitute it. [59] A multiplepoinding to determine whether the real raiser is entitled to claim

[50] *N.B. Ry.* v. *White* (1881) 9 R. 97.
[51] *Fraser's Exrx.* v. *Wallace's Trs.* (1893) 20 R. 374.
[52] *Mackenzie's Trs.* v. *Sutherland* (1895) 22 R. 233; *Davidson* v. *Ewen* (1895) 3 S.L.T. 162 (O.H.).
[53] *Taylor* v. *Noble* (1836) 14 S. 817, 819, *per* L.P. Hope; *McClement's Trs.* v. *Lord Advocate,* 1949 S.L.T.(Notes) 59.
[54] *MacGillivray's Trs.* v. *Dallas* (1905) 7 F. 733, 738, *per* Lord McLaren.
[55] *Orr Ewing* v. *Orr Ewing's Trs.* (1884) 11 R. 600, 627, *per* L.P. Inglis; *MacGillivray's Trs.* v. *Dallas, supra.*
[56] *Paterson's Trs.* v. *Paterson* (1899) 7 S.L.T. 134.
[57] *Mackenzie's Trs.* v. *Sutherland* (1895) 22 R. 233.
[58] *Glen's Trs.* v. *Miller,* 1911 S.C. 1178.
[59] *Blair's Trs.* v. *Blair* (1863) 2 M. 284; *Glen's Trs.* v. *Miller, supra,* p. 1185, *per* Lord Johnston.

legitim is incompetent, the proper remedy being a direct action against the estate.[60] If the multiplepoinding is raised to determine the validity of the trust, the trustees should lodge a claim as trustees for the whole fund for the purpose of administration.[61]

The trustees can deal with the funds notwithstanding that there is a multiplepoinding relating to them.[62] The fact that the fund is the subject of a multiplepoinding will not exonerate the trustees from discharging the duty of having accounts furnished to them and audited periodically.[63]

Summary trial

A petition for summary trial under the Administration of Justice (Scotland) Act 1933, s. 10, has been brought by trustees to determine the validity of a bequest of heritage.[64]

General

The court will not entertain an application by trustees to have their accounts audited by an accountant appointed by the court in terms of a direction in the deed that, on this being done, and approved by the court, the trustees would be exonerated and discharged.[65] Similarly, in England, it is ineffectual to provide that trustees may do an act with the consent of a judge of the Chancery Division.[66] An ordinary person has not the power, as the legislature has, to impose upon a judge a jurisdiction which is not given to him by the procedure of the courts or by any statute.

If a testator provides that there is to be no litigation upon certain points and arranges for their determination in another manner, the provision will receive effect.[67] It may be different if he declares that there is to be no litigation about his succession whatever.

Forum [68]

The Court of Session has jurisdiction over all Scottish trusts.

" What constitutes a Scottish trust arises from a variety of circumstances which may or may not concur, thus (1) if the trust originates in the testamentary writings of a Scotsman; (2) if the truster declares that the powers and immunities of his trustees are to be ruled by the law of Scotland; (3) if some or all of the trustees are Scotsmen and (4) if the greater part of the trust estate is in Scotland then the trust is a Scottish trust. But it is clear that if all these conditions do not concur it may be difficult to determine which of them or what combination of

---

60 Scott's J.F. v. Richardson (1905) 13 S.L.T. 537.
61 Hall's Trs. v. Macdonald (1892) 19 R. 567.
62 Miller's Trs. v. Miller (1848) 10 D. 765.
63 Gordon's Trs. v. Gordon (1882) 19 S.L.R. 549.
64 MacLaren's Trs. v. Mitchell and Brattan, 1959 S.C. 183. See also Munro v. Munro, 1962 S.C. 599.
65 Dundas (1869) 7 M. 670.
66 Re Hooker's Settlement, Heron v. Public Trustee [1955] Ch. 55.
67 Low's Trs. (1871) 8 S.L.R. 638, approved Board of Management for Dundee General Hospitals v. Bell's Trs., 1952 S.C.(H.L.) 78.
68 For a fuller treatment, see Anton, Private International Law, 470 et seq.

them is essential to constitute the nationality of the trust. If either the presence of the trustees, one or more, or the presence of trust funds in the territory gives jurisdiction there is no need to consider further the local character of the trust; while if both these elements be absent, it is doubtful how far the others in combination would suffice to give jurisdiction." [69]

A trust which falls within that definition of a Scottish trust may, however, be a trust of another system as well. The question is resolved by applying the principle of convenience. " The true principle upon which jurisdiction in such cases should depend is, that every person beneficially interested ought to seek his remedy in that Court in which it is most for the benefit of the trust and all concerned that the litigation should be carried on." [70]

Under the *nobile officium*, the Court of Session will assist the administration of an English trust in an ancillary role. Where the sole trustee in an English trust became *incapax* and the Chancery Division appointed new trustees the Court of Session authorised the necessary alterations to the titles to a bank account and investments held in Scotland. [71]

SUPERINTENDENCE ORDER

Trustees (or one or more of them) may apply to the court for an order on the Accountant of Court to superintend their administration of the trust in so far as it relates to the investment of the trust funds and the distribution thereof among the creditors and beneficiaries. If the court grants the order the accountant annually examines and audits the accounts and at any time, if he thinks fit, he may report to the court upon any question that may arise in the trust administration with regard to the investment and distribution of funds and obtain the directions of the court thereupon. [72] A minority of trustees can apply. [73] The court will give under this section the same assistance which they give to judicial factors and other officers of the court. Advice will not be given on the exercise of a purely discretionary power. Investment is usually of a purely administrative nature but some questions as to distribution may be controversial and the court will relegate them for decision *in foro contentioso*. [74] The question of when heritage should be sold in compliance with the truster's direction to sell when " advantageous or expedient " was held in the circumstances not to be a matter of investment or distribution. [74] The sale of an ordinary

[69] Duncan and Dykes, *The Principles of Civil Jurisdiction*, 213. Appvd. by L.P. Clyde, *Clarke's Trs.*, 1966 S.L.T. 249, 251.
[70] *Orr Ewing's Trs.* v. *Orr Ewing* (1885) 13 R.(H.L.) 1, 31, *per* Lord Watson. See also *Clarke's Trs., supra; Betts Brown Trust Fund Trs.*, 1968 S.C. 170.
[71] *Evans-Freke's Trs.*, 1945 S.C. 382.
[72] 1921 Act, s. 17, replacing Judicial Factors (Scotland) Act 1889, s. 18, which replaced Bankruptcy (Scotland) Act 1856, s. 166.
[73] The law was different prior to the 1921 Act: *Coulson* v. *Murison's Trs.*, 1920 S.C. 322.
[74] *Earl of Stair's Trs.* (1896) 23 R. 1070; *Coulson* v. *Murison's Trs.*, 1920 S.C. 322; *Liddell's Trs.* v. *Liddell*, 1929 S.L.T. 169.

investment, however, is within the section just as much as is the purchase of one.[75]

The section is intended to deal with matters of present or future administration and not to clear up stale matters in dispute.[76]

On occasion, the appointment of new trustees on a lapsed trust has been made conditional upon an undertaking to apply for a superintendence order.[77]

Disagreement among the trustees may be a ground for making an order.[78]

The order does not remove the trustees' obligation to account for their intromissions, and the audit does not necessarily give immunity from all liability in respect of improper investment.[79] It is no doubt different if a direction has been obtained from the court. The superintendence order does not prevent a beneficiary from bringing an action against the trustees on a question which is not one of investment or distribution without first laying the matter before the Accountant.[80]

In the early history of the legislation the court was reluctant to make an order on the ground that if the section was brought into operation generally the administration of private trusts would be carried out at public expense [81]—but

> " I am not aware of any reason, in regard to expense or otherwise, which should deter honest administrators of a trust from coming under the supervision of the Accountant of Court, and thereby obtaining protection from that responsibility about investments which has frightened so many men away from the office of trustee." [82]

As has already been indicated, the immunity given is perhaps not as wide as this dictum would suggest.

---

[75] *Donaldson's Trs.*, 1932 S.L.T. 463.
[76] *Liddell's Trs.* v. *Liddell*, 1929 S.L.T. 169.
[7] *Milroy* v. *Tawse* (1905) 12 S.L.T. 777; *Pattullo* (1908) 16 S.L.T. 637; McLaren, II, 1135. See p. 275, *supra*.
[78] *Turnbull* v. *Turnbull's Trs.* (1905) 13 S.L.T. 145.
[79] *Hutton* v. *Annan* (1898) 25 R.(H.L.) 23; Menzies, 168.
[80] *Bonnar* (1893) 1 S.L.T. 57.
[81] *Tweedie's Trs.* (1858) 20 D. 438; *Raeburn's Trs.* (1888) 15 R. 740.
[82] *Earl of Stair's Trs.*, *supra*, 1072, *per* L.P. Robertson. It appears from Lord Pitman's opinion in *Donaldson's Trs.*, *supra*, that the decision in *Stair's Trs.* in fact inhibited further use of the section. See also Menzies, 167.

CHAPTER 21

THE POWERS OF TRUSTEES

GENERAL ADMINISTRATION

THE administrative powers of trustees are regulated primarily by the terms of the trust deed which may confer powers expressly or by implication.

> " The trust-deed is the foundation and the measure of the powers of the trustees. Whatever is directed or permitted by the trust-deed cannot be in breach of the trust, for the truster was entitled to direct or permit as he pleased, and the expression of his will in the trust-deed constitutes the law of the trust." [1]

In most trusts there is an implied power to do acts of ordinary administration. Then there are the provisions of the 1921 Act. Section 3 confers specified minimal powers such as power to resign and power to assume new trustees " unless the contrary be expressed " in the deed; these are treated elsewhere.[2] Section 4 confers power to do specified acts if they are not " at variance with the terms or purposes of the trust." Section 5 empowers the court to authorise the trustees to do the acts specified in section 4 notwithstanding that the act is at variance with the terms or purposes of the trust, on being satisfied that such act is " in all the circumstances expedient for the execution of the trust." Lastly, resort may be made to the *nobile officium* for special powers.

Section 4

Section 3 of the Trusts (Scotland) Act 1867 enabled trustees to apply to the court for authorisation to sell, feu, excamb and borrow money on the security of the trust estate if such act was " expedient for the execution of the trust and not inconsistent with the intention thereof." [3] In the 1921 Act, by section 4, trustees are given power to sell, feu, grant leases, borrow on security, and do certain other acts without prior application to the court where such acts " are not at variance with the terms or purposes of the trust." Such acts when done are as effectual as if powers had been contained in the trust deed. The terms and the purposes of the trust must be considered separately; an act can be at variance with the purposes of the

---

[1] *Goodsir* v. *Carruthers* (1858) 20 D. 1141, 1145, *per* Lord Ardmillan.
[2] See Chaps. 16 and 19.
[3] See as to the effect of the 1867 Act, *Malcolm* v. *Goldie* (1895) 22 R. 968, 972, *per* Lord Kinnear; *Tosh's J.F.*, 1913 S.C. 242, 244, *per* Lord Dunedin; *Hall's Trs.* v. *McArthur*, 1918 S.C. 646, 654, *per* Lord Skerrington. See, as to the difference between the wording of the two Acts, *Leslie's J.F.*, 1925 S.C. 464.

trust even although it is not at variance with its terms.[4] The purpose of the trust may be to preserve the estate until a certain event occurs.

" Section 4 of the Act of 1921 is not very happily expressed and has given rise to certain difficulties in the past. Even if an ' act ' is not forbidden by the ' trust,' it may still be ' at variance with the . . . purposes of the trust,' and these words I read as equivalent to ' involving a variation of the purposes of the trust.' Of the fourteen ' general powers ' enumerated in the section, some are of a type which, in any normal case, could easily enough be described as being either at variance, or not at variance, with the terms or purposes of the trust, e.g., the power to sell or feu the heritable estate in whole or in part; while others are of such a type that it is exceedingly difficult to figure how they could ever be at variance with the purposes of the trust, e.g., the power to appoint law agents, or to uplift debts due to the estate, or to grant deeds necessary for carrying into effect the powers vested in the trustees." [5]

An act can be " at variance " with the terms of a trust although it is not specially prohibited. When the Act refers to a special prohibition it uses appropriate words, as in section 10—" unless specially prohibited by the constitution or terms of the trust." [6] " Not at variance with the purposes " does not mean " necessary for the purposes." [7] Decisions on the wording of the 1867 Act may still be relevant in considering the 1921 Act.

If trustees enter into a transaction with any person (the second party) under which the trustees purport to do in relation to the trust estate or any part thereof any of the acts specified in the first six heads of section 4, i.e. selling, feuing, leasing, borrowing, excambing and purchasing residential accommodation, the validity of the transaction and of any title acquired by the second party under the transaction is not challengeable by the second party or any other person on the ground that the act in question is at variance with the terms or purposes of the trust.[8] This applies to a transaction entered into by trustees acting under the supervision of the Accountant of Court only if the Accountant consents to the transaction. The provision does not affect any question of liability or otherwise between any of the trustees on the one hand and any co-trustee or any of the beneficiaries on the other hand.

Section 5

The court, on the petition of trustees under any trust, can grant authority to do any of the acts mentioned in section 4 notwithstanding that such act is at variance with the terms or purposes of the trust, on being

---

[4] *Marquess of Lothian's C.B.*, 1927 S.C. 579, 584, *per* L.P. Clyde; *Christie's Trs.*, 1946 S.L.T. 309.
[5] *Tennent's J.F.* v. *Tennent*, 1954 S.C. 215, 225, *per* L.P. Cooper.
[6] *Marquess of Lothian's C.B.*, 1927 S.C. 579, 585, *per* L.P. Clyde, *contra per* Lord Blackburn, p. 587.
[7] *Marquess of Lothian's C.B.*, *supra*; p. 586, *per* Lord Sands.
[8] 1961 Act, s. 2. See *Barclay*, 1962 S.C. 594.

satisfied that the act is " in all the circumstances expedient for the execution of the trust." [9]

The section does not apply to any trust constituted by private or local
Act of Parliament. A question has been raised as to whether the General
Trustees of the Church of Scotland incorporated under the Church of
Scotland (General Trustees) Order Confirmation Act 1921, could competently apply under the section.[10] Lord Mackay opined that they could
not. Lord Blackburn thought that the words " trust constituted by private
or local Act of Parliament " could not apply to a trust constituted by
private Act of Parliament only for the purpose of administering property
belonging to an already existing trust.

An endowment vested in a hospital board of management under a
scheme approved by statutory instrument is not a trust to which the 1921
Act applies so an application under section 5 in respect thereof is incompetent.[11]

The petition will be dismissed as unnecessary if there is power by
virtue of section 4.[12] However, in a doubtful case, the trustees act properly in applying to the court, even although the petition is dismissed.[13]

The nobile officium

If neither the trust deed nor the 1921 Act confers the desired power
resort may be made to the *nobile officium* of the court—" an extraordinary
equitable jurisdiction, the exercise of which has always been scrupulously
guarded, and rarely carried beyond precedent." [14] In relation to trusts
resort to the doctrine is " practically confined to cases where something
administrative or executive is wanting in the constituting document to
enable the trust purposes to be effectually carried out." [14] It can be used
only in cases of necessity or strong expediency.[15]

The court will not grant to trustees powers higher than those defined
by the trust-deed.[16]

> " The petition is not presented under the Trusts Acts; it is an
> appeal to the *nobile officium*, and the view hitherto taken and applied
> has been that the powers of trustees are defined by the trust-deed and
> that the Court will give no higher powers. It follows from this that,
> if the trustees have the power, then a petition such as this is unneces-
> sary; and, if they have not the power, it is not competent for the
> Court to give it." [17]

The provisions of the Trusts Acts constitute another constraint on the
exercise of the court's powers.

---

[9] s. 5.   [10] *Church of Scotland General Trustees,* 1931 S.C. 704.
[11] *Board of Management for Edinburgh Royal Infirmary,* 1959 S.C. 393.
[12] *Christie's Trs.,* 1946 S.L.T. 309.
[13] *Leslie's J.F.,* 1925 S.C. 464; *Cunningham's Tutrix,* 1949 S.C. 275.
[14] *Hall's Trs.* v. *McArthur,* 1918 S.C. 646, 650, *per* Lord Johnston. See also *Scott's Hospital
Trs.,* 1913 S.C. 289; *Anderson's Trs.,* 1921 S.C. 315.
[15] *Gibson's Trs.,* 1933 S.C. 190.   [16] *Berwick* (1874) 2 R. 90.
[17] *Hall's Trs.* v. *McArthur,* 1918 S.C. 646, 652, *per* Lord Mackenzie.

" While I admit that there still persists a certain residuum of common law powers in this Court in dealing with trusts and judicial factories and that in suitable circumstances these powers may be resorted to, I do not consider it feasible to accept the argument that, in relation to matters which have been made the subject of specific regulation in statute, we are at liberty to regard ourselves as free either to comply with the express injunctions of the statute or to fall back upon the vague and indeterminate decisions which date from nearly a century ago and which gave rise to doubts and difficulties which the later statutes were passed to resolve." [18]

This view probably requires modification so far as investment powers are concerned because the Trustee Investments Act 1961, s. 15, provides:

" The enlargement of the investment powers of trustees by this Act shall not lessen any power of a court to confer wider powers of investment on trustees or affect the extent to which any such power is to be exercised."

Foreign trusts

The Trusts Acts do not apply to an English or foreign trust.[19] If English trustees have power of sale under the deed or by statute, no further power is needed from the Scottish court.[20] If the trustees of such a trust, not having the necessary powers, wish to deal with heritage in Scotland they should apply to the court having jurisdiction over the trust for an order to the effect that the transaction is competent and expedient. Thereafter an application is made to the *nobile officium* to authorise the sale in the exercise of an auxiliary or ancillary jurisdiction.[21] A general authority to feu or lease lands comprised in the order of the foreign court can be granted so that there is no need to return to the court to seek powers for each transaction.[22] The court required the deletion from the prayer of a petition of a proviso: " provided every sale shall be made for the best consideration in money that can reasonably be obtained." [23] This was an attempt to incorporate the effect of certain sections of the Settled Land Act 1925.

In the absence of compelling reasons, the court will not give retrospective sanction to *ultra vires* acts.[24]

Power to alienate heritage: (a) the trust deed

The question of whether the trustees have power of sale under the

---

[18] *Tennent's J.F.* v. *Tennent*, 1954 S.C. 215, 225, *per* L.P. Cooper. See also *Tod* v. *Marshall* (1895) 23 R. 36; *Mitchell Bequest Trs.*, 1959 S.C. 395.
[19] *Hall* (1869) 7 M. 667; *Brockie* (1875) 2 R. 923; *Carruthers' Trs.* (1896) 24 R. 238.
[20] *Phipps* v. *Phipps' Tr.*, 1914, 1 S.L.T. 239.
[21] *Allan's Trs.* (1897) 24 R. 718; *Harris's Trs.*, 1919 S.C. 432. See also *Blundell* (1893) 1 S.L.T. 125.
[22] *Pender's Trs.*, 1907 S.C. 207; *Campbell, Petitioner*, 1958 S.C. 275.
[23] *Campbell, Petitioner, supra. Campbell-Wyndham-Long's Trs.*, 1951 S.C. 685, was a special case and is not to be followed.
[24] *Horne's Trs.*, 1952 S.C. 70.

trust-deed can competently be decided in a special case to which the trustees and the beneficiaries are parties.[25]

A direction to divide the residue of an estate comprising heritable and moveable property was construed as conferring by implication power to sell heritage.[26] A power under the will of a testator domiciled in England to sell English real estate implies a power to sell Scottish heritage acquired after the date of the will.[27] A direction to pay the truster's debts can imply a power of sale if the moveable estate is insufficient to meet the debts.[28] The nature and character of the estate itself may imply a power of sale.[29] A trustee without an express power of sale can sue an action of division of common property.[30]

A power to sell does not imply a power to excamb.[31] " Excambion is a peculiar transaction, and is attended with some consequences which do not accompany an out-and-out sale. For instance, mutual rights of real warrandice attach to excambed lands . . ." [32]

A provision that the subjects are not to be " sold or disposed of " or let on long lease imports a prohibition against feuing.[33] Feuing can be regarded as an act of administration rather than of alienation so trustees of a charitable mortification have power at common law to feu.[34]

(b) 1921 Act

Under the Trusts (Scotland) Act 1867, s. 3,[35] the court could authorise trustees to sell, feu or excamb the trust estate if the alienation was " expedient for the execution of the trust and not inconsistent with the intention thereof," [36]—as for example, where the buildings had become unsuitable for the purposes of the trust.[37] " Inconsistent with the intention of the trust " was construed to mean " inconsistent with the main design and object " of the trust.[38] A power to sell the heritage with certain specified exceptions is an implied prohibition against selling the excepted

[25] *Galloway* v. *Campbell's Trs.* (1905) 7 F. 931; *Mitchell Innes' Trs.* v. *Mitchell Innes*, 1912 S.C. 228.

[26] *Boag* v. *Walkinshaw* (1872) 10 M. 872; *Thomson's Trs.* v. *Thomson* (1897) 25 R. 19.

[27] *Phipps* v. *Phipps' Tr.*, 1914, 1 S.L.T. 239.

[28] *McKinnon Campbell's Trs.* v. *Campbell* (1838) 1 D. 153; *Graham* v. *Graham's Trs.* (1850) 13 D. 420. *Cf. Allan* v. *Glasgow's Trs.* (1835) 2 S. & McL. 333.

[29] *Thomson's Trs.* v. *Thomson* (1897) 25 R. 19, 22, *per* Lord Young.

[30] *Craig* v. *Fleming* (1863) 1 M. 612.

[31] *Bruce* v. *Stewart* (1900) 2 F. 948.

[32] p. 953, *per* Lord Moncreiff. Real warrandice is now abolished (Conveyancing (Scotland) Act 1924, s. 14).

[33] *Oliver's Trs.* (1876) 3 R. 639.

[34] *Merchant Company of Edinburgh* (1765) Mor. 5750; *Mags. of Elgin* v. *Morrison* (1882) 10 R. 342; *Jamieson* (1884) 21 S.L.R. 541.

[35] As to the relation of the section to the prior law see *Brownlie* v. *Brownlie's Trs.* (1879) 6 R. 1233, 1237, *per* Lord Deas, p. 1241, *per* Lord Shand.

[36] See *Hay's Trs.* v. *Hay Miln* (1873) 11 M. 694; *Anderson* (1876) 3 R. 639; *Weir's Trs.* (1877) 4 R. 876; *Deacons of the Incorporated Trades of Perth* v. *Hunt* (1881) 18 S.L.R. 585; *Molleson* v. *Hope* (1888) 15 R. 665; *Fiddes' Trs.* (1899) 7 S.L.T. 67; *Pottie* (1902) 4 F. 876; *Christie's Trs.* (1904) 11 S.L.T. 786; *Hiddleston's Trs.* (1906) 13 S.L.T. 705; *Old Meldrum U.F. Church Managers* (1908) 15 S.L.T. 913; *Jamieson's Trs.*, 1909, 1 S.L.T. 36.

[37] *Downie* (1879) 6 R. 1013.

[38] *Weir's Trs.* (1877) 4 R. 876.

lands [39] but a *direction* to sell with exceptions does not imply that there is no power to sell the excepted subjects.[40] A direction not to sell before a certain date [41] and an express prohibition against selling any part of the heritage [42] were grounds for refusal of petitions. A wish is not a prohibition.[43] It was decided that a sale which was of advantage to the liferenter but which prejudiced the fiar was not expedient.[44]

The court refused to ratify under the 1867 Act a sale which had already taken place.[45]

The acts specified in section 4 of the 1921 Act include selling the trust estate or any part thereof, heritable as well as moveable, and granting feus of the heritable estate or any part thereof. There is also power to excamb heritable estate. These powers can accordingly be exercised if the act is not at variance with the terms or purposes of the trust.

It has been suggested that, so far as sale is concerned, there is no difference between heritable and moveable property.[46]

The feuing of a small plot of ground forming a very small part of a large estate might not be at variance with the purposes of the trust although the conversion of the whole estate into a superiority might be.[47] If the testator has himself feued part of the estate, further feuing is probably not at variance with the trust purposes.[48]

Most of the reported cases under section 5 relate to tutors.[49] Where the truster had directed his trustees to use part of his estate to found a hospital and to invest the rest of the estate in heritage the revenue of which was to be applied to maintain the hospital, authority was given to sell the heritage notwithstanding an express prohibition in the deed, on the ground that the revenue from the heritage was insufficient and that the proceeds of sale could be more productively invested elsewhere.[50]

In *Darwin's Trs.*,[51] the testatrix directed her trustees to convey heritage to A whom failing B on A's (or B's) attaining the age of twenty-five. The surplus income of the heritage could be applied in making advances for the education and maintenance of A (whom failing B). The court gave the trustees authority to sell the heritage and invest the proceeds in a form giving a higher return so that suitable advances could be made to the minor beneficiary for maintenance. Although the sale was at variance with the

[39] *Whyte's Factor* v. *Whyte* (1891) 18 R. 376.
[40] *Sutherland's Trs.* (1892) 29 S.L.R. 903.
[41] *Marshall's Trs.* (1897) 24 R. 478; *Pratt* (1897) 4 S.L.T. 249. *Cf. Richardson* (1898) 6 S.L.T. 241.
[42] *Hay's Trs.* v. *Hay Miln* (1873) 11 M. 694.
[43] *Jamieson* v. *Allardice* (1872) 10 M. 755.
[44] *Molleson* v. *Hope* (1888) 15 R. 665.
[45] *Clyne* (1894) 21 R. 849. See also *Hall's Trs.* v. *McArthur*, 1918 S.C. 646; *Drummond's J.F.* (1894) 21 R. 932.
[46] *Marquess of Lothian's C.B.*, 1927 S.C. 579, 587, *per* Lord Sands.
[47] *Marquess of Lothian's C.B.*, *supra.*
[48] *Pettigrew's Exrs.* (1890) 28 S.L.R. 14. See also *Campbell* (1880) 7 R. 1032.
[49] *Dempster*, 1926 S.L.T. 157; *Brunton*, 1928 S.N. 112; *Cunningham's Tutrix*, 1949 S.C. 275; *Conage's J.F.*, 1948 S.L.T.(Notes) 11.
[50] *Chalmers Hospital (Banff) Trs.*, 1923 S.C. 220.
[51] 1924 S.L.T. 778.

express provision of the trust deed as to conveyance of the heritage, the conversion affected " only the form or method " of carrying out the trust provision. While the heritage was retained, the return was so low that the trustees were unable to make adequate advances for maintenance. The sale was therefore expedient for the execution of the trust.

If the trust deed confers adequate powers of sale the petition under section 5 will be refused as unnecessary.[52]

(c) Nobile officium

It is thought that power to sell can still be granted under the *nobile officium* where there is " urgency to avoid loss " or " the highest possible expediency " in granting the power craved and the trustee cannot take advantage of the Trusts Acts.[53]

Mode of sale

Powers of sale conferred by the deed or the 1921 Act may be exercised by public roup or private bargain unless the deed, or the authority given by the court, directs otherwise.[54] It has been suggested that a valuation should be obtained to determine the upset price,[55] but it is doubtful if this is necessary in every case. If the trustees sell by public roup, one of the beneficiaries may lawfully purchase.[56] It is lawful to sell subject to or under reservation of a feu-duty or ground annual at such rate and on such conditions as may be agreed upon and in such sales or feus it is lawful to reserve the mines and minerals.[54] Unnecessarily depreciatory conditions of sale should not be made.[57] In England, it has been held that, as trustees are under a duty to obtain the best possible price, they are not entitled to decide on grounds of commercial morality not to break off negotiations with one prospective purchaser on receipt of a better offer.[58] The opinion has been expressed that trustees are not entitled to sell at a price to be fixed by arbitration.[59] In certain circumstances they can participate in a joint sale.[60]

Purchase of heritage

There is no general statutory power to purchase heritage; the power must be derived from the trust deed or the *nobile officium*. Power to pur-

---

[52] *The Hamilton Trs.* (1919) 56 S.L.R. 555; *Campbell's Trs.*, 1935 S.N. 109.
[53] *Shearer's Tutor*, 1924 S.C. 445; *Ferrier's Tutrix*, 1925 S.C. 571. See *Mackenzie* (1855) 17 D. 314; *Presbytery of Aberdeen* v. *Cooper* (1860) 22 D. 1053; *Lord Clinton* (1875) 3 R. 62; *Campbell* (1880) 7 R. 1032; *Logan* (1897) 25 R. 51; *Gilligan's Factor* v. *Fraser* (1898) 25 R. 876; *Stranraer Original Secession Congregation*, 1923 S.C. 722.
[54] 1921 Act, s. 6.
[55] Menzies, 215.
[56] *Shiell* v. *Guthrie's Trs.* (1874) 1 R. 1083.
[57] Menzies, 217. There is no statutory provision in Scotland corresponding to Trustee Act 1925, s. 13. See Lewin, 582.
[58] *Buttle* v. *Saunders* [1950] W.N. 255.
[59] Menzies, 215.
[60] Menzies, 219–222.

chase superiorities was granted to trustees who had power to acquire
" lands." [61]

Section 4 now [62] includes power, if it is not at variance with the terms
or purposes of the trust, to acquire with funds of the trust estate any
interest in residential accommodation (whether in Scotland or elsewhere)
reasonably required to enable the trustees to provide a suitable residence
for occupation by any of the beneficiaries. Power to purchase heritage
has been granted under the *nobile officium* in exceptional circumstances.[63]
Authority can be given if the deed contains no power and if the purchase is
necessary or strongly expedient in the interests of the trust.[64] Retrospective authorisation will be given only in exceptional circumstances and
for compelling reasons.[65]

Leases

Trustees have no power at common law to alienate the property or to
grant long leases.[66] A lease not of extraordinary length is within the
trustees' power as an ordinary act of administration.

> " In Scotland the powers of trustees to grant leases have not been
> very strictly defined; but the limit which has always been placed upon
> these powers may be described thus: They have been permitted to use
> all those administrative powers and faculties which are necessary to
> the extrication and fulfilment of the purposes of the trust-deed, but
> not to use administrative rights and powers which instead of giving
> effect to and carrying out the purposes of the truster would tend to
> defeat or confuse those purposes as appearing from the deed itself." [67]

A lease of twenty-one years of property held for investment is *intra
vires*.[68]

> " But where the property is a mere investment for the purpose of
> profit, it is the duty of the trustees to administer that item of the trust
> estate to the best advantage; and if they think that a twenty-one years'
> lease of it is to the advantage of the estate, they certainly have power
> to grant it." [69]

A lease of 999 years was held not to be contrary to the testator's intention although he had directed the trustees to hold the trust fund until the
death of the last survivor of his children.[70] It was said that a power of
sale in a certain event did not imply a prohibition of the granting of such a
lease.

---

[61] *Sharpe* (1823) 2 S. 203.
[62] head (ee) added by 1961 Act, s. 4. See *Bristow*, 1965 S.L.T. 225.
[63] *Anderson's Trs.*, 1921 S.C. 315. See also *Wardlaw's Trs.* (1902) 10 S.L.T. 349.
[64] *Fletcher's Trs.*, 1949 S.C. 330.
[65] *Dow's Trs.*, 1947 S.C. 524.
[66] *Petrie's Trs.* v. *Ramsay* (1868) 7 M. 64.
[67] *Campbell* v. *Wardlaw* (1883) 10 R.(H.L.) 65, 69, *per* Lord Watson.
[68] *Noble's Trs.*, 1912 S.C. 1230.
[69] *per* Lord Johnston, p. 1234.
[70] *Birkmyre* (1881) 8 R. 477.

Trustees have an implied power to continue the estate in the condition in which it was at the testator's death. So if the testator had granted a lease which was running at his death, the trustees can enter into a new lease when it expires.[71]

If the trust deed directs the trustees " not to sell or dispose of " heritage there is no power to grant a lease of ninety-nine years because such a lease amounts in law to an alienation of the subjects.[72]

Section 4 specifies " to grant leases of any duration (including mineral leases) of the heritable estate or any part thereof and to remove tenants." [73]

The granting of a mineral lease may be an ordinary act of administration. As a lease of minerals is really a sale of a portion of the *solum*, a general power to sell heritage imports a power to grant such a lease.[74] Under the 1867 Act [75] trustees could grant a lease of minerals for not more than thirty-one years if such an act was not at variance with the terms or purposes of the trust.[76] It was doubted whether this included power to open up new mineral fields.[77] Mineral leases of any duration are now covered by section 4.

If a lease is granted *ultra vires* it can be reduced at the instance of the trustees.[78] There is statutory power to accept a renunciation of a lease.[79]

Borrowing

Although they can borrow on personal credit,[80] trustees as a general rule have no power at common law to borrow on security of the estate.[81] A power to borrow on security may be implied by the deed if full and extensive powers of administration and management are conferred.[82]

Where the testator has left his estate burdened with bonds, the trustees have an implied power to effect a transmission of the debt from one creditor to another by means of a discharge of a bond and the granting of a new bond. This is a matter of administration and not one of alienation.[83] The statutory power does not contemplate a case of this kind.

Section 4 specifies " to borrow money on the security of the trust estate or any part thereof, heritable as well as moveable " [84]; and accord-

---

[71] *Dick's Trs.* v. *Robertson* (1901) 3 F. 1021.
[72] *Petrie's Trs.* v. *Ramsay* (1868) 7 M. 64.
[73] As to advisability of granting a lease, see *Tosh's J.F.*, 1913 S.C. 242. Lord President Dunedin suggested that s. 3 of the 1867 Act was limited in its terms to leases of agricultural lands and minerals and did not relate to urban subjects. However, he went on to opine that trustees had a common law power. The trustees must now bear in mind that a protected tenancy may be created.
[74] *Naismith's Trs.* v. *Naismith*, 1909 S.C. 1380.   [75] s. 2.
[76] *Naismith's Trs.* v. *Naismith*, 1909 S.C. 1380.
[77] *Campbell* v. *Wardlaw* (1883) 10 R. (H.L.) 65, 67, *per* Lord Blackburn, p. 70, *per* Lord Watson.
[78] *Eliott's Trs.* v. *Eliott* (1893) 31 S.L.R. 36.
[79] 1921 Act, s. 4 (1) (*m*). See also *Berwick* (1874) 2 R. 90.
[80] McLaren, II, 1189.
[81] *Ralston* v. *McIntyre's Factor* (1882) 10 R. 72.
[82] *Christie's Trs.*, 1946 S.L.T. 309.
[83] *Henderson's Trs.* (1901) 8 S.L.T. 431.
[84] The following were applications under the 1867 Act, s. 3, for authority to borrow: *McNeill* (1883) 21 S.L.R. 168; *Sturrock's Trs.* (1897) 4 S.L.T. 228; *Ross's Trs.* (1901) 9 S.L.T. 122; *Pottie* (1902) 4 F. 876; *Grant's Trs.* (1904) 12 S.L.T. 144; *Kerr's Trs.* v. *Kerr's Curator*, 1907 S.C. 678.

ingly this can be done if it is not at variance with the terms or purposes of the trust.

It has been said that if the trust deed does not by construction or implication empower the trustees to borrow on security of the trust estate, the court cannot confer such power under the *nobile officium*.[85] Such a power is a higher one than power to sell.[86] But under the *nobile officium*, the court authorised trustees, who had otherwise no power to borrow, to charge heritage in security for estate duty paid.[87]

If trustees grant a security which is *ultra vires* it can be reduced at the instance of the beneficiaries except in so far as the money lent has been applied for the benefit of the beneficiaries.[88]

Where the trust deed contained an express power to borrow together with an immunity clause to the effect that " parties paying moneys to my trustees . . . shall not be entitled to inquire into or see to the application of the same," it was held that a bond could not be reduced on the ground that the trustees had applied the money to an improper purpose unless the lender had knowledge of the breach of trust.[89]

Compromise and submission

Prior to the 1867 Act, trustees, in the absence of express provisions in the deed,[90] had no power to refer to arbitration an important claim, *e.g.* the question of whether the truster was a member of a firm and whether his estate was consequently under a substantial liability.[91] There was power to refer matters arising in the course of the ordinary administration of the estate but not to refer something which was not a question of mere management of the estate but the question whether there was an estate to administer. So a compromise relating to a debt due to the estate was competent at common law.[92]

Section 4 includes—" (i) To compromise or to submit and refer all claims connected with the trust estate." Lord Cooper opined that the power to compromise lay between the extremes of his classification in *Tennent's J.F.* v. *Tennent*.[93] He said:

> " In the vast majority of cases the ' claims connected with the trust estate ' which it may be desirable to compromise will, I imagine, be claims by or against persons independent of the trust, and only connected therewith by the relationship of debtor and creditor. In such cases it must be very seldom indeed that the compromise of such claims can reasonably be said to be at variance with the purposes of

---

[85] *Kinloch* (1859) 22 D. 174.
[86] *Ker* (1855) 17 D. 565.
[87] *Harris' Trs.* v. *Harris* (1904) 6 F. 470.
[88] *McMillan* v. *Armstrong* (1848) 11 D. 191. See also *Heriot's Trs.* v. *Fyffe* (1836) 14 S. 670.
[89] *Buchanan* v. *Glasgow University Court*, 1909 S.C. 47.
[90] *Mackintosh* v. *Mackintosh* (1863) 2 M. 48.
[91] *Thomson's Trs.* v. *Muir* (1867) 6 M. 145. See Bell, *Prin.*, s. 1998.
[92] *City of Glasgow Bank* v. *Geddes' Trs.* (1880) 7 R. 731. See also *Anderson* (1855) 17 D. 596; *Hadden* v. *Bryden* (1899) 1 F. 710.
[93] *Supra*, p. 319.

the trust, except in the unduly narrow sense that all compromises may be said to involve a departure from strict legal rights on the part of one or both of the parties. No encouragement should therefore be given to any idea that a trustee, in any normal case, requires to apply to the Court for special powers to perform such an act of what must normally be ordinary trust administration, e.g., where a trustee accepts a composition payment from a debtor, or buys off a doubtful litigation by a settlement. Given good faith and the prudence that the ordinary reasonable man would employ in his own affairs, no successful challenge could be taken against the performance of such an act by a trustee. . . . But then the ' compromise ' may be of a different kind, in respect that the claim in question is one which arises between the trust and a beneficiary, or affects the rights of beneficiaries, and the compromise involves that some variation is thereby made in the trust purposes to the effect of doing appreciable violence to the scheme of division directed by the truster, e.g., where it is proposed under the compromise to give the claimant more or less, and therefore to give other beneficiaries less or more, than the truster directed according to some *prima facie* reasonable interpretation of the language used in the trust deed. In such a case it appears to me that it can fairly be said that the compromise is at variance with the purposes of the trust, and it is intelligible enough that such a compromise should not be allowed to be carried through on the authority of the trustee or factor alone, but that the Court should require to be satisfied that the proposal is ' in all the circumstances expedient for the execution of the trust,' the transaction being not one of ordinary trust administration but involving exceptionally a variation of the purposes of the trust." [94]

Section 5

" In cases in which the Court's sanction to a compromise of this exceptional type is required, all that the Court does is to approve or disapprove of the compromise *as a compromise*, the propriety of which falls to be determined by weighing the pros and cons of an immediate settlement of doubtful claims without the delays, expense and uncertainty of litigation, due consideration being given to ' all the circumstances of the case,' many of which may be of a speculative nature and all of which have to be viewed *ab ante* in the light of such information as is reasonably available at the time. There is no question, as was suggested in argument, of ascertaining by proof the whole of the facts bearing upon the rights of parties, for that could much better be done not by compromising but by fighting the claims to a finish regardless of the consequences. The question is whether, on a prudent weighing up of the facts so far as known, and of the

[94] 1954 S.C. 215, 225.

inevitable imponderable and incalculable factors, the bird in the hand is better than two in the bush." [95]

Where the trustees have compromised with a debtor, a beneficiary cannot sue the debtor.[96]

Managing business

Trustees who are unable to let on satisfactory terms a farm forming part of the trust estate are entitled to take it into their own hands and manage it for the trust as an ordinary act of administration. They do not require the authority of the court to manage the farm or to borrow money on security of the trust estate for purposes of the business.[97] Trustees with power to " continue " a business may convert it into, and conduct it as, a limited liability company.[98]

Miscellaneous powers

Under section 4, there is power to do the following where the act is not at variance with the terms or purposes of the trust:

(f) To appoint factors and law agents and to pay them suitable remuneration.

(g) To discharge trustees who have resigned and the representatives of trustees who have died.

(h) To uplift, discharge, or assign debts due to the trust estate.

(j) To refrain from doing diligence for the recovery of any debt due to the truster which the trustees may reasonably deem irrecoverable.

(k) To grant all deeds necessary for carrying into effect the powers vested in the trustees.

(l) To pay debts due by the truster or by the trust estate without requiring the creditors to constitute such debts where the trustees are satisfied that the debts are proper debts of the trust.

(m) To make abatement or reduction, either temporary or permanent, of the rent, lordship, royalty, or other consideration stipulated in any lease of land, houses, tenements, minerals, metals, or other subjects, and to accept renunciations of leases of any such subjects.

(n) To apply the whole or any part of trust funds which the trustees are empowered or directed by the trust deed to invest in the purchase of heritable property in the payment or redemption of any debt or burden affecting heritable property which may be destined to the same series of heirs and subject to the same conditions as are by the trust deed made applicable to heritable property directed to be purchased.

Further powers are added to the section by the Agriculture Act 1970, s. 33 (3) (execution of deeds relating to amalgamation and boundary

[95] *Tennent's J.F.* v. *Tennent*, 1954 S.C. 215, 226, *per* L.P. Cooper.

[96] *Hannah* v. *Sharp* (1901) 9 S.L.T. 333.

[97] *Dunbar's Trs.*, 1915 S.C. 860.   [98] *MacKechnie's Trs.* v. *Macadam*, 1912 S.C. 1059.

adjustments of agricultural land), Forestry Act 1967, Sched. 2, para. 4 (2) (entering into forestry dedication agreements) the Countryside (Scotland) Act 1967, s. 13 (5) (entering into access agreements) and the Field Monuments Act 1972, Sched. para. 2 (2) (entering into acknowledgment payment agreements).

ADVANCES

(a) The trust deed

The trust deed may give the trustees power to make advances to a beneficiary of the whole or part of his prospective share of capital.

Where there was a power to make advances to fiars during the currency of the liferent, the expediency of doing so being left to " the exclusive judgment " of the trustees, it was held that the liferentrix had no right to interfere with the trustees in the exercise of their discretion.[99]

Where there was power to advance to

" any of the beneficiaries, whether such beneficiary's interest shall be vested or not (provided that where such interest shall not be vested my trustees shall make reasonable insurance against possible defeasance, at the expense of such beneficiary . . .) sums not exceeding in all one-half of the amount to which such beneficiary may be prospectively entitled,"

it was held that advances could be made to a person who had a mere *spes successionis* and that " prospectively entitled " did not apply only to a beneficiary who had at least a vested right subject to defeasance.[1] In the ordinary sense " prospective beneficiary " means a beneficiary who may take, but has not yet taken, a vested interest but this may yield to indications that the testator intended to include beneficiaries who had a vested right but had not yet received payment.[2] " Beneficiary " may be interpreted to exclude a person who may never take any part of the income or capital of the estate.[3] Power " to make advances " to children on their marriage does not authorise the making of annual allowances.[4]

Where trustees were directed to apply income to the maintenance of children but in fact for some years the father supported them himself, it was held that the father was entitled to reimbursement from the trustees.[5] Assumed trustees can normally exercise a power to make advances.[3]

(b) Statutory power

Section 16 of the 1921 Act provides:

" The court may from time to time under such conditions as they see fit, authorise trustees to advance any part of the capital of a fund

[99] *Caithness' Trs.* v. *Caithness* (1877) 4 R. 937.
[1] *Moss's Trs.* v. *King*, 1952 S.C. 523.
[2] *Pattinson's Trs.* v. *Motion*, 1941 S.C. 290.
[3] *Maclachlan's Trs.* v. *Gingold*, 1928 S.L.T. 409.
[4] *Baird's Trs.* v. *Duncanson* (1892) 19 R. 1045.
[5] *Hutcheson* v. *Hoggan's Trs.* (1904) 6 F. 594.

destined either absolutely or contingently to beneficiaries who at the date of the application to the court are not of full age, if it shall appear that the income of the fund is insufficient or not applicable to, and that such advance is necessary for, the maintenance or education of such beneficiaries or any of them, and that it is not expressly prohibited by the trust deed, and that the rights of such beneficiaries, if contingent, are contingent only on their survivance."

This replaced the Trusts (Scotland) Act 1867, s. 7, under which advances could be made only to beneficiaries who were minor descendants of the truster who had " a vested interest " [6] and it was provided that the rights of parties other than the heirs or representatives of the minor beneficiaries were not to be prejudiced by the making of the advance.[7] In interpreting section 16 of the 1921 Act it is legitimate to keep in view the terms of section 7 of the 1867 Act.[8]

The petitioner must be a trustee within the meaning of the Act.[9] The application must be made when the beneficiary is in minority but the court can authorise advances which fall to be operative after the applicant has attained majority.[10] The words " at the date of the application " were inserted to make this clear.

The advances must be made from capital.[11] Advances can be authorised from unappropriated income which is to be added to the capital of the fund.[12] " Accumulation of income with capital fixes accumulated income with the character of capital." [13] Heritable subjects converted into money answer the description of capital because " fund " is equivalent to " property." [14]

Necessity is to be treated as a question of degree depending on the condition of the beneficiaries.[15] The words " expressly prohibited " mean that the trust deed must contain " a clear and specific provision that advances of capital shall not be made to a minor beneficiary." [16]

Where advances were authorised by the trust deed in the event of the death of the beneficiaries' father, it was held that this was an express prohibition of the making of advances in the father's lifetime.[17] It has been

---

[6] In *Pattison* (1870) 8 M. 575, it was held that these words were not to be read literally but meant " a primary interest " which might be contingent. See *Latta* (1880) 7 R. 881; *Baillie's Trs.* (1896) 4 S.L.T. 30; *Martin* (1904) 6 F. 592; *Hodgson's Trs.* (1904) 12 S.L.T 532.

[7] *Ross's Trs.* (1894) 21 R. 995; *Clark's Trs.* (1895) 22 R. 706.

[8] *Macfarlane* v. *Macfarlane's Trs.*, 1931 S.C. 95, 98, *per* Lord Ormidale.

[9] *Rigg* (1905) 13 S.L.T. 144.

[10] *Macfarlane* v. *Macfarlane's Trs.*, 1931 S.C. 95; *Anderson's Trs.*, 1936 S.C. 460; *cf. Craig's Trs.*, 1934 S.C. 34, 38, *per* Lord Hunter. " Full age " is now eighteen (Age of Majority (Scotland) Act 1969, s. 1 (2)).

[11] *Main* v. *Clark's Trs.*, 1909, 2 S.L.T. 375.

[12] *Ross's Trs.* (1894) 21 R. 995; *Anderson's Trs.*, 1936 S.C. 460.

[13] *Per* L.P. Normand, *Anderson's Trs., supra*, p. 463.

[14] *Weir's Trs.* (1877) 4 R. 876.

[15] *Clark's Trs.* (1895) 22 R. 706.

[16] *Paton's Trs.*, 1953 S.L.T. 276, 277, *per* Lord Guthrie. See also *Anderson's Trs.*, 1957 S.L.T.(Notes) 5.

[17] *Thomson* v. *Miller's Trs.* (1883) 11 R. 401.

suggested [18] that the decision is suspect because a further petition by the same applicant was granted subsequently,[19] but in granting the subsequent petition the court may have been acting under the *nobile officium* and not under the statutory power. Although *Thomson* v. *Miller's Trs.* may be suspect, Lord Young's dictum that " An express direction to do something else inconsistent is just the same as an express prohibition against doing the thing that is in question," [20] seems to have been approved by Lord President Clyde.[21] Neither an express [22] nor an implied [23] direction to accumulate income is an express prohibition of the making of advances. " In my opinion, accumulation merely results in enlarging the capital fund out of which advances may be made under the Act, and is not of itself a prohibition against making advances." [24] Provision for an alimentary liferent is not an express prohibition.[25] A direction that the capital was not to be paid to the beneficiary until she was twenty-one was held not to be an express prohibition.[26]

The court will not authorise advances if to do so would be contrary to the obvious intention of the testator.[27] The attitude and financial circumstances of an alimentary liferenter of the fund will be taken into consideration.[28] The court will be reluctant to authorise advances of large sums for a long period of years.[28] The petition is remitted to a reporter for independent verification of the facts averred. The reporter should not proceed only on a certificate by the petitioner's solicitors that the facts are correct.[29] An order may be made for a period of years reserving to the parties the right to apply for variation on a change of circumstances and for a further order on the expiry of the period.[30]

The court has no power under the statute to sanction advances which have already been made,[31] but approval can be given by the Inner House under the *nobile officium*.[32]

(c) Nobile officium

It is clearly established that the court in the exercise of the *nobile officium* can authorise advances for the maintenance and education of minor beneficiaries out of estate which has vested in them.[33]

---

[18] *Macfarlane* v. *Macfarlane's Trs.*, 1931 S.C. 95, 99, *per* Lord Ormidale.
[19] See *Webster* v. *Miller's Trs.* (1887) 14 R. 501 and note at 503.
[20] *Thomson* v. *Miller's Trs.* (1883) 11 R. 401, 403.
[21] *Anderson's Trs.*, 1932 S.C. 226, 231.
[22] *Anderson's Trs.*, 1936 S.C. 460. *Cf. I.R.C.* v. *Bernstein* [1961] Ch. 399.
[23] *Macfarlane* v. *Macfarlane's Trs.*, *supra*.
[24] *Per* L.P. Normand, 1936 S.C. at p. 463.
[25] *Ballantyne*, Nov. 10, 1937, unreported; *Paton's Trs.*, 1953 S.L.T. 276. See also *Pattison* (1870) 8 M. 575.
[26] *Anderson's Trs.*, 1957 S.L.T.(Notes) 5.
[27] *Thomson* v. *Miller's Trs.* (1883) 11 R. 401.
[28] *Paton's Trs.*, 1953 S.L.T. 276.
[29] *Paton's Trs.*, 1953 S.L.T. 276.
[30] *Macfarlane* v. *Macfarlane's Trs.*, 1931 S.C. 95; *Paton's Trs.*, 1953 S.L.T. 276.
[31] *Young's Trs.* (1895) 3 S.L.T. 192.
[32] *Christie's Trs.*, 1932 S.C. 189.
[33] *Hamilton* (1860) 22 D. 1095.

" But this power is exercised only when the maintenance and education of the children is unprovided for in the settlement, or hampered by a direction to accumulate, or the like. The situation is really in the nature of a *casus improvisus*, in which the legal right of the testator's children to be maintained out of his estate has been unintentionally defeated or left unprovided for." [34]

Under the *nobile officium*, it is competent to sanction advances already made,[35] but such retrospective validation will be granted only in exceptional circumstances and for very compelling reasons.[36]

The beneficiary need not be a relative. In *Stewart* v. *Brown's Trs.*,[37] in circumstances stated to be exceptional, an advance was authorised to the testator's former housekeeper who had only a contingent right. The court took the view that, as the statutory power under the 1921 Act could be invoked in favour of a stranger, it was not extending the *nobile officium* unduly. In *Mundell* [38] it was decided that the court had no power under the *nobile officium* to authorise advances out of capital to beneficiaries who did not have a vested right. It is now settled, however, that such advances can be made, whether from capital [39] or from accumulations of income,[40] and whether to major [41] or minor beneficiaries.

An advance for maintenance was authorised out of the general capital of the estate and not from the individual shares of the beneficiaries on the consideration that the testator's children were entitled to be alimented out of their father's estate.[42] But the interlocutor authorising advances does not necessarily regulate their incidence and this may be determined once vesting has occurred.[43]

Payment can be authorised only if the children have a legal guardian [44] capable of giving a valid discharge.[45] A maintenance allowance should be paid to the person charged with the minor's custody and not to the minor's factor *loco tutoris*.[46] A father domiciled in England cannot apply to the equitable jurisdiction of the court as their administrator-at-law because in

[34] *Anderson's Trs.*, 1932 S.C. 226, 231, *per* L.P. Clyde. See also *Gibson's Trs.*, 1933 S.C. 190, 201. The severity of Lord Clyde's dictum was somewhat modified in subsequent decisions.

[35] *Christie's Trs.*, 1932 S.C. 189.

[36] *Dow's Trs.*, 1947 S.C. 524. See also *Horne's Trs.*, 1952 S.C. 70.

[37] 1941 S.C. 300.

[38] (1862) 24 D. 327. Followed in *Baillie's Trs.* (1896) 33 S.L.R. 589.

[39] *Robertson's Trs.*, 1909 S.C. 236; *Milne's Trs.* (1919) 57 S.L.R. 112; *Christie's Trs.*, 1932 S.C. 189; *Craig's Trs.*, 1934 S.C. 34.

[40] *Muir* v. *Muir's Trs.* (1887) 15 R. 170; *Sinclair's Trs.*, 1921 S.C. 484.

[41] *Frew's Trs.*, 1932 S.C. 501. See Mackenzie Stuart, " The *Nobile Officium* and Trust Administration," 1935 S.L.T.(News) 1.

[42] *Bett's Trs.*, 1922 S.C. 21. See also *Gilmour's Trs.* (1872) 44 Sc.Jur. 555. *Cf. Baillie's Trs.* (1896) 33 S.L.R. 589, where it was said that it was for the trustees to deal with a claim for aliment on their own responsibility and that the court would not authorise advances from capital in name of aliment.

[43] *Muir's Trs.* v. *Muir* (1899) 37 S.L.R. 257.

[44] *Seddon* (1891) 19 R. 101; (1893) 20 R. 675.

[45] *Atherstone's Trs.* (1896) 24 R. 39.

[46] *Ferguson* v. *Robertson* (1869) 41 Sc.Jur. 212.

that capacity he is a creditor and must proceed by ordinary action.[47] The trustees may make payment to an English administrator-at-law.[48]

INCOME

Under the *nobile officium* the court can authorise the payment of income to be applied for the maintenance and education of beneficiaries.[49]

Payment from income which the testator has directed to be accumulated can continue after the expiry of the lawful period of accumulation.[50]

The following cases have to be distinguished:

(a) where the court has ordered payment of aliment to children from the trust fund [51];

(b) where the court has held that there was an implied direction in the trust deed for payment of income for the maintenance of children [52];

(c) where it has been held that advances could properly be made to minor beneficiaries from the income of a fund vested in them, there being no direction to accumulate [53];

(d) where the trust deed gives a discretion to trustees to make a payment of income and the court has assisted them in, or interfered with, the exercise of that discretion.[54]

DISCRETIONARY POWERS

Some general considerations apply to the exercise of discretionary powers which have been conferred on trustees expressly or impliedly. *In limine*, it should be noted that what appears at first sight to be a power may be a direction. " When a testator ' authorises and empowers ' his trustees to do a certain thing in such circumstances that failure to do it will result in intestacy, the power is, to all intents and purposes, a direction." [55] In Scotland the cardinal principle is that the courts will not control the exercise of a discretion which has been conferred on trustees. " The great principle in the administration of Scotch testamentary trusts is, to leave the administration where the testator himself has placed it, unless from fault or accident the trust has become unworkable." [56]

At one time the courts defined their powers of intervention " some-

---

[47] *Edmiston* v. *Miller's Trs.* (1871) 9 M. 987.
[48] *Mackintosh* v. *Wood* (1872) 10 M. 933.
[49] *Latta* (1880) 7 R. 881; *Colquhoun* (1894) 21 R. 671; *Walker* (1905) 13 S.L.T. 141.
[50] *Muir's Trs.* v. *Jameson* (1903) 10 S.L.T. 701.
[51] *Spalding* v. *Spalding's Trs.* (1874) 2 R. 237.
[52] *Briggs' Trs.* (1869) 8 M. 242; *Baird* v. *Baird's Trs.* (1872) 10 M. 482; *Christie* v. *Christie's Trs.* (1877) 4 R. 620.
[53] *Normand's Trs.* v. *Normand* (1900) 2 F. 726; *Mackintosh* v. *Wood* (1872) 10 M. 933; *Duncan's Trs.* (1877) 4 R. 1093.
[54] *Allan* (1869) 8 M. 139; *Ferguson's Trs.* (1869) 8 M. 155; *Douglas* v. *Douglas's Trs.* (1872) 10 M. 943; *Spears's Trs.* v. *Spears* (1873) 11 M. 731; *Thomson* v. *Davidson's Trs.* (1888) 15 R. 719; *Ritchie* v. *Davidson's Trs.* (1890) 17 R. 673. But see *Board of Management for Dundee General Hospitals* v. *Bell's Trs.*, 1950 S.C. 406, 438, *per* L.P. Cooper.
[55] *Brown's Trs.* v. *Young* (1898) 6 S.L.T. 32. See also *Re Courtier* (1886) 34 Ch.D. 136; *Tempest* v. *Lord Camoys* (1882) 21 Ch.D. 571.
[56] *Orr Ewing* v. *Orr Ewing's Trs.* (1884) 11 R. 600, 627, *per* L.P. Inglis.

what elastically " [57] but after the decision in *Gisborne* v. *Gisborne* [58] the law perceptibly stiffened. The trustees " are to decide upon this principle, that it is to be such part as they shall think expedient . . . and upon the question of what is expedient it is their discretion which is to decide, and that discretion according to which they are to decide is to be uncontrolled." [59]

The trustees are not entitled to come to the court for advice as to the exercise of their powers.[60]

"I see no reason whatever to doubt that the petitioners take a judicious view of what is for the interests of the trust-estate. But it is for them to exercise their own discretion in that matter. If they do so rightly they will be safe. But it is a pure question of management, in which we cannot aid them, and I think we must refuse the petition as incompetent." [61]

"It is a matter entirely for their discretion, and therefore they cannot come here to ask us for powers, because that would be simply to ask the Court to put its *imprimatur* upon an exercise of the trustees' discretion, where they have the power already." [62]

"If trustees possess a power, however difficult and delicate may be its exercise, and however serious the responsibility which they may incur either by exercising it or refusing to exercise it, the Court will not lift a finger to help them." [63]

A multiplepoinding cannot be used to obtain the court's advice as to the exercise of the trustees' powers.[64] " When trustees have powers, they must act for themselves." [65]

Illustrations

Where a beneficiary was to be paid " either the whole or only a portion of the annual revenue " of a fund " and that subject to such conditions and restrictions, all as my trustees in their sole and absolute discretion think fit," the court refused to interfere with the exercise of the trustees' discretion.[66]

"I am not doubting that the trustees are not entitled simply to button their pockets and say that they will not exercise any discretion whatever; and if they did take up that impossible attitude, certainly I think the Court would find a remedy by managing to give an order

---

[57] *Board of Management for Dundee General Hospitals* v. *Bell's Trs.*, 1950 S.C. 406, 438, *per* L.P. Cooper.

[58] (1877) 2 App.Cas. 300. As to English law, see *Re Steed's Will Trusts* [1960] Ch. 407.

[59] *Per* Lord Cairns L.C., p. 305.

[60] *Berwick* (1874) 2 R. 90.

[61] *Per* Lord Deas, p. 92. See also, as to the different approach of the English courts, *Orr Ewing's Trs.* v. *Orr Ewing* (1885) 13 R.(H.L.) 1, 7, *per* Lord Selborne L.C.

[62] *Noble's Trs.*, 1912 S.C. 1230, 1234, *per* Lord Johnston.

[63] *Hall's Trs.* v. *McArthur*, 1918 S.C. 646, 654, *per* Lord Skerrington.

[64] *Gregorson* v. *Macdonald* (1842) 4 D. 678.

[65] *Per* L.J.-C. Hope, p. 682.

[66] *Train* v. *Clapperton*, 1907 S.C. 517; 1908 S.C.(H.L.) 26.

for the money; but the Court will never take upon themselves the exercise of a discretion which the testator particularly stipulates is to be exercised by trustees." [67]

Where legacies were to be paid " when my trustees shall find it suitable and convenient " and were to be secured " as my trustees may consider best," the court refused to interfere with the exercise of the trustees' discretion.[68] The court will not interfere with the trustees' discretion as to whether the estate should be realised or conveyed to the beneficiaries *in forma specifica*,[69] or as to the amount of capital to be retained to provide an annuity.[70] One reason given for a refusal to intervene was that it would not be for the benefit of the beneficiaries as the trustees would then be relieved of their responsibility.[71]

Mode of exercise

" The discretion of trustees may be unlimited, but it must be exercised in a reasonable manner; it is a discretion, not caprice." [72] A discretion cannot be exercised *nunc pro tunc* [72]; it must be exercised according to the circumstances at the proper time.[73] The trustees must inform themselves as to the facts which appear to be relevant and they must address themselves to their duty carefully, seriously and impartially, and with a real desire to perform their duty to the best of their ability.[74] The fact that trustees were guided by counsel's advice is evidence of the reasonableness of their decision. The considerations which apply to the exercise of statutory powers by a statutory commission may be different and may not be a safe guide as to the duty of trustees.[75]

A trustee should not participate in the exercise of a discretion if he has an interest in the results. He should retire from the trustees' meeting when the subject is discussed.[76]

Consultation

Trustees having a discretion to exercise can consult the views of the beneficiaries—

" It would be extremely dangerous to hold that trustees, having such a discretion to exercise, might not freely discuss with the beneficiaries the reasons for and against a particular decision, without

---

[67] *Per* L.P. Dunedin, 1907 S.C. 524. See also *Dick's Trs.* v. *Dick*, 1907 S.C. 953, 961.
[68] *Cuninghame's Trs.* v. *Duke* (1873) 11 M. 543.
[69] *Brown* v. *Elder's Trs.* (1906) 13 S.L.T. 837.
[70] *Chivas' Trs.* v. *Stewart*, 1907 S.C. 701.
[71] *Taylor* v. *Adam's Trs.* (1876) 13 S.L.R. 268.
[72] *Dunn* v. *Flood* (1885) 28 Ch.D. 586, 592, *per* Bowen L.J.
[73] Lewin, 394; *Re Gulbenkian's Settlements (No. 2)* [1970] Ch. 408.
[74] *Board of Management for Dundee General Hospitals* v. *Bell's Trs.*, 1950 S.C. 406.
[75] *Board of Management for Dundee General Hospitals* v. *Bell's Trs.*, *supra*, p. 438, *per* L.P. Cooper, p. 427, *contra per* Lord Russell. These dicta were uttered with reference to the dissenting opinion of L.P. Clyde in *Donaldson's Hospital*, 1932 S.C. 585, 599, in which it was said that all discretionary powers must be exercised " reasonably and according to law."
' *Caldwell's Trs.* v. *Caldwell*, 1923 S.L.T. 694; Mackenzie Stuart, 251.

running the risk of being held to act against their own judgment, if they should disregard, in the end, objections to which they had thought it right, in the first instance, to direct attention." [77]

In deciding the detailed means by which the truster's directions are to be carried out, the trustees are permitted to look at letters written by the truster prior to the execution of the deed, at least when they are expressly empowered by the deed to do this.[78]

Grounds for interference

The court cannot review, or even examine, the grounds on which trustees have exercised their discretion unless there are definite and precise averments of *mala fides*.[79] There may be interference when one trustee is willing to exercise the discretion and the other has refused to exercise it.[80]

Reasons

The court has no greater liberty to examine the decision if the trustees give reasons.

" The principles upon which the Courts must proceed are the same whether the reasons for the trustees' decision are disclosed or not, but, of course, it becomes easier to examine a decision if the reasons for it have been disclosed." [81]

Reasons need not be stated but if they are stated, and are wrong, the court will correct the decision unless the testator has indicated that the trustees' decision on a point is to be final and conclusive.[82]

" Trustees who are appointed to execute a trust according to discretion . . . are not bound to go into a detail of the grounds upon which they come to their conclusion, their duty being satisfied by shewing that they have considered the circumstances of the case, and have come to their conclusion accordingly. . . . If, however, as stated by Lord Ellenborough in *The King* v. *The Archbishop of Canterbury*,[83] trustees think fit to state a reason, and the reason is one which does not justify their conclusion, then the Court may say that they have acted by mistake and in error, and that it will correct their decision; but if, without entering into details, they simply state, as in many cases it would be most prudent and judicious for them to do, that they have met and considered and come to a conclusion, the Court has

---

[77] *Robinson* v. *Fraser's Tr.* (1881) 8 R.(H.L.) 127, 129, *per* Lord Selborne L.C.

[78] *Milne's Trs.* v. *Cowie* (1853) 15 D. 321.

[79] *MacTavish* v. *Reid's Trs.* (1904) 12 S.L.T. 404; *Dick* v. *Audsley*, 1908 S.C.(H.L.) 27, 28, *per* Lord Loreburn L.C.

[80] *Klug* v. *Klug* [1918] 2 Ch. 67.

[81] *Per* Lord Normand, *Board of Management for Dundee General Hospitals* v. *Bell's Trs.*, 1952 S.C.(H.L.) 78, 85.

[82] *Board of Management for Dundee General Hospitals* v. *Bell's Trs.*, 1952 S.C.(H.L.) 78. See, as to the beneficiary's right to recover documents relating to the exercise of the discretion, *Re Londonderry's Settlement* [1964] Ch. 594; [1965] Ch. 918.

[83] (1812) 15 East 117.

then no means of saying that they have failed in their duty, or to consider the accuracy of their conclusion." [84]

Where trustees had to be satisfied in their " sole and absolute discretion " as to a matter before paying a legacy, it was held that their decision was intended to be final and conclusive and not subject to correction by the courts. The trustees could construe the testator's words rightly or wrongly and it seems that their decision could not be attacked on any ground other than *mala fides* or *ultra vires*. [85]

[84] *Beloved Wilkes's Charity* (1851) 3 Mac. & G. 440, 447, *per* Lord Truro L.C.
[85] *Board of Management for Dundee General Hospitals* v. *Bell's Trs.*, 1952 S.C.(H.L.) 78.

CHAPTER 22

THE INVESTMENT OF THE TRUST ESTATE

POWERS OF INVESTMENT

THE powers and liabilities of trustees as to investment depend primarily on the trust deed, if there is a deed, and otherwise on the rules of common or statute law.[1]

> " Of course in anything that is decided in this case there is no suggestion that a testator may not, if he think fit, give the largest possible powers of investment to his trustees, enabling them to put and leave money at hazard if he pleases . . ." [2]

A clause extending powers of investment beyond what is authorised by the general law ought to be construed strictly.[3] In the case cited, Cozens-Hardy M.R. went so far as to say: " It is for those who seek to include a particular investment to prove beyond all reasonable doubt that the words of the clause cover it."

Where the trust deed conferred the " usual powers " conferred by law on gratuitous trustees and went on to grant power to invest only in a list of investments much more restricted than what was permissible under common or statute law, it was held that there was no repugnancy and the trustees were confined to the investments specified.[4]

It was said that a power to invest " in such stocks, funds, and securities as they should think fit," must be read as " shall honestly think fit." [5] A power in such terms does not restrict the trustees to trustee investments.[6] A direction to invest in specified investments does not exclude investments authorised by the statute.[7] Even if there is a direction to appropriate certain investments towards a settled legacy the trustees can sell the specified investments and invest in investments authorised by the statute.[8] The words " but on no other investment whatsoever " constitute an express prohibition.[9] " But not otherwise " occurring after a list of types of investment was construed to mean " not in any other class or mode of investment " and not " not in any other investment whatsoever." [10]

---

[1] *Brownlie* v. *Brownlie's Trs.* (1879) 6 R. 1233.
[2] *Brownlie* v. *Brownlie's Trs., supra,* p. 1242, *per* Lord Shand.
[3] *Re Maryon-Wilson's Estate* [1912] 1 Ch. 55. See also *Re Peczenik's Settlement Trusts* [1964] 1 W.L.R. 720.
[4] *McMillan's Trs.* v. *Children's Catholic Refuge, Glasgow* (1908) 16 S.L.T. 236.
[5] *Re Smith* [1896] 1 Ch. 71.
[6] *Re Harari's Settlement Trusts* [1949] 1 All E.R. 430; *Re Peczenik's Settlement Trusts* [1964] 1 W.L.R. 720.
[7] *Re Burke* [1908] 2 Ch. 248; *Re Warren* [1939] Ch. 684.
[8] *Re Warren, supra. Cf. Re Owthwaite* [1891] 3 Ch. 494.
[9] *Re Hill* [1914] 1 W.N. 132.
[10] *Re Rider's Will Trusts* [1958] 3 All E.R. 135.

Where the trustees were given " the fullest powers of and in regard to realisation, investment, administration, management and division as if they were beneficial owners," it was said that the clause could not be read literally and did not affect the trustees' overriding fiduciary obligation; its effect could not be greater than to relieve the trustees from the restrictions normally applicable to the detailed execution of the trust in such matters as realisation, investment, administration, management and division amongst the beneficiaries.[11] If the trustees are under a duty to consult a beneficiary about investments and he fails to act they are free to act themselves. If the beneficiary is empowered to direct the trustees as to the purchase of investments, the trustees are bound to comply with his directions but, if there is no open market in the shares, they must satisfy themselves that the price is reasonable and proper.[12]

" Investment "

To " invest " *prima facie* means " to apply money in the purchase of some property from which interest or profit is expected and which property is purchased in order to be held for the sake of the income which it will yield." [13] Accordingly, the purchase of a house to be let to a beneficiary rent-free or on uneconomic terms is not permissible under a power to invest in the usual form.[14] Trustees who have been given " the fullest powers of investment " can purchase real estate in England.[11]

If the money has to be in the trustees' hands for a short period pending distribution, it is a sufficient discharge of their duty to put it on deposit-receipt. If the money has to remain under administration for a period more or less prolonged, they must invest it so as to yield an investment return.[15] But the trustees may not incur liability on this ground if it is shown that they did apply their minds to the question of whether the sum on deposit-receipt should be invested and decided not to invest.[16]

Heritable security

Where money is lent on heritable security, and part of the security subjects is occupied by the owner, that fact ought to be taken into consideration in estimating the amount of the rental available for payment of interest on the loan.[17] Trustees may take a postponed heritable security but only after deliberate and very careful consideration of the circumstances affecting the security.[18] The fact that the buildings on the security subjects are not completed does not *per se* make the investment improper if an independent valuation is obtained and due inquiry made as to the letting history of the site and the estimated rentals to be obtained.[19]

---

[11] *Moss's Trs.* v. *King*, 1952 S.C. 523.
[12] *Re Hart's Will Trusts* [1943] 2 All E.R. 557.
[13] *Re Wragg* [1919] 2 Ch. 58, 65, *per* P. O. Lawrence J.
[14] *Moss's Trs.* v. *King*, 1952 S.C. 523. See also *Re Power* [1947] Ch. 572.
[15] *Melville* v. *Noble's Trs.* (1896) 24 R. 243; *Clarke* v. *Clarke's Trs.*, 1925 S.C. 693.
[16] *Manners* v. *Strong's J.F.* (1902) 4 F. 829.
[17] *Maclean* v. *Soady's Tr.* (1888) 15 R. 966.
[18] *Ibid.*; *Boyd* v. *Greig*, 1913, 1 S.L.T. 398.
[19] *Raes* v. *Meek* (1889) 16 R.(H.L.) 31. But see *Guild* v. *Glasgow Educational Endowments Board* (1887) 14 R. 944; *Crabbe* v. *Whyte* (1891) 18 R. 1065.

Personal security

A power to lend on personal security includes lending on a personal bond and is not restricted to lending on the security of personal property,[20] but it has been said:

" The power to lend trust money on personal credit may prove very useful to trustees who are in search of a permanent investment, but trustees who make a permanent loan on that footing must, in my opinion, if any loss results from it, justify their action by shewing that no safer investment was open to them." [21]

The onus is on the party challenging the investment to show that the personal security was not " good." [22] Bank deposit-receipts are loans on personal security.[23] Power to lend on " heritable or good personal security " was held not to permit investment in bank-stock.[24]

Where an unpunctuated clause gave power to invest " in good heritable moveable or personal security in the Government or Parliamentary funds in the stock of any chartered or incorporated bank or on debentures or mortgages by railway or other joint stock companies or trusts or corporations of a public nature," it was held that the words " good heritable moveable or personal security " were separable from the rest of the clause and defined one of the separate classes of authorised investment.[25]

Banks

" Public stocks of the Bank of England " means " public stocks forming part of the National Debt of this country, and transferable at the Bank of England." [26] " Bank-stock " is not restricted to stock of the Bank of England or chartered or limited banks and means the stock of any bank in good repute for the time.[27] " Chartered banks " are those established by Act of Parliament or royal charter and do not include joint stock banks with unlimited liability.[28]

Types of company

" Any company incorporated by Act of Parliament " includes a company incorporated by a charter granted under a statute,[29] but not a company incorporated by registration under the Companies Acts.[30] " Any company in the United Kingdom " includes a company registered in England and having a head office there at which the directors meet to manage its affairs even although the property is situated abroad and its

---

20 *Knox* v. *Mackinnon* (1888) 15 R.(H.L.) 83. See also *Lamb* v. *Cochran* (1883) 20 S.L.R. 575; *Sim* v. *Muir's Trs.* (1906) 8 F. 1091.
21 *Per* Lord Watson, 15 R.(H.L.) 86.
22 *Cathcart* v. *Baxter's Trs.*, 1921, 1 S.L.T. 150.
23 *Sim* v. *Muir's Trs.*, *supra.*
24 *Grant* v. *Baillie* (1869) 8 M. 77.
25 *Cathcart* v. *Baxter's Trs.*, *supra.*
26 *Re Hill* [1914] 1 W.N. 132.
27 *Cuningham* v. *Montgomerie* (1879) 6 R. 1333.
28 *Sanders* v. *Sanders' Trs.* (1879) 7 R. 157.
29 *Elve* v. *Boyton* [1891] 1 Ch. 501.
30 *Re Smith* [1896] 2 Ch. 590.

operations are carried on abroad.[31] " Any corporation or company, municipal, commercial or otherwise " is not restricted to companies registered in the United Kingdom and can include unincorporated bodies.[32] " Public company," in the context, was taken to mean a United Kingdom company.[33] An express prohibition of investment in an unlimited company does not impliedly permit investment in the stocks or shares of limited companies.[34] " South African trustee securities " means investments regarded by the courts of South Africa or any province thereof as suitable for investment of trust funds.[35] Dominion government stocks are covered by stock of " a British colony or dependency " where the will was made before 1931.[36]

Types of security

" Stock " may not include shares in a limited liability company.[37] " Preference stock " has been held not to include preference shares.[38] " Ordinary preferred stock " means a sub-class of ordinary stock having some preference or priority over another sub-class of ordinary stock.[39] " Deferred stock " prima facie means a class postponed to ordinary stock.[39] " Securities " may be construed to mean " investments " and not as being confined to secured investments.[40] " Blue chips " is not a sufficiently certain description of a class of investments.[41]

Power to retain

The trustees must sell investments held by the truster within a reasonable time if they are not authorised by the trust deed to retain them.[42] " They are just as little entitled to continue the truster's imprudence as to commit it themselves." [43]

Where the testator gave a special direction to his trustees to retain investments held by him at his death, it was held that such an imperative direction in relation to Stock Exchange securities could never absolutely relieve trustees from their basic duty to preserve the trust estate and the trustees were not bound to continue to hold the investments if they thought that to do so would imperil the safety of the trust estate.[44] Lord Cooper

[31] Re Hilton [1909] 2 Ch. 548.
[32] Re Stanley [1906] 1 Ch. 131.
[33] Re Castlehow [1903] 1 Ch. 352.
[34] Hardie v. Fulton's Trs. (1895) 2 S.L.T. 534.
[35] Re Sebba, decd. [1959] Ch. 166.
[36] Re Rider's Will Trusts [1958] 1 W.L.R. 974. Cf. Re Brassey's Settlement [1955] 1 W.L.R. 192, where the settlement was made in 1936.
[37] Henderson v. Henderson's Trs. (1900) 2 F. 1295. But see Re McEacharn's Settlement Trusts [1939] Ch. 858; Re Boys, decd. [1950] W.N. 134.
[38] Re Willis [1911] 2 Ch. 563.
[39] Re Powell-Cotton's Resettlement [1957] Ch. 159.
[40] Re Rayner [1904] 1 Ch. 176; Re Gent and Eason's Contract [1905] 1 Ch. 386; Re Douglas' Will Trusts [1959] 1 W.L.R. 744.
[41] Re Kolb's Will Trusts [1962] Ch. 531.
[42] Brownlie v. Brownlie's Trs. (1879) 6 R. 1233.
[43] Per L.P. Inglis, p. 1236.
[44] Thomson's Trs. v. Davidson, 1947 S.C. 654 (approving Mackenzie Stuart, 275); Thomson's Trs. v. Henderson (1890) 18 R. 24; Scott's Trs. v. Scott (1895) 23 R. 52, 59, per Lord Trayner; Stevenson's Trs., 1924 S.L.T. 792.

reserved his opinion as to the holding of heritage subject to a similar direction.

Power to retain does not imply a power to purchase.[45]

The fact that the truster, after the constitution of an irrevocable trust, has approved of the making of a particular investment does not render it a proper investment if it was not already so.[46] At common law, a power to retain did not authorise trustees on the reconstruction and winding up of a company and the formation of a new one, to take up shares in the new one in lieu of the holding authorised by the trust deed, but this is now permissible under the 1921 Act unless it is at variance with the terms or purposes of the trust.[47] Power to continue the truster's business authorises the trustees to carry it on in the form of a limited company with substantially the same capital and control.[48]

Power to lend funds to a firm of which the testator had been a partner, does not permit the continuance of the loan after a change in the constitution of the partnership.[49]

The general law

At common law the power to invest was restricted to British Government Consolidated Stock and loans on heritable security.[50] In the short term, bank deposits were permissible. The Acts of 1884[51] and 1921[52] conferred additional powers and the position is now regulated by the Trustee Investments Act 1961.

In applications to the *nobile officium*, the court will not extend the trustees' powers of investment beyond what is authorised by the trust deed and what is authorised by the Trustee Investments Act.[53]

The 1961 Act

The 1921 Act authorised only a limited range of investments, nearly all of which have a fixed rate of interest and were repayable at par. In an age of inflation, this proved to be unduly restrictive and the powers of investment were extended by the Trustee Investments Act 1961 which authorised trustees on certain conditions to acquire and hold the investments specified in the First Schedule to the Act. The Schedule is divided into three parts. The significant change is effected by Part III (Wider-Range Investments) which includes certain shares and debentures of United Kingdom incorporated companies. Part IV imposes restrictions on the investments which can be held.

[45] Menzies, 353.
[46] *Mauchline* v. *Cranston*, 1910, 2 S.L.T. 428.
[47] *Thomson's Trs.* v. *Thomson* (1889) 16 R. 517; Trustee Investments Act 1961, s. 10.
[48] *MacKechnie's Trs.* v. *Macadam*, 1912 S.C. 1059.
[49] *Smith* v. *Patrick* (1901) 3 F.(H.L.) 14.
[50] Menzies, 340.
[51] Trusts (Scotland) Amendment Act 1884, s. 3.
[52] ss. 10, 11.
[53] *Mitchell Bequest Trs.*, 1959 S.C. 393; *Inglis*, 1965 S.L.T. 326; Mackenzie Stuart, 256. See also *Re Kolb's Will Trusts* [1962] Ch. 531; *Re Cooper's Settlement* [1962] Ch. 826; *Re University of London Charitable Trusts* [1964] Ch. 282.

Additions may be made to the Parts by Order in Council.[54] The Schedule is as follows:

" FIRST SCHEDULE

Manner of Investment

Part I

Narrower-Range Investments Not Requiring Advice

1. In Defence Bonds, National Savings Certificates and Ulster Savings Certificates, Ulster Development Bonds,[55] National Development Bonds,[56] British Savings Bonds.[57]

2. In deposits in the National Savings Bank,[58] ordinary deposits in a trustee savings bank and deposits in a bank or department thereof certified under subsection (3) of section nine of the Finance Act 1956.

Part II

Narrower-Range Investments Requiring Advice

1. In securities issued by Her Majesty's Government in the United Kingdom, the Government of Northern Ireland or the Government of the Isle of Man, not being securities falling within Part I of this Schedule and being fixed-interest securities registered in the United Kingdom or the Isle of Man, Treasury Bills or Tax Reserve Certificates.

2. In any securities the payment of interest on which is guaranteed by Her Majesty's Government in the United Kingdom or the Government of Northern Ireland.

3. In fixed-interest securities issued in the United Kingdom by any public authority or nationalised industry or undertaking in the United Kingdom.

4. In fixed-interest securities issued in the United Kingdom by the government of any overseas territory within the Commonwealth or by any public or local authority within such a territory, being securities registered in the United Kingdom.

References in this paragraph to an overseas territory or to the government of such a territory shall be construed as if they occurred in the Overseas Service Act 1958.

5. In fixed-interest securities issued in the United Kingdom by the International Bank for Reconstruction and Development, being securities registered in the United Kingdom. In fixed-interest securities issued in the United Kingdom by the Inter-American

---

[54] s. 12.
[55] Trustee Investments (Additional Powers) (No. 2) Order 1962, S.I. 1962 No. 2611.
[56] Trustee Investments (Additional Powers) Order 1964, S.I. 1964 No. 703.
[57] Trustee Investments (Additional Powers) Order 1968, S.I. 1968 No. 470.
[58] Post Office Act 1969, Sched. 6, Pt. III.

Development Bank. In fixed-interest securities issued in the United Kingdom by the European Investment Bank or by the European Coal and Steel Community being securities registered in the United Kingdom.[59]

6. In debentures issued in the United Kingdom by a company incorporated in the United Kingdom, being debentures registered in the United Kingdom.

7. In stock of the Bank of Ireland. In Bank of Ireland 7 per cent. Loan Stock 1986/91.[60]

8. In debentures issued by the Agricultural Mortgage Corporation Limited or the Scottish Agricultural Securities Corporation Limited.

9. In loans to any authority to which this paragraph applies charged on all or any of the revenues of the authority or on a fund into which all or any of those revenues are payable, in any fixed-interest securities issued in the United Kingdom by any such authority for the purpose of borrowing money so charged, and in deposits with any such authority by way of temporary loan made on the giving of a receipt for the loan by the treasurer or other similar officer of the authority and on the giving of an undertaking by the authority that, if requested to charge the loan as aforesaid, it will either comply with the request or repay the loan.

This paragraph applies to the following authorities, that is to say—

(a) any local authority in the United Kingdom;

(b) any authority all the members of which are appointed or elected by one or more local authorities in the United Kingdom;

(c) any authority the majority of the members of which are appointed or elected by one or more local authorities in the United Kingdom, being an authority which by virtue of any enactment has power to issue a precept to a local authority in England and Wales, or a requisition to a local authority in Scotland, or to the expenses of which, by virtue of any enactment, a local authority in the United Kingdom is or can be required to contribute;

(d) the Receiver for the Metropolitan Police District or a combined police authority (within the meaning of the Police Act 1946);

(e) The Belfast City and District Water Commissioners;

(f) the Great Ouse Water Authority and river authorities under the Water Resources Act 1963.[61]

(g) any district council in Northern Ireland. [61a]

[59] Trustee Investments (Additional Powers) (No. 2) Order 1964, S.I. 1964 No. 1404; Trustee Investments (Additional Powers) Order 1972, S.I. 1972 No. 1818.
[60] Trustee Investments (Additional Powers) Order 1966, S.I. 1966 No. 401.
[61] Trustee Investments (Additional Powers) Order 1962, S.I. 1962 No. 658.
[61a] Trustee Investments (Additional Powers) Order 1973, S.I. 1973 No. 1332.

10. In debentures or in the guaranteed or preference stock [60] of any incorporated company, being statutory water undertakers within the meaning of the Water Act 1945, or any corresponding enactment in force in Northern Ireland, and having during each of the ten years immediately preceding the calendar year in which the investment was made paid a dividend of not less than $3\frac{1}{2}$ per cent.[61b] on its ordinary shares.

11. In deposits by way of special investment in a trustee savings bank or in a department (not being a department certified under subsection (3) of section nine of the Finance Act 1956) of a bank any other department of which is so certified.

12. In deposits in a building society designated under section one of the House Purchase and Housing Act 1959.

13. In mortgages of freehold property in England and Wales or Northern Ireland and of leasehold property in those countries of which the unexpired term at the time of investment is not less than sixty years, and in loans on heritable security in Scotland.

14. In perpetual rent-charges charged on land in England and Wales or Northern Ireland and fee-farm rents (not being rent-charges) issuing out of such land, and in feu-duties or ground annuals in Scotland.

Part III

Wider-Range Investments

1. In any securities issued in the United Kingdom by a company incorporated in the United Kingdom, being securities registered in the United Kingdom and not being securities falling within Part II of this Schedule.

2. In shares in any building society designated under section one of the House Purchase and Housing Act 1959.

3. In any units, or other shares of the investments subject to the trusts, of a unit trust scheme in the case of which there is in force at the time of investment an order of the Board of Trade under section seventeen of the Prevention of Fraud (Investments) Act 1958, or of the Ministry of Commerce for Northern Ireland under section sixteen of the Prevention of Fraud (Investments) Act (Northern Ireland) 1940.

Part IV

Supplemental

1. The securities mentioned in Parts I to III of this Schedule do not include any securities where the holder can be required to accept

---

[61b] Trustee Investments (Water Companies) Order 1973, S.I. 1973 No. 1393.

repayment of the principal, or the payment of any interest, otherwise than in sterling.

2. The securities mentioned in paragraphs 1 to 8 of Part II, other than Treasury Bills or Tax Reserve Certificates, securities issued before the passing of this Act by the Government of the Isle of Man, securities falling within paragraph 4 of the said Part II issued before the passing of this Act or securities falling within paragraph 9 of that Part, and the securities mentioned in paragraph 1 of Part III of this Schedule, do not include—

(a) securities the price of which is not quoted on a recognised stock exchange within the meaning of the Prevention of Fraud (Investments) Act 1958, or the Belfast stock exchange;

(b) shares or debenture stock not fully paid up (except shares or debenture stock which by the terms of issue are required to be fully paid up within nine months of the date of issue).

3. The securities mentioned in paragraph 6 of Part II and paragraph 1 of Part III of this Schedule do not include—

(a) shares or debentures of an incorporated company of which the total issued and paid up share capital is less than one million pounds;

(b) shares or debentures of an incorporated company which has not in each of the five years immediately preceding the calendar year in which the investment is made paid a dividend on all the shares issued by the company, excluding any shares issued after the dividend was declared and any shares which by their terms of issue did not rank for the dividend for that year.

For the purposes of sub-paragraph (b) of this paragraph a company formed—

(i) to take over the business of another company or other companies, or

(ii) to acquire the securities of, or control of, another company or other companies,

or for either of those purposes and for other purposes shall be deemed to have paid a dividend as mentioned in that sub-paragraph in any year in which such a dividend has been paid by the other company or all the other companies, as the case may be.

4. In this Schedule, unless the context otherwise requires, the following expressions have the meanings hereby respectively assigned to them, that is to say—

" debenture " includes debenture stock and bonds, whether constituting a charge on assets or not, and loan stock or notes;

" enactment " includes an enactment of the Parliament of Northern Ireland;

" fixed-interest securities " means securities which under their terms of issue bear a fixed rate of interest;

" local authority " in relation to the United Kingdom, means any of the following authorities—

(a) in England and Wales, the council of a county, a borough, an urban or rural district or a parish, the Common Council of the City of London, the Greater London Council and the Council of the Isles of Scilly;

(b) in Scotland, a local authority within the meaning of the Local Government (Scotland) Act, 1947;

(c) in Northern Ireland, the council of a county, a county or other borough, or an urban or rural district;

" ordinary deposits " and " special investment " have the same meanings respectively as in the Trustee Savings Banks Act 1954;

" securities " includes shares, debentures, Treasury Bills and Tax Reserve Certificates;

" share " includes stock;

" Treasury Bills " includes bills issued by Her Majesty's Government in the United Kingdom and Northern Ireland Treasury Bills.

5. It is hereby declared that in this Schedule " mortgage," in relation to freehold or leasehold property in Northern Ireland, includes a registered charge which, by virtue of subsection (4) of section forty of the Local Registration of Title (Ireland) Act 1891, or any other enactment, operates as a mortgage by deed.

6. References in this Schedule to an incorporated company are references to a company incorporated by or under any enactment and include references to a body of persons established for the purpose of trading for profit and incorporated by Royal Charter.

7. The references in paragraph 12 of Part II and paragraph 2 of Part III of this Schedule to a building society designated under section one of the House Purchase and Housing Act 1959, include references to a permanent society incorporated under the Building Societies Acts (Northern Ireland) 1874 to 1940 for the time being designated by the Registrar for Northern Ireland under subsection (2) of that section (which enables such a society to be so designated for the purpose of trustees' powers of investment specified in paragraph (a) of subsection (1) of that section).

Scope of powers

The power to invest includes a power to vary the investment once made.[62]

The power relates to " property " in the trustee's hands, whether at the

[62] s. 1 (1).

time in a state of investment or not.[63] "Property" includes property of any description, whether heritable or moveable, corporeal or incorporeal, which is presently enjoyable, but does not include a future interest, whether vested or contingent.[64]

The powers conferred by the Act are not limited by any provision relating to the trustee's powers contained in any instrument made before the passing of the Act (August 3, 1961).[65] This does not hold when the instrument is an enactment or an instrument made under an enactment and the powers are exercisable only in so far as a contrary intention is not expressed in any Act or instrument made under an enactment. The phrase " if and so far only as a contrary intention is not expressed " in section 69 (2) of the Trustee Act 1925 was held to mean the same as " unless expressly forbidden " in section 1 of the Trustee Act 1893.[66] The powers are also affected by a contrary intention in any instrument made after August 3, 1961. In this connection, any rule of Scots law whereby a testamentary writing may be deemed to be made on a date other than that on which it was actually executed is to be disregarded.

The powers conferred by the Act are in addition to and not in derogation from any other power of investment or postponing conversion exercisable by the trustees.[67] Such a power is referred to in the Act as a " special power."

Where a power to invest property in any investment for the time being authorised by law for the investment of trust property was conferred on the trustees before the passing of the Act or was conferred by any enactment passed before the passing of the Act, that power shall have effect as a power to invest in the manner and under the conditions provided by the Act.[68] Before exercising the power the trustee must obtain " proper advice." [69] The Act does not lessen any power of a court to confer wider powers of investment on trustees or affect the extent to which any such power is to be exercised.[70]

No special conditions apply to investment in Part I investments.

Obtaining advice

Before acquiring Part II or III investments, however, a trustee must obtain and consider " proper advice " on the question whether the investment is satisfactory having regard to two criteria—

    (a) the need for diversification of investments of the trust, in so far as is appropriate to the circumstances of the trust, and

[63] See *Hume* v. *Lopes* [1892] A.C. 112; *Re Pratt's Will Trusts* [1943] Ch. 326.
[64] s. 4 (4).
[65] s. 1 (3).
[66] *Re Warren* [1939] Ch. 684.
[67] s. 3 (1).
[68] s. 3 (2).
[69] See below. It seems that the trustee has no duty to obtain advice if a power of this kind was conferred after the passing of the Act (Underhill, 398).
[70] s. 15. See Note 53, *supra*.

(b) the suitability to the trust of investments of the description of investment proposed and of the investment proposed as an investment of that description.[71]

This duty to obtain advice does not extend to advice as to the suitability of a particular loan on heritable security.[72] " Proper advice " is the advice of a person who is reasonably believed by the trustee to be qualified by his ability in and practical experience of financial matters. It may be given by a person in the course of his employment as an officer or servant.[73] This means that a bank or other corporate trustee can obtain advice from its own employees if they are qualified. The advice must be given or subsequently confirmed in writing.[74]

The trustee who has exercised his powers of investment in this way has a duty to determine at what intervals the circumstances, and in particular the nature of the investment, make it desirable to obtain proper advice and a duty to obtain and consider advice at such intervals.[75]

The duty to obtain advice does not apply to a trustee who is the person giving the advice to his co-trustees. Nor does it apply where the powers of a trustee are lawfully exercised by an officer or servant who is qualified to give proper advice.[76] It seems that a sole trustee who is qualified to give advice must nevertheless obtain advice.

Division of the fund

The condition for investment in Part III investments is that the trust fund is divided into two parts—the narrower-range part and the wider-range part.[77]

For this purpose, the " trust fund " is so much of the property in the hands of the trustee as is held on trusts which as respects the beneficiaries or their respective interests or the purposes of the trust or as respects the powers of the trustee are not identical with those on which any other property in his hands is held.[78]

The division must be into two parts equal in value at the time of the division.[79] The Treasury can direct by an order made by statutory instrument that any division of a trust fund made during the continuance in force of the order shall be made so that the value of the wider-range part bears to the value of the narrower-range part such proportion, greater than one but not greater than three to one, as may be prescribed by the order.[80] Such an order may be revoked by a subsequent order prescribing a greater proportion.[81]

[71] s. 6 (2).
[72] s. 6 (7).
[73] s. 6 (4).
[74] s. 6 (5).
[75] s. 6 (3).
[76] s. 6 (6).
[77] s. 2 (1).
[78] s. 4 (2).
[79] s. 2 (1).
[80] s. 13 (1).

[81] s. 13 (4).

If the trustee obtains, from a person reasonably believed by the trustee to be qualified to make it, a valuation in writing of any property, the valuation shall be conclusive in determining whether the division has been duly made.[82] This is so notwithstanding that the valuation is made by an officer or servant in the course of his employment.[83]

The property in the narrower-range part can be invested only in narrower-range investments.[84] If any property invested outwith the narrower-range investments becomes comprised in the narrower-range part, it must either be reinvested in narrower-range investments as soon as may be or transferred to the wider-range part in exchange for narrower-range investments of equal value.[84] The wider-range part may be invested in Part III investments. Where property (other than a dividend or interest) accrues to the trustee as owner or former owner of property comprised in either part of the fund, it is to be treated as belonging to that part of the fund.[85] In other cases where property accrues to a divided trust fund, the trustee must secure by apportionment or transfer that the value of each part of the fund is increased by the same amount.[86] This presumably applies to income which is being accumulated.

The acquisition of property for a money payment is treated as investment and not as an accrual to the trust fund even if the amount of the consideration is less than the value of the property.[87]

The division of the fund does not restrict the trustee's discretion as to the choice of property to be taken out of the trust fund in the course of the administration of the trust.[88] This provides an important loophole in the scheme of the Act as trustees who have to pay out capital can realise narrower-range investments for the purpose and thus reduce that part of the fund without making a compensating transfer.

If property is appropriated from a divided trust fund to form a separate fund, then if the separate fund is to be divided, it can be divided in such a way that the two parts are either equal in value [89] or bear to each other the same proportion as the values at the time of appropriation of the two corresponding parts of the fund out of which the appropriation was made or some intermediate proportion.[90] For example, if the trust fund was originally divided into two equal parts but at the time of the appropriation the values of the parts are in the proportion of three to one, then the appropriated fund can be divided into any proportions not greater than three to one and not less than one to one.

[82] s. 5 (1).
[83] s. 5 (2).
[84] s. 2 (2).
[85] s. 2 (3) (a).
[86] s. 2 (3) (b). If an order is made altering the proportion into which the fund should be divided, the increases should bear the altered proportion to each other (s. 13 (3) (a)).
[87] s. 2 (3).
[88] s. 2 (4).
[89] If an order has been made altering the proportion into which the fund should be divided, the altered proportion is substituted for equality.
[90] s. 4 (3).

Once a division has been made property cannot be transferred from one part of the fund to the other unless the transfer is authorised or required by the Act or there is made at the same time a compensating transfer, *i.e.* a transfer in the opposite direction of property of equal value.[91]

Once a division has been made the fund cannot be divided again,[92] except that if the Treasury makes an order altering the proportions laid down in the Act a fund which had been divided before the order came into operation can be redivided in the new proportion on one occasion during the continuance in force of the order.[93]

Special-range property

" Special-range property " [94] is property including wider-range but not including narrower-range investments which either (a) a trustee is authorised to hold apart from (i) the provisions of the Act, or (ii) the provisions of the 1921 Act, or (iii) a power to invest property in any investment for the time being authorised by law,[95] *or* (b) became part of the trust fund in consequence of the trustee's exercise, as owner of the property, of the powers conferred by paragraphs (o) or (p) of section 4 (1) of the 1921 Act (which enable trustees to concur in certain schemes or arrangements and to exercise conditional or preferential rights to subscribe for securities). This category is intended to cover investments which the trustee is specifically empowered to make under the terms of the trust deed.

Special-range property is not divided and is carried to a separate part of the fund. If the remainder of the fund is divided, property belonging to the narrower-range or wider-range part which is converted into special-range property and special-range property which accrues to a part of a divided fund is to be carried to the separate fund.[96] Where property in the separate fund is converted into property other than special-range property, it is transferred to the narrower-range part or wider-range part or apportioned between them and any transfer from one part to the other is to be made which is necessary to secure that the value of each part is increased by the same amount [97] (or where an order altering the pro-

---

[91] s. 2 (1).
[92] s. 2 (1).
[93] s. 13 (2).
[94] s. 3 (3); Sched. 2, para. 1.
[95] It has been pointed out (Underhill, 394) that there is an ambiguity in s. 3 (3). S. 3 (2) refers to " any special power . . . to invest property in any investment for the time being authorised by law for the investment of trust property, being a power conferred on a trustee before the passing of this Act or conferred on him under any enactments passed before the passing of this Act . . . ."
S. 3 (3) when taken with the Second Schedule defines " special-range property " as property, including wider-range but not including narrower-range investments, which a trustee is authorised to hold apart from, *inter alia*, " any such power to invest in authorised investments as is mentioned in the foregoing subsection." The question is whether the reference is only to such powers conferred before the passing of the Act or whether it is intended to cover powers of whatever date. The former is the literal reading but the latter seems to achieve a more reasonable result.
[96] Sched. 2, para. 2.
[97] Sched. 2, para. 3.

portion of the parts has been made, that the wider-range part is increased by an amount which bears the prescribed proportion to the amount by which the value of the narrower-range part is increased).[98]

Obviously, the trustees who have the necessary powers under the trust deed can convert the funds of the wider-range part into special-range investments. It is not clear whether they are free to treat the narrower-range fund in this way. Such a result would seem to be contrary to the intention of the Act as it would be possible to convert the whole of the narrower-range fund into special range investments.[99]

The provisions as to special-range property do not apply where the powers of the trustee to invest or postpone conversion have been conferred or varied by an order of any court made within the ten years ending on August 3, 1961 or by any enactment passed, or instrument having effect under an enactment made within that period, which relates specifically to the trusts in question or by an enactment contained in certain local Acts.[1] In such cases, if property belonging to the narrower-range part of the fund is invested otherwise than in a narrower-range investment or is so invested and is retained and not transferred to the wider-range part or as soon as may be reinvested, section one of the Act does not authorise the making or retention of any wider-range investment.[2] Where an investment ceases to be authorised in this way, the trustee cannot take advantage of the relief provided by section 33 of the 1921 Act.[3]

The effect of this is that if the trustees have exercised a power of investment conferred in the ways specified, and wish to utilise the machinery of the Act, they must divide the whole fund into two parts and until the narrower-range part consists entirely of narrower-range investments, they cannot acquire or hold wider-range investments by virtue of section 1 of the Act.

Rights offers

If it is not at variance with the terms or purposes of the trust, trustees may, to the extent they think fit, exercise conditional or preferential rights to subscribe for securities which are offered in respect of a trust holding in the company, to apply capital of the trust estate in payment therefor and to retain the securities for any period for which, and on the same conditions as, they have power to retain the original holding.[4] They may also renounce such rights or assign them for the best consideration that can reasonably be obtained to any person, including a beneficiary.

Reconstructions

If it is not at variance with the terms or purposes of the trust, the trustees have power, in like manner as if they were entitled to the securities

[98] s. 13 (3).   [99] Lewin, 344
[1] s. 3 (4).
[2] Sched. 3, para. 1.
[3] Sched. 3, para. 2. See p. 356, *infra*.
[4] 1921 Act, s. 4 (1) (*p*) added by T.I.A. 1961, s. 10. The corresponding provision in England is the Trustee Act 1925, s. 10 (4) as amended by T.I.A. 1961, s. 9 (2).

beneficially, to concur in respect of securities of a company held by the trust in a scheme or arrangement for reconstruction, or amalgamation of the company or for the acquisition of the securities by another company or the sale of the company's property or undertaking or the release, modification or variation of rights attaching to the securities.[5] They can accept in exchange for the securities held, securities of the reconstructed, purchasing or new company and retain them for any period for which they could have properly retained the original securities.

Miscellaneous provisions

Some provisions of the 1921 Act relating to investments are still in force but are of minor importance. A trustee having power to invest in real securities, unless expressly forbidden by the trust deed, can invest in any charge or mortgage on such charge under the Improvement of Land Acts 1864 and 1899, or on any charge created for payment of estate or other government duty under the Finance Act 1894, or the Finance (1909–10) Act 1910.[6]

A trustee having power to invest in the mortgages or bonds of any railway company or of any other description of company may, unless the contrary is expressed in the trust deed, invest in the debenture stock of a railway company or such other company.[7] A trustee having power to invest in the purchase of land or on heritable security may invest in the purchase of, or on heritable security over, any land notwithstanding that the same is charged with a rent under the Public Money Drainage Acts 1846 to 1856, or by an absolute order made under the Improvement of Land Act 1864, unless the terms of the trust expressly provide that the land to be purchased or taken in security shall not be subject to any such prior charge.[8]

Unless authorised by the terms of the trust, trustees must not apply for, purchase, acquire or hold beyond a reasonable time for realisation or conversion into registered or inscribed stock any certificate to bearer or debenture or other bond or document payable to bearer.[9]

Exercise of powers

In the exercise of his powers of investment a trustee must have regard to the need for diversification of investments of the trust, in so far as is appropriate to the circumstances of the trust and to the suitability to the trust of investments of the description of investment proposed and of the investment proposed as an investment of that description.[10]

---

[5] 1921 Act, s. 4 (1) (o) added by T.I.A. 1961, s. 10. The corresponding English provision is Trustee Act 1925, s. 10 (3) as amended by T.I.A. 1961, s. 9 (1).

[6] 1921 Act, s. 12 (1). See Trustee Act 1925, s. 5 (1) (b).

[7] 1921 Act, s. 12 (2). See Trustee Act 1925, s. 5 (3).

[8] 1921 Act, s. 13. See Trustee Act 1925, s. 6.

[9] 1921 Act, s. 15 (1). English trustees can hold such securities unless expressly prohibited from doing so—Trustee Act 1925, s. 7.

[10] T.I.A. 1961, s. 6 (1).

" A trustee does not adequately discharge his duty by placing trust funds upon an investment falling within the class or classes of investments specified in an investment clause—it is also his duty ' to avoid all investments of that class which are attended with hazard.' " [11]

The discretion must be exercised in good faith. Trustees are not entitled to make an investment within an authorised class merely to accommodate the borrower.[12] " Trustees are not entitled to accommodate their friends, or the members of the truster's family, with the funds entrusted to their care." [13] Similarly, they must not invest in such a way as to favour the liferenter at the expense of the fiar.

The suitability of the investment to the purposes of the trust must be borne in mind.[14] The times of payment of dividends and the security and liquidity of the investment must be considered in relation to the income rights of beneficiaries and the probable dates of distribution of capital. Where an annuity is to be paid the requirements are " in the first place, that the security should be ample; secondly, that the rate of interest should be sufficient to satisfy the annuity; thirdly, that such rate of interest should endure to the termination of the annuities." [15]

Shares which are not fully paid up are not, as a rule, a suitable investment for trustees.[16]

Improper investment

In a continuing trust, the trustees are under a duty to invest the estate and they will be liable for breach of trust if they make an *ultra vires* investment or an improper investment.[17] The fact that the investments were generally held and reputed by business men and others to be sound and safe and that large sums of trust and other moneys were invested in them does not exonerate the trustees.[18]

The trustee's duty is not discharged by merely investing within a specified class.

" As a general rule the law requires of a trustee no higher degree of diligence in the execution of his office than a man of ordinary prudence would exercise in the management of his own private affairs. Yet he is not allowed the same discretion in investing the moneys of the trust as if he were a person *sui juris* dealing with his own estate. Business men of ordinary prudence may, and frequently do, select investments which are more or less of a speculative character; but it is the duty of a trustee to confine himself to the class of investments

[11] *Henderson* v. *Henderson's Trs.* (1900) 2 F. 1295, 1307, *per* L.P. Balfour.
[12] *Millar's Factor* v. *Millar's Trs.* (1886) 14 R. 22.
[13] *Per* Lord McLaren, p. 29.
[14] Menzies, 387.
[15] *Forsyth* v. *Kilgour* (1854) 17 D. 207, 213, *per* L.P. McNeill. See also *Maclean* v. *Soady's Tr.* (1888) 15 R. 966.
[16] Menzies, 384.
[17] See Chap. 25.
[18] *Alexander* v. *Johnstone* (1899) 1 F. 639.

which are permitted by the trust, and likewise to avoid all investments of that class which are attended with hazard." [19]

Breach of trust in respect of an *intra vires* investment is more difficult to establish if it is shown that the trustees did apply their minds to the question of suitability.[20]

When the primary purpose of the trust is to secure an alimentary provision, the trustee is bound to be specially careful that the security is sufficient to ensure payment of the interest on a loan.[21]

In one case,[22] where the investment clause was complicated and difficult to interpret, it was decided that the trustees were not liable for the loss incurred on an unauthorised investment because they had acted *in bona fide*. The loss was small and the court did not expressly decide that the investment was not authorised. The decision should therefore be regarded as special.

A trustee is not liable for breach of trust by reason only of his continuing to hold an investment which has ceased to be authorised by the trust deed or by statute.[23]

APPROPRIATION

A question may arise as to whether trustees have power to appropriate particular investments to particular legacies. As a rule all the legatees are entitled to the security of the whole estate and of the massed trust investments and any appreciation or depreciation in the value of the investment enures to the benefit or prejudice of the estate as a whole and is shared according to their several rights and interests by all the beneficiaries.[24] If a power to appropriate is exercised, particular investments are set aside to meet particular legacies and any appreciation of a particular investment enures to, and any depreciation is borne by, the beneficiary in right of the legacy to which the investment has been appropriated.[25] In effect, the trust is subdivided into a number of subordinate trusts. If the trustees have power to appropriate, a question may arise as to whether they have exercised it.[26]

In the absence of an express or implied direction by the truster, trustees are not entitled to appropriate particular investments to particular legacies.[27]

---

[19] *Learoyd* v. *Whiteley* (1887) 12 App.Cas. 727, 733, *per* Lord Watson; *Henderson* v. *Henderson's Trs.* (1900) 2 F. 1295.

[20] *Melville* v. *Noble's Trs.* (1896) 24 R. 243; *Manners* v. *Strong's J.F.* (1902) 4 F. 829.

[21] *Maclean* v. *Soady's Tr.* (1888) 15 R. 966.

[22] *Warren's J.F.* v. *Warren's Exrx.* (1903) 5 F. 890.

[23] 1921 Act, s. 33.

[24] *Lynch's J.F.* v. *Griffin* (1900) 2 F. 653.

[25] *Gordon* v. *Douglas* (1868) 41 Sc.Jur. 43.

[26] *Smith's Trs.* v. *Smith* (1900) 2 F. 713. See also *Warrack's Trs.* v. *Warrack*, 1919 S.C. 522.

[27] *Scott's Trs.* v. *Scott* (1895) 23 R. 52, 58, *per* Lord Trayner; *Colville's Trs.* v. *Colville*, 1914 S.C. 255, 258, *per* Lord Mackenzie. Appropriation has, of course, to be distinguished from making an investment in the name of the beneficiary which amounts to payment of the legacy (Menzies, 433).

" In the general case trustees have no power to subdivide their trust into a number of subordinate trusts by appropriating particular investments to particular legacies (the vesting or payment of which is postponed) and so tying the fortunes of each beneficiary or group of beneficiaries to particular investments. Normally all the legatees are entitled to the security of the whole estate and of the massed trust investments, and any appreciation or depreciation in the value of these investments should enure to the benefit or prejudice of the estate as a whole and should be shared according to their several rights and interests by all the beneficiaries ultimately entitled thereto. This general rule suffers exception if, but only if, such an appropriation is either expressly or impliedly directed by the truster." [28]

Although there are in the books frequent references to a " power " of appropriation it is more correct to regard it as a duty imposed upon the trustees.

" I do not think that the ' power ' was regarded as a mere faculty or option which the trustees could at any time exercise or not at their own discretion; for it would be very difficult to infer by implication that trustees were authorised at their own hand to adopt or reject an irrevocable expedient which might have the most serious results on the benefits eventually taken by the beneficiaries, these results usually depending upon the course of future events which in the general case would be unpredictable when the decision of the trustees was taken." [29]

Express direction

Grosset v. *Birrell's Trs.*[30] is an example of an express direction. The trustees were directed " to invest, hold or set aside and retain and administer " a specific sum for each of the truster's daughters and to pay to each daughter the income " arising upon the sum so set aside for each of them " and, on the death of each daughter, to pay the capital of " the sums so held and set apart for each of my said daughters " to the daughter's children. It was held that the trustees were under a duty to appropriate investments to each legacy and that they were not entitled to hold one massed fund for the several legacies.

Implied direction

Robinson v. *Fraser's Trs.*[31] is the leading case of an implied direction to appropriate. The trustees were to pay " the interest or annual-rent of £2,000 " to the testatrix's daughter and on her death to pay the fee to her children. There was a similar provision for another daughter and, after provision was made for the two legacies, the residue was to be divided among the testatrix's children. Power was given " to lend or place out on

[28] *Duncan's Trs.*, 1951 S.C. 557, 561, *per* L.P. Cooper.
[29] *Duncan's Trs.*, *supra*, p. 563, *per* L.P. Cooper.
[30] 1920 S.C. 231.
[31] (1881) 8 R.(H.L.) 127.

such securities, heritable or moveable, as they shall consider advantageous, the foresaid legacies of £2,000 and £2,000 respectively." The trustees allocated investments to form two separate funds to meet the two legacies and then distributed the residue. One particular stock was retained by the trustees at the request of one daughter as part of her legacy fund. The trustees later had to pay heavy calls on this stock and they sought relief from the trust estate generally, that is to say, from both legacy funds. The House of Lords held that as the stock had been appropriated to the one legacy fund the trustees were not entitled to relief from the other legacy fund. As to the propriety of the severance of the fund, Lord Selborne L.C. said: " And not only was such a severance legally possible, but it also appears to me to have been the most proper (if not the only proper) mode of fulfilling the directions of the will." [32] Lord Watson stated that the authority to lend out upon securities " the foresaid legacies of £2,000 and £2,000 respectively " conferred upon the trustees " by plain implication, a right to make the severance if they chose." [33]

In a later case,[34] Lord Trayner explained the decision in *Robinson* thus

> " In that case appropriation of special funds to meet certain legacies was sustained, although such appropriation had not been directed to be made by the trust-deed. That such a course was intended by the truster in that case might very reasonably be inferred because such appropriation was necessary to enable the residue to be divided without undue delay, which was the truster's object and, indeed, direction."

A direction to appropriate was held to be implied where a specified fund was to be held for a person in liferent and his issue in fee and the residue was to be paid to other persons " as it accrues and becomes available." Investments were appropriated to the liferented fund and from time to time payments were made from residue. On the liferenter's death the value of the appropriated investment had increased and the appreciation was claimed by the residuary legatees. It was held, however, that it fell to the fiars because there had been a lawful appropriation.[35] Lord Dunedin said:

> " I can quite understand that where a trust is, in all its terms, a continuing trust but for the benefit of different individuals, it might be necessary to have a special power of appropriation conferred upon trustees in order to allow them to separate up the investments of the trust and tie the fortunes of each beneficiary or set of beneficiaries to particular investments. But it seems to me that when a trust is of a composite character and is partly for holding and partly for distribution, there is of necessity an implied power upon trustees to set

---

[32] p. 129.
[33] p. 138.
[34] *Scott's Trs.* v. *Scott* (1895) 23 R. 52, 58, appvd. by L.P. Dunedin in *Vans Dunlop's Trs.* v. *Pollok*, 1912 S.C. 10, 14.
[35] *Vans Dunlop's Trs.* v. *Pollok, supra.*

apart the whole, at the time when they have to part with some of the trust for distribution." [36]

This dictum, however, does not mean that a distribution of part enables the trustees to appropriate funds against each of the provisions for which they continue to hold. Appropriation of a part does not imply appropriation of the whole.[37]

In several cases it has been held that there was no express or implied power to appropriate.

In *Teacher's Trs.* v. *Teacher*,[38] the trustees were directed to divide the residue of the estate into equal shares corresponding to the number of the testator's children. Two of the sons, C and D, were to be entitled to immediate payment of their shares provided that they paid specified interest thereon to the testator's widow during her life; the share of another son, W, would be lent to him without security during the widow's life provided that he paid her interest thereon. During the widow's lifetime, the amount of the residue was estimated and one share was paid to W on his granting a bond for the interest which contained a declaration that if it should be ascertained that he had received more or less than his share of the residue he should repay or receive the difference; C's share was similarly paid to him " subject to rectification "; D received payments on account of his share. Subsequently, it was ascertained that there had been a considerable loss on the investments held by the trust. The sons contended that as they had received the bulk of their shares, the loss should be borne exclusively by the residue held by the trustees for the daughters. It was held, however, that the sons had received merely interim loans or payments which did not result in an appropriation of the remainder of the trust fund; the loss had therefore to fall equally on all the beneficiaries.

In *Scott's Trs.* v. *Scott*,[39] the residue was to be divided into a number of portions some of which were to be retained and invested and the income paid to various beneficiaries. The trustees appropriated a number of deposit-receipts for each set of the beneficiaries. A loss accrued on some of the deposit-receipts. It was held that the loss must be borne by the whole of the retained fund because there was no ground for inferring that the truster had ever contemplated an appropriation of the kind which had been made.

Similarly, in *Colville's Trs.* v. *Colville*,[40] an appropriation to a particular legacy was held *ultra vires*, it being conceded in the special case that when the appropriation was made " the trustees were not constrained thereto by any necessity for immediate distribution of the trust-estate, or any part thereof, and they came to it merely because they considered it expedient so to set aside and secure in such investments a sum to meet the legacy."

[36] p. 14.
[37] *Duncan's Trs.*, 1951 S.C. 557, 563, *per* L.P. Cooper.
[38] (1890) 17 R. 303.
[39] (1895) 23 R. 52.
[40] 1914 S.C. 255.

In *Duncan's Trs.*,[41] five of eight equal shares of residue were to be paid over immediately to the testator's son and the remaining three were to be apportioned to each of his daughters and held for them in liferent and their issue in fee. For twenty years after the testator's death the three shares were held for the daughters but there was no appropriation of particular investments to each share. One daughter who was resident abroad then called upon the trustees to appropriate a particular investment to her share so that the interest could be paid to her without deduction of tax. It was held that there was no implied power to appropriate because (a) the will directed that securities were to be set aside to meet a postponed annuity and these retained securities were to be brought into computation in the division of the residue into shares, a direction which pointed to a paper calculation and not to an actual severance, (b) the testator had directed that certain bonds forming part of his estate were not to be called up until seven years after his death, a restriction which would have made appropriation difficult without complicated book-keeping. Lord Cooper, in his opinion, went on to suggest that even if there had been power to appropriate at the commencement of the trust administration it would be impracticable to sever after twenty years because the operation would have to be carried out on the basis of the state of the fund at the date of the commencement of the trust.

If all the interested beneficiaries so request the trustees may appropriate funds to each legacy even although the trust deed confers no express or implied power to do so. They cannot, however, accede to such a request from *some* of the beneficiaries if compliance might result in prejudicing other of the beneficiaries.[42]

41 1951 S.C. 557.
42 *Scott's Trs.* v. *Scott* (1895) 23 R. 52.

CHAPTER 23

AUCTOR IN REM SUAM

General principle

A trustee is not allowed to enter into transactions in which he has, or can have, a personal interest which conflicts, or may possibly conflict, with the interests of those whom he is bound by fiduciary duty to protect.[1] " It appears to me that from first to last the rule of the law of Scotland has been that anyone holding a fiduciary character, whether that of guardian or trustee, cannot lawfully become *auctor in rem suam*." [2]

" Equity goes farther; it prohibits a trustee from making any profit by his management directly or indirectly. An act of this nature may in itself be innocent; but is poisonous with respect to consequences; for if a trustee be permitted, even in the most plausible circumstances, to make profit, he will soon lose sight of his duty, and direct his management chiefly for making profit to himself." [3]

" The fiduciary duty may arise not only from trust but also *ex lege* and *ex conventione*. The duty was recognized by the Civil Law and it is, I think, acknowledged in the jurisprudence of all civilized communities. The duty is, to use the Latin phrase, that the person subject to it must not become *auctor in rem suam*. It applied to tutors and curators in the civil law; and it applies to tutors and curators in the Scots law. It applies also to judicial factors appointed by the courts in Scotland, and to partners, to agents under a contract of agency, and, of course, to trustees under a settlement or under a will." [4]

" It would be profitless to quote the many cases which have arisen to illustrate the doctrine. They may all be referred to the same root idea, that equity will not allow a person, who is in a position of trust, to carry out a transaction where there is a conflict between his duty and his interest." [5]

Conflict of interest is not the only reason for the prohibition.

" Nor is it only on account of the conflict between his interest and his duty to the trust that such transactions are forbidden. The knowledge which he acquires as trustee is of itself a sufficient ground of disqualification, and of requiring that such knowledge be not only

---

[1] *Aberdeen Ry.* v. *Blaikie Bros.* (1853) 1 Macq. 461; *Mags. of Aberdeen* v. *University of Aberdeen* (1877) 4 R.(H.L.) 48. See also *York Buildings Co.* v. *Mackenzie* (1795) 3 Pat. App. 378.
[2] *Aitken* v. *Hunter* (1871) 9 M. 757, 762, *per* Lord Neaves.
[3] Kames, *Principles of Equity*, 3rd ed., Bk. II, Chap. I., cited by Lord Macmillan in *Regal (Hastings) Ltd.* v. *Gulliver* [1942] 1 All E.R. 378, 391.
[4] *Dale* v. *I.R.C.* [1954] A.C. 11, 26, *per* Lord Normand.
[5] *Wright* v. *Morgan* [1926] A.C. 788, 797, *per* Lord Dunedin.

361

not used to the detriment of the trust, but be not used for his own benefit, because it may, by possibility, injure the trust, rather than because it may give him an undue advantage over others." [6] " There are two reasons for the rule of law that trustees cannot be allowed to traffic in their own interest in the trust-estate under their administration. The first is, that their duty and their interest must not conflict. It is the duty of the trustees to obtain the highest price for any item of the trust property which it becomes necessary to sell. It is the interest of the individual trustee, if he becomes an offerer, to buy the property at the lowest price possible. Were any one of the trustees to be both seller and buyer, his duty and his interest would conflict. The second reason is that a trustee, in his position as administrator of the trust-estate, has opportunities of knowledge regarding the property of which the estate consists which are not open to outsiders, and that this gives him an advantage in dealing with the trust-estate, which he may turn to his own profit, even unconsciously. But in particular, if the sale be by auction and one of the exposers appears openly and with notice as a bidder, members of the public may reasonably consider that they are not entering on the competition on equal terms, and may be choked off, to the detriment of the trust-estate and to the advantage of the trustee bidding. If, on the other hand, an exposer appears and bids without notice or prior disclosure, his doing so is a breach of faith with the public and his action may be effectually challenged." [7]

No question can be raised as to the fairness or unfairness of the transaction; it is enough that the parties interested object. [8]

" There cannot be a greater mistake than to suppose . . . that a trustee is only prevented from doing things which bring an actual loss upon the estate under his administration. It is quite enough that the thing which he does has a tendency to injure the trust, a tendency to interfere with his duty." [9]

" No Court is equal to the examination and ascertainment of the truth in much the greater number of cases." [10] " But when he comes to make the purchase, having had all these circumstances in his power—whether used or not to the disadvantage of the party is of no consequence—the law looks with jealousy to these things, for it cannot discover whether they have been used prejudicially or not." [11] " The criterion, however, is not what was done, but what might be done." [12]

---

6   *Hamilton* v. *Wright* (1842) 1 Bell's App.Cas. 574, 591, *per* Lord Brougham.
7   *Hall's Trs.* v. *McArthur*, 1918 S.C. 646, 651, *per* Lord Johnston.
8   *Aberdeen Ry.* v. *Blaikie Bros.* (1853) 1 Macq. 461; *Laird* v. *Laird* (1855) 17 D. 984.
9   *Hamilton* v. *Wright* (1842) 1 Bell's App.Cas. 574, 590, *per* Lord Brougham.
10   *Ex p. James* (1803) 8 Ves.Jun. 337, 345, *per* Lord Eldon L.C.
11   *Elias* v. *Black* (1856) 18 D. 1225, 1230, *per* L.P. McNeill.
12   *Wright* v. *Morgan* [1926] A.C. 788, 798, *per* Lord Dunedin.

Prospective trustees

A contract is not affected merely because one party, at the time it was entered into, could, at his option, have become one of the trustees but in fact did not do so. There may be an effect if it is shown that in fact he used his power so as to render it inequitable that the sale should be upheld.[13]

A bank which had been appointed an executor was entitled to exercise after the testator's death an option to purchase property which had been conferred on it by a contract with the testator. The right had been created before the fiduciary relationship arose and the exercise of the option did not create any fresh contractual relationship.[14]

Former trustees

A trustee who has resigned from the trust is not entitled to take as an individual a lease of premises the proprietors of which had refused to renew the prior lease to the trustees.[15]

In England, it has been said that there is no reason why a man who has once been a trustee, twelve years before the sale, should not purchase trust property.[16]

Connected persons

There is no absolute rule that the wife of a trustee cannot purchase the trust estate but the court will be astute to examine the true nature of the transaction to ascertain whether the husband was truly the party concerned.[17]

> " Trustees expose themselves to great peril in allowing their own relatives to intervene in any matter connected with the execution of the trust; for the suspicion which that circumstance is calculated to excite, where there is any other fact to confirm it, is one which it would require a very strong case to remove." [18]

There is no absolute rule that a person who is a trustee under one trust cannot contract with himself as a trustee under another trust—" the rule that a trustee cannot be *auctor in rem suam* cannot be extended to a case where he is *auctor in rem alienam*." [19] But the transaction may be liable to be set aside if it appears to be prejudicial to one or other of the trusts.

A sale of trust estate to a firm of which a trustee is a partner [20] or to a company of which he is managing director [21] is reducible. However in an English case it was held that where a mortgagee sold the property to a

---

13 *Clark* v. *Clark* (1884) 9 App.Cas. 733.
14 *Re Mulholland's Will Trusts* [1949] 1 All E.R. 460.
15 *Halley's Trs.* v. *Halley*, 1920, 2 S.L.T. 343.
16 *Re Boles and British Land Company's Contract* [1902] 1 Ch. 244.
17 *Burrell* v. *Burrell's Trs.*, 1915 S.C. 333. *Cf.* Underhill, 459. See Lewin, 695.
18 *Ferraby* v. *Hobson* (1847) 2 Phillips 255, 261, *per* Lord Cottenham L.C.
19 *Templeton* v. *Burgh of Ayr*, 1912, 1 S.L.T. 421. See also *Hickley* v. *Hickley* (1876) 2 Ch.D. 190.
20 *Ex p. Moore* (1881) 51 L.J.Ch. 72.
21 *Dunn* v. *Chambers* (1897) 25 R. 247.

company in which he had a substantial interest, this was not a sale to himself [22]:

> " A sale by a person to a corporation of which he is a member is not, either in form or in substance, a sale by a person to himself. To hold that it is, would be to ignore the principle which lies at the root of the legal idea of a corporate body, and that idea is that the corporate body is distinct from the persons composing it." [23]

Circuitous transactions

If there is a sale by the trustees to a third party, a trustee can subsequently acquire the property from the third party [24] provided that the sale to the third party was complete and not merely executory.[25] Where the will gave one trustee an option to purchase a part of the estate which he assigned to another trustee, who exercised it, it was held that the transaction could be set aside.[26]

Types of contract

" The inability to contract depends not on the subject matter of the agreement, but on the fiduciary character of the contracting party." [27]

The trustee cannot purchase the trust estate even at an auction where he could probably give as good a price as anyone else.[28] The principle has been applied to an assignation of a registered lease.[29] A trustee can take a lease of an estate in which the trust has a contingent interest.[30]

A trustee cannot obtain a loan, secured or unsecured, from the trust.[31]

> " The lending of trust money by trustees to one of their own number is unquestionably an illegal proceeding. It is much more than a mere breach of trust in the ordinary sense, because such a breach of trust covers and includes small acts of negligence which may infer very little blame on the part of those concerned in them. But to lend trust money to one of their own number is an absolutely illegal proceeding." [32]

He cannot lend to the trust; the loan is voidable but the trustee is not bound to repay the interest.[32] The purchase of a debt due by the trust is

---

[22] *Farrar* v. *Farrars Ltd.* (1888) 40 Ch.D. 395. The court did, however, examine the transaction.
[23] *Per* Lindley L.J., p. 409.
[24] *Wright* v. *Morgan* [1926] A.C. 788, 796, *per* Lord Dunedin.
[25] *Williams* v. *Scott* [1900] A.C. 499; *Delves* v. *Gray* [1902] 2 Ch. 606.
[26] *Wright* v. *Morgan* [1926] A.C. 788.
[27] *Aberdeen Ry.* v. *Blaikie Bros.* (1853) 1 Macq. 461, 472, *per* Lord Cranworth L.C.
[28] *Hamilton* v. *Wright* (1842) 1 Bell's App.Cas. 574, 591, *per* Lord Brougham. See also *Ex p. James* (1803) 8 Ves.Jun. 337, 349, *per* Lord Eldon L.C.; *Thorburn* v. *Martin* (1853) 15 D. 845.
[29] *Meff* v. *Smith's Trs.*, 1930 S.N. 162.
[30] *Montgomerie* v. *Vernon* (1895) 22 R. 465.
[31] *Perston* v. *Perston's Trs.* (1863) 1 M. 245; *Ritchies* v. *Ritchie's Trs.* (1888) 15 R. 1086; *Templeton* v. *Burgh of Ayr*, 1912, 1 S.L.T. 421.
[32] *Croskery* v. *Gilmour's Trs.* (1890) 17 R. 697, 700, *per* L.P. Inglis; *Wilson* v. *Smith's Trs.*, 1939 S.L.T. 120.

void.[33] It is not illegal for a trustee to obtain an assignation of a bond due to the trust on his paying the full amount.[34]

A contract to supply goods to a business conducted by the trustees is struck at.[35] Where the trustees have become entitled to the deceased's interest in a partnership and are empowered to continue the business, they can renew the partnership arrangement with one of their own number but they cannot transact with him to the effect of giving him a larger share of the profits than he previously had.[36] Where a business carried on by the trustees was converted into a limited company, the trustees were not entitled to take an allotment of shares.[37]

A trustee is not disqualified from acting as solicitor for persons holding bonds over the trust heritage.[38]

The trustee cannot purchase the interest of the liferenter in the trust because his personal interest would then conflict with that of the person entitled to the fee.[39]

Where the repairer of a vessel arrested it in his own hands and brought it to a judicial sale, he could not purchase it himself because he had a fiduciary relationship to the owner.[40]

A mandatary for a debtor to the trust cannot act as a trustee.[41]

In an English case, a trustee was restrained from setting up in business as a yacht-broker because he would have been competing with the similar business carried on by the trust.[42]

Leases

A trustee cannot renew in his own name a lease previously held by the trust.[43] In England, this is known as the rule in *Keech* v. *Sandford*[44] in which it was applied even although the lessor had refused to renew the lease to the trust.

> " This may seem hard, that the trustee is the only person of all mankind who might not have the lease; but it is very proper that rule should be strictly pursued, and not in the least relaxed; for it is very obvious what would be the consequence of letting trustees have the lease, on refusal to renew to *cestui que* use." [45]

Generally, where a person in a fiduciary position renews a lease in his own name, he is held to have taken it in trust for the beneficiaries.[46]

[33] *Hamilton* v. *Wright* (1842) 1 Bell's App.Cas. 574.
[34] *Fleming* v. *Imrie* (1868) 6 M. 363 (Mackenzie Stuart (187) points out that there was no challenge by the beneficiaries who alone could have taken objection).
[35] *Cherry's Trs.* v. *Patrick*, 1911, 2 S.L.T. 313. *Cf. Re Sykes* [1909] 2 Ch. 241.
[36] *Mackie's Trs.* v. *Mackie* (1875) 2 R. 312; *Lawrie* v. *Lawrie's Trs.* (1892) 19 R. 675. See also *Lister* v. *Marshall's Tr.*, 1927 S.N. 55.
[37] *Taylor* v. *Hillhouse's Trs.* (1901) 9 S.L.T. 31.
[38] *Pott* v. *Stevenson*, 1935 S.L.T. 106. See also *Sleigh* v. *Sleigh's J.F.*, 1908 S.C. 1112.
[39] *Davis* v. *Davis* (1908) 16 S.L.T. 380.
[40] *Elias* v. *Black* (1856) 18 D. 1225.
[41] *Foggo* (1893) 20 R. 273.
[42] *Thomson* v. *Allen* [1930] 1 Ch. 203.
[43] *Wilsons* v. *Wilson* (1789) Mor. 16376; *McNiven* v. *Peffers* (1868) 7 M. 181.
[44] (1726) Sel.Cas.Ch. 61.
[45] *Per* Lord King L.C., p. 62.
[46] McLaren, II, 1046–1050 and the cases there cited. See also *Biss* v. *Biss* [1903] 2 Ch. 40.

Transactions with beneficiaries

A trustee can purchase the interest of a beneficiary in the trust but he must give the beneficiary all the information as to its value which is in his possession.[47] The onus is on the trustee to prove that the beneficiaries assented to the transaction with full knowledge of the circumstances.[48]

> " I will not say that in all cases beneficiaries and trustees may not bargain with each other, provided it be clear beyond all doubt that it is with a view to the benefit of the beneficiaries and of the trust-estate. I think, however, that that must be shewn by the trustee." [49]

Effect

As a general rule, the court will not give authority under the *nobile officium* for a trustee to bid for the trust-estate [50] but such authority was given in one highly exceptional case.[51] Normally, when a conflict arises the trustee must resign.[52] If he does not do so, the court may sequestrate the estate and appoint a judicial factor.[53]

If the transaction has been effected the contract is not an absolute nullity; it is reducible but it is valid until it is set aside.[54] The challenge must be made within a reasonable time.[55] The beneficiary can elect whether he will have the transaction set aside or will adopt it.[56]

Co-trustees have a title to challenge.[57] So do the creditors of the truster.[58] But where trustees had exposed heritage for sale by auction and the successful bid was made on behalf of one of the trustees, it was said that, while the purchase might have been set aside by a beneficiary, a third party who had been an unsuccessful bidder could not challenge the transaction.[59]

In one case, the sale of the liferent interest to the trustee was reduced at the instance of the liferenter but on the ground that the fiars would be prejudiced.[60]

A judicial factor appointed on the trust estate has a duty to recover fees which have been paid unlawfully to a trustee.[61]

Defences

The consent of the truster, his creditors and the beneficiaries is a defence.[62] But the onus is on the trustee to show that the beneficiary's

---

[47] *Dougan* v. *Macpherson* (1902) 4 F.(H.L.) 7.
[48] *Williams* v. *Scott* [1900] A.C. 499.
[49] *Buckner* v. *Jopp's Trs.* (1887) 14 R. 1006, 1023, *per* L.J.-C. Moncreiff.
[50] *Hall's Trs.* v. *McArthur*, 1918 S.C. 646.
[51] *Coats's Trs.*, 1914 S.C. 723.
[52] *Maclean* (1895) 22 R. 872; *Mills* v. *Brown's Trs.* (1900) 2 F. 1035. But see *Caldwell's Trs.* v. *Caldwell*, 1923 S.L.T. 694, 698.
[53] *Foggo* (1893) 20 R. 273; *Cherry* v. *Patrick*, 1910 S.C. 32.
[54] *Ashburton* v. *Escombe* (1892) 20 R. 187, 198, *per* Lord Kinnear.
[55] *Mackie's Trs.* v. *Mackie* (1875) 2 R. 312, 316, *per* Lord Neaves.
[56] *Gillies* v. *Maclachlan's Reps.* (1846) 8 D. 487; *Taylor* v. *Hillhouse's Trs.* (1901) 9 S.L.T. 31.
[57] *Wilson* v. *Smith's Trs.*, 1939 S.L.T. 120.
[58] *Bon-Accord Marine Assurance Co.* v. *Souter's Trs.* (1850) 12 D. 1010; *Meff* v. *Smith's Trs.*, 1930 S.N. 162.
[59] *Aberdein* v. *Stratton's Trs.* (1867) 5 M. 726.
[60] *Davis* v. *Davis* (1908) 16 S.L.T. 380.
[61] *Henderson* v. *Watson*, 1939 S.C. 711.   [62] *Browning* v. *Hamilton* (1837) 15 S. 999.

consent was true and informed. " When trustees in defence of a breach of trust, especially when it is one by which they profit, plead the consent of the beneficiaries, I think they must show that the beneficiaries were aware of the breach of trust and the legal wrong, and condoned it." [63]

There may be an exception to the general rule where the truster has foreseen the conflict of interest but has nevertheless made the appointment —for example, where the truster's son or partner is appointed specially for the purpose of carrying on a business.[64]

It is no answer that the trustee concerned withdrew from the counsels of the other trustees while the transaction was under consideration.[65]

Remuneration

The second aspect of the doctrine is that in the absence of a special provision in the trust deed, a trustee must act gratuitously.[66]

" The principle is this: It is the duty of an executor and a trustee to be the guardian of an estate, and to watch over the interests of the estate committed to his charge. If he be allowed to perform the duties connected with the estate, and to claim compensation for his services, his interest would then be opposed to his duty, and, as a matter of prudence, the Court does not allow the executor or trustee to place himself in that situation. If he chooses to perform those duties or services on that estate, he is not entitled to receive compensation. The case applies as strongly to an attorney as to that of any other person; for if an attorney, who is an executor, performs business that was necessary to be transacted—if this attorney, being an executor, performs those duties himself, he, in my opinion, is not entitled to be paid for the performance of those duties; it would be placing his interests at variance with the duties he has to discharge." [67] " It is not that reward for services is repugnant to the fiduciary duty, but that he who has the duty shall not take any secret remuneration or any financial benefit not authorized by the law, or by his contract, or by the trust deed under which he acts, as the case may be." [68] " A man is not to be the judge of what is proper remuneration for himself." [69]

" It does not appear to me that this rule is, as has been said, founded upon principles of morality. I regard it rather as based on

---

[63] *Taylor* v. *Hillhouse's Trs.* (1901) 9 S.L.T. 31, 33, *per* Lord Kincairney; see *Phipps* v. *Boardman* [1965] Ch. 992, C.A.

[64] *Maclean* (1895) 22 R. 872, 875, *per* Lord McLaren.

[65] *Perston* v. *Perston's Trs.* (1863) 1 M. 245, 254, *per* L.J.-C. Inglis. But see *Holder* v. *Holder* [1968] Ch. 353, where an auction bid by an executor whose interference with the administration of the estate had been minimal was upheld.

[66] *Fegan* v. *Thomson* (1855) 17 D. 1146. Prior to the decision of the House of Lords in *Home* v. *Pringle* (1841) 2 Rob.App. 384, it appears to have been the practice to allow remuneration to a trustee who had been appointed to act by his co-trustees (see *Miller's Trs.* v. *Miller* (1848) 10 D. 765; *Aitken* v. *Hunter* (1871) 9 M. 756, 762, *per* Lord Neaves).

[67] *New* v. *Jones*, 1 H. & Tw. 632, 634, *per* Lord Lyndhurst C.B., cited by L.J.-C. Hope in *Lord Gray and Others* (1856) 19 D. 1, 5.

[68] *Dale* v. *I.R.C.* [1954] A.C. 11, 27, *per* Lord Normand.

[69] *Fegan* v. *Thomson* (1855) 17 D. 1146, 1148, *per* L.J.-C. Hope.

the consideration that, human nature being what it is, there is danger, in such circumstances, of the person holding a fiduciary position being swayed by interest rather than by duty, and thus prejudicing those whom he was bound to protect." [70]

The principle applies to a trustee acting as auctioneer [71] and to a trustee who received commission in respect of business introduced to a stockbrokers' firm by which he was employed.[72]

Solicitors

A trustee who is a solicitor is not entitled to payment of anything more than his outlays nor can he employ for remuneration a firm of which he is a partner.[73] It is different if there is an express provision in the trust deed or if the beneficiaries have acquiesced.[74]

It is not an answer that the account has to be taxed—" the estate has a right not only to the protection of the taxing officer, but also to the vigilance and guardianship of the executor, in addition to the check of the taxing officer." [75]

In general a firm of which a trustee is a partner cannot be paid remuneration for acting on behalf of the trust. This is so even where all the business is transacted by the partners of the solicitor trustee and not by the trustee himself [76]; even where under the partnership agreement the trustee is entitled only to a fixed sum in each year from the profits of the firm [77]; and even where there is an agreement that the trustee should not have a share of the profits accruing to the firm from the trust business.[78]   In *Clack* v. *Carlon* [79] it was decided that charges could be made if a solicitor trustee employed his partners to act for the trust so that the partners alone received the profits. The partners were in effect acting as independent solicitors and *quoad* the trust business the solicitor trustee was not in partnership with the others. This seems a narrow distinction and it is doubtful if it would be accepted in Scotland.

The solicitor trustee can of course employ an independent solicitor to act for him but he cannot receive agency in respect of the work.[80]

Express provisions

Authority in the trust deed " to appoint agents and factors either of their own number or other fit persons " has been held to imply an inten-

[70] *Bray* v. *Ford* [1896] A.C. 44, 51, *per* Lord Herschell.
[71] *Matthison* v. *Clarke* (1854) 3 Drew. 3.
[72] *Williams* v. *Barton* [1927] 2 Ch. 9.
[73] *Lord Gray and Others* (1856) 19 D. 1; *Wellwood's Trs.* v. *Hill* (1856) 19 D. 187; *Lauder* v. *Millars* (1859) 21 D. 1353.
[74] *Ommanney* v. *Smith* (1854) 16 D. 721; *Dixon* v. *Rutherford* (1863) 2 M. 61; *Scott* v. *Handyside's Trs.* (1868) 6 M. 753; *Henderson* v. *Watson*, 1939 S.C. 711.
[75] *Per* Lord Lyndhurst C.B., *New* v. *Jones, supra,* p. 635.
[76] *Christophers* v. *White* (1847) 10 Beav. 523.
[77] *Claremont* v. *Hill* [1934] Ch. 623, C.A.
[78] *Arnold* v. *Gates* [1933] Ch. 913.
[79] (1861) 30 L.J.Ch. 639. See also *Re Doody* [1893] 1 Ch. 129.
[80] *Re Taylor* (1854) 18 Beav. 165.

tion that a trustee so appointed should receive remuneration.[81] An appointment under an authority in the trust deed should be made formally and recorded in the trust minutes.[82] Whether a trustee who is acting as solicitor to the trust can charge as much for attendance at meetings as a solicitor who was not a trustee could is a question of circumstances.[83]

Where a solicitor trustee was to be entitled to charge for all business transacted by him " including all business of whatever kind not strictly professional, but which might have been performed, or would necessarily have been performed in person by a trustee not being a solicitor," he was held to be entitled to charge for his trouble as well as for his professional costs.[84] But where the wording was " any business ... whether in the ordinary course of his profession or business or not, and although not of a nature strictly requiring the employment of a solicitor or other professional person " the trustee was held entitled to charge for work done in the course of his profession or business, whether done in the ordinary course thereof or not, but he could not charge for work done outside the profession or business.[85]

Authority to appoint one of the trustees as a " factor or cashier " with remuneration does not permit the appointment of one trustee as salaried manager of a business conducted by the trust.[86]

Where a trustee was given a legacy it was held that he was also entitled to professional remuneration under an authority in the will.[87]

Cradock v. Piper

In England, the rule in *Cradock* v. *Piper* [88] forms a curious exception to the general principle. If a solicitor trustee acts in an action or matter on behalf of himself and a co-trustee, he may receive his costs provided that the expense is no greater than would have been incurred if he had appeared only for his co-trustee. This exception is regarded with some suspicion in England [89] and forms no part of the law of Scotland.

Directors' fees

In a number of English cases, the right of trustees to retain remuneration paid by a company in which the trust holds shares has been discussed. The test is: Did the trustee acquire the position in respect of which he drew the remuneration by virtue of his position as a trustee? Where trustees used their powers as shareholders to appoint themselves as directors, they were liable to account to the trust estate for remuneration received as

81 *Goodsir* v. *Carruthers* (1858) 20 D. 1141. See also *Cameron's Trs.* v. *Cameron* (1864) 3 M. 200.
82 *Lewis's Trs.* v. *Pirie*, 1912 S.C. 574.
83 *Turner* v. *Fraser's Trs.* (1897) 24 R. 673.
84 *Re Fish* [1893] 2 Ch. 413.
85 *Clarkson* v. *Robinson* [1900] 2 Ch. 722.
86 *Mills* v. *Brown's Trs.* (1900) 2 F. 1035.
87 *Re Fish* [1893] 2 Ch. 413.
88 (1850) 1 Mac. & G. 664.
89 See *Manson* v. *Baillie* (1855) 2 Macq. 80; *Re Doody* [1893] 1 Ch. 129.

directors.[90] But if the resolution making the appointment would have been
carried even although the voting power of the trust holding had been
exercised against it, the trustees are not liable to account [91]; and where
individuals held shares in company A as trustees for company B in order
to be qualified to act as directors of company A, it was held that the
directors' remuneration was not derived by the use of the shares.[92]

In Scotland, there is some authority for the view that trustees are not
required to communicate directors' fees notwithstanding that they qualified for office as holders of shares belonging to the trust.[93]

90 *Re Macadam* [1946] Ch. 73. See also *Re Francis* (1905) 74 L.J.Ch. 198.
91 *Re Gee, decd.* [1948] Ch. 284.
92 *Re Dover Coalfield Extension, Ltd.* [1907] 2 Ch. 76 (the headnote is misleading).
93 *Elliot* v. *Mackie & Sons*, 1935 S.C. 81, 87, *per* Lord Moncrieff (Ordinary), p. 92, *per* Lord
Morison.

Chapter 24

PAYMENT AND DISCHARGE

PAYMENT

Powers of restriction

If the trustees in the exercise of a discretion resolve to restrict the share of a beneficiary to an alimentary liferent or to reduce the amount of income payable, this affects the right of any assignee or arrester of the share [1] and the trustee in the beneficiary's sequestration.[2] In *Adam* v. *Forsyth's Trs.*,[3] it was held that a discretionary power to render a share " alimentary and inalienable " must be exercised within a reasonable time of the date of distribution, at least where the claim of an assignee of the share has been in some way recognised by the trustees. But in a later House of Lords case, in which *Adam* was not cited, it was held that an arrestment of a share does not affect the power of trustees to exercise a discretion conferred by the trust deed to postpone payment and render the income alimentary.[4]

A discretion to withhold payment of an alimentary liferent or of a share of capital can be exercised on the sequestration of the beneficiary.[5]

Where trustees, who had power to decide whether the testator's son's share should be paid over to him or placed under some restriction, decided that there should be some restriction but, as a curator *bonis* had been appointed to the son, conveyed the share to the son absolutely, it was held that they had acted *ultra vires*.[6]

> " They have no discretion to resolve that a son is not in a position to have the uncontrolled command and disposal of his interest, and then to proceed on that resolution to hand over his share to him. The only condition on which they are entitled to do that is when they have resolved that the share of succession falling to the son should be unrestricted, and without any limitation whatever." [7]

A power to withhold payment can be exercised even although the trustees have not minuted a resolution that this should be done.[8]

It is not competent to withhold income from the liferenter in order to

---

[1] *Chambers' Trs.* v. *Smiths* (1878) 5 R.(H.L.) 151; *Train* v. *Clapperton*, 1908 S.C.(H.L.) 26.
[2] *White's Tr.* v. *White's Trs.*, 1917, 1 S.L.T. 272; *Cox's Trs.* v. *Rainie* (1899) 6 S.L.T. 370.
[3] (1867) 6 M. 31.
[4] *Chambers' Trs.* v. *Smiths* (1878) 5 R.(H.L.) 151.
[5] *White's Tr.* v. *White's Trs.*, 1917, 1 S.L.T. 272; *Cox's Trs.* v. *Rainie* (1899) 6 S.L.T. 370.
[6] *McNicol's Exrx.* v. *McNicol* (1893) 20 R. 386.
[7] p. 395, *per* Lord Kinnear.
[8] *White's Trs.* v. *White* (1896) 23 R. 836. The power cannot be validly exercised by a majority of trustees without notice to the minority (*Slimon* v. *Slimon's Trs.*, 1915, 2 S.L.T. 19).

create a sinking fund to provide against loss of capital arising on the redemption at par of securities properly bought at a premium.[9]

Discretionary trusts

Lord Wilberforce has described the duty of a trustee with a discretion to distribute among a class of beneficiaries as follows:

> " He would examine the field, by class and category; might indeed make diligent and careful inquiries, depending on how much money he had to give away and the means at his disposal, as to the composition and needs of particular categories and of individuals within them; decide upon certain priorities or proportions, and then select individuals according to their needs or qualifications. If he acts in this manner, can it really be said that he is not carrying out the trust ? " [10]

Form of payment

Whether the estate should be handed over to the beneficiaries *in forma specifica* is a question for the discretion of the trustees but it is a discretion which must be exercised reasonably.[11]

A beneficiary entitled to the liferent of heritable property cannot compel the trustees to grant him a conveyance of the property in liferent. The trustees have to hold the estate for behoof of the fiars as well as the liferenter and they cannot be required to denude of the liferent when they could not denude of the fee.[12]

The residuary legatee is entitled to the whole property of the deceased remaining undisposed of after satisfying the other provisions of the will. This includes, where the deceased was a solicitor, his business books.[13]

Options

The trustees may be directed to give a beneficiary an option to purchase a specific asset of the estate at a fixed price. If, before the sale can be made, compulsory acquisition or other third party intervention substitutes a sum of money for the specified asset in the trust estate, the beneficiary is not deprived of his option and the sum of money is treated as a *surrogatum* for the asset. The position is quite different where the trustees are given a discretion to sell, and are directed to give a beneficiary an option to purchase if they do decide to sell. If some third party intervention then prevents the trustees from exercising their power of sale, the beneficiary has no claim to a *surrogatum*. So where trustees had been directed to offer shares in a company to A at a certain price if, " in their uncontrolled sole

---

[9] *Heath* v. *Baxter's Trs.* (1902) 10 S.L.T. 462.

[10] *McPhail* v. *Doulton* [1971] A.C. 424, 449. See also pp. 334–338, *supra*. See, as to the beneficiary's right to recover documents relating to the exercise of the discretion, *Re Londonderry's Settlement* [1965] Ch. 918.

[11] See *Center's Tr.* v. *Center's Exrx.*, 1948 S.L.T.(Notes) 83; *Conage's J.F.*, 1948 S.L.T. (Notes) 11. See also *Stewart's Trs.* v. *Stewart* (1897) 25 R. 302; *Brown* v. *Elder's Trs.* (1906) 13 S.L.T. 837.

[12] *Ker's Trs.* v. *Justice* (1868) 6 M. 627.

[13] *Robertson* v. *Robertson's Exors.*, 1925 S.C. 606.

discretion," they decided to sell them, and the company subsequently went into voluntary liquidation before any decision to sell had been taken, it was held that A was not entitled to the difference between the sum received by the trustees on liquidation and the price he would have paid if the shares had been offered to him.[14]

An option to purchase " at a reasonable valuation " is valid.[15]

The payee

The trustee has a duty to pay over the estate to the right person. The duty is of a high order.

> " I consider it to be a settled principle of our law that trustees, in distributing the trust-estate, are bound to pay it away to the party in right to receive it, and are liable to that party if they pay it away to any other. There is no hardship to trustees in so holding, for if the matter is one of difficulty, they can always have recourse to judicial authority, and refrain from paying without the warrant of a Court. The case of distribution herein differs essentially from that of realisation. I do not hold it of any moment what the precise blunder is. The payment may be to the wrong beneficiary, or may be to the beneficiary and not to the creditors, or it may be, as here, to the secondary creditors, and not the primary. In all such cases it is the rule of law that the wrong-paying trustee is responsible." [16]

Where the trustee had taken the erroneous view that the trust deed was revocable and had made payments of capital to the trusters, he had to account therefor to the beneficiaries who had a vested right to the trust fund.[17] A trustee for creditors who paid an unfounded claim had to account for the amount to the truster.[18]

If payment to the wrong person is made because of an error of law, it is not a defence that the trustees acted on the advice of counsel.[19] Where the error is one of fact the payment is recoverable by a *condictio indebiti*; if the error is as to the general law—as distinct from an error in construction of a document—the payment is not recoverable.[20]

There are, however, some situations in which there is not liability for payment made in error. " Cases may undoubtedly occur in which the facts necessary to be known, in order to point out the true person entitled, may be beyond the knowledge, and fairly possible discovery of the trustees; and in such cases responsibility may be modified." [21] It has been suggested that

---

14 *Smith* v. *Cotton's Trs.*, 1956 S.C. 338; *Re Flint* [1927] 1 Ch. 570. *Cf. Re Fison's Will Trusts* [1950] Ch. 394.
15 *Talbot* v. *Talbot* [1968] A.C. 1.
16 *Lamond's Trs.* v. *Croom* (1871) 9 M. 662, 671, *per* Lord Kinloch.
17 *Morrisons* v. *Allan* (1886) 13 R. 1156.
18 *Buttercase and Geddie's Tr.* v. *Geddie* (1897) 24 R. 1128.
19 *National Trustees Co. of Australasia Ltd.* v. *General Finance Co. of Australasia Ltd.* [1905] A.C. 373; *Buttercase and Geddie's Tr.* v. *Geddie* (1897) 24 R. 1128; McLaren, II, 1254.
20 *Credit Lyonnais* v. *George Stevenson & Co. Ltd.* (1901) 9 S.L.T. 93; *Glasgow Corporation* v. *Lord Advocate*, 1959 S.C. 203; *British Hydro-Carbon Chemicals Ltd.*, 1961 S.L.T. 280.
21 *Lamond's Trs.* v. *Croom* (1871) 9 M. 662, 671, *per* Lord Kinloch.

the trustee's liability is not absolute where the mistake is as to foreign law and there is nothing in the deed to put the trustee on his inquiry.[22] Another exception is where the beneficiary is personally barred from insisting on payment.[23]

Assignations

The trustees must ascertain whether any assignations of a beneficiary's interest have been intimated. Once an assignation of a beneficiary's interest has been intimated, the assignee has an absolute and preferable right to the subject of the assignation as it stands at the date of intimation. If the trustees continue thereafter to make advances to the beneficiary under a power conferred in the will, they will be personally liable if they do not retain sufficient funds to pay the amount assigned.[24] The assignee must, of course, produce his title.

Title

The trustee is bound to pay the holder of an *ex facie* good title. The title must be regular and complete. Trustees who paid a sum due to a minor to his *curator bonis* who had neither extracted his appointment nor found caution and who soon after left the country in a state of insolvency were found liable to pay the sum over again to the minor.[25]

Difficulties arise where a title is *ex facie* valid but is in the course of being questioned or impugned. Where a woman became entitled to income from a trust when she obtained a decree of divorce, it was held that the trustees should have ceased to make payment to her when the former husband's trustee in bankruptcy raised an action for reduction of the divorce decree which was in the event successful.[26]

Mackenzie Stuart [27] distinguishes three situations where a title, *ex facie* good, is known by the trustee to be open to challenge:

(1) Where the title is voidable and the trustee knows that the person with the right to challenge is *sui juris* and aware of his rights; the trustee must pay the beneficiary.

(2) Where the title is not merely challengeable but the holder must justify his right to it—*e.g.* where a legacy has been left to the truster's solicitor; the trustee should see that those entitled to challenge have full knowledge of their rights and independent legal advice.

(3) Where there is reasonable doubt as to whether the title has any validity at all—*e.g.* doubt as to whether an appointment is within a power; the trustee should seek the guidance of the court.

---

[22] Mackenzie Stuart, 224; *Leslie* v. *Baillie* (1843) 2 Y. & Coll.C.C. 91; Underhill, 424.

[23] *Ibid.* p. 225. See, as to the situation where the trustee holds two different funds for the same beneficiary, *Beith* v. *Mackenzie* (1875) 3 R. 185.

[24] *Macpherson's J.F.* v. *Mackay*, 1915 S.C. 1011. This is subject to what is said as to Powers of Restriction, *supra.*

[25] *Donaldson* v. *Kennedy* (1833) 11 S. 740.

[26] *Corbidge* v. *Fraser*, 1915, 1 S.L.T. 67.

[27] p. 228. See also Underhill, 425.

In England, it has been held that the trustee is not protected if he has paid on a forged title.[28]

Illegitimacy

The executor is entitled to treat a child as legitimate if there is produced an entry of the child in the register of births as legitimate which has not been challenged.[29]

An executor or trustee may distribute the estate without having ascertained that no illegitimate person is entitled to an interest therein and that no illegitimate person exists or has existed, the fact of whose existence is relevant to the ascertainment of the persons entitled to an interest. The executor is not personally liable to any person so entitled of whose claim he has not had notice at the time of distribution but the right of the person so entitled to recover the payment or property from the person who has received it is not affected by this provision.[30]

Adoption orders

A trustee or executor may distribute the estate without having ascertained that no adoption order has been made by virtue of which any person is or may be entitled to any interest therein and is not liable to any such person of whose claim he has not had notice at the time of the distribution.[31] There would seem to be no protection in relation to adoption orders by virtue of which a person ceases to be entitled to an interest in the estate.

Presumed death

The estate can be distributed on the basis established by a decree under the Presumption of Life Limitation (Scotland) Act 1891, subject to the obligation of the beneficiaries to repay any sums necessary in the event of the presumption being afterwards proved to have been incorrect.[32]

Extent of duty

In the case of a bequest to an existing body to be applied to a charitable purpose, the trustees have no duty to see to the administration of the bequest and can pay over the sum to the body on their receipt.[33] Where trustees had to pay over a legacy which was subject to something in the nature of a clause of return it was held that they were not under a duty to ensure that the destination was effective.[34]

---

[28] Underhill, 421. But see Menzies, 402.
[29] *Flett* v. *Brown's Exor.*, 1915, 2 S.L.T. 261.
[30] Law Reform (Miscellaneous Provisions) (Scotland) Act 1968, s. 7.
[31] 1964 Act, s. 24 (2). The right of the person concerned to recover the property from the person who has received it is not affected.
[32] 1891 Act, ss. 3, 6; *Barr* v. *Campbell*, 1925 S.C. 317.
[33] *Milne's Exors.* v. *Aberdeen University* (1905) 13 S.L.T. 45.
[34] *Masson* v. *Scott's Trs.*, 1910, 2 S.L.T. 28.

Recovery of payments

If a legacy has been paid to the wrong person, the trustees can demand repetition thereof.[35] They cannot, however, recover overpayments of income which have been made because of an error in construing the trust deed.[36] The doctrine of *fruges bona fide perceptae et consumptae* is applicable. In *Darling's Trs.* v. *Darling's Trs.*[37] it was suggested that as that principle applies only to the disposal of the fruits of a subject which has been given to a wrong person *in bona fide*, it cannot operate where the thing given was an independent gift of annual income such as a liferent— " The liferent here paid was not a fruit it was the thing itself." [38] This view was doubted in *Rowan's Trs.* v. *Rowan*[39] but it does seem more consistent with principle. Indeed, it is difficult to reconcile the rule as to overpayments with the principle.

DISCHARGE

Trustees are not bound to denude until they are " validly and effectually freed from challenge " [40] not only in respect of their intromissions but also in respect of contingent and future claims.[41] Generally, the court will not order trustees to denude unless at the same time a decree of exoneration and discharge can be pronounced.[42] Trustees are bound to denude on receiving a discharge covering their own intromissions. They are not entitled to require a full and final discharge of the intromissions of their predecessors.[43] The existing trustees are liable to account for the intromissions of previous trustees but they are not liable for those intromissions.

Methods

The trust deed may provide for the method of discharge of the trustees.[44] It may provide that exoneration is to be given by someone who is not a beneficiary [45]; or, for example, that a sufficient discharge can be given by the parent of a minor legatee.[46]

By trustees

If it is not at variance with the terms or purposes of the trust, trustees have power to discharge trustees who have resigned and the representa-

---

[35] *Armour* v. *Glasgow Royal Infirmary*, 1909 S.C. 916.
[36] *Hunter's Trs.* v. *Hunter* (1894) 21 R. 949; *Rowan's Trs.* v. *Rowan*, 1940 S.C. 30. See also *Ferguson* v. *Lord Advocate* (1906) 14 S.L.T. 52.
[37] 1909 S.C. 445.
[38] p. 451, *per* L.P. Dunedin.
[39] p. 39, *per* L.P. Normand; p. 48, *per* Lord Moncrieff.
[40] *Edmond* v. *Dingwall's Trs.* (1860) 23 D. 21, 25, *per* L.J.-C. Inglis. See also *Blair's Trs.* v. *Blair* (1863) 2 M. 284.
[41] *Elliott's Trs.* v. *Elliott* (1828) 6 S. 1058.
[42] *Elliott's Trs.* v. *Elliott* (1828) 6 S. 1058. See also *Edmond* v. *Dingwall's Trs.* (1860) 23 D. 21.
[43] *Mackenzie's Exor.* v. *Thomson's Trs.*, 1965 S.C. 154.
[44] *Bunten* v. *Muir* (1894) 21 R. 370.
[45] *Tod* v. *Tod's Trs.* (1842) 4 D. 1275.
[46] *Lumsden's Trs.* v. *Lumsden*, 1921, 1 S.L.T. 155. See also *Egg* v. *Devey* (1847) 10 Beav. 444, where a person accepting benefit under the will was prohibited from impugning the execution of another trust.

tives of trustees who have died.[47] Such a discharge is as valid as one granted by the beneficiaries.[48] If the trustees have wrongly discharged a resigned trustee they may be liable to the beneficiaries for breach of trust but a creditor cannot sue a resigned trustee for his debt.[49]

A provision in the trust deed might make a settlement between the trustees conclusive against the beneficiaries.[50]

By court

Section 18 [51] of the 1921 Act provides:

> " When a trustee who resigns or the representatives of a trustee who has died or resigned cannot obtain a discharge of his acts and intromissions from the remaining trustees, and when the beneficiaries of the trust refuse, or are unable from absence, incapacity or otherwise to grant a discharge, the court may, on petition to that effect at the instance of such trustee or representative and after such intimation and inquiry as may be thought necessary, grant such discharge."

If either the trustees or the beneficiaries are available and willing to grant a discharge the court cannot intervene.[52]

Beneficiary's obligation

The trustees cannot demand a discharge of their intromissions with the estate from the legatee on payment of a legacy of a specific amount. Only a simple receipt can be required.[53] If, however, the subject of the specific legacy constitutes the whole estate the trustees are entitled to a discharge of their intromissions and not merely a receipt.[54] The position is the same where the estate is insufficient to meet the specific legacies in full; the specific legacies are then similar to residue.

A discharge can be required of a residuary legatee because the residue depends on the administration of the trust and the trustees are entitled to exoneration in respect of their management.[55] Where a beneficiary was entitled to one third of the free surplus rents of the estate in each year, it was held in the Outer House that only a simple receipt could be demanded from the beneficiary and it could not be a condition of payment that he would annually examine the accounts and acknowledge that they were correct.[56]

When paying a legacy, trustees are not entitled to demand a discharge from the legatee to exclude a possible alternative claim against the estate.[57]

---

[47] 1921 Act, s. 4 (g).
[48] Menzies, 584.
[49] Town and County Bank Ltd. v. Walker (1904) 12 S.L.T. 411; (1905) 13 S.L.T. 287.
[50] Re Fish [1893] 2 Ch. 413, 421, per Lindley L.J.
[51] Substantially re-enacting Trusts (Scotland) Act 1867, s. 9.
[52] Matthews' Trs. (1894) 2 S.L.T. 122.
[53] Fleming v. Brown (1861) 23 D. 443.
[54] Davidson's Tr. v. Cooper (1895) 3 S.L.T. 28.
[55] Fleming v. Brown, supra. But see Edie v. Cairns' Trs., 1947 S.L.T.(Notes) 14.
[56] Bonnar (1893) 1 S.L.T. 57. Johnstone's Trs. v. Smith Clark (1896) 4 S.L.T. 180, concerned a factor and law agent.
[57] Laing v. Laing (1895) 22 R. 575.

It seems that, in England, if the beneficiary has assigned his interest, the assignee cannot be required to give more than a receipt.[58] Where the same trustee holds two different trust funds for the same beneficiary he is not entitled to refuse to pay over the one fund until all questions relating to the second have been settled.[59] On denuding, the trustee has no right to a copy of the document constituting the title of the recipient of the fund.[60]

Form of discharge

A holograph document is a sufficient receipt for a specific legacy; a deed with a clause of registration is not necessary.[61]

A discharge may be presumed from circumstances.[62] The presence of the beneficiary at a meeting of trustees is not sufficient to imply her assent to an arrangement recorded in a minute of the meeting not signed by her.[63] The trustee's possession of the back-bond implies that the trust is discharged.[64]

Capacity to discharge

If there is doubt as to whether a legatee can give a valid discharge, the trustees are entitled to the expenses of bringing the question before the court.[65] If a legacy is due to a pupil, the father as its administrator is entitled to demand payment but in certain circumstances he may be required to find caution.[66] If the beneficiary is a minor he can grant a receipt with the concurrence of his curator. A discharge granted by a minor or by a tutor on behalf of his pupil is never conclusive because it can be reduced at the instance of the minor or pupil during the *quadriennium utile*. Even the authority of the court does not render a transaction exempt from subsequent challenge in this way.[67] The court will not authorise payment to a father who, under the law of the domicile, is not the guardian of the child.[68]

If the beneficiaries have no capacity under the law of their domicile to grant a discharge and have no legal guardians capable of giving a binding discharge, the trustees cannot safely make payment[69] unless the testator has provided in the will as to the form of discharge.[70] If a guardian can grant an effectual discharge under the law of the domicile, Scottish trustees are bound to accept it.[71] But a guardian appointed under a foreign law

[58] *Re Cater's Trusts (No. 2)* (1858) 25 Beav. 366.
[59] *Price* v. *Loaden* (1856) 21 Beav. 508.
[60] *Warter* v. *Anderson* (1853) 11 Hare 301; *Re Palmer* [1907] 1 Ch. 486.
[61] *Fleming* v. *Brown* (1861) 23 D. 443; *McLaren* v. *Howie* (1869) 8 M. 106.
[62] *Stuart* v. *Maconochie* (1836) 14 S. 412. See also *Scott* v. *Mitchell* (1830) 8 S. 820.
[63] *Cameron* v. *Panton's Trs.* (1891) 18 R. 728.
[64] *Charteris* v. *Charteris* (1712) Mor. 11413.
[65] *Neilson's Trs.* v. *Peacock* (1822) 2 S. 89; *Freeman* v. *Bruce's Exors.* (1905) 13 S.L.T. 97.
[66] *Dumbreck* v. *Stevenson* (1861) 4 Macq. 86; *Murray's Trs.* v. *Bloxsom's Trs.* (1887) 15 R. 233.
[67] *White* (1855) 17 D. 599, 602, *per* Lord Deas.
[68] *Atherstone's Trs.* (1896) 24 R. 39; *Seddon* (1891) 19 R. 101.
[69] *Atherstone's Trs.* (1896) 24 R. 39; *Freeman* v. *Bruce's Exors.* (1905) 13 S.L.T. 97.
[70] *Lumsden's Trs.* v. *Lumsden*, 1921, 1 S.L.T. 155.
[71] *Seddon* (1893) 20 R. 675.

has no power to grant a valid discharge to trustees in respect of the transfer of heritable property in Scotland; the only solution is to appoint a factor *loco tutoris* in Scotland.[72]

Agent

If payment is made to the beneficiary's agent, the trustees should ascertain that he has authority to receive payment and discharge them.[73] Similarly, payment should not be made to a curator *bonis* who has not extracted his appointment.[74]

Foreign beneficiaries

Where a national of certain states is entitled to a payment or delivery of property from the estate and is not resident in Scotland a consular officer of the state has the like right and power to give a valid discharge, to complete title thereto and administer or dispose of it as if he had been authorised by power of attorney. This does not apply if the person authorised or required to pay knows that a person in Scotland other than the consular officer has been expressly authorised to receive the money or property.[75]

There is a similar right and power where the national is a person to whom money or property comprised in an estate may be paid or delivered in pursuance of any enactment rule or regulation without production of confirmation.

Construction

A discharge in general terms covers only items in contemplation of the parties at the time at which it was granted. " General clauses are always to be interpreted with reference to the matter immediately on hand." [76] " General words used in a discharge are subject to construction with reference to the particular transaction to which it relates." [77] " One cannot read into a general discharge such as we have here a specific discharge of a claim which was clearly not in the contemplation of the parties at the time the discharge was granted." [78]

A discharge granted on payment of legitim does not bar a claim to estate which later falls into intestacy.[79] Where a beneficiary with a right of occupancy of heritage had paid rates and burdens for eight years, it was held that she was not barred from claiming repayment from the trustees by a discharge in which she had exonered the trustees of their intromissions. There was nothing to show that she knew of the matter in dispute when she signed the discharge and she was not seeking to enforce personal liability

[72] *Ogilvy* v. *Ogilvy's Trs.*, 1927 S.L.T. 83.
[73] *Kennedy* v. *Kennedy* (1843) 6 D. 40; *Cameron* v. *Panton's Trs.* (1891) 18 R. 728.
[74] *Donaldson* v. *Kennedy* (1833) 11 S. 740.
[75] Consular Conventions Act 1949, s. 2 (3). For the states to which the section applies see p. 439, *infra*, Note 18.
[76] *Dickson* v. *Halbert* (1854) 16 D. 586, 597, *per* Lord Ivory.
[77] *Burns' Trs.* v. *Burns' Trs.*, 1911, 2 S.L.T. 392, 394, *per* Lord Cullen.
[78] *Dickson's Trs.* v. *Dickson's Trs.*, 1930 S.L.T. 226.
[79] *Symmers's Trs.* v. *Symmers*, 1918 S.C. 337.

against the trustees.[80] A discharge granted on payment of *jus relicti* did not bar a claim to a conventional provision after the operation of equitable compensation.[81]

Effect of discharge

Once a formal discharge has been granted, the intromissions covered by the discharge cannot be challenged unless the discharge is reduced.[82] Fraud, misrepresentation and essential error are possible grounds of reduction. In an action for reduction the beneficiary must aver the specific facts with which he was not acquainted at the date of the discharge.[83]

A discharge of the trustees and of their solicitor was held not to preclude the raising by a beneficiary of an action of accounting against the trustees on the ground that the account of the solicitor was excessive. The case is odd because the trustees had failed to have the account taxed and the item in the trust accounts was prima facie incorrect.[84] A trustee who has been discharged by the beneficiaries can be sued in order to constitute a claim against the trust-estate.[85]

The validity of a discharge which has been granted before the completion of the trust depends upon completion being effected.[86] A discharge in favour of the trustees is not a discharge by the beneficiaries of their claims *inter se*.[87]

Judicial exoneration

If trustees cannot obtain a valid extrajudicial discharge they are entitled to seek judicial exoneration. The process normally appropriate is a multiplepoinding.[88] Delay or vacillating and inconstant conduct on the part of the beneficiaries will justify the trustees in taking this course.[89] Judicial exoneration is not granted in respect of intromissions after the date of the raising of the action unless the sanction of the court for the subsequent actings is specially obtained.[90] Trustees are entitled to raise an action of multiplepoinding for their exoneration notwithstanding that the person claiming the legacy has obtained a decree under the Presumption of Life Limitation (Scotland) Act 1891.[91]

---

[80] *Johnstone* v. *Mackenzie's Trs.*, 1911 S.C. 321.
[81] *Burns' Trs.* v. *Burns' Trs.*, 1911, 2 S.L.T. 392.
[82] *Macpherson* v. *Macpherson* (1841) 3 D. 1242.
[83] *Campbell* v. *Montgomery* (1822) 1 S. 484.
[84] *McFarlane* v. *McFarlane's Trs.* (1897) 24 R. 574.
[85] *Assets Co. Ltd.* v. *Falla's Tr.* (1894) 22 R. 178.
[86] *Mayne* v. *McKeand* (1835) 13 S. 870.
[87] *Halbert* v. *Dickson* (1851) 13 D. 667; *Armour* v. *Glasgow Royal Infirmary*, 1909 S.C. 916.
[88] See p. 314, *supra*.
[89] *Fothringham* v. *Salton* (1852) 14 D. 427.
[90] *Barnet's Trs.* v. *Barnet* (1872) 10 M. 730.
[91] *Davidson* v. *Ewen* (1895) 3 S.L.T. 162.

One trustee can bring an action although the other disclaims it.[92] A trustee is entitled to exoneration even although he has not taken an active part in the management of the estate.[93]

It seems that a possible alternative procedure is for the trustee to raise an action against the beneficiaries for declarator that he has accounted for his whole intromissions.[94]

---

[92] *Taylor* v. *Noble* (1836) 14 S. 817.
[93] *Dunbar* v. *Sinclair* (1850) 13 D. 54.
[94] *Davidson's Tr.* v. *Simmons* (1896) 23 R. 1117; *Dickson's Tr.* v. *Dickson*, 1959 S.L.T.(Notes) 55. The trustee can apparently ask for discharge for a co-trustee who has died or resigned.

CHAPTER 25

BREACH OF TRUST

Liability to account

The existing trustees, whether original or assumed, are obliged to account, not only for their own intromissions, but also for those of their predecessors as trustees.[1] Liability to account does not necessarily involve liability for losses incurred. It is no answer to a claim for an accounting for the representatives of the last surviving trustee to say that for a period the trust management had been in the hands of other trustees.[2] " I hold it a principle in our law of trust that a beneficiary is entitled at any time to demand from a surviving trustee or trustees, or from the representatives of the last survivor, a full production of accounts." [3]

In general the right to call for an accounting from existing trustees is restricted to the beneficiaries and the truster's creditors. A trustee who is also a beneficiary can demand an accounting.[4] A beneficiary who has been paid his interest has no title.[5]

Liability to account is not subject to the long negative prescription but a discharge granted to a trustee must be reduced before he can be required to account.[6]

Breach of trust

" Where trustees resist the execution of their duty or are guilty of *culpa lata* in neglecting their duty, they will be personally liable to the beneficiaries so injured." [7] " Where personal liability is to be attached to a trustee, the grounds of that personal liability must be clearly established." [8]

" A breach of trust may consist of embezzlement, or it may arise simply from failure to account, or it may consist, as alleged here, of some act or default which amounts only to some irregularity or error of judgment for which, nevertheless, there may be personal liability. But in all such cases the result is simply to create a liability by the trustee to make good to the trust estate the loss which he has caused." [9]

---

[1] *Sommerville's Trs.* v. *Wemess* (1854) 17 D. 151; *Mackenzie's Exor.* v. *Thomson's Trs.*, 1965 S.L.T. 410.

[2] *Pearson* v. *Houstoun's Trs.* (1868) 6 M. 286.

[3] *Pearson* v. *Houstoun's Trs.* (1868) 6 M. 286, 292, *per* Lord Neaves.

[4] *Sawer* (1873) 10 S.L.R. 249.

[5] *Bain* v. *Black* (1849) 11 D. 1286, 1310, *per* Lord Fullerton.

[6] *Hastie's J.F.* v. *Morham's Exors.*, 1951 S.C. 668; Prescription and Limitation (Scotland) Act 1973, ss. 7, 8, Sched. 3.

[7] Bell, *Prin.* s. 2000.

[8] *Dawson* v. *Stirton* (1863) 2 M. 196, 204, *per* Lord Cowan; *Moffat* v. *Kirk Session of Canonbie*, 1936 S.C. 209.

[9] *Town and County Bank Ltd.* v. *Walker* (1904) 12 S.L.T. 411, 412, *per* Lord Kyllachy.

It is a breach of trust to fail to carry out instructions [10] or to fail to pursue for recovery of a debt [11] or to convey part of the estate to a purchaser without receiving the price therefor.[12] While failure in business promptitude may easily turn into breach of trust, it is not necessarily and in all circumstances such.[13] Trustees were held not to have been negligent in failing to claim a tax repayment due to the trust by virtue of an English decision which was not averred to be widely known in Scotland.[14]

In *Hood* v. *Macdonald's Tr.*,[15] the testator provided in his will that his business was to " be put up for sale and first chance of it given to " A. It was further provided that if A could not find sufficient capital to purchase it was to be sold to the person " who gives the best price that can be accepted by my trustees." The trustees did not inform A of the provision and sold the business to another party. It was held without difficulty that this was relevantly averred as a breach of trust. It was indicated that the assessment of damages would be a more complex question and that it was possible that A would not be able to prove that he had suffered damage by the loss of the opportunity to purchase—he would have to show that he could have obtained the necessary capital and that the business would have been a lucrative profit-making subject.

The fact that the trustees acted or failed to act in ignorance of their duty is not material. " People who undertake a duty are bound to know what their duty requires." [16]

If his co-trustee is guilty of misconduct, a trustee is guilty of *culpa lata* if he does not prevent the co-trustee intromitting further with the funds and attempt to recover any sums misappropriated.[17] " A trustee is not entitled to purchase a quiet life at the expense of the estate, or to act as good-natured men sometimes do in their own affairs, in letting things slide and losing money rather than create ill-feeling." [18]

It will be an answer to an allegation of breach of trust that what was done was directed or permitted by the trust-deed.[19]

Beneficiaries who, as trustees, were parties to the breach of trust cannot hold their co-trustees liable.[20] An alimentary beneficiary has no power to homologate an unauthorised investment.[21]

A claim in respect of a breach of trust is subject to the long negative

[10] *Morrison* v. *Miller* (1827) 5 S. 322.
[11] *Forman* v. *Burns* (1853) 15 D. 362.
[12] *Thomson* v. *Christie* (1852) 1 Macq. 236.
[13] *Clarke* v. *Clarke's Trs.*, 1925 S.C. 693, 709, *per* L.P. Clyde. There is no rule that loss resulting from borrowing falls on the trustees (*Binnie* v. *Binnie's Trs.* (1889) 16 R.(H.L.) 23).
[14] *Free Church of Scotland* v. *MacKnight's Trs.*, 1916 S.C. 349.
[15] 1949 S.C. 24.
[16] *Ferguson* v. *Paterson* (1900) 2 F.(H.L.) 37, 40, *per* L.C. Halsbury.
[17] *Millar's Trs.* v. *Polson* (1897) 24 R. 1038.
[18] p. 1043, *per* L.P. Robertson.
[19] *Goodsir* v. *Carruthers* (1858) 20 D. 1141, 1145, *per* Lord Ardmillan.
[20] *Raes* v. *Meek* (1889) 16 R.(H.L.) 31. But see *Lees' Trs.* v. *Dun*, 1912 S.C. 50, in which it was held that the rights of a beneficiary who is also a trustee cannot be decided in an action to which he, as an individual, is not a party.
[21] *Sanders* v. *Sanders' Trs.* (1879) 7 R. 157.

prescription.[22] The prescription does apply to a claim against the representatives of a deceased trustee for a sum alleged to be due under the trust because that is a claim for debt and not for an accounting.[23] The positive prescription does not avail a trustee who has retained property in breach of trust. " No trustee of such an endowment as this can by any course of time prescribe a right to perpetuate a breach of trust." [24]

Enforcement of liability

The liability on the part of a former trustee should be enforced by the existing trustees, or, if there are none, by a judicial factor.[25] An individual beneficiary or creditor can sue only if the existing trustees refuse either to sue or to lend their names for the purpose of suing.[26]

The fact that the negligence of one of the existing trustees contributed towards the loss does not prevent them bringing an action for recovery against their predecessors because they are entitled to prosecute the action for behoof of the beneficiaries [27]: " a claim by the beneficiaries whose rights are being maintained, and can only be maintained, by the trustees now in office." [28]

> " The present action is not at the instance of the pursuers as individuals, for it has been dismissed so far as it was brought at the instance of individuals on the ground of no title. It is brought by them as administrators of the trust-estate, to recover trust-funds which, but for the negligence of the previous trustees, would now have been in the pursuers' possession. It might equally well have been brought at the instance of a judicial factor who had superseded the pursuers, and I can see no reason for holding that an action at the instance of such a factor would have been excluded because of the intervening negligence of the trustees whom he superseded." [29]

An action for breach of trust can be brought by only one of several beneficiaries but, as the action might be *res judicata* against the other beneficiaries, the dependence of the action should be intimated to them.[30]

In an action for breach of trust, it is competent to sue one or more of the trustees without calling all.[31] The liability is *ex delicto* or *ex quasi delicto*. The action need not be at the instance of the other trustees and

---

[22] *Barns* v. *Barns' Trs.*, (1857) 19 D. 626. See Prescription and Limitation (Scotland) Act 1973, ss. 7, 8, Sched. 3.

[23] *Murray* v. *Mackenzie* (1897) 34 S.L.R. 571.

[24] *University of Aberdeen* v. *Mags. of Aberdeen* (1876) 3 R. 1087, 1094, *per* L.P. Inglis.

[25] *Town and County Bank Ltd.* v. *Walker* (1904) 12 S.L.T. 411; *affd.* (1905) 13 S.L.T. 287.

[26] *Watt* v. *Roger's Trs.* (1890) 17 R. 1201. See *Sproat's J.F.* v. *McLellan* (1877) 14 S.L.R. 454.

[27] *Lees's Trs.* v. *Dun*, 1912 S.C. 50; 1913 S.C.(H.L.) 12.

[28] *Per* Lord Salvesen, 1912 S.C., 67, appvd. by Lord Shaw of Dunfermline, 1913 S.C.(H.L.) 14.

[29] *Per* Lord Salvesen, 1912 S.C. 66.

[30] *Allen* v. *McCombie's Trs.*, 1909 S.C. 710.

[31] *Allen* v. *McCombie's Trs.*, 1909 S.C. 710.

can be brought by the beneficiaries.[32] This does not affect any right of relief as between the trustees.[33]

Duty of care

The trustees must bring to the trust management the same care and diligence which a man of ordinary prudence may be expected to use in his own concerns—*secundum arbitrium boni viri*. It is not the law that, in the absence of any special dispensation by the truster, a gratuitous trustee's responsibility must be tested by reference to the degree of care and prudence which he uses in the management of his own private affairs.[34]

> " In applying this rule we must of course assume parallel cases. A prudent man of business may be a builder by profession, or a dealer in subjects which are more or less speculative, but which on the average of all his transactions yield him a profitable return. Such an illustration is evidently not at all to the point. We must suppose a prudent man desirous of placing a sum of money in a state of safe investment, such as will produce only the ordinary interest of a loan on heritable security." [35]

A trustee who is remunerated is expected to show a higher standard of diligence and knowledge than an unpaid trustee.[36]

Loans to trustees

Trustees cannot make a loan to one of their own number even if there is heritable security,[37] and even if he is a beneficiary.[38]

> " The lending of trust money by trustees to one of their own number is unquestionably an illegal proceeding. It is much more than a mere breach of trust in the ordinary sense, because such a breach of trust covers and includes small acts of negligence which may infer very little blame on the part of those concerned in them. But to lend trust money to one of their own number is an absolutely illegal proceeding. . . . No circumstances will justify such a proceeding, as it is quite *ultra vires* of any body of trustees so to act." [39]

Investments

If an *ultra vires* investment has been made, the beneficiaries have a right to demand that it should be immediately realised and invested in accordance with the provisions of the trust deed.[40]

If a profit has been made on the *ultra vires* investment it enures to all

---

[32] *Aitkenhead* v. *Oliver*, 1933 S.N. 18.

[33] *Croskery* v. *Gilmour's Trs.* (1890) 17 R. 697.

[34] *Knox* v. *Mackinnon* (1888) 15 R.(H.L.) 83; Stair, I,12,10. See *Kennedy* v. *Kennedy* (1884) 12 R. 275, 287, *per* L.J.-C. Moncreiff; *Buchanan* v. *Eaton*, 1911 S.C.(H.L.) 40, 55, *per* Lord Shaw.

[35] *Crabbe* v. *Whyte* (1891) 18 R. 1065, 1068, *per* Lord McLaren.

[36] *Re Waterman's Will Trusts* [1952] 2 All E.R. 1054.

[37] *Perston* v. *Perston's Trs.* (1863) 1 M. 245; *Templeton* v. *Burgh of Ayr*, 1912, 1 S.L.T. 421.

[38] *Ritchies* v. *Ritchie's Trs.* (1888) 15 R. 1086.

[39] *Croskery* v. *Gilmour's Trs.* (1890) 17 R. 697, 700, *per* L.P. Inglis.

[40] *Grant* v. *Baillie* (1869) 8 M. 77.

the beneficiaries in proportion to their respective interests.[40] The trustees are entitled to charge the expenses necessarily incurred in obtaining the profit.[41] Where there is a loss on the transaction as a whole the trustees are liable only for the net loss and can take credit for incidental profits received while the investment was held.[42]

If there has been a loss on an imprudent *ultra vires* investment the trustees must make good the deficit.[43] They must pay interest from the date of failure of the security at the rate obtainable on a safe investment and they cannot take into account the income received by the beneficiaries prior to the failure albeit that they had received a higher payment because of the hazardous nature of the security.[44]

If there has been a failure to invest, the trustees must debit themselves with the return which could have been obtained from a safe investment in the relevant period consistently with sound trust management.[45] This is not fixed by taking the lowest rate of return among those investments which were open to them.[45] They may take some credit in respect of the expenses of investment saved.[45]

Trustees who have lent funds to themselves are obliged to pay to the beneficiaries the highest rate of interest the trustees could presumably have made by the use of the trust money for their own purposes.[46] Where trustees use the trust-funds in their own business, they must account for the full profits made thereby and not merely for legal interest.[47]

Where trustees are liable to repay sums lost through negligence, they are also liable to pay simple, not compound, interest thereon.[48] A judicial factor appointed to supersede trustees can recover from them the capital of a sum lost to the estate because of *ultra vires* investment but he cannot recover interest where the trust income has been paid to a liferenter.[49]

Causation of loss

A trustee in default is not liable for a loss suffered by the estate which is not caused by his default but the *onus* is on him to show that loss has not resulted from the default.[50] If his fault is failure to pursue a debt he may be able to show that the debt could never have been recovered[50]; if he failed to take proper advice, he may be able to show that even if advice had been taken, the investment could still have been made and the loss would still have occurred.[51]

[41] *Currie* (1901) 9 S.L.T. 170.
[42] *Henderson* v. *Henderson's Trs.* (1900) 2 F. 1295.
[43] *Pollexfen* v. *Stewart* (1841) 3 D. 1215.
[44] *Learoyd* v. *Whiteley* (1887) 12 App. Cas. 727; *Boyd* v. *Greig*, 1913, 1 S.L.T. 398.
[45] *Melville* v. *Noble's Trs.* (1896) 24 R. 243. See *Malcolm's Exors.* v. *Malcolm* (1869) 8 M. 272.
[46] *Templeton* v. *Burgh of Ayr*, 1912, 1 S.L.T. 421.
[47] *Torrie* v. *Munsie* (1832) 10 S. 597; *Cochrane* v. *Black* (1855) 17 D. 321; (1857) 19 D. 1019; *Laird* v. *Laird* (1855) 17 D. 984; (1858) 20 D. 972.
[48] *Lees's Trs.* v. *Dun*, 1912 S.C. 50; 1913 S.C.(H.L.) 12.
[49] *Macfarlane's Trs.* v. *Macarthur* (1900) 8 S.L.T. 111.
[50] *Carruthers* v. *Cairns* (1890) 17 R. 769, 777, *per* Lord Kincairney; *Millar's Trs.* v. *Polson* (1897) 24 R. 1038.
[51] *Crabbe* v. *Whyte* (1891) 18 R. 1065, 1069, *per* Lord McLaren.

The principle was not applied in a rather special case where the trustees were prohibited by statute from purchasing local authority stocks at a price above the redemption value although purchase of the stock at par was allowed. The trustees purchased at a price over par but, under an arrangement with the liferenter, received payment of the premium from him. At the liferenter's death, the stock stood below par and the trustees were held liable to repay to the trust the difference between the redemption value and the price realised. The argument that the mischief struck at by the statute had not arisen was rejected; the investment was *ultra vires* and the loss thereby sustained had to be restored to the estate.[52]

The representatives of a deceased trustee are liable to make good a loss caused by improper investment even although he died some time before the loss occurred and the investment had been retained by the surviving trustee during that period.[53]

Advice

A trustee is not required to exercise personal judgment in matters of professional skill. He is entitled to act on the opinion of a conscientious and skilful valuator selected by himself as to the suitability of a security. If he does this and acts according to the best of his judgment he is not responsible for supervening loss.

> " But unless one examines with reference to what question the skilled person gives advice it is possible to confuse the reliance which may be properly placed upon the skill of a skilled person with the judgment which the trustee himself is bound to form on the subject of the performance of his trust." [54]

But even if he does not take advice and loss occurs, if he satisfies the court that he would have been advised to accept the investment he will not be held responsible for his negligence has not caused the loss.[55]

If the trust estate is large, the trustees should take legal advice and not rely on their own interpretation of legal terms.[56] The agent should not be employed outside the scope of his business.[57] A trustee is not entitled to rely on the advice of an agent who is also acting for the other party to the transaction.[58] Nor can he rely on general inquiries made by a co-trustee.[59] If the valuation has not been made on behalf of the trust the trustees should independently inquire into facts which upon the face of the valuation appear to call for investigation.[60]

---

[52] *Beveridge's Tr.* v. *Beveridge*, 1908 S.C. 791.

[53] *Duncan* v. *Newlands* (1882) 20 S.L.R. 8.

[54] *Learoyd* v. *Whiteley* (1887) 12 App. Cas. 727, 731, *per* L.C. Halsbury.

[55] *Crabbe* v. *Whyte* (1891) 18 R. 1065, 1068, *per* Lord McLaren.

[56] *Clarke* v. *Clarke's Trs.*, 1925 S.C. 693, 711, *per* L.P. Clyde.

[57] *Fry* v. *Tapson* (1884) 28 Ch.D. 268.

[58] *Knox* v. *Mackinnon* (1888) 15 R.(H.L.) 83, 87, *per* Lord Watson, p. 88, *per* Lord Macnaghten.

[59] *Alexander* v. *Johnstone* (1899) 1 F. 639.

[60] *Boyd* v. *Greig*, 1913, 1 S.L.T. 398. See also *Shaw* v. *Cates* [1909] 1 Ch. 389.

Sufficiency of security

The 1921 Act, s. 30, provides:

" (1) Any trustee lending money on the security of any property shall not be chargeable with breach of trust by reason only of the proportion borne by the amount of the loan to the value of such property at the time when the loan was made, provided that it shall appear to the court that in making such loan the trustee was acting upon a report as to the value of the property made by a person whom the trustee reasonably believed to be an able practical valuator instructed and employed independently of any owner of the property, whether such valuator carried on business in the locality where the property is situated or elsewhere, and that the amount of the loan by itself or in combination with any other loan or loans upon the property ranking prior to or pari passu with the loan in question does not exceed two equal third parts of the value of the property as stated in such report, and this section shall apply to a loan upon any property on which the trustees can lawfully lend.

(2) This section shall apply to transfers of existing securities as well as to new securities, and in its application to a partial transfer of an existing security the expression ' the amount of the loan ' shall include the amount of any other loan or loans upon the property ranking prior to or pari passu with the loan in question."

" The court " means any court of competent jurisdiction in which a question relative to the actings, liability or removal of a trustee comes to be tried.

The section grants relief to trustees and does not impose a duty upon them.[61] It has been said that the words " believed to be " do not govern " instructed and employed independently of any owner of the property " but there are expressions of the contrary opinion.[62]

The relation between the trustees and the valuator must be that of employer and employed so that the valuator looks for his remuneration only to the trustees and is responsible only to them for the due performance of his duty.[63] The trustees need not inquire whether the valuator has in the past acted for the owner of the property.[63] Where the valuator was suggested by the mortgagor, instructed by the mortgagor's solicitors, referred to the mortgagor both as to his fee and the properties he was to value, and was accompanied by the mortgagor when he made his survey, it was held that he was not independent.[64] The valuator's fee should not depend upon the transaction being carried through.[65] The report should state not only the actual value of the property but the proportion which, in

---

[61] *Palmer* v. *Emerson* [1911] 1 Ch. 758.
[62] *Re Somerset* [1894] 1 Ch. 231. *Cf. Re Stuart* [1897] 2 Ch. 583; *Re Solomon* [1912] 1 Ch. 261.
[63] *Re Solomon* [1912] 1 Ch. 261.
[64] *Shaw* v. *Cates* [1909] 1 Ch. 389.
[65] *Marquis of Salisbury* v. *Keymer* (1909) 25 T.L.R. 278.

the valuator's opinion, the trustees would in the particular case be justified in advancing, quite independently of the two-thirds proportion.[63] It is not correct that *prima facie* an advance of two-thirds of the value can be advised.[64] Each property must be treated separately.[64]

Section 29 of the 1921 Act provides that where a trustee has improperly advanced trust money on a heritable security which would, at the time of the investment, have been a proper investment in all respects for a less sum than was actually advanced thereon, the security shall be deemed an authorised investment for such less sum, and the trustee shall only be liable to make good the sum advanced in excess thereof with interest.

Acts of co-trustee

McLaren summarises the law by saying that trustees are liable for the obligations of their co-trustees " to the extent to which they have authorised them, either expressly or by acquiescence." [66]

In *Wilkins* v. *Hogg*,[67] Lord Westbury declared that there are three ways in which a trustee can become liable for the acts of his co-trustees:

   (a) where, having received trust assets, he hands them over to the co-trustees without securing their due application;

   (b) where he permits a co-trustee to receive assets and makes no inquiry as to their application;

   (c) when he becomes aware of a misapplication by his co-trustee and wilfully abstains from noticing it.

Trustees who signed a receipt for sums of money due to the trust estate but left the fund in the hands of one trustee for eight years without making inquiry as to its disposal were held to be guilty of gross negligence.[68] The result was different where the fund was entrusted to one trustee for immediate distribution [69] or in the ordinary course of management.[70]

Directors who were not present at the relevant meetings and did not sign the relevant documents were not held liable for a fraud perpetrated by their colleagues [71] and it is suggested that gratuitous trustees cannot have a greater liability [72]—*culpa tenet suos auctores*.

Trustees assumed seventeen years after the commencement of the trust were entitled to presume that their predecessors had completed title to an item of estate.[73]

   " It is impossible to hold that they were guilty of gross negligence in taking this for granted, in reference to such a fund as a policy of insurance, to which a title might be completed so easily, and to which

---

[66] II, 1217.
[67] (1861) 31 L.J.Ch. 41. See also *Kennedy* v. *Kennedy* (1884) 12 R. 275; *Millar's Trs.* v. *Polson* (1897) 24 R. 1038.
[68] *Sym* v. *Charles* (1830) 8 S. 741; *Moffat* v. *Robertson* (1834) 12 S. 369; *Blain* v. *Paterson* (1836) 14 S. 361; *Seton* v. *Dawson* (1841) 4 D. 310.
[69] *Urquhart* v. *Brown* (1843) 5 D. 1142. See also *McNair* v. *Broomfields* (1830) 8 S. 968.
[70] *Thomson* v. *Campbell* (1838) 16 S. 560.
[71] *Inglis* v. *Douglas* (1861) 23 D. 561.
[72] McLaren, II, 1220.
[73] *Scott* v. *Gray* (1862) 1 M. 57.

it was so necessary that it should be completed." [74] " There is a material difference between the position of trustees appointed at the original constitution of such a trust and that of trustees assumed or added to keep the trust going after an interval of time." [75]

Unless the contrary is expressed a trust is held to include a provision that each trustee shall be liable only for his own acts and intromissions and shall not be liable for those of his co-trustees and shall not be liable for omissions. [76] This is merely declaratory of the common law. [77]

Immunity clauses

A common form of immunity clause in trust deeds is:

" The said trustees shall not be answerable for errors, omissions, or neglect of diligence, nor for the insufficiency of securities, insolvency of debtors, or depreciation in the value of purchases, nor *singuli in solidum*, or for the intromissions of each other or of their factor, but each for his or her actual intromissions only."

A clause of this type does not give protection against a " positive breach of duty "—*crassa negligentia* or *culpa lata* or any conduct which is inconsistent with *bona fides*. [78] It may give some protection to trustees who have *bona fide* abstained from closely superintending the trust administration or " who have committed mere errors of judgment whilst acting with a single eye to the benefit of the trust and of the persons whom it concerns." [79]

It seems that a clause of this kind will not confer immunity where there has been imprudent investment [80]; or failure to consider the advisability of retaining an investment [81]; or a failure to invest. [82] Indeed, in one of the more recent cases, Lord President Clyde said: " It is difficult to imagine that any clause of indemnity in a trust settlement could be capable of being construed to mean that the trustees might with impunity neglect to execute their duty as trustees, in other words, that they were licensed to perform their duty carelessly." [83]

Where the clause read that " trustees shall not be liable for neglect of any sort, but only for actual intromissions," it was held that failure to secure payment of the price of a trust asset was an intromission for which

---

[74] p. 63, *per* L.J.-C. Inglis.

[75] p. 65, *per* Lord Neaves.

[76] 1921 Act, s. 3 (*d*), replacing Trusts (Scotland) Act 1861, s. 1.

[77] McLaren, II, 1219.

[78] *Seton* v. *Dawson* (1841) 4 D. 310, 318, *per* Lords Ivory, Gillies and Murray; *Knox* v. *Mackinnon* (1888) 15 R.(H.L.) 83; *Raes* v. *Meek* (1889) 16 R.(H.L.) 31; *Ferguson* v. *Paterson* (1900) 2 F.(H.L.) 37; *Carruthers* v. *Carruthers* (1896) 23 R.(H.L.) 55. See as to trustees for debenture holders, Companies Act 1948, s. 88. In *Rae* v. *Meek* (1888) 15 R. 1033, 1057, Lord Young said that there would be a great deal to be said for the indemnity clause but for the decisions. In *Inglis*, 1965 S.L.T. 326, L.P. Clyde said of such clauses " their inclusion only creates a false sense of security in the minds of the trustees."

[79] *Knox* v. *Mackinnon*, *supra*, p. 86, *per* Lord Watson.

[80] *Alexander* v. *Johnstone* (1899) 1 F. 639.

[81] *Clarke* v. *Clarke's Trs.*, 1925 S.C. 693.

[82] *Melville* v. *Noble's Trs.* (1896) 24 R. 243.

[83] *Clarke* v. *Clarke's Trs.*, *supra*, p. 707.

the trustee was liable.[84] If the result of the trustees' actings is the adoption of a course of administration which is authorised neither by the general law nor by the trust deed, this cannot be regarded as a mere omission.[85]

Where a clause in the general form contained the addition " they shall be liable for wilful default, and no further," it was held that to allow funds to remain in the hands of a debtor whose personal estate was worth nothing was a wilful failure of duty and it was said that this wording did not differ in effect from the clause in the more usual form.[86] The result was the same where the words were " wilful and intentional misdoings." [87]

" Wilful neglect or default " means that the person has consciously acted, or failed to act, in a reprehensible manner or has failed to give any consideration at all to the question of his duties or has acted recklessly and without caring whether he was fulfilling his duties or not.[88] The expression does not cover mere inadvertence or error of judgment.

The immunity from liability for the intromissions of a factor or agent extends only to the acts of a factor or agent properly appointed and acting within the legitimate scope of his agency. It does not cover actings of an agent whom the trustees have improperly allowed to retain trust funds in his hands.[89]

Statutory relief

The 1921 Act, s. 32 (1), provides:

> " If it appears to the court that a trustee is or may be personally liable for any breach of trust, whether the transaction alleged to be a breach of trust occurred before or after the passing of this Act, but has acted honestly and reasonably, and ought fairly to be excused for the breach of trust, then the court may relieve the trustee either wholly or partly from personal liability for the same." [90]

" The court " means any court of competent jurisdiction in which a question relative to the actings, liability or removal of a trustee comes to be tried. In order to give relief it is not necessary for the court to decide that the trustee is under any personal liability; it is sufficient that in the opinion of the court he may be under liability.[91]

It has been said that the application of the section is always a question of circumstances.[92] It is also a matter of discretion and an appellate court should be slow to reverse a decision on the question.[93] " Reasonably "

---

[84] *Thomson* v. *Christie* (1852) 1 Macq. 236.
[85] *Carruthers* v. *Carruthers* (1896) 23 R.(H.L.) 55.
[86] *Carruthers* v. *Cairns* (1890) 17 R. 769.
[87] *Wilson* v. *Guthrie Smith* (1894) 2 S.L.T. 338.
[88] *Re City Equitable Fire Insurance Co. Ltd.* [1925] Ch. 407; *Re Munton* [1927] 1 Ch. 262; *Re Vickery* [1931] 1 Ch. 572.
[89] *Ferguson* v. *Paterson* (1900) 2 F.(H.L.) 37; *Lees' Trs.* v. *Dun*, 1912 S.C. 50.
[90] The corresponding English provision is Trustee Act 1925, s. 61, which replaced Judicial Trustees Act 1896, s. 3. See also Companies Act 1948, s. 448.
[91] *Re Mackay* [1911] 1 Ch. 300.
[92] *Re Turner* [1897] 1 Ch. 536.
[93] *Marsden* v. *Regan* [1954] 1 W.L.R. 423.

means reasonably as trustees.[94] The onus of proof is on the trustee.[95] " The provisions of the section were intended to enable the Court to excuse breaches of trust where the circumstances of the particular case show reasonable conduct, but it was never meant to be used as a sort of general indemnity clause for honest men who neglect their duty." [96]

In considering whether trustees acted reasonably the court must look only at their conduct in regard to the particular matter which has given rise to the alleged breach of trust and not at their conduct of the trust administration as a whole.[97]

In considering reasonableness, any obscurity of the language of the trust deed and the smallness of the sum involved can be taken into account.[98] The fact that the trustee acted in exactly the same way with respect to his own money does not show that he acted reasonably—" the fact that he has acted with equal foolishness in both cases will not justify relief under this statute." [99] Where trustees had failed to consider the propriety of retaining an investment held by the testator and had left a large sum on deposit receipt, the court refused to grant relief under the section because the trustees could not be said to have acted reasonably.[1] Payment to the wrong person is a breach of a trust in respect of which relief can be given under the section,[2] as is an unauthorised sale of a trust asset.[3] Relief can be granted when the claim is by a creditor.[4]

A trustee was held not to have acted reasonably where " if he had with reasonable care considered the authority under which he was acting, he would have found that it did not authorise that which he was doing." [5] Failure to take advice or to seek directions from the court may be failure to act reasonably.[6] In considering reasonableness of actings relating to investment, the requirements of section 30 of the 1921 Act constitute a standard by which conduct is to be judged although failure to comply with them is not a fatal obstacle to relief.[7] It is not sufficient that the trustee has acted honestly and reasonably; if these facts are established the court must then proceed to consider if he ought fairly to be excused.[8]

Where a banker undertakes to act as a paid trustee of a settlement created by a customer, and so deliberately places himself in a position

[94] *Re Grindey* [1898] 2 Ch. 593, 601, *per* Chitty L.J.
[95] *Wynne* v. *Tempest* (1897) 13 T.L.R. 360.
[96] *Evans Williams* v. *Byron* (1901) 18 T.L.R. 172, 176, *per* Byrne J.
[97] *Palmer* v. *Emerson* [1911] 1 Ch. 758.
[98] *Re Grindey* [1898] 2 Ch. 593; *Re Mackay* [1911] 1 Ch. 300.
[99] *Re Lord De Clifford's Estate* [1900] 2 Ch. 707, 716, *per* Farwell J.
[1] *Clarke* v. *Clarke's Trs.*, 1925 S.C. 693. See also *Khoo Tek Keong* v. *Ch'ng Joo Tuan Neoh* [1934] A.C. 529, P.C.; *Breckney* v. *Nicol* (1942) 58 Sh.Ct.Rep. 133 (a trustee appointed under the Workmen's Compensation Acts).
[2] *Re Allsop* [1914] 1 Ch. 1.
[3] *Perrins* v. *Bellamy* [1899] 1 Ch. 797.
[4] *Re Kay* [1897] 2 Ch. 518.
[5] *Re Dive* [1909] 1 Ch. 328.
[6] *Chapman* v. *Browne* [1902] 1 Ch. 785; *Re Kay* [1897] 2 Ch. 518; *Re Windsor Steam Coal Co.* (1901) *Ltd.* [1929] 1 Ch. 151.
[7] *Re Stuart* [1897] 2 Ch. 583.
[8] *National Trustees Co. of Australasia Ltd.* v. *General Finance Co. of Australasia Ltd.* [1905] A.C. 373.

where his duty as trustee conflicts with his interest as a banker, the court should be slow to relieve such a trustee.[9]

In one case the Court of Appeal assumed without deciding that a liquidator could rely on the provision.[10]

Relief against beneficiary

A beneficiary at whose request or instigation the trustee committed a breach of trust cannot claim against the trustee in respect of the breach.[11]

Section 31 of the 1921 Act [12] provides:

" Where a trustee shall have committed a breach of trust at the instigation or request or with the consent in writing of a beneficiary, the court may, if it shall think fit, make such order as to the court shall seem just for applying all or any part of the interest of the beneficiary in the trust estate by way of indemnity to the trustee or person claiming through him."

" The court " is any court of competent jurisdiction in which a question relative to the actings, liability, or removal of a trustee comes to be tried.

The words " in writing " qualify only " consent " and not " instigation " or " request." [13] The subject of the request must be something which the beneficiary knows or ought to know is a breach of trust. Relief was not allowed where the beneficiary acquiesced in the retention of an improper investment but did so in reliance on the judgment of the trustees as to the investment being *intra vires* and prudent.[14] It must be something which is in itself a breach of trust and not merely something which becomes a breach because of the carelessness of the trustee.[15] The court is not bound to exercise its discretion.[16]

Relief against co-trustees

If a breach has been committed by several trustees and one has paid damages, he has a right of relief rateably against his co-trustees who were also in breach.[17] It may be possible for one trustee to obtain complete indemnity from another.[18]

---

[9] *Re Pauling's Settlement Trusts* [1964] Ch. 303. See also *National Trustees Co. of Australasia Ltd.* v. *General Finance Co. of Australasia Ltd.* [1905] A.C. 373.

[10] *Re Windsor Steam Coal Co.* (*1901*) *Ltd.* [1929] 1 Ch. 151. It has been suggested that a liferenter could take advantage of the section but *quaere* (*Fogo's J.F.* v. *Fogo,* 1929 S.C. 546, 555).

[11] *Raes* v. *Meek* (1889) 16 R.(H.L.) 31; *City of Glasgow Bank* v. *Parkhurst* (1880) 7 R. 749.

[12] Replacing Trusts (Scotland) Amendment Act 1891, s. 6. The corresponding English provision is Trustee Act 1925, s. 62, replacing Trustee Act 1888, s. 6.

[13] *Griffith* v. *Hughes* [1892] 3 Ch. 105.

[14] *Henderson* v. *Henderson's Trs.* (1900) 2 F. 1295. See also *Re Somerset* [1894] 1 Ch. 231.

[15] *Cathcart's Trs.* v. *Cathcart* (1907) 15 S.L.T. 646.

[16] *Henderson* v. *Henderson's Trs., supra.*

[17] *Pearson* v. *Houstoun's Trs.* (1868) 6 M. 286; *Croskery* v. *Gilmour's Trs.* (1890) 17 R. 697.

[18] *Bahin* v. *Hughes* (1886) 31 Ch.D. 390, 394, *per* Cotton L.J.

CHAPTER 26

LIABILITY TO THIRD PARTIES

QUESTIONS may arise as to whether trustees incur personal liability to third parties by their actings in the course of administration of the trust estate. The general principle is that, in the absence of express stipulation to the contrary, trustees are personally liable to parties with whom they transact. " Perhaps there are no funds of the bankrupt, but a third party has nothing to do with that." [1]

> " In regard to debts originating with the truster, and devolving on the trustees only by the force of the trust, there can be no doubt that trustees are bound only in their fiduciary character, consequently not *ultra valorem* of the trust estate. But, in regard to debts contracted by the trustees themselves, although it may be bona fide for the trust purposes, they will be personally bound to third parties, unless it appear clearly from the terms of the transaction that the creditor expressly took the trust-estate, as distinct from the individual trustees, as his debtor. In such cases it is held, and justly held, that the trustees who are supposed to know their own trust affairs, are bound to warrant the sufficiency of the trust-funds to the persons with whom they deal, and who have no such means of information." [2]

The existence of personal liability on the part of the trustees does not mean that the creditor cannot recover from the trust estate if the trustees are not themselves able to pay.[3] The liability of the trust estate is not restricted to the amount for which the trustees seek relief. Otherwise, the liability would be measured entirely by the solvency or insolvency, total or partial, of the trustees. The creditor can proceed against the whole estates of the trustees, including their rights of relief against the trust estate, and he can therefore compel the trustees to grant him an assignation of their rights against the estate and the beneficiaries, if any.

If the trustees are personally liable to repay advances made to them they are liable jointly and severally.[4]

Personal liability may be incurred through the actings of a servant or agent as where their factor has sold heritage [5] or their manager has drawn

---

[1] *Scott* v. *Patison* (1826) 5 S. 172, 173, *per* L.P. Hope. As a corollary, the other party to the contract cannot rely on limitations in the trust deed. It is *res inter alios acta* (*Dalgety's Trs.* v. *Drummond*, 1938 S.C. 709).

[2] *Cullen* v. *Baillie* (1846) 8 D. 511, 522, *per* Lord Fullerton.

[3] *Cuninghame* v. *Montgomerie* (1879) 6 R. 1333.

[4] *Commercial Bank of Scotland* v. *Sprot* (1841) 3 D. 939; *Oswald's Trs.* v. *City of Glasgow Bank* (1879) 6 R. 461, 466, *per* L.P. Inglis.

[5] *Thomas* v. *Walker's Trs.* (1832) 11 S. 162.

bills [6] or incurred debts.[7] Personal liability cannot be incurred through a co-trustee unless he was authorised to act on behalf of the trustees.[8]

Contracts

A trustee is personally liable on a contract which he has made with a third party unless there is an express or implied agreement that only the trust estate is to be liable.[9]

" By the law of England, as by the law of Scotland, trustees in dealing with third persons may so contract as to exempt themselves from personal responsibility, and to confine those with whom they are dealing to such relief as they can obtain from the trust-funds; whether this is the true effect of any contract into which they are entering, must in every case be a question of construction. . . . The true question to be resolved in every case is, whether the circumstances do fairly shew that the contracting parties were dealing only as trustees, and were not intending to incur liability beyond the amount of the trust funds." [10]

" Whether in any particular case the contract of an executor or trustee is one which binds himself personally, or is to be satisfied only out of the estate of which he is the representative, is, as it seems to me, a question of construction, to be decided with reference to all the circumstances of the case, the nature of the contract, the subject-matter on which it is to operate, and the capacity and duty of the parties to make the contract in the one form or in the other. I know of no reason why an executor, either under English or Scotch Law, entering into a contract for payment of money with a person who is free to make the contract in any form he pleases, should not stipulate by apt words that he will make the payment, not personally, but out of the assets of the testator. If, for example, AB, the executor of X, contracted to make a payment as executor of X, and as executor only, to CD, it would be difficult to suppose that any obligation except an obligation to pay out of the testator's assets was intended." [11]

The use of the word " trustee " in the contract is not in itself sufficient to prevent personal liability. The word may have been used descriptively.

" Whenever a man means to bind another and not himself he should take care to say so. I think this is never to be implied. Even if a trust character is mentioned it will be held in general that this is merely descriptive of the obligant, but does not exempt him from personal liability." [12]

---

[6] *Murray & McGregor* v. *Campbell* (1827) 6 S. 147.
[7] *Macphail & Son* v. *Maclean's Tr.* (1887) 15 R. 47; *Ford & Sons* v. *Stephenson* (1888) 16 R. 24.
[8] *Higgins* v. *Livingstone* (1816) 6 Paton's App.Cas. 243.
[9] *Jeffrey* v. *Brown* (1824) 2 Shaw's App.Cas. 349.
[10] *Lumsden* v. *Buchanan* (1865) 3 M.(H.L.) 89, 95, *per* Lord Cranworth.
[11] *Muir* v. *City of Glasgow Bank* (1879) 6 R.(H.L.) 21, 22, *per* Lord Cairns L.C.
[12] *Brown* v. *Sutherland* (1875) 2 R. 615, 621, *per* Lord Gifford.

On the other hand, " as trustees " or " *qua* trustees " will normally suffice
to elide personal liability. Trustees who in a bond bound themselves as
trustees and their successors as trustees were held not to have incurred
personal liability [13]—" The style and form of words adopted throughout
the instrument were such as properly belong to a dealing in a fiduciary
character alone." [14]

The solicitors to the trust are in an exceptional position.

" For they have notice of everything. They are, or are presumed
to be, conversant not only with the terms of the trust-deed, but with
the whole circumstances of the trust-estate, its amount, the claims
upon it, actual or anticipated, and the results, probable or possible, of
unsuccessful litigations. They are not, therefore, in the position of
tradesmen or other persons employed in the ordinary course of the
trust management. Unlike such ordinary employees, they cannot, if
the trust funds prove inadequate, proceed against the trustee personally on the ground of his implied warranty of the adequacy of the
trust funds. On the contrary, knowing all that the trustee knows, they
are held, with respect to their charges, to take their chance of recovering from the trust-estate." [15]

A trustee who becomes a creditor of the trust is also in a special
position as he knows the value of the estate and he therefore cannot hold
his co-trustees personally liable.[16]

Particular contracts

If the document is a bill or other negotiable instrument, the signatures
bind the parties as individuals unless they are expressly qualified.[17]

" Where a person signs a bill as drawer, indorser, or acceptor, and
adds words to his signature, indicating that he signs . . . in a representative character, he is not personally liable thereon; but the mere
addition to his signature of words describing him . . . as filling a
representative character, does not exempt him from personal liability." [18] " In the case of a commercial document like a bill or
promissory-note, which passes freely from hand to hand, it is a
reasonable requirement that, if the actual signatory is to bind a third
party and not himself, the obligation should unambiguously bear that
meaning." [19]

In contracts for the supply of goods or services, the presumption is
that the trustees are personally liable. As McLaren points out,[20] they know

---

[13] *Gordon* v. *Campbell* (1842) 1 Bell's App.Cas. 428.
[14] *Lumsden* v. *Buchanan* (1865) 3 M.(H.L.) 89, 93, *per* Lord Westbury L.C.
[15] *Ferme, Ferme & Williamson* v. *Stephenson's Tr.* (1905) 7 F. 902, 905, *per* Lord Kyllachy.
[16] *Cullen* v. *Baillie* (1846) 8 D. 511, 522, *per* Lord Fullerton.
[17] *Brown* v. *Sutherland* (1875) 2 R. 615. See also *Eaton* v. *Macgregor's Exors.* (1837) 15 S. 1012.
[18] Bills of Exchange Act 1882, s. 26 (1).
[19] *Brebner* v. *Henderson*, 1925 S.C. 643, 647, *per* L.P. Clyde.
[20] II, 1333.

the value of the trust estate which forms their security but the other party
does not.

Trustees who carried on an omnibus business were held personally
liable to a passenger injured by the negligence of a driver employed by
them because the claim arose out of a contract of carriage with regard to
which they had not given due notice that any liability attaching to them
would be limited to that of persons acting in the capacity of trustees.[21]

A trustee in a sequestration who continued to trade with a ship which
formed an asset of the estate was held liable to a cargo-owner for breach of
a contract of carriage.[22]

Warrandice

Trustees who have contracted to sell heritage *qua* trustees can be
required only to give warrandice from their own facts and deeds.[23] If they
have not contracted as trustees, they must grant absolute warrandice.[24]
Warrandice from fact and deed infers a protection against eviction by
reason of the granter's own act or omission, past or future.[25] A party who
has given as trustee warrandice from fact and deed cannot do as an individual what he could not do as a trustee. So a trustee who had let a farm
could not make alterations on an adjacent estate owned by him as an
individual which would injuriously affect the subjects let.[26] Where a disposition was granted "as trustee" and contained the clause "I grant
warrandice," the trustee was held to be bound in warrandice from fact and
deed and it was suggested that he might be personally liable in absolute
warrandice.[27] In the sale of debts, trustees must, in the absence of express
stipulation, warrant the subsistence of the debt.[28]

Calls on shares [29]

If trustees are entered on the register of a company they are personally
liable for calls on the shares held.[30] This is so even if they appear on the
register "as trustees." Any limitation of liability for calls would be inconsistent with the principles of the Companies Acts. If trustees do not wish
to incur liability they should merely intimate their title to the company so

[21] *Johnston* v. *Waddell*, 1928 S.N. 81.
[22] *Mackessack & Son* v. *Molleson* (1886) 13 R. 445.
[23] *Forbes's Trs.* v. *McIntosh* (1822) 1 S. 535. McLaren (II, 1332) points out that this rule rests
on usage.
[24] *Mackenzie* v. *Neill* (1899) 37 S.L.R. 666.
[25] *Horsbrugh's Trs.* v. *Welch* (1886) 14 R. 67.
[26] *Hill* v. *Kinloch* (1856) 18 D. 722.
[27] *Horsbrugh's Trs.* v. *Welch, supra.*
[28] McLaren, II, 1332.
[29] For a full discussion of this topic, which is not now of great practical importance, see
McLaren, II, 1343–1350.
[30] *Buchan* v. *City of Glasgow Bank* (1879) 6 R.(H.L.) 44. See also *Wishart* v. *City of Glasgow
Bank* (1879) 6 R. 1341, 1349, per Lord Shand; *Elliot* v. *Mackie & Sons*, 1935 S.C. 81;
Companies Act 1948, s. 76, Sched. I, Table A, Arts. 29–32. The company has no right of
lien or retention over the shares for a debt due by the beneficiary (*Robertson* v. *General
Accident Assurance Corpn. Ltd.* (1905) 21 Sh.Ct.Rep. 339).

that they are not entered on the register and they will then be allowed a reasonable time in which to dispose of the holding.

The solicitor of the trust has no implied authority to have the trustees' names placed on the register and, if he does this without authority, the trustees can subsequently petition to have their names removed.[31]

Partnership

Trustees who purchased shares in a trading partnership without expressly limiting their liability by special stipulation were held personally liable in the liquidation.[32] In the nature of the contract of partnership, a trustee cannot become a partner in such a way as to restrict his liability to third parties for the partnership debts but he can restrict his liability to his co-partners by using appropriate terms.[33]

Truster's contracts

Where the truster was party to a continuing contract, such as a lease, a question may arise as to whether the trustee incurs personal liability for any of the truster's outstanding obligations thereunder. The principle is that the trustee incurs personal liability under the contract only if he adopts it. If the trustee adopts a lease he becomes personally liable to fulfil the conditions thereof [34] and, in particular, he becomes personally liable for the arrears of rent,[35] unless the landlord has expressly or impliedly waived his claim.[36]

It may be difficult to determine whether a trustee has adopted a lease or is merely intromitting with the subjects for the purpose of winding up the lease.[37] In the absence of agreement, the question must be decided by examining the conduct of the parties.[38] A trustee by raising an action, founded on a contract, in which he is unsuccessful because he is not prepared to implement the obligations under the contract, does not adopt the contract so as to become personally liable thereon.[39]

Delicts

Trustees who carry on a business will be personally liable in respect of delicts committed by them or by their servants or agents in the course of

---

[31] Stott v. City of Glasgow Bank (1879) 6 R. 1126; Wishart v. City of Glasgow Bank (1879) 6 R. 1341.

[32] Lumsden v. Buchanan (1865) 3 M.(H.L.) 89. See also Muir v. City of Glasgow Bank (1879) 6 R.(H.L.) 21.

[33] Lumsden v. Buchanan (1864) 2 M. 695. There may be a question as to whether trustees were partners of a business—Morrison (1870) 8 M. 500.

[34] Ross v. Monteith (1786) Mor. 15290; Nisbet & Co.'s Tr. (1802) Mor. 15268; Gibson v. Kirkland and Sharpe (1833) 6 W. & S. 340; Bertram v. Guild (1880) 7 R. 1122; Sturrock v. Robertson's Tr., 1913 S.C. 582, 586; Campbell Paton and Cameron, Law of Landlord and Tenant in Scotland, 185–186, 195–197.

[35] Dundas v. Morison (1857) 20 D. 225.

[36] Maclean's Tr. v. Maclean of Coll's Tr. (1850) 13 D. 90.

[37] McGavin v. Sturrock's Tr. (1891) 18 R. 576; Imrie's Tr. v. Calder (1897) 25 R. 15.

[38] Taylor's Tr. v. Paul (1888) 15 R. 313.

[39] Sturrock v. Robertson's Tr., 1913 S.C. 582.

the business.[40] If trustees induced the purchase of shares by means of fraudulent statements, they would be personally liable in damages.[41]

Form of summons

If an action is brought against trustees in which they are cited " as trustees," the decree can only be against them as trustees and they cannot be made personally liable.[42] Decree for payment of a principal sum can pass only under the conclusions of the summons. The position with regard to expenses is different.

Litigation

It is a question of circumstances whether a trustee who litigates unsuccessfully with a stranger to the trust is personally liable for the expenses of the successful party.[43] In this matter the form of the summons is not conclusive and persons who are cited as trustees can be found personally liable for the expenses.[44]

A decree for expenses against an individual " as trustee " or " qua trustee " cannot be construed so as to make him personally liable.[45] If a majority of trustees decide to defend an action, the minority can avoid liability for expenses by lodging a minute of disclamation.[46]

If the trustee sists himself as a party to an action against the deceased and is unsuccessful he is personally liable in expenses, not because he has adopted the contract of litiscontestation (" this so-called contract is a mere legal fiction for which no doubt there is respectable authority "), but because he has elected to sist himself as a party and so must incur all the risks of an ordinary litigant.[47] He becomes liable for the expenses incurred by the other party before, as well as after, he has sisted himself.[48] He must sist himself unconditionally or not at all.[49]

A finding of expenses against trustees carries liability against the trust-estate.[50]

[40] McLaren II, 1342; *Mulholland* v. *Macfarlane's Trs.*, 1928 S.L.T. 251.
[41] This was assumed in *Allan* v. *Wright* (1853) 15 D. 725.
[42] *Mulholland* v. *Macfarlane's Trs.*, 1928 S.L.T. 251. As to sequestration of persons *qua* trustees, see *J. & W. Campbell & Co.* (1899) 6 S.L.T. 406; and *Bain* (1901) 9 S.L.T. 14.
[43] *Barrie* v. *Barrie's Tr.*, 1933 S.C. 132. In *Gorrie's Tr.* v. *Stiven's Exrx.*, 1952 S.C. 1, expenses in the Inner House were awarded against the trustee personally. *Cf. Craig* v. *Hogg* (1896) 24 R. 6.
[44] *Mitchell* v. *Baird* (1902) 4 F. 809; *Mulholland* v. *Macfarlane's Trs.*, 1928 S.L.T. 251.
[45] *Beadie* v. *Carr* (1850) 12 D. 1069; *Craig* v. *Hogg* (1896) 24 R. 6.
[46] *Fairlie* v. *Fairlie's Trs.* (1903) 11 S.L.T. 51.
[47] *Sturrock* v. *Robertson's Tr.*, 1913 S.C. 582.
[48] *Torbet* v. *Borthwick* (1849) 11 D. 694.
[49] *Sandeman* v. *Shepherd* (1835) 13 S. 1037.
[50] *Merrilees* v. *Leckie's Trs.*, 1908 S.C. 576.

CHAPTER 27

REIMBURSEMENT

THE trustee has a right to be reimbursed in respect of all expenses properly incurred by him in the administration of the estate. "The contract between the author of a trust and his trustees entitles the trustees, as between themselves and their *cestuis que trust*, to receive out of the trust estate all their proper costs incident to the execution of the trust." [1] So, for example, they are entitled to reimbursement in respect of travelling expenses properly incurred [2]; calls on shares held by the trust [3]; claims for damages incurred in the conduct of a business forming part of the trust-estate [4]; in the case of a trustee for creditors, the costs of completing an executory contract [5]; costs incurred in opposing a private Bill which affected the trust-estate.[6] They are also entitled to reimbursement of the fees of solicitors and other agents properly employed by them.[7]

If a private trust is superseded by a sequestration or the appointment of a judicial factor, the private trustee has a right of retention of the trust-estate for his necessary outlay in the fair administration of the trust. An agent employed by the trust should make his claim against his employer, the private trustee, who in turn will obtain payment by exercising his right of retention. Once the estate has been handed over without reservation, it seems that the private trustee is entitled only to an ordinary ranking.[8]

Trustees may be reimbursed for expenditure incurred after they have resigned. Marriage-contract trustees, after they had resigned and a judicial factor had been appointed on the estate, were entitled to retain the extra-judicial expenses incurred by them in successfully defending an action brought by the judicial factor in which they had to account for their intromissions.[9] Expenditure incurred before the trustee's appointment can be reimbursed.[10]

The trustees are entitled to relief before they have made payment. Lord President Inglis, after opining that a trustee was a mandatary, said:

" There can be no doubt whatever that the mandant is bound to relieve his mandatary not only of all expenses incurred by him in

---

[1] *Cotterell* v. *Stratton* (1872) L.R. 8 Ch.App. 295, 302, *per* Lord Selborne L.C., cited by Lord Hunter, *Jackson* v. *Jackson's Trs.*, 1918, 1 S.L.T. 119, 120.
[2] *Young* v. *Naval etc. Society of South Africa Ltd.* [1905] 1 K.B. 687. *Cf. Malcolm* v. *O'Callaghan* (1837) 3 Myl. & Cr. 52.
[3] *Cuningham* v. *Montgomerie* (1879) 6 R. 1333.
[4] *Benett* v. *Wyndham* (1862) 4 De G.F. & J. 259; *Re Raybould* [1900] 1 Ch. 199.
[5] *Thomson* v. *Tough's Tr.* (1880) 7 R. 1035.
[6] *Re Ormrod's Settled Estate* [1892] 2 Ch. 318; *Re Nicoll's Estates* [1878] W.N. 154.
[7] *Goodsir* v. *Carruthers* (1858) 20 D. 1141.
[8] *MacGregor* v. *MacLennan's Tr.* (1898) 25 R. 482.
[9] *Erentz's Trs.* v. *Erentz's J.F.* (1897) 25 R. 53.
[10] Underhill, 596; *Re Dee Estates Ltd.* [1911] 2 Ch. 85.

the execution of his mandate, but of all liability incurred by him in the exercise of his powers as mandatary, and in the administration of the affairs of the mandant, and this obligation of relief on the part of the mandant may be enforced not merely upon the occasion of each payment that the mandatary is compelled to make on behalf of the mandant, but if any liability has been incurred by the mandatary in the due execution of his power, and if liability is threatened to be enforced against him, he is quite entitled to fall back upon the mandant's obligation of relief and demand that he shall stand between him and the creditor who is demanding the performance of this obligation. It is not mere reimbursement of money spent that the mandatary is entitled to have, but it is relief of obligation." [11]

The trustee is not entitled to interest, except, possibly, where interest was running on the claim which he paid.[12]

There is no right of relief in respect of an obligation undertaken as a beneficiary and not as a trustee.[13] If a trustee is remunerated he cannot be reimbursed for expenditure which the remuneration is intended to cover.[14]

The trustee is entitled to retain the estate until he has been reimbursed and his claim is preferred to those of creditors and beneficiaries.[15]

Funds liable

If part of the trust fund has been lawfully appropriated to a particular provision, the trustees cannot obtain relief from that part in respect of a liability arising from the remainder of the fund.[16]

Reimbursement cannot as a general rule be sought outwith the trust estate.

" The trustee voluntarily accepts the trust, and can only incur liability in consequence of his own act in so accepting; unless there be an express or implied bargain for indemnity from the maker of the trust, he must be taken to accept the trust, relying on the trust-funds. He has, no doubt, a right to charge the trust-funds with all just allowances." [17]

In England, a beneficiary under a simple trust who is *sui juris* has been placed under obligation to indemnify the trustee against calls on shares.[18] But the beneficiary must either have created the trust himself or have

---

[11] *Cuningham* v. *Montgomerie* (1879) 6 R. 1333, 1337. See, as to the extent to which the potential liability has to be established, *Hughes-Hallett* v. *Indian Mammoth Gold Mines Co.* (1882) 22 Ch.D. 561.

[12] *Wilson* v. *Smith's Trs.*, 1939 S.L.T. 120; *Re Beulah Park Estate* (1872) L.R. 15 Eq. 43; *Finch* v. *Pescott* (1874) L.R. 17 Eq. 554.

[13] *Henderson* v. *Norrie* (1866) 4 M. 691.

[14] *Young* v. *Naval etc. Society of South Africa Ltd.* [1905] 1 K.B. 687.

[15] *MacGregor* v. *MacLennan's Tr.* (1898) 25 R. 482; Bell, *Comm.*, II, 117.

[16] *Robinson* v. *Fraser's Tr.* (1881) 8 R.(H.L.) 127.

[17] *Robinson* v. *Fraser's Tr.* (1881) 8 R.(H.L.) 127, 135, *per* Lord Blackburn.

[18] *Hardoon* v. *Belilios* [1901] A.C. 118; *Robinson* v. *Fraser's Tr.* (1881) 8 R.(H.L.) 127, 134, *per* Lord Blackburn.

accepted a transfer of the beneficial interest with full knowledge of the facts.[19]

If the testator directs the trustees to employ only a specific portion of the estate for the purpose of carrying on the testator's business, the trustee's indemnity in respect of debts incurred in carrying on the business is restricted to these specific assets.[20]

Where trustees carry on the testator's business, they are entitled to indemnification from the estate in respect of the liabilities they incur in the conduct of the business but not in priority to the creditors of the testator at death [21] unless such creditors have assented to the continuance of the business.[22]

A trustee who has paid insurance premiums out of his own pocket may have a lien over the policy to the extent that the estate is *lucratus* by the expenditure but he cannot demand that the policy should be surrendered prematurely in order to reimburse him.[23]

Trustees of a club who have incurred liabilities on its behalf are entitled to indemnity out of the club's property but they have no right of relief against the club members. An ordinary club is formed on the tacit understanding that no member as such becomes liable to pay to its funds or otherwise any money beyond the subscriptions required by its rules.[24]

Expenses of litigation

Trustees are entitled to reimbursement of the expenses of litigation properly incurred.

> " I think that trustees are, as a rule, very much harassed and bullied by beneficiaries and courts of law and everybody else, but fortunately they have this decided in their favour that if they expend money in litigation in the discharge of their duty as trustees, they are entitled to take their expenses out of the trust if they are successful, or even if they are unsuccessful." [25]

The right to reimbursement is not dependent upon success in the litigation.

> " It is always understood that where trustees, acting in the discharge of their duty, litigate in the name of the trust-estate and for the protection of the interests of the trust, they are entitled to charge the trust with the account for expenses, upon the principle that representative persons are entitled to the costs necessarily incurred in the interests of their constituents. It would, I think, be unfair that their right should depend upon the circumstances of their being successful

---

[19] Underhill, 600. *Cf. City of Glasgow Bank* v. *Parkhurst* (1880) 7 R. 749.
[20] *Re Johnson* (1880) 15 Ch.D. 548.
[21] *Re Oxley* [1914] 1 Ch. 604.
[22] As in *Dowse* v. *Gorton* [1891] A.C. 190.
[23] *Brown* v. *Meek's Trs.* (1896) 4 S.L.T. 46.
[24] *Wise* v. *Perpetual Trustee Co. Ltd.* [1903] A.C. 139, J.C.
[25] *Wemyss* v. *Kennedy* (1906) 14 S.L.T. 237, 238, *per* Lord Ardwall. See also *Johnstone* v. *Beattie* (1856) 18 D. 343, 349.

in the litigation; and if such a rule were established, I imagine that it would be difficult to find persons willing to become trustees." [26] " The general rule is, that they are never to litigate with such gross unreasonableness as implies a disregard of their duty. But, in judging whether they have actually done so or not, we can rarely determine merely from the result. A reasonable action may have an unfortunate issue. We must look to the whole circumstances. And where a trustee, though not perhaps proceeding with perfect wisdom, appears, upon the whole, to have acted substantially according to his warrant, and with a sincere desire to do right, a court is not called upon to visit him personally with loss which his honest and reasonable view of his duty may have occasioned to the estate." [27]

If the trustees acted in good faith and there was " a fair question for discussion," they are entitled to their expenses although they were wrong in law.[28]

A trustee under a marriage-contract trust who had unsuccessfully resisted an action at the instance of the spouses calling on him to denude the estate was allowed his expenses from the estate—he was " doing nothing but his duty." [29]

If trustees enter into a litigation on counsel's advice that is normally enough to entitle them to reimbursement.[30] " Really, if trustees cannot go to the Dean of Faculty and follow his advice without having it afterwards said that they have done something improper and must forfeit their expenses and pay personally, nobody would be a trustee at all." [31]

It is in favour of the trustees getting their expenses that they entered the litigation to defend the interests of minors, or insane or absent persons.[32]

In England, trustees have been given the costs of intervening in a petition for a declaration of legitimacy brought by a person who, if he had been declared legitimate, would have had an interest in the estate [33]; and the costs of a litigation which has been abandoned.[34]

The expenses of an appeal may raise a different issue. Where there is a question between the trustees and a beneficiary, the trustees should normally abide by the decision of the court of first instance which in itself gives them protection.[35] In questions with third parties, the trustees should take and follow counsel's opinion as to whether an appeal should be taken.

If the trustees do not see that they are in safety in defending an action,

[26] *Gibson* v. *Caddall's Trs.* (1895) 22 R. 889, 893, *per* Lord McLaren.
[27] *Cameron* v. *Anderson* (1844) 7 D. 92, 103, *per* Lord Cockburn.
[28] *Gibson* v. *Caddall's Trs.* (1895) 22 R. 889.
[29] *Laidlaws* v. *Newlands* (1884) 11 R. 481.
[30] *Buckle* v. *Kirk* (1908) 15 S.L.T. 1002.
[31] *Per* L.P. Dunedin at p. 1004.
[32] *Craig* v. *Hogg* (1896) 24 R. 6, 20, *per* Lord McLaren. See also *McLauchlan* v. *McLauchlan's Trs.*, 1941 S.L.T. 43.
[33] *Cleave* v. *Att.-Gen.* [1952] W.N. 346.
[34] *Re Wilkie's Settlement* [1914] 1 Ch. 77.
[35] *Stewart* v. *Bruce's Trs.* (1898) 25 R. 965.

they can ask the beneficiaries to furnish them with funds if they wish the action to be defended.[36] But there is no obligation on trustees to take this course.[37] In the case of a public trust, where the beneficiaries cannot be called on in this way, the trustees may have a higher duty to defend.

A minority of trustees who do not wish to incur the expenses of an action which is being defended by a majority should disclaim the defence.[38]

Defence of the trust deed

It is a question of circumstances whether testamentary trustees who have unsuccessfully defended the trust deed in an action of reduction will be allowed their expenses out of the estate.[39] An important factor is whether the character of the trustees has been impugned.

> " While I am far from wishing to countenance the idea that when a will is challenged trustees are entitled to defend at the expense of the trust-estate no matter what the circumstances may be, there is one consideration which will weigh with the Court, and it is this, ' What is said about the trustees ? ' "[40]

Trustees who successfully defended their characters were allowed expenses from the estate although the will was reduced on another ground.[41]

Trustees who unsuccessfully defended an action of reduction of the testamentary deed were allowed the expenses up to the date of the verdict from the trust estate but not the expenses of a motion to set aside the verdict.[42] Trustees who were accessory to impetrating the deed which has been reduced will not be allowed expenses.[43] Where a trust deed was reduced at the instance of creditors on the ground that it contravened an antenuptial marriage-contract, the trustees under the deed were refused their expenses from the estate, apparently on the ground that by accepting the trust they had endeavoured to perpetrate a wrong against the creditors.[44] On the other hand, trustees who defend the trust against the maker of the deed are normally allowed expenses from the estate.[45]

Construction of the deed

If the difficulty giving rise to the litigation was created by the testator himself, the expenses should be borne by the estate.[46] " Where the question arises as to the meaning of the trust-deed, and is fairly brought before

[36] *Graham* v. *Marshall* (1860) 23 D. 41; *Crichton* v. *Henderson's Trs.* (1898) 1 F. 24.
[37] *Barrie* v. *Barrie's Tr.*, 1933 S.C. 132.
[38] Menzies, 760.
[39] *Watson* v. *Watson's Trs.* (1875) 2 R. 344. See also *Watt* v. *Watson* (1897) 24 R. 330; *Crichton* v. *Henderson's Trs.* (1898) 1 F. 24; *Sutherland* v. *Hamilton's Trs.*, 1917, 2 S.L.T. 173. *Cf. Mags. of Leith* v. *Leith Dock Commissioners* (1899) 1 F.(H.L.) 65, 68, *per* Lord Watson.
[40] *Merrilees* v. *Leckie's Trs.*, 1908 S.C. 576, 579, *per* L.P. Dunedin.
[41] *Ross* v. *Ross's Trs.* (1898) 25 R. 897.
[42] *Munro* v. *Strain* (1874) 1 R. 1039.
[43] *Watson* v. *Watson's Trs.* (1875) 2 R. 344.
[44] *Graham* v. *Marshall* (1860) 23 D. 41.
[45] *Watt* v. *Watson* (1897) 24 R. 330; *Stevenson* v. *Stevenson's Trs.* (1905) 13 S.L.T. 457.
[46] *Hickling's Trs.* v. *Garland's Trs.* (1898) 1 F.(H.L.) 7, 22.

the Court, we are entitled to deal with the expenses as we would in ordinary actions, and make the testator's estates pay for the ambiguities to which this trust-deed has given rise." [47] Trustees seeking guidance as to what the testamentary instruments consisted of would be entitled to expenses even although they were unsuccessful in the view maintained by them. [48]

Formal appearance

It may be proper in certain cases for the trustees to appear only for the purpose of stating the facts known to them and explaining that they have no interest in the decision. [49] In applications under the 1921 Act the court must determine all questions of expenses and may direct that the expenses shall be paid out of the trust estate where the court considers this reasonable. [50] Trustees who appeared to state their position with regard to, but did not oppose, a petition on behalf of minor beneficiaries for advances out of income were allowed the expenses of appearance. [51] If trustees are called as defenders for their interest and enter appearance formally the pursuer ought to inform them if he does not intend to proceed further against them. [52] A trustee may be allowed watching fees to enable him to be present at every stage of a litigation and to consider whether overt intervention is necessary. [53] Expenses of a petition to appoint new trustees where the trust has become unworkable will be allowed. [54]

Refusal of expenses

Expenses may be refused where trustees " from over-scrupulousness or obstinacy, engage in litigation, occasioning great and unnecessary expense which it would be unjust to impose on those holding the beneficial interest in the trust," [55] or display in the conduct of the case " an animus unnecessary for any legitimate object which they could have in view." [56] An executor who conducted litigation unreasonably, as, for example, by proponing defences which he must have known to be untrue, was found personally liable in expenses. [57] Expenses will not be allowed if the action was of a speculative nature [58] or concerned a matter which could have been raised in a process already in court [59] or if the trustees were intervening in a dispute between beneficiaries with which they were not concerned.

---

[47] *Wright's Trs.* (1870) 8 M. 708, 713, *per* Lord Cowan. See also *Grieve's Trs.* v. *Bethune* (1830) 8 S. 896; *Rigg* v. *Ramsay* (1836) 14 S. 472; *Ramsay's Trs.* v. *Ramsay* (1876) 4 R. 243; *Tennent* v. *Dunsmure* (1878) 6 R. 150; *Hamilton's Trs.* v. *Hamilton* (1879) 6 R. 1216; *Whyte* v. *Hamilton* (1881) 8 R. 940; *Brooks* v. *Brooks's Trs.* (1902) 4 F. 1014, 1045.
[48] *Fairbairn* v. *Neville* (1897) 25 R. 192, 211.
[49] *Buckle* v. *Kirk* (1908) 15 S.L.T. 1002.
[50] s. 34.
[51] *Edmiston* v. *Miller's Trs.* (1871) 9 M. 987.
[52] *Paterson's J.F.* v. *Paterson's Trs.* (1897) 24 R. 499, 510.
[53] *Martin & Co.* v. *Hunter's Tr.* (1897) 25 R. 125.
[54] *Aikman* (1881) 9 R. 213.
[55] *Smith* v. *Telford* (1838) 16 S. 1223. See also *Farquharson* v. *King* (1823) 2 S. 230; *Re England's Settlement Trusts* [1918] 1 Ch. 24.
[56] *Morrison* v. *Morrison's Trs.* (1848) 11 D. 297.
[57] *Law* v. *Humphrey* (1876) 3 R. 1192.
[58] *Re Yorke* [1911] 1 Ch. 370.
[59] *Cruickshank's Exor.* v. *Cruickshank's Trs.* (1907) 14 S.L.T. 761.

Again, expenses will be refused if the litigation is caused by the fault or neglect of the trustees themselves. Trustees who had delayed unduly to account to beneficiaries were not allowed to charge against the estate the expenses of an action of accounting brought against them.[60] If the trustee has improperly allowed trust papers out of his hands he is not entitled to the expenses of recovering them.[61] Trustees are not entitled to the expenses occasioned by what is in substance a dispute between them.[62]

Trustees who unsuccessfully oppose a petition for their removal and the appointment of a judicial factor will be found personally liable in expenses except, perhaps, where they assent to the factor's appointment but object to their removal as involving some stigma on them.[63] Where the trustees initially opposed a petition for sequestration of the trust estate but later agreed to apply for an order placing the trust administration under the superintendence of the Accountant of Court, they were refused their expenses from the estate although they had acted in good faith and in accordance with the advice of their solicitor.[64]

Where one trustee undertakes the defence of an action without the consent of his co-trustees, he does not fall under the general rule and he can obtain reimbursement of his expenses only if he can show that his intervention resulted in benefit to the trust estate.[65]

The terms of the statute under which a petition has been presented to the court may preclude an award of expenses.[66]

Effect of award

If the action is unsuccessful but was properly brought the trustees can recover not only the expenses incurred to the adversary but also what they have had to pay their own solicitor.[67] If the action is successful and the trustees are awarded expenses but these are not recoverable from the other party, the trustees will be given their expenses from the estate.[68] If the trustees are awarded expenses from the estate, the expenses then become expenses of administration and not expenses of litigation. They are therefore expenses as between agent and client " in the fullest sense." [69] This is so even if the trustee has been awarded only half of the expenses; he is entitled to indemnity to that extent.[70]

---

60 *Jackson* v. *Jackson's Trs.*, 1918, 1 S.L.T. 119. See *Edie* v. *Cairns' Trs.*, 1947 S.L.T.(Notes) 14.
61 *Hill* v. *Tait* (1856) 18 D. 316.
62 *Fothringham* v. *Salton* (1852) 14 D. 427.
63 *Stewart* v. *Morrison* (1892) 19 R. 1009. See also *Thomson* v. *Dalrymple* (1865) 3 M. 336; *Jackson* v. *Welch* (1865) 4 M. 177. *Cf. Baxter & Mitchell* v. *Wood* (1864) 2 M. 915.
64 *Neilson* v. *Stewart's Trs.* (1905) 12 S.L.T. 785.
65 *Stewart* v. *Dobie's Trs.* (1899) 1 F. 1183.
66 *Stewart Menzies* (1903) 10 S.L.T. 636; *Chaplin*, 1926 S.L.T. 422. *Cf. Mackechnie* (1898) 6 S.L.T. 242; *Orr-Ewing*, 1920, 1 S.L.T. 259; *Hope Vere*, 1921, 2 S.L.T. 271; *Bedell-Sivright's C.B.*, 1924 S.L.T. 17.
67 *Lord Lovat* v. *Fraser* (1866) 4 M.(H.L.) 32, 39, *per* Lord Kingsdown.
68 *Train* v. *Clapperton*, 1908 S.C.(H.L.) 26.
69 *Mackenzie Stuart*, 327; *Merrilees* v. *Leckie's Trs.*, 1908 S.C. 576; *McGregor's Trs.* v. *Kimbell*, 1912 S.C. 261.
70 *Davidson's Tr.* v. *Simmons* (1896) 23 R. 1117. *Cf. Fletcher's Trs.* v. *Fletcher* (1888) 15 R. 862. For the English position see *Re Grimthorpe* [1958] Ch. 615.

A finding that trustees are entitled to expenses from the estate is binding only on the parties before the court. The finding does not bind a beneficiary who is not a party to the action.[71]

A residuary legatee who had been unsuccessfully sued by the trustees for a debt due to the trust-estate was held to be entitled to a finding that no part of the expenses of litigation should be paid out of her share of the residue.[72]

If the trustee has been refused his expenses from the trust estate, the solicitors employed by him in the litigation cannot rank for their account in the subsequent sequestration of the trust estate.[73] Solicitors are not in the same position as other persons contracting with a trustee. They know the circumstances of the trust estate and they take the risk of the contingencies involved in the litigation in which they act.

---

[71] *Paterson's J.F.* v. *Paterson's Trs.* (1897) 24 R. 499, 510.
[72] *Easson's Trs.* v. *Mailer* (1901) 3 F. 778. See also *Anderson* v. *Anderson's Tr.* (1901) 4 F. 96; *North of Scotland Bank Ltd.* v. *Cumming*, 1939 S.L.T. 391.
[73] *Ferme, Ferme & Williamson* v. *Stephenson's Tr.* (1905) 7 F. 902.

PART III—EXECUTORS

CHAPTER 28

THE OFFICE OF EXECUTOR

The office

" Moveable subjects are upon the death of the owner, whether dying testate, or intestate, put under the administration of persons authorized by law to execute either the actual or the presumed will of the deceased, who are therefore styled executors; and hence the subject of moveable succession is called executry." [1]

He " is called Executor because he executes and performs the Defunct's will." [2] An executor appointed by the deceased is an executor-nominate; one appointed by the court is an executor-dative. The executor now administers both the heritable and the moveable estate. [3]

In the early law, an appointment as executor-nominate was in effect a legacy of the whole estate of the deceased subject to payment of pecuniary legacies and legal rights—" the Executor was in effect universal Legator where there was no other Legators; albeit in reason the Executor should only have had some small acknowledgment for executing the Defunct's will." [4] The Executors Act 1617 [5] compelled an executor to account for the whole estate to the widow and children and restricted the beneficial right of an executor-nominate who was a stranger to one third of the dead's part under deduction of debts, legacies and any legacy left to the executor. [6] The Intestate Moveable Succession (Scotland) Act 1855, s. 8, provided that executors-nominate, as such, were to have no right to any part of the estate.

Originally, confirmation was required to vest the moveable estate in the executor-dative but the 1823 Act provided that in cases of intestacy the moveable estate vested *ipso jure* in the surviving next-of-kin to the effect of being either assignable or arrestable. [7]

Powers etc.

Executors-nominate, unless the contrary is expressed in the trust deed, have the whole powers, privileges and immunities and are subject to all the

---

[1] Ersk. III, 9, 1. See also *Regiam Majestatem*, 2. 38. 2, 3; Craig, *Ius Feudale*, 2. 17. 1; Balfour, *Practicks*, I, 219; Hope, *Major Practicks*, IV, 4; Stair, III, 8, 29; Hume, *Lect.* V, 195; Anton, " Medieval Scottish Executors and the Courts Spiritual " (1955) 67 J.R. 129.
[2] Mackenzie, *Inst.* III, 8.
[3] Succession (Scotland) Act 1964, s. 14.
[4] Mackenzie, *Observations, Collected Works*, II, 378.
[5] 1617, c. 14. See *Nasmyth* v. *Hare*, Feb. 17, 1819, F.C.; *Finnie* v. *Lords of the Treasury* (1836) 15 S. 165.
[6] Stair, III, 8, 53; *Wilson* v. *Tinto* (1631) Durie 593; *Paton* v. *Leishman* (1674) 2 Stair Dec. 253; *Lowndes* v. *Douglas* (1862) 24 D. 1391.
[7] See *Mann* v. *Thomas* (1830) 8 S. 468; *Frith* v. *Buchanan* (1837) 15 S. 729; *Elder* v. *Watson* (1859) 21 D. 1122. In the case of testate succession, confirmation was not necessary at common law to take the moveables out of the *hereditas jacens* (Bell, *Prin.* s. 1891; *Robertson* v. *Gilchrist* (1828) 6 S. 446.)

411

limitations and restrictions which gratuitous trustees have, or are subject
to, under the Trusts Acts and the statute and common law.[8] Executors-
dative are in the same position except that they must find caution for their
intromissions and do not have power to resign or assume new trustees.[9]
Both types of executor are " trustees " within the meaning of the Trusts
(Scotland) Acts 1921 and 1961. " An executor well confirmed stands in
the position of a trustee. It is a judicial trust." [10]

The office of executor is not now regarded as a benefit; it is an administrative office.[11] " The office of executor has long ceased to be a
beneficial one. It is an administrative one. Somebody must administer the
estate, and acceptance of office does not disturb the distribution provided.
The considerations are of propriety and convenience, not of abstract legal
right.".[12] So a widow who has been appointed executrix is not bound to
elect between accepting the office and claiming her legal rights.[11]

The right of an executor to claim *ius relictae* in right of the deceased is
not barred by the fact that the executor as an individual has accepted a
conventional provision from the estate from which the *ius relictae* is
claimed. This is so even if the executor is also universal legatory of the
estate of which he is executor.[13]

Trustees and executors

The provisions already mentioned have assimilated the position of an
executor to that of a trustee but some differences still exist.

(1) The executor's duty is to ingather the estate and distribute it
among the beneficiaries; the trustee's duty is to hold the estate for the
purposes of the trust. " An executor is one who winds up the estate of a
person deceased. On the other hand, a trustee is one who holds it for
further purposes." [14] In theory it is possible for one of several trustees to
be nominated and confirmed as executor and, then he, after realising the
estate and paying the debts, can transfer the free executry funds to the
whole body of trustees, including himself, to be administered by them for
the purposes of the trust.[15] In the case cited, Lord Watson said that where
trustees were also appointed executors, this was merely an ancillary
appointment " made with the view of giving them an active title to recover,
if necessary, his moveable estate in order to its being administered by
them as his trustees." [16] This now needs modification as the whole estate
vests for administration in the executors by virtue of the confirmation.[17]

---

[8] 1900 Act, s. 2. See *Reid's Exors.* v. *Reid*, 1954 S.L.T.(Notes) 20.
[9] Succession (Scotland) Act 1964, s. 20.
[10] *Fulton* v. *Fulton* (1864) 2 M. 893, 900, *per* Lord Cowan. But see *Fogo's J.F.* v. *Fogo's Trs.*,
     1929 S.C. 546.
[11] *Smart* v. *Smart*, 1926 S.C. 392.   [12] *Per* Lord Sands, p. 402.
[13] *MacGregor's Exrx.* v. *MacGregor's Trs.*, 1935 S.C. 13.
[14] Wood, *Lectures*, 718. See also *Fogo's J.F.* v. *Fogo's Trs.*, 1929 S.C. 546. The appointment
     of executors alone indicates immediate vesting (*Hay's Trs.* v. *Hay* (1890) 17 R. 961;
     Davidson's Exors. (1900) 8 S.L.T. 239).
[15] *Orr Ewing's Trs.* v. *Orr Ewing* (1885) 13 R.(H.L.) 1, 25, *per* Lord Watson. See also
     Malcolm's Exrs. v. *Malcolm* (1869) 8 M. 272; *Martin* v. *Ferguson's Trs.* (1892) 19 R. 474;
     Allan's Exor. v. *Allan*, 1908 S.C. 807; *Reid's Exors.* v. *Reid*, 1954 S.L.T.(Notes) 20.
[16] *Loc. cit.*   [17] 1964 Act s. 14 (1).

Lord President Inglis said of persons who were appointed trustees and executors: " They were thus clothed with a double character—the character of executors for the purposes of realising and converting the estate, and the character of trustees under a trust which was contemplated to endure for a very considerable period." [18] In the same opinion, in discussing the retention of certain stock by the persons, he said:

" at all events it was certainly not in their character of executors nor with a view to the performance of any duty of executors that they retained this stock; it could only be in their character of trustees because it was with a view to securing a better permanent investment than they could command at the time that they kept on the stock. If they had been executors only they could not consistently with their duty have kept on this stock; it would have been their imperative duty certainly to have sold it and realised it." [19]

(2) The executor's title is a factorial one in that he acts, in a sense, as a representative of the deceased; the trustee's title is proprietary in character. " Trustees have not, in any proper sense of the word, a representative character, but executors have." [20] Where the estate includes shares in a limited company, executors may choose whether to have the shares transferred to their names as owners or merely make up a title by confirmation and dispose of the shares without going on the register.[21] Another aspect of this is that the executor is *eadem persona cum defuncto*. His title is subject to all pleas which could be taken against the deceased and there is compensation between a debt due to the executor and one due by the deceased.[22] Another consequence is that, in general, an executor's liability is limited to the amount of the inventory; a trustee can be personally liable to creditors.

Persons referred to as executors in the testamentary writing may be held to have been appointed trustees because of the nature of the duties imposed upon them.

" All executors are in a certain sense trustees; they are charged with the realisation and distribution of the deceased's estate, and, though they are not properly speaking trustees, but mere debtors to the deceased's creditors, yet it is easy to engraft on them duties which no one but a trustee can carry out." [23]

Administration

If there are differences of opinion between co-executors, the majority prevails. The court will intervene only if the majority's proposals are likely to injure or dilapidate the estate or prejudice the interests of the

[18] *Gordon* v. *City of Glasgow Bank* (1879) 7 R. 55, 56.
[19] p. 58.
[20] *Buchan* v. *City of Glasgow Bank* (1879) 6 R.(H.L.) 44, 50, *per* Lord Selborne.
[21] *Ibid.*, p. 46, *per* Lord Cairns L.C.
[22] *Mitchell* v. *Mackersy* (1905) 8 F. 198.
[23] *Ainslie* v. *Ainslie* (1886) 14 R. 209, 211, *per* L.P. Inglis. See also *Bannatyne* v. *Dunlop* (1894) 1 S.L.T. 484. *Cf. Fogo's J.F.* v. *Fogo's Trs.*, 1929 S.C. 546.

beneficiaries or the executors as a whole.[24] So where the majority entered
into an agreement binding them to further the interests of one claimant,
the court, on a petition at the instance of, *inter alios*, the minority, sequestrated the estate and appointed a judicial factor.[25]

A majority of executors may bring an action and may settle an action.[26]
Normally, however, all executors should concur in an action against a
debtor to the estate but this does not apply if one co-executor is the debtor
or one refuses to concur from some personal motive or from caprice.[27]

Remuneration

In the absence of express provision in the will an executor is not
entitled to remuneration. An executor who managed a farm for the estate
was not entitled to commission.[28] An executor-dative *qua* factor for pupil
children who is later appointed curator *bonis* to the children to receive a
legacy for them cannot, when petitioning for his discharge as curator,
deduct losses he has sustained as executor.[29]

Jurisdiction

An executor is not subject to the jurisdiction of a sheriff court only on
the ground that it is the court which granted confirmation.[30] It is thought
that a sheriff court has jurisdiction over executors if one of them is resident
within the sheriffdom and some sheriff court has jurisdiction over each of
the others.[31] It seems that the Court of Session cannot grant decree
against executors unless jurisdiction has been constituted against the whole
body of executors, or at least a majority of them.[32]

A domiciled Englishman who has been decerned executor-dative by the
Scottish courts but has not given up an inventory or been confirmed and
has no property in Scotland is not subject to the jurisdiction of the Scottish
courts in an action at the instance of a creditor of the deceased.[33] Personal
service in Scotland upon one of two executors of a domiciled Englishman
was held not to subject the executors to the jurisdiction of the Court of
Session in an action of damages in respect of a delict committed in Scotland.[34]

---

[24] *Mackenzies* v. *Mackenzie* (1886) 13 R. 507.
[25] *Birnie* v. *Christie* (1891) 19 R. 334.
[26] *Scott* v. *Craig's Representatives* (1897) 24 R. 462; *Graham* v. *Graham*, 1968 S.L.T.(Notes)
       42.
[27] *Rogerson* v. *Barker* (1833) 11 S. 563; *Torrance* v. *Bryson* (1841) 4 D. 71; *Ballantyne* v.
       Ballantyne (1899) 7 S.L.T. 3.
[28] *Malcolm's Exors.* v. *Malcolm* (1869) 8 M. 272.
[29] *Matheson's C.B.* v. *Mathesons* (1889) 16 R. 701.
[30] *Halliday's Exor.* v. *Halliday's Exors.* (1886) 14 R. 251. For a fuller discussion of this topic,
       see Anton, *Private International Law*, 470.
[31] See Dobie, *Sheriff Court Practice*, 59.
[32] *Dalziel* v. *Coulthurst's Exors.*, 1934 S.C. 564.
[33] *Robson* v. *Walsham* (1867) 6 M. 4.
[34] *Dalziel* v. *Coulthurst's Exors.*, 1934 S.C. 564. See now Law Reform (Jurisdiction in
       Delict) (Scotland) Act 1971.

Death of executor

Where more than one executor-dative has been confirmed, and one subsequently fails, the survivor or survivors can continue to act.[35] While more than two survive a majority is a quorum. Executors-nominate are in the same position as trustees.

When a sole or last surviving executor dies with property in Scotland vested in him as such executor, confirmation by his executors, noting his Scottish domicile, or the English or Irish probate granted to his executors and noting his English or Irish domicile, is valid and available to the executors for recovering the property and transferring it to the persons entitled to continue the administration thereof, or, if no act of administration remains to be performed, to the beneficiaries entitled thereto, or their nominees.[36] A note of the property must be appended to the inventory of the estate of the deceased executor and must be referred to in the confirmation.[37] The note must include a reference to the deed, confirmation or other document whereby any property referred to in the note and not standing or invested in the name of the trustee or executor or to which he had not completed title, became vested in him and such a description as will be sufficient to identify any heritable property or interest referred to in the note.[38] The executors are not bound to make up title to the property.

Where a sole or surviving executor dies with property in England and Wales or Northern Ireland held in trust by him, a confirmation or additional confirmation granted in respect of his property in Scotland and noting his Scottish domicile may contain or have appended thereto a note or statement of the property in England and Wales or Northern Ireland which has been set forth in the inventory.[39] The confirmation or additional confirmation can then be treated as a grant of representation to the executors in England and Wales or Northern Ireland in respect of the property specified in the note or statement. It does not in itself entitle the executors to act as executors of the original deceased.[40]

An alternative procedure available on the executor's death is by way of confirmation *ad non executa* to any estate contained in the original confirmation which remains unuplifted or untransferred to the persons entitled thereto. Such confirmation is a sufficient title to continue and complete the administration of the estate contained therein.[41]

---

[35] 1900 Act, s. 4; *Anderson* v. *Kerr* (1866) 5 M. 32.

[36] 1900 Act, s. 6, as amended by the Succession (Scotland) Act 1964, Sched. 2, para. 13. In its original form the section applied only to " any funds in Scotland standing or invested in his name as trustee or executor " and where both executors were executors-nominate. (See *Metcalfe* v. *Bank of Scotland* (1930) 46 Sh.Ct.Rep. 43; Currie, 250.) The section does not apply to letters of administration (Currie, 251).

[37] See *Landale's Tr.* v. *Nicol*, 1918, 2 S.L.T. 10.

[38] Act of Sederunt (Confirmation of Executors) 1964 as amended by Act of Sederunt (Confirmation of Executors Amendment) 1966.

[39] Administration of Estates Act 1971, s. 5.

[40] Administration of Estates Act 1971, ss. 1 (3), 2 (4).

[41] 1900 Act, s. 7. See Chap. 19.

Removal of executors

It is not a ground for displacing executors that they have personal interests conflicting with their duty as executors. Until the contrary is proved, it is presumed that the interest and the duty can be reconciled. But where a majority of the executors entered into an agreement binding themselves to use their powers to further the interests of one of the claimants to the estate, the court sequestrated the estate and appointed a judicial factor.[42] If a person accepts office as executor and then asserts his legal rights against the executry estate, his adverse interest would entitle, and probably compel, the other beneficiaries to apply to have his administration superseded by a judicial factor.[43] The court will remove an executor from office in the same circumstances in which it will remove a trustee, *e.g.* where there is a deadlock in administration caused by the failure of one of the executors to co-operate.[44]

Resignation

An executor-nominate can resign; an executor-dative cannot do so. The resignation of a trustee who is also an executor infers resignation as an executor unless where otherwise expressly declared.[45]

Discharge

It has never been the practice for an executor to obtain a formal discharge of his intromissions.

" It has never been in use for an executor to obtain a discharge, because it is held he cannot get a discharge until he has administered the whole estate; and conversely, that, after he has administered the whole estate, he needs no discharge, because his office has come to an end." [46]

Liability

It has been held competent to sequestrate a body of executors-dative *qua* executors [47] but the process cannot be used to equalise diligence used by a creditor of the deceased with that of creditors in debts incurred by the executors themselves.[47] It is not competent to arrest the private funds of the executor on the dependence of an action brought against him as executor in which he could not be made personally liable.[48]

[42] *Birnie* v. *Christie* (1891) 19 R. 334. See also *MacGregor* (1934) 50 Sh.Ct.Rep. 268.
[43] *Smart* v. *Smart*, 1926 S.C. 392.
[44] *Wilson* v. *Gibson*, 1948 S.C. 52. *Cf. Fleming* v. *Anderson*, 1948 S.L.T.(Notes) 43.
[45] 1921 Act, s. 28.
[46] *Johnston's Exor.* v. *Dobie*, 1907 S.C. 31, 34, *per* Lord McLaren.
[47] *Bain* (1901) 9 S.L.T. 14, 15.
[48] *Macfarlane* v. *Sanderson and Muirhead* (1868) 40 Sc.Jur. 189. See as to the arrester's liability, *Wilson* v. *Mackie* (1875) 3 R. 18.

Ultimus haeres

If the deceased has no known heirs, his estate becomes caduciary and as such belongs to the Crown as *ultimus haeres*.[49] The Queen's and Lord Treasurer's Remembrancer takes possession of the estate without confirmation, pays the debts and retains the balance.[50] The Queen's and Lord Treasurer's Remembrancer has the like right to uplift and ingather estate which has fallen to the Crown as *ultimus haeres* in Scotland and England and Wales as an executor-nominate to whom confirmation has been granted noting the deceased's Scottish domicile.[51] The persons in possession of the estate are possessors *custodiae causa tantum* and their only right of intromission is for preservation. If they know of an heir they have a duty to intimate to him. If they do not know of an heir they should give intimation to the Queen's and Lord Treasurer's Remembrancer. They are under no duty to find an heir but they may properly incur reasonable expenses in making the usual inquiries and in using the ordinary channels of publicity.[52] The Queen's and Lord Treasurer's Remembrancer makes no objection to the incurring of such reasonable expenses and after taking possession of the estate he may supplement the investigations by advertisement in the *Edinburgh Gazette* and in newspapers.

If the Queen's and Lord Treasurer's Remembrancer has not taken possession of the estate, he cannot prevent an executor-creditor confirming to items thereof.[53]

" Heirs and executors "

Where a destination in a testamentary disposition is expressed to " heirs and executors " or " heirs, executors and successors whomsoever," it is presumed in the absence of any indication to the contrary that the testator intended to designate generally the parties entitled to take on intestacy.[54] In *Scott's Exors.* v. *Methven's Exors.*,[55] a contrary indication was found and a gift to " executors and representatives whomsoever " was held to carry the subject to executors-nominate.

---

[49] Dig. 49. 14. 1, 2; Stair, III, 3, 47; IV, 13; Ersk. III, 10, 2; *Goldie* v. *Murray* (1753) Mor. 3183; *Finnie* v. *Lords of the Treasury* (1836) 15 S. 165; Succession (Scotland) Act 1964, s. 7. The Crown cannot take as *ultimus haeres* under a conditional institution of " heirs " (*Torrie* v. *Munsie* (1832) 10 S. 597). See also McMillan, *Bona Vacantia*, 17–31.

[50] Ersk. III, 9, 53.

[51] Law Reform (Miscellaneous Provisions) (Scotland) Act 1940, s. 6 (1); Administration of Estates Act 1971, Sched 1, para. 4.

[52] *Rutherford* v. *Lord Advocate*, 1932 S.C. 674.

[53] *Irvine* v. *King's and Lord Treasurer's Remembrancer* (1949) 65 Sh.Ct.Rep. 53.

[54] *Lady Kinnaird's Trs.* v. *Ogilvy*, 1911 S.C. 1136; *Mackenzie's Trs.* v. *Georgeson*, 1923 S.C. 517.

[55] (1890) 17 R. 389.

CHAPTER 29

THE CONFIRMATION OF EXECUTORS

THE administrative title of an executor must be completed by a judicial proceeding known as confirmation:

" A sentence of the judge competent, authorising an executor, one or more, upon making inventory of the moveable estate, and debts due to the deceased, to sue for, recover, possess and administer the whole, either for the behoof of themselves, or of others interested therein." [1]

Heritable estate is now included in the inventory and confirmation is granted thereto [2] and, provided the deceased died domiciled in Scotland, real estate in England and Wales or Northern Ireland may also be included.

The inventory

The executor must, before confirmation, exhibit upon oath a full and true inventory of all the estate, heritable and moveable, real and personal, of the deceased already recovered or known to be existing; distinguishing what is situated in Scotland and what elsewhere. [3] If the deceased died domiciled in Scotland real and personal estate situated in England and Wales or Northern Ireland must be included in the inventory. [4] The inventory should include such a description of any heritable property which forms part of the estate, or an interest in which forms part of the estate, as will be sufficient to identify the property or interest therein as a separate item in the estate. [5]

The confirmation

Confirmation cannot be granted to any estate not included in the inventory. [6] Every person requiring confirmation must confirm to the whole estate known at the time, apart from estate subject to a special assignation [7] or a special destination [8] and the special case of confirmation by an executor-creditor. [9]

---

[1] Ersk. III, 9, 27.
[2] Succession (Scotland) Act 1964, s. 14.
[3] Probate and Legacy Duties Act 1808, s. 38. As to the earlier history of the inventory, see *Lord Advocate* v. *Meiklam* (1860) 23 D. 57, 64, *per* L.J.-C. Inglis.
[4] Confirmation of Executors (Scotland) Act 1858, ss. 9, 15; Administration of Estates Act 1971, s. 6.
[5] Act of Sederunt (Confirmation of Executors Amendment) 1966 (S.I. 1966 No. 593 (S. 37)) (1966 S.L.T.(News) 112), amending the Act of Sederunt (Confirmation of Executors) 1964, which required " such a description, including a description by reference, as is acceptable by present law and practice for a conveyance of lands or of an estate in land."
[6] Probate and Legacy Duties Act 1808, s. 42.
[7] Confirmation of Executors (Scotland) Act 1823 (4 Geo. 4, c. 98), s. 3.
[8] See Succession (Scotland) Act 1964, s. 18.   [9] 1823 Act, s. 4. See Chap. 32.

If the deceased died domiciled in Scotland real and personal estate situated in England and Wales or Northern Ireland may be confirmed to. If the fact of Scottish domicile is set forth in the oath that is sufficient warrant for the sheriff clerk to insert in the confirmation, or to note thereon and sign, a statement that the deceased died domiciled in Scotland.[10] Estate outwith the United Kingdom cannot be confirmed.

Confirmation may be granted by the sheriff court of the county in which the deceased died domiciled and, where he was domiciled outwith Scotland, or without any fixed or known domicile, and left property in Scotland, by the Edinburgh Commissary Court.[11] The confirmation bears that the sheriff approves of and confirms the executors and gives and commits to them full power as appropriate to take possession of, make up title to, uplift or receive the estate and effects of the deceased, " administer and dispose of the same, grant discharges thereof, if needful to pursue therefor, and generally every other thing concerning the same to do that to the office of executor . . . . is known to belong: Providing always that the said executors shall render just count and reckoning for Intromissions therewith when and where the same shall be legally required." [12]

Certificates of confirmation

A certificate relating to one item of property in the confirmation can be issued which is as valid and effectual for anyone acting on the faith thereof to the same effect as if the confirmation had been exhibited.[13] Issue is not restricted to executors or those acting on their behalf.[14] The certificate can be issued in respect of an item of real or personal property situated in England and Wales or Northern Ireland.[15]

The Commissary Court [16]

The Commissary Court of Edinburgh was established in 1563 and inferior commissaries were later appointed in the principal towns to deal with, *inter alia*, the appointment and confirmation of executors. The Edinburgh Commissaries, in addition to their jurisdiction over the Lothians, Peebles and part of Stirlingshire (*i.e.* the former bishopric of Edinburgh), dealt with the confirmation of estates of persons dying domiciled furth of Scotland *tanquam commune forum* and reviewed the pro-

10 Sheriff Courts (Scotland) Act 1876, s. 41.
11 1858 Act, s. 8.
12 Act of Sederunt (Confirmation of Executors) 1967 (S.I. 1967 No. 789 (S. 58)).
13 Act of Sederunt, February 3, 1933 (S.R. & O. 1933 No. 48), para. 5 (amended by A.S., December 11, 1936); Act of Sederunt (Confirmation of Executors) 1964, para. 5; Act of Sederunt (Confirmation of Executors Amendment) 1971 (1971 S.L.T.(News) 187); Act of Sederunt (Confirmation of Executors Amendment No. 2) 1971.
14 *Watt*, 1942 S.C. 214.
15 Administration of Estates Act 1971, ss. 1 and 2.
16 For a more detailed account, see Fergusson, *Consistorial Law in Scotland*, chap. II; Alexander, *The Practice of the Commissary Courts in Scotland*, 1859, chap. 1; Fraser, *Treatise on Husband and Wife*, 2nd ed., 14–18; Donaldson, " The Church Courts," *Introduction to Scottish Legal History*, chap. XXVII, 368–371. See also Balfour, *Practicks*, 655; Hope, *Major Practicks* V. 13; Dirleton, s.v. " Consistories "; Ersk. I, 5, 26–31; Hume *Lect.* V. 281.

ceedings of the inferior commissaries. They also had a consistorial jurisdiction. In 1823 the inferior commissariots were abolished and each county was made a commissariot with the sheriff as commissary. In 1836, the Edinburgh Commissary Court was abolished and the jurisdiction transferred to the sheriff of the county of Edinburgh as commissary. In 1876, the commissary courts were abolished and their powers and jurisdiction transferred to the sheriff, the duties of the commissary clerk being transferred to the sheriff clerk except in Edinburgh. It was provided that it should still be competent to use the seal of office of a commissariot and the seals are still attached to documents. The offices of the sheriff clerk of Midlothian and commissary clerk of Edinburgh are now united to the effect that they are held and the duties thereof are discharged by one and the same person.[17]

The executor-nominate

An executor appointed by the deceased himself is styled an executor-nominate. To complete his title he must obtain a confirmation which was formerly known as a " testament-testamentar." A preliminary application for special authority to issue confirmation may be necessary if, for example, the executors are not appointed by name in the will, or the execution of the will is defective or one of the executors is abroad or cannot be found.[18]

The oath

The oath must state the date and place of death, the domicile, and the testamentary writings containing the nomination. Where several executors were nominated, those who are not seeking confirmation must be accounted for. If the executors are not named but described as " heirs " or " my children " the facts relevant to identification must be set forth.[19] If the appointment is conditional, facts showing the fulfilment of the condition must be stated.[20] Finally, the deponent must state that the inventory is a full and complete inventory and whether confirmation is or is not required.[21]

The oath [22] may be taken before the sheriff principal or sheriff, any commissioner appointed by the sheriff, any sheriff clerk or his depute, any notary public, magistrate, or Justice of the Peace, in the United King-

---

[17] Sheriff Courts (Scotland) Act 1876, ss. 35–40; Sheriff Courts and Legal Officers (Scotland) Act 1927, s. 11 (1).

[18] For styles of writ, see Currie, 445–448. An affidavit as to identity should not be sworn before the petitioner's solicitor—*Mrs. A. Barr, Ptnr.* (1959) 75 Sh.Ct.Rep. 169. For examples, see *Briggs' Exor.* (1927) 43 Sh.Ct.Rep. 141; *Campbell* (1931) 47 Sh.Ct.Rep. 162 (effect of writing); *Dickerson* (1959) 75 Sh.Ct.Rep. 126.

[19] Currie, 81.

[20] Currie, 86.

[21] See Currie, 192.

[22] A solemn affirmation may be taken instead of the oath if the deponent states that he has no religious belief, or that the taking of the oath is contrary to his religious belief or if it is not reasonably practicable without inconvenience or delay to administer an oath in the manner appropriate to his religious belief. (Oaths Act 1888: Oaths Act 1961 (c. 21).)

dom, and also, if taken in England or Ireland, before any Commissioner of Oaths appointed by the courts of these countries, or if taken at any place out of the United Kingdom, before any British consul or local magistrate, or any notary public practising in such foreign country, or admitted and practising in Great Britain or Ireland.[23]

Productions

Any testament or other writing relating to the disposal of the estate must be exhibited with the inventory.[24] If the applicant's name has altered since the date of the will evidence vouching the change must be produced.[25]

If one of the nominated persons is *incapax* or unwilling to act, a medical certificate or, as the case may be, a minute or other evidence of declinature must be produced.[26]

If a corporation or other body is to be confirmed, a certified copy of a resolution or minute nominating the officer appointed to take the oath must be produced with the inventory and referred to in the oath.[27]

Contentious cases

" The duty of the Sheriff as Commissary is to determine who is entitled to the office of executor on the face either of the deeds which are put before the Court, or of the relation to the deceased which is set out as the title of the applicant." [28]

The court is not concerned with the comparative capacities of the parties claiming right to administer the estate.[29] The mere proponing of averments in support of a reduction of the testamentary deed cannot stop the application for confirmation where the will containing the nomination is *ex facie* valid and effectual.[30] A dispute as to the validity of a testamentary deed cannot be determined in a competition between parties seeking confirmation because the decision would not be *res judicata* in a question with the beneficiaries who are not represented.[31]

Where there are testaments of different dates appointing different persons as executors and a dispute as to which is the valid deed, the court may, without deciding the question of validity, confirm the persons named in all the deeds as executors-nominate [32] or confirm the executors in the will last in date who have *prima facie* a good title to claim confirmation.[33] Where there is an obvious objection to the will and the executors named

[23] Executors (Scotland) Act 1900, s. 8.
[24] Probate and Legacy Duties Act 1808, s. 38 (48 Geo. 3, c. 149).
[25] Currie, 85.
[26] Currie, 93.
[27] Currie, 84.
[28] *Martin* v. *Ferguson's Trs.* (1892) 19 R. 474, 478, *per* L.P. Robertson.
[29] *Lady Denman* v. *Torry* (1899) 1 F. 881. But see *Crolla*, 1942 S.C. 21.
[30] *Grahame* v. *Bannerman* (1822) 1 S. 403; *Hamilton* v. *Hardie* (1888) 16 R. 192; *Young* v. *Bell* (1924) 40 Sh.Ct.Rep. 221.
[31] *MacHardy* v. *Steele* (1902) 4 F. 765.
[32] *Jones* v. *Pursey* (1886) 23 S.L.R. 628.
[33] *MacHardy* v. *Steele, supra.*

therein are persons of no means, who might dissipate the estate after getting possession of it, the court may refuse to confirm them, and may appoint a judicial factor instead.[34] Where, on the objector's averments, there was a *prima facie* risk of injury to the estate if the administration was left in the petitioner's hands, the court took the same course.[35] And where the trustees under a former settlement and the testator's next-of-kin raised an action of reduction of the will on the ground of facility, fraud and circumvention and averred that the applicant, who was a general disponee and executor-nominate, was a person of no substance and that there was a danger of loss to the estate, a factor was appointed.[36] Where the divorced wife of the deceased applied for confirmation as general disponee under a will which the next-of-kin maintained was inoperative, the court in its discretion appointed a judicial factor to administer the estate.[37]

The practice of the Edinburgh Commissary Court is to refuse confirmation on the will if the testator is survived by a minor child who may be able to invoke the *conditio si testator sine liberis decesserit* to impugn the validity of the will.[38]

The testament

A testamentary writing must be attested by two witnesses or be holograph of the testator or be adopted as holograph.[39] If a writing has been subscribed by the granter and bears to be attested by two witnesses, certain informalities of execution can be remedied by a proof under section 39 of the Conveyancing (Scotland) Act 1874.[40]

Holograph testaments

The practice of the commissary court was that when an unattested testamentary writing which contained *in gremio* a statement that it was holograph of the writer was produced by the person named therein as executor, confirmation was granted *de plano* if there was no opposition.[41] Where the document did not contain such a statement, the practice was that confirmation was granted on presentation of affidavits of two witnesses who deponed that the handwriting was that of the testator.[42]

Where there was opposition in the commissary court, and in all cases outwith the commissary court, the authenticity of the document had to be established by the normal methods of proof,[43] but any writing of a testa-

34 *Hamilton* v. *Hardie* (1888) 16 R. 192.
35 *Campbell* v. *Barber* (1895) 23 R. 90.
36 *Simpson's Exor.* v. *Simpson's Trs.*, 1912 S.C. 418.
37 *Henderson* v. *Henderson*, 1930 S.L.T. 23.
38 Currie, 80.
39 In certain circumstances, a will may be treated as properly executed if it is validly executed according to the laws of another territory—Wills Act 1963—see p. 423, *infra*.
40 See Burns, *Conveyancing Practice*, 4th ed. 1957, pp. 2–4.
41 *Cranston* (1890) 17 R. 410.
42 *Frederick* v. *Craig*, 1932 S.L.T. 315.
43 *Anderson* v. *Gill* (1858) 20 D. 1326; *affd.* (1858) 3 Macq. 180; *Harper* v. *Green*, 1938 S.C. 198. There was provision for evidence by affidavit in Sheriff Court actions for declarator that a testamentary writing was holograph (Act of Sederunt, July 19, 1935). The Wills

mentary character on which confirmation of executors-nominate had been issued prior to July 1, 1938 was deemed to be probative.[44]

Now, in all cases, the court must be satisfied by evidence consisting at least of an affidavit by each of two persons that the writing and signature of the disposition are in the handwriting of the testator.[45]

For the purpose of any question arising as to entitlement to any property by virtue of a testamentary disposition, the disposition is treated as probative if confirmation of an executor to property disposed of in the disposition has been granted in Scotland or probate, letters of administration or other grant of administration has been issued in England and Wales or Northern Ireland in respect of property disposed of in the disposition and notes the domicile of the deceased in England and Wales or Northern Ireland, as the case may be, or probate or letters of administration issued outwith the United Kingdom in respect of such property has been sealed in Scotland under section 2 of the Colonial Probates Act 1892.[46]

Where the will is partly printed and partly holograph, confirmation cannot be granted if the nomination of executors is contained in the printed portion even although the holograph portion may contain sufficient material to give the document testamentary effect.[47]

Wills Act 1963 [48]

A will is treated as properly executed if its execution conforms to the internal law of (i) the place of execution, or (ii) the place of the testator's domicile or habitual residence at the time of its execution or at the time of his death, or (iii) of a state of which he was, at either of those times, a national.[49] The Act applies if the testator died on or after January 1, 1964.[50]

The appointment of executors-nominate

The appointment can be express, by reference, or implied. Executors can be nominated by reference—for example, reference to another

Act 1963, s. 5 which came into force on January 1, 1964 provided that any testamentary instrument should be treated as probative for the purpose of the conveyance of heritable property if confirmation of property disposed of in the instrument had been issued in Scotland or probate, letters of administration or other grant of representation had been certified or sealed in Scotland. The section was repealed by the Succession (Scotland) Act 1964 (s. 34 (2), Sched. 3). See Meston, 82.

[44] Conveyancing Amendment (Scotland) Act 1938 (1 & 2 Geo. 6, c. 24), s. 11.

[45] 1964 Act, s. 21. It is the practice to follow the procedure established by the Act of Sederunt of July 19, 1935 (S. R. & O. 1935 No. 756 (s. 34)).

[46] 1964 Act, s. 32; Administration of Estates Act 1971, Sched. 1, para. 5.

[47] Dr. H. Campbell (1963) 79 Sh.Ct.Rep. 15. See also Bridgeford's Exor. v. Bridgeford, 1948 S.C. 416, 423, per Lord Mackay.

[48] c. 44.

[49] s. 1. S. 2 deals with execution aboard vessels or aircraft, immoveable property, revocation of wills and the exercise of powers of appointment. To obtain confirmation of a will the validity of which depends on foreign law, an opinion of a person qualified in that law must be produced.

[50] s. 7 (4). The repeal of the Wills Act 1861 by s. 7 (3) is not to invalidate a will executed before January 1, 1964.

man's will.[51] The holder of a specified office can be nominated.[52] An appointment may be conditional or for only a limited period.[53] If there is a substitution as " A whom failing B," the confirmation cannot be issued in these terms and the substitute cannot be confirmed until the institute has failed.[54]

A sentence in a holograph will—" I leave and bequeath to B £200 with power to see this will executed " was treated as an appointment of B as executor.[55] The naming of a person as " judicial factor, to carry out the purposes of this trust " was held to be a nomination as executor.[56] Where the testator, who owned a valuable library, in his will named his two daughters and a son as his executors and in a letter to his son instructed him to take out confirmation as soon as possible and added " you will of course consider it prudent to sell the library as soon as possible " it was held that the letter contained merely a suggestion to the executors and was not a nomination of the son as sole executor to carry out the sale of the library.[57]

A bequest to " my executor, Mr. Torry," there being no nomination in the will, was held not to be a sufficiently clear nomination.[58] A nomination of a person as " heir " followed by bequests of legacies and the residue to other persons was regarded as being neither an appointment as executor-nominate nor a nomination as general disponee and universal legatory.[59]

Where the appointment was " A, B and C or their representatives, namely, the successors of each, as representing their respective families " and B predeceased the testator, B's eldest son was treated as an executor-nominate.[60]

Where parties were appointed in the will as " sole executors and universal legatories " but the beneficial interest was withdrawn from all except one of them by a codicil which ratified the will in all other respects, it was held that there was no implied revocation of the appointment as executors.[61]

Special cases

A corporation can be an executor.[62] Confirmation can be granted in favour of minors and insane persons on the application of the curator but the preferable course where the incapax is a beneficiary is for the curator to seek confirmation as executor-dative.[63] Where the person named cannot

---

[51] Martin v. Ferguson's Trs. (1892) 19 R. 474.
[52] Currie, 84.
[53] Currie, 86.
[54] Currie, 85.
[55] Dundas v. Dundas (1837) 15 S. 427.
[56] Tod (1890) 18 R. 152.
[57] Mackenzie v. Mackenzie (1886) 13 R. 507.
[58] Lady Denman v. Torry (1899) 1 F. 881.
[59] Jerdon v. Forrest (1897) 24 R. 395. For other cases of implied appointment, see Currie, 65.
[60] Michie's Exors. v. Michie (1905) 7 F. 509.
[61] Scott v. Peebles (1870) 8 M. 959.
[62] Currie, 84.
[63] Currie, 90–91.

be found, confirmation may be granted in favour of the remaining executors but if the absentee has a beneficial interest, caution may have to be
found.[64] An executor resident abroad can grant a factory or power of
attorney authorising the factor to expede confirmation in the executor's
name. It is not competent for confirmation to be expede in the factor's
name.[65]

Where the appointment is stated to be " joint " the nomination fails if
all do not accept and act.[66] Where one nominee is a *sine quo non*, he must
make the oath and the qualification will appear in the confirmation. If
he declines, it seems that the other executors can be confirmed but this
may turn on the wording of the appointment.[67] There is a presumption
that an executor appointed in the will is appointed to carry out all the
provisions of the will but partial appointments are competent.[68] Where
different executors are nominated for different parts of the estate, the
whole estate in Scotland must nevertheless be included in one confirmation.[69] An executor-nominate can be appointed by someone who has been
empowered by the testator to do so.[70]

Constructive appointment

Under the 1900 Act if the testator has not appointed an executor, or
failing any person so appointed, the testator's testamentary trustees,
original or assumed, or appointed by the court (if any) are held to be
executors-nominate and entitled to confirmation.[71] Failing such trustees
any general disponee or universal legatory or residuary legatee appointed
by the testator shall be held to be his executor-nominate and entitled to
confirmation in that character. In practice, the view taken is that if all the
general disponees or universal or residuary legatees survive the deceased
they are all held to be executors-nominate but one or more can decline. If,
however, one or more predecease the deceased and there is no survivorship clause and partial intestacy results, in Edinburgh Commissary Court
the surviving general disponees may be confirmed only in a dative
character.[72]

" After this citation [73] it is impossible for anyone to contend, that
the term universal legatory means, in the law of Scotland, anything
else than the party who has, by the testament of the defunct, right to
the entire dead's part; or that a universal legacy is more than the

[64] Currie, 94.
[65] p. 92.
[66] McLaren, II, 896.
[67] Currie, 87. See " Non-acceptance of Sine Quo Non Executor " (1935) 51 *Scottish Law
Review* 178.
[68] *Allan's Exor.* v. *Allan*, 1908 S.C. 807, 812, *per* Lord Kinnear.
[69] Currie, 89.
[70] Currie, 68.
[71] Executors (Scotland) Act 1900, s. 3. As to the common law, see *Martin* v. *Ferguson's Trs.*
(1892) 19 R. 474.
[72] Currie, 73. If some have predeceased the testator the others may be confirmed as executors-dative.
[73] Stair, III, 8, 38.

legacy of the entire legacy fund—the whole of the dead's part, the whole of that of which the testator had power to dispose by his testament." [74]

The beneficiary must have a vested right but he need not have an immediate right to payment.[75] It seems that a liferenter cannot be confirmed under the section.[76] A substitute general disponee can be, but an executor or assignee of the legatee or disponee must be, confirmed as an executor-dative.[77] In a case prior to the Act, a widow who was given the liferent of the whole of her husband's estate with power to test on £2,000 thereof if she did not re-marry but was restricted to an annuity of £100 if she did, was held not to be a general disponee.[78] A bequest of " all siller and stock " was held to constitute the legatee a universal legatory.[79] In one case a person described by the testator as " executor " and " universal intromitter with my goods and money " was held to be a universal legatory.[80] A person named as " heir " was held, in the circumstances, not to be a clear nominee as universal legatee.[81]

In this connection, there are numerous decisions on whether, in the particular context, an expression covered the whole estate including heritage, the whole moveable estate or the residue of the estate [82]: " money " [83]; " all moneys and goods " [84]; " any other capital " [85]; " funds " [86]; " means and effects " [87]; " means and substance " [88]; " belongings " [89]; " estate and effects " [90]; " all my estate " [91]; " everything else " [92]; " residue of my property " [93]; " whole residue of my estate." [94]

Where the will read " All I possess I leave to my husband, T. D., and after him to my sister, M. H. R., and her heirs," it was held that the husband was a full fiar, not merely a liferenter, and was entitled to confirmation under the section.[95]

[74] White v. Finlay (1861) 24 D. 38, 49, per L.J.-C. Inglis.
[75] Currie, 74.
[76] Reid v. Dobie, 1921 S.C. 662; Currie, 74.
[77] Currie, 75.
[78] McGown v. McKinlay (1835) 14 S. 105.
[79] Christison v. Christison (1881) 18 S.L.R. 528.
[80] Jamieson v. Clark (1872) 10 M. 399.
[81] Jerdon v. Forrest (1877) 24 R. 395.
[82] For commissary decisions, see Currie, 72.
[83] Easson v. Thomson's Trs. (1879) 7 R. 251; Keith v. Fraser (1883) 20 S.L.R. 785; Ord v. Ord, 1927 S.C. 77; Fraser's Exrx. v. Fraser's C.B., 1931 S.C. 536.
[84] Dunsmure v. Dunsmure (1879) 7 R. 261.
[85] Auld's Trs. v. Auld's Trs., 1933 S.C. 176.
[86] Sibbald v. Lord's Trs., 1913, 2 S.L.T. 86.
[87] Forsyth v. Turnbull (1887) 15 R. 172.
[88] Maclagan's Trs. v. Lord Advocate (1903) 11 S.L.T. 227.
[89] Macintyre v. Miller (1900) 7 S.L.T. 435; Dunlop v. McCrorie, 1909, 1 S.L.T. 544; Simson's Trs. v. Simson, 1922 S.C. 14.
[90] Bryden v. Cormack, 1913 S.C. 209.
[91] Jack's Exor. v. Downie, 1908 S.C. 718; Smith's Exors. v. Smith, 1918 S.C. 772.
[92] Crowe v. Cook, 1908 S.C. 1178.
[93] Craw's Trs. v. Blacklock, 1920 S.C. 22.
[94] Bell v. Bell (1906) 14 S.L.T. 244. See also Millar v. Morrison (1894) 21 R. 921.
[95] Reid v. Dobie, 1921 S.C. 662.

The executor-dative

If there is no person who can be confirmed as executor-nominate or if the executor-nominate takes no steps to expede confirmation [96] it is necessary to apply to the court for the appointment of an executor-dative. " Executors not named by the deceased are called *dative*, because they are given by the judge, and derive their authority solely from him." [97]

A person cannot be appointed as executor-dative merely on the grounds of expediency; the person appointed must have a legal title to the office.[98] Interest in the succession is the general ground of confirmation.[99] As the executor has to find caution, an averment that an applicant is *vergens ad inopiam* is not a relevant objection to appointment.[1]

Instructions to the commissaries

The basis of the present law and practice is the instructions given by the archbishops and bishops to the Commissaries in 1666 [2]:

> " If there be no Nomination or Testament made by the Defunct, or if the Testament-Testamentar shall not be desired to be confirmed, ye shall confirm the nearest of kin desiring to be confirmed; and if the nearest of kin shall not desire to be confirmed, ye shall confirm such of the creditors as desire to be confirmed as Creditors, they instructing their Debts; and if neither nearest of Kin, Executor, or Creditor, shall desire to be confirmed, you shall confirm the Legators such of them as desire to be confirmed, and instruct that they are Legators. And if no other Person having Interest foresaid shall confirm, you shall confirm your Procurator-fiscal, Datives always being duly given thereto before; and if after the said Datives but before Confirmation any Person having Interest shall desire to be surrogate in Place of the Procurator-fiscal, ye shall confirm them as Executors surrogate in place of the Procurator-fiscal." [3]

The widow is not mentioned in the instructions but the possibility of the widow being confirmed as executor-dative appears in earlier decisions.[4]

In the earlier law the next-of-kin was appointed in preference to a universal disponee but in *Crawfurd* v. *Ure* [5] it was held that general disponees were entitled to the office in preference to the next-of-kin because

> " the next of kin who cannot figure to herself any advantage by the office, ought not to be admitted; especially in competition with the disponee; who has a well-founded interest to be admitted to the

---

[96] *Fernie* v. *Fernie* (1893) 1 S.L.T. 108; *Wilson, Ptnr.* (1957) 73 Sh.Ct.Rep. 237.
[97] Ersk. III, 9, 32.
[98] *Whiffin* v. *Lees* (1872) 10 M. 797, 800, *per* L.P. Inglis.
[99] *Muir* (1876) 4 R. 74.
[1] *Chrystal* v. *Chrystal*, 1923 S.L.T.(Sh.Ct.) 69.
[2] The instructions are printed in Stair's Decisions Vol. I. As to the earlier practice, see *Bones* v. *Morrison* (1866) 5 M. 240, 243, *per* L.J.-C. Inglis.
[3] See *Muir* (1876) 4 R. 74, 75, *per* Lord Deas.
[4] *E.g. Steven* v. *Govan* (1622) Mor. 3843.
[5] (1755) Mor. 3818; Ersk. III, 9, 32.

management of effects, which, after payment of the debts, are wholly to be applied to his use."

This decision did not, however, prevent the appointment of next-of-kin not having a beneficial interest where there was no competition for the office.[6] " The order of executors has long been settled: The universal legatee is preferred to the office; (2) the next of kin; (3) the widow; (4) a creditor; (5) a legatee; (6) the procurator-fiscal of Court." [7]

The next-of-kin

Under the old law, the moveable estate went to the " next of kin " or " nearest of kin " who were " the Defunct's whole agnates, Male or Female, being the Kinsmen of the Defunct's Fathers side, of the nearest Degree, without Primogeniture or Right of Representation." [8]

So the order of succession was (1) children, (2) their descendants degree by degree, (3) brothers and sisters, (4) their descendants degree by degree, (5) the father,[9] (6) the father's brothers and sisters, (7) their descendants— and so on. The full blood and the descendants of the full blood excluded the half-blood consanguinean.[10] The half-blood uterine and relations on the mother's side generally were excluded from the succession as were relatives by affinity.

The Intestate Moveable Succession (Scotland) Act 1855 made the following changes:

(1) representation was introduced among the intestate's descendants and among his brothers and sisters [11] and their descendants [12];

(2) the father was given a right to one half of the estate in preference to brothers and sisters of the intestate [13];

(3) the mother was given a right to one-third of the estate in preference to brothers and sisters, if the father had predeceased [14];

(4) brothers and sisters of the half-blood uterine and their descendants were given a right to one half of the estate where the intestate was not survived by parents or brothers or sisters german or consanguinean or their descendants.[15]

The Act therefore extended the class of heirs *in mobilibus ab intestato* but it adopted the common law meaning of " next-of-kin " which accordingly was not altered by the Act.[16] It was provided that the surviving

---

[6] *Bones* v. *Morrison* (1866) 5 M. 240.

[7] *Stewart* v. *Kerr* (1890) 17 R. 707, 708, *per* Lord Rutherfurd Clark.

[8] Stair, III, 8, 31. See also Balfour, *Practicks*, 218; Bankton, III, 4, 28; Ersk. III, 9, 2.

[9] Stair (*loc. cit.*) mentions a doubt as to whether the father excluded his collaterals.

[10] *Gemmil* v. *Gemmils* (1729) Mor. 14877. Erskine (III, 9, 2) illogically regards the preference of the descendants as an instance of representation—see Hume, *Lects.* V, 176.

[11] Including the half-blood consanguinean (*Finlayson's Exor.* v. *Hastie*, 1916, 1 S.L.T. 123).

[12] s. 1; *Ormiston* v. *Broad* (1862) 1 M. 10; *Turner* (1869) 8 M. 222; *Macmillan* v. *Macmillan*, 1909, 1 S.L.T. 35; *Colville's J.F.* v. *Nicoll*, 1914 S.C. 62.

[13] s. 3.

[14] s. 4. This was increased to one half by the Intestate Moveable Succession (Scotland) Act 1919, s. 1.

[15] s. 5.

[16] *Gregory's Trs.* v. *Alison* (1889) 16 R.(H.L.) 10; *Young's Trs.* v. *Janes* (1880) 8 R. 242; *Murray's Factor* v. *Melrose*, 1910 S.C. 924; *Steedman's Trs.* v. *Steedman*, 1916 S.C. 857.

next-of-kin would have exclusive right to the office of executor in pre-ference to persons taking by representation.[17] After the Act, the right of the father [18] and the mother [19] to the office of executor was recognised. The practice was to confirm such persons " qua father " etc., and not qua next-of-kin.[20]

The surviving spouse

The widow was entitled to be decerned qua relict but she was not entitled to the office in competition with the next-of-kin,[21] except where she had right to the whole estate under the Intestate Husband's Estate (Scot-land) Acts 1911 to 1959.[22] After the institution of ius relicti by the Married Women's Property Act 1881, s. 6, the husband was in the same position.[23]

Intestate Husband's Estate (Scotland) Acts

In 1911, the widow was given a prior right, where the intestate was not survived by issue, to the first five hundred pounds of the estate, borne rateably by the heritable and moveable estate.[24] In 1940, a surviving husband was given a similar right and the Acts were extended to cases of partial intestacy, it being provided that any legacy received by the sur-viving spouse was to be deducted from the five hundred pounds.[25] In 1959, the sum was increased to five thousand pounds.[26]

Illegitimacy

In 1926 an illegitimate child was given the same right as he would have had if he had been legitimate in his mother's estate where she died in-testate and without lawful issue. The mother was given the same right to the estate of her intestate illegitimate child as she would have had if the child had been legitimate and she had been the only surviving parent.[27]

The present order

If the death occurred on or after September 10, 1964, the order of preference to the office of executor-dative is:

(1) General disponees, universal legatories or residuary legatees who cannot or do not seek confirmation as executors-nominate.

---

[17] s. 1. See Webster v. Shiress (1878) 6 R. 102, 108, per Lord Gifford; Dowie v. Barclay (1871) 9 M. 726.
[18] Webster v. Shiress (1878) 6 R. 102.
[19] Muir (1876) 4 R. 74.
[20] Currie, 106.
[21] Scott v. Cook (1887) 3 Sh.Ct.Rep. 301; Murray v. Murray (1888) 4 Sh.Ct.Rep. 129.
[22] Intestate Husband's Estate (Scotland) Act 1919, s. 3.
[23] Stewart v. Kerr (1890) 17 R. 707; Campbell v. Falconer (1892) 19 R. 563. The husband, of course, had no right under the Intestate Husband's Estate (Scotland) Acts until 1940— see next paragraph.
[24] Intestate Husband's Estate (Scotland) Act 1911.
[25] Law Reform (Miscellaneous Provisions) (Scotland) Act 1940, s. 5. In Taylor's Exors. v. Taylor, 1918 S.C. 207, it had been held that the 1911 Act did not apply to partial intestacies.
[26] Intestate Husband's Estate (Scotland) Act 1959.
[27] Legitimacy Act 1926, s. 9. See Osman v. Campbell, 1946 S.C. 204.

(2) If a spouse has right to the whole of the intestate estate by virtue of a prior right under section 9 of the 1964 Act, he or she has the right to be appointed executor.[28] Where the prior rights do not take up the whole estate the spouse nevertheless has a claim to be appointed along with the persons entitled to the remainder of the estate.

(3) The heirs *ab intestato*, that is to say:

(a) children including adopted [29] and (where the death occurred on or after November 25, 1968) illegitimate children;

(b) their legitimate issue, degree by degree [30];

(c) if the deceased was illegitimate, the mother, or (where the death occurred on or after November 25, 1968) the surviving parent or parents [31];

(d) the surviving parent or parents if any, *and*

(i) brothers and sisters of the full blood, whom failing,

(ii) legitimate issue of brothers and sisters of the full blood,[32] degree by degree,[30] whom failing,

(iii) brothers and sisters of the half-blood, ranking without distinction between consanguinean and uterine, whom failing,

(iv) the legitimate issue of brothers and sisters of the half-blood, degree by degree [30];

(e) the surviving spouse;

(f) collaterals of the deceased's parents [33];

(g) their legitimate issue, degree by degree;

(h) the grandparents;

(i) collaterals of grandparents [33];

(j) their legitimate issue, degree by degree;

(k) ancestors generation by generation successively, the brothers and sisters [33] of any failing ancestor and their legitimate issue having right before the ancestors of the next more remote generation.

Although there is provision for infinite representation—for example, the child of a predeceasing child of the deceased can take along with the surviving children—it is provided that the right of persons taking by representation to be appointed to the office of executor is postponed to the

---

[28] 1964 Act, s. 9 (4).

[29] 1964 Act, s. 23; Adoption Act 1968, s. 4 (2).

[30] See the following paragraph on the effect of representation.

[31] 1964 Act, s. 4, as amended by Law Reform (Miscellaneous Provisions) (Scotland) Act 1968, s. 1.

[32] Where a person is adopted by two spouses jointly he is deemed to be related as a brother or sister of the full blood to the children or adopted children of both spouses and of the half blood to the children or adopted children of one of the spouses. If the adoption is not by spouses jointly, he is treated as a collateral of the half blood of the children or adopted children of the adopters or of either of the adopters (1964 Act, s. 24).

[33] Again the full blood and their issue are preferred to the half-blood.

right of persons taking directly who apply for appointment.[34] It is probably still competent to appoint an executor *qua* next-of-kin even although the beneficial succession is now regulated by the 1964 Act and not by the common law.[35] The Act does not expressly alter the prior law as to the appointment of executors and the schedules to the Act of Sederunt (Confirmation of Executors) 1964 provide for decerniture *qua* next-of-kin. Moreover, under the prior law a next-of-kin had a good title to the office of executor although he had no beneficial interest in the succession.[36]

In the Edinburgh Commissary Court, where a person such as a surviving spouse had a right to the office of executor the court has appointed a next-of-kin if the spouse declined the office and consented to the procedure but where the spouse was *incapax* the court refused to appoint a next-of-kin unless a curator was appointed to the spouse who could decline and consent on her behalf (*Jack*, March 2, 1967, unreported).

The Confirmation of Executors (Scotland) Act 1823, s. 1,[37] provided that where one of the next-of-kin died before confirmation was expede, his right would transmit to his representatives and confirmation could be granted to the representatives in the same manner as it might have been granted to the next-of-kin. In practice the representatives are required to confirm to the estate of the deceased next-of-kin. This provision can presumably still operate where the deceased person was one of the next-of-kin. It may be that the same principle would be applied even where the deceased was entitled to the estate but was not one of the next-of-kin on the ground that beneficial interest is the primary criterion.

(4) the surviving spouse *qua* relict.

(5) special legatees including liferenters.

(6) the procurator-fiscal.[38]

(7) the funerator. In practice, this can be done only where, in a small estate, the next-of-kin are unknown or incapacitated or decline to act. The applicant must be the undertaker or the person who paid the undertaker's account. There must be advertisement in the *Edinburgh Gazette* and, if there are no known next-of-kin, by virtue of an official instruction, intimation must be made to the Queen's and Lord Treasurer's Remembrancer.

Two persons may be confirmed either in the same character or in different characters.[39] An application to be confirmed can be lodged after an appointment has been made but before confirmation has been issued.[40] An assignee of the only person having an interest in the estate can be confirmed as executor-dative.[41]

[34] 1964 Act, s. 5. There was a corresponding provision in the Intestate Moveable Succession (Scotland) Act 1855, s. 1—see p. 429, *supra*.
[35] Meston, 77.
[36] *Bones* v. *Morrison* (1866) 5 M. 240.
[37] See *Webster* v. *Shiress* (1878) 6 R. 102; *Chrystal* v. *Chrystal*, 1923 S.L.T.(Sh.Ct.) 69.
[38] Such confirmations are now rare. As to the procedure see Currie, 120.
[39] *Muir* (1876) 4 R. 74; *Webster* v. *Shiress* (1878) 6 R. 102.
[40] Dobie, *Sheriff Court Practice*, 440.
[41] *Macpherson* v. *Macpherson* (1855) 17 D. 357.

Special cases

The following can be appointed executor-dative—a corporation; a company [42]; an undischarged bankrupt [43]; an enemy alien.[44] The court refused to appoint as executor-dative a person who had been appointed to collect and hold during the dependence of a suit the personal estate in England of a person who had died domiciled in Paraguay.[45]

A factor may confirm in his own name as executor-dative and as factor for the use and behoof of his ward unless some other person having a title offers to confirm.

> " Where it is necessary by law, that such money, or effects, or moveables, should be confirmed, the said factor may confirm the same in his own name as executor-dative, and as factor appointed by the Lords of Council and Session, on the estate of such a person, and for the use and behoof of the said person and of all that have, or shall have interest, unless some other person having a title offer to confirm...." [46]

Accordingly, where other persons were willing to confirm, appointment of a curator *bonis* to an insane person was refused.[47] Approval has been given to a procedure whereby a minor was decerned executrix-dative, the minor's mother was then appointed as factrix to the minor and the mother was confirmed *qua* factrix for the executrix.[48] Pupils and minors can be confirmed in their own names as executor-dative but this course is undesirable.[49]

The appointment of an executor-dative *qua* factor to a pupil or minor does not terminate on the attainment of majority by the ward.[50] The appointee is not a mere *locum tenens* but is clothed with the full office and powers of an executor.

The petition

The essential averments of the petition [51] are as to the place and date of death, the intestacy, the domicile of the deceased at death, and the relationship of the pursuer [52] or other facts giving him right to apply. If the deceased died testate, the testamentary writings must be referred to and the originals or extracts produced. Any person who, if he had survived the deceased, would have had a prior claim to the office of executor must be

---

[42] Currie, 132.

[43] Currie, 123.

[44] *Schulze*, 1917 S.C. 400. See also *Crolla*, 1942 S.C. 21 (detainee under emergency powers).

[45] *Whiffin* v. *Lees* (1872) 10 M. 797.

[46] Act of Sederunt, February 13, 1730, s. 7. See *Judicial Factors*, 88, 151.

[47] *Martin* v. *Ferguson's Trs.* (1892) 19 R. 474.

[48] *Johnstone* v. *Lowden* (1838) 16 S. 541.

[49] Currie, 121. As to commissary factors, see Currie, 121–123; *Accountant of Court*, 1907 S.C. 909; *Haston* (1930) 46 Sh.Ct.Rep. 141.

[50] *Johnston's Exor.* v. *Dobie*, 1907 S.C. 31.

[51] The form is prescribed by the Act of Sederunt (Confirmation of Executors), 1964 (1964 S.L.T.(News) 158) S.I. 1964 No. 1143 (s. 77) (Sched. 2,)

[52] Although the application is by petition, the applicant is referred to as the pursuer. The prior practice was to head the application as an Initial Writ but the form given in the 1858 Act is a petition brought by a petitioner.

eliminated. If the deceased was survived by a spouse who is not the pursuer, the reason must be given why the petition is not brought by the surviving spouse unless (a) the deceased died prior to 10 September, 1964, leaving no issue and it is averred that the net estate exceeds £5,000 [53] or (b) the deceased died on or after that date and it is averred that the estate of the deceased exceeds the prior rights of the surviving spouse.[54] If the deceased was domiciled outwith Scotland there should be an averment that the pursuer is entitled to decerniture under the law of the domicile. An opinion of a qualified person as to foreign law will be required.

Procedure

A petition for appointment as executor-dative is presented in the sheriff court of the county in which the deceased died domiciled or if he died domiciled furth of Scotland, or without any fixed or known domicile, having property in Scotland, to the Edinburgh Commissary Court.[55] Intimation must be effected by affixing a full copy of the petition on the door of the sheriff court house or in some conspicuous place of the court or of the office of the sheriff clerk in such manner as the sheriff shall direct.[56] The sheriff clerk must certify that it has been intimated by endorsing the petition " Intimated in terms of the statute." [57] The certificate dated and signed by the sheriff clerk is sufficient evidence of intimation. Special intimation must be made of any subsequent petition in respect of the estate of the same deceased to all executors already decerned or confirmed.[57]

On the expiration of nine clear days from the date of certification of intimation, if neither answers nor a competing petition nor a caveat have been lodged, the petition may be laid before the sheriff in chambers without the calling of the petition in court and without the attendance of the pursuer or his solicitor and if the sheriff is satisfied that the petition is in proper form and that the proceedings have been regular, he may, without hearing any party, decern the pursuer executor or may, in his discretion, direct the petition to be called and heard in court *quam primum*.[58] Where the averments do not disclose any objection to the appointment of the pursuer and there is no competing petition, the sheriff must grant decree *de plano*.[59]

The decree-dative may be extracted three lawful days after it has been pronounced [60] unless there has been a competition in which event, as a

[53] This is to exclude the spouse's absolute right under the Intestate Husband's Estate (Scotland) Acts.

[54] This is to exclude the spouse's right under s. 9 (4) of the Succession (Scotland) Act 1964.

[55] Confirmation of Executors (Scotland) Act 1858 (21 & 22 Vict. c. 56) ss. 2, 3.

[56] Act of Sederunt (Edictal Citations, Commissary Petitions and Petitions of Service) 1971 (1971 S.L.T.(News) 187).

[57] Sheriff Courts (Scotland) Act 1876, s. 44, as amended by Act of Sederunt (Confirmation of Executors Amendment No. 2) 1971 (1971 S.L.T.(News) 228).

[58] Act of Sederunt (Unopposed Executry Petitions) 1948 (1948 S.L.T.(News) 44) (S.I. 1948 No. 621 (s. 44)).

[59] *Henderson* (1906) 22 Sh.Ct.Rep. 186.

[60] 1858 Act, s. 6. For the form of extract, see Act of Sederunt (Confirmation of Executors) 1964, Sched. 1. (S.I. 1964 No. 1143) (1964 S.L.T.(News) 158).

matter of practice, extract is not issued until the time for appeal has elapsed.[61] Where a decree has been extracted but confirmation has not been obtained, it is competent to present a petition for recall of the decree and for decerniture of another person as executor-dative.[62] Once confirmation has been issued, it is incompetent to grant a second decerniture or confirmation until the first has been reduced in the Court of Session.[63]

Caution

An executor-dative must find caution [64] even if he is acting as a judicial factor and has already found caution in that capacity. An individual acting as cautioner must satisfy the court of his ability to guarantee the necessary amount. A company is accepted if it has been accepted by the Court of Session under section 27 of the Judicial Factors (Scotland) Act 1849. Two or more cautioners may be conjoined. The amount required is in the court's discretion. If it is not restricted by the court,[65] it must be for the gross amount of the estate without deduction for debts. The bond, which may be partly printed and partly written,[66] must be executed by the executor and the cautioner. It is exempt from stamp duty.[67] It is not subject to the septennial prescription.[68] In practice, the bond of caution is never given up.[69] The cautioner is bound jointly and severally with the executor to make forthcoming the estate given up in the inventory. The maximum amount of his liability is ascertained by the inventory. A beneficiary can sue the cautioner for the value of his share in the estate.[70]

Executor's position

An executor-dative has the whole powers, privileges and immunities and is subject to the same obligations, limitations and restrictions which gratuitous trustees have or are subject to under statute or common law.[71] He is a " trustee " for purposes of the Trusts (Scotland) Acts 1921 and 1961.[71] He must, however, find caution and he does not have power to resign or to assume new trustees.[71] After he has been decerned the executor-dative must expede confirmation of the estate in the same way as an executor-nominate.[72] The oath must narrate the decree-dative. The confirmation of an executor-dative was formerly known as a " testament-dative."

[61] Currie, 130.
[62] *Webster* v. *Shiress* (1878) 6 R. 102; *Murray* v. *Murray* (1888) 4 Sh.Ct.Rep. 129.
[63] *Todd* v. *Todd* (1886) 2 Sh.Ct.Rep. 83; *Johnstone* v. *Johnstone* (1904) 20 Sh.Ct.Rep. 50.
[64] Confirmation of Executors (Scotland) Act 1823, s. 2. An executor-nominate need not find caution.
[65] As to applications for restriction, see Currie, 230–232 and " Restriction of Caution," 1966 S.L.T.(News) 11. A separate petition is necessary—*Girdwood* (1930) 46 Sh.Ct.Rep. 115.
[66] 1858 Act, s. 6.
[67] Finance Act 1949, s. 35 (1).
[68] *Gallie* v. *Ross* (1836) 14 S. 647.
[69] Currie, 133.
[70] *Scott* v. *McNab* (1902) 10 S.L.T. 288.
[71] 1964 Act, s. 20.
[72] For the form of the confirmation, see the Act of Sederunt (Confirmation of Executors) 1967 (S.I. 1967 No. 789 (S. 58)).

Eiks

There may be an eik to a confirmation of any part of the estate which is afterwards discovered.[73] The whole of the additional estate must be confirmed. An additional inventory specifying the amounts comprised in any former inventory should be submitted within two calendar months after the discovery.[74] If any inventories have already been lodged with the Estate Duty Office containing items which are confirmable but to which an eik was not required, they must be submitted to the sheriff clerk and the items must be included in the eik.[75]

An eik can also be used by lodging a corrective additional inventory where an item has been wrongly described in the original inventory.

Confirmation ad non executa [76]

If all the executors are dead or incapable of acting, confirmation *ad non executa* may be granted to any estate contained in the original confirmation which remains unuplifted or has not been transferred to the persons entitled thereto.[77] It is granted to the same persons and according to the same rules as confirmations *ad omissa*. So, when the deceased's father had confirmed as executor-dative and died before the estate was distributed, the father's executors were entitled to be appointed executors *ad non executa* along with a brother of the deceased.[78]

The confirmation is a sufficient title to continue and complete the administration of the estate.[79] It may be specified as a midcouple or link of title for the purposes of any deduction of title from the former executors.[77]

Executors ad omissa vel male appretiata [80]

Confirmation *ad omissa vel male appretiata* is competent where an item of estate has been omitted from, or undervalued in, the original confirmation and the original executors decline to obtain an eik or are not available to do so. An inventory *ad omissa* must be submitted unless the items have already been included in a recorded inventory.[81] The person entitled to apply is the person who would have been entitled to the original confirmation if the first executor had declined. So where the first to be confirmed was an executor-nominate, the general disponee can be confirmed as executor *ad omissa*. It is important to observe, however, that the governing principle is beneficial interest in the succession and so, where the first executor had a beneficial interest in the whole succession—as heir

---

[73] Confirmation of Executors (Scotland) Act 1823, s. 3. For the form of eik, see Act of Sederunt (Confirmation of Executors) 1967 (S.I. 1967 No. 789 (S. 58)).
[74] Probate and Legacy Duties Act 1808, ss. 38 and 40.
[75] Currie, 279.
[76] See Stair, III, 8, 61; Ersk., III, 9, 38; *Nicol and Carny* v. *Wilson* (1856) 18 D. 1000.
[77] Executors (Scotland) Act 1900, s. 7, as amended by the Succession (Scotland) Act 1964, Sched. 2, para. 14.
[78] *Chrystal* v. *Chrystal*, 1923 S.L.T.(Sh.Ct.) 69.
[79] A standard form of inventory is now supplied by sheriff clerks—J.L.S. 1967, 236. The executor *ad non executa* is entitled to delivery of the papers relating to the estate (*Grant* v. *Gordon Falconer & Fairweather* (1932) 48 Sh.Ct.Rep. 155).
[80] Stair, III, 8, 62; Ersk. III, 9, 36.
[81] A standard form of inventory is now supplied by sheriff clerks—J.L.S. 1967, 236.

ab intestato, for example—and has died, *his* executor is entitled to the confirmation.

Ad omissa

Before confirmation *ad omissa* can be obtained there must be special intimation to any executor already appointed so that he may himself take up the estate by an eik, or move that the two appointments be conjoined.[82]

> " The general rule . . . is that the executor who has confirmed is the party who is cited in the confirmation *ad omissa*, and has an opportunity of adding to his inventory, and it is only if he does not add to his inventory that there is granted to the party seeking it a separate confirmation *ad omissa*." [83]

This does not apply where the first executor is an executor-creditor because he is not confirming for behoof of all concerned.[84] Nor does the rule apply where there are allegations of fraud against the first executor.

Small estates

The basic legislation on this subject comprises the Intestates Widows and Children (Scotland) Act 1875, and the Small Testate Estates (Scotland) Act 1876, which now apply to all applicants for confirmation, wherever the deceased may have died domiciled, where the value of the net estate is less than £1,000 *and* that of the gross estate is less than £3,000.[85] The gross estate is the aggregate of the heritable and moveable property, excluding property settled otherwise than by the will of the deceased, in respect of which estate duty would be payable if the duty were payable in respect of estates however small the principal value thereof.[86] The value of the net estate is the value of the gross estate less the aggregate of the funeral expenses, debts and incumbrances for which an allowance falls to be made under section 7 (1) of the Finance Act 1894 in determining the value of the estate for the purpose of estate duty.

Where a person dies intestate leaving an estate within the statutory limits, a separate petition for appointment as executor-dative is not necessary. The sheriff clerk will prepare an inventory and oath, take the applicant's oath thereto, and, on caution being found, will record the inventory and expede confirmation.[87] Sufficient proof of the identity and relationship of the applicant may be required.[88]

---

[82] *Johnston's Exor.* v. *Dobie*, 1907 S.C. 31, 36, *per* Lord Pearson.
[83] *Smith's Trs.* v. *Grant* (1862) 24 D. 1142, 1164, *per* Lord President McNeill.
[84] *Ibid.*; *Lee* v. *Jones*, F.C. May 17, 1816.
[85] Customs and Inland Revenue Act 1834; Small Estates (Representation) Act 1961, s. 1, which applied to deaths on or after April 10, 1946 (Small Estates (Representation) Act (Commencement) Order 1961). The limit for deaths prior to that date was £500 (Finance Act 1894, s. 16 (1)).
[86] The sum can accordingly include *inter vivos* gifts made by the deceased.
[87] 1875 Act, s. 3. Formerly, under the Executors (Scotland) Act 1900, s. 9, the inventory could alternatively be lodged with certain Inland Revenue officers but they no longer have these functions (Finance Act 1967, s. 10; S.I. 1968 No. 361 (c. 6)).
[88] 1875, s. 4. In practice two witnesses attend with the applicant and their depositions are recorded with the inventory and oath (Currie, 226).

Where a person dies testate leaving estate within the limits, the executor may apply to the sheriff clerk who, on production of the will [89] and sufficient proof of the executor's identity, will prepare an inventory, take the oath and take the necessary steps to have confirmation issued.[90]

The statutory procedure cannot be used if there is competition for the office of executor.[91] Nor can it be used in a case of presumed death.[92]

The same rules and procedure govern the issue of eiks and confirmations *ad omissa* where estate has been omitted and *ad non executa* where estate remains unadministered provided the total value of estate does not exceed the statutory limits. Where additional estate is discovered which brings the total value of estate above the statutory limits and the original executor is still acting, the practice is to issue a confirmation *ad omissa* under the normal procedure albeit that it is being issued to an executor who has already been confirmed. An executor-dative is required first to petition for decerniture as executor-dative *ad omissa*.[93]

English and Irish estate

Formerly, the confirmation to the estate of a person dying domiciled in Scotland had to be resealed in the High Court before it had force and effect in England.[94] Now, the confirmation to the estate of a person dying domiciled in Scotland which notes his Scottish domicile is, without being resealed, treated for the purposes of the law of England and Wales as a grant of representation to the executors named in the confirmation in respect of the property of the deceased of which according to the terms of the confirmation they are executors.[95] The grant of representation is treated as a grant of probate where it appears from the confirmation that the executors named are executors-nominate and in any other case it is treated as a grant of letters of administration.[96] Section 7 of the Administration of Estates Act 1925, under which an executor of an executor represents the original testator, does not apply on the death of an executor named in the confirmation.[97] The executor cannot be compelled to deliver up his grant to the High Court.[98] The provision applies to additional confirmations in relation to the items of property specified therein, and to certificates of confirmation, provided always that the Scottish domicile is noted.

A document purporting to be a confirmation, additional confirmation or certificate of confirmation given under the seal of office of any commissariot in Scotland shall, except where the contrary is proved, be taken in

---

[89] Witnesses are required to attend to set up a holograph will.
[90] 1876 Act, s. 3.
[91] Currie, 223.
[92] Currie, 226.
[93] Currie, 228.
[94] For the prior law, see *Orr Ewing's Trs.* v. *Orr Ewing* (1885) 13 R.(H.L.) 1.
[95] Administration of Estates Act 1971, s. 1. The provision applies to confirmations expede before as well as after the commencement of the Act (January 1, 1972).
[96] s. 1 (2).
[97] s. 1 (3).
[98] s. 1 (5).

England and Wales and Northern Ireland, to be such document without further proof. A document purporting to be a duplicate of such a document and to be given under such a seal is receivable in evidence in like manner and for the like purposes as the document of which it purports to be a duplicate.[99]

There is a corresponding provision for Northern Ireland.[1] There is no machinery for the recognition or resealing of confirmations in Eire, the Channel Islands or the Isle of Man.

A confirmation or additional confirmation granted in respect of property situated in Scotland of a person who died domiciled there, which notes that domicile, may contain or have appended thereto and signed by the sheriff clerk a note or statement of property in England and Wales or Northern Ireland held by the deceased in trust, being a note or statement which has been set forth in any inventory recorded in the books of the court of which the sheriff clerk is clerk.[2] The provisions of the 1971 Act apply in relation to such property as they apply to property specified in the confirmation or additional confirmation i.e. the executor is treated as if he had a grant of representation in respect of the trust property.

English and Irish grants

Formerly, an English or Irish grant had to be certified in the Edinburgh Commissary Court before it had effect in Scotland.[3] Now, a grant of probate or letters of administration of the estate of a person dying domiciled in England and Wales or Northern Ireland, from the High Court in England and Wales or Northern Ireland, as the case may be, which notes the domicile, has, without being resealed, the like force and effect and the same operation in relation to property in Scotland as a confirmation given under the seal of office of the Commissariot of Edinburgh to the executor or administrator named in the probate or letters of administration.[4] A document purporting to be a grant of probate or of letters of administration issued under the seal of the High Court in England and Wales or Northern Ireland, is to be taken, except when the contrary is proved, to be such a grant without further proof. A document purporting to be a copy of such a grant and to be sealed with such a seal is receivable in evidence in like manner and for the like purposes as the grant of which it purports to be a copy.[5]

The Colonial Probates Act 1892

Under the Colonial Probates Act 1892 [6] probate or letters of administration granted by a court of probate in a British possession to which the

---

[99] s. 4 (1).   [1] s. 2.
[2] s. 5.
[3] For the common law, see Bell v. Elliot (1686) Mor. 9860.
[4] Administration of Estates Act 1971, s. 3. The section applies to probates and letters of administration granted before as well as after the commencement of the Act (January 1, 1972).   [5] s. 4 (2), (3).
[6] 55 & 56 Vict. c. 6. The Act was extended to protected, mandated and trust territories by the Colonial Probates (Protected States and Mandated Territories) Act 1927 (17 & 18 Geo. 5, c. 43) and the Mandated and Trust Territories Act 1947 (11 & 12 Geo. 6, c. 8).

Act applies can be sealed in the Edinburgh Commissary Court. The document then has the like form and effect and the same operation in the United Kingdom as if granted by the Scottish court.[7] The grant or a sealed duplicate or certified copy [8] must be produced with a copy for deposit. In practice, an inventory and oath must be produced. The court may require such evidence, if any, as it thinks fit as to the deceased's domicile. The court must be satisfied that United Kingdom estate duty has been paid. If the grant is not in favour of an executor-nominate the court must be satisfied that security has been given to cover the property in the United Kingdom.[9] The court may also, if it thinks fit, on the application of any creditor require that adequate security be given for the payment of debts due from the estate to creditors residing in the United Kingdom.[10] The court may refuse sealing if it is doubtful whether the persons to whom the grant was issued would be entitled to confirmation in Scotland.[11] If one of the persons to whom the grant was issued has died, sealing is not possible.[12] The Act applies to a limited grant.[13] The countries and territories to which the Act applies were set forth in Schedule 1 to the Colonial Probates Act Application Order 1965 [14] which consolidated most of the prior orders but (i) South Africa has to be added [15]; (ii) the Act ceased to apply to Aden on November 30, 1967; (iii) grants of representation made by the High Court of Rhodesia after September 13, 1968 will not be resealed.[16] The Act is based on reciprocity and a Scottish confirmation can be resealed in the courts of the countries to which the Act applies. Certified extracts of the confirmation and the testamentary writings are usually necessary.[17]

Consular Conventions Act 1949

The Consular Conventions Act 1949 [18] applies where a national of a State to which the Act applies has been named as executor in the will of a deceased person disposing of property in Scotland or is otherwise a person who may be appointed or confirmed as executor on the estate in Scotland

[7] s. 2 (1).
[8] s. 2 (4).
[9] s. 2 (2).
[10] s. 2 (3).
[11] Currie, 260.
[12] Currie, 259.
[13] *Smith* [1904] P. 114.
[14] S.I. 1965 No. 1530. The following statutes preserve the position of the countries concerned:—Lesotho Independence Act 1966 (c. 24) s. 2; Botswana Independence Act 1966 (c. 23) s. 2; Malawi Republic Act 1966 (c. 22) s. 1; Swaziland Independence Act 1968 (c. 56); Guyana Republic Act 1970 (c. 18) s. 1; Sierra Leone Republic Act 1972 (c. 1) s. 1; Sri Lanka Republic Act 1972 (c. 55) s. 1; Bangladesh Act 1973 (c. 49) s. 1.
[15] South Africa Act 1962 (10 & 11 Eliz. 2, c. 23) s. 2 (1) and Sched. 2, para. 1; S.R. & O. 1914 No. 144.
[16] 1970 S.L.T.(News) 84.
[17] Currie, 261.
[18] 12, 13 & 14 Geo. 6, c. 29, s. 2. The foreign states specified by Order in Council are: Austria, Belgium, Bulgaria, Denmark, Estonia, Federal Republic of Germany, Finland, France, Greece, Hungary, Italy, Japan, Mexico, Norway, Poland, Spain, Sweden, Thailand, Turkey, U.S.A., U.S.S.R., and Yugoslavia. For Orders see Index to Government Orders *s.v.* Administration of Estates 3.

of a deceased person. A consular officer of the State, if satisfied that the
national is not resident in Scotland and is not represented by a person
authorised by power of attorney to act for him in the matter, may make
application for the national to be appointed or confirmed as executor on
the estate of the deceased as if he had been authorised by a power of
attorney. If the application is granted, the officer and his successors in
office are entitled to receive and administer the estate and to do all things
necessary in that behalf as if authorised by power of attorney.

CHAPTER 30

THE EXECUTOR'S TITLE

The estate

The heritable and moveable estate falling to be administered under the law of Scotland which has been included in the confirmation vests by virtue of the confirmation in the executor for purposes of administration. The estate to which the executor can confirm—the estate *in bonis defuncti* —consists of the heritable and moveable estate belonging to the deceased at the time of his death or over which the deceased had power of appointment and includes any interest held by the deceased immediately before his death as a tenant under a tenancy or lease which was not expressed to expire on his death.[1] Heritable property which belongs to the deceased and is subject to a special destination in favour of another person which could not be, or has in fact not been, evacuated by the deceased, does not vest in the executor for administration as estate of the deceased but the executor can confirm thereto and it then vests in the executor only for the purpose of enabling it to be conveyed to the person next entitled thereto under the destination, if such conveyance is necessary.[2] Where any heritable property over which the deceased had a power of appointment was not disposed of in the exercise of that power and is then subject to a power of appointment by another person, the property is not treated as estate of the deceased.[3]

The confirmation including a heritable security or a description of heritable property is a valid title to the heritable security or heritage and is a warrant for the executor dealing with it and completing title thereto.[4] Probate or letters of administration or other grant of representation issued by any court in England and Wales or Northern Ireland and noting the domicile of the deceased in England and Wales or Northern Ireland, as the case may be, or issued by any court outwith the United Kingdom and sealed in Scotland under the Colonial Probates Act 1892 is an implied confirmation and has the same effect as a title to securities and heritage but it need not contain a reference to the heritable security or a description of the heritage.[4]

On the death of the heir of entail in possession of property subject to an entail, the entailed property, if it is included in the confirmation, vests in

[1] 1964 Act, ss. 14 (1), 36 (2).
[2] s. 18 (2). A conveyance is not necessary in the case of a survivorship destination: McDonald (1965) 10 J.L.S. 73; Meston, 83.
[3] s. 36 (2).
[4] Conveyancing (Scotland) Act 1924, s. 5 (2); Administration of Estates Act 1971, Sched. 1, para. 3.

441

the deceased's executor for the sole purpose of enabling it to be conveyed to the heir of entail next entitled thereto if such conveyance is necessary.[5]

Where a partnership contract provided that, if one of the partners died during the continuance of the partnership leaving a widow or children surviving him, the surviving partner should for six months thereafter pay a share of profits to the executors for the benefit of the widow and children, it was held that the share of profits did not form part of the deceased partner's executry estate.[6] A gratuity payable to the representatives of a deceased civil servant under the Superannuation Act 1909 was held, on a construction of the statute, to form part of the executry estate although it was not *in bonis* of the deceased at the time of his death.[7] Where the deceased had been sequestrated twelve years before his death but no trustee had been appointed in the sequestration, it was held that his executor had no title to recover an item of the estate because there was no *prima facie* case that the creditors had abandoned the property.[8]

Rights of action

The executor is always entitled to be sisted in an action raised by the deceased, without prejudice to the question of whether he will be allowed to proceed further with the action.[9] Where the executor had no interest in the merits of the action and the defenders' conduct had not been unreasonable, the executor was not allowed to continue with the action merely for the purpose of recovering expenses.[9] An executor can raise an action of damages in respect of patrimonial loss sustained by the deceased.[10] Loss of wages constitutes patrimonial loss.[11] He cannot, however, recover solatium in respect of injuries sustained by the deceased because the claim is personal to the party injured.[12] If the deceased had raised an action, however, the executor can continue it and recover the pecuniary damages to which the deceased was entitled.[13]

Where the deceased had brought an action for declarator of an irregular marriage with an alternative conclusion for damages for breach of promise and seduction, the executor was allowed to pursue the conclusion for damages.[14] Where the deceased had obtained a decree of divorce against his wife who had reclaimed, it was held that his executors were entitled to sist themselves as respondents in the reclaiming note to support

[5] 1964 Act, s. 18 (1).
[6] *Adamson's Trs.* v. *Adamson's Exors.* (1891) 18 R. 1133. See also *Ventisei* v. *Ventisei's Exors.*, 1966 S.C. 21.
[7] *Beveridge* v. *Beveridge's Exrx.*, 1938 S.C. 160. *Cf. Craigie's Trs.* v. *Craigie* (1904) 6 F. 343.
[8] *Milne* v. *British Linen Bank*, 1937 S.L.T. 419.
[9] *Martin's Exrx.* v. *McGhee*, 1914 S.C. 628.
[10] *Auld* v. *Shairp* (1874) 2 R. 191.
[11] *Smith* v. *Stewart & Co.*, 1961 S.C. 91.
[12] *Bern's Exor.* v. *Montrose Asylum* (1893) 20 R. 859; *Stewart* v. *London Midland & Scottish Ry.* 1943 S.C.(H.L.) 19. Intimation of a claim by the deceased does not give the executor a title to sue for solatium. (*Smith* v. *Stewart & Co.*, 1960 S.C. 329; overruling *Leigh's Exrx.* v. *Caledonian Ry.*, 1913 S.C. 838).
[13] *Neilson* v. *Rodger* (1853) 16 D. 325; *Darling* v. *Gray & Sons* (1892) 19 R.(H.L.) 31.
[14] *Green or Borthwick* v. *Borthwick* (1896) 24 R. 211.

the decree.[15] The executor of the mother of an illegitimate child cannot insist in an action raised by the deceased for custody of the child.[16]

The executor can raise an action to eject intruders from property forming part of the estate and has a duty to protect the moveable estate on such property.[17] A husband has no right to retain moveables belonging to his deceased wife's estate against the executor on account of his claim as relict or as having paid the funeral expenses.[18] The executor has a title to sue a poinding of the ground.[19]

As there is no passive representation in crime, the executors of a person who dies after having appealed against conviction by stated case cannot be sisted as parties to the appeal.[20]

Where executors granted an assignation of a copyright before they had obtained confirmation, it was held that the assignee had a title to sue for infringement but could not extract a decree for payment before confirmation was expede.[21] Similarly, executors not yet confirmed may appoint a mandatary to vote at meetings of creditors in a sequestration.[22] " A general disposition unconfirmed is a license to sue, and so is a decree dative." [23] It is not necessary to confirm to a right of reduction because the right of raising necessary actions is part of the office of executor which is a general title of administration.[24]

Recovery of debts

If the deceased had not pursued the debt and if it is transmissible, his executors may raise an action for its recovery. This may be done before they have confirmed to the debt but confirmation must be obtained before the decree is extracted.[25] A summons which was served by the deceased but had not been called, can be called in the name of his representatives.[26] If the deceased had raised an action for recovery of the debt which is in dependence, his executors are entitled to be sisted in his place,[27] even after judgment has been given.[28] If the deceased had obtained a decree which had not been extracted before his death, the executors, before they can proceed with diligence, must present in the Petition Department a bill for letters of horning and poinding together with proof of their title. On the bill being passed, the letters can be signeted and they

15 *Ritchie* v. *Ritchie* (1874) 1 R. 826.
16 *Brand* v. *Shaws* (1888) 15 R. 449.
17 *McPhail* v. *McGregor* (1920) 36 Sh.Ct.Rep. 177.
18 *Bell* v. *Scott* (1894) 11 Sh.Ct.Rep. 220.
19 *Crabb's Exors.* v. *Laurie* (1917) 33 Sh.Ct.Rep. 143.
20 *Keane* v. *Adair*, 1941 J.C. 77. L.J.-C. Cooper at p. 80 discusses *Cathcart* v. *Houston*, 1915 S.C.(J.) 5, in relation to active transmission in a private prosecution.
21 *Mackay* v. *Mackay*, 1914 S.C. 200. See also *Crabb's Exors.* v. *Laurie* (1917) 33 Sh.Ct.Rep. 143.
22 *Chalmers' Trs.* v. *Watson* (1860) 22 D. 1060.
23 p. 1064, *per* Lord Ivory.
24 *Johnston's Exor.* v. *Dobie*, 1907 S.C. 31.
25 *Mackay* v. *Mackay*, 1914 S.C. 200.
26 *Gallie* v. *Lockhart* (1840) 2 D. 445; Maclaren, *Court of Session Practice*, 350.
27 *Martin's Exrx.* v. *McGhee*, 1914 S.C. 628.
28 *Scott* v. *Mills's Trs.*, 1923 S.C. 726; *Cumming* v. *Stewart*, 1928 S.C. 709.

then constitute a warrant for diligence.[29] If the deceased had extracted a
decree in his favour, the executors present the extract together with the
confirmation and a minute to the Petition Department.[30] A deliverance is
written on the extract which then forms a warrant for diligence.[31] If a
charge had been served prior to death, the execution of the charge is
presented to the Petition Department in the same way. If a poinding had
been executed, the executors can obtain a warrant for sale on production
of the confirmation.[32] If the warrant had been obtained prior to death the
executors may carry out the sale without further procedure.[33] Where an
arrestment had been executed before death, the executors can raise a
furthcoming.[34] An inhibition which has been served transmits to the
executors if they sist themselves as pursuers in the relevant action.[35] If the
deceased was creditor under a deed which could have been registered for
execution, but was in fact not so registered, the executors must proceed by
letters of horning and poinding.[36] If the deed had been registered, the
executors present the extract together with the confirmation to the Petition
Department and deliverance is written on the extract which forms a
warrant for diligence.[37]

Liability to account

The executor must account for his own intromissions and for the
amount of the funds in the inventory.[38] If he has not intromitted with the
estate concerned, he is not under an obligation to account for the deceased's intromissions as executor or universal legatee of the estate of
another deceased.[39] The remedy of a creditor of the first deceased is to
sequestrate the estate of that deceased and possibly that of the deceased
executor as well. The executor is liable to account for estate liferented by
the deceased of which the deceased had possession as executor.[40]

Other dispositions

Deeds other than wills may have a testamentary effect and may operate
to transfer property *in bonis* of the deceased at the date of death to someone
other than the executor. Such property is nevertheless available for payment of the deceased's debts.[41]

---

[29] J. Graham Stewart, *Law of Diligence* (1898), 284.
[30] In the case of a sheriff court decree, the sheriff clerk.
[31] Personal Diligence Act 1838, ss. 7, 12.
[32] Graham Stewart, 363.
[33] Graham Stewart, 363.
[34] Ersk. III, 6, 11; Graham Stewart, 134.
[35] Bankton, I, 7, 140; Graham Stewart, 552.
[36] Graham Stewart, 284.
[37] Personal Diligence Act 1838, ss. 7, 12.
[38] Bell, *Prin.* s. 1900; *Renton* v. *Renton* (1851) 14 D. 35.
[39] *Hutcheson & Co.'s Administrator* v. *Taylor's Exrx.*, 1931 S.C. 484.
[40] *Dingwall* v. *Dow*, 1909, 2 S.L.T. 311.
[41] *Renouf's Trs.* v. *Haining*, 1919 S.C. 497, 507, *per* Lord Dundas.

Special assignations

The Confirmation Act 1690 [42] provides that special assignations and dispositions made by the deceased shall constitute good and valid rights even although the money or goods contained therein have not been confirmed. This is without prejudice to the rights and diligence of creditors.

Nominations

Under several statutes a nomination has testamentary effect in relation to a particular sum of money. [43] The following funds are affected: sums payable by a trade union [44] or friendly society [45] on the death of a member; deposits in the National Savings Bank [46] or a trustee savings bank [47]; shares, loans or deposits in a co-operative society. [48] The maximum sum is in general £500. [49] In some instances there is provision for payment to creditors or persons entitled to legal rights from the estate of the deceased.

For example, a depositor in a trustee savings bank of the age of sixteen or upwards can nominate any person to receive any sum not exceeding £500 due to the depositor at his decease but a depositor cannot have more than one nomination in force at any time and the trustees may in their absolute discretion refuse to accept or register any nomination. [50] The nomination must be in writing, witnessed and registered by the trustees. [51] It may be in favour of several persons. [52] It is revoked by, *inter alia*, notice in writing, the nominee's death or the nominator's marriage but not by a subsequent will. [53] On the depositor's death, payment is made to the nominee but the trustees have a discretion to satisfy the claim of a creditor [54] or to apply the amount nominated towards satisfaction of a claim for legal rights. [55]

Where the nomination is not regulated by statute, but is made in terms of the rules of an association, it is a question of construction whether the nominee is given a beneficial interest or whether he is merely the person who has the legal title to receive payment and must account to the executor. [56]

---

[42] The effect of the statute is expressly preserved by the 1823 Act, s. 3. See also Ersk. III. 9, 30; Bell, *Prin.* s. 1892; *Robertson* v. *Gilchrist* (1828) 6 S. 446; *Bell* v. *Willison* (1831) 9 S. 266; *Innerarity* v. *Gilmore* (1840) 2 D. 813; *Lyle* v. *Falconer* (1842) 5 D. 236; *Duff's Trs.* v. *Phillips*, 1921 S.C. 287, 298, *per* Lord Skerrington.

[43] *Gill* v. *Gill*, 1938 S.C. 65; *Ford's Trs.* v. *Ford*, 1940 S.C. 426. As to authentication of nominations, see *Morton* v. *French*, 1908 S.C. 171.

[44] Industrial Relations (Nominations) Regulations 1971 (S.I. 1971 No. 2085).

[45] Friendly Societies Act 1896 (59 & 60 Vict. c. 25), ss. 56, 57.

[46] National Savings Bank Regulations 1972 (S.I. 1972 No. 764).

[47] Trustee Savings Bank Regulations 1972 (S.I. 1972 No. 583), regs. 11–15.

[48] Industrial and Provident Societies Act 1965, ss. 23–24. See also The Great Western Railway Act 1885 (48 & 49 Vict. c. cxlvii), s. 45 (7); The Taff Vale Railway Act 1895 (58 & 59 Vict. c. cxxii), s. 18 (9); The London, Midland and Scottish Railway Act 1924 (14 & 15 Geo. 5, c. liv), s. 61 (9); The Southern Railway Act 1924 (14 & 15 Geo. 5, c. lxvi), s. 99 (10).

[49] Administration of Estates (Small Payments) Act 1965, s. 2.

[50] Trustee Savings Bank Regulations 1972 (S.I. 1972 No. 583), regs. 11–15.

[51] Reg. 11.

[52] Reg. 11 (9).

[53] Reg. 12.

[54] Reg. 14.

[55] Reg. 21 (2).

[56] *Young* v. *Waterson*, 1918 S.C. 9. *Campbell* v. *Campbell*, 1917, 1 S.L.T. 339, seems to have been decided on a misunderstanding of the facts.

Special destinations

The title to property, heritable or moveable may be held on a special destination, *e.g.* " A whom failing B," " A and B and the survivor." [57] Heritable property subject to a special destination is not part of the deceased's estate for purposes of the 1964 Act unless the destination is one which could competently be, and has in fact been, evacuated by the deceased by testamentary disposition or otherwise.[58]

The first question which arises is whether the deceased had power to evacuate the destination. Where the property was the subject of a gift to the deceased, and the destination was in terms instructed by the donor, the deceased has no power to evacuate it by gratuitous testamentary settlement.[59] Accordingly where the destination is taken to the donor, the donee and the survivor, the donor can, but the donee cannot, evacuate the destination in respect of his half share.[60]

It seems, however, that this principle applies only to survivorship destinations and does not operate where the destination is " to A whom failing B." It is trite law that a substitution can be defeated by the institute's gratuitous disposition of the property, by *inter vivos* deed or testamentary settlement.[61] Moreover, it is implied in the rules about to be stated as to whether a destination which could be revoked has been revoked, that a testator can in some circumstances revoke a destination made by another party.

If the destination is taken as a result of a contractual arrangement, where, for example, each party has contributed cash or property rights to the acquisition of the property and takes the chance of getting the other's half, the destination cannot be evacuated.[62] In ascertaining whether a contractual arrangement was made, the court is not bound by any statement in the narrative of the disposition and can proceed on extrinsic evidence contradicting the narrative.[63]

The second question which can arise is whether a destination which could have been evacuated by the deceased has been evacuated by him. This is a question of intention. Prior to the 1964 Act the presumption was that a general testamentary disposition and settlement which recalled all other testamentary writings and was a general conveyance, did not revoke special destinations taken prior to the date of the will by the testator himself but did operate to revoke a destination made by another person. A second presumption was that a special destination taken by the testator

---

[57] *Perrett's Trs.* v. *Perrett*, 1909 S.C. 522; *Hay's Tr.* v. *Hay's Trs.*, 1951 S.C. 329. See Walker, 1832.

[58] 1964 Act, s. 36 (2).

[59] *Renouf's Trs.* v. *Haining*, 1919 S.C. 497; *Taylor's Exors.* v. *Brunton*, 1939 S.C. 444.

[60] *Brown's Tr.* v. *Brown*, 1943 S.C. 488; *Hay's Tr.* v. *Hay's Trs.*, 1951 S.C. 329.

[61] *Baine* v. *Craig* (1845) 7 D. 845; Candlish Henderson, 53.

[62] *Brown* v. *Advocate-General* (1852) 1 Macq. 79; *Perrett's Trs.* v. *Perrett*, 1909 S.C. 522; *Chalmers's Trs.* v. *Thomson's Exrx.*, 1923 S.C. 271; *Shand's Trs.* v. *Shand's Trs.*, 1966 S.C. 178.

[63] *Hay's Tr.* v. *Hay's Trs.*, *supra.*

after the date of his testament was not affected by the terms of the testament.[64] Both presumptions could be redargued by circumstances.[65]

Section 30 of the 1964 Act provides that a testamentary disposition executed on or after September 10, 1964, shall not have effect so as to evacuate a special destination (being a destination which could competently be evacuated by the testamentary disposition) unless it contains " a specific reference to the destination and a declared intention on the part of the testator to evacuate it."

Heritable property subject to an unevacuated special destination does not pass to the executor but he may confirm thereto for the purpose of conveying it to the person next entitled.[66] A destination in a deposit-receipt has no testamentary effect.[67]

Donation mortis causa

A donation *mortis causa* is:

" a conveyance of an immoveable or incorporeal right, or a transference of moveables or money by delivery, so that the property is immediately transferred to the grantee, upon the condition that he shall hold for the granter so long as he lives, subject to his power of revocation, and, failing such revocation, then for the grantee on the death of the granter." [68]

If the grantee predeceases the granter the property reverts to the granter and the qualified right of property which was vested in the grantee is extinguished by his predecease.

Solicitors' client accounts

On the death of a solicitor who immediately before his death was practising as a solicitor in his own name or as a sole solicitor in a firm name the right to operate on or otherwise deal with any " client account " in the name of the solicitor or his firm vests in the Law Society of Scotland to the exclusion of any personal representatives of the solicitor. The right is exercisable as from the death of the solicitor.[69] A " client account " is a current, deposit or savings account, or a deposit receipt, at a bank in the title of which the word " client," " trustee," " Trust " or other fiduciary term appears. It includes an account or a deposit receipt for a client whose name is specified in the title of the account or deposit receipt.

[64] *Campbell* v. *Campbell* (1880) 7 R.(H.L.) 100; *Perrett's Trs.* v. *Perrett, supra*; *Cunningham's Trs.* v. *Cunningham*, 1922 S.C. 581; *Drysdale's Trs.* v. *Drysdale*, 1922 S.C. 741; *Murray's Exors.* v. *Geekie*, 1929 S.C. 633.

[65] As in *Turnbull's Trs.* v. *Robertson*, 1911 S.C. 1288; *Dennis* v. *Aitchison*, 1924 S.C.(H.L.) 122.

[66] See p. 441, *supra*.

[67] *Connell's Trs.* v. *Connell's Trs.* (1886) 13 R. 1175. A cheque has no testamentary effect (*Stewart's Trs.*, 1953 S.L.T.(Notes) 25).

[68] *Morris* v. *Riddick* (1867) 5 M. 1036, 1041, *per* L.P. Inglis. See McLaren, I, 434; Walker, 1830; *Gray's Trs.* v. *Murray*, 1970 S.L.T. 105; *Forrest-Hamilton's Tr.* v. *Forrest-Hamilton*, 1970 S.L.T. 338.

[69] Solicitors (Scotland) Act 1965, s. 3.

Payment to executor

A person or corporation who, in reliance on any instrument purporting to be a confirmation (or any instrument purporting to be a probate or letters of administration issued by any court in England and Wales or Northern Ireland and noting the domicile of the deceased as being in England and Wales or Northern Ireland, as the case may be,[70]) has made or has permitted to be made a payment or transfer bona fide upon such document, shall be indemnified and protected in so doing, notwithstanding any defect or circumstance whatsoever affecting the validity of the document.[71] The executor or his agent is the only person entitled to uplift the estate.[72] The debtor cannot safely pay the executor a sum larger than that appearing in the confirmation.[73] A debtor who has paid the executor is not concerned with the application of the money unless he knows of the executor's intention to misapply it.[74]

Vitious intromission

A person who, without lawful title, takes possession of the deceased's property—known as a vitious intromitter—may incur a general liability for all the debts of the deceased which is not limited to the value of the estate.[75] Innocent continuance of possession while confirmation is being obtained is not vitious intromission.[76] Liability may be elided:

(a) if the intermeddler subsequently is confirmed as an executor other than an executor-creditor;

(b) if the intermeddler can show that he has a probable title of some kind other than confirmation.[77] Moreover, if a fraudulent intention is excluded, "equity interposes" and the intermeddler may not be held liable if he has accounted for his intromissions.[78]

Payment without confirmation

Under a large number of statutes, provision has been made for payments of small sums to the relatives of a deceased person without the necessity of confirmation. A degree of uniformity was achieved by the Administration of Estates (Small Payments) Act 1965 which amended most of the statutes to make the maximum amount five hundred pounds and extended the provisions to cover testate cases where they did not already do so.

---

[70] Administration of Estates Act 1971, Sched. 1, para. 1.
[71] Confirmation and Probate Amendment Act 1859 (22 Vict. c. 30), s. 1.
[72] *Barnet* v. *Duncan* (1831) 10 S. 128.
[73] *Buchanan* v. *Royal Bank of Scotland* (1842) 5 D. 211.
[74] *Taylor* v. *Forbes* (1830) 4 W. & S. 444.
[75] Bell, *Prin.* s. 1921; *Wood* v. *Stewart* (1915) 31 Sh.Ct.Rep. 133. See also *Forbes* v. *Forbes* (1823) 2 S. 395; *Wilson* v. *Taylor* (1865) 3 M. 1060; *Greig* v. *Christie*, 1908 S.C. 370. It would seem that the principle extends to heritable as well as moveable estate by virtue of the Succession (Scotland) Act 1964.
[76] *Thomson* v. *Jones* (1834) 13 S. 143.
[77] *Chalmers* v. *Dalgarno* (1662) Mor. 9857.
[78] Ersk. III, 9, 53; *Adam* v. *Campbell* (1854) 16 D. 964; *Pringle & Alexander* v. *Semple* (1913) 29 Sh.Ct.Rep. 187; *Lees* v. *Reid & Campbell* (1913) 29 Sh.Ct.Rep. 191.

Government annuities

Sums not exceeding five hundred pounds due in respect of government or savings bank annuities may be paid without confirmation if the National Debt Commissioners so direct to or among the persons appearing to the Commissioners to be beneficially entitled to the estate of the deceased or to one or more of these persons.[79]

Trade union funds

Where a member of a registered trade union was entitled to a sum not exceeding five hundred pounds from the union funds and had made no nomination, payment can be made without confirmation to the person who appears to a majority of the directors, upon such evidence as they may deem satisfactory, to be entitled by law to receive the same.[80]

Friendly societies

If a member of a friendly society dies entitled to a sum not exceeding five hundred pounds from the funds thereof without having made a nomination, the society may, without confirmation or probate, distribute the sum among such persons as appear to the committee, upon such evidence as they may deem satisfactory, to be entitled by law to receive that sum. If the member is illegitimate, the society may pay the sum which that member might have nominated to or among the persons who, in the opinion of the committee, would have been entitled thereto if that member had been legitimate, or if there are no such persons, the society shall deal with the money as the Treasury may direct.[81]

Co-operative societies

Where a member of a registered industrial and provident society leaves property in the society in shares, loans or deposits not exceeding in the whole five hundred pounds and there has been no nomination, the committee of the society may pay the amount due without confirmation to such persons as appear to the committee on such evidence as they deem satisfactory to be entitled by law to receive it.[82] It is provided that if the member was illegitimate, left no widow, widower or issue (including any illegitimate child), and neither of his parents survived him, the committee shall deal with his property in the society as the Treasury shall direct.[83]

Building societies

Where a member of, or depositor with, a building society has a sum of money in the funds of the society not exceeding five hundred pounds, the amount due may be paid without confirmation to the person who appears to the directors to be entitled to receive it under the law for the time being

---

[79] Government Annuities Act 1929 (19 & 20 Geo. 5, c. 29), ss. 21, 57.
[80] Industrial Relations (Nominations) Regulations 1971 (S.I. 1971 No. 2085).
[81] Friendly Societies Act 1896 (59 & 60 Vict. c. 25), s. 58.
[82] Industrial and Provident Societies Act 1965 (c. 12), s. 25 (1).
[83] s. 25 (2), am. by Family Law Reform Act 1969 (c. 46), s. 19 (2).

in force in England and Wales or in Scotland. The society must receive satisfactory evidence of the death and a statutory declaration that the member or depositor has died and that the person claiming the amount is entitled to receive it. Where payment has been made to the person who at that time appeared to be entitled to the deceased's effects, the payment shall be valid and effectual with respect to any demand against the funds of the society from any other person as next-of-kin or as the lawful representative of the deceased but the next-of-kin or representative nevertheless has a remedy against the person who received it.[84]

Seamen's estates

If the value of the residue of the assets of a deceased merchant seaman in the hands of the Board of Trade does not exceed five hundred pounds, the Board, unless confirmation or representation has to the Board's knowledge been granted, may pay or deliver it or distribute it among any person appearing to the Board to be a person named as the next-of-kin in the crew agreement or list of the crew in which the seaman's name last appeared, any person appearing to the Board to be the deceased's widow or child (including an adopted and an illegitimate child) any person appearing to the Board to be beneficially entitled, under a will or on intestacy, to the seaman's estate or any part of it, or any person appearing to the Board to be a creditor of the deceased.[85] If the person is resident abroad, payment may be made to a consular officer of the foreign state.[86] On payment the Board is discharged from any further liability.

Similar provisions apply to trustee savings bank deposits[87]; national savings bank deposits[88]; premium savings bonds[89]; national health service superannuation[90]; teachers' superannuation[91]; police[92] and fire service[93] pensions.

The effect of provisions of this type was considered in Symington's

---

[84] Building Societies Act 1962 (10 & 11 Eliz. 2, c. 37), s. 46.
[85] Merchant Shipping Act 1970 (c. 36), s. 66.
[86] s. 66 (4).
[87] Trustee Savings Banks Regulations 1972 (S.I. 1972 No. 583), reg. 18.
[88] National Savings Bank Regulations 1972 (S.I. 1972 No. 764), reg. 40.
[89] Premium Savings Bonds Regulations 1972 (S.I. 1972 No. 765), reg. 12.
[90] Superannuation (Miscellaneous Provisions) Act 1967 (c. 28), s. 6 (2).
[91] Teachers (Superannuation) (Scotland) Regulations 1957 (S.I. 1957 No. 356), reg. 58.
[92] Police Pensions Regulations 1962 (S.I. 1962 No. 2756), reg. 57 (3).
[93] Firemen's Pension Scheme 1964 (S.I. 1964 No. 1148), art. 47 (3). For other statutory instruments, see Administration of Estates (Small Payments) Act 1965, Sched. 1, Part III. See also: Friendly Societies Act 1829 (10 Geo. 4, c. 56), s. 24. Army Pensions Act 1830 (11 Geo. 4 & 1 Will. 4, c. 41), s. 5. Loan Societies Act 1840 (3 & 4 Vict. c. 110), s. 11. Navy and Marines (Property of Deceased) Act 1865 (28 & 29 Vict. c. 111), ss. 5, 6, 8. Great Western Railway Act 1885 (48 & 49 Vict. c. cxlvii), s. 45 (8). Regimental Debts Act 1893 (56 & 57 Vict. c. 5.), ss. 7, 9, 16. Taff Vale Railway Act 1895 (58 & 59 Vict. c. cxxii), s. 18 (10). Superannuation (Ecclesiastical Commissioners and Queen Anne's Bounty) Act 1914 (4 & 5 Geo. 5, c. 5), s. 7. London, Midland and Scottish Railway Act 1924 (14 & 15 Geo. 5, c. liv), s. 61 (11). Southern Railway Act 1924 (14 & 15 Geo. 5, c. lxvi), s. 99 (12). Superannuation (Various Services) Act 1938 (1 & 2 Geo. 6, c. 13), s. 2. Greenwich Hospital Act 1942 (5 & 6 Geo. 6, c. 35), s. 2. London and North Eastern Railway Act 1944 (7 & 8 Geo. 6, c. x), s. 3 (12) (b). U.S.A. Veterans' Pensions (Administration) Act 1949 (12, 13 & 14 Geo. 6, c. 45), s. 1 (3) (c). Local Government Superannuation Act 1953 (1 & 2 Eliz. 2, c. 25), s. 25 (1).

Exor. v. *Galashiels Co-operative Store Co. Ltd.*[94] where the society's committee had paid to one of the next-of-kin under a power contained in the Industrial and Provident Societies Act 1876, s. 11 (6), to pay to "the persons who appear to a majority of the committee, upon such evidence as they may deem satisfactory, to be entitled by law to receive the same." In an action brought by another of the next-of-kin who had been appointed executor-dative, it was held that the society had acted *ultra vires* in making the payments because the person to whom they had paid was not the person entitled by law.

Lord President Robertson said [95]:

"That provision is plainly intended to save the expense of requiring strict legal evidence of propinquity or title in the case of small successions which could not well afford such expense. It in no way at all alters the legal succession, or allows the society to alter it, or authorises them to pick and choose among those known to them to be the legal successors of the deceased. If they find the legal representatives, or think they have found them, on such evidence as satisfies a majority of the committee, then they may pay to those persons without liability to pay over again in case of mistake. But, if they first find the legal representatives, and then do not pay to them, but only to some of them without authority of the rest, such a proceeding is, in my judgment, wholly unauthorised by the section."

[94] (1894) 21 R. 371.
[95] p. 376.

CHAPTER 31

THE DUTIES OF THE EXECUTOR ·

DUTY TO INGATHER

THE executor's primary duty is to ingather the estate so that he may pay the debts due by the deceased and then distribute the remainder among the persons entitled thereto. An executor has by virtue of his office power to realise the whole moveable estate.[1] As regards heritage, he is in the same position as a trustee.[2]

An executor is liable to be debited with the value of any estate which he fails to realise.[3] The fact that the executor has a beneficial interest in the estate is not an excuse for his failure to use due diligence in ingathering it.[4] If a beneficiary claims that the executor has not realised an asset of the estate, his usual remedy is to raise an action against him calling on him to realise and account for the asset.[5] The alternative of the beneficiary having himself confirmed as executor-dative *ad omissa et non executa* and suing the person in possession of the asset is open to objection.[6] A legatee under a special bequest can sue the person in possession of the subject if he calls the executor as well.[7] A residuary legatee, however, as a rule, cannot sue the testator's debtor.[8] A beneficiary will be allowed to sue a debtor to the estate in the executor's name if the executor refuses to do so.[9] He must, however, keep the executor *indemnis* by finding caution for expenses. A beneficiary was allowed to bring an action against one trustee as an individual and the other trustees as trustees concluding that the individual should account to the trustees for a sum alleged to be due by him to the trust.[10]

If the executor holds as an individual a document of debt granted by the deceased, a beneficiary can bring an action against the executor to reduce the document.[11] Beneficiaries cannot normally sue solicitors employed by

[1] *Brownlie* v. *Brownlie's Trs.* (1879) 6 R. 1233, 1241, *per* Lord Shand.
[2] See Chap. 21.
[3] *Donald* v. *Hodgart's Trs.* (1893) 21 R. 246.
[4] *Forman* v. *Burns* (1853) 15 D. 362.
[5] *Donald* v. *Hodgart's Trs.*, *supra*; *Smith* v. *Smith* (1880) 7 R. 1013. See *Reid* v. *Reid*, 1938 S.L.T. 415.
[6] *Thatcher* v. *Thatcher* (1904) 11 S.L.T. 605. See also *Donald* v. *Hodgart's Trs.* (1893) 21 R. 246.
[7] *Blair* v. *Stirling* (1894) 1 S.L.T. 599; *Morrison* v. *Morrison's Exrx.*, 1912 S.C. 892. See also *Aitken* v. *Taylor* (1912) 28 Sh.Ct.Rep. 297; *Young* v. *Young* (1930) 47 Sh.Ct.Rep. 102. *Cf. Inglis' Tr.* v. *Kellar* (1900) 8 S.L.T. 323.
[8] *Hinton* v. *Connell's Trs.* (1883) 10 R. 1110.
[9] *Morrison* v. *Morrison's Exrx.*, *supra*.
[10] *Watt* v. *Roger's Trs.* (1890) 17 R. 1201. *Teulon* v. *Seaton* (1885) 12 R. 971, was another exceptional case.
[11] *Strachan* v. *Strachan* (1894) 1 S.L.T. 498.

the trustees in respect of a breach of duty.[12] The duty is to the trustees and not to the beneficiaries. But if the trustees fail to act, the beneficiaries may compel them to do so or even enforce the right themselves.

The executor has no title to represent a creditor of the deceased to the effect of enforcing a claim which that creditor may have to a fund which does not form part of the executry estate.[13]

PAYMENT OF DEBTS

In distributing the estate, the first duty of the executor is to pay the debts due by the deceased. It has been laid down on several occasions that the executor is not a trustee for the creditors of the deceased.

> " An executor is not a trustee for either creditors or legatees, though he is bound to satisfy the claims of both, just as a testator is bound to satisfy the claims of his creditors during his lifetime. He is in the shoes of the testator deceased, and his capacity being representative, and not fiduciary, is the ground of all the duties imposed on him, and all the equities against him." [14]

> " An executor is not a trustee in the sense of being a depositary. A trustee has to hold as a depositary; not so an executor, who has to administer, not to hold. An executor must pay legacies and debts within a certain time, and is liable in interest if he does not. An executor is nothing else than a debtor to the legatees or next of kin. He is a debtor with a limited liability; but he is nothing else than a debtor; and the creditors of the deceased and the legatees who claim against him do so as creditors." [15]

These dicta must however be considered in their context and it must be kept in mind that an executor is now subject to the limitations and restrictions which gratuitous trustees have under statute and common law.

On the principle set forth in these dicta, it has been held that it is sufficient if an executor retains funds of the value of the deceased's estate at the date of death and is ready to pay debts to the extent of the value, and that he is not bound to segregate the estate and is not liable to account for the profits he may make from the use of the estate.[16] However these propositions must be treated with caution and it is not clear that they can apply beyond the circumstances of the cases in which they were laid down.

Time of payment

The executor cannot be compelled to pay an ordinary debt until the expiry of six months from the date of death. The six months period derives

---

[12] *Raes* v. *Meek* (1889) 16 R.(H.L.) 31.

[13] *Livie* v. *Anderson* (1903) 11 S.L.T. 229.

[14] *Globe Insurance Co.* v. *McKenzie* (1850) 7 Bell's App.Cas. 296, 319, *per* Lord Brougham; *Lawson's Tr.* v. *Lawson*, 1938 S.C. 632.

[15] *Jamieson* v. *Clark* (1872) 10 M. 399, 405, *per* L.P. Inglis.

[16] *Stewart's Tr.* v. *Stewart's Exrx.* (1896) 23 R. 739; *Morrison's Tr.* v. *Morrison*, 1915, 2 S.L.T. 296. But see *Lawrence* (1872) 2 Couper 168.

from the Act of Sederunt of February 28, 1662,[17] which provided that all creditors citing the executors before the expiry of half a year from the date of death were to rank *pari passu*. The object of the provision is to prevent the creditors who heard of the death first gaining an advantage over those who were at a distance.

Privileged debts

Most modern writers assert that the executor can safely pay within the six-months period certain privileged debts—expenses of confirmation, funeral and deathbed expenses, reasonable family mournings,[18] the current term's board and wages of the deceased's domestic and farm servants.[19] Some add rates and taxes and rates payable under the Ministers' Widows' Fund Act 1779. The institutional writers explain that these debts could be paid because they were preferable.[20]

The Bankruptcy (Scotland) Act 1913 [21] has extended the category of preferential debts in a sequestration and has reformulated the preference for servants' wages and for taxes. It would appear that the category of privileged debts should either extend to all the debts preferred in a sequestration or, as seems more logical, be restricted to expenses of confirmation and funeral (including cremation [22]) and deathbed expenses. The position of funeral and deathbed expenses is expressly preserved by the 1913 Act and they rank prior to other preferential debts.[23] From a practical point of view, it might be difficult for an executor to know whether all claims for debts preferred under the 1913 Act had been lodged.

The privileged debts rank *pari passu*.[24]

Interim aliment

A widow who has no means of her own and who has been given no other provision is entitled to interim aliment for herself and the children from the date of death except, perhaps, where the estate is manifestly insolvent.[25] She is not obliged to wait for payment until six months have expired. This is so notwithstanding the decision in *Lindsay's Creditors* v. *His Relict* [26] that interim aliment is not a privileged debt.

After six months

After the expiry of the six months, if the executor is satisfied on reasonable grounds that the estate is solvent, he can pay *primo venienti*. But

---

[17] Re-enacting the Acts 1654, cc. 16 and 18. See Stair, III, 8, 68; Bell, *Comm.* II, 83; *Sanderson* v. *Lockhart-Mure*, 1946 S.C. 298.

[18] See *Morrison* v. *Cornfoot* (1930) 46 Sh.Ct.Rep. 74; *Griffiths' Trs.* v. *Griffiths*, 1912 S.C. 626.

[19] Gloag & Henderson, 628; Walker, 1867; Encyclopaedia, s.v. " Executor," Vol. 6, p. 507.

[20] Stair, III, 8, 72; Ersk. III, 9, 43; Bankton, III, 8, 86; Bell, *Comm.* II, 147. See also Instructions to the Commissaries, January 21, 1666; *Kelhead* v. *Irvine* (1674) Mor. 11826; *Dunipace* v. *Watson and Vert* (1750) Mor. 11852.

[21] s. 118, as amended by Companies Act 1947, s. 115 (1).

[22] Cremation Act 1902, s. 9.

[23] s. 118 (5); Goudy, *Bankruptcy*, 4th ed., 514, 515.

[24] *Peter* v. *Monro* (1749) Mor. 11852.

[25] *Barlass* v. *Barlass's Trs.*, 1916 S.C. 741. See also *Harkness* v. *Graham* (1836) 14 S. 1015.

[26] (1714) Mor. 11847. Lord Johnston distinguishes this case in *Barlass, supra*, p. 748.

although he is not a trustee for the creditors the executor does owe a duty to them. He is not entitled to pay a deferred creditor and leave a preferred creditor unsatisfied; and if, at the expiry of the six months, creditors come forward in such numbers that it is obvious that the estate is insolvent, he must give notice to the creditors and refrain from paying more to one than to another.

> " I can scarcely suppose that an executor with creditors (who cannot claim payment before the six months) is entitled, so to speak, to get up early in the morning of the day of the elapse of the six months and pay the creditor who is his friend, and say to the other creditors, ' Well, I have paid away the money, and I have nothing more to say to you.' " [27]

If a creditor with a contingent claim does nothing for a period he takes the risk that the estate will be disposed of by the executor.[28]

An executor against whom claims are made which are greater than the estate in his hands may raise an action of multiplepoinding to obtain exoneration. A similar action may be brought at the instance of the creditors with the assent of the executor.[29] The limit of liability is the estate of the deceased which is in the executor's hands or which he can recover by the exercise of reasonable diligence. He has no duty to the creditors as regards estate which he cannot ingather.[30] A creditor cannot sue a trustee or executor who has lawfully resigned for payment of a debt which was due by the deceased.[31]

Payment to beneficiaries

The executor is not entitled to make payment to the beneficiaries without first providing for payment of the debts.[32] If he fails to pay the debts before disposing of the estate, he is liable to the creditors and is not protected by an immunity clause.[33] It is a defence that the payment was made bona fide in excusable and legitimate ignorance of the existence of the claim.[34] The executor is not freed from liability because he thought that reasonable provision had been made to meet the debt.

> " It is therefore not doubtful in point of law that if trustees and executors, after six months, pay away the funds, even to legatees, in the reasonable belief that all debts have been satisfied, they cannot be made personally responsible, although if there was from the first a deficiency of funds the legatees may be obliged to pay back what they have got to the unpaid creditor. Creditors are bound to make their

[27] *Laird* v. *Hamilton*, 1911, 1 S.L.T. 27, 29, *per* L.P. Dunedin.
[28] *Taylor & Ferguson Ltd.* v. *Glass's Trs.*, 1912 S.C. 165.
[29] *Jamieson* v. *Robertson* (1888) 16 R. 15.
[30] *Lawson's Tr.* v. *Lawson*, 1938 S.C. 632.
[31] *Town & County Bank Ltd.* v. *Walker* (1904) 12 S.L.T. 411; (1905) 13 S.L.T. 287.
[32] *Lamond's Trs.* v. *Croom* (1871) 9 M. 662; *Heritable Securities Investment Association Ltd.* v. *Miller's Trs.* (1893) 20 R. 675.
[33] *Ibid.* Lord Kinloch (p. 672) was not prepared to say that such a clause could never be pleadable against creditors.
[34] *Stewart's Trs.* v. *Evans* (1871) 9 M. 810; *Beith* v. *Mackenzie* (1875) 3 R. 185.

claim in reasonable time; and if they so act as to induce executors to believe that the debt is abandoned or discharged they cannot make them responsible for acting on a belief they have themselves created, although their debt may remain entire against the estate." [35]

Recourse against beneficiaries

If the executor has properly paid out the estate to the beneficiaries, the creditor's remedy is to sue them, although it seems that the claim should be constituted against the executor first.[36] The creditor cannot recover from a legatee if at the time of payment of the legacy there were sufficient funds in the hands of the executor and the creditor has failed *debito tempore* to claim against the executor.[37] If the creditor proceeds against the executor or a beneficiary and the estate of the person concerned is sequestrated, the creditor has a preference in competition with the bankrupt's creditors over the deceased's assets which can be identified and distinguished. This now rests on the common law.[38] The preferential right is subject to the long negative prescription and may be extinguished in a shorter period by personal bar or acquiescence.[39]

Validity of claims

The executor can pay a debt without requiring a decree to be obtained against him.[40]

As a trustee, he has implied power under section 4 (1) (*l*) of the 1921 Act, if it is not at variance with the terms or purposes of the trust, to pay debts due by the deceased without requiring the creditors to constitute the debts if he is satisfied that the debts are proper debts of the deceased. But if the estate is small and the amount of the claims uncertain and the existence or amount of the alleged debt doubtful, he is entitled to protect himself and the estate by requiring formal constitution.[41] There is no absolute rule that a creditor must constitute his debt at his own expense.[42] If the executor puts forward an unreasonable defence he may be held personally liable in expenses with a right of relief against the estate.[43] In some circumstances he may be justified in raising an action of multiple-poinding.[44]

---

[35] *Stewart's Trs.* v. *Evans* (1871) 9 M. 810, 813, *per* L.J.-C. Moncreiff.
[36] *Poole* v. *Anderson* (1834) 12 S. 481; *Clelland* v. *Baillie* (1845) 7 D. 461; *Stewart's Trs.* v. *Evans* (1871) 9 M. 810; *Beith* v. *Mackenzie* (1875) 3 R. 185.
[37] Ersk. III, 9, 46; *Robertson* v. *Strachans* (1760) Mor. 8087; *Wyllie* v. *Black's Tr.* (1853) 16 D. 180; *Threipland* v. *Campbell* (1855) 17 D. 487; *Magistrates of St. Andrews* v. *Forbes* (1893) 31 S.L.R. 225.
[38] Bell, *Comm.* II, 85; McLaren, II, 866, 1299; Graham Stewart, *Diligence*, 681; *Menzies* v. *Poutz*, 1916 S.C. 143. The Act 1661, c. 24, which applied to heritable estate, has been repealed (Succession (S.) Act 1964, Sched. 3). The Confirmation Act 1695 applies only where an executor has not been confirmed.
[39] *Traill's Trs.* v. *Free Church of Scotland*, 1915 S.C. 655.
[40] *Laird* v. *Hamilton*, 1911, 1 S.L.T. 27; *Taylor & Ferguson Ltd.* v. *Glass's Trs.*, 1912 S.C. 165; 1921 Act, s. 4 (1) (*l*). The older law was different—*Johnston* v. *Kincaide* (1664) Mor. 3853; *Binning* v. *Hamilton* (1675) Mor. 3853; *Andrew* v. *Anderson* (1677) Mor. 3854.
[41] *McGaan* v. *McGaan's Trs.* (1883) 11 R. 249.
[42] *Barclays Bank Ltd.* v. *Lawton's Trs.*, 1928 S.L.T. 298. *Cf. Harper* v. *Connor's Trs.* (1927) 43 Sh.Ct.Rep. 138.
[43] *Law* v. *Humphrey* (1876) 3 R. 1192.
[44] *Jamieson* v. *Robertson* (1888) 16 R. 15. *Cf. Mackenzie's Trs.* v. *Sutherland* (1895) 22 R. 233.

An executor is entitled to make payment of sums due to himself as an individual unless the estate is apparently insolvent or there is a dispute about the validity of the claim.[45] If the executor's personal claim is seriously disputed by the beneficiaries he must be replaced by a judicial factor, so that the claim may be determined by some form of judicial process.

A solicitor employed by the executor to ingather the estate which is found to be insolvent is entitled to retain the proceeds of the estate realised by him in extinction of a debt due to him by the deceased because the executor is *eadem persona cum defuncto*.[46] The executor is not *eadem persona cum defuncto* to the effect of making a debt which he incurs in the course of the administration a debt due by the defunct.[47] A sum due to the widow under an antenuptial marriage-contract may be a debt.[48] The deathbed and funeral expenses of the deceased's widow are a proper charge on the estate if she has died in indigent circumstances.[49]

There may be a claim by the widow or children of the deceased in respect of future aliment. If it is a valid existing claim it must be met [50] and may be paid out of capital.[51] It is not, however, in the same position as the claim of an ordinary creditor and it can be enforced against the trustees only so long as they stand possessed of the estate. Once the time for distribution of the estate has arrived, the trustees are not bound to retain sufficient funds to meet the claim.[52] The claim can then be enforced only against the deceased's special representatives who are *lucrati* by the succession.[53]

Incidence of debts

Although a creditor is entitled to payment of his debt from any part of the debtor's estate, in questions between the debtor's representatives, heritable debts must be paid from the heritable estate and moveable debts from the moveable estate.[54] The distinction can still be of importance where legal rights are claimed and in some cases of intestacy. The testator may, of course, alter the incidence of debt by express direction or clear implication.[55]

---

[45] *Salaman* v. *Sinclair's Tr.*, 1916 S.C. 698; *Watson* v. *British Linen Bank*, 1941 S.C. 43. Where the executor's claim as an individual creditor exhausted the estate, he was held entitled to raise a multiplepoinding to obtain exoneration (*Ironside* v. *Ironside* (1911) 27 Sh.Ct.Rep. 321).

[46] *Mitchell* v. *Mackersy* (1905) 8 F. 198.

[47] *Macdonald Fraser & Co.* v. *Cairns's Exrx.*, 1932 S.C. 699.

[48] *Dowager Countess of Galloway* v. *Stewart* (1903) 11 S.L.T. 188.

[49] *Heriot* v. *Blyth* (1681) Mor. 5924; *Wardhaugh* v. *Baldie* (1922) 38 Sh.Ct.Rep. 39.

[50] *Spalding* v. *Spalding's Trs.* (1874) 2 R. 237.

[51] *Anderson* v. *Grant* (1899) 1 F. 484.

[52] *Edinburgh Parish Council* v. *Couper*, 1924 S.C. 139.

[53] *Mackintosh* v. *Taylor* (1868) 7 M. 67; *Howard's Exor.* v. *Howard's C.B.* (1894) 21 R. 787; *Davidson's Trs.* v. *Davidson*, 1907 S.C. 16; *Edinburgh Parish Council* v. *Couper*, 1924 S.C. 139.

[54] *Carnousie* v. *Meldrum* (1630) Mor. 5204; McLaren, II, 1305; 1964 Act, s. 14 (3).

[55] *Douglas's Trs.* v. *Douglas* (1868) 6 M. 223; *Macleod's Trs.* (1871) 9 M. 903; *Muir's Trs.* v. *Muir*, 1916, 1 S.L.T. 372.

As a general rule, debts vesting *in obligatione* are moveable *quoad debitorem*. The following moveable debts require special mention: the unpaid price of heritage [56]; arrears of feu-duty [57] and rent [58]; an obligation of warrandice.[59] Debts secured over heritage, real burdens and annuities [60] are heritable. Annual sums of aliment are not heritable debts.[61] Where the security subjects are insufficient in value to satisfy the heritable debt secured, the other heritable estate is liable for the balance.[62]

Where heritable property or a heritable bond which is heritable *quoad ius relictae* has been disponed or assigned in security by the deceased, the debt constituted by the advances made on the security falls to be charged against the subject of the security.[63] The rule is the same where the deceased has given a specific legacy of heritable or moveable property which is subject to a security: the legacy is taken *cum onere*.[64]

The general debts falling to be charged against the moveable estate should be deducted from the gross moveable estate as ascertained for the purpose of computing legal rights. Heritable bonds which are heritable *quoad ius relictae* need not bear a rateable share of the general debts.[63]

There may also be a question as to the incidence of debts between the beneficiaries entitled to capital and those entitled to income. This can arise where the payment of the debts has been postponed and they are eventually paid in part from accumulated income. The solution reached in an Outer House case [65] was that the debts fall to be paid out of such sum of capital as, with simple interest thereon at the net rate earned by the trust estate from the date of death of the testator till the respective dates of payment, was sufficient to satisfy these debts. The net interest is the rate earned after deducting any interest paid on the debts.[66]

Interest does not run on general legacies during a period in which the estate is insolvent, there is in the estate no asset available to meet the legacies and the return on the estate is going to the creditors.

Estate duty

The executor is liable to pay the estate duty in respect of all moveable property wheresoever situate of which the deceased was competent to dispose at his death on exhibiting and recording the inventory and may pay the duty on any other property passing on death which by virtue of any testamentary disposition of the deceased is under control of the executor or, in the case of property not under his control, if the persons accountable

[56] *Clayton* v. *Lothian* (1826) 2 W. & S. 40; *Ramsay* v. *Ramsay* (1887) 15 R. 25.
[57] *Johnston* v. *Cochran* (1829) 7 S. 226.
[58] *Kinloch's Exors.* v. *Kinloch,* (1811) Hume 178.
[59] *Duchess of Montrose* v. *Stuart* (1887) 15 R.(H.L.) 19.
[60] *Crawford's Trs.* v. *Crawford* (1867) 5 M. 275.
[61] *Countess de Serra Largo* v. *Largo's Trs.,* 1933 S.L.T. 391.
[62] *Bell's Trs.* v. *Bell* (1884) 12 R. 85.
[63] *Heath* v. *Grant's Trs.,* 1913 S.C. 78.
[64] *Stewart* v. *Stewart* (1891) 19 R. 311.
[65] *Wilson's Tr.* v. *Morton,* 1938 S.L.T. 215. But see Dobie, *Liferent and Fee,* 166–174, where it is argued that this was an abnormal case.
[66] *Waddell's Trs.* v. *Crawford,* 1926 S.C. 654.

for the duty thereon request him to make payment.[67] If he does not know
the value of any property passing on death he may state in the inventory
that it exists and undertake to submit an account and pay the appropriate
duty when the amount and value of the property is ascertained.[68] The
executor is also accountable for estate duty in respect of heritable property
which vests in him.[69] He has all the powers which are conferred by any
enactment for raising the duty.[70] He is not liable for any duty in excess of
the assets, heritable or moveable, which he has received as executor or
might but for his own neglect or default have received.[71] The executor may
obtain from the Commissioners of Inland Revenue a certificate that he has
paid or commuted, or will pay or commute, all estate duty for which he is
accountable in respect of heritable property vested in him or any part
thereof. The certificate discharges the property to which it extends from
any further claim for estate duty.[72] A certificate can also be obtained in
respect of other property.[73]

DISTRIBUTION

Time for distribution

It has been said that after a period of twelve months from the date of
death, the executor, after paying or providing for such of the deceased's
debts as due and reasonable inquiry has disclosed, may proceed to distribute the estate to the persons beneficially entitled thereto. However, the
authority establishing the twelve-month period is not strong [74] and
McLaren states that it is " rather to be understood as a maximum." [75]
There are now no material differences between distribution by executors
and distribution by trustees.[76]

If the executor receives payment of a sum under a court order against
which, to his knowledge, an appeal will probably be taken, he should not
distribute it to the beneficiaries; if he does so and the order is reversed he
may be liable to the party found to be entitled to the fund.[77]

A general legatee seeking payment should normally sue the executor as
executor and not as an individual.[78] A legatee can proceed to constitute
his debt against the executor before the expiry of six months from the
date of death.[79] An action of accounting within the six months is pre-

---

[67] Finance Act 1894, s. 6 (2).
[68] s. 6 (3).
[69] 1964 Act, s. 19 (1).
[70] 1964 Act, s. 19 (2).
[71] Finance Act 1894, s. 8 (3); 1964 Act, s. 19 (6).
[72] 1964 Act, s. 19 (7).
[73] Finance Act 1894, s. 11 (2); Finance Act 1907, s. 14.
[74] *Stair* v. *Stair's Trs.* (1827) 2 W. & S. 614, 618, *per* Lord Redesdale; McLaren, II, 1161;
Howat's Trs. v. *Howat* (1869) 8 M. 337.
[75] McLaren, II, 1164.
[76] See Chap. 24.
[77] *Pattisson* v. *McVicar* (1886) 13 R. 550.
[78] *Kirsop* v. *Kirsop* (1949) 65 Sh.Ct.Rep. 4.
[79] *McPherson* v. *Cameron* (1941) 57 Sh.Ct.Rep. 64.

mature.[80] A claim against an executor for payment of a legacy is subject to the long negative prescription.[81]

Unpaid beneficiaries cannot normally recover from persons who have been paid in error but an action for this purpose was held competent where the executors were called as additional defenders.[82]

The executors are entitled to refuse to distribute the estate to the beneficiaries if it is not clear that the funds remaining are sufficient to meet the debts. It cannot be assumed that heritable creditors will be content to rely on their security and will not subsequently proceed against the executors.[83] The fact that estate duty is being paid by instalments does not in every case mean that the trustees or executors are entitled to retain the estate in their own hands until all the instalments have been paid.[84]

In some circumstances, the title to a legacy is dependent upon the consent of the executor being obtained. Where a testatrix left a bequest: " My Dog to the party who will take care of it £25 per year also £10 per year for each of my Cats as long as they live," it was held that persons who, on the testatrix's death had taken possession of the dog and cats and maintained them were not entitled to the legacies because they had not obtained the consent of the executor.[85]

Transfer by docket

If it is necessary for the executor in distributing the estate to transfer heritage to a person in respect of a prior right, a claim to legal rights, a right on intestacy or a right under a testamentary disposition, the executor can effect the transfer by endorsing on the confirmation, or a certificate of confirmation, a docket in the statutory form.[86] The docket can be used as a midcouple or link in deducing title. Other modes of transfer are, of course, still competent. The docket procedure can be used to transfer entailed property and heritable property subject to a special destination to the person entitled thereto.[87] A docket cannot be executed in favour of a deceased beneficiary. The docketed confirmation or certificate can be registered for preservation but clearly cannot be registered in the Register of Sasines.[88]

Protection of purchasers

Section 17 of the 1964 Act provides:

" Where any person has in good faith and for value acquired title to any interest in or security over heritable property which has vested in an executor as aforesaid directly or indirectly from:

---

[80] *Wallace* v. *Wallace* (1894) 10 Sh.Ct.Rep. 142.
[81] *Jamieson* v. *Clark* (1872) 10 M. 399; Walker, 1869.
[82] *Armour* v. *Glasgow Royal Infirmary*, 1909 S.C. 916.
[83] *Heritable Securities Investment Association Ltd.* v. *Miller's Trs.* (1893) 20 R. 675; *Campbell* v. *Lord Borthwick's Trs.*, 1929 S.N. 131; 1930 S.N. 156; *City of Glasgow Friendly Society* v. *McHugh's Trs.*, 1936 S.L.T.(Sh.Ct.) 34 (Interdict by creditor).
[84] *De Robeck* v. *Inland Revenue*, 1928 S.C.(H.L.) 34.
[85] *Robson's J.F.* v. *Wilson*, 1922 S.L.T. 640.
[86] 1964 Act, s. 15 (2) Sched. 1.
[87] 1964 Act, s. 18 (4).   [88] Journal of the Law Society of Scotland, 1966, 36.

(*a*) the executor, or

(*b*) a person deriving title directly from the executor,

the title so acquired shall not be challengeable on the ground that the confirmation was reducible or has in fact been reduced, or, in a case falling under paragraph (*b*) above, that the title should not have been transferred to the person mentioned in that paragraph."

The section applies to entailed property and heritable property subject to a special destination to which the executor has confirmed as if the person next entitled to the property were a person entitled to share in the estate of the deceased.[89]

Leases

If the estate includes the interest of a tenant under a lease or tenancy which has not been effectually disposed of by the deceased, either because there was no bequest, or the bequest was not accepted or, in the case of an agricultural lease, was declared null and void, and the lease contains an express or implied prohibition of assignation, the executor can nevertheless transfer the interest to a person entitled to the estate by virtue of a right on intestacy, a prior right or legal rights.[90] He cannot transfer it to any other person without the consent of the landlord or, in the case of the lease of a croft, of the Crofters Commission.

In the case of a croft, the executor must as soon as may be furnish particulars of the transferee to the landlord, who must accept the transferee as tenant and notify the Crofters Commission accordingly.[91]

If the executor is satisfied that the interest in a lease cannot be disposed of according to law and so informs the landlord, either the landlord or the executor may, on giving appropriate notice, terminate the lease notwithstanding any provision therein or rule of law to the contrary effect.[92] In agricultural leases the period of notice is to be as may be agreed or, failing agreement, a period of not less than one and not more than two years ending with such term of Whitsunday or Martinmas as may be specified in the notice. In other leases, the period is six months unless there is a shorter period prescribed by statute in relation to the lease in question.[93]

Either party can terminate the lease in the same way if the interest is not disposed of within a year or such longer period as may be fixed by agreement, or failing agreement, by the sheriff on the executor's application.[94] The period runs from the date of the deceased's death except that:

(a) if the lease is agricultural and there is a petition to the Land Court

---

[89] 1964 Act, s. 18 (4). As the executor is a trustee, s. 2 of the 1961 Act also applies (see p. 319, *supra*).

[90] 1964 Act, s. 16 (2) as amended by Law Reform (Miscellaneous Provisions) (Scotland) Act 1968, Sched. 2.

[91] Crofters (Scotland) Act 1955, s. 11 (1) as amended by Law Reform (Miscellaneous Provisions) (Scotland) Act 1968, Sched. 2, para. 4. If notice is not given within three months of the death, the Commission may proceed to nominate a successor (s. 11 (4), (4A), (4B), (4C), (5).)

[92] 1964 Act, s. 16 (3).

[93] 1964 Act, s. 16 (4).

[94] 1964 Act, s. 16 (3).

under the Crofters Holdings (Scotland) Act 1886, s. 16, or an application under the Agricultural Holdings (Scotland) Act 1949, s. 20, it runs from the date of determination or withdrawal of the petition or application;

(b) if the lease is agricultural and there is an application by the legatee to the Crofters Commission under the Crofters (Scotland) Act 1955, s. 10 (1), it runs from the date of any refusal by the Commission to determine that the bequest shall not be null and void;

(c) if the lease is agricultural and is the subject of an intimation of objection by the landlord to the legatee and the Crofters Commission under s. 10 (3) of the 1955 Act, it runs from the date of any decision of the Commission upholding the objection.

This provision does not affect any claim for damages or compensation in respect of the termination but an award in respect of termination at the instance of the executor is enforceable only against the deceased's estate and not against the executor personally.[95]

If the landlord under a non-agricultural lease brings an action of removing against the executor in respect of a breach of a condition of the lease, the court is not to grant decree unless it is satisfied that the condition is one which it is reasonable to expect the executor to have observed, having regard to the fact that the interest is vested in him in his capacity as an executor.[96] Similarly, in the case of an agricultural lease, the Land Court cannot make an order for removal from a croft or smallholding, and an arbiter considering a question[96a] in connection with a notice to quit an agricultural holding cannot make an award in favour of the landlord, unless the court or arbiter is satisfied that it is reasonable, having regard to the fact that the interest is vested in the executor in his capacity as executor, that it should be made.[97]

Where there is a valid bequest of an interest under an agricultural lease, the fact that the interest is vested in the executor for the purposes of administration does not prevent the operation, in relation to the legatee, of the various statutory procedures[98] by which the landlord can have the bequest declared null and void.[99]

---

[95] s. 16 (5).
[96] s. 16 (7).
[96a] The question whether in terms of s. 25 (2) (f) of the Agricultural Holdings (Scotland) Act 1949 the landlord's interest has been prejudiced by an irremediable breach of the conditions of tenancy.
[97] s. 16 (6).
[98] i.e. Crofters Holdings (Scotland) Act 1886, s. 16; Agricultural Holdings (Scotland) Act 1949, s. 20; Crofters (Scotland) Act 1955, s. 10
[99] s. 16 (8).

CHAPTER 32

THE EXECUTOR-CREDITOR

CONFIRMATION as executor-creditor is a species of diligence by which the creditor satisfies his debt out of the estate to which he confirms—" his confirmation is no more than a form of diligence established by law, by which he, as creditor, may be enabled to recover payment out of the executry effects." [1] Formerly, the diligence affected only the moveable estate of the deceased but it seems that the heritable estate can now be confirmed.[2]

The appointment of an executor-creditor is null if an executor-nominate or dative has already confirmed to the item of estate,[3] but the executor-creditor is not excluded by a foreign title.[4] A grant of representation in England or Northern Ireland containing the appropriate statement as to domicile will exclude.[5] The granting of a decree dative does not exclude [6]; nor does a decree of preference in a multiplepoinding.[7] The executor-creditor is excluded from assets of which such possession has been taken by the deceased's trustee or executor-nominate or dative or assignee as to remove them ex bonis defuncti.[8] Intimation of a special assignation excludes the executor-creditor.[9]

Before applying for decerniture, a creditor who does not already hold a decree or liquid document of debt must obtain a decree *cognitionis causa tantum.* The personal obligation in a heritable bond is sufficient.[10] A bill drawn and accepted in India, and indorsed to a creditor in London, fortified by the opinion of an English barrister with knowledge of Indian law that the bill was valid under that law, was sufficient constitution.[11]

Decree cognitionis causa tantum

Where the debt is not liquid, the creditor must proceed against the *hereditas jacens* by raising an action against all the known heirs of the deceased for the decree *cognitionis causa tantum.*[12] It is not now necessary to charge the heirs to give them an opportunity to protect their rights of succession,[13] but all the known heirs must be called for their interests,

[1] Ersk. III, 9, 34. See Kames, *Elucidations*, Art. 16; Bell, *Prin.* s. 1895, *Comm.* II, 81.
[2] Succession (Scotland) Act 1964, s. 14.
[3] *Lees* v. *Dinwidie* (1706) 5 B.S. 35.
[4] *Smith's Trs.* v. *Grant* (1862) 24 D. 1142.
[5] Currie, 145; Administration of Estates Act 1971.
[6] Bell, *Comm.* II, 81; *Willison* v. *Dewar* (1840) 3 D. 273.
[7] *Anderson* v. *Stewart* (1831) 10 S. 49.
[8] *Smith's Trs.* v. *Grant* (1862) 24 D. 1142.
[9] *Bell* v. *Willison* (1831) 9 S. 266.
[10] *A.* v. *B.* (1686) Mor. 3933; *Trent*, January 28, 1887, Edinburgh Commissary Court.
[11] *Tod*, November 20, 1885, Edinburgh Commissary Court.
[12] Confirmation Act 1695 (formerly called the Act anent Executry and Moveables).
[13] *Forrest* v. *Forrest* (1863) 1 M. 806; *Ferrier* v. *Crockart*, 1937 S.L.T. 205.

whether or not they are subject to the jurisdiction of the Scottish courts.[14] Executors who have not confirmed need not be called.[15]

It is competent to bring an action against two defenders jointly and severally and to restrict the decree sought against one to a decree *cognitionis causa tantum*.[16]

Confirmation procedure

The creditor must in the first place apply for decerniture. The petition narrates the debt and the document of debt or decree must be produced. The domicile of the deceased is immaterial. Notice of the application must be inserted in the *Edinburgh Gazette* immediately after its presentation.[17]

All those decerned as joint executors-creditor must concur in applying for confirmation.[18] To obtain confirmation, a full and complete inventory of the estate must be given up. It seems to be competent to include estate situated in England or Northern Ireland.[19] The oath relates to the inventory and need not relate to the verity of the debt.[20] The confirmation may be limited to the amount of the debt.[21]

The confirmation process is not appropriate for determining whether certain property deponed to in the inventory should be taken out of the confirmation.[22] If the deceased was a pledgee his creditor can confirm to the articles held.[23]

Effect

The effect of the confirmation is to give a complete title to the executor.[24] The confirmation creates a nexus on the assets specified therein which is limited by (a) the amount of the debt, and (b) the value in the confirmation.[25] If there are two successive confirmations to the same asset and the asset is put at a higher value in the second confirmation, the creditor first confirming has no preference beyond the value in his confirmation.[26]

The executor must use due diligence to ingather the assets in the confirmation and must account for any surplus.[27]

The executor-creditor has a good title to pursue an action before confirmation has been obtained but he must confirm before extracting the

---

[14] *Smith* v. *Tasker*, 1955 S.L.T. 347. See also *Davidson Pirie & Co.* v. *Dihle's Reps.* (1900) 2 F. 640; *Stevens* v. *Thomson*, 1971 S.L.T. 136.
[15] *Smith's Trs.* v. *Grant* (1862) 24 D. 1142.
[16] *Smith* v. *Tasker, supra.*
[17] 1823 Act, s. 4. For details of the practice and procedure, see Currie, Chap. 7.
[18] *Willison* v. *Dewar* (1840) 3 D. 273.
[19] Currie, 149.
[20] *Greig* v. *Christie* (1837) 15 S. 697.
[21] Confirmation of Executors (Scotland) Act 1823, s. 4. This continued the rule established by the Act of Sederunt of November 14, 1679 " that creditors be not unnecessarily intangled in the execution of defunct's debts."
[22] *Wm. Tait's Exy.* (1918) 34 Sh.Ct.Rep. 306.
[23] *Bridges* v. *Ewing* (1836) 15 S. 8.
[24] *Dickson* v. *Barbour* (1828) 6 S. 856.
[25] *Smith's Trs.* v. *Grant* (1862) 24 D. 1142, 1169, *per* Lord Curriehill.
[26] *Smith's Trs.* v. *Grant, supra.*
[27] *Lee* v. *Donald*, May 17, 1816, F.C. See *Harlow* v. *Hume* (1671) Mor. 3932.

decree.[28] The executor can sist himself as a party to an action begun by the deceased to recover an asset included in the confirmation.[29] If the executor dies without having received payment of his debt, his representatives can proceed with its recovery.[30]

Competition

Sequestration of the deceased's estates within seven months of the death renders any confirmation as executor-creditor of no effect in competition with the trustee except that the creditor has a preference for payment out of the effects for the expenses bona fide incurred in such confirmation.[31] Confirmation cannot be granted after the date of the first deliverance on the petition for sequestration.[32] Another creditor who appears before the confirmation has been granted can be conjoined in the confirmation.[33] Another creditor who cites the executor-creditor after confirmation but within six months of the death is, on paying a proportion of the expenses, entitled to rank *pari passu* on the assets confirmed to.[34] The executor-creditor is preferred to any creditor appearing after the expiry of the six-month period.[35]

If an executor nominate or dative is himself a creditor, his confirmation gives him the same preference he would have had if he had been executor-creditor.[36]

The confirmation, being a completed diligence, is preferred to a prior arrestment which until followed by a furthcoming is merely inchoate [37]; similarly, confirmation prevails over a poinding if there has been no sale.[38]

Privileged debts are preferred to the confirmation.[39]

Creditors of next-of-kin

The creditors of the deceased's next-of-kin may confirm as executors-creditor.[40] The deceased's creditors doing diligence within a year and a day of the death are, however, preferred to the diligence of the creditors of the next-of-kin. Such a creditor can confirm even although the next-of-kin has died.[41] The trustee in the sequestrated estate of the next-of-kin can be confirmed executor-creditor to the estate of the deceased.[42]

---

[28] *Maitland* v. *Cockerell* (1827) 6 S. 109.
[29] *Mein* v. *McCall* (1844) 6 D. 1112.
[30] *Mitchel* v. *Mitchel* (1737) Mor. 3935.
[31] Bankruptcy (Scotland) Act 1913, s. 106.
[32] s. 29.
[33] Bell, *Comm.* II, 82; *Gibbon* v. *Johnston* (1787) Hume 276.
[34] *Ramsay* v. *Nairn* (1708) Mor. 3934; Bell, *Comm.* II, 84; Act of Sederunt, February 28, 1662.
[35] Bell, *Comm.* II, 85.
[36] *Macleod* v. *Wilson* (1837) 15 S. 1043.
[37] *Wilson & McLellan* v. *Fleming* (1823) 2 S. 430.
[38] Graham Stewart, *Law of Diligence*, 452.
[39] *Crawford* v. *Hutton* (1680) Mor. 11832.
[40] Confirmation Act 1695.
[41] *Smith's Trs.* v. *Grant* (1862) 24 D. 1142.
[42] *Davidson*, April 19, 1866, Edinburgh Commissary Court.

APPENDIX

Executors (Scotland) Act 1900
(63 *and* 64 *Vict. c.* 55)

An Act to amend the Law relating to Executors in Scotland
[8th August, 1900]

1. *Short title.*—This Act may be cited as the Executors (Scotland) Act, 1900.

2. *Executors-nominate to have the powers and privileges of trustees.*—All executors-nominate shall, unless the contrary be expressly provided in the trust deed, have the whole powers, privileges, and immunities, and be subject to all the limitations and restrictions, which from time to time gratuitous trustees have, or are subject to, under the Trusts (Scotland) Acts, 1861 to 1898, or this Act, or any Act amending the same, and otherwise under the statute and common law of Scotland.

3. *Who may be confirmed executors-nominate.*—Where a testator has not appointed any person to act as his executor, or failing any person so appointed, the testamentary trustees of such testator, original or assumed, or appointed by the Supreme Court (if any), failing whom any general disponee or universal legatory or residuary legatee appointed by such testator, shall be held to be his executor-nominate, and entitled to confirmation in that character.

4. *Powers, etc., of executors-dative where more than one.*—In all cases where confirmation is, or has been, granted in favour of more executors-dative than one, the powers conferred by it shall accrue to the survivors or survivor, and while more than two survive a majority shall be a quorum, and each shall be liable only for his own acts and intromissions.

5. *Confirmation to contain inventory.*—All confirmations of personal estate shall have embodied therein, or appended thereto, the inventory of estate confirmed, and the forms of confirmation prescribed by the Confirmation of Executors (Scotland) Act 1858, s. 10, Scheds. D and E, shall be amended accordingly, by the insertion of words referring to the inventory as being embodied therein or appended thereto, or words to that effect.

6.[1] *Transmission of trust property by executors of sole or last surviving trustee.*—When any sole or last surviving trustee or executor has died with any property (whether heritable or moveable) in Scotland vested in him as trustee or executor, confirmation by his executors (if any) to the proper estate of such trustee or executor, or the probate granted in England and Wales or Northern Ireland to his executors and noting his domicile in England and Wales or in Northern Ireland, as the case may be, shall, whether granted before or after the passing of this Act, be valid, and available to such executors for recovering such property, and for assigning and transferring the same to such person or persons as may be legally authorised to continue the administration thereof, or, where no other act of administration remains to be performed, directly to the beneficiaries entitled thereto, or to any person or persons whom the beneficiaries may appoint to receive and discharge, realise and distribute the same, provided always that a note or statement of such property shall have been appended to any inventory or additional inventory of the estate of such deceased trustee or executor given up by his executors in Scotland, and duly confirmed; and provided further that nothing herein contained shall bind executors of a deceased trustee or executor to make up title to such property, nor prejudice or exclude the right of any other person to complete a title to such property by any proceedings otherwise competent.

7.[1] *Where confirmation ad non executa may be granted.*—Where any confirmation has become inoperative by the death or incapacity of all the executors in whose favour it has been granted, no title to intromit with the estate confirmed therein shall, otherwise than in the circumstances and to the extent authorised by the preceding section, transmit to the representatives of any such executors whatever may be the extent of their beneficial interest therein, but it shall be competent to grant confirmation *ad non executa* to any estate contained in the original confirmation which may remain unuplifted or untransferred to the persons entitled thereto, and such confirmation *ad non executa* shall be granted to the same persons, and according to the same rules as confirmations *ad omissa* are at present granted, and shall be a sufficient title to continue and complete the administration of the estate contained therein, and it shall be competent to specify such confirmation as a midcouple or link of title for the purposes of any deduction of title in relation to such estate from the former executors, provided always that nothing herein contained shall be held to affect the rights and preferences at present conferred by confirmation on executors-creditors.

8. *Before whom oaths may be taken.*—Oaths and affirmations to inventories of personal estate given up to be recorded in any Sheriff Court and to revenue statements appended thereto may be taken before the Sheriff or Sheriff-Substitute, or any Commissioner appointed by the Sheriff, or before any Commissary Clerk or his Depute, or where the office of Commissary Clerk has been abolished before any Sheriff Clerk or his Depute, or before any Notary Public, Magistrate, or Justice of the Peace, in the United Kingdom, and also if taken in England or Ireland before any Commissioner for Oaths appointed by the Courts of these countries, or if taken at any place out of the United Kingdom, before any British Consul, or local Magistrate, or any Notary Public practising in such foreign country, or admitted and practising in Great Britain or Ireland.

---

[1] As amended by the Succession (Scotland) Act 1964 (Sched. 2, para. 13) and the Administration of Estates Act 1971, Sched. 1, para. 2.

9. *Amendment of Small Estates Acts.*—Repealed by the Finance Act 1967, s. 10, which was brought into operation with effect from April 1, 1968, by the Finance Act 1967 (s. 10) Appointed Day Order 1968.

Trusts (Scotland) Act 1921

(11 *and* 12 *Geo.* 5, *c.* 58)

An Act to consolidate and amend the Law relating to Trusts in Scotland
[19th August, 1921][2]

1. *Citation.*—This Act may be cited as the Trusts (Scotland) Act 1921.

2. *Definitions.*—In the construction of this Act unless the context otherwise requires—

" Trust " shall mean and include—
  (a) any trust constituted by any deed or other writing, or by private or local Act of Parliament, or by Royal Charter, or by resolution of any corporation or public or ecclesiastical body, and
  (b) the appointment of any tutor, curator, or judicial factor by deed, decree, or otherwise;

" Trust deed " shall mean and include—
  (a) any deed or other writing, private or local Act of Parliament, Royal Charter, or resolution of any corporation or ecclesiastical body, constituting any trust, and
  (b) any decree, deed, or other writing appointing a tutor, curator, or judicial factor;

  [3] " Trustee " shall mean and include any trustee under any trust whether nominated, appointed, judicially or otherwise, or assumed, whether sole or joint, and whether entitled or not to receive any benefit under the trust or any remuneration as trustee for his services, and shall include any trustee ex officio, executor nominate, tutor, curator, and judicial factor;

  [4] " Judicial factor " shall mean any person holding a judicial appointment as a factor or curator on another person's estate;

" Local authority " and " rate " shall have respectively the meanings assigned to these expressions by the Local Authorities Loans (Scotland) Act 1891 (54 & 55 Vict. c. 34).

" The court " shall mean the Court of Session;

" East India Stock " shall mean India $3\frac{1}{2}$ per cent. stock, India 3 per cent. stock, India $2\frac{1}{2}$ per cent. stock, or any other capital stock which may, at any time hereafter, be issued by the Secretary of State in Council of India under the authority of Act of Parliament and charged on the revenues of India.

3. *What trusts shall be held to include.*—All trusts shall be held to include the following powers and provisions unless the contrary be expressed (that is to say):—

---

[2] " References in the Trusts (Scotland) Act 1921 to section ten or eleven of that Act, or to provisions which include either of those sections, shall be construed respectively as references to section one of this Act and as including references to that section "—Trustee Investments Act 1961, Sched. 4. para. 1 (2).

[3] Now also includes an executor-dative—Succession (Scotland) Act 1964, s. 20.

[4] Substituted by the Trusts (Scotland) Act 1961, s. 3.

(a) Power to any trustee to resign the office of trustee;

(b) Power to the trustee, if there be only one, or to the trustees, if there be more than one, or to a quorum of the trustees, if there be more than two, to assume new trustees;

(c) A provision that a majority of the trustees accepting and surviving shall be a quorum;

(d) A provision that each trustee shall be liable only for his own acts and intromissions and shall not be liable for the acts and intromissions of co-trustees and shall not be liable for omissions:

Provided that—

(1) A sole trustee shall not be entitled to resign his office by virtue of this Act unless either (1) he has assumed new trustees and they have declared their acceptance of office, or (2) the court shall have appointed new trustees or a judicial factor as hereinafter in this Act provided; and

(2) A trustee who has accepted any legacy or bequest or annuity expressly given on condition of the recipient thereof accepting the office of trustee under the trust shall not be entitled to resign the office of trustee by virtue of this Act, unless otherwise expressly declared in the trust deed, nor shall any trustee appointed to the office of trustee on the footing of receiving remuneration for his services be entitled so to resign that office in the absence of an express power to resign; but it shall be competent to the court, on the petition of any trustee to whom the foregoing provisions of this proviso apply, to grant authority to such trustee to resign the office of trustee on such conditions (if any) with respect to repayment or otherwise of his legacy as the court may think just; and

(3) A judicial factor shall not, by virtue of this Act, have the power of assumption, nor shall he have the power by virtue of this Act to resign his office without judicial authority.

Nothing in this section shall affect any liability incurred by any trustee prior to the date of any resignation or assumption under the provisions of this Act or of any Act repealed by this Act.

⁵ **4.** *General powers of trustees.*—(1) In all trusts the trustees shall have power to do the following acts, where such acts are not at variance with the terms or purposes of the trust, and such acts when done shall be as effectual as if such powers had been contained in the trust deed, viz.:—

(a) To sell the trust estate or any part thereof, heritable as well as moveable.

(b) To grant feus of the heritable estate or any part thereof.

(c) To grant leases of any duration (including mineral leases) of the heritable estate or any part thereof and to remove tenants.

(d) To borrow money on the security of the trust estate or any part thereof, heritable as well as moveable.

(e) To excamb any part of the trust estate which is heritable.

(ee) To acquire with funds of the trust estate any interest in residential accommodation (whether in Scotland or elsewhere) reasonably required to enable the trustees to provide a suitable residence for occupation by any of the beneficiaries.

⁵ Extended. See Forestry Act 1947, s. 4 (2); National Parks, etc., Act 1949; Agriculture Act 1970, s. 33. Amended by the Trusts (Scotland) Act 1961, s. 4. See also Field Monuments Act 1972, s. 1 (4) and Sched., para. 2 (2).

(*f*) To appoint factors and law agents and to pay them suitable remuneration.

(*g*) To discharge trustees who have resigned and the representatives of trustees who have died.

(*h*) To uplift, discharge, or assign debts due to the trust estate.

(*i*) To compromise or to submit and refer all claims connected with the trust estate.

(*j*) To refrain from doing diligence for the recovery of any debt due to the truster which the trustees may reasonably deem irrecoverable.

(*k*) To grant all deeds necessary for carrying into effect the powers vested in the trustees.

(*l*) To pay debts due by the truster or by the trust estate without requiring the creditors to constitute such debts where the trustees are satisfied that the debts are proper debts of the trust.

(*m*) To make abatement or reduction, either temporary or permanent, of the rent, lordship, royalty, or other consideration stipulated in any lease of land, houses, tenements, minerals, metals, or other subjects, and to accept renunciations of leases of any such subjects.

(*n*) To apply the whole or any part of trust funds which the trustees are empowered or directed by the trust deed to invest in the purchase of heritable property in the payment or redemption of any debt or burden affecting heritable property which may be destined to the same series of heirs and subject to the same conditions as are by the trust deed made applicable to heritable property directed to be purchased.

[6] (*o*) To concur, in respect of any securities of a company (being securities comprised in the trust estate), in any scheme or arrangement—

(i) for the reconstruction of the company,

(ii) for the sale of all or any part of the property and undertaking of the company to another company,

(iii) for the acquisition of the securities of the company, or of control thereof, by another company,

(iv) for the amalgamation of the company with another company, or

(v) for the release, modification, or variation of any rights, privileges or liabilities attached to the securities or any of them,

in like manner as if the trustees were entitled to such securities beneficially; to accept any securities of any denomination or description of the reconstructed or purchasing or new company in lieu of, or in exchange for, all or any of the first mentioned securities; and to retain any securities so accepted as aforesaid for any period for which the trustees could have properly retained the original securities.

[6] (*p*) To exercise, to such extent as the trustees think fit, any conditional or preferential right to subscribe for any securities in a company (being a right offered to them in respect of any holding in the company), to apply capital money of the trust estate in payment of the consideration, and to retain any such securities for which they have subscribed for any period for which they have power to

[6] Added by the Trustee Investments Act 1961, s. 10.

retain the holding in respect of which the right to subscribe for the
securities was offered (but subject to any conditions subject to
which they have that power); to renounce, to such extent as they
think fit, any such right; or to assign, to such extent as they think
fit and for the best consideration that can reasonably be obtained,
the benefit of such right or the title thereto to any person, in-
including any beneficiary under the trust.

(2) This section shall apply to acts done before as well as after the
passing of this Act, but shall not apply so as to affect any question relating
to an act enumerated in head (a), (b), (c), (d), or (e) of this section which
may, at the passing of this Act, be the subject of a depending action.

5. *Powers which may be granted to trustees by the court.*—It shall be
competent to the court, on the petition of the trustees under any trust, to
grant authority to the trustees to do any of the acts mentioned in the
section of this Act relating to general powers of trustees, notwithstanding
that such act is at variance with the terms or purposes of the trust, on
being satisfied that such act is in all the circumstances expedient for the
execution of the trust.

In this section the expression " trust " shall not include any trust
constituted by private or local Act of Parliament, and the expression
" trustees " shall be construed accordingly.

6. *Method of sale by trustees.*—All powers of sale conferred on
trustees by the trust deed or by virtue of this Act may be exercised either by
public roup or private bargain unless otherwise directed in the trust deed
or in the authority given by the court, and when the estate is heritable it
shall be lawful in the exercise of such powers to sell subject to or under
reservation of a feu-duty or ground annual at such rate and on such
conditions as may be agreed upon, and in such sales and feus it shall be
lawful to reserve the mines and minerals.

7. *Deeds granted by trustees.*—Any deed bearing to be granted by the
trustees under any trust, and in fact executed by a quorum of such trustees
in favour of any person other than a beneficiary or a co-trustee under the
trust where such person has dealt onerously and in good faith shall not be
void or challengeable on the ground that any trustee or trustees under the
trust was or were not consulted in the matter, or was or were not present
at any meeting of trustees where the same was considered, or did not
consent to or concur in the granting of the deed, or on the ground of any
other omission or irregularity of procedure on the part of the trustees or
any of them in relation to the granting of the deed.

Nothing in this section shall affect any question of liability or otherwise
between any trustee under any trust on the one hand and any co-trustee or
beneficiary under such trust on the other hand. This section shall apply
to deeds granted before as well as after the passing of this Act, but shall not
apply so as to affect any question which may, at the passing of this Act, be
the subject of a depending action.

In this section the expression " quorum " means a quorum of the
trustees under any trust entitled to act in terms of the trust deed or in
virtue of this Act, or of any Act repealed by this Act, as the case may be.

8. *Conveyances to non-existing or unidentifiable persons.*—(1) Where in
any deed, whether inter vivos or mortis causa, heritable or moveable
property is conveyed to any person in liferent, and in fee to persons who,

when such conveyance comes into operation, are unborn or incapable of ascertainment, the person to whom the property is conveyed in liferent shall not be deemed to be beneficially entitled to the property in fee by reason only that the liferent is not expressed in the deed to be a liferent allenarly; and all such conveyances as aforesaid shall, unless a contrary intention appears in the deed, take effect in the same manner and in all respects as if the liferent were declared to be a liferent allenarly; provided always that this subsection shall not apply to any conveyance which has come into operation before the passing of this Act.

For the purposes of this subsection, the date at which any conveyance in liferent and fee as aforesaid comes into operation shall be deemed to be the date at which the person to whom the liferent is conveyed first becomes entitled to receive the rents or income of the property.

(2) Where under any conveyance, whether coming into operation before or after the passing of this Act, any property is conveyed to one person in liferent and in fee to persons who, when such conveyance comes into operation, are unborn or incapable of ascertainment, it shall be competent to the court, on the application of the liferenter, whether or not he would, according to the existing law, be deemed to be fiduciary fiar, or of any person to whom the fee or any part thereof bears to be presumptively destined, or who may have an interest under such conveyance notwithstanding that such interest is prospective or contingent, or of the Accountant of Court:—

(a) To grant authority to the fiduciary fiar to exercise all or such of the powers, or to do all or such of the acts, competent to a trustee at Common Law or under this Act, as to the court may seem fit:

(b) To appoint a trustee or trustees (of whom the liferenter or fiduciary fiar may be one) with all the powers of trustees at Common Law and under this Act, or a judicial factor, to hold the said property in trust in place of the liferenter or fiduciary fiar; and to authorise and ordain the fiduciary fiar to execute and deliver all such deeds as may be necessary for the completion of title to the said property by such trustee or trustees or judicial factor; or otherwise, to grant warrant to such trustee or trustees or judicial factor to complete a title to the said property in the same manner and to the same effect as under a warrant in favour of a trustee or trustees granted in terms of the section of this Act relating to the appointment of new trustees by the court, or a warrant in favour of a judicial factor granted in terms of section twenty-four of the Titles to Land Consolidation (Scotland) Act 1868 (31 & 32 Vict. c. 101), or section forty-four of the Conveyancing (Scotland) Act 1874 (37 & 38 Vict. c. 94), as the case may be. The expense of completing the title as aforesaid shall, unless the court otherwise directs, be a charge against the capital of the estate.

(3) For the purposes of this section, all references to a trust deed in this Act contained shall be read and construed as a reference to the conveyance of the property in liferent and fee as aforesaid.

[7] 9. *Liferents of personal estate beyond certain limits prohibited.*—It shall be competent to constitute or reserve by means of a trust or otherwise

---

[7] Amended by Conveyancing (S.) Act 1924, s. 45 (termination of perpetual trusts of moveables).

". . . section 9 of the Trusts (Scotland) Act 1921 shall not have effect in relation to any deed executed after the commencement of this Act "—Law Reform (Miscellaneous Provisions) (Scotland) Act 1968, s. 18 (4).

a liferent interest in moveable and personal estate in Scotland in favour only of a person in life at the date of the deed constituting or reserving such liferent, and, where any moveable or personal estate in Scotland shall, by virtue of any deed dated after the thirty-first day of July, eighteen hundred and sixty-eight, (the date of any testamentary or mortis causa deed being taken to be the date of the death of the granter, and the date of any contract of marriage being taken to be the date of the dissolution of the marriage) be held in liferent by or for behoof of a person of full age born after the date of such deed, such moveable or personal estate shall belong absolutely to such person, and, where such estate stands invested in the name of any trustees, such trustees shall be bound to deliver, make over, or convey such estate to such person: Provided always that, where more persons than one are interested in the moveable or personal estate held by trustees as hereinbefore mentioned, all the expenses connected with the transference of a portion of such estate to any of the beneficiaries in terms of this section shall be borne by the beneficiary in whose favour the transference is made.

10. [Repealed by the Trustee Investments Act 1961, Sched. 5.]

11. [Repealed by the Trustee Investments Act 1961, Sched. 5.]

[8] **12.** *Investment on charges under Improvement of Land Acts, etc.*— (1) A trustee having power to invest in real securities, unless expressly forbidden by the trust deed, may invest, and shall be deemed to have always had power to invest, on any charge or on any mortgage on such charge made under the Improvement of Land Acts 1864 (27 & 28 Vict. c. 114) and 1899 (62 & 63 Vict. c. 46), or on any charge created for payment of estate or other Government duty under the Finance Act 1894 (57 & 58 Vict. c. 30), or the Finance (1909–10) Act 1910 (10 Edw. 7 & 1 Geo. 5. c. 8).

(2) A trustee having power to invest in the mortgages or bonds of any railway company or of any other description of company may, unless the contrary is expressed in the trust deed, invest in the debenture stock of a railway company or such other company as aforesaid.

13. *Power to invest notwithstanding drainage charges.*—A trustee having power to invest in the purchase of land or on heritable security may invest in the purchase of or on heritable security over any land notwithstanding that the same is charged with a rent under the powers of the Public Money Drainage Acts, 1846 to 1856, or by an absolute order made under the Improvement of Land Act 1864 (27 & 28 Vict. c. 114), unless the terms of the trust expressly provide that the land to be purchased or taken in security shall not be subject to any such prior charge.

14. *Powers of investment in trust deeds not to be restricted.*—(1) The powers of investment conferred upon trustees by the four immediately preceding sections of this Act shall not be held or construed as restricting or controlling any powers of investment of trust funds expressly contained in any trust deed.

(2) In the aforesaid sections and in this section the expression " trustee " includes any person holding funds in a fiduciary capacity, and the expressions " trust " and " trust deed " shall be construed accordingly.

[8] As amended by the Trustee Investments Act 1961, Sched. 5.

15. *Trustees not to hold certificates or bonds payable to bearer.*—(1) A trustee, unless authorised by the terms of his trust, shall not apply for, purchase, acquire, or hold beyond a reasonable time for realisation or conversion into registered or inscribed stock any certificate to bearer or debenture or other bond or document payable to bearer.

(2) Nothing in this section shall impose on the Bank of England or the Bank of Ireland or on any person authorised by or under any Act of Parliament to issue any such certificate, bond, or document any obligation to inquire whether a person applying for such a certificate, bond, or document is or is not a trustee, or subject them to any liability in the event of their granting any such certificate, bond, or document to a trustee, nor invalidate any such certificate, bond or document if granted.

16. *The court may authorise the advance of part of the capital of a trust fund.*—The court may, from time to time under such conditions as they see fit, authorise trustees to advance any part of the capital of a fund destined either absolutely or contingently to beneficiaries who at the date of the application to the court are not of full age, if it shall appear that the income of the fund is insufficient or not applicable to, and that such advance is necessary for, the maintenance or education of such beneficiaries or any of them, and that it is not expressly prohibited by the trust deed, and that the rights of such beneficiaries, if contingent, are contingent only on their survivance.

17. *Trustees may apply to court for superintendence order as to investment and distribution of estate.*—It shall be competent for the trustees under any trust deed or one or more of them to apply to the court for an order on the accountant of court to superintend their administration of the trust in so far as it relates to the investment of the trust funds and the distribution thereof among the creditors interested and the beneficiaries under the trust, and the court may grant such order accordingly, and if such order be granted the accountant of court shall annually examine and audit the accounts of such trustees, and at any time, if he thinks fit, he may report to the court upon any question that may arise in the administration of the trust with regard to any of the foresaid matters and obtain the directions of the court thereupon.

18. *Discharge of trustees resigning and heirs of trustees dying during the subsistence of the trust.*—When a trustee who resigns or the representatives of a trustee who has died or resigned cannot obtain a discharge of his acts and intromissions from the remaining trustees, and when the beneficiaries of the trust refuse or are unable from absence, incapacity or otherwise to grant a discharge, the court may, on petition to that effect at the instance of such trustee or representative and after such intimation and inquiry as may be thought necessary, grant such discharge.

19. *Form of resignation of trustees.*—(1) Subject to the provisions of subsection (2) of this section, any trustee entitled to resign his office may do so by minute of the trust entered in the sederunt book of the trust and signed in such sederunt book by such trustee and by the other trustee or trustees acting at the time, or he may do so by signing a minute of resignation in the form of Schedule A to this Act annexed or to the like effect, and may register the same in the books of council and session, and in such case he shall be bound to intimate the same to his co-trustee or trustees, and the resignation shall be held to take effect from and after the date of the receipt of such intimation, or the last date thereof if more than one, and in case after inquiry the residence of any trustee to whom intimation should be given under this provision cannot be found, such intimation shall be sent by post in a registered letter [9] addressed to the Keeper of the Register of Edictal Citations.

(2) A sole trustee desiring to resign his office may apply to the court stating such desire and praying for the appointment of new trustees or of a judicial factor to administer the trust, and the court, after intimation to the beneficiaries under the trust, or such of them as the court may direct, may thereafter appoint either a judicial factor or new trustees, and if the court appoint new trustees the court may grant warrant to complete title as provided in the section of this Act relating to appointment of new trustees by the court.

20. *Effect of resignation.*—Where a trustee entitled to resign his office shall have resigned in either of the modes provided by the immediately preceding section or otherwise, and his resignation shall have been duly completed, such trustee shall be thereby divested of the whole property and estate of the trust, which shall accrue to or devolve upon the continuing trustees or trustee without the necessity of any conveyance or other transfer by the resigning trustee, but without prejudice to the right of the continuing trustee or trustees to require the resigning trustee to execute and deliver to the continuing trustees or trustee at the expense of the trust a conveyance or transfer (or conveyances or transfers) of the property or estate belonging to the trust, or any part thereof if the continuing trustees or trustee shall consider this expedient, and the resigning trustee when so required shall be bound at the expense of the trust to execute and deliver such conveyance or conveyances, transfer or transfers accordingly.

21. *Appointment of new or additional trustees by deed of assumption.*— When trustees have the power of assuming new trustees, such new trustees may be assumed by deed of assumption executed by the trustee or trustees acting under the trust deed or by a quorum of such trustees, if more than two, in the form of Schedule B to this Act annexed or to the like effect, and a deed of assumption so executed, in addition to a general conveyance of the trust estate, may contain a special conveyance of heritable property belonging to the trust estate, and in such case shall be effectual as a conveyance of such heritable property in favour of the existing trustees and the trustees so to be assumed, and such deed of assumption shall also be effectual as an assignation in favour of such existing and assumed trustees of the whole personal property belonging to the trust estate, and in the event of any trustee acting under any trust deed being insane or incapable of acting by reason of physical or mental disability or by continuous absence from the United Kingdom for a period of six months or upwards, such deed of assumption may be executed by the remaining trustee or trustees acting under such trust deed: Provided that, when the signatures of a quorum of trustees cannot be obtained, it shall be necessary to obtain the consent of the court to such deed of assumption on application either by the acting trustee or trustees or by any one or more of the beneficiaries under the trust deed.

22. *Appointment of new trustees by the court.*—When trustees cannot be assumed under any trust deed, or when any person who is the sole

---

[9] Now also recorded delivery service.

trustee appointed in or acting under any trust deed is or has become insane or is or has become incapable of acting by reason of physical or mental disability, or by being absent continuously from the United Kingdom for a period of at least six months, or by having disappeared for a like period, the court may, upon the application of any party having interest in the trust estate, after such intimation and inquiry as may be thought necessary, appoint a trustee or trustees under such trust deed with all the powers incident to that office, and, on such appointment being made in the case of any person becoming insane or incapable of acting as aforesaid, such person shall cease to be a trustee under such trust deed, and the court may, on such application, grant a warrant[10] to complete a title to any heritable property forming part of the trust estate in favour of the trustee or trustees so appointed, which warrant shall specify and describe the heritable property to which it is applicable, or refer in terms of law to a recorded deed containing a description thereof, and shall also specify the moveable or personal property, or bear reference to an inventory appended to the petition to the court in which such moveable or personal property is specified, and such warrant shall be effectual as a conveyance of such heritable property in favour of the trustee or trustees so appointed in like manner and to the same effect as a warrant in favour of a judicial factor granted under the authority of section twenty-four of the Titles to Land Consolidation (Scotland) Act 1868, or section forty-four of the Conveyancing (Scotland) Act 1874, and shall also be effectual as an assignation of such moveable or personal property in favour of the trustee or trustees so appointed.

23. *Court may remove trustees in certain cases.*—In the event of any trustee being or becoming insane or incapable of acting by reason of physical or mental disability or being absent from the United Kingdom continuously for a period of at least six months, or having disappeared for a like period, such trustee, in the case of insanity or incapacity of acting by reason of physical or mental disability, shall, and in the case of continuous absence from the United Kingdom or disappearance for a period of six months or upwards, may, on application in manner in this section provided by any co-trustee or any beneficiary or other person interested in the trust estate, be removed from office upon such evidence as shall satisfy the court to which the application is made of the insanity, incapacity, or continuous absence or disappearance of such trustee. Such application in the case of a mortis causa trust may be made either to the court of session or to the sheriff court from which the original confirmation of the trustees as executors issued, and in the case of a marriage contract may be made either to the court of session or to the sheriff court of the district in which the spouses are or the survivor of them is domiciled, and in all other cases shall be made to the court of session.

24. *Completion of title by the beneficiary of a lapsed trust.*—Any person who shall be entitled to the possession for his own absolute use of any heritable property or moveable or personal property the title to which has been taken in the name of any trustee who has died or become incapable of acting without having executed a conveyance of such property, or any other person deriving right whether immediately or otherwise from the person entitled as aforesaid, may apply by petition to the court for

---

[10] A warrant to complete title is no longer necessary in the case of a trustee appointed by the court: Conveyancing Amendment (Scotland) Act 1938, s. 1.

authority to complete a title to such property in his own name, and such petition shall specify and describe the heritable property, or refer to a description thereof in terms of law, and refer to an inventory in which the moveable or personal property is specified to which such title is to be completed, and after such intimation and inquiry as may be thought necessary it shall be lawful for the court to grant a warrant for completing such title as aforesaid, which warrant shall specify and describe the heritable property to which it is applicable, or refer in terms of law to a description thereof, and shall also specify the moveable or personal property or shall bear reference to an inventory appended to the petition in which such moveable or personal property is specified, and such warrant shall be effectual as a conveyance of such heritable property in favour of the petitioner in like manner and to the same effect as a warrant in favour of a judicial factor granted under the authority of section twenty-four of the Titles to Land Consolidation (Scotland) Act 1868, or section forty-four of the Conveyancing (Scotland) Act 1874, and shall also be effectual as an assignation of such moveable or personal property in favour of the petitioner.

25. *Completion of title of judicial factors.*—Application for authority to complete the title of a judicial factor to any trust property or estate may be contained in the petition for the appointment of such factor, and such application may include moveable or personal property.

[11] **26.** *Powers of court under this Act to be exercised by Lord Ordinary.*— Applications to the court under the authority of this Act shall be by petition addressed to the court, and shall be brought in the first instance before one of the Lords Ordinary officiating in the Outer House, who may direct such intimation and service thereof and such investigation or inquiry as he may think fit, and the power of the Lord Ordinary before whom the petition is enrolled may be exercised by the Lord Ordinary on the Bills during vacation, and all such petitions shall, as respects procedure, disposal and review, be subject to the same rules and regulations as are enacted with respect to petitions coming before the Junior Lord Ordinary in virtue of the Court of Session Act 1857 (20 & 21 Vict. c. 56): Provided that, when in the exercise of the powers pertaining to the court of appointing trustees and regulating trusts, it shall be necessary to settle a scheme for the administration of any charitable or other permanent endowment, the Lord Ordinary shall, after preparing such scheme, report to one of the divisions of the court, by whom the same shall be finally adjusted and settled, and in all cases where it shall be necessary to settle any such scheme, intimation shall be made to His Majesty's Advocate, who shall be entitled to appear and intervene for the interests of the charity or any object of the trust or the public interest.

[12] **27.** *Court may pass Acts of Sederunt.*—The court shall be and is hereby empowered from time to time to make such regulations by Act or Acts of Sederunt as may be requisite for carrying into effect the purposes of this Act.

28. *Resignation of trustee who is also executor to infer resignation as executor.*—In all cases where a trust deed appoints the trustees to be also executors the resignation of any such trustee shall infer, unless where

---

[11] See Law Officers Act 1944, s. 2.
[12] As amended by the Trustee Investments Act 1961, Sched. 5.

otherwise expressly declared, his resignation also as an executor under such trust deed.

29. *Extent of liability of trustee.*—Where a trustee shall have improperly advanced trust money on a heritable security which would, at the time of the investment, have been a proper investment in all respects for a less sum than was actually advanced thereon, the security shall be deemed an authorised investment for such less sum, and the trustee shall only be liable to make good the sum advanced in excess thereof with interest.

[13] **30.** *Trustee not to be chargeable with breach of trust for lending money on security of any property on certain conditions.*—(1) Any trustee lending money on the security of any property shall not be chargeable with breach of trust by reason only of the proportion borne by the amount of the loan to the value of such property at the time when the loan was made, provided that it shall appear to the court that in making such loan the trustee was acting upon a report as to the value of the property made by a person whom the trustee reasonably believed to be an able practical valuator instructed and employed independently of any owner of the property, whether such valuator carried on business in the locality where the property is situated or elsewhere, and that the amount of the loan by itself or in combination with any other loan or loans upon the property ranking prior to or pari passu with the loan in question does not exceed two equal third parts of the value of the property as stated in such report, and this section shall apply to a loan upon any property on which the trustees can lawfully lend.

(2) This section shall apply to transfers of existing securities as well as to new securities, and in its application to a partial transfer of an existing security the expression " the amount of the loan " shall include the amount of any other loan or loans upon the property ranking prior to or pari passu with the loan in question.

31. *Power of court to make orders in case of breach of trust.*—Where a trustee shall have committed a breach of trust at the instigation or request or with the consent in writing of a beneficiary, the court may, if it shall think fit, make such order as to the court shall seem just for applying all or any part of the interest of the beneficiary in the trust estate by way of indemnity to the trustee or person claiming through him.

32. *Court may relieve trustee from personal liability.*—(1) If it appears to the court that a trustee is or may be personally liable for any breach of trust, whether the transaction alleged to be a breach of trust occurred before or after the passing of this Act, but has acted honestly and reasonably, and ought fairly to be excused for the breach of trust, then the court may relieve the trustee either wholly or partly from personal liability for the same.

(2) In this section and in the two immediately preceding sections the expression " the court " shall mean any court of competent jurisdiction in which a question relative to the actings, liability, or removal of a trustee comes to be tried.

[14] **33.** *Investment ceasing to be an authorised investment.*—A trustee shall not be liable for breach of trust by reason only of his continuing to

---

[13] See also Trustee Investments Act 1961, s. 6 (7).
[14] See also Trustee Investments Act 1961, s. 3 (4) and Sched. 3, para. 2.

hold an investment which has ceased to be an investment authorised by the trust deed or by or under this Act.

34. *Expenses of applications under this Act.*—(1) The court shall determine all questions of expenses in relation to any application made under this Act, and may direct that any such expenses shall be paid out of the trust estate where the court considers this reasonable.

(2) In this section the expression " the court " shall include any court to which an application may be made under this Act.

35. *Application of Act.*—Save as in this Act expressly otherwise provided—

(1) This Act shall apply to trusts which have come into operation before as well as to trusts coming into operation after the passing of this Act.

(2) Nothing in this Act contained shall be held to extend the liability of trustees.

36. [Repealed S.L.R. 1950.]

SCHEDULES

SCHEDULE A

(Section 19)

FORM OF MINUTE OF RESIGNATION

I, *A.B.*, do hereby resign the office of trustee under the trust disposition and settlement (*or other deed*) granted by *C.D.* dated the   day of   . [15] (*If the trustee was assumed add*, and to which office of trustee I was assumed by deed of assumption granted by *E.F.* and *G.H.*, dated   day of   .[15]) (*To be attested.*)

SCHEDULE B

(Section 21)

FORM OF DEED OF ASSUMPTION

I, *A.B.* (*or* we, *A.B.* and *C.D.*), the accepting and surviving (*or* remaining) trustee (*or* trustees, *or* a majority and quorum of the accepting and surviving trustees), acting under a trust disposition and settlement (*or other deed*) granted by *E.F.*, dated the   day of   (*if recorded, specify register and date of recording*), do hereby assume *G.H.* (*or G.H. and I.K.*) as a trustee (*or* trustees) under the said trust disposition and settlement (*or other deed*); and I (*or* we) dispone and convey to myself (*or* ourselves) and the said *G.H.* (*or G.H. and I.K.*) as trustees under the said trust disposition and settlement (*or other deed*), and the survivors or survivor, and the heir of the last survivor, the majority, while more than two are acting, being a quorum (*or otherwise in accordance with the terms*

---

[15] If recorded specify register and date of recording.

of the trust deed), all and sundry the whole trust, estate and effects, heritable and moveable, real and personal, of every description and wherever situated, at present belonging to me (*or* us) or under my (*or* our) control as trustee (*or* surviving trustees, *or otherwise as the case may be*), under the said trust disposition and settlement (*or other deed*), together with the whole vouchers, titles, and instructions thereof. (*Then may follow, if wished, special conveyances of heritable or personal property, with the usual clauses of a conveyance applicable to such property, and as the case may require.*) (*To be attested.*)

Trusts (Scotland) Act 1961

(9 & 10 *Eliz.* 2, *c.* 57)

An Act to amend the law of Scotland relating to trusts

[27th July, 1961]

1. *Jurisdiction of court in relation to variation of trust purposes.*—(1) In relation to any trust taking effect, whether before or after the commencement of this Act, under any will, settlement or other disposition, the court may if it thinks fit, on the petition of the trustees or any of the beneficiaries, approve on behalf of—

(*a*)   any of the beneficiaries who by reason of nonage or other incapacity is incapable of assenting, or

(*b*)   any person (whether ascertained or not) who may become one of the beneficiaries as being at a future date or on the happening of a future event a person of any specified description or a member of any specified class of persons, so however that this paragraph shall not include any person who is capable of assenting and would be of that description, or a member of that class, as the case may be, if the said date had fallen or the said event had happened at the date of the presentation of the petition to the court, or

(*c*)   any person unborn,

any arrangement (by whomsoever proposed, and whether or not there is any other person beneficially interested who is capable of assenting thereto) varying or revoking all or any of the trust purposes or enlarging the powers of the trustees of managing or administering the trust estate:

Provided that the court shall not approve an arrangement under this subsection on behalf of any person unless it is of the opinion that the carrying out thereof would not be prejudicial to that person.

[16] (2) For the purposes of the foregoing subsection a person who is over the age of pupillarity but has not attained the age of eighteen years (whether acting with the concurrence of a curator, administrator-at-law, or other guardian or not) shall be deemed to be incapable of assenting; but before approving an arrangement under that subsection on behalf of any such person the court shall take such account as it thinks appropriate of his attitude to the arrangement.

(3) Where the court has approved an arrangement on behalf of any person under subsection (1) of this section, or that subsection as extended by the last foregoing subsection, the arrangement shall not be reducible by that person on grounds of minority and lesion.

(4) Where under any trust such as is mentioned in subsection (1) of this section a trust purpose entitles any of the beneficiaries (in this sub-

---

[16]   As amended by Age of Majority (Scotland) Act 1969, Sched. 1.

section referred to as " the alimentary beneficiary ") to an alimentary liferent of, or any alimentary income from, the trust estate or any part thereof, the court may if it thinks fit, on the petition of the trustees or any of the beneficiaries, authorise any arrangement varying or revoking that trust purpose and making new provision in lieu thereof, including, if the court thinks fit, new provision for the disposal of the fee or capital of the trust estate or, as the case may be, of such part thereof as was burdened with the liferent or the payment of the income:

Provided that the court shall not authorise an arrangement under this subsection unless—

(a) it considers that the carrying out of the arrangement would be reasonable, having regard to the income of the alimentary beneficiary from all sources, and to such other factors, if any, as the court considers material, and

(b) the arrangement is approved by the alimentary beneficiary, or, where the alimentary beneficiary is a person on whose behalf the court is empowered by subsection (1) of this section or that subsection as extended by subsection (2) of this section to approve the arrangement, the arrangement is so approved by the court under that subsection.

(5) Nothing in the foregoing provisions of this section shall be taken to limit or restrict any power possessed by the court apart from this section under any Act of Parliament or rule of law.

(6) In this section the expression " beneficiary " in relation to a trust includes any person having, directly or indirectly, an interest, whether vested or contingent, under the trust.

2. *Validity of certain transactions by trustees.*—(1) Where, after the commencement of this Act, the trustees under any trust enter into a transaction with any person (in this section referred to as " the second party "), being a transaction under which the trustees purport to do in relation to the trust estate or any part thereof an act of any of the descriptions specified in paragraphs (a) to (ee) of subsection (1) of section four of the Act of 1921 (which empowers trustees to do certain acts where such acts are not at variance with the terms or purposes of the trust) the validity of the transaction and of any title acquired by the second party under the transaction shall not be challengeable by the second party or any other person on the ground that the act in question is at variance with the terms or purposes of the trust:

Provided that in relation to a transaction entered into by trustees who are acting under the supervision of the Accountant of Court this section shall have effect only if the said Accountant consents to the transaction.

(2) Nothing in this section shall affect any question of liability or otherwise between any of the trustees on the one hand and any co-trustee or any of the beneficiaries on the other hand.

[17] **5.** *Accumulations of income.*—(1) The following provisions of this

---

[17] " **6.** *Amendment of s. 5 of Trusts (Scotland) Act* 1961.—(1) The periods for which accumulations of income under a settlement or other disposition are permitted by section 5 of the Trusts (Scotland) Act 1961 shall include—

(a) a term of twenty-one years from the date of the making of the settlement or other disposition, and

(b) the duration of the minority or respective minorities of any person or persons living or in utero at that date,

and a direction to accumulate income during a period specified in paragraph (a) or paragraph (b) of this subsection shall not be void, nor shall the accumulation of the income be

section shall have effect in substitution for the provisions of the Accumulations Act, 1800, and that Act is hereby repealed.

(2) No person may by any will, settlement or other disposition dispose of any property in such manner that the income thereof shall be wholly or partially accumulated for any longer period than one of the following, that is to say—

(*a*) the life of the grantor; or

(*b*) a term of twenty-one years from the death of the grantor; or

(*c*) the duration of the minority or respective minorities of any person or persons living or in utero at the death of the grantor; or

(*d*) the duration of the minority or respective minorities of any person or persons who, under the terms of the will, settlement or other disposition directing the accumulation, would for the time being, if of full age, be entitled to the income directed to be accumulated.

(3) In every case where any accumulation is directed otherwise than as aforesaid, the direction shall, save as hereinafter provided, be void, and the income directed to be accumulated shall, so long as the same is directed to be accumulated contrary to this section, go to and be received by the person or persons who would have been entitled thereto if such accumulation had not been directed.

(4) For avoidance of doubt it is hereby declared that, in the case of a settlement or other disposition inter vivos, a direction to accumulate income during a period specified in paragraph (*d*) of subsection (2) of this section shall not be void, nor shall the accumulation of the income be contrary to this section, solely by reason of the fact that the period begins during the life of the grantor and ends after his death.

(5) The restrictions imposed by this section apply to wills, settlements and other dispositions made on or after the twenty-eighth day of July, eighteen hundred, but, in the case of wills, only where the testator was living and of testamentary capacity after the end of one year from that date.

(6) In this section " minority " in relation to any person means the period beginning with the birth of the person and ending with his attainment of the age of twenty-one years, and " grantor " includes settlor and, in relation to a will, the testator.

6. *Interpretation.*—(1) In this Act, unless the context otherwise requires,—

" Act of 1921 " means the Trusts (Scotland) Act 1921;

" the court " means the Court of Session; and

"trust" and "trustee"[18] have the same meanings respectively as in the Act of 1921.

(2) Unless the context otherwise requires references in this Act to any other Act are references to that Act as amended, modified or extended by any Act including this Act.

contrary to the said section 5, solely by reason of the fact that the period begins during the life of the grantor and ends after his death.

(2) The restrictions imposed by the said section 5 shall apply in relation to a power to accumulate income whether or not there is a duty to exercise that power, and they shall apply whether or not the power to accumulate extends to income produced by the investment of income previously accumulated.

(3) This section shall apply only in relation to instruments taking effect after the passing of this Act, and in the case of an instrument made in the exercise of a special power of appointment shall apply only where the instrument creating the power takes effect after the passing of this Act."—Law Reform (Miscellaneous Provisions) (Scotland) Act 1966.

18 Now also includes an executor-dative: see Succession (Scotland) Act 1964, s. 20.

7. *Short title, citation, application and commencement.*—(1) This Act may be cited as the Trusts (Scotland) Act 1961, and this Act and the Act of 1921 may be cited together as the Trusts (Scotland) Acts 1921 and 1961.

(2) This Act shall apply to trusts which have come into operation before, as well as to trusts coming into operation after, the commencement of this Act.

(3) This Act shall come into operation on the expiration of the period of one month beginning with the date of the passing thereof.

Trustee Investments Act 1961
(9 & 10 *Eliz.* 2, *c.* 62)

An Act to make fresh provision with respect to investment by trustees and persons having the investment powers of trustees, and by local authorities, and for purposes connected therewith.

[3rd August, 1961.]

1. *New powers of investment of trustees.*—(1) [19] A trustee may invest any property in his hands, whether at the time in a state of investment or not, in any manner specified in Part I or II of the First Schedule to this Act or, subject to the next following section, in any manner specified in Part III of that Schedule, and may also from time to time vary any such investments.

(2) The supplemental provisions contained in Part IV of that Schedule shall have effect for the interpretation and for restricting the operation of the said Parts I to III.

(3) No provision relating to the powers of the trustee contained in any instrument (not being an enactment or an instrument made under an enactment) made before the passing of this Act shall limit the powers conferred by this section, but those powers are exerciseable only in so far as a contrary intention is not expressed in any Act or instrument made under an enactment, whenever passed or made, and so relating or in any other instrument so relating which is made after the passing of this Act.

For the purposes of this subsection any rule of the law of Scotland whereby a testamentary writing may be deemed to be made on a date other than that on which it was actually executed shall be disregarded.

(4) In this Act " narrower-range investment " means an investment falling within Part I or II of the First Schedule to this Act and " wider-range investment " means an investment falling within Part III of that Schedule.

2. *Restrictions on wider-range investment.*—(1) A trustee shall not have power by virtue of the foregoing section to make or retain any wider-range investment unless the trust fund has been divided into two parts (hereinafter referred to as the narrower-range part and the wider-range part), the parts being, subject to the provisions of this Act, equal in value at the time of the division; and where such a division has been made no subsequent division of the same fund shall be made for the purposes of this section, and no property shall be transferred from one part of the fund to the other unless either—

(a) the transfer is authorised or required by the following provisions of this Act, or

(b) a compensating transfer is made at the same time.

[19] S. 1 (1) explained: see Trustee Savings Banks Act 1964, s. 12.

In this section " compensating transfer," in relation to any transferred property, means a transfer in the opposite direction of property of equal value.

(2) Property belonging to the narrower-range part of a trust fund shall not by virtue of the foregoing section be invested except in narrower-range investments, and any property invested in any other manner which is or becomes comprised in that part of the trust fund shall either be transferred to the wider-range part of the fund, with a compensating transfer, or be reinvested in narrower-range investments as soon as may be.

(3) Where any property accrues to a trust fund after the fund has been divided in pursuance of subsection (1) of this section, then—

(a) if the property accrues to the trustee as owner or former owner of property comprised in either part of the fund, it shall be treated as belonging to that part of the fund;

(b) in any other case, the trustee shall secure, by apportionment of the accruing property or the transfer of property from one part of the fund to the other, or both, that the value of each part of the fund is increased by the same amount.

Where a trustee acquires property in consideration of a money payment the acquisition of the property shall be treated for the purposes of this section as investment and not as the accrual of property to the trust fund, notwithstanding that the amount of the consideration is less than the value of the property acquired; and paragraph (a) of this subsection shall not include the case of a dividend or interest becoming part of a trust fund.

(4) Where in the exercise of any power or duty of a trustee property falls to be taken out of the trust fund, nothing in this section shall restrict his discretion as to the choice of property to be taken out.

3. *Relationship between Act and other powers of investment.*—(1) The powers conferred by section one of this Act are in addition to and not in derogation from any power conferred otherwise than by this Act of investment or postponing conversion exerciseable by a trustee (hereinafter referred to as a " special power ").

(2) Any special power (however expressed) to invest property in any investment for the time being authorised by law for the investment of trust property, being a power conferred on a trustee before the passing of this Act or conferred on him under any enactment passed before the passing of this Act, shall have effect as a power to invest property in like manner and subject to the like provisions as under the foregoing provisions of this Act.

(3) In relation to property, including wider-range but not including narrower-range investments,—

(a) which a trustee is authorised to hold apart from—

(i) the provisions of section one of this Act or any of the provisions of Part I of the Trustee Act, 1925, or any of the provisions of the Trusts (Scotland) Act, 1921, or

(ii) any such power to invest in authorised investments as is mentioned in the foregoing subsection, or

(b) which became part of a trust fund in consequence of the exercise by the trustee, as owner of property falling within this subsection, of any power conferred by subsection (3) or (4) of section ten of the Trustee Act 1925, or paragraph (o) or (p) of subsection (1) of section four of the Trusts (Scotland) Act 1921,

the foregoing section shall have effect subject to the modifications set out in the Second Schedule to this Act.

(4) The foregoing subsection shall not apply where the powers of the trustee to invest or postpone conversion have been conferred or varied—

(a) by an order of any court made within the period of ten years ending with the passing of this Act, or

(b) by any enactment passed, or instrument having effect under an enactment made, within that period, being an enactment or instrument relating specifically to the trusts in question; or

(c) by an enactment contained in a local Act of the present Session;

but the provisions of the Third Schedule to this Act shall have effect in a case falling within this subsection.

4. *Interpretation of references to trust property and trust funds.*—(1) In this Act " property " includes real or personal property of any description, including money and things in action:

Provided that it does not include an interest in expectancy, but the falling into possession of such an interest, or the receipt of proceeds of the sale thereof, shall be treated for the purposes of this Act as an accrual of property to the trust fund.

(2) So much of the property in the hands of a trustee shall for the purposes of this Act constitute one trust fund as is held on trusts which (as respects the beneficiaries or their respective interests or the purposes of the trust or as respects the powers of the trustee) are not identical with those on which any other property in his hands is held.

(3) Where property is taken out of a trust fund by way of appropriation so as to form a separate fund, and at the time of the appropriation the trust fund had (as to the whole or a part thereof) been divided in pursuance of subsection (1) of section two of this Act, or that subsection as modified by the Second Schedule to this Act, then if the separate fund is so divided the narrower-range and wider-range parts of the separate fund may be constituted so as either to be equal, or to bear to each other the same proportion as the two corresponding parts of the fund out of which it was so appropriated (the values of those parts of those funds being ascertained as at the time of appropriation), or some intermediate proportion.

(4) In the application of this section to Scotland the following subsection shall be substituted for subsection (1) thereof:—

> " (1) In this Act ' property ' includes property of any description (whether heritable or moveable, corporeal or incorporeal) which is presently enjoyable, but does not include a future interest, whether vested or contingent."

5. *Certain valuations to be conclusive for purposes of division of trust fund.*—(1) If for the purposes of section two or four of this Act or the Second Schedule thereto a trustee obtains, from a person reasonably believed by the trustee to be qualified to make it, a valuation in writing of any property, the valuation shall be conclusive in determining whether the division of the trust fund in pursuance of subsection (1) of the said section two, or any transfer or apportionment of property under that section or the said Second Schedule, has been duly made.

(2) The foregoing subsection applies to any such valuation notwithstanding that it is made by a person in the course of his employment as an officer or servant.

6. *Duty of trustees in choosing investments.*—(1) In the exercise of his powers of investment a trustee shall have regard—

(a) to the need for diversification of investments of the trust, in so far as is appropriate to the circumstances of the trust;

(b) to the suitability to the trust of investments of the description of investment proposed and of the investment proposed as an investment of that description.

(2) Before exercising any power conferred by section one of this Act to invest in a manner specified in Part II or III of the First Schedule to this Act, or before investing in any such manner in the exercise of a power falling within subsection (2) of section three of this Act, a trustee shall obtain and consider proper advice on the question whether the investment is satisfactory having regard to the matters mentioned in paragraphs (a) and (b) of the foregoing subsection.

(3) A trustee retaining any investment made in the exercise of such a power and in such a manner as aforesaid shall determine at what intervals the circumstances, and in particular the nature of the investment, make it desirable to obtain such advice as aforesaid, and shall obtain and consider such advice accordingly.

(4) For the purposes of the two foregoing subsections, proper advice is the advice of a person who is reasonably believed by the trustee to be qualified by his ability in and practical experience of financial matters; and such advice may be given by a person notwithstanding that he gives it in the course of his employment as an officer or servant.

(5) A trustee shall not be treated as having complied with subsection (2) or (3) of this section unless the advice was given or has been subsequently confirmed in writing.

(6) Subsections (2) and (3) of this section shall not apply to one of two or more trustees where he is the person giving the advice required by this section to his co-trustee or co-trustees, and shall not apply where powers of a trustee are lawfully exercised by an officer or servant competent under subsection (4) of this section to give proper advice.

(7) Without prejudice to section eight of the Trustee Act 1925, or section thirty of the Trusts (Scotland) Act 1921 (which relate to valuation, and the proportion of the value to be lent, where a trustee lends on the security of property) the advice required by this section shall not include, in the case of a loan on the security of freehold or leasehold property in England and Wales or Northern Ireland or on heritable security in Scotland, advice on the suitability of the particular loan.

7. *Application of ss. 1–6 to persons, other than trustees, having trustee investment powers.*—(1) Where any persons, not being trustees, have a statutory power of making investments which is or includes power—

(a) to make the like investments as are authorised by section one of the Trustee Act 1925, or section ten of the Trusts (Scotland) Act 1921, or

(b) to make the like investments as trustees are for the time being by law authorised to make,

however the power is expressed, the foregoing provisions of this Act shall with the necessary modifications apply in relation to them as if they were trustees:

Provided that property belonging to a Consolidated Loans Fund or any other fund applicable wholly or partly for the redemption of debt shall not by virtue of the foregoing provisions of this Act be invested or held invested in any manner specified in paragraph 6 of Part II of the First Schedule to this Act or in wider-range investments.

(2) Where, in the exercise of powers conferred by any enactment, an authority to which paragraph 9 of Part II of the First Schedule to this Act applies uses money belonging to any fund for a purpose for which the authority has power to borrow, the foregoing provisions of this Act, as applied by the foregoing subsection, shall apply as if there were comprised in the fund (in addition to the actual content thereof) property, being narrower-range investments, having a value equal to so much of the said money as for the time being has not been repaid to the fund, and accordingly any repayment of such money to the fund shall not be treated for the said purposes as the accrual of property to the fund:

Provided that nothing in this subsection shall be taken to require compliance with any of the provisions of section six of this Act in relation to the exercise of such powers as aforesaid.

(3) In this section " Consolidated Loans Fund " means a fund established under section fifty-five of the Local Government Act 1958, and includes a loans fund established under section two hundred and seventy-five of the Local Government (Scotland) Act 1947, and "statutory power" means a power conferred by an enactment passed before the passing of this Act or by any instrument made under any such enactment.

8. *Application of ss. 1–6 in special cases.*—(1) In relation to persons to whom this section applies—

(*a*) notwithstanding anything in subsection (3) of section one of this Act, no provision of any enactment passed, or instrument having effect under an enactment and made, before the passing of this Act shall limit the powers conferred by the said section one;

(*b*) subsection (1) of the foregoing section shall apply where the power of making investments therein mentioned is or includes a power to make some only of the investments mentioned in paragraph (*a*) or (*b*) of that subsection.

(2) This section applies to—

(*a*) the persons for the time being authorised to invest funds of the Duchy of Lancaster;

(*b*) any persons specified in an order made by the Treasury by statutory instrument, being persons (whether trustees or not) whose power to make investments is conferred by or under any enactment contained in a local or private Act.

(3) An order of the Treasury made under the foregoing subsection may provide that the provisions of sections one to six of this Act (other than the provisions of subsection (3) of section one) shall, in their application to any persons specified therein, have effect subject to such exceptions and modifications as may be specified.

9. *Supplementary provisions as to investments.*—(1) In subsection (3) of section ten of the Trustee Act 1925, before paragraph (*c*) (which enables trustees to concur in any scheme or arrangement for the amalgamation of a company in which they hold securities with another company, with power to accept securities in the second company) there shall be inserted the following paragraph:—

" (*bb*) for the acquisition of the securities of the company, or of control thereof, by another company."

(2) It is hereby declared that the power to subscribe for securities conferred by subsection (4) of the said section ten includes power to retain them for any period for which the trustee has power to retain the holding

in respect of which the right to subscribe for the securities was offered, but subject to any conditions subject to which the trustee has that power.

[20] **11.** *Local Authority investment schemes.*—(1) Without prejudice to powers conferred by or under any other enactment, any authority to which this section applies may invest property held by the authority in accordance with a scheme submitted to the Treasury by any association of local authorities [or by the London County Council] [21] and approved by the Treasury as enabling investments to be made collectively without in substance extending the scope of powers of investment.

(2) A scheme under this section may apply to a specified authority or to a specified class of authorities, may make different provisions as respects different authorities or different classes of authorities or as respects different descriptions of property or property held for different purposes, and may impose restrictions on the extent to which the power conferred by the foregoing subsection shall be exerciseable.

(3) In approving a scheme under this section, the Treasury may direct that the Prevention of Fraud (Investments) Act 1958, or the Prevention of Fraud (Investments) Act (Northern Ireland) 1940, shall not apply to dealings undertaken or documents issued for the purposes of the scheme, or to such dealings or documents of such descriptions as may be specified in the direction.

(4) The authorities to which this section applies are—

[22] (a) in England and Wales, the council of a county, a [county metropolitan or other] [23] borough a district or a parish [a river authority], [24] the Common Council of the City of London [the Greater London Council] [25] and the Council of the Isles of Scilly;

(b) in Scotland, a local authority within the meaning of the Local Government (Scotland) Act 1947;

[26] (c) in any part of Great Britain, a joint board or joint committee constituted to discharge or advise on the discharge of the functions of any two or more of the authorities mentioned in the foregoing paragraphs (including a joint committee established by those authorities acting in combination in accordance with regulations made under section 7 of the Superannuation Act 1972);

(d) in Northern Ireland, the council of a county, a county or other borough, or an urban or rural district, and the Northern Ireland Local Government Officers' Superannuation Committee established under the Local Government (Superannuation) Act (Northern Ireland) 1950.

12. *Power to confer additional powers of investment.*—(1) Her Majesty may by Order in Council extend the powers of investment conferred by section one of this Act by adding to Part I, Part II or Part III of the First Schedule to this Act any manner of investment specified in the Order.

---

[20] See also Local Authorities Mutual Investment Trust Act 1968, s. 1.
[21] Words repealed as from 1st April, 1965, by London Government Act 1963, Sched. 18, Pt. II.
[22] As amended (prosp.) by Local Government Act 1972, Sched. 30.
[23] Words repealed as from April 1, 1965, by London Government Act 1963, Sched. 18, Pt. II.
[24] Words added by Water Resources Act 1963, Sched. 13, para. 16.
[25] Words added by London Government Act 1963, Sched. 17, para. 25 (a).
[26] As amended by the Superannuation Act 1972, Sched. 6.

(2) Any Order under this section shall be subject to annulment in pursuance of a resolution of either House of Parliament.

13. *Power to modify provisions as to division of trust fund.*—(1) The Treasury may by order made by statutory instrument direct that, subject to subsection (3) of section four of this Act, any division of a trust fund made in pursuance of subsection (1) of section two of this Act during the continuance in force of the order shall be made so that the value of the wider-range part at the time of the division bears to the then value of the narrower-range part such proportion, greater than one but not greater than three to one, as may be prescribed by the order; and in this Act " the prescribed proportion " means the proportion for the time being prescribed under this subsection.

(2) A fund which has been divided in pursuance of subsection (1) of section two of this Act before the coming into operation of an order under the foregoing subsection may notwithstanding anything in that subsection be again divided (once only) in pursuance of the said subsection (1) during the continuance in force of the order.

(3) If an order is made under subsection (1) of this section, then as from the coming into operation of the order—

(*a*) paragraph (*b*) of subsection (3) of section two of this Act and sub-paragraph (*b*) of paragraph 3 of the Second Schedule thereto shall have effect with the substitution, for the words from " each " to the end, of the words " the wider-range part of the fund is increased by an amount which bears the prescribed proportion to the amount by which the value of the narrower-range part of the fund is increased ";

(*b*) subsection (3) of section four of this Act shall have effect as if for the words " so as either " to " each other " there were substituted the words " so as to bear to each other either the prescribed proportion or ".

(4) An order under this section may be revoked by a subsequent order thereunder prescribing a greater proportion.

(5) An order under this section shall not have effect unless approved by a resolution of each House of Parliament.

14. *Amendment of s. 27 of Trusts (Scotland) Act 1921.*—So much of section twenty-seven of the Trusts (Scotland) Act 1921, as empowers the Court of Session to approve as investments for trust funds any stocks, funds or securities in addition to those in which trustees are by that Act authorised to invest trust funds shall cease to have effect.

15. *Saving for powers of court.*—The enlargement of the investment powers of trustees by this Act shall not lessen any power of a court to confer wider powers of investment on trustees, or affect the extent to which any such power is to be exercised.

16. *Minor and consequential amendments and repeals.*—(1) The provisions of the Fourth Schedule to this Act (which contain minor amendments and amendments consequential on the foregoing provisions of this Act) shall have effect.

(2) The enactments mentioned in the Fifth Schedule to this Act are hereby repealed to the extent specified in the third column of that Schedule.

17. *Short title, extent and construction.*—(1) This Act may be cited as the Trustee Investments Act 1961.

(2) Sections eleven and sixteen of this Act shall extend to Northern Ireland, but except as aforesaid and except so far as any other provisions of the Act apply by virtue of subsection (1) of section one of the Trustee Act (Northern Ireland) 1958, or any other enactment of the Parliament of Northern Ireland, to trusts the execution of which is governed by the law in force in Northern Ireland, this Act does not apply to such trusts.

[27] (3) So much of section sixteen of this Act as relates to the National Savings Bank and to trustee savings banks shall extend to the Isle of Man and the Channel Islands.

(4) Except where the context otherwise requires, in this Act, in its application to trusts the execution of which is governed by the law in force in England and Wales, expressions have the same meaning as in the Trustee Act, 1925.

(5) Except where the context otherwise requires, in this Act, in its application to trusts the execution of which is governed by the law in force in Scotland, expressions have the same meaning as in the Trusts (Scotland) Act 1921.

SCHEDULES

Section 1.

FIRST SCHEDULE

Manner of Investment

Part I

Narrower-Range Investments not Requiring Advice

[28] 1. In Defence Bonds, National Savings Certificates and Ulster Savings Certificates, Ulster Development Bonds, National Development Bonds, British Savings Bonds.

[27] 2. In deposits in the National Savings Bank, ordinary deposits in a trustee savings bank and deposits in a bank or department thereof certified under subsection (3) of section nine of the Finance Act 1956.

Part II

Narrower-Range Investments Requiring Advice

1. In securities issued by Her Majesty's Government in the United Kingdom, the Government of Northern Ireland or the Government of the Isle of Man, not being securities falling within Part I of this Schedule and being fixed-interest securities registered in the United Kingdom or the Isle of Man, Treasury Bills or Tax Reserve Certificates.

2. In any securities the payment of interest on which is guaranteed by Her Majesty's Government in the United Kingdom or the Government of Northern Ireland.

3. In fixed-interest securities issued in the United Kingdom by any public authority or nationalised industry or undertaking in the United Kingdom.

4. In fixed-interest securities issued in the United Kingdom by the government of any overseas territory within the Commonwealth or by any

---

[27] As amended by Post Office Act 1969, Sched. 6.
[28] Ulster Development Bonds added by S.I. 1962 No. 2611; National Development Bonds by S.I. 1964 No. 703; British Savings Bonds by S.I. 1968 No. 470.

public or local authority within such a territory, being securities registered in the United Kingdom.

References in this paragraph to an overseas territory or to the government of such a territory shall be construed as if they occurred in the Overseas Service Act 1958.

[29] 5. In fixed-interest securities issued in the United Kingdom by the International Bank for Reconstruction and Development, being securities registered in the United Kingdom. In fixed-interest securities issued in the United Kingdom by the Inter-American Development Bank. In fixed-interest securities issued in the United Kingdom by the European Investment Bank or by the European Coal and Steel Community, being securities registered in the United Kingdom.

6. In debentures issued in the United Kingdom by a company incorporated in the United Kingdom, being debentures registered in the United Kingdom.

7. In stock of the Bank of Ireland. In Bank of Ireland 7 per cent Loan Stock 1986/91.[30]

8. In debentures issued by the Agricultural Mortgage Corporation Limited or the Scottish Agricultural Securities Corporation Limited.

9. In loans to any authority to which this paragraph applies charged on all or any of the revenues of the authority or on a fund into which all or any of those revenues are payable, in any fixed-interest securities issued in the United Kingdom by any such authority for the purpose of borrowing money so charged, and in deposits with any such authority by way of temporary loan made on the giving of a receipt for the loan by the treasurer or other similar officer of the authority and on the giving of an undertaking by the authority that, if requested to charge the loan as aforesaid, it will either comply with the request or repay the loan.

This paragraph applies to the following authorities, that is to say—

    (a) any local authority in the United Kingdom;

    (b) any authority all the members of which are appointed or elected by one or more local authorities in the United Kingdom;

    (c) any authority the majority of the members of which are appointed or elected by one or more local authorities in the United Kingdom, being an authority which by virtue of any enactment has power to issue a precept to a local authority in England and Wales, or a requisition to a local authority in Scotland, or to the expenses of which, by virtue of any enactment, a local authority in the United Kingdom is or can be required to contribute;

    (d) the Receiver for the Metropolitan Police District or a combined police authority (within the meaning of the Police Act 1946);

    (e) the Belfast City and District Water Commissioners;

  [31](f) the Great Ouse Water Authority;

  [32](g) any district council in Northern Ireland.

[29] As amended by S.I. 1964 No. 1404 and S.I. 1972 No. 1818.

[30] Added by S.I. 1966 No 401

[31] Added by S.I. 1962 No. 658. "Any river authority which, apart from this paragraph, would not be included among the authorities to which paragraph 9 of Part II of Schedule I to the Trustee Investments Act, 1961 applies shall by virtue of this Act be included among those authorities "—Water Resources Act 1963, Sched. 4, para. 33.

[32] Added by S.I. 1973 No. 1332.

10. In debentures or in the guaranteed or preference stock of any incorporated company, being statutory water undertakers within the meaning of the Water Act, 1945, or any corresponding enactment in force in Northern Ireland, and having during each of the ten years immediately preceding the calendar year in which the investment was made paid a dividend of not less than $3\frac{1}{2}$ per cent.[33] on its ordinary shares.

11. In deposits by way of special investment in a trustee savings bank or in a department (not being a department certified under subsection (3) of section nine of the Finance Act, 1956) of a bank any other department of which is so certified.

12. In deposits in a building society designated under section one of the House Purchase and Housing Act, 1959.

13. In mortgages of freehold property in England and Wales or Northern Ireland and of leasehold property in those countries of which the unexpired term at the time of investment is not less than sixty years, and in loans on heritable security in Scotland.

14. In perpetual rent-charges charged on land in England and Wales or Northern Ireland and fee-farm rents (not being rent-charges) issuing out of such land, and in feu-duties or ground annuals in Scotland.

PART III

WIDER-RANGE INVESTMENTS

1. In any securities issued in the United Kingdom by a company incorporated in the United Kingdom, being securities registered in the United Kingdom and not being securities falling within Part II of this Schedule.

2. In shares in any building society designated under section one of the House Purchase and Housing Act 1959.

3. In any units, or other shares of the investments subject to the trusts, of a unit trust scheme in the case of which there is in force at the time of investment an order of the Board of Trade under section seventeen of the Prevention of Fraud (Investments) Act, 1958, or of the Ministry of Commerce for Northern Ireland under section sixteen of the Prevention of Fraud (Investments) Act (Northern Ireland) 1940.

PART IV

SUPPLEMENTAL

1. The securities mentioned in Parts I to III of this Schedule do not include any securities where the holder can be required to accept repayment of the principal, or the payment of any interest, otherwise than in sterling.

2. The securities mentioned in paragraphs 1 to 8 of Part II, other than Treasury Bills or Tax Reserve Certificates, securities issued before the passing of this Act by the Government of the Isle of Man, securities falling within paragraph 4 of the said Part II issued before the passing of this Act or securities falling within paragraph 9 of that Part, and the securities mentioned in paragraph 1 of Part III of this Schedule, do not include—

(*a*) securities the price of which is not quoted on a recognised stock exchange within the meaning of the Prevention of Fraud (Investments) Act 1958, or the Belfast stock exchange;

[33] Amended by S.I. 1973 No. 1393.

(b) shares or debenture stock not fully paid up (except shares or debenture stock which by the terms of issue are required to be fully paid up within nine months of the date of issue).

3. The securities mentioned in paragraph 6 of Part II and paragraph 1 of Part III of this Schedule do not include—

(a) shares or debentures of an incorporated company of which the total issued and paid up share capital is less than one million pounds;

(b) shares or debentures of an incorporated company which has not in each of the five years immediately preceding the calendar year in which the investment is made paid a dividend on all the shares issued by the company, excluding any shares issued after the dividend was declared and any shares which by their terms of issue did not rank for the dividend for that year.

For the purposes of sub-paragraph (b) of this paragraph a company formed—

(i) to take over the business of another company or other companies, or

(ii) to acquire the securities of, or control of, another company or other companies,

or for either of those purposes and for other purposes shall be deemed to have paid a dividend as mentioned in that sub-paragraph in any year in which such a dividend has been paid by the other company or all the other companies, as the case may be.

4. In this Schedule, unless the context otherwise requires, the following expressions have the meanings hereby respectively assigned to them, that is to say—

" debenture " includes debenture stock and bonds, whether consti-tuting a charge on assets or not, and loan stock or notes;

" enactment " includes an enactment of the Parliament of Northern Ireland;

" fixed-interest securities " means securities which under their terms of issue bear a fixed rate of interest;

" local authority " in relation to the United Kingdom, means any of the following authorities—
    [34] (a) in England and Wales, the council of a county, a borough, an urban or rural district or a parish, the Common Council of the City of London the Greater London Council,[35] and the Council of the Isles of Scilly;
    (b) in Scotland, a local authority within the meaning of the Local Government (Scotland) Act 1947;
    (c) in Northern Ireland, the council of a county, a county or other borough, or an urban or rural district;

" ordinary deposits " and " special investment " have the same mean-ings respectively as in the Trustee Savings Banks Act 1954;

" securities " includes shares, debentures, Treasury Bills and Tax Reserve Certificates;

" share " includes stock;

" Treasury Bills " includes bills issued by Her Majesty's Government in the United Kingdom and Northern Ireland Treasury Bills.

[34] As amended (prosp.) by Local Government Act 1972, Sched. 30.
[35] Words added as from April 1, 1965 by London Government Act, 1963, Sched. 17, para. 25 (b).

5. It is hereby declared that in this Schedule " mortgage " in relation to freehold or leasehold property in Northern Ireland, includes a registered charge which, by virtue of subsection (4) of section forty of the Local Registration of Title (Ireland) Act 1891, or any other enactment, operates as a mortgage by deed.

6. References in this Schedule to an incorporated company are references to a company incorporated by or under any enactment and include references to a body of persons established for the purpose of trading for profit and incorporated by Royal Charter.

7. The references in paragraph 12 of Part II and paragraph 2 of Part III of this Schedule to a building society designated under section one of the House Purchase and Housing Act 1959, include references to a permanent society incorporated under the Building Societies Acts (Northern Ireland) 1874 to 1940 for the time being designated by the Registrar for Northern Ireland under subsection (2) of that section (which enables such a society to be so designated for the purpose of trustees' powers of investment specified in paragraph (a) of subsection (1) of that section).

Section 3.   SECOND SCHEDULE

MODIFICATION OF S. 2 IN RELATION TO PROPERTY FALLING WITHIN S. 3 (3)

1. In this Schedule " special-range property " means property falling within subsection (3) of section three of this Act.

2.—(1) Where a trust fund includes special-range property, subsection (1) of section two of this Act shall have effect as if references to the trust fund were references to so much thereof as does not consist of special-range property, and the special-range property shall be carried to a separate part of the fund.

(2) Any property which—

    (a) being property belonging to the narrower-range or wider-range part of a trust fund, is converted into special-range property, or

    (b) being special-range property, accrues to a trust fund after the division of the fund or part thereof in pursuance of subsection (1) of section two of this Act or of that subsection as modified by sub-paragraph (1) of this paragraph,

shall be carried to such a separate part of the fund as aforesaid; and subsections (2) and (3) of the said section two shall have effect subject to this sub-paragraph.

3. Where property carried to such a separate part as aforesaid is converted into property other than special-range property,—

    (a) it shall be transferred to the narrower-range part of the fund or the wider-range part of the fund or apportioned between them, and

    (b) any transfer of property from one of those parts to the other shall be made which is necessary to secure that the value of each of those parts of the fund is increased by the same amount.

THIRD SCHEDULE

Section 3.

PROVISIONS SUPPLEMENTARY TO S. 3 (4)

1. Where in a case falling within subsection (4) of section three of this Act, property belonging to the narrower-range part of a trust fund—

    (a) is invested otherwise than in a narrower-range investment, or

    (b) being so invested, is retained and not transferred or as soon as may be reinvested as mentioned in subsection (2) of section two of this Act,

then, so long as the property continues so invested and comprised in the narrower-range part of the fund, section one of this Act shall not authorise the making or retention of any wider-range investment.

2. Section four of the Trustee Act 1925, or section thirty-three of the Trusts (Scotland) Act 1921 (which relieve a trustee from liability for retaining an investment which has ceased to be authorised), shall not apply where an investment ceases to be authorised in consequence of the foregoing paragraph.

FOURTH SCHEDULE

Section 16.

MINOR AND CONSEQUENTIAL AMENDMENTS

1.—(1) References in the Trustee Act 1925, except in subsection (2) of section sixty-nine of that Act, to section one of that Act or to provisions which include that section shall be construed respectively as references to section one of this Act and as including references to section one of this Act.

(2) References in the Trusts (Scotland) Act 1921, to section ten or eleven of that Act, or to provisions which include either of those sections, shall be construed respectively as references to section one of this Act and as including references to that section.

2.—[Repealed by Building Societies Act 1962, Sched. 10, Pt. I.]

3. The following enactments and instruments, that is to say—

    (a) subsection (3) of section seventy-four of the Third Schedule to the Water Act 1945, and any order made under that Act applying the provisions of that subsection;

    (b) any local and personal Act which, or any order or other instrument in the nature of any such Act, which, modifies paragraph (l) of subsection (1) of section one of the Trustee Act 1925,

shall have effect as if for any reference to the said paragraph (l) there were substituted a reference to paragraph 10 of Part II of the First Schedule to this Act.

4 and 5. [Repealed by National Savings Bank Act 1971, Sched. 2.]

6. For the reference in subsection (2) of section one of the House Purchase and Housing Act 1959, to paragraph (a) of subsection (1) of that section there shall be substituted a reference to paragraph 12 of Part II and paragraph 2 of Part III of the First Schedule to this Act.

FIFTH SCHEDULE

Section 16.

REPEALS

Session and Chapter	Short Title	Extent of Repeal
63 & 64 Vict. c. 62.	The Colonial Stock Act 1900.	Section two.
2 Edw. 7. c. 41	The Metropolis Water Act 1902.	In section seventeen, subsection (4).
11 & 12 Geo. 5. c. 58.	The Trusts (Scotland) Act 1921.	Sections ten and eleven. In section twelve, subsections (3) and (4). In section twenty-seven, the words from "including such regulations" to the end of the section.
15 & 16 Geo. 5. c. 19.	The Trustee Act 1925.	Section one. In section two, the proviso to subsection (1). In section five, paragraph (a) of subsection (1) and subsections (4) to (6).
18 & 19 Geo. 5. c. 43.	The Agricultural Credits Act 1928.	Section three.
19 & 20 Geo. 5. c. 13.	The Agricultural Credits (Scotland) Act 1929.	Section three.
20 & 21 Geo. 5. c. 5.	The Colonial Development Act 1929.	In section three, subsection (3).
24 & 25 Geo. 5. c. 47.	The Colonial Stock Act 1934.	The whole Act.
8 & 9 Geo. 6. c. 12.	The Northern Ireland (Miscellaneous Provisions) Act 1945.	Sections four to six.
11 & 12 Geo. 6. c. 7.	The Ceylon Independence Act 1947.	In the Second Schedule, paragraph 4.
12, 13 & 14 Geo. 6. c. 1.	The Colonial Stock Act 1948	In section two, subsection (3).
2 & 3 Eliz. 2. c. 62.	The Post Office Savings Bank Act 1954.	In section four, subsection (4).
5 & 6 Eliz. 2. c. 6.	The Ghana Independence Act 1957.	In the Second Schedule, paragraph 4.
5 & 6 Eliz. 2. c. 60.	The Federation of Malaya Independence Act 1957.	In the First Schedule, paragraph 8.
6 & 7 Eliz. 2. c. 47.	The Agricultural Marketing Act 1958.	In section sixteen, in paragraph (a), the words from "or for the time" to "Act."
6 & 7 Eliz. 2. c. 55.	The Local Government Act 1958.	Section fifty-four.
6 & 7 Eliz. 2. c. 64.	The Local Government and Miscellaneous Financial Provisions (Scotland) Act 1958.	Section sixteen.
7 & 8 Eliz. 2. c. 33.	The House Purchase and Housing Act 1959.	In section one, paragraph (a) of subsection (1), and subsection (5).
8 & 9 Eliz. 2. c. 52.	The Cyprus Act 1960.	In the Schedule, in paragraph 9, sub-paragraphs (1), (3) and (4).
8 & 9 Eliz. 2. c. 55.	The Nigeria Independence Act 1960.	In the Second Schedule, paragraph 4.
9 & 10 Eliz. 2. c. 16.	The Sierra Leone Independence Act 1961.	In the Third Schedule, paragraph 5.

Administration of Estates Act 1971
(c. 25)

An Act to provide for the recognition, without resealing, of certain grants of administration and confirmations throughout the United Kingdom; to allow for the inclusion of real estate in any part of the United Kingdom in the inventory of the estate of a person dying domiciled in Scotland; to amend the law with respect to the grant of administration by the High Court and resealing by that Court of administration granted outside the United Kingdom and to exempt from stamp duty guarantees given under the law so amended; to make provision with respect to the duties and rights of personal representatives; and for connected purposes.

[May 12th, 1971]

Reciprocal recognition of grants

1.—(1) Where a person dies domiciled in Scotland—

(a) a confirmation granted in respect of all or part of his estate and noting his Scottish domicile, and

(b) a certificate of confirmation noting his Scottish domicile and relating to one or more items of his estate,

shall, without being resealed, be treated for the purposes of the law of England and Wales as a grant of representation (in accordance with subsection (2) below) to the executors named in the confirmation or certificate in respect of the property of the deceased of which according to the terms of the confirmation they are executors or, as the case may be, in respect of the item or items of property specified in the certificate of confirmation.

(2) Where by virtue of subsection (1) above a confirmation or certificate of confirmation is treated for the purposes of the law of England and Wales as a grant of representation to the executors named therein then, subject to subsections (3) and (5) below, the grant shall be treated—

(a) as a grant of probate where it appears from the confirmation or certificate that the executors so named are executors nominate; and

(b) in any other case, as a grant of letters of administration.

(3) Section 7 of the Administration of Estates Act 1925 (executor of executor represents original testator) shall not, by virtue of subsection (2) (a) above, apply on the death of an executor named in a confirmation or certificate of confirmation.

(4) Subject to subsection (5) below, where a person dies domiciled in Northern Ireland a grant of probate of his will or letters of administration in respect of his estate (or any part of it) made by the High Court in Northern Ireland and noting his domicile there shall, without being resealed, be treated for the purposes of the law of England and Wales as if it had been originally made by the High Court in England and Wales.

(5) Notwithstanding anything in the preceding provisions of this section, a person who is a personal representative according to the law of England and Wales by virtue only of those provisions may not be required, under section 25 of the Administration of Estates Act 1925, to deliver up his grant to the High Court.

(6) This section applies in relation to confirmations, probates and letters of administration granted before as well as after the commencement of this Act, and in relation to a confirmation, probate or letters of

administration granted before the commencement of this Act, this section shall have effect as if it had come into force immediately before the grant was made.

(7) In this section " confirmation " includes an additional confirmation, and the term " executors," where used in relation to a confirmation or certificate of confirmation, shall be construed according to the law of Scotland.

2.—(1) Where a person dies domiciled in England and Wales a grant of probate of his will or letters of administration in respect of his estate (or any part of it) made by the High Court in England and Wales and noting his domicile there shall, without being resealed, be treated for the purposes of the law of Northern Ireland as if it had been originally made by the High Court in Northern Ireland.

(2) Where a person dies domiciled in Scotland—

(a) a confirmation granted in respect of all or part of his estate and noting his Scottish domicile, and

(b) a certificate of confirmation noting his Scottish domicile and relating to one or more items of his estate,

shall, without being resealed, be treated for the purposes of the law of Northern Ireland as a grant of representation (in accordance with subsection (3) below) to the executors named in the confirmation or certificate in respect of the property of the deceased of which according to the terms of the confirmation they are executors or, as the case may be, in respect of the item or items of property specified in the certificate of confirmation.

(3) Where by virtue of subsection (2) above a confirmation or certificate of confirmation is treated for the purposes of the law of Northern Ireland as a grant of representation to the executors named therein then, subject to subsection (4) below, the grant shall be treated—

(a) as a grant of probate where it appears from the confirmation or certificate that the executors so named are executors nominate; and

(b) in any other case, as a grant of letters of administration.

(4) Notwithstanding anything in any enactment or rule of law, subsection (3) (a) above shall not operate to entitle an executor of a sole or last surviving executor of a testator, whose will has been proved in Scotland only, to act as the executor of that testator.

(5) This section applies in relation to probates, letters of administration and confirmations granted before as well as after the commencement of this Act, and—

(a) in relation to a probate, letters of administration or confirmation granted, and resealed in Northern Ireland, before the commencement of this Act, this section shall have effect as if it had come into force immediately before the grant was so resealed; and

(b) a probate, letters of administration or confirmation granted but not resealed in Northern Ireland before the commencement of this Act shall, for the purposes of this section, be treated as having been granted at the commencement of this Act.

(6) In this section " confirmation " includes an additional confirmation, and the term " executors," where used in relation to a confirmation or certificate of confirmation shall be construed according to the law of Scotland.

3.—(1) Where a person dies domiciled in England and Wales or in Northern Ireland a grant of probate or letters of administration

(*a*) from the High Court in England and Wales and noting his domicile there, or

(*b*) from the High Court in Northern Ireland and noting his domicile there

shall, without being resealed, be of the like force and effect and have the same operation in relation to property in Scotland as a confirmation given under the seal of office of the Commissariot of Edinburgh to the executor or administrator named in the probate or letters of administration.

(2) This section applies in relation to probates and letters of administration granted before as well as after the commencement of this Act, and in relation to a probate or letters of administration granted before the commencement of this Act, this section shall have effect as if it had come into force immediately before the grant was made.

4.—(1) In England and Wales and in Northern Ireland—

(*a*) a document purporting to be a confirmation, additional confirmation or certificate of confirmation given under the seal of office of any commissariot in Scotland shall, except where the contrary is proved, be taken to be such a confirmation, additional confirmation or certificate of confirmation without further proof; and

(*b*) a document purporting to be a duplicate of such a confirmation or additional confirmation and to be given under such a seal shall be receivable in evidence in like manner and for the like purposes as the confirmation or additional confirmation of which it purports to be a duplicate.

(2) In England and Wales and in Scotland—

(*a*) a document purporting to be a grant of probate or of letters of administration issued under the seal of the High Court in Northern Ireland or of the principal or district probate registry there shall, except where the contrary is proved, be taken to be such a grant without further proof; and

(*b*) a document purporting to be a copy of such a grant and to be sealed with such a seal shall be receivable in evidence in like manner and for the like purposes as the grant of which it purports to be a copy.

(3) In Scotland and in Northern Ireland—

(*a*) a document purporting to be a grant of probate or of letters of administration issued under the seal of the High Court in England and Wales or of the principal or a district probate registry there shall, except where the contrary is proved, be taken to be such a grant without further proof; and

(*b*) a document purporting to be a copy of such a grant and to be sealed with such a seal shall be receivable in evidence in like manner and for the like purposes as the grant of which it purports to be a copy.

5.—(1) A confirmation or additional confirmation granted in respect of property situated in Scotland of a person who died domiciled there, which notes that domicile, may contain or have appended thereto and signed by the sheriff clerk a note or statement of property in England and Wales or in Northern Ireland held by the deceased in trust, being a note or statement which has been set forth in any inventory recorded in the books of the court of which the sheriff clerk is clerk.

(2) Section 1 or, as the case may be, section 2 of this Act shall apply in relation to property specified in such a note or statement as is mentioned in subsection (1) above as it applies in relation to property specified in the confirmation or additional confirmation concerned.

6.—(1) It shall be competent to include in the inventory of the estate of any person who dies domiciled in Scotland any real estate of the deceased situated in England and Wales or Northern Ireland, and accordingly in section 9 of the Confirmation of Executors (Scotland) Act 1858, the word " personal " wherever it occurs is hereby repealed.

(2) Section 14 (2) of the Succession (Scotland) Act 1964 (act of sederunt to provide for description of heritable property) shall apply in relation to such real estate as aforesaid as it applies in relation to heritable property in Scotland.

INDEX

TRUSTS, TRUSTEES
AND EXECUTORS